PSYCHOLOGY AND LAW

PSYCHOLOGY AND LAW
An Empirical Perspective

Edited by

NEIL BREWER
KIPLING D. WILLIAMS

THE GUILFORD PRESS
New York   London

© 2005 The Guilford Press
A Division of Guilford Publications, Inc.
72 Spring Street, New York, NY 10012
www.guilford.com

Printed in the United States of America

This book is printed on acid-free paper.

Last digit is print number: 9 8 7 6 5 4 3 2 1

Library of Congress Cataloging-in-Publication Data

Psychology and law : an empirical perspective / edited by Neil Brewer, Kipling
D. Williams.
     p. cm.
   Includes bibliographical references and index.
   ISBN 1-59385-122-7 (hardcover : alk. paper)
  1. Forensic psychology. 2. Forensic psychiatry. I. Brewer, Neil. II.
Williams, Kipling D.
  RA1148.P78 2005
  614′.1—dc22
                                                    2004029585

About the Editors

Neil Brewer, PhD, is Professor of Psychology at Flinders University in South Australia, where he teaches an upper-level undergraduate course on experimental psychology and law. The research programs in his laboratory span both cognitive and social psychology, focusing on issues such as confidence-accuracy and decision time-accuracy relationships in eyewitness identification, identification decision processes, eyewitness recall, eyewitness confidence effects on juror judgments, and improving comprehension of judicial instructions. Dr. Brewer's recent publications include articles in *Journal of Applied Psychology, Journal of Experimental Psychology: Applied, Journal of Personality and Social Psychology, Law and Human Behavior,* and *Applied Cognitive Psychology.* He is a current member of the editorial boards of *Journal of Experimental Psychology: Applied* and *Legal and Criminological Psychology.*

Kipling D. Williams, PhD, is Professor of Psychological Sciences at Purdue University. He is an experimental social psychologist and teaches undergraduate courses on psychology and law. Dr. Williams has conducted research on various topics focusing on psychology and law, including the biasing effects of judges' instructions, eyewitness accuracy and testimony, stealing thunder as a courtroom tactic, homonymic priming, and the effects of crime heinousness on lowering thresholds of beyond a reasonable doubt. He has also conducted research on social loafing and, more recently, on ostracism. His recent publications include articles in *Science, Journal of Personality and Social Psychology, Journal of Experimental Social Psychology,* and *Law and Human Behavior.* He is also author of *Ostracism: The Power of Silence* and coeditor of several social psychology books, including the upcoming *The Social Outcast: Effects of Ostracism, Social Exclusion, Rejection, and Bullying.*

Contributors

Robert M. Bray, PhD, Research Triangle Institute, Research Triangle Park, North Carolina

Neil Brewer, PhD, School of Psychology, Flinders University, Adelaide, South Australia, Australia

Brian L. Cutler, PhD, Department of Psychology, University of North Carolina, Charlotte, Charlotte, North Carolina

Erin M. Danielsen, MS, Department of Psychology, Florida International University, Miami, Florida

Jason J. Dickinson, PhD, Department of Psychology, Montclair State University, Upper Montclair, New Jersey

Ronald P. Fisher, PhD, Department of Psychology, Florida International University, Miami, Florida

Lynne ForsterLee, PhD, School of Psychology and Sociology, Central Queensland University, Rockhampton, Australia

Robert ForsterLee, MA, School of Psychology and Sociology, Central Queensland University, Rockhampton, Australia

Maryanne Garry, PhD, School of Psychology, Victoria University of Wellington, Wellington, New Zealand

Matthew P. Gerrie, BSc(Hons), School of Psychology, Victoria University of Wellington, Wellington, New Zealand

Morris Goldsmith, PhD, Department of Psychology, University of Haifa, Haifa, Israel

Jane Goodman-Delahunty, JD, PhD, School of Psychology, University of New South Wales, Sydney, Australia

Pär Anders Granhag, PhD, Department of Psychology, Göteborg University, Göteborg, Sweden

Andrew Jones, BSc(Hons), Department of Psychology, Macquarie University, Sydney, Australia

Norbert L. Kerr, PhD, Department of Psychology, Michigan State University, East Lansing, Michigan

Asher Koriat, PhD, Department of Psychology, University of Haifa, Haifa, Israel

Margaret Bull Kovera, PhD, Department of Psychology, John Jay College of Criminal Justice, The City University of New York, New York, New York

Rachel L. Laimon, MS, Department of Psychology, Central Michigan University, Mt. Pleasant, Michigan

Lora M. Levett, MS, Department of Psychology, John Jay College of Criminal Justice, The City University of New York, New York, New York

Elizabeth F. Loftus, PhD, Department of Psychology and Social Behavior, University of California, Irvine, Irvine, California

James R. P. Ogloff, JD, PhD, Monash University and Victorian Institute of Forensic Mental Health, Thomas Embling Hospital, Fairfield, Victoria, Australia

Ainat Pansky, PhD, Department of Psychology, University of Haifa, Haifa, Israel

Steven D. Penrod, JD, PhD, Department of Psychology, John Jay College of Criminal Justice, The City University of New York, New York, New York

Debra A. Poole, PhD, Department of Psychology, Central Michigan University, Mt. Pleasant, Michigan

Martine B. Powell, PhD, School of Psychology, Deakin University, Burwood, Victoria, Australia

V. Gordon Rose, LLM, PhD, Department of Psychology, Simon Fraser University, Burnaby, British Columbia, Canada

Carolyn Semmler, PhD, School of Psychology, Flinders University, Adelaide, South Australia, Australia

Christina A. Studebaker, PhD, MLS, The Chicago School of Professional Psychology, Chicago, Illinois

Aldert Vrij, PhD, Department of Psychology, University of Portsmouth, Portsmouth, United Kingdom

Nathan Weber, PhD, School of Psychology, Flinders University, Adelaide, South Australia, Australia

Gary L. Wells, PhD, Department of Psychology, Iowa State University, Ames, Iowa

Kipling D. Williams, PhD, Department of Psychological Sciences, Purdue University, West Lafayette, Indiana

Rebecca Wright, BA(Hons), School of Psychology, Deakin University, Burwood, Victoria, Australia

Acknowledgments

Preparation of this volume was helped considerably by the following research grants: ARC Large Grant (A00104516) to Neil Brewer and Gary L. Wells; ARC Discovery Grant (A00104516) to Neil Brewer, Kipling D. Williams, and Lynne ForsterLee; and a Flinders University Small Grant to Neil Brewer and Kipling D. Williams.

We gratefully acknowledge the support of Flinders University (Neil Brewer) and Macquarie University (Kipling D. Williams) during the preparation of this volume; the assistance of Sarah Hollitt for her diligent reference checking and formatting of all chapters; all of the contributors for their cooperation; and Seymour Weingarten, Editor-in-Chief of The Guilford Press, for his interest in the project.

Contents

Contents

CHAPTER ONE

Psychology and Law Research

An Overview

NEIL BREWER
KIPLING D. WILLIAMS
CAROLYN SEMMLER

This volume explores the contributions of psychological theory and empirical research to advancing our understanding of a diverse array of practices and processes within the criminal justice system. Underpinning this exploration is the basic premise that such understanding is crucial for the development of effective practices within the legal system. Much of the research described is firmly based in the traditions of experimental psychology. This approach reflects the view that carefully controlled experimental work is crucial for the advancement of psychological knowledge and understanding—and, in turn, for meaningful practical progress.

Our hope is that this book will serve a number of purposes for the reader. At a general level, it is intended to (1) illustrate how theoretical advances in the broad fields of experimental psychology can provide valuable directions for applied research, (2) highlight many of the methodological difficulties with which applied researchers are confronted, and (3) show how carefully controlled experimental research can be used to make meaningful contributions to the solution of everyday or real-world problems. At a more specific level, this volume is designed to provide readers with an up-to-date knowledge base on developments in diverse areas of experimental psychology (e.g., cognitive, developmental, and social psychology) that is relevant to practices within the various sectors of the criminal justice system. Furthermore, some of the major contemporary research developments in psychology and law are highlighted, and readers are acquainted with the specific practical possibilities that are sug-

1

gested by recent research. We should warn, however, that the contributors do not take a clinical–forensic perspective; offender characteristics, offender assessment and management, or other related issues are not discussed. This book is not a legal text; it is, quite simply, an examination of the application of psychological science to issues and problems within the criminal justice system.

We hope that a diverse array of readers will find the book useful. Certainly we believe that it should be a valuable resource for advanced-level undergraduate and postgraduate students undertaking coursework and research in psychology and law. Additionally, we believe that the mixture of comprehensive overviews of theory and research, and the challenges laid out for future research, should stimulate more experienced researchers in the various fields covered in these pages. Finally, we are just a little hopeful that the breadth of coverage and the general readability will allow the book to serve as a useful resource for students in various criminal justice, police science/administration, legal studies and law programs, as well as for various professionals within the criminal justice system, including senior police, lawyers, and the judiciary.

The sequence of chapters roughly parallels the sequence of events that occur between the commission of a crime and the judge's sentencing of a defendant. In Chapter 2, Martine B. Powell, Ronald P. Fisher, and Rebecca Wright focus on two major aspects of investigative interviewing. First, they examine the four most widely agreed-upon features for the successful interviewing of witnesses: (1) the establishment of good rapport with the interviewee; (2) clear descriptions of the rules of the interview process; (3) the use of an open-ended questioning style; and (4) the interviewer's willingness to explore alternative hypotheses regarding the events under consideration. Powell et al. describe in detail the reasoning behind the use of each practice, using evidence from research and anecdotal reports from interviewers and witnesses. Second, they consider the extent to which police personnel adhere to these principles of good interviewing and review studies that have evaluated the effectiveness of training programs designed to teach these principles. In general, they conclude that police seldom strictly observe the good principles of interviewing. Evidence gathered from around the world shows that the use of the open-ended-question format is rare and that interviewers are often biased toward particular hypotheses in their investigations. The authors recommend that training programs should use highly structured training protocols, incorporate multiple opportunities for practice, and provide supervision feedback on interviewing techniques. They also draw on research from other organizational settings and instructional contexts as a basis for their suggestions about the most efficacious training regimes.

In Chapter 3 Pär Anders Granhag and Aldert Vrij explore the literature on the detection of deception. They examine people's beliefs regarding deception, gleaned from surveys of experts (e.g., police and judges) and laypeople that highlight a focus on behaviors associated with nervousness. The major reason identified for the overwhelming tendency to rely on nervous behavior as an indicator of deception is that, in many contexts, there is a paucity of balanced feedback about the accuracy of lie detection. They review (1) the use of verbal or content-based methods for detecting deception (e.g., Statement Validity Assessment and Criteria-Based Content Analysis), techniques that demonstrate high accuracy but await support from real-life cases; (2) a promising technique for assessing verbal veracity, based on principles of Reality Monitoring (from memory research); and (3) the most popular polygraph techniques (Control Questions Technique and Guilty Knowledge Test), including reasons for their differing rates of classifying guilty-versus-innocent suspects. Granhag and Vrij's examination of objective indicators of deception and truth focuses on the three major emotional states that people may experience when telling the truth and lying, highlighting the absence of objective cues that are systematically related to lying. Verbal cues to lying are also discussed (including the consistency of the story presented and the order in which the events are reported). The strategies of liars and truth tellers have a central role in determining the content and behavior associated with their communications, so that understanding how memory is involved in deception may improve the accuracy of detection. Finally, Granhag and Vrij review the effectiveness of training strategies for improving detection of deception, highlighting useful approaches for increasing accuracy rates.

Although eyewitness memory is probably considered by many to be one of the most substantial research areas in the psychology–law domain, a detailed breakdown of existing research is likely to reveal heavy emphases on the topics of eyewitness identification and false memory (or misinformation), topics covered in Chapters 6 and 7 of this volume, but not a great deal of systematic coverage of many other important memory issues. In Chapter 4, Ainat Pansky, Asher Koriat, and Morris Goldsmith took up the editors' challenge to provide us with a broader direction for research on eyewitness recall and testimony, producing a framework that is much more representative of the broad field of memory theory and research. Pansky et al. emphasize the distinction between quantity-oriented and accuracy-oriented approaches to the study of memory, arguing that the accuracy-based approach to memory is particularly important in the forensic or legal setting. They make the key point that most real-world situations allow the individual to determine the type and amount of information they report. Variables affecting encoding and, hence, the quantity and quality of information remembered, such as the physical characteristics of the stimulus, distinctiveness of the stimulus, amount of attention allocated to the stimulus at study, and whether the stimulus is learned intentionally or incidentally, are reviewed. Likewise, variables such as elaboration and schema-based processing of stimuli, which can increase memory quantity but also reduce accuracy, are considered. Factors affecting the retention of information are examined, including effects on quantity and quality of retention interval, the interpolation or retelling of events, and repeated testing. Retrieval related factors are divided into those that play a role in forced versus free reporting of information. Pansky et al. show that retrieval cues—that is, aspects of the rememberers' environment that drive the retrieval process—can improve the quantity of information retrieved, but can both enhance and inhibit accuracy.

Finally, the authors devote considerable attention to witnesses' subjective monitoring of their own memory and how it operates during encoding, storage, and retrieval phases, emphasizing that witnesses' ability to differentiate between correct and incorrect information and to regulate the reporting of that information is of pivotal importance for accuracy. They discuss some of the clues that individuals use when monitoring the correctness of recalled information (i.e., their confidence), including the content of the information recalled, perceptual fluency, and retrieval fluency, and discuss the way in which witnesses may control the reporting of recalled information (e.g., whether to volunteer the remembered information or withhold it; what level of detail they choose to report). In conclusion, the chapter focuses on the joint contribution that research into memory quantity and accuracy and metacognitive control can make toward advancing our understanding of eyewitness testimony. Although much of the research presented in this chapter was not conducted in the eyewitness domain, the principles outlined have broad application to eyewitness reports and provide a necessary framework for future research.

Chapter 5 highlights how research can dispel some common misconceptions regarding children's eyewitness testimony and recall. Jason J. Dickinson, Debra A. Poole, and Rachel L. Laimon review two major aspects of the literature on children's testimony: (1) children's recall ability when no misinformation has been introduced, and (2) children's susceptibility to misinformation. Using research findings from the many studies of children's testimony and selected interview transcripts from studies conducted in their own laboratory, Dickinson et al. illustrate the complexities of the variables that are controlled by interviewers (e.g., question format) and the changing abilities of the child (e.g., the child's ability to comprehend the questions asked by interviewers and to maintain rules set down by the interviewers). Among the misconceptions addressed here are the ideas that (1) preschool children are more suggestible than school-age children to the effects of misinformation on their memory accuracy, (2) children who report more details are necessarily more accurate than children who report less, and (3) "off-topic" talk and omission of details are indicative of children's memory repression or embarrassment regarding abuse. The authors suggest that broad generalizations about the accuracy of children's memory cannot be applied to specific cases, because there are difficulties in reducing and applying the often complex research findings. Instead, they suggest that psychologists can best offer a balanced view of children's abilities and alternative explanations for the type of information that children typically give to interviewers, rather than "rules of thumb" about the likely accuracy of specific reports.

In Chapter 6, Neil Brewer, Nathan Weber, and Carolyn Semmler consider the topic of eyewitness identification. Their examination of the relevant literature covers the various stages of the identification process that unfold in the real world—although this process is conducted against the backdrop of important methodological shortfalls in the extant research. These shortfalls include the restricted set of stimulus and lineup conditions that characterize most studies, the often underpowered experiments, and the importance of having some reasonable real-world estimates of the proportion of perpetrator- or target-absent lineups that occur. Brewer et al. examine issues that surround the witnessed event: that is, variables related to offender (e.g., changed appearance, distinctiveness), witness (e.g., age), and situation (e.g., viewing conditions, cross-race identifications). Then they focus on a number of the experiences that can intervene between the event and the identification test. Subsequently they consider the conduct of the identification test itself, examining the influence of social factors, lineup instructions, lineup composition, and lineup presentation mode. Characteristics of the identification decision that can serve as markers of likely identification accuracy—namely, identification latency and confidence—are examined. Finally, the authors consider the influence of events that occur subsequent to the identification test—for example, postidentification feedback—that can exert an important influence on witnesses' posttest assessments of their identification confidence and on various other perceptions of the witnessed event. One dominant theme pervades their review of the empirical research. Despite the relatively large volume of research on eyewitness identification, it is clear that theoretical issues have taken a backseat to practical considerations, with the consequence that even after many years of research, we do not have any particularly well-developed theories of the identification decision process. This deficiency means that we have a relatively poor understanding of how key variables interact, particularly with regard to the shaping of eyewitness choosing behavior at the time of the identification test. But it also means that some of the paths for future research are obvious.

Matthew P. Gerrie, Maryanne Garry, and Elizabeth F. Loftus review and analyze the literature on false memories in Chapter 7. Coverage includes the effects of suggestive questioning, introduction of nonexistent objects into memory, and transformation of specific details for an event in memory. Cognitive and social moderators of the misinformation effect are considered. The former include quality of memory for the event (particularly for central details), attention to the postevent information, and the extent to which the misinformation fits with witnesses' event schemas; the latter include the credibility, power, and social attractiveness of the source of the information. Gerrie et al. also examine the debate over the appropriate theoretical accounts of the misinformation effect, outlining evidence suggesting that the effect has a memory component and is not simply a matter of the conscious acceptance of the misinformation—that is, witnesses tend to accept the "planted" memories as real and retain them as memories over time. Finally, the authors explore issues surrounding false memories, with a particular focus on the controversy sur-

rounding recovered memories for sexual abuse. They present research showing that vivid, detailed false memories for highly significant childhood events
(e.g., being lost in a shopping mall, having a balloon ride, and seeing someone
being possessed by demons) can be fairly easily created, and they review research from neuroimaging studies that suggest that the parts of the brain involved in imagining are the same as those used when actually experiencing
events.

Considerable publicity often accompanies a crime and the defendant, in
the lead-up to a trial, and this publicity often leads to conjecture about how
such publicity may affect jurors' judgments. In Chapter 8, Christina A. Studebaker and Steven D. Penrod examine the effects of pretrial publicity on juror
judgments. First they describe the type and amount of pretrial publicity that
may exist (particularly in the United States), using content analyses of newspapers and surveys of jurors as a basis for their conclusions. They demonstrate
that the amount of pretrial publicity can be high in the immediate locality
where the events took place, although surrounding areas may be relatively
protected from such publicity. They then examine existing research on the impact of pretrial publicity on the pretrial and trial judgments, research involving both field studies and experimental methods. The studies reveal that information that casts doubt on the character of the defendant can affect the
likelihood that jurors will return a guilty verdict. Studebaker and Penrod review the effectiveness of various "safeguards" for preventing or reducing the
impact of pretrial publicity. These include the use of legal sanctions on the
media to limit the information that can be published, extensions of the delay
before the trial begins, extended questioning of jurors and the provision of judicial instructions to potential jurors pretrial, and the moderating effects of
the presentation of the actual trial evidence on the impact of prejudicial information. In general, sanctions and safeguards have been largely ineffective and
sometimes even inflate the effect of prejudicial information on jurors' judgments. The authors then present a theoretical framework, loosely based on
research in social persuasion, to understand the reasons why pretrial publicity
has an impact on juror judgments. They divide the variables into three categories: those that characterize the source of the pretrial information (e.g., expertise and credibility), the message content (e.g., information about the defendant's prior convictions or the type of charge being brought against the
defendant), and the medium in which the message is presented (e.g., print or
video). Studebaker and Penrod highlight the lack of systematic research on
many of these key issues.

Chapter 9 is concerned with trial strategy and tactics, with Kipling D.
Williams and Andrew Jones applying social persuasion theory to the courtroom context to illustrate when lawyers' persuasion attempts are likely to be
effective. The chapter is largely organized around Petty and Cacciopo's elaboration likelihood model, which proposes two routes to persuasion: the central
route, which involves effortful processing of the available information, and
the peripheral route, which is less effortful and involves the use of "rules of

thumb." Short-term attitudes are considered most relevant to the trial tactician because they are specific and more predictive of behavior, easier to
change, and not limited by legal sanctions. The most effective route to persuasion is likely to depend on the strength of the argument. Weak arguments may
be best presented using tactics that encourage peripheral route persuasion,
whereas strong arguments may be best presented to encourage central-route
processing. Williams and Jones also examine tactics likely to enable and dis-
able central-route processing. The chapter also reviews research on several
other issues: the effects of peripheral cues (e.g., source credibility, trustworthiness and expertise, or number of arguments presented); how jury deliberation
may affect processing routes; and tactics used to influence jurors and discredit
opponents. In sum, the chapter provides a wide-ranging exposition of how social persuasion theory and research can be applied to understand the tactics
and outcomes of jury trials, and it highlights an array of interesting research
issues.

Researchers conducting experimental investigations in the psychology
and law domain are regularly confronted with the criticism that their research
lacks external validity. Furthermore, it is often suggested that experimental or
laboratory studies are so far removed from the complexities of the justice system that their findings have limited applicability. The general themes of these
criticisms are that (1) typical jury simulations are highly artificial, (2) the ecological validity of such studies can be called into question, (3) field research on
juries is likely to be much more informative and ecologically valid than simulation research, and (4) if experimental jury simulations are to be employed at
all, they must achieve a much higher level of realism. In 1982, Norbert L. Kerr
and Robert M. Bray explored these and an array of related issues in depth.
Here, in Chapter 10, they revisit and update that discussion, providing a comprehensive analysis of the criticisms of experimental simulations of jury behavior. These authors provide an overview of the type of methods most commonly used by researchers on the jury decision-making process, noting that
the majority of studies has been unrealistic (e.g., students as jurors, trial materials that are brief written summaries or audiotaped excerpts of trials, use of
both continuous and categorical verdict measures, and the primary unit of
analysis focused on individual jurors rather than juries). Nevertheless, Kerr
and Bray discuss the potential advantages and contributions of experimental
methods and unrealistic trial simulations compared with field studies and
more realistic trial simulations (and the disadvantages). They point out how
some of these limitations can be overcome and show that empirical comparisons of various methodological distinctions (e.g., student-vs.-juror-based samples, mode of presentation of materials) do not produce changes in important
dependent variables, nor do they show realism by treatment interactions.

In Chapter 11, Lora M. Levett, Erin M. Danielsen, Margaret Bull Kovera,
and Brian L. Cutler offer a wide-ranging review of the research on juror decision making. They examine the way that jurors and juries make decisions: using an evidence-based focus or a verdict-based focus; the use of informational-

vs.-normative influence during deliberations; the influence of jury size; and whether the jury is required to reach a unanimous or a majority verdict. They also review the two major theoretical models of juror decision making: mathematical models (including probabilistic, algebraic, and stochastic models) and explanation or cognitive models (namely, the story model developed by Pennington and Hastie). They conclude that the story model provides a better fit to describe what jurors actually do in trials (because it can, among other things, account for multiple elements considered within a trial). The chapter then considers whether jurors, in criminal cases, are competent at evaluating different types of evidence (including eyewitness, hearsay, confession, statistical, complex, and expert evidence) and examines extraevidential influences on juror decision making in criminal trials (e.g., defendant characteristics, such as attractiveness, race, and socioeconomic status, and factors that can produce interactions between the defendant and the jurors). Decision making of juries in civil trials is also considered, with the evidence again showing that juries are sometimes influenced by extralegal factors when they must render liability judgments and award damages. Levett et al. conclude that there is generally good agreement between juries and the alternative decision maker (a judge), and that research should focus on ways of improving the ability of jurors to make good decisions, rather than dwelling on areas in which they lack good judgment.

James R. P. Ogloff and V. Gordon Rose discuss the comprehension of jury instructions in Chapter 12. They assess research that has examined actual jurors' ability to understand instructions (through posttrial questionnaires, field studies of jurors' queries of judges during trials, and judges' reports of their impressions of jurors' comprehension) and mock jurors' ability to understand actual instructions. Their conclusion is that jurors (actual and mock) have very poor levels of comprehension regarding jury instructions (in both criminal and civil law cases). Although the legal profession often rejects the usefulness of simulation studies—because they focus on juror, not jury, behavior—and suggests that, collectively, jurors will get it right, Ogloff and Rose argue that deliberation may actually harm comprehension of instructions and certainly does not improve it. The authors carefully examine various strategies used in an effort to improve comprehension of jury instructions—strategies that have met with mixed success. These strategies include the redrafting of instructions into "plain language," allowing juror note taking, providing preliminary instructions to juries, and providing copies of instructions during deliberations. Finally, Ogloff and Rose review studies that have used flow-charts or decision trees to improve comprehension, and they underscore the potential application of these tools in the courtroom.

Dealing with the guilty offender is the focus of Chapter 13, authored by Jane Goodman-Delahunty, Lynne ForsterLee, and Robert ForsterLee. They review different approaches to punishment in sentencing: specifically, incapacitation (to prevent the criminal from reoffending), retribution, deterrence, rehabilitation, and restorative justice. The effects of these sentencing strategies on recidivism and perceptions of fairness of the victim and the community are examined (although the psychological aspects of these approaches have not been fully researched), with rehabilitation and restorative justice programs considered to be more effective at reducing recidivism and less costly than incarceration. Models of legal decision making in sentencing offenders are the other major focus of the chapter. Here, for example, Goodman-Delahunty et al. cover research on the effects of victim-impact statements on sentencing decisions and gender biases in sentencing. They show that heuristic biases can operate in judges' sentencing decisions, despite the requirement for impartiality, and that judges' individual decision styles have a strong effect and can help to explain discrepancies in sentencing decisions across judges. Psychological research on models of judicial sentencing is examined. Although there is no accepted model of judicial information processing, various models, based on decision making in other domains of cognitive and social psychology that have been used to elucidate judicial decision making, are reviewed.

Chapters 2–13 review psychological theory and research covering a number of substantive topics in psychology and law. The final chapter is a little different in focus: Chapter 14 considers how the outcomes of experimental psychological research can be brought to bear to influence legal policy. Gary L. Wells, using extensive experience gained from his involvement with the recent reforms to lineup procedures in several states in the United States, highlights some of the difficulties that social scientists may experience in applying their research. Wells concentrates on his own area of expertise, eyewitness identification tests, but many of the points are likely to be more generally applicable to other subareas of the field. The first issue discussed is the frequent poor fit between researchers' focus on the single effects of particular lineup practices on a dependent variable and the practical implications for the investigation and legal process more generally. For example, researchers may focus on the rate of mistaken identifications, without consideration of concerns for public safety and the rights of individuals to be quickly cleared of suspicion in an investigation. Wells uses the example of the "showup" (i.e., witness is shown a single suspect and asked whether or not he or she is the perpetrator): It may increase the rate of mistaken identifications compared to lineups, but its value lies in quickly clearing innocent suspects of suspicion and in detaining (and not re-releasing) perpetrators. Researchers are encouraged to study the full set of issues or constraints that policymakers must consider when formulating guidelines. Wells also urges researchers to consider who makes the reforms to procedures in the justice system. For example, in the eyewitness identification domain, there may be a focus on judges as policymakers, but it tends to be prosecutors who are most influential in changing the way that police collect evidence. The perceptions that the criminal justice community may hold about academic psychologists are also considered. The fact that eyewitness researchers often frame their research in terms of reducing rates of mistaken identifications, rather than on increasing correct identification decisions, has almost certainly led police and prosecutors to pay less attention to this research. Wells also provides suggestions on influencing policymakers. He reminds us that, in the eyewitness identification domain, the biggest influence on policymakers is provided by single cases of mistaken identification (i.e., the DNA exoneration cases) rather than by statistics quoted from experiments. Furthermore, for researchers to have an impact, they must not only show that current procedures are flawed but must also provide clear recommendations for a better procedure—and Wells provides specific suggestions for how to go about doing this.

Overall, this volume contains a variety of chapters that demonstrate that experimental psychology is making a rich contribution to a range of important issues for the criminal justice system. Such research has already advanced our understanding in a number of areas and provided guidelines for meaningful practical developments. Our hope is that the contributions in this volume will encourage researchers to continue this trend, thereby consolidating the interaction between psychological science and various levels of the legal system.

ACKNOWLEDGMENTS

This research was supported by Grant No. A00104516 from the Australian Research Council to Neil Brewer, Kipling D. Williams, and Lynne ForsterLee, and by a Flinders University Small Grant to Neil Brewer and Kipling D. Williams.

CHAPTER TWO

Investigative Interviewing

MARTINE B. POWELL
RONALD P. FISHER
REBECCA WRIGHT

Interviews are conducted at various stages of the investigative process, ranging from the initial police interview of a victim, witness, or suspect to an in-court interview in front of a judge or other decision maker. Interviews conducted during the initial phase of the police investigation are usually the most critical in determining whether a criminal case is solved (Fisher, Geiselman, & Raymond, 1987), especially when there is little or no physical evidence and only one witness to guide the investigation. At this point in the investigation, there is considerable potential to extract extensive, accurate information, because the event is still fresh and, hence, relatively accessible in the witnesses' memory. Furthermore, witnesses have had little time to think about the event, so their immediate perceptions are likely to be pristine, untainted by later influences. Properly conducted interviews may thus advance the police investigation immeasurably by eliciting thorough, accurate records of the crime details. On the other hand, poorly conducted interviews have the potential to distort the witnesses' memories and contaminate the entire investigative process. For this reason, initial police interviews with vulnerable witnesses (e.g., children or people with intellectual disabilities) are often recorded on videotape and presented as evidence-in-chief during the trial (Davies, Wilson, Mitchell, & Milsom, 1995).

Eliciting reliable and detailed information from a person about an alleged offense is a unique and complex process in which both the interviewer and interviewee play integral roles. Ultimately, the quality of any forensic interview is determined by a wide range of interrelated factors, which can be conceptualized broadly as (1) factors relating to the interviewee (i.e., the physical, mental, and emotional state of the interviewee at the time of the event and the interview), (2) factors relating to the interview, per se (e.g., the interview setting and the purpose of the interview), and (3) factors relating to the interviewer (e.g., questioning techniques, social status, degree of bias). Irrespective of the interview context and the interviewee's abilities, however, the onus always rests on the interviewer to maximize both the *quantity* and the *quality* of information that the interviewee can potentially provide. Maximizing the quantity and quality of information increases the likelihood of obtaining corroborative evidence to support the interviewee's account, thereby increasing the likelihood that successful prosecution will result. Although there is considerable variability in the abilities of individual interviewees, research over the past few decades has clearly defined the elements of all interviews that lead to best performance by each interviewee.

Several distinct interviewing protocols are currently used by police and other investigative interviewers; these have been developed for different interview populations and situations. For instance, the Step-wise Approach (Yuille, 1996; Yuille, Marxsen, & Cooper, 1999), the National Institute of Child Health and Human Development (NICHD) protocol (Sternberg, Lamb, Esplin, Orbach, & Hershkowitz, 2002), and the Guidance for Achieving Best Evidence in Criminal Proceedings (Home Office, 2002) were developed principally for interviewing child witnesses as young as 3 years of age as well as other vulnerable or intimidated witnesses (e.g., persons with intellectual disabilities, persons from different cultural backgrounds). Conversation Management (Shepherd, 1988) was designed to provide interviewers with the skills needed to elicit more information from a hostile witness (e.g., alleged offender). Specifically, it assists the interviewer to understand the witness's motivational blocks to volunteer information and to parry the witness's conversation-diverting tactics by redirecting the conversation to the task at hand. In contrast, the Cognitive Interview was developed mainly for the interviewing of cooperative adults (Fisher & Geiselman, 1992); however, it does contain some provisions for interviewing children. It is used primarily in situations in which the witness is genuinely attempting to recall and describe what he or she knows, but needs assistance to overcome the difficulties of remembering and describing the alleged offense in detail. Thus the Cognitive Interview is designed to assist the witness by providing memory-enhancing techniques (e.g., context reinstatement and imagery) and by facilitating communication (e.g., by encouraging the witness to convey his or her knowledge in a nonverbal output format).

Although each of the protocols has unique components specifically designed to suit its targeted psychological processes and interviewee populations, there is still considerable overlap in their approaches because the protocols are based on a common, public pool of knowledge derived from interviewing respondents. Some of this knowledge arises from experimental laboratory research and reflects controlled testing of specific interview techniques (e.g., context reinstatement). Typically, this research is conducted by cognitive and social psychologists and is directed toward the testing of formal theories of memory and communication. Other knowledge is more experiential and reflects the personal insights gained from conducting many interviews or from modeling the differences between effective and ineffective interviewers. This knowledge typically is the product of interviews conducted in real-world (uncontrolled) settings and reflects a more global and retroactive analysis of interview styles. In other words, the knowledge is more eclectic because it is collected from experts in a variety of interviewing disciplines in addition to criminal investigations (e.g., oral history, journalism, social work, medicine). Irrespective of the data-gathering technique, there has been considerable agreement across the experimental and experiential approaches about the most effective methods of conducting interviews. The first section of this chapter provides a brief summary of the four central areas of agreement among the protocols and provides a rationale for the importance of each element. Practical recommendations and further reading are also provided.

Finally, despite the presence of clearly defined "best-practice" guidelines in investigative interviewing, numerous concerns have been voiced over the past decade regarding the inappropriate questioning styles of investigative interviewers. These concerns have led several researchers in recent years to focus on the content, structure, and efficacy of training courses in investigative interviewing, as distinct from formal evaluations of the effect of various interview techniques. In the second section of this chapter, we review research regarding the effectiveness of investigative interviewers in adhering to best-practice guidelines. Furthermore, we describe the elements of professional training programs that are likely to maximize the ability of investigative interviewers to adhere to these guidelines.

COMMON ELEMENTS OF A GOOD
INVESTIGATIVE INTERVIEW PROTOCOL

Interview protocols are intended for use as guiding frameworks to support interviewers through the various stages of conducting an investigative interview with a specific population. The common elements inherent in each of the aforementioned protocols include (1) a good rapport between the interviewer and the interviewee, (2) a clear description of the interviewer's investigative needs, (3) an open-ended questioning style, and (4) a willingness to explore alternative hypotheses. The importance of each of these elements within the forensic context (including related research) is reviewed below.

Good Rapport between the Interviewer and Interviewee

Most clinicians and researchers agree that the more at ease the interviewee feels in the interview setting, the more information the person is likely to impart (Fisher & Geiselman, 1992; Wilson & Powell, 2001). This principle is especially true when the topic is sensitive or traumatic (e.g., when the interviewee is recalling a robbery or violent crime), or when the interviewee is fearful of the consequences that could arise from reporting the offense. When recalling emotional or personal events, respondents of all ages report that their principal concern is to feel heard, understood, and believed by the investigator (Federal Law Enforcement Training Center, 1992). Although an investigative interview is not designed to be therapeutic, eliciting a detailed account from an interviewee requires the development of a trusting relationship in which the interviewee knows that his or her "story" will be heard, accepted, and not judged. The importance of building a trusting relationship is especially relevant when interviewing people from cultural groups such as Australian Aborigines or Native Americans, who depend heavily on the existence of personal relationships and respect among others in their own society (Powell & Bartholomew, 2003). Building rapport is considered so important that it is listed as a discrete training phase in most prominent investigative interview protocols (see Poole & Lamb, 1998). In other words, the initial phase of most interview protocols is devoted solely to developing a positive interviewer–interviewee relationship.

Establishing good rapport with an interviewee should not compromise professionalism or impartiality (Gudjonsson, 1992). Even among people from vulnerable minority groups, those police officers who earn the most respect and cooperation are described as courteous, fair, honest, and respectful of their different traditions and value systems (Powell, 2000). An interviewer who shows acceptance of the interviewee's background and cultural/ethnic differences reduces the interviewee's subjective experience of threat, thereby increasing his or her willingness to cooperate in the interview process. Evidence of this acceptance is displayed by a sensitive and flexible response to the interviewee's needs (when appropriate), showing goodwill (without being patronizing), listening carefully to the interviewee (i.e., showing the interviewee that he or she has been heard and understood), and not assuming that the interviewee is familiar with various legal or interview procedures (Powell, 2000).

Establishing rapport within a single interview is difficult, especially when the interviewer and interviewee have no prior relationship. The problem is compounded by an obvious power imbalance that characterizes most police interviews. Difficulties also arise in response to the interviewer's status or authority, which may be inherently associated with fear (e.g., fear of punishment or fear of being taken away from one's community or family). Such fears are heightened in young children and people from social minority groups (see Powell & Bartholomew, 2003; Powell, Wilson, Croft, & Gibbons, 2003).

There is little empirical research to indicate precisely how interviewers should establish rapport, mainly because of the ethical considerations entailed in experimentally manipulating whether a witness is made to feel comfortable or intimidated. The primary contribution of research has thus been to define the three aims of the rapport-building phase:

1. The interviewee does most of the talking.
2. The interviewer conveys understanding, acceptance, noncoerciveness, and a nonjudgmental perspective.
3. The interviewer creates an informal and relaxed context.

First, during the rapport-building phase of the interview it is important that the interviewee does most of the talking. For instance, in the NICHD and Step-wise interview protocols, interviewers are instructed to elicit a detailed free-narrative account from a child witness about an innocuous event such as a holiday or birthday party (McCauley & Fisher, 1995; Poole & Lamb, 1998). An open-ended style of interaction in this phase conveys the impression that the interview is interviewee-focused. This impression, in turn, promotes more elaborate responses to subsequent questions during the main part of the interview about the alleged offense (see Sternberg et al., 1997). From a linguistic perspective, an open-ended style of questioning also has the advantage of providing the interviewer with a reliable gauge of the interviewee's verbal fluency and ability to describe prior experiences (Cooke, 1996; Walker, 1999). This gauge is especially important when the interviewee has significant cognitive or language deficits, or may require the assistance of an interpreter. Questions that elicit brief or stereotypical responses (e.g., "What's your favorite subject at school?", "Who is your teacher?") may mask language weaknesses that are likely to surface during the main phase of the interview, when the linguistic task demands are more pronounced. Indeed, recent research has shown that juvenile offender populations have significant oral language impairment compared to mainstream age-matched control samples, and this impairment is not usually detected when interviewers ask specific (i.e., short-answer) questions—which, unfortunately, is the more common technique used during the rapport-building phase of forensic interviews (Snow & Powell, in press).

Second, in the initial phase of the interview a relationship needs to be established in which the interviewer is understanding and accepting of the interviewee's responses and conveys a noncoercive and nonjudgmental perspective. Due to the heightened social status and power of police, many interviewees have a strong desire to please the interviewer and to provide whatever information is desired. This is especially the case with witnesses who have low social status or communication barriers—for example, children (Ceci & Bruck, 1993), people with intellectual disabilities (Agnew & Powell, 2004; Henry & Gudjonsson, 1999), and people from cultural minority groups (Cooke, 1996; Powell, 2000). Interviewers may reduce the detrimental effect of social demand characteristics by being friendly and attentive, avoiding emotional reactions to comments, and avoiding any display of attitudes or beliefs about the interviewee (Ceci, Powell, & Principe, 2002).

Third, good interviewer–interviewee rapport is just as dependent on the interview context as it is on the qualities and questioning style of the individual interviewer. Any diminution in formality of manner and language is likely to decrease intimidation and anxiety, particularly when the interview is conducted at a relaxed pace in which silence is tolerated and the interviewee is free to respond without pressure. Indeed, research has shown that memory performance is improved when the person interviewed is in a relaxed, as opposed to a tense, environment (de Quervain, Roozendaal, Nitsch, McGaugh, & Hock, 2000; Saywitz & Nathanson, 1993). Anecdotally, anthropologists and linguists have noted that persons from cultural minority groups perform better when interviewed in familiar environments (Eades, 1992). Creating an ideal interview environment involves considering, in advance, the relevant cultural, cognitive, and linguistic factors that may affect the interview. Establishing the proper interview environment also involves (1) recognizing signs of awkwardness, intimidation, embarrassment, and discomfort, and (2) eliciting from interviewees ideas about how to make the interview process easier for them (Powell, 2000).

A Clear Description of the "Rules" of the Interview Process

Investigative interviewers often report frustration that witnesses do not volunteer much specific information (Kebbell & Milne, 1998), even in those interviews where good rapport is established. There are at least two reasons why this reticence occurs. First, the forensic interview procedure is alien to many people because it contains rules that violate normal conversational processes (e.g., the importance of reporting highly specific details). In most interviews with professionals (e.g., doctors and other health professionals), the interviewer usually knows more about the topic than does the interviewee, and the interviewer directs the content of the interview in order to elicit information required for a specific diagnosis. This process is different from a forensic interview, where the goal is to minimize interviewer input and to encourage the witness to tell everything he or she knows about an event, about which the interviewer knows little or nothing.

The second reason why witnesses do not convey as much information as they possess in investigative interviews is that the kinds of detail usually required for police investigations (e.g., descriptions of people's appearance and clothing, contextual and temporal details) are difficult to provide. For example, adult witnesses to crimes are usually asked to provide detailed descriptions of a person's appearance (particularly, facial details). Although adults can discriminate among many different details (e.g., face shapes, skin tone), most languages contain few words to adequately describe variations in these aspects. The same limitation occurs in other domains, for example, movements and intervals in time. Adults can often make very accurate perceptual discriminations, even though they have difficulty describing these experiences (Leibowitz, Guzy, Peterson, & Blake, 1993). Not surprisingly, this problem is compounded when witnesses have cognitive limitations and poor verbal skills, such as occurs with children or recent immigrants who are asked to describe an event in their second or third language. It is well established that when vulnerable interviewees are pressured to recall highly specific details, they are more prone to fabrication or an acceptance of false details—perhaps to appear competent or to complete the interview (Ceci & Bruck, 1993; Eades, 1995). Yes/no and forced-choice questions are particularly problematic, because interviewees can merely choose an answer to please the interviewer. Similar concepts can be found among linguists and anthropologists (referred to as "gratuitous concurrence"; Eades, 1995), and child eyewitness memory researchers (referred to as "affirmation bias" or "acquiescence bias"; Poole & Lindsay, 1995).

The implication of these findings is that, irrespective of the interviewee, all interviewers need to convey their investigative needs clearly. If investigative interviewers require detailed descriptions of events (more detailed than normally expected in casual social exchanges), then they need to instruct witnesses explicitly to adopt a different level of discourse than is the norm. That is, witnesses need to be instructed to volunteer *all* information and not to edit or withhold information because they believe it is irrelevant or because it contradicts an earlier response. At the same time, interviewers need to caution witnesses about the dangers of guessing or fabricating. Other important rules include instructing witnesses to indicate when they do not know an answer or do not understand a question, to use any words they want to use (including slang or swear words), and to correct the interviewer if he or she says something that is wrong. The most common instructions recommended by trainers are summarized in Table 2.1.

Providing simple instructions regarding the rules of the interview (such as those presented in Table 2.1) are important, but their effectiveness should not be overestimated. Simple instructions are particularly limited with young children, who often require the use of intensive and multifaceted training packages (including repeated, elaborate instructions accompanied by practice and feedback in the use of the strategies) to alter their patterns of responding so that they are more in line with the rules of the investigative interview process (Ellis, Powell, Thomson, & Jones, 2003). The downside of such intensive training and instruction is that it is time consuming and it forces the interviewee to play a more passive role, which is opposite to the social dynamic that should be achieved at the beginning of the interview. Furthermore, training children not to guess responses can lead them to answer "I don't know" to questions that they might otherwise have answered correctly (Gee, Gregory, & Pipe, 1999; Nesbitt & Markham, 1999; Saywitz & Moan-Hardie, 1994). For these reasons, most trainers in the investigative interviewing of children recommend that interviewers use simple instructions rather than multifaceted training packages (Poole & Lamb, 1998; Wilson & Powell, 2001). Although we encourage interviewers to offer these instructions at the beginning of the interview, it is even more important for interviewers to follow up with proper questioning techniques, because much of the value of proper initial instructions will be undermined by poor questioning technique.

TABLE 2.1. Common Misunderstandings in Investigative Interviews

Misunderstanding	Instruction for overcoming misunderstanding
Interviewees (particularly children and people with an intellectual disability) may be hesitant to correct the interviewer because they believe the interviewer knows best.	The interviewer needs to stress that he or she does not know what has happened and that, if the interviewer says something wrong, the interviewee should correct him or her.
Interviewees often do not know the level of detail that is required in investigative interviews and may believe that minor descriptive details are not important.	The interviewer should explicitly state that he or she was not there when the alleged event happened and that the more the interviewee can report, the better. Anything the interviewee remembers could be useful, even little things that the interviewee does not think are important, and even if something is not the "whole" answer.
Interviewees may believe that it is acceptable to make up a response.	The interviewee should be encouraged to say "I don't know" or "I don't remember" when applicable.
When a question, or part thereof, is repeated in an interview, the interviewee may assume that his or her initial response was incorrect and should be changed.	The interviewer should say, "If I ask a question again, it doesn't mean I want you to change your answer. Just tell me what you remember the best you can."
The interviewee may believe that it is not acceptable to use slang or swear words or sexually explicit language, even when these words are the only words available to describe the offense.	The interviewee should be informed that he or she can use any words that work, and that the interviewer will not be shocked, angry, or upset.
Sometimes interviewees will say they do not know the answer to a question when, in fact, they do not understand the question.	The interviewer should explicitly state that he or she does not mind rephrasing questions.
Interviewees may not report information if they think the interviewer knows the information already.	The interviewer should say, "Even if you think I already know something, please tell me anyway."

Open-Ended Questioning Style

All prominent interview protocols acknowledge that the most useful information obtained in any forensic interview is that which is given in a free narrative response (see Milne & Bull, 1999, for a review). Furthermore, they state that a free-narrative account should be obtained prior to asking any specific questions. A free narrative is obtained when interviewees are encouraged to provide an account of the event or situation in their own words, at their own pace, and without interruption (Fisher, 1995). The account generally proceeds with the interviewer asking a broad, open-ended question (e.g., "Tell me everything you can remember about [the event]. Start at the beginning. What was the first thing that happened?"). The interviewer then uses minimal nonverbal encouragers (e.g., head nods, pauses, silence, "Mmmm," "Uh-huh") and additional open-ended statements or questions (e.g., "Tell me more about that," "What happened then?" "What else can you remember about?") to steer the interviewee to the next point in the story or to gently encourage the interviewee to provide additional narrative information. *Open-ended* questions refer to questions that require multiple-word responses and allow interviewees the flexibility to choose which aspects of the event they will describe. Once the interviewee has reached the end of the story, he or she is usually guided back to parts of the narrative and provided with the opportunity for further recall (e.g., "You said Billy touched you; tell me more about that"). The importance of these prompts is that they are general. They focus the interviewee on a particular part of the account but do not dictate or imply which specific information is required. In contrast, specific questions ask about a particular detail or concept and can be answered in one or two words (e.g., "What was that man's name?"). Closed questions are specific questions that have a limited number of response alternatives; these include multiple-choice (option posing) and yes/no questions (Poole & Lamb, 1998).

The benefits of eliciting a free narrative compared to more focused or brief responses are fourfold. First, responses to open-ended questions are usually more accurate than responses to specific or closed questions (Lipton, 1977). The heightened accuracy of responses to open-ended questions has been demonstrated empirically in research using unstructured interviews that mimic the pattern of real-world interviews (Fisher, Falkner, Trevisan, & McCauley, 2000), as well as experimentally controlled interviews that equate for the specific items being probed (Phillips, Fisher, & Schwartz, 1999; see Fisher, 1995, for a methodological analysis). The greater accuracy of answers to open-ended questions may occur because the resulting free-narrative format allows the witness to use a more stringent metacognitive level of control, or because the retrieval process is less influenced by external contamination (i.e., the interviewer). Second, specific questions (to which responses generally require fewer words compared to open-ended questions) can lead interviewers to underestimate the witness's language limitations, especially when the witness adopts strategies to conceal those limitations. For example, interviewees may repeat phrases or words used by the interviewer, provide stereotypical responses, or give affirmative answers to yes/no questions even when they do not understand the questions (Snow & Powell, in press).

Third, open-ended questioning, which is conducted at the interviewee's own pace, allows the interviewee time to collect his or her thoughts and consequently promotes more elaborate memory retrieval. Given that witnesses have only limited mental resources with which to process information, any distraction or deflection of these mental resources may impair the ability to remember the critical event (Broadbent, 1958; Kahneman, 1973). Excessive questioning—as opposed to asking fewer, but open-ended questions—is therefore distracting for witnesses, because the questions redirect their attention from searching internally through memory to focusing externally on the interviewer's next question. Formulating many short-answer questions also is likely to take its toll on the interviewer, who also has limited mental resources (Fisher, 1999). Directing those limited mental resources to formulating many questions—rather than listening intently to the witness's narrative response to open-ended questions—ought to increase the difficulty of understanding or notating the witness's responses (Briggs, Peters, & Fisher, 1972). In this light, it is not surprising that interviewers who ask fewer, but open-ended, questions elicit the greatest amount of information from witnesses (Fisher, Geiselman, & Amador, 1989).

Although free-narrative reports typically provide the most accurate information, they invariably do not provide all the information that the investigator needs. Hence, interviewers usually follow up free-narrative reports with more focused questions to elicit as-yet-unreported details (e.g., where and when the event took place, exacting descriptions of perpetrators, and precisely what happened: George & Clifford, 1992). Although these follow-up specific questions are required to elicit a more complete description of the event, they are more prone to elicit erroneous answers than open-ended questions, especially when the interviewer does not phrase questions appropriately. Recommended strategies for the interviewer to minimize error include (1) making the topic or information that is requested clear at all times, (2) using the interviewee's terminology, (3) simplifying the language, (4) watching carefully for signs of fatigue and poor concentration—and scheduling frequent breaks, and (5) using meaningful labels for concepts related to distance, time, and number (see Fisher & Geiselman, 1992; Walker, 1999). Generally, the less restricted the answer to a question, or the less the interviewer imposes a view of what happened, the lower the potential for errors or misunderstanding. Chapters 4 and 5 of this book provide a more detailed description of the impact of various types of specific questions on memory.

Willingness to Explore Alternative Hypotheses

Any interview conducted for the purpose of gathering accurate and reliable information about an event or situation should be regarded as an exercise in testing alternative hypotheses. Just as scientists try to arrive at the truth by ruling out rival hypotheses or by falsifying favored hypotheses, interviewers should also attempt to rule out alternative hypotheses, rather than simply trying to confirm what they already believe (Ceci & Bronfenbrenner, 1991; Dawes, Faust, & Meehl, 1989). Interviewers are particularly susceptible to interviewer bias when they acquire prior information about the case from colleagues, parents, or other case workers *and* assume that this information is true. The detrimental impact of bias is threefold. First, biased interviewers tend to inaccurately report the contents of the interview so that these contents are consistent with their own a priori beliefs (Langer & Abelson, 1974). Second, when interviewers believe they know the truth about an event or an individual, they tend to overlook, screen out, or ignore relevant and vital information (i.e., information that may produce negative or inconsistent evidence, Ceci & Bruck, 1993; Loftus, 1975). Third, biased interviewers tend to shape witnesses' reports (through the use of misleading or closed questions that restrict the range of possible answers) to be consistent with their hypotheses about what happened (Jones & Powell, 2004; Thompson, Clarke-Stewart, & Lepore, 1997; White, Leichtman, & Ceci, 1997). The potential damage of misleading the witness should not be underestimated. Misinformation has been shown to be detrimental to interviewees' later testimony, regardless of whether the false details were initially rejected (Warren, Hulse-Trotter, & Tubbs, 1991).

Interviewers who are not open-minded risk losing their professional credibility and also risk the inadmissibility of the information obtained. To guide professionals in detecting biased interviewers, experts have identified several characteristics or styles of interaction that tend to characterize interviewers who are not willing to explore alternative hypotheses about an event. Specifically, biased interviewers tend to (1) gather predominantly confirmatory evidence and avoid avenues that may produce negative or inconsistent evidence, (2) engage in a rigid form of questioning, interrupt the interviewee's account, and fail to summarize the interviewee's responses, (3) ignore information that does not fit with their perceptions or assumptions, (4) fail to encourage interviewees to say "I don't know" or establish a relationship in which interviewees feel they can correct misunderstandings in the interview, (5) overlook or ignore the degree to which the interviewee's responses are constrained by limited language skills or a desire to please the interviewer, (6) fail to establish the source of reported information (i.e., whether it was actually observed or learned firsthand by the interviewee or was merely talked about), and (7) ask leading and other questions that control the interviewee's answers by implying an answer or assuming facts that might be in dispute. See Ceci and Bruck (1995) for further discussion of these issues.

THE ESSENTIAL ELEMENTS OF A GOOD INVESTIGATIVE INTERVIEWER TRAINING PROGRAM

There is strong international consensus about which interviewing skills yield the most accurate eyewitnesses accounts. An important goal of researchers, therefore, is to determine how effectively these skills are taught in training programs provided for investigative interviewers. To date, the majority of evaluation research has focused solely on measuring the degree to which interviewers adhere to the use of open-ended questions. This skill has been isolated, in part, because (1) it is one of the main components that distinguishes effective and ineffective police interviewers (Fisher et al., 1987); (2) there is abundant experimental research supporting the effectiveness of these questions; (3) open-ended questions should be relatively easy to implement, because they can be memorized and do not require much ad hoc decision making; and (4) when used properly, they reduce the negative consequences of other interviewer errors (e.g., confirmation bias) and they promote other desirable interviewing skills (e.g., encouraging the witness to play an active role in the interview process).

In summary, much of the evaluation research converges on the discouraging conclusion that investigative interviewers tend to use predominantly short-answer questions with few pauses and an excessive number of closed and leading questions (Cederborg, Orbach, Sternberg, & Lamb, 2000; Fisher et al., 1987; Mildren, 1997; Moston, Stephenson, & Williamson, 1993). Furthermore, the pattern is widespread. This pattern occurs internationally (e.g., United States, United Kingdom, Australia, Sweden, and Israel), across different interviewee groups (e.g., children, adults), and for different kinds of interviewer (e.g., police, social workers). For example, Fisher et al. (1987) analyzed field transcripts with eyewitnesses who ranged from 11 years old to middle-aged and found that for every open-ended question, nine additional short-answer questions were posed. Research focusing on interviews with child witnesses has revealed similar results, with approximately 10% or less of interviewers' questions being open-ended invitations to describe the event (Aldridge & Cameron 1999; Cederborg et al., 2000; Clarke & Milne, 2001; Freeman & Morris, 1999; Sternberg, Lamb, Orbach, Esplin, & Mitchell, 2001; Warren et al., 1999).

Research shows no association between interviewers' knowledge of best-practice interviewing guidelines and actual interview practice (Cederborg et al., 2000; Freeman & Morris, 1999; Lamb, Sternberg, Orbach, Hershkowitz, et al., 2002; Orbach et al., 2000; Powell, 2002; Warren, Woodall, Hunt, & Perry, 1996). For example, Warren et al. (1999) found no significant improvement in the use of open-ended questions by experienced investigative interviewers (M = 11 years) following a comprehensive 10-day program on how to interview children. The program (developed at Cornell University, titled "What Kids Can Tell Us") focused on the acquisition of knowledge and skills in four key areas: child development, self-assessment of practice, critical thinking, and interview protocols and procedures. Learning activities included (1) lectures and training activities about children's development, legal issues, and various interview protocols, (2) two 15-minute practice interviews with children, ages 3–5 years, about an innocuous event, and (3) critical feedback in small groups regarding the interviewers' first practice interview. The practice interviews were conducted on the second and eighth day of the training program and were followed by an exercise in generating alternative hypotheses about what the child may have experienced.

The results of the 10-day training program showed that the interviewers had increased their declarative knowledge about children's abilities and appropriate interview practices. However, the interviewers' questioning styles did not change much as a result of training. There was no significant increase in the frequency of open-ended questions across the two practice interviews: 17% at Time 1 (T1) to 25% at Time 2 (T2). Nor was there a significant change in the frequency of misleading (8% at T1 to 13% at T2) or correctly leading questions (8% at T1 to 6% at T2) used posttraining. Although the interviewers significantly reduced the percentage of yes/no questions from 74% at T1 to 66% at T2, this decline merely resulted in a significant increase in the percentage of specific *wh* questions (i.e., who, what, where, when) (24% at T1 to 36% at T2).

Larger-scale evaluations conducted in the United Kingdom and United States have also demonstrated the ineffectiveness of short-term intensive training in improving the effectiveness of investigative interviewers. Davies et al. (1995) evaluated the quality of field interviews conducted in the United Kingdom following the implementation of the Memorandum of Good Practice. The Memorandum of Good Practice refers to guidelines introduced by the Home Office and Department of Health (U.K.) in 1992, specifying how to interview children and other vulnerable witnesses who are involved, or might be involved, in criminal proceedings. Although the elicitation of a free-narrative account is the central focus of the Memorandum of Good Practice (Home Office and Department of Health, 1992), in 28% of the cases reviewed interviewers did not attempt to elicit narrative responses from children. In an additional 43% of cases, interviewers did not exhaust the child's free narrative before rushing unnecessarily into the more direct questioning phase of the interview. In fact, the average time spent in the free-narrative phase was 1 minute, 44 seconds compared with 18 minutes, 36 seconds in the questioning phase—that is, a phase composed of predominantly direct questioning (Davies et al., 1995). These findings are similar to those of an evaluation study by Berliner and Lieb (2001), who reviewed a total of 92 interviews obtained from three offices of the Division of Children and Family Services (Washington, DC) between January and October 2000.

In contrast to these disappointing findings, some researchers have demonstrated that improved interviewing techniques *can* be achieved through formal training. The first major demonstrations of the positive effects of training on interviewer skills examined the Cognitive Interview (Fisher et al., 1989; George & Clifford, 1992). Because these studies are reviewed elsewhere (e.g., Fisher & McCauley, 1995), we mention them only briefly, concentrating instead on the more recent studies conducted by Lamb and colleagues at the National Institute of Child Health and Human Development (Washington, DC: Lamb, Sternberg, Orbach, Esplin, & Mitchell, 2002; Lamb, Sternberg, Orbach, Hershkowitz, et al., 2002; Orbach et al., 2000; Sternberg, Lamb, Esplin, & Baradaran, 1999; Sternberg et al., 1997; Sternberg et al., 2001). Given the important contribution of this small group of studies, we briefly describe each study in turn. Subsequently, we draw tentative conclusions about the training strategies used in these studies, which may have led to improvements in interview performance. A summary of the studies is provided in Table 2.2.

Cognitive Interview Studies

Both Fisher et al. (1989) and George and Clifford (1992) monitored experienced police officers' interviews with victims and witnesses of crime, before and after training on the Cognitive Interview. In both studies, prior to training, the interviewers asked primarily closed questions and offered witnesses few opportunities to elaborate on their answers. Some of the police investigators were then trained to conduct the Cognitive Interview. Training was provided by experts over multiple sessions (four sessions in Fisher et al.; two sessions in George & Clifford). The training entailed background lectures on good and poor interviewing techniques. More important, the lectures were punctuated with tape-recorded samples of good and poor interviewing techniques taken from actual police interviews of witnesses. The trainees went through several role-playing exercises and received individual feedback on their technique. In Fisher et al., the police also conducted and tape-recorded several posttraining field interviews and received individualized feedback. For several weeks following training, the police tape-recorded several witness interviews. Both Fisher et al. and George and Clifford found that, compared to their pretraining performance (and also to a control group, untrained), posttrained interviews contained more open-ended questions, fewer closed questions, and fewer leading questions. For instance, in George and Clifford, the number of open-ended questions increased almost 10-fold, from 0.5 (per 10 questions asked) to 4.7; and the number of closed questions decreased by twofold, from 7.1 to 3.3. More important, posttrained interviewers collected significantly more crime-relevant facts from witnesses (e.g., 50–60% increase in Fisher et al.) in comparison to their pretrained interviews and to their nontrained colleagues. Interestingly, of the seven police officers who received training on the Cognitive Interview, only one did not increase witness output—and he was the only interviewer who did not change his questioning style in response to the training.

Sternberg et al. (1997)

The first study in the Lamb et al. series to demonstrate improvement in the use of open-ended questioning by investigative interviewers was conducted by Sternberg et al. (1997). They created two prescribed interviews that differed on the basis of the question type that was asked during the rapport-building phase. Either open-ended questions were used (e.g., "Tell me about your teacher"; "Tell me about the children in your class") or direct questions were used (e.g., "Do you celebrate [holiday] at school?"; "Did you dress up?").

TABLE 2.2. Description of the Training Programs and Study Demographics in Research Examining the Effectiveness of Interviewer Training

Reviewed studies	Elements inherent in training programs	Number of trainees	Number of interviews	
			Pre	Post
Fisher et al. (1989)	4 1/2 day sessions of initial training program on Cognitive Interview by expert • Formal instruction on principles of cognition, memory enhancement, witness–interviewer communication, and sequence of interview • Tape-recorded samples of good/bad interviewing techniques • Role-playing exercises plus individual and group feedback by expert • Personal feedback of posttraining interviews by expert	7	42	24
George & Clifford (1992)	2 full-day sessions of initial training program on Cognitive Interview by expert • Formal instruction on principles of cognition, memory enhancement, witness–interviewer communication, and sequence of interview • Tape-recorded samples of good/bad interviewing techniques • Role-playing exercises plus individual and group feedback by expert	7	7	7
Sternberg et al. (1997)	Length of training unspecified • Instruction and practice in utilizing two rapport-building scripts (open-ended introduction and direct introduction)	14	N/a	N/a
Sternberg et al. (1999)	5-day initial training program with follow-up supervision and feedback • Instruction and practice in utilizing two rapport-building scripts (open-ended introduction and direct introduction) • Formal instruction on children's memory, linguistic abilities, suggestibility, and the step-wise interview • Videotaped illustrations of appropriate and inappropriate interviewing techniques • Review of appropriate and inappropriate techniques evident within participants' field interviews • Group supervision every 2 months • Expert feedback on field transcripts and individual telephone consultations	7	15	29

TABLE 2.2. (*continued*)

Reviewed studies	Elements inherent in training programs	Number of trainees	Number of interviews	
			Pre	Post
Orbach et al. (2000)	3-day initial training program with follow-up supervision and feedback • Formal instruction on research literature and recommended interviewing techniques • Monthly group sessions in instruction and practice in utilizing the NICHD scripted protocol • Monthly group in-depth discussions of recurring problems and rehearsal of more appropriate alternatives • Individual expert feedback on field transcripts every month	6	50	55
Sternberg et al. (2001)	5-day initial training program with follow-up supervision and feedback • Instruction and practice in utilizing the NICHD scripted protocol • Expert feedback on participants' adherence to the protocol • Group and individual training sessions reemphasizing adherence to the NICHD protocol every 6–8 weeks • Expert written feedback of field interviews throughout duration of study (unspecified) • Videotaped illustrations of appropriate and inappropriate interviewing techniques	6	50	50
Lamb, Sternberg, Orbach, Esplin, et al. (2002)	5-day initial training program with follow-up supervision and feedback • Instruction and practice in utilizing the NICHD scripted protocol • Expert feedback on participants' adherence to the protocol • Group and individual training sessions reemphasizing adherence to the NICHD protocol every 4–8 weeks • Expert written feedback of field interviews throughout duration of study (12 months) • Videotaped illustrations of appropriate and inappropriate interviewing techniques	8	37	37
Lamb, Sternberg, Orbach, Hershkowitz, et al. (2002)	1. Validation condition. 5-day session: • Formal instruction on child development and individual variations among children in abilities to describe experiences, child's credibility, and how interviewers affect the quality of interview • Videotaped examples of appropriate and inappropriate interviewing techniques 2. Rapport-building condition. Elements inherent in validation condition, as well as: • Formal instruction on importance of interview structure and motivating interviewee to be informative (2 days)	6 5	25 24	25 24

• Instruction and practice in utilizing two rapport-building scripts (open-ended introduction and direct introduction)			
3. Victims' protocol. 2-day training seminar outlining the conceptual and empirical support for all phases of investigative interviews	5	30	30
• Videotaped illustrations of appropriate and inappropriate interviewing techniques			
• Instruction and practice in utilizing the NICHD scripted protocol			
• Interviewers observed conducting both simulated and field interviews using the protocol, followed by provision of written feedback (until the end of the study; unspecified)			
• Group and individual training sessions reemphasizing adherence to the NICHD protocol every 4 weeks			
• Group review of problematic cases and alternative strategies discussed			
4. Suspects' protocol. Training seminar comparable to victims' protocol condition except for instruction and practice in interviewing alleged juvenile perpetrators	5	17	17
• Uses a fully structured interview protocol similar to the NICHD protocol (i.e., both emphasize the value of recall memory retrieval; however, the suspects' protocol includes coercive strategies to elicit information from less motivated interviewees)			
• No individual supervision or feedback on interviewers' field interviews was provided			

Following the rapport-building phase, one single statement was made (for both scripts) at the beginning of the substantive phase of the interview: "Please tell me everything that happened, every detail, from the very beginning to the very end." Fourteen Israeli youth investigators were trained to implement each script. After they learned the protocols, all investigators were instructed to alternate between the open-ended and direct prescripted questions in subsequent field interviews, which were then used as a posttest measure. In total, 51 interviews (26 using the direct script and 25 using the open-ended script) were collected during a 3-year period, allowing for pre- and posttest comparisons.

Analysis of responses to the interviewers' first substantive question about the alleged offense indicated that two-and-a-half times as many details and words were provided by children exposed to the open-ended script than to the direct script (90.56 vs. 38.32, respectively). The overall beneficial effect was short lived, however, because use of the open-ended script during the rapport-building phase did not encourage interviewers to ask more open-ended questions during the remainder of the interview. These results suggest that when presented with a structured script, interviewers *can* ask open-ended questions, which is clearly favorable in light of the greater detail elicited from the children in the study. However, the results do not imply that interviewers can utilize open-ended questions without a script.

Sternberg et al. (1999)

Given these encouraging findings on the benefit of scripted protocols, Sternberg, Lamb, Esplin, and Baradaran (1999) extended their use beyond the rapport-building phase to include the substantive phase as well. After completing the introductory phase of the interview using either the open-ended or direct-scripted protocols (see Sternberg et al., 1997), both protocols outlined a series of identical questions for use during the entire substantive phase of the interview. A baseline sample of 15 interviews was collected from seven investigative interviewers in the United States. Interviewers then participated in a week-long training course in which they received (1) formal instruction on children's memory, linguistic abilities, suggestibility, and the Step-wise Approach interview protocol; (2) videotaped exemplars, including the participants' field interviews, of appropriate and inappropriate interviewing techniques; (3) instruction and practice in using the rapport-building scripts (as discussed above); and (4) group supervision every 2 months, supplemented by individual written feedback on field transcripts and individual telephone consultations.

Upon completing the training, the interviewers were requested to alternate between the open-ended and direct scripted protocols in subsequent investigative interviews; of these, a total of 29 posttraining field interviews were analyzed. Similar to their preceding study (Sternberg et al., 1997), this study revealed that interviewers using the open-ended protocol asked significantly more open-ended questions (during the entire interview) than comparative interviews featuring the direct protocol and those obtained at baseline (10.20, 6.50, 4.28, respectively). Furthermore, all of the interviewers, whether they followed the open-ended or the closed protocols, performed better than they had performed at baseline (pretraining): They asked (1) fewer direct questions than at baseline (33.13, 34.43, and 55.87 for the open-ended protocol, direct protocol, and baseline conditions, respectively), and (2) fewer leading questions than at baseline (16.33, 16.36, and 35.53 for the open-ended protocol, direct protocol, and baseline conditions, respectively).

Orbach et al. (2000)

Based on their initial research, which demonstrated the relative effectiveness of a scripted protocol in improving the performance of investigative interviewers, subsequent studies by Lamb and colleagues assessed the value of using a fully structured formal interview: the National Institute of Child Health and Human Development (NICHD) protocol. In particular, the study by Orbach et al. (2000) compared the questioning styles of six senior youth Israeli investigators before and after training. The pretraining ($N = 50$) and posttraining interviews ($N = 55$) were conducted in the field and were matched, when possible, for the child's age, type of offense, and relationship between child and alleged perpetrator. The interviewing protocol was introduced in a training program that consisted of (1) detailed practice and instruction in the use of the NICHD scripted protocol, (2) monthly feedback by an expert on individual transcripted interviews, and (3) in-depth discussions about recurring problems and rehearsal of more appropriate alternatives. The results of the study revealed that posttraining interviewers conducted superior interviews during the substantive phases of the interview. Specifically, they asked significantly more open-ended questions and fewer focused, option-posing (i.e., questions that offer the interviewee a range of possible responses regarding details not previously disclosed) and suggestive questions. These results are consistent with the next study in the series (Sternberg et al., 2001), which used a revised version of the NICHD protocol.

Sternberg et al. (2001)

Sternberg et al. (2001) compared six experienced youth investigators in the United States across a sample of 50 pretraining field interviews and 50 posttraining field interviews, and found that the frequency of open-ended questions increased with training. The training program consisted of a 5-day introduction incorporating formal instruction in the format and application of the NICHD protocol, multiple practice opportunities, as well as expert feedback on the participants' adherence to the protocol. Group and individual training sessions, which were provided on a 6- to 8-week basis, reemphasized adherence to the protocol and provided critical written feedback about the participants' field interviews. Furthermore, videotaped illustrations of appropriate and inappropriate techniques were provided.

The six investigative interviewers improved dramatically over the course of the training program. Collectively, they asked three times more open-ended questions and significantly fewer option-posing and suggestive questions after training. Open-ended questions accounted for 18% of the total questions asked by interviewers prior to training; this figure increased to 47% of total questions asked after training in the NICHD protocol. These findings suggest that training that incorporates individual supervision and feedback can increase investigative interviewers' reliance on open-ended questions.

The remaining two studies examined different training methods to facilitate interviewers' acquisition of the open-ended-question format (Lamb, Sternberg, Orbach, Esplin, et al., 2002; Lamb, Sternberg, Orbach, Hershkowitz, et al., 2002). These studies focused primarily on the value of ongoing supervision and critical feedback, and examined the durability of the training effect: Would the training effect endure after formal supervision had ended?

Lamb, Sternberg, Orbach, Esplin, et al. (2002)

Lamb, Sternberg, Orbach, Esplin, et al. (2002) trained eight experienced police officers and compared the frequency of open-ended questions during and after supervision. Supervision for each officer comprised group and individual training sessions every 4–8 weeks, as well as individual written feedback on every field interview conducted during the study period. The training was similar to the former studies, as summarized in Table 2.2 (Orbach et al., 2000; Sternberg et al., 2001). Thirty-seven interviews were collected during the supervision phase of the study and a subsequent 37 interviews during the 6-month period immediately following the supervision. During the supervision phase of training, the interviewers improved their skills: They asked more open-ended questions and fewer option-posing and suggestive prompts. (We cannot calculate the degree to which performance changed relative to pretraining techniques, because no baseline measurements were reported.) After the supervision phase ended, however, the interviewers' performance declined dramatically. Specifically, the percentage of open-ended invitations declined significantly from 34.22% during supervision to 19.72% after supervision. Furthermore, interviewers increased their use of "risky practices," such as option-posing and suggestive questions, from 24.46% and 6.77% during supervision to 32.61% and 10.78% after supervision, respectively. Thus, although training had the desired effect, its value was short lived.

Lamb, Sternberg, Orbach, Hershkowitz, et al. (2002)

The final study in this series provides a direct comparison of several training techniques (Lamb, Sternberg, Orbach, Hershkowitz, et al., 2002). Twenty-one experienced youth investigators were exposed to one of four training conditions (see Table 2.2). The first two conditions (i.e., validation and rapport building) included didactic workshops and formal instruction in areas such as child development and the influence of the interviewer on the interview quality. The second condition also included highly structured presubstantive (rapport building) interview procedures (examined in Sternberg et al., 1997, 1999). The third and fourth conditions incorporated ongoing supervision and feedback opportunities. Specifically, participants in the third condition received (1) feedback on both simulated and field interviews using the NICHD protocol, (2) written feedback on individual transcripts (until the study ended), and (3) individual and group sessions every 4 weeks, reemphasizing adherence to the NICHD protocol. Participants in the fourth condition received a similar package to that of the third condition, with the following exceptions: (1) they did not receive individual supervision and feedback on individual transcripts, and (2) they were trained initially to interview alleged juvenile perpetrators (who are typically less motivated to participate in the investigative interview) using the suspects' protocol (similar to the NICHD, except for the inclusion of coercive strategies to elicit information from less-motivated interviewees).

The conclusions are based on a comparison of the 92 pre- and 92 posttraining field interviews, which were matched with regard to the child's age and gender, relationship between the victim and alleged perpetrator, and type and frequency of abuse. Providing only didactic instructions had no beneficial effects: Conditions 1 and 2 had negligible impact on the number of open-ended prompts asked by investigative interviewers. Fortunately, the results were more encouraging for the conditions that incorporated ongoing group supervision and training in the use of a structured interview protocol. Trainees in Condition 3 (the victims' protocol condition) asked an average of 8.02 open-ended invitations pretraining, compared with an average of 11.04 posttraining. Likewise, trainees in Condition 4 (the suspects' protocol condition) asked an average of 5.12 open-ended questions pretraining, compared with 14.27 posttraining. Significant posttraining improvements in the use of open-ended questions were observed irrespective of whether the analyses were performed on absolute or proportion scores.

Why were these researchers more successful than earlier police efforts to improve investigators' interviewing skills? On the basis of existing research, it is not possible to ascertain the independent contribution of the precise elements that made these training programs successful. However, we believe that successful long-term improvement depends on (1) the operationalization of training principles via use of a highly structured protocol, *and* (2) the incorporation of multiple opportunities for practice (supplemented by detailed expert feedback) and continuing supervision. However, trainers in investigative interviewing argue that it is too costly to implement the type of training offered by Lamb and colleagues on a global scale (Powell, 2002). In particular, the provision of ongoing supervision by experts and detailed written feedback on field interviews is clearly beyond the capabilities of many large-scale police services, which are typically plagued by tight budgets and high staff turnover rates. By identifying the *relative* impact of the various elements within these studies, however, it may be possible to develop more cost-effective programs that improve interviewing skills.

When considering the precise nature of the training programs in the two Cognitive Interview studies (Fisher et al., 1989; George & Clifford, 1992), and those conducted by Lamb and colleagues (Lamb, Sternberg, Orbach, Esplin, et al., 2002; Lamb, Sternberg, Orbach, Hershkowitz, et al., 2002; Orbach et al., 2000; Sternberg et al., 1997, 1999, 2001), it is likely that four elements related to the delivery of these programs contributed to their success in improving interviewers' performance in the long term: (1) distribution of training (incorporating practice) over time, (2) expert instruction and feedback, (3) exemplars of good practice, and (4) participants' motivation to improve their own performance. In the remainder of this section we review the existing empirical evidence to support the potential independent contribution of each of these distinct training elements, followed by recommendations for future research.

Training Distributed over Separate Sessions

In the most successful training studies, training (incorporating practice and critical feedback) was typically distributed over several day-long forums separated by a break of several weeks and extending over an expansive period (e.g., 12 months). Given the independent evidence supporting the use of distributed practice, we strongly suspect that this factor contributed significantly to the success of these programs. Donovan and Radosevich (1999) conducted a meta-analytic review of the effect of the distribution of practice over 63 studies. Studies were included in the meta-analysis provided that (1) they contained both a spaced and massed practice condition, (2) some form of skill or knowledge acquisition was required by participants, (3) the acquisition or retention of the skill learned by participants was measured in a standardized manner, and (4) the participants did not include children or persons with a mental illness. This last requirement was intended to ensure that the findings of the meta-analysis were as generalizable to the workplace training setting as possible. The analysis revealed that spaced practice conditions (i.e., practice sessions interspersed with rest intervals) were superior to massed practice conditions (i.e., continuous practice sessions without rest intervals). This finding was evident for both simple and complex tasks. For relatively simple tasks, performance was nearly half a standard deviation greater among participants in the spaced practice conditions, yielding an overall effect size of 0.46. Although the acquisition of more complex tasks yielded smaller effect sizes, the superiority of spaced practice conditions was still evident (Donovan & Radosevich, 1999).

Despite the obvious benefit of spaced training sessions, most training programs for investigative interviewers are structured so that participants learn about the process of interviewing over a single intensive session spanning 1 or several days (see Davies, Marshall, & Robertson, 1998; Powell, 2002). This common structure has not gone uncriticized. Formal evaluations of prominent training courses around the globe have typically criticized programs for attempting to teach "too much too quickly" (Aldridge & Cameron, 1999; Clarke & Milne, 2001; Davies et al., 1995; Powell, 2002). The scheduling of one-off (i.e., single, not ongoing) programs seems to be a practical issue related to (1) the need to service rural as well as regional trainees, (2) heavy workloads, (3) high turnover of staff, as well as (4) the limited time and financial assistance available for in-house training (Davies et al., 1998).

Although some regions do claim to offer "in-house" posttraining supervision or support for investigative interviewers, such professional development is at the discretion of supervisory personnel, and police trainees often claim that these persons often hold negative attitudes about the value of training. For example, Cioccarelli (1989, as cited in Christie, Petrie, & Timmins, 1996) reported that new police recruits often receive advice from more experienced officers to "forget that academy stuff." Such advice implies that "real training" is learned "on the job" and not in the classroom. Police officers mandated to investigate complaints of child abuse express concern that the nature and skill required to perform their job is poorly understood by colleagues in other areas of the police force (Aarons, Powell, & Browne, 2004). Indeed, many of the participants interviewed in Aaron and colleagues' qualitative inquiry mentioned that their role was perceived by other police officers as similar to that of "social workers," characterized by an "airy-fairy, touchy-feely" quality, rather than operating as a specialized unit comprised of highly trained and skilled officers. Consequently, participants felt that their supervisors believed it was not beneficial to invest training resources to enhance interviewing skills and that their unit was "stand alone"—and isolated from other departments within the police force.

Expert Instruction and Feedback

In the most successful studies reviewed, the participants received expert feedback and instruction in group as well as individual sessions. According to Ericsson, Krampe, and Tesch-Romer (1993), expert instruction plays a critical role in maintaining skill acquisition. Irrespective of the specific skill domain (e.g., violin, piano, figure skating, wrestling, soccer), experts and laypeople alike consistently rate instruction from an authority figure as being more relevant than any other domain-specific practice activity (Ericsson et al., 1993; Helsen, Starkes, & Hodges, 1998; Hodges & Starkes, 1996). For example, violin players consider taking lessons with an expert to be more relevant to their ongoing performance than practice with others, giving lessons, studying music theory, or giving solo performances (Ericsson et al., 1993).

The fact that expert instruction is frequently overlooked by police services may contribute, in part, to the weak impact of training on interviewing performance. An Australian study by Brewer, Wilson, and Beck (1994) demonstrated (through unobtrusive observation and objective classification procedures) that performance monitoring, in the form of instructional feedback of subordinates by patrol sergeants, was strongly associated with effective team performance. However, the patrol sergeants spent 30–40% less time than other managers (e.g., insurance managers, newspaper managers, bank and theatre managers) in providing feedback to subordinates. Widespread concerns about the lack of supervision expressed by the participants in Brewer et al.'s (1994) study seem to characterize many sectors of police organizations. With regard to training in investigative interviewing, corrective posttraining feedback from experts is currently not a typical feature of these programs (see Cornford & Athanasou, 1995; Powell, 2002)—even though interview quality is higher among investigative interviewers who operate under a workplace "interview supervision policy" (Clarke & Milne, 2001).

Supervision has obvious benefits, although certainly the effectiveness of "in-house supervision" (as is the case with any professional supervision) is directly dependent on the ability of supervisors to provide constructive feedback (Baldwin, 1992; Warren et al., 1999). In fact, a review conducted by the U.K. Social Services Inspectorate noted that "few supervisors or managers were trained to the same extent as front line workers . . . raising concerns about the adequacy of supervision and support for those conducting evidential interviews" (Social Services Inspectorate Survey, 1994, as cited in Davies et al., 1995, p. 17). Warren et al. (1999, p. 135) noted that a common complaint among trainees was that "collegial and instructor feedback was not specific enough to learn new skills." Similarly, a recent qualitative inquiry of 20 Australian police interviewers of children revealed that senior officers were often not equipped with the appropriate skills and knowledge base to offer appropriate feedback on staff interviewing performance (Aarons et al., 2004). It may be that better selection of, and/or training of, supervisors responsible for providing feedback and the use of standardized evaluation tools are required to improve the quality and consistency of feedback.

Exemplars of Good Practice

As discussed above, the usefulness of feedback is related to the skills and knowledge of instructors and supervisors, and their ability to demonstrate good practice. Accordingly, exemplars of good practice may offer supervisors and trainees a useful tool for demonstrating appropriate interviewing techniques (Brewer, 1995). In the successful training studies we reviewed, modeling behavior was achieved through a variety of different methods, including written structured protocols (e.g., NICHD structured interview protocol), role-playing exercises using confederates, and audio/video training tapes. Currently we do not know how much these methods independently improved the performance of the investigative interviewers. However, feedback from police trainers and trainees suggests that the demonstration of videotaped material taken from real-world field interviews is particularly useful in providing a representation of recently learned skills in practice. Furthermore, as we outline below, prior research in related disciplines suggests that training videos are particularly beneficial. Training videos can provide a clear demonstration, through visual comparisons and analogy, of the appropriate structure of an interview along with specific and attainable goals to assist learning (Berger, 1970).

Video training aids have been shown, in many domains, to improve the quality of performance of trainees compared to control groups who are taught under typical learning conditions (e.g., verbal instruction only). In a study by Arnspiger (1933), only three showings of a 10-minute "talking picture" led to improvements, over standard teaching methods, in objective tests on knowledge of course materials in both natural sciences and music units. These improvements were maintained for 4 weeks postinstruction by both intellectually superior and inferior pupils. Video exemplars have also been shown to play an important role in improving performance in practical communication-based skills (as opposed to the acquisition of knowledge, per se; Bashman & Treadwell, 1995; Walter, 1975).

Walter (1975) compared a variety of training methods used to enhance students' performance in a brainstorming problem-solving activity. In this study, 135 university students were randomly assigned to one of five conditions: (1) no experimental input and no time allowed for discussion among group members; (2) brief verbal instructions about how the brainstorming should be conducted and general group discussion about that information; (3) videotaped presentation of the participants partaking in a brainstorming exercise, coupled with verbal feedback; (4) presentation of a videotaped "model" group demonstrating how the brainstorming exercise *should* be undertaken, coupled with verbal instruction; and (5) the provision of both Conditions 3 and 4, wherein comparisons could be made directly between ideal (model) and actual group performance. The results showed that students exposed to the videotaped model presentation (Condition 4) performed significantly better than those in Conditions 1, 2, and 3. Videotaped feedback (Condition 3) did not improve performance, however, unless it was coupled with videotaped model presentation (Condition 5). These findings are consistent with a recent study (comparing similar training conditions to that above) involving the teaching of psychodrama to university students (Bashman & Treadwell, 1995). Furthermore, they are consistent with the findings of Warren et al. (1999), who showed that providing feedback (via video), per se, on investigative interview performance did not improve performance.

The effectiveness of video instruction (as is the case with supervision or instruction) is dependent on the quality of individual training videos. Currently there are few published training videos, and these videos contain actors rather than actual witnesses (for ethical reasons), which may limit the degree to which they are comparable to actual field interviews. Since the effectiveness of modeling as a training technique is enhanced by the presentation of "realistic" or "real-world" exemplars, mock scenarios or interviews with actors about innocuous events may not be considered by investigative interviewers to be directly relevant to their practice (Aarons et al., 2004; Brewer, 1995).

Participant Motivation

The last factor that we believe contributed to the success of the cited training programs is the voluntary status of the participants. Due to the ongoing and intensive nature of the research design, it is reasonable to assume that the participants in these studies (1) were internally motivated to enhance their performance in investigative interviewing, and (2) had faith in the researchers' ability to improve their performance. The role of motivation in sustaining prolonged periods of practice is one of the central premises proposed in Ericsson et al.'s (1993) theory of deliberate practice. Because practice is not inherently enjoyable and there are often no short-term rewards, individuals must retain a certain degree of motivation in order to engage in practice over extended periods (Ericsson et al., 1993). Most workplaces often fail to provide external motivators (i.e., rewards, incentives, recognition, promotion), the role of intrinsic motivation within investigative interviewers becomes vital.

This important role of intrinsic motivation in enhancing the development of specific skills is potentially problematic in light of the pervasive cultural and organizational issues that confront investigative interviewers. For example, analysis of in-depth interviews with investigative interviewers of children and adolescents reveals that within the wider police force, the investigation of child abuse is often devalued, and there is little opportunity for promotion (Aarons et al., 2004; Adams & Hendry, 1996). Furthermore, investigative interviewers (social workers as well as police) frequently complain of high workloads, staff turnover, and inadequate support from supervisors and colleagues (Aarons et al., 2004). Clearly, the low profile, high stress, and limited promotion opportunities of the job would create barriers to maintaining effective intrinsic motivation to improve one's interviewing skills. Some research suggests that, when there is limited supervision and external training, goal setting and self-regulatory processes (e.g., self-monitoring, self-evaluation, and self-reactions) may be critical motivational techniques for enhancing task performance (see Altman, 1976; Kanfer & Ackerman, 1989; Langan-Fox, Armstrong, Balvin, & Anglim, 2002; Langan-Fox, Waycott, & Galna, 1997; Wood, Mento, & Locke, 1987; Zimmerman & Kitsantas, 1996).

An alternative approach to improving interviewer performance is to recruit professionals who exhibit (or have the potential to maintain) high levels of intrinsic motivation (O'Bryen, Clark, & Malakuti, 1997). Unfortunately, there is currently little basis for predicting which interviewers will be driven toward maintaining professional enhancement, because intrinsic motivation is associated with a diverse array of individual and situational factors (Langan-Fox et al., 2002).

SUMMARY AND CONCLUSION

There is strong international consensus about which interviewing skills are most responsible for eliciting extensive, accurate accounts. Two of the most critical skills are (1) the use of open-ended questions, and (2) refraining from the use of closed and/or specific leading questions. Although these skills can be learned, as evidenced by the success reported in laboratory-based training studies, most police (and other investigative interviewers) do not use these skills reliably in their real-world criminal investigations. Given the critical role of investigative interviewers in the criminal justice system and the large amount of resources currently invested in training, more research is needed to identify the factors responsible for facilitating the acquisition of best-practice skills in interviewing.

It is not yet clear which specific training elements (or combination of elements) best promote significant improvements in interviewer performance. After comparing the elements of those training protocols that were the most successful with those of most other (unsuccessful) training programs, we believe that the core elements of success include the use of structured interview protocols, multiple opportunities to practice over an extended period, expert feedback and ongoing supervision, and internal trainee motivation to enhance individual performance. Further support for the importance of these elements is found in related research that has examined the acquisition of other practical skills. The aim of future research, therefore, should be to establish the relative effectiveness of these elements with investigative interviewers and the most cost-effective strategies for promoting change on a broad scale. This level of change will require a greater understanding of the individual and organizational factors that facilitate and hinder the implementation of appropriate interviewing techniques among investigative interviewers. Organizational change in line with specialized training (that incorporates empirically proven and cost-effective strategies) would thereby maximize the acquisition and transferability of learned skills to the police workplace environment.

REFERENCES

Aarons, N. M., Powell, M. B., & Browne, J. (2004). Changing cultures: Police perceptions of interviews involving children with intellectual disabilities. *Policing and Society, 14*(3), 269–278.

Adams, C., & Hendry, E. (1996). Challenges to police training on child protection. *Child Abuse Review, 5,* 70–72.

Agnew, & Powell, M. B. (2004). The effect of intellectual disability on children's recall of an event across different question types. *Law and Human Behavior, 28*(3), 273–294.

Aldridge, J., & Cameron, S. (1999). Interviewing child witnesses: Questioning techniques and the role of training. *Applied Developmental Science, 3,* 136–147.

Altman, J. (1976). *Transferability of vocational skills: Review of literature and research information* (Series No. 103). Ohio: Center for Vocational Education.

Arnspiger, V. C. (1933). *Measuring the effectiveness of sound pictures as teaching aids.* New York: Teachers College, Columbia University.

Baldwin, J. (1992). *Videotaping police interviews with suspects: An evaluation.* London: Home Office Police Department.

Bashman, J. G., & Treadwell, T. W. (1995). Assessing the effectiveness of a psychodrama training video. *Journal of Group Psychotherapy, Psychodrama and Sociometry, 48,* 61–69.

Berger, M. M. (1970). *Videotape techniques in psychiatric training and treatment.* New York: Brunner/Mazel.

Berliner, L., & Lieb, R. (2001). *Child sexual abuse investigations: Testing documentation methods.* Washington State Institute for Public Policy.

Brewer, N. (1995). Leadership and supervision. In N. Brewer & C. Wilson (Eds.), *Psychology and policing* (pp. 291–316). Hillsdale, NJ: Erlbaum.

Brewer, N., Wilson, C., & Beck, K. (1994). Supervisory behaviour and team performance amongst police patrol sergeants. *Journal of Occupational and Organizational Psychology, 67,* 69–78.

Briggs, G. E., Peters, G. L., & Fisher, R. P. (1972). On the locus of the divided attention effects. *Perception and Psychophysics, 11,* 315–320.

Broadbent, D. E. (1958). *Perception and communication.* London: Pergamon Press.

Ceci, S. J., & Bronfenbrenner, U. (1991). On the demise of everyday memory: The rumors of my death are greatly exaggerated. *American Psychologist, 46,* 27–31.

Ceci, S. J., & Bruck, M. (1993). Suggestibility of the child witness: A historical review and synthesis. *Psychological Bulletin, 113,* 403–439.

Ceci, S. J., & Bruck, M. (1995). *Jeopardy in the courtroom: A scientific analysis of children's testimony.* Washington, DC: American Psychological Association.

Ceci, S. J., Powell, M. B., & Principe, G. F. (2002). The scientific status of children's memory and testimony. In D. L. Faigman, D. H. Kaye, M. J. Saks, & J. Sanders (Eds.), *Modern scientific evidence: The law and science of expert testimony* (Vol. 2, pp. 144–205). St. Paul, MN: West.

Cederborg, A. C., Orbach, Y., Sternberg, K. J., & Lamb, M. E. (2000). Investigative interviews of child witnesses in Sweden. *Child Abuse and Neglect, 24,* 1355–1361.

Christie, G., Petrie, S., & Timmins, P. (1996). The effect of police education, training and socialisation on conservative attitudes. *Australian and New Zealand Journal of Criminology, 29,* 299–314.

Clarke, C., & Milne, R. (2001). National evaluation of the PEACE investigative interviewing course. Retrieved December 3, 2003, from the Home Office website: *http://www.homeoffice.gov.au.uk/docs/peaceinterviewingcourse.pdf.*

Cooke, M. (1996). A different story: Narrative versus "question and answer" in Aboriginal evidence. *Forensic Linguistics, 3,* 273–288.

Cornford, I. R., & Athanasou, J. (1995). Developing expertise through training. *Industrial and Commercial Training, 27,* 10–18.

Davies, G., Marshall, E., & Robertson, N. (1998). *Child abuse: Training investigative of-*

ficers (Police Research Series Paper No. 94). London: Policing and Reducing Crime Unit.

Davies, G. M., Wilson, C., Mitchell, R., & Milsom, J. (1995). *Videotaping children's evidence: An evaluation.* London: Home Office.

Dawes, R. M., Faust, D., & Meehl, P. E. (1989). Clinical versus actuarial judgement. *Science, 243,* 1668–1674.

de Quervain, D. J., Roozendaal, B., Nitsch, R. M., McGaugh, J. L., & Hock, C. (2000). Acute cortisone administration impairs retrieval of long-term declarative memory in humans. *Nature Neuroscience, 3,* 313–314.

Donovan, J. J., & Radosevich, D. J. (1999). A meta-analytic review of the distribution of practice effect: Now you see it, now you don't. *Journal of Applied Psychology, 84,* 795–805.

Eades, D. (1992). *Aboriginal English and the law.* Queensland: Queensland Law Society.

Eades, D. (1995). Cross examination of Aboriginal children: The Pinkenba case. *Aboriginal Law Bulletin, 3,* 10–11.

Ellis, L., Powell, M. B., Thomson, D. M., & Jones, C. (2003). The usefulness of conversational "groundrules" in reducing preschoolers' suggestibility about experienced and nonexperienced events. *Psychiatry, Psychology and Law, 10,* 334–345.

Ericsson, K. A., Krampe, R. T., & Tesch-Romer, C. (1993). The role of deliberate practice in the acquisition of expert performance. *Psychological Review, 100,* 363–406.

Federal Law Enforcement Training Center. (1992). *Validation of 9-week basic law enforcement for land management agencies (9-PT) report.* Glynco, GA: Department of the Treasury.

Fisher, R. P. (1995). Interviewing victims and witnesses of crime. *Psychology, Public Policy, and Law, 1,* 732–764.

Fisher, R. P. (1999). Probing knowledge. In D. Gopher & A. Koriat (Eds.), *Attention and performance* (Vol. 17, pp. 537–556). Cambridge, MA: MIT Press.

Fisher, R. P., Falkner, K. L., Trevisan, M., & McCauley, M. R. (2000). Adapting the cognitive interview to enhance long-term (35 years) recall of physical activities. *Journal of Applied Psychology, 85,* 180–189.

Fisher, R. P., & Geiselman, R. E. (1992). *Memory-enhancing techniques in investigative interviewing: The cognitive interview.* Springfield, IL: Thomas.

Fisher, R. P., Geiselman, R. E., & Amador, M. (1989). Field test of the cognitive interview: Enhancing the recollection of actual victims and witnesses of crime. *Journal of Applied Psychology, 74,* 722–727.

Fisher, R. P., Geiselman, R. E., & Raymond, D. S. (1987). Critical analysis of police interview techniques. *Journal of Police Science and Administration, 15,* 177–185.

Fisher, R. P., & McCauley, M. L. (1995). Information retrieval: Interviewing witnesses. In N. Brewer & C. Wilson (Eds.), *Psychology and policing* (pp. 81–99). Hillsdale, NJ: Erlbaum.

Freeman, K. A., & Morris, T. L. (1999). Investigative interviewing with children: Evaluation of the effectiveness of a training program for child protective service workers. *Child Abuse and Neglect, 23,* 701–713.

Gee, S., Gregory, M., & Pipe, M. (1999). "What colour is your pet dinosaur?" The impact of pre-interview training and question type on children's answers. *Legal and Criminological Psychology, 4,* 11–128.

George, R., & Clifford, B. (1992). Making the most of witnesses. *Policing, 8,* 185–198.

Gudjonsson, G. (1992). *The psychology of interrogations, confessions and testimony.* Chichester, UK: Wiley.

Helsen, W. F., Starkes, J. L., & Hodges, N. J. (1998). Team sports and the theory of deliberate practice. *Journal of Sport and Exercise Psychology, 20,* 12–34.

Henry, L. A., & Gudjonsson, G. H. (1999). Eyewitness memory and suggestibility in children with in mental retardation. *American Journal on Mental Retardation, 104,* 491–508.

Hodges, N. J., & Starkes, J. L. (1996). Wrestling with the nature of expertise: A sport specific test of Ericsson, Krampe and Tesch-Romer's (1993) theory of deliberate practice. *International Journal of Sport Psychology, 27,* 400–424.

Home Office. (2002). *Achieving best evidence in criminal proceedings: Guidance for vulnerable or intimidated witnesses including children.* London: HMSO.

Home Office and Department of Health. (1992). *Memorandum of good practice for videorecorded interviews with child witnesses for criminal proceedings.* London: HMSO.

Jones, C. H., & Powell, M. B. (2004). *The effect of bias on the questioning style of police interviews.* Manuscript in preparation.

Kahneman, D. (1973). *Attention and effort.* Englewood Cliffs, NJ: Prentice-Hall.

Kanfer, R., & Ackerman, P. L. (1989). Motivation and cognitive abilities: An integrative/aptitude-treatment interaction approach to skill acquisition. *Journal of Applied Psychology, 74,* 657–690.

Kebbell, M., & Milne, R. (1998). Police officers' perception of eyewitness factors in forensic investigations. *Journal of Social Psychology, 138,* 323–330.

Lamb, M. E., Sternberg, K. J., Orbach, Y., Esplin, P. W., & Mitchell, S. (2002). Is ongoing feedback necessary to maintain the quality of investigative interviews with allegedly abused children? *Applied Developmental Science, 6,* 35–41.

Lamb, M. E., Sternberg, K. J., Orbach, Y., Hershkowitz, I., Horowitz, D., & Esplin, P. W. (2002). The effects of intensive training and ongoing supervision on the quality of investigative interviews with alleged sex abuse victims. *Applied Developmental Science, 6,* 114–125.

Langan-Fox, J., Armstrong, K., Balvin, N., & Anglim, J. (2002). Process in skill acquisition: Motivation, interruptions, memory, affective states, and metacognition. *Australian Psychologist, 37,* 104–117.

Langan-Fox, J., Waycott, J., & Galna, C. (1997). Ability–performance relations during skill acquisition. *Australian Psychologist, 32,* 153–158.

Langer, E. J., & Abelson, R. (1974). A patient by any other name: Clinician group difference in labeling bias. *Journal of Consulting and Clinical Psychology, 42,* 4–9.

Leibowitz, H. W., Guzy, L. T., Peterson, E., & Blake, P. T. (1993). Quantitative perceptual estimates: Verbal versus nonverbal retrieval techniques. *Perception, 2,* 1051–1060.

Lipton, J. P. (1977). On the psychology of eyewitness testimony. *Journal of Applied Psychology, 62,* 90–93.

Loftus, E. F. (1975). Leading questions and the eyewitness report. *Cognitive Psychology, 7,* 560–572.

McCauley, M. R., & Fisher, R. P. (1995). Facilitating children's recall with the revised cognitive interview. *Journal of Applied Psychology, 80,* 510–516.

Mildren, J. D. (1997). Redressing the imbalance against Aboriginals in the criminal justice system. *Criminal Law Journal, 21,* 7–22.

Milne, B., & Bull, R. (1999). *Investigative interviewing: Psychology and practice.* Chichester, UK: Wiley.

Moston, S., Stephenson, G. M., & Williamson, T. (1993). The incidence, antecedents and consequences of the use of the right to silence during police questioning. *Criminal Behaviour and Mental Health, 3,* 30–47.

Nesbitt, M., & Markham, R. (1999). Improving young children's accuracy of recall for an eyewitness event. *Journal of Applied Developmental Psychology, 20,* 449–459.

O'Bryen, K., Clark, R. E., & Malakuti, R. (1997). Expert and novice performance: Implications for clinical training. *Educational Psychology Review, 9,* 321–332.

Orbach, Y., Hershkowitz, I., Lamb, M. E., Sternberg, K. J., Esplin, P. W., & Horowitz, D. (2000). Assessing the value of structured protocols for forensic interviews of alleged child abuse victims. *Child Abuse and Neglect, 24,* 733–752.

Phillips, M. R., Fisher, R. P., & Schwartz, B. L. (1999, July). *Metacognitive control in eyewitness memory.* Paper presented at the meeting of the Society for Applied Research in Memory and Cognition, Boulder, CO.

Poole, D. A., & Lamb, M. E. (1998). *Investigative interviews of children.* Washington, DC: American Psychological Association.

Poole, D. A., & Lindsay, D. S. (1995). Interviewing preschoolers: Effects of non-suggestive techniques, parental coaching, and leading questions on reports of nonexperienced events. *Journal of Experimental Child Psychology, 60,* 129–154.

Powell, M. B. (2000). P.R.I.D.E.: The essential elements of a forensic interview with an Aboriginal person. *Australian Psychologist, 35,* 186–192.

Powell, M. B. (2002). Specialist training in investigative and evidential interviewing: Is it having any effect on the behaviour of professionals in the field? *Psychiatry, Psychology and Law, 9,* 44–55.

Powell, M. B., & Bartholomew, T. (2003). Interviewing and assessing clients from different cultural backgrounds: Guidelines for all forensic professionals. In R. Bull & D. Carson (Eds.), *Handbook of psychology in legal contexts* (pp. 625–643). Chichester, UK: Wiley.

Powell, M. B., Wilson, C. J., Croft, C. M., & Gibbons, C. (2003). *Children's conception of the boundaries of police authority.* Manuscript submitted for publication.

Saywitz, K. J., & Moan-Hardie, S. (1994). Reducing the potential for distortion of childhood memories. *Consciousness and Cognition, 3,* 408–425.

Saywitz, K. J., & Nathanson, R. (1993). Children's testimony and their perceptions of stress in and out of the courtroom. *Child Abuse and Neglect, 17,* 613–622.

Shepherd, E. (1988). Developing interview skills. In P. Southgate (Ed.), *New directions in police training* (pp. 170–188). London: HMSO.

Snow, P., & Powell, M. B. (in press). What's the story? An exploration of narrative language abilities in male juvenile offenders. *Psychology, Crime and Law.*

Sternberg, K. J., Lamb, M. E., Esplin, P. W., & Baradaran, L. P. (1999). Using a scripted protocol in investigative interviews: A pilot study. *Applied Developmental Science, 3,* 70–76.

Sternberg, K. J., Lamb, M. E., Esplin, P. W., Orbach, Y., & Hershkowitz, I. (2002). Using a structured protocol to improve the quality of investigative interviews. In M. Eisen, J. Quas, & G. Goodman (Eds.), *Memory and suggestibility in the forensic interview* (pp. 409–436). Mahwah, NJ: Erlbaum.

Sternberg, K. J., Lamb, M. E., Hershkowitz, I., Yudilevitch, L., Orbach, Y., Esplin, P. W., et al. (1997). Effects of introductory style on children's abilities to describe experiences of sexual abuse. *Child Abuse and Neglect, 21,* 1133–1146.

Sternberg, K. J., Lamb, M. E., Orbach, Y., Esplin, P. W., & Mitchell, S. (2001). Use of a structured investigative protocol enhances young children's responses to free-recall prompts in the course of forensic interviews. *Journal of Applied Psychology, 86,* 997–1005.

Thompson, W. C., Clarke-Stewart, K. A., & Lepore, S. (1997). What did the janitor do? Suggestive interviewing and the accuracy of children's accounts. *Law and Human Behavior, 21,* 405–426.

Walker, A. G. (1999). *Handbook on questioning children: A linguistic perspective.* Washington, DC: American Bar Association Center on Children and the Law.

Walter, G. A. (1975). Effects of videotape training inputs on group performance. *Journal of Applied Psychology, 60,* 308–312.

Warren, A. R., Hulse-Trotter, K., & Tubbs, E. C. (1991). Inducing resistance to suggestibility in children. *Law and Human Behavior, 15,* 273–285.

Warren, A. R., Woodall, C. E., Hunt, J. S., & Perry, N. W. (1996). It sounds good in theory, but . . . ": Do investigative interviewers follow guidelines based on memory research? *Child Maltreatment, 1,* 231–245.

Warren, A. R., Woodall, C., Thomas, M., Nunno, M., Keeney, J., Larson, S., et al. (1999). Assessing the effectiveness of a training program of interviewing child witnesses. *Applied Developmental Science, 3,* 128–135.

White, T. L., Leichtman, M. D., & Ceci, S. J. (1997). The good, the bad and the ugly: Accuracy, inaccuracy and elaboration in preschoolers' reports about a past event. *Applied Cognitive Psychology, 11,* 37–54.

Wilson, C. J., & Powell, M. B. (2001). *A guide to interviewing children: Essential skills for counsellors, police, lawyers and social workers.* Crows Nest, New South Wales: Allen & Unwin.

Wood, R. E., Mento, A. J., & Locke, E. A. (1987). Task complexity as a moderator of goal effects: A meta-analysis. *Journal of Applied Psychology, 72,* 416–425.

Yuille, J. C. (1996). *Improving investigations into allegations of child sexual abuse.* Province of British Columbia, Ministry of Social Services, Research Evaluation and Statistics Branch.

Yuille, J. C., Marxsen, D., & Cooper, B. (1999). Training investigative interviewers: Adherence to the spirit, as well as the letter. *International Journal of Law and Psychiatry, 22,* 323–336.

Zimmerman, B. J., & Kitsantas, A. (1996). Self-regulated learning of a motoric skill: The role of goal setting and self-monitoring. *Journal of Applied Sport Psychology, 8,* 60–75.

CHAPTER THREE

Deception Detection

PÄR ANDERS GRANHAG
ALDERT VRIJ

Many people are fascinated by deception. Grand liars often become famous (e.g., Nick Leeson, who destroyed the 200-year-old Barings Bank), and a lie told by an already-famous person is often considered grand (e.g., Bill Clinton lying about his affair with Monica Lewinsky). Books with covers that promise some easy tricks to reveal liars may sell well, although the cover promises more than the authors can deliver. This general interest in deception is mirrored in the field of psychology and law, and intense research efforts over recent years have resulted in an impressive corpus of knowledge on deception and its detection (for recent overviews, see Granhag & Strömwall, 2004a; Vrij, 2000a). In this chapter we examine some of the latest research findings and explore what scientific psychology can tell us about the detection of deception. We focus mainly on research that has been conducted within the framework of "psychology and law" and pay less attention to related topics, such as deception in everyday life (DePaulo, Kashy, Kirkendol, Wyer, & Epstein, 1996), and deception in close relations (DePaulo & Bell, 1996).

The study of deception spans many of psychology's subdisciplines. For example, to understand why a liar's internal states might translate into certain nonverbal behaviors, it is necessary to study emotion and physiological psychology; to be able to argue why the verbal content of a true statement might differ from a false statement, we must study memory; in order to explain why people with a certain facial appearance are judged as liars more often than others, we must study social psychology. The full list is much longer, but the point is that a student of human deception needs to be acquainted with different domains within psychology.

Almost on a daily basis, people are forced to reflect and decide upon questions of truth and deception. The outcome of these reflections and decisions may or may not be important. Most people accept white lies and might even confess to have uttered a few themselves, but will feel hurt or angry if lied to on serious matters. For professionals working within the field of law enforcement (e.g., police officers, judges), it is of paramount importance to assess veracity accurately. The consequences of failing to do so can be very severe.

We have structured the chapter as follows: First, we set the stage by defining deception and providing an overview of the different lines of research found within the field. Then we explore the underlying core beliefs that people hold about the cues to deception, mainly by examining the beliefs of presumed experts, and identify where these beliefs originate and where they might lead. In the next section we focus on people's ability to detect deception, both laypeople's and presumed experts'. We review research on the accuracy of the most commonly used lie detection methods (i.e., speech, physiological, and behavioral analysis), and take a closer look at how different factors, such as high-stake situations, repeated interrogations, and multiple suspects, affect people's ability to detect deception. We then turn to objective indicators of deception, differentiating the verbal and nonverbal cues that are, to some extent, diagnostic of deception from those that are not. In addition, we discuss liars' and truth tellers' strategies and how these might translate into verbal and nonverbal behavior. We end the section by arguing that human memory plays an important role in deception—for liars, truth tellers, and those trying to distinguish between them. Finally, we examine the attempts made to train people to detect deception and discuss the so-far promising results of the more indirect techniques (i.e., implicit lie detection), as well as a few new, promising, but not yet fully investigated ways to detect deceit. We close the chapter by summarizing the most important findings and highlighting some of the future challenges.

DEFINING DECEPTION

To define *deception* is not an easy task, and many scholars have made more or less successful attempts to conceptualize the phenomenon. We use a definition formulated by Vrij (2000a), wherein deception is seen as "a successful or unsuccessful deliberate attempt, without forewarning, to create in another a belief which the communicator considers to be untrue" (p. 6). Note that a person who unintentionally misremembers is not lying, because lying requires an intentional act. Note also that someone should be called a liar only if he or she lies without prior warning about his or her intention, and that even an unsuccessful attempt to deceive is a lie.

There are many different types of lies. Basic distinctions can be made between falsifications, distortions, and concealments. *Falsifications* are total falsehoods, wherein everything communicated is contradictory to the truth (also called "outright lies"). *Distortions* are departures from the truth to fit the liar's goal; *exaggerations* are classified in the distortion category. Finally, the truth can be *concealed*, in that a liar can say that he or she does not know (even if he or she does) or that he or she does not remember (although he or she does).

In this chapter we focus on the more serious lies, not the "social lies" (white lies) that most people tell on a daily basis in order to place themselves ("I never dream about anyone but you") or others ("I wouldn't call you fat") in a more positive light. Furthermore, we focus exclusively on lies told by adults; for a recent overview of studies on deception by children, see Vrij (2002).

BELIEFS REGARDING CUES TO DECEPTION

To define *belief* is also a difficult task. For the present context, it suffices to say that a belief is a feeling that something is true or real. A belief can be strong or weak, correct or incorrect. The beliefs that a person holds are often reflected in his or her behavioral dispositions: that is, beliefs guide action. Hence, if we want to learn about deception detection, it is important to study people's beliefs about cues to deception.

Traditionally, two different methods have been used to investigate people's beliefs about cues to deception: surveys and controlled, laboratory-based studies. In the surveys, participants typically have been asked to rate the extent to which they believe that a particular behavior (e.g., gaze aversion and finger movements) on a list of prespecified verbal and nonverbal behaviors is indicative of deception. The basic idea is that the participants are asked to indicate how they think that liars behave.

The second source of information on how people believe liars behave is studies wherein participants watch videotapes of liars and truth tellers, then judge these "suspects" in terms of their veracity. One way to map the participants' beliefs is to ask them to justify their veracity judgments in writing; another way is to calculate correlations between the (objective) behaviors of the suspects and the types of judgments made by the participants (Zuckerman, DePaulo, & Rosenthal, 1981). None of these methods is perfect, however. In brief, the prespecified behaviors that participants are asked to rate in surveys might not be the behaviors they would observe and act upon if faced with a real-life situation. When analyzing self-reported cues to deception, we need to keep in mind that there is a large number of psychological studies showing that people are rather poor at pinpointing all (or sometimes even the most significant) factors that led to an impression, for example, that a person is lying (Yzerbyt, Dardenne, & Leyens, 1998). Investigating cues to perceived deception provides insight into which cues participants actually use to signify deception, but it is not certain whether they themselves are aware of which cues they act upon. Nevertheless, a brief summary of the research conducted on beliefs about cues to deception serves as an important platform for the later sections in this chapter.

Surveys on Presumed Experts' Beliefs about Deception

The majority of the surveys investigating people's beliefs about cues to deception has been conducted with college students as participants. However, in this chapter we turn to the surveys conducted on professional "lie catchers," such as police officers, judges, and customs officers. To date, such studies have been conducted in the United Kingdom (Akehurst, Köhnken, Vrij, & Bull, 1996), Sweden (Strömwall & Granhag, 2003), The Netherlands (Vrij & Semin, 1996), and Spain (Garrido & Masip, 1999). Most surveys of experts' beliefs have contrasted the beliefs of police officers and students (Akehurst et al., 1996); students, prisoners, and professional lie catchers, such as police officers, customs officers and prison guards (Vrij & Semin, 1996); police officers, prosecutors, and judges (Strömwall & Granhag, 2003); and students and immigration officers handling asylum cases (Granhag, Strömwall, & Hartwig, in press).

These surveys show that the beliefs held by experts and laypeople (i.e., college students) are highly similar. In terms of nonverbal cues, the converging evidence is that both experts and laypeople consider nervous behaviors to indicate deception (Vrij, 2000a). For example, both presumed experts and laypeople believe that eye contact decreases when lying. However, research on objective cues to deception (reviewed later in the chapter) shows that this particular cue is an unreliable predictor of deception (DePaulo et al., 2003). Furthermore, both presumed experts and laypeople seem to believe that there is a strong link between deceptive behavior and an increase in body movements; research on objective cues shows that this belief also is incorrect (DePaulo et al., 2003). In terms of verbal indicators of deception, presumed experts and laypeople seem to believe that truthful accounts are more detailed than fabricated accounts; to some extent, research on objective cues to deception supports this belief. In addition, both groups express a strong belief that truthful consecutive statements are more consistent, over time, than are fabricated consecutive statements (Strömwall & Granhag, 2003). However, research on objective verbal cues questions this belief (Granhag & Strömwall, 1999). For a recent review on professionals' beliefs about deception, see Strömwall, Granhag, and Hartwig (2004). In sum, the results from these surveys on subjective cues to deception show that (1) the beliefs are highly similar for experts and laypeople, and (2) that these beliefs, to a large extent, are misconceptions of how liars actually behave.

Self-Reported Cues to Deception

As mentioned earlier, an alternative way to elicit information on people's beliefs about cues to deception is to ask lie catchers to justify the veracity assessments they have made. Mann, Vrij, and Bull (2004) showed police officers fragments of videotaped real-life police interviews with suspects and asked them to try to detect deceit. In addition, the police officers were asked which cues they had used to make their assessments. The results showed that the most commonly reported cue was "gaze," and the second was "movements." That is, they tended to go for nonverbal cues more than verbal. In contrast, in a study conducted by Hartwig, Granhag, Strömwall, and Vrij (2004b), experienced police officers reported relying on verbal cues (e.g., details and plausibility) and nonverbal cues (e.g., gaze and movements) to an equal extent, when assessing students who acted as suspects. The explanation for this inconsistency is probably very simple. In the study by Mann et al., the police officers watched videotapes—that is, they had no opportunity to ask questions, and they had no access to facts about the case. In the study by Hartwig et al., the police officers were given a brief case file and were free to conduct the interrogations with the suspects in whatever manner they found appropriate. In conclusion, the cues to deception that police officers report using are very much in line with the stereotypical cues that laypeople report. In the same study, Mann et al. (2004) also examined cues to perceived deception and found that the more gaze aversive the suspects were, the more likely they were to be judged deceptive. This finding suggests an overlap between beliefs about cues associated with deception and cues to perceived deception. It should be noted, however, that the distribution of the cues to deception reported is moderated by the situation in which the officers are tested (at least, to some extent).

Investigating a different aspect of subjective cues to deception, Granhag and Strömwall (2000) showed the same videotaped suspect, interrogated on three different occasions, to 125 undergraduate students. The students were asked to assess the suspect's veracity and to provide arguments in support of their assessment. In short, two types of interobserver disagreements were found. The first type of disagreement pertained to how a particular cue was perceived. For example, 40 observers perceived the suspect's three statements as being inconsistent over time, whereas an equal number of observers perceived the same three statements to be consistent over time. The second type of disagreement pertained to how a particular cue was used. For example, the cue "low confidence" was used about equally often to justify that the suspect was lying and to justify why he was telling the truth. Overall, the study showed that there was relatively more disagreement about how cues were to be perceived than about how they were to be used. Granhag and Strömwall (2000) argued that both types of disagreements contribute to the low averages of deception-detection accuracy commonly found for groups.

Why Do We Have Such Misconceptions about Deceptive Behavior?

Several explanations have been proposed to elucidate why people hold such incorrect beliefs about how liars behave. One explanation highlights the importance of feedback. DePaulo, Stone, and Lassiter (1985b) suggested that feedback often is inadequate and unsystematic in occupations where lie detection is a central task. Consider, for example, the working environment of customs officers: From the travelers they decide not to search they get no feedback at all, and they will never know whether it was correct to let those travelers pass without visitation. They can only learn something from the travelers they do search, but the feedback they receive from this group may not be as valid as it might seem. If a customs officer decides to search a traveler and indeed finds smuggled goods, he or she may regard this as a validation of his or her beliefs about the relation between behavior and deception. However, it might be that the customs officer relied on the wrong cues but managed to catch the smuggler by chance. Furthermore, if a customs officer neglects to try to find systematic patterns in his or her "false alarms" (i.e., travelers he or she decides to search but who have not smuggled anything), he or she will learn little or nothing from these mistakes.

Critically, the working environment of customs officers, as well as many other groups within law enforcement, contains learning structures in which feedback is lacking or even misleading (Hogarth, 2001). Hence, such learning structures may lead to erroneous beliefs about deceptive behavior that are then cemented, rather than corrected, through experience. This line of reasoning suggests that the mere experience of judging veracity is not sufficient to learn the correct beliefs about deception or to fine-tune the beliefs already held (DePaulo & Pfeifer, 1986; Ekman & O'Sullivan, 1991; Vrij, 2000a; Vrij & Semin, 1996). Instead, the development of valid decision-making rules (in this case, beliefs about deceptive behavior) demands feedback that is frequent, reliable, and preferably immediate (Allwood & Granhag, 1999; Einhorn, 1982).

In line with Hogarth (2001), we argue that feedback is the key to learning the right lesson from experience. To find empirical support for the idea that feedback moderates beliefs about cues to deception, we need to investigate groups of persons that are provided with regular feedback. One such group may be experienced criminals. Speculatively, criminals live in a more deceptive environment than most other people—something that may make them aware of deceptive strategies that work. For example, being repeatedly interrogated by the police and thus receiving feedback on deception success and failure might increase a person's knowledge about which deceptive strategies are useful in convincing others. In addition, and importantly, survival in such a deceptive culture is also dependent on a general alertness in order not to be deceived by others.

The idea that criminals might have more accurate beliefs about deception was first tested in a study by Vrij and Semin (1996). Indeed, the results from this study showed that prison inmates had a better notion about the relationship between nonverbal behavior and deception than other presumed lie experts (in this study, customs officers, police detectives, patrol police officers, and prison guards). This finding was further supported in a study by Granhag, Andersson, Strömwall, and Hartwig (2004), which found that criminals' beliefs about verbal as well as nonverbal cues to deception were less stereotypical than the ones held by prison personnel and students.

Further support for the idea that feedback is important to achieve a certain degree of expertise in the deception area comes from the fact that criminals have been shown to detect lies significantly more accurately than chance (Hartwig, Granhag, Strömwall, & Andersson, 2004), and, on demand, and with little or no time for preparation, produce very convincing false confessions (Norwick, Kassin, Meissner, & Malpass, 2002). In addition, Bugental et al. (as cited in Ekman, 2001) showed that abused children living in an institutional environment were better at detecting lies from demeanor than were other children. In sum, these studies show that living in an environment that demands high alertness to possible betrayal and deceit can improve the individual's knowledge about cues to deception. One implication of these findings is that law enforcement personnel should avoid questionable interrogation tactics, such as lying and manipulation, for other than ethical reasons: Such deceptive tactics might simply be an easy "catch" for the "expert" sitting on the opposite side of the table.

It should be noted that the learning structures that characterize the working situation of many presumed deception-detection experts is but one of several possible explanations as to why they hold such stereotypical beliefs about deception. Reasonably, people's tendency to remember those instances that support their beliefs and forget those in conflict with their beliefs (i.e., selective memory and confirmation bias) may contribute to the perseverance of misconceptions. Vrij, Edward, and Bull (2001a) reported that people who lied in an interview and who later were asked to indicate how they thought they had behaved, incorrectly believed that they had behaved in a nervous manner (e.g., fidgeting). Such misconceptions about a person's own behavior during deception might add to the cementing of the stereotypical beliefs he or she has regarding other people's lying behavior. Yet another source of misconceptions about cues to deception is to be found in so-called police interrogation manuals.

Cues to Deception in Police Interrogation Manuals

In many interrogation manuals, it is suggested that the interrogator should pay close attention to the suspects' behavioral responses, and that the suspects' nonverbal behavior provides important information regarding his or her truthfulness. For example, the most influential interrogation manual suggests that posture shifts, grooming gestures, and placing a hand over the mouth are reliable cues to deception (Inbau, Reid, & Buckley, 1986; Inbau, Reid, Buckley, & Jayne, 2001). In another influential manual, it is claimed that liars' movements are jerky, abrupt, and swift and that their hands are cold and clammy (Zulawski & Wicklander, 1993). In the same manual it is stated that liars are gaze aversive, that they stutter and mumble, and that they fidget and scratch themselves. As we outline later, there is no empirical support whatsoever for these claims. Instead, research suggests that the cues reported in police interrogation manuals often reflect *common misconceptions* about the link between demeanor and deception. To trust the information that these manuals provide in terms of cues to deception might result in misinterpretations of the verbal and nonverbal behaviors that a suspect shows. Such misinterpretations might, in turn, fuel suspect-driven investigations that might ultimately result in miscarriages of justice.

Research by Kassin and Fong (1999) demonstrates this point. They trained students in the technique recommended by John E. Reid and his associates (Inbau et al., 2001). The researchers then compared the deception-detection performance of the trained group against the performance of an untrained group. They found that *the untrained group outperformed the trained group*. In support of this result, Mann et al. (2004) found, in a study of real-like police interviews, that the more the officers endorsed the views recommended by Inbau et al. (2001), the worse they became at distinguishing between truths and lies. In short, passing through a training program that teaches cues that are nondiagnostic of deception can impair people's ability to detect lies.

THE ABILITY TO DETECT DECEPTION

In this section, we review research on the accuracy of the different deception-detection methods. First, however, a few words on experimental procedure, evaluation, and terminology are warranted.

Ground Truth and Evaluation

The paradigmatic task for people participating in studies on deception detection is to view a number of video clips and after each clip, make a dichotomous judgment as to whether the person just viewed is lying or telling the truth. That is, the participants are asked to circle either "This person is lying" or "This person is telling the truth" (this dichotomous scale is sometimes complemented by a Likert scale running from, for example, 1—"No, definitely not lying"—to 7—"Yes, definitely lying"). Before showing the first video, the experimenter commonly informs the participants that exactly (or about) half of the people on the videotape are lying.

To be able to determine the accuracy of a judgment, it is necessary to have a criterion for comparison. Translated into studies on deception-detection performance, researchers need to ensure that some (often half) of the videotaped "suspects" really are lying, and that the others really are telling the truth (sometimes each "suspect" is asked to lie in one interview and to tell the truth in another). In controlled, laboratory-based studies, this requirement is seldom problematic. Liars are simply instructed to lie, and truth tellers are instructed to tell the truth about, for example, a mock theft from a wallet placed in a nearby room. Some "suspects" steal money from the wallet and then deny their action (i.e., they lie), whereas other "suspects" take no money and tell the truth in the interview. The experimenter knows who is lying and who is not, because he or she knows to whom the money was given. However, in real-life situations it is often difficult to know whether a certain suspect is telling the truth or not. That is, studies using real-life material are often faced with problems in terms of "ground truth."

Truth and Lie Biases

In most studies, deception-detection accuracy is captured by an overall measure: number of correct judgments in relation to the total of number of judgments made. Some researchers conduct separate computations for detecting accuracy of truthful and deceptive statements, with the former exceeding the latter (Levine, Sun Park, & McCornack, 1999). This "veracity effect" follows from the fact that subjects participating in a deception-detection task tend to go for "This statement is true" more often than "This statement is deceptive" (even though they are told that the set of video clips contains an equal number of liars and truth tellers). This "truth bias" is well documented within the deception-detection paradigm and has proven to be especially strong for laypeople (Vrij, 2000a). In studies testing police officers, however, the truth bias is often less pronounced and sometimes even lacking (Hartwig et al., 2004b; Porter, Woodworth, & Birt, 2000; Vrij, 2003). This finding is not surprising, given the fact that many police officers have considerable experience with interrogating suspects, presumably encounter a different base rate of liars, and thus have a different frame of mind when facing the task of assessing veracity (Kassin & Fong, 1999).

Hartwig, Granhag, Strömwall, and Andersson (2004) tested prison inmates' deception-detection ability and found that this group exhibited a very pronounced lie bias. That is, the inmates chose to circle "This statement is deceptive" much more often than "This statement is truthful." Consequently, the inmates had a very high accuracy in identifying statements that were, in fact, deceptive, but were less successful in identifying truthful statements. Hartwig et al. proposed two complementary explanations for this unusual lie bias. First, most prison inmates probably have extensive experience with lying and/or being lied to, which might create a "false consensus" bias (Ross, Greene, & House, 1977) that deception is as frequent in the lives of other people as it is in their own lives. Second, the consequences of being duped, or failing to dupe, are probably more severe in the criminal environment than in other contexts. This severity may lead to a more suspicious attitude toward others. (For a discussion on judgmental biases in deception-detection contexts, see also Meissner and Kassin, 2002.)

Confidence

Some deception researchers have asked their participants not only to decide whether a suspect is lying or telling the truth, but also to reflect on the decision made with respect to the person's degree of certainty. To gain knowledge about how realistic people are about their own ability to detect deception is important, because the felt or expressed level of confidence can influence both their own and other people's actions.

Subjective estimates of confidence are typically elicited after a participant has seen a video clip and selected one of the two answer alternatives ("The suspect is lying" or "The suspect is telling the truth"). Then the participant is asked to rate his or her choice on a half-range confidence scale, where 50% means "guess" and 100% means "absolutely sure" that the chosen alternative is correct. Research on deception has found that there is a very weak relationship between accuracy and confidence and that people tend to be overconfident in their judgment. That is, they think they are more correct than, in fact, they are. The meta-analysis by DePaulo, Charlton, Cooper, Lindsay, and Muhlenbruck (1997) showed that the degree of confidence was correlated with type of veracity judgment made, with higher confidence for statements judged as truthful (independent of whether the veracity judgment made was correct or not).

Ekman and O'Sullivan (1991) used a somewhat different method to investigate the relationship between confidence and performance. Before taking the actual test of watching 10 videotaped interviews (five liars and five truth tellers), the lie catchers (e.g., Secret Service, FBI, and CIA agents) were asked to estimate their ability to tell when other people are lying. Computed over all tested occupational groups, these general predictions turned out to be nonsignificantly related to accuracy. In addition, immediately after taking the test the presumed experts were asked to indicate how well they thought they had done in detecting deceit. This correlation between estimated and actual performance also turned out to be nonsignificant. In sum, people's estimates about their own ability and performance seem to be unrelated to their actual lie-detection ability and performance.

The Accuracy of Lie Detection Methods

There are, in principle, three ways to catch a liar: (1) by analyzing his or her speech, (2) by measuring his or her physiological responses, and (3) by observing his or her behavior. Psychologists have developed various lie- and truth-detection methods, and several of them—Statement Validity Analysis, Comparison Question Test, and Guilty Knowledge Test—are used in criminal investigations. These methods, and others, are discussed in this section.

Speech Analyses

Statement Validity Analysis (SVA) is probably the most popular technique for assessing the veracity of verbal statements. The technique was developed in Germany to determine the credibility of children's testimony in trials for sexual offenses. It is perhaps not surprising that a technique has been developed to verify whether sexual abuse has taken place with a child. It is usually difficult to determine the facts of a sexual abuse case, because often there is no medical or physical evidence. Frequently, the alleged victim and the defendant give contradictory testimonies, with no independent witnesses available to confirm or deny what happened. Therefore, the perceived credibility of the defendant and alleged victim are important. The alleged victims are in a disadvantageous position if they are children, because adults have a tendency to mistrust statements made by children (Ceci & Bruck, 1995). SVA results are accepted as evidence in criminal courts in several countries, including Germany, The Netherlands, and Sweden (Vrij, 2000a). According to Undeutsch (1967), a child's statement, derived from memory of an actual experience, differs in content and quality from a statement based on invention or fantasy. This is known as the "Undeutsch hypothesis" (Steller, 1989). Undeutsch (and others) has developed various content criteria which could be used to check the veracity of statements (Undeutsch, 1967, 1982).

Based on his work, Steller and Köhnken (1989) compiled a list of 19 criteria to be used in credibility assessment. The SVA consists of three stages (Vrij, 2000a). In the first stage, children are interviewed in a semistructured format wherein they provide their own account of the allegation, without any influence from the interviewer. Psychologists have designed special interview techniques, based on psychological principles, to obtain as much information as possible from children in a free-narrative style, unhindered by inappropriate prompts or suggestions (Davies, Westcott, & Horan, 2000; Memon, Vrij, & Bull, 2003; Milne & Bull, 1999; Sternberg, Lamb, Esplin, Orbach, & Hershkowitz, 2002). These interviews are audiotaped and then transcribed. In the second stage, using the written transcripts, a systematic assessment of the credibility of the statement given during the interview is conducted. This assessment, the Criteria-Based Content Analysis (CBCA), is based on the list of 19 criteria compiled and discussed by Steller and Köhnken (1989). (Several of these criteria are discussed in a later section on objective indicators of deception and truth.) Trained CBCA experts score the absence or presence of each of these 19 criteria in each statement—for example, on a 3-point scale, where 0 is assigned if the criterion is absent, 1 if the criterion is present, and 2 if the criterion is strongly present. The presence of each criterion enhances the quality of the statement and strengthens the hypothesis that the account is based on a genuine personal experience.

In the third stage, alternative explanations for the CBCA outcomes are considered, because CBCA scores might be affected by factors other than the veracity of the statement, such as the cognitive abilities of the interviewee (Buck, Warren, Betman, & Brigham, 2002) or the style and approach of the interviewer (Köhnken, Schimossek, Aschermann, & Höfer, 1995). For this purpose, a so-called Validity Checklist, consisting of issues that are thought to be relevant and so worth considering, has been developed (Raskin & Esplin, 1991; Steller, 1989).

The core of the SVA procedure is Stage 2, the CBCA, and most SVA research has focused on this aspect of the instrument. Vrij (in press) has recently reviewed 37 CBCA studies, 16 of which have explicitly addressed the question of how many truths and lies could be correctly classified on the basis of CBCA scores. In most of these studies, truthful and deceptive statements of adults, rather than children, were assessed. This procedure might be problematic because CBCA was developed to assess the veracity of children's statements and, in criminal investigations, CBCA evaluations are only used for children's statements. However, several authors have argued that CBCA analyses could be used to evaluate the testimonies of adult suspects or witnesses who talk about issues other than sexual abuse (Köhnken et al., 1995; Ruby & Brigham, 1997; Steller & Köhnken, 1989), because, as they pointed out, the underlying Undeutsch hypothesis is not restricted to children, witnesses, victims, or to sexual abuse. In agreement with this argument, Vrij's (in press) review revealed that accuracy rates for children's statements did not seem to differ from accuracy rates for adults' statements.

In order to test whether CBCA actually works in discriminating between truthful and fabricated accounts, both laboratory studies and field studies have been conducted. In laboratory studies, statements of people who lied or told the truth about certain issues, for the sake of the experiment, are assessed. As discussed later, laboratory studies have inherent problems concerning ecological validity. In real life, CBCA assessments are made on statements that describe highly emotional events (e.g., sexual abuse). Obviously, in laboratory studies those type of experiences can never be simulated. In field studies, CBCA assessments in real sexual abuse cases are examined. The advantage of a field study is that it is realistic. However, the disadvantage is that in most criminal cases, it is virtually impossible to check "ground truth"—that is, to know, with certainty, which statements were truthful and which were fabricated. Ground truth (also called "basic reality") is often based on confessions: that is, on whether or not the person accused of sexual abuse by the child confessed to having committed the crime.

To base the ground truth on confessions, however, generates problems. As Steller and Köhnken (1989) pointed out, CBCA statements are usually obtained in cases where no other evidence is available. If a statement is judged as truthful under such conditions, the chances of the defendant obtaining an acquittal are decreased. If there is a reduced chance of the defendant avoiding a guilty verdict, it may be a beneficial strategy for the defendant to falsely confess to the crime, because confession may result in a considerably milder punishment. On the other hand, there is no reason for the guilty defendant to confess to the crime if the CBCA outcome suggests that the witness's statement is not about a genuinely experienced event. As a result, the defendant's decision to confess may be influenced by the outcome of the CBCA assessment. An attempt to validate CBCA assessments by confessions may therefore be circular, at least, partly.

This ground-truth issue makes conducting field studies difficult, and very few field studies have addressed this issue satisfactorily. As a result, no reliable data on the accuracy of CBCA assessments in real-life cases are currently available (Vrij, in press). Vrij's (in press) review, based solely on laboratory studies, revealed a 73% average accuracy rate for detecting truths (i.e., correctly classifying a truthful statement as truthful) and a 72% average accuracy rate for detecting lies (i.e., correctly classifying a deceptive statement as deceptive). The overall accuracy rate (combined accuracy scores for detecting lies and truths) was 73% (see Table 3.1). These accuracy rates are above the 50% level of chance (guessing whether someone is lying or not has a 50% chance of being correct); however, they are not high enough to justify using CBCA evaluations as the main evidence in criminal courts. SVA experts argue that they use SVA rather than CBCA evaluations in criminal cases. However, there are several problems with using the Validity Checklist, the third stage of the SVA procedure, making it at least uncertain whether SVA evaluations are more accurate than CBCA evaluations (see Vrij, in press, for a discussion of this issue).

Recently, Reality Monitoring has been used as an alternative method to examine verbal differences between responses believed to be true and false (Alonso-Quecuty, 1992, 1996; Alonso-Quecuty, Hernandez-Fernaud, & Campos, 1997; Höfer, Akehurst, & Metzger, 1996; Manzanero & Diges, 1996; Roberts, Lamb, Zale, & Randall, 1998; Sporer, 1997; Strömwall, Bengtsson, Leander, & Granhag, 2004; Vrij, Edward, & Bull, 2001b; Vrij, Edward, Roberts, & Bull, 2000). At the core of Reality Monitoring is the premise that memories of experienced events differ in quality from memories of imagined (e.g., fabricated) events. Memories of real experiences are obtained through perceptual processes and are therefore likely to contain various types of information, including perceptual information (details of vision, audition, smell, taste, and touch), contextual information (spatial details about where the event took place and where objects and people were situated in relation to each other), and temporal information (details about the timing sequence of the events). Accounts of imagined events are derived from an internal source and are therefore likely to contain cognitive operations, such as thoughts and reasoning ("I must have had my coat on, because it was very cold that night"; Johnson, Hashtroudi, & Lindsay, 1993; Johnson & Raye, 1981, 1998). It might be argued that experienced events reflect truth telling whereas imagined events reflect deception. Therefore, differences between truth tellers and liars could be expected on the Reality Monitoring criteria. Table 3.1 presents all the Reality Monitoring studies that reported accuracy rates. These rates for detecting truths vary from a modest 61 to a high 88%, and for detecting lies, from 61 to 76%. Overall accuracy rates range from 66 to 81%. The average truth accuracy rate is somewhat higher (75%) than the average lie accuracy rate (70%). The average overall accuracy rate is 73%. These accuracy rates are comparable with the rates reported for CBCA evaluations (see Table 3.1). This finding is encouraging, because Reality Monitoring analyses are much easier to conduct than CBCA evaluations (Sporer, 1997). Unlike CBCA evaluations, however, Reality Monitoring assessments are not used in criminal investigations.

TABLE 3.1. Accuracy Rates for Lies and Truths Using Different Lie/Truth Detection Methods

	Truth	Lie	Overall
CBCA (review)			
Vrij (in press)	73%	72%	72%
Reality Monitoring (individual studies)			
Höfer et al. (1996)	61%	70%	66%
Sporer (1997)	75%	68%	72%
Vrij et al. (2000)	71%	65%	67%
Vrij et al. (2004a)[a]	81%	73%	77%
Vrij et al. (2004b)	88%	61%	74%
Comparison Question Technique (reviews)			
Ben-Shakhar & Furedy (1990, N = 9)	72%	84%	
Carroll (1991, N = 3)	53%	83%	
Honts & Perry (1992, N = 3)	59%	86%	
Iacono & Patrick (1997, N = 3)	56%	84%	
OTA report (Saxe et al., 1985, N = 10)	78%	88%	
Lykken (1998, N = 4)	61%	86%	
Raskin & Honts (2002, N = 4)	59%	89%	
Guilty Knowledge Technique (individual studies)			
Elaad (1990)	98%	42%	
Elaad et al. (1992)	94%	76%	
Behavioral analyses (reviews, individual study, and systematic analyses)			
Vrij (2000, review, laypersons)	67%	44%	57%
Vrij & Mann (2003, review, professionals)	55%	55%	55%
Mann, Vrij, & Bull (2004, individual study, professionals)	64%	66%	65%
Ekman et al. (1991, systematic analysis)			86%
Frank & Ekman (1997, systematic analysis)			80%
Vrij et al. (2000, systematic analysis)	71%	85%	78%
Vrij et al. (2004a, systematic analysis)	65%	77%	71%

[a] Adult participants only.

Physiological Analyses

Throughout history it has been assumed that lying is accompanied by physiological activity within the liar's body. For example, the Chinese used to force suspected liars to chew rice powder and then to spit it out. If the resultant powder was dry, then the person was judged to have been lying (Kleinmuntz & Szucko, 1984). The modern way of detecting physiological activity in liars is to use a polygraph (from two Greek words: *poly* = many; *grapho* = to write), a scientific measuring device that can display (via ink-pen motions on charts or a computer visual display unit) a direct and valid representation of various types of bodily activity (Bull, 1988). The most commonly measured activities are sweating of the fingers, blood pressure, and respiration. Polygraph tests are currently used in criminal investigations in countries all over the world, including Belgium, Canada, Israel, Japan, Turkey, Mexico, Pakistan, the Philippines, Singapore, South Korea, Taiwan, Thailand, and the United States (Lykken, 1998; Vrij, 2000a). A polygraph is sometimes called a lie detector, but this term is misleading. A polygraph does not detect lies but, rather, the arousal that is assumed to accompany telling a lie. Polygraph examiners have no other option than to measure deception in such an indirect way, because a pattern of physiological activity directly related to lying does not exist (Saxe, 1991). Many different polygraph tests exist; we restrict our coverage to briefly describing only the Comparison Question Test (CQT) and the Guilty Knowledge Test (GKT). The CQT could be considered the standard polygraph test, and it is mostly used in criminal investigations. However, the test is also fiercely criticized by its opponents. The GKT is considerably less disputed among scientists (Iacono & Patrick, 1997; for more detailed descriptions and critical discussions of these two and other polygraph tests, see Kleiner, 2002; Lykken, 1998; Vrij, 2000a).

The CQT (sometimes called the Control Questions Test) compares responses to relevant questions with responses to control questions. Relevant questions are specific questions about the crime: for example, in a murder investigation, "On March 12, did you shoot Scott Fisbee?" (Iacono & Patrick, 1997, p. 254). Control questions deal with acts that are related to the crime under investigation, but do not relate specifically to the crime. They are general in nature, deliberately vague, and cover long periods of time. They are meant to embarrass the suspects (both guilty and innocent) and to evoke arousal. These goals are facilitated, on the one hand, by giving suspects no choice but to lie when answering the control questions, and, on the other hand, making it clear to suspects that the polygraph will detect these lies. Examiners formulate a control question for which, in their view, a denial is deceptive. The exact formulation of the question depends on the examinee's circumstances; a control question in an examination regarding a murder might be "Have you ever tried to hurt someone to get revenge?" (Iacono & Patrick, 1997, p. 255), in a case where the examiner believes that the examinee has indeed hurt someone at some point in his or her life. Under normal circumstances, some examinees might admit this wrongdoing. However, during a polygraph examination they are unlikely to do so, because the examiner tells the examinee that admitting to this behavior would cause the examiner to conclude that the examinee is the type of person who would commit the crime in question and is therefore likely to be considered guilty. The examinee feels that he or she has no other choice than to deny this earlier wrongdoing and thus give an untruthful answer to the control question.

The CQT is based on the assumption that control questions will generate more arousal than the relevant questions in the innocent suspect. The innocent examinee will become more concerned with regard to his or her answers to the control questions because (1) the examiner puts so much emphasis on the control questions, and (2) the examinee knows he or she is lying in response to the control questions but answering the relevant questions truthfully. However, the same control questions are expected to elicit less arousal in guilty suspects than the relevant questions. A guilty suspect gives deceptive responses to both types of question, which, in principle, should produce similar physiological reactions to both types of question. However, because relevant questions represent the most immediate and serious threat to the examinee, they will lead to a stronger physiological response than the control questions.

The aim of the GKT is to ascertain whether examinees possess knowledge about a particular crime which they do not want to reveal. For example, suppose that the examinee is a man who killed somebody with a knife, left the knife at the murder scene, and tells the police that he is not involved in the crime in any way. The police might then use the Guilty Knowledge Test to determine if the suspect is telling the truth when he denies any involvement in the crime. In this test the examiner shows the suspect several types of knives, including the one used in the murder (assuming it has been recovered). For each knife, the examinee is asked whether he recognizes it as one he used. Both innocent and guilty examinees deny that they have used such a knife. A guilty examinee, however, recognizes the knife he has used. It is assumed that this so-called guilty knowledge will produce a heightened physiological response that will be detected by the polygraph. Lykken (1998) described how the GKT could have been used in the O.J. Simpson murder trial. Questions that could have been used in a GKT administered immediately after the body of Simpson's wife was found included the following:

> (1) "You know that Nicole has been found murdered, Mr. Simpson. How was she killed?—Was she drowned? Was she hit on the head with something? Was she shot? Was she beaten to death? Was she stabbed? Was she strangled?" and (2) "Where did we find her body? Was it—in the living room? In the driveway? By the side gate? In the kitchen? In the bedroom? By the pool?" (Lykken, 1998, p. 298)

Similar to testing the accuracy of CBCA assessments, the accuracy of polygraph tests has been tested both in laboratory and field studies. Laboratory studies in polygraph testing often use a "mock crime" paradigm, in which "guilty participants" are instructed to commit a mock crime and "innocent participants" are told that they are suspected of the crime. Both "innocent" and "guilty" participants are then given a polygraph test. These studies, which generally show favorable results for polygraph testing (for recent reviews of laboratory-based polygraph studies, see Ben-Shakhar & Elaad, 2003; MacLaren, 2001; Raskin & Honts, 2002; Vrij, 2000a), are fiercely attacked by polygraph opponents. One issue raised by opponents is that the "guilty" participants have little incentive to try to beat the test, and the "innocent" participants are unlikely to be concerned about the relevant questions (Iacono & Patrick, 1997).

Numerous field studies have been published, but they are subject to debate. The problem is that the quality of polygraph field studies conducted or published is low (Committee to Review the Scientific Evidence on the Polygraph, 2003). Similar to CBCA field studies, one of the main issues is establishing the ground truth; that is, establishing with certainty whether the suspect is actually innocent or guilty. Ideally, this certainty would be established with corroborative and conclusive evidence (e.g., DNA evidence) that is gathered independent of the polygraph test. However, this type of evidence is typically not available in cases where polygraph tests are conducted. Typically, polygraph tests are conducted when no corroborative evidence is available. Therefore, in most field studies confessions are used to establish the ground truth. A suspect is considered guilty when he or she confesses to the crime under investigation, and innocent when another suspect confesses to the crime. The problem with confessions is that they are not independent of polygraph outcomes. For example, a guilty suspect who passes the test is unlikely to confess, because there is no further evidence against him or her. Since that suspect is the culprit, it is unlikely that anyone else will confess to that crime. In other words, in this case a confession will typically not occur, and the case will not be included in the field study, because only cases in which someone made a confession are included. The incorrect polygraph decision will therefore not be noted, and the result is that accuracy percentages reported in field studies that are based on confessions (almost all field studies) are likely to be inflated. (For a further discussion of this issue, see Fiedler, Schmid, and Stahl, 2002.)

Several reviews have been published regarding the accuracy of CQT (see Table 3.1). The outcomes differ because of different inclusion criteria. Perhaps the most lenient criteria were set by Saxe, Dougherty, and Cross (1985). Their review was initiated by the U.S. Congressional Office of Technology Assessment (OTA) to advise President Reagan about polygraph testing, and included 10 studies that met the OTA standards. As can be seen in Table 3.1, their review presented the most favorable outcomes for CQT polygraph testing. Taking all CQT reviews into account, Table 3.1 shows that there is reasonable agreement among the reviews regarding guilty suspects. Correct classifications were made in 83–89% of the cases. There is less agreement regarding innocent suspects, and findings are less positive than for guilty suspects: between 53 and 78% of innocent suspects were correctly classified. These relatively low accuracy rates for innocent suspects imply that, despite being innocent, they nevertheless might have experienced arousal when answering the relevant questions. For example, arousal may occur (1) when the relevant questions are generally arousal-evoking questions (e.g., when an innocent man, suspected of murdering his beloved wife, is asked questions about his wife in a polygraph test, and the memory of her triggers his strong feelings for her); and (2) when the innocent examinee experiences fear of detection, which may occur when the person is afraid that his or her honest answers will not register as true on the polygraph.

Only two field studies regarding the accuracy of the GKT have been published (see Table 3.1), and their findings differed considerably. Both tests revealed very good results regarding the classification of innocent suspects (94% and 98% of innocent suspects were correctly classified) but rather poor results regarding the classification of guilty suspects (76% and 42% of guilty suspects were correctly classified). One explanation for these poor results on guilty suspects is a possible lack of "guilty knowledge." This situation occurs when the questions used in the GKT test are not carefully selected: These could be questions about minor details that the guilty suspect simply has forgotten or perhaps has never known. (e.g., The culprit stole the laptop from a room where a TV was also located. Where exactly was the TV located? Next to the door? Next to the window? Next to the bed?).

Behavioral Analyses

Lie-detection tools based on analyses of nonverbal behavior are less developed than those based on verbal or physiological assessments. Police manuals typically emphasize the importance of examining nonverbal behavior and specify where to pay attention, but this information is never systematic and often inaccurate. In scientific studies concerning the detection of deception on the basis of nonverbal analyses, observers are typically given videotapes or audiotapes and asked to judge whether the people in the scenario are lying or telling the truth. (In fact, in those studies, observers could pay attention to a mixture of nonverbal behavior and speech content.) Statements from liars and truth tellers are usually taken from laboratory studies (i.e., liars and truth tellers produced statements for the sake of the experiment) and rarely from real-life situations. Vrij (2000a) examined the percentages of correct truth and lie detection across 37 studies. Included were studies in which observers were laypersons (typically, university students) who tried to detect lies and truths told by people they did not know. The overall accuracy rate was 57% (see also Table 3.1). The accuracy rate for detecting truths (67%) was higher than for detecting lies (44%), with the latter percentage falling below the level of chance. This high accuracy rate for detecting truths can partly be explained by the truth bias.

It could be argued that university students do not habitually detect deception. Perhaps professional lie catchers, such as police officers or customs officers, would obtain higher accuracy rates than laypersons. It might be that professional lie catchers' experiences with interviewing people have a positive influence on their skills to detect deceit. Vrij and Mann (2003) reviewed studies in which professional lie catchers participated as observers. The overall accuracy rate found in those studies was 55%, as were the accuracy rates for detecting lies and detecting truths, separately. However, some groups of lie detectors seem to be better than others. Ekman and O'Sullivan (1991) and

Ekman, O'Sullivan, and Frank (1999) found that Secret Service agents (64% overall accuracy rate), CIA agents (73% overall accuracy rate) and sheriffs (67% overall accuracy rate) were better lie detectors than personnel from other divisions of police officers. Due to the artificial nature of these lie detection studies, however, we might wonder whether they truly measured professional lie catchers' ability to distinguish between truths and lies.

In all the studies reviewed above, police officers' and other professional lie catchers' performances were investigated by the use of noninteractive designs; that is, the presumed experts watched video clips. Such designs do not mirror real-life situations very well. To remedy this mismatch, Hartwig et al. (2004b) placed experienced police officers in a face-to-face situation with a suspect and let the officers conduct the interrogations in whatever manner they found appropriate. This design was an attempt to investigate the lie-detection ability of experienced police officers in a more ecologically valid fashion. The suspects were undergraduates, half of whom had committed a mock crime and later denied it (liars), and half of whom had committed no such crime (truth tellers). The result was discouraging in terms of deception-detection performance, with experienced police officers unable to detect deception any better than expected by chance alone (overall accuracy rate 56.7%). Critically, almost every second time that police officers assessed a suspect as a liar, the suspect was actually innocent and had told the truth during the interrogation. The study by Hartwig et al. also highlighted the great extent to which interrogation styles differed, despite the fact that all police officers faced the same task. For example, the total number of questions asked by the police officers during the interrogation ranged from 17 to 69; the number of times the suspect was interrupted ranged from 0 to 11 times; and in half of the interrogations the police officer spoke more than the suspect. No covariation was found between lie-detection ability and interrogation characteristics (e.g., number and type of questions).

Another way to increase the ecological validity of this type of study is to examine police officers' skills when they attempt to detect truths and lies told by real suspects during police interviews. Mann et al. (2004) showed 99 police officers a total of 54 video clips of suspects who were lying and telling the truth during their police interviews. The suspects were all being interviewed in connection with serious crimes such as murder, rape, and arson. None of the sample of police officers belonged to the specific groups that were identified by Ekman and his colleagues as being superior lie detectors. The overall accuracy rate was 65%, with a 64% truth accuracy rate and a 66% lie accuracy rate.

Although these accuracy rates were higher than generally found in previous studies, incorrect classifications were still frequently made. One problem lie detectors face is that nonverbal differences between liars and truth tellers are typically small and therefore hard to spot (Vrij, 1994). Another factor that hampers lie detection is that people often have incorrect beliefs about how liars behave (Akehurst et al., 1996; Mann et al., 2004; Strömwall & Granhag,

2003; Strömwall, Granhag, & Hartwig, 2004; Taylor & Vrij, 2000; Vrij & Semin, 1996; Vrij & Taylor, 2003). This information suggests that people could become better lie detectors by conducting detailed analyses of diagnostic nonverbal cues displayed by liars and truth tellers. Research has supported this view. For example, Ekman, O'Sullivan, Friesen, and Scherer (1991) analyzed liars' and truth tellers' smiles and pitch of voice and correctly classified 86% of liars and truth tellers on the basis of these measurements (see also Table 3.1). Frank and Ekman (1997) examined signs of emotions that emerged via (micro) facial expressions and correctly classified around 80% of liars and truth tellers on the basis of these facial expressions. Vrij, Akehurst, Soukara, and Bull (2004) and Vrij et al. (2000) examined nonverbal cues that indicate cognitive demand (e.g., pauses in speech, decrease in subtle movements) and correctly classified between 71 and 78% of the truths and lies told.

Further Factors Affecting Deception-Detection Performance and Strategy

Repeated Interrogations

In real-life situations lie catchers rarely base their final assessment of veracity on one statement only. Instead, suspects often have to go through repeated interrogations. However, very few studies have focused on the effects of repeated interrogations. Granhag and Strömwall (2001a) conducted a study in which the suspects were interrogated three times over a period of 11 days (each interrogation was videotaped). The "suspects" were undergraduates who either lied or told the truth about a scenario in which a man was assaulted. In the next stage other undergraduates watched the videotapes and were asked to assess veracity. The main finding was that judges who assessed veracity after seeing only one interrogation (55.6% correct judgments) performed in line with judges who had seen all three interrogations (56.9% correct judgments). It was also found that judges who assessed veracity after seeing one interrogation (55.6% accuracy) and then, again, after seeing the additional two interrogations, significantly increased their performance (69.4% accuracy). This finding indicates that a step-by-step response mode (i.e., repeated assessments of veracity) may facilitate the use of a more effective information-processing strategy than an end-of-sequence response mode (i.e., one final assessment of veracity). However, much more research is needed on how lie catchers integrate this kind of sequential information.

Granhag and Strömwall (2002) also showed that when lie catchers assessed veracity after watching one interrogation only, the frequencies of the subjective cues reported were evenly distributed across a number of different categories (e.g., "details," "completeness"). But as the basis for assessing veracity was altered from one statement to three consecutive statements (i.e., three interrogations with the same "suspect"), the distribution of the reported subjective cues to deception changed dramatically. That is, a new category had to be added to the list of categories: "consistency." This category turned out to be the most commonly used, irrespective of whether the suspect was assessed as a liar ("The statements are inconsistent over time, therefore he [or she] is lying") or as a truth teller ("The statements are consistent over time, therefore he [or she] is telling the truth"). In a later section we return to the consistency cue and explain why a stereotypical use of this heuristic may be problematic.

Partners in Crime

In real-life cases, lie catchers often have to try to detect deceit on the basis of statements derived from multiple suspects, and sometimes those suspects have been interrogated repeatedly. Similar to the questions pertaining to repeated interrogations, questions regarding how to assess statements from multiple suspects have been overlooked. Strömwall, Granhag, and Jonsson (2003) conducted a study in which each member of 10 truth-telling and 10 lying pairs of "suspects" was interrogated twice about an alibi. In the next stage, the videotaped interrogations were shown to judges who tried to assess veracity. Again, both the suspects and the judges were undergraduates. The overall deception-detection performance was modest (from 58.3 to 62.5%). Furthermore, lie catchers given access to a larger number of statements did not outperform lie catchers given access to a lesser number of statements.

An analysis of the subjective cues reported to justify the assessments showed that the judges were very occupied with the extent to which the different statements were consistent or not. Specifically, the results showed that the judges paid more attention to whether the two suspects were consistent *between* themselves, than to whether each of them was consistent *within* him- or herself. The cue "consistency within pairs of suspects" was reported to be used more than twice as often as the cue "consistency within single suspects." Collapsed, these two types of consistency cues constituted no less than one-third of all cues reported.

In sum, research on the subjective cues to deception suggests that lie catchers faced with a single statement from a suspect will report a wide range of different subjective cues. But if faced with consecutive statements from a single suspect and/or statements from multiple suspects, the pattern of the reported cues becomes much less scattered, in that many judges tend to go for consistency (either within a suspect or between suspects).

Effects of Presentation Mode (Live vs. Video)

The material on which lie catchers base their veracity assessments may come in different forms (presentation modes). A lie catcher may, for example, meet the suspect in a-face-to-face situation, watch a videotaped interrogation, listen to an audiotape, or read the protocol of a transcribed interrogation. Research shows that the type of presentation mode may affect both deception-detection accuracy and judgmental biases. For the current context, we focus mainly on differences between live and video presentation modes. Strömwall and Granhag (2003) showed that police officers, prosecutors, and judges strongly believe that it is easier to detect deception during a face-to-face interrogation than when watching the very same interrogation on video. In contrast, research shows that those who observe an interrogation on video are more accurate (Buller, Strzyzewski, & Hunsaker, 1991; Feeley & deTurck, 1997; Granhag & Strömwall, 2001a) or as accurate (Hartwig et al., 2004b) in detecting lies as those who actually conduct the interrogation. This finding may be explained by the fact that an interrogator must spend cognitive effort on monitoring him- or herself and the suspect, posing the correct questions, and making the appropriate conversational extensions for different segments of the interrogation (Feeley & deTurck, 1997). In contrast, a lie catcher who watches the videotaped version of the same interrogation can allocate all resources to watching and listening to the suspect.

In terms of judgmental biases it has been found that interrogators exhibit more truth bias than do those who watch the same interrogations on video (Feeley & deTurck, 1997; Granhag & Strömwall, 2001b). It can be speculated that the physical appearance and the proximity of the suspect increases the difficulty of disbelieving him or her. It should be noted that this increased truth bias in the context of a live presentation mode seems to hold for laypeople but not for police officers (Hartwig et al., 2004b).

Why Such Poor Deception Detection Performance?

It is intriguing to reflect upon why people perform so poorly in deception-detection tests, and many scholars have suggested many different explanations. O'Sullivan (2003) summarized much of what has been said on the topic and lists no less than 12 different reasons for the mediocre lie-detection ability found. All reasons listed are formulated from the perspective of the person trying to distinguish between truth and deception, and some reasons have more bearing than others on forensic contexts. Here we highlight six of these reasons. First, it might be that lie catchers underutilize the nonverbal behaviors involved in emotional and cognitive reactions to lying; that is, they do not know which nonverbal cues to attend to when trying to detect deceit (Ekman et al., 1991). Second, lie catchers may overrely on the content of the speech, instead of, for example, paying attention to *how* a suspect speaks (DePaulo, Rosenthal, Rosenkrantz, & Green, 1982). Third, the detection performance of lie catchers may be impeded by truth (Vrij, 2000a) or lie biases (Ekman, 2001; Hartwig et al., 2004b). Fourth, lie catchers might hold incorrect beliefs about cues to deception; for example, in many Western societies it is believed that eye-gaze aversion is a sign of deception (Vrij, 2000a). Fifth, research shows that lie catchers tend to misinterpret deviations from the norm as signs of deception (Bond, Omar, Pitre, & Lashley, 1992); hence, a baby-faced, extraverted, and "nonweird" person is likely to be judged as truthful. (For recent findings supporting this idea, see Bull and Vine, 2003; for a recent review, see Bull, 2004.) Finally, O'Sullivan argues that it is reasonable to propose that lie-catching ability is moderated by social–emotional intelligence, which, in turn, varies among people (Riggio, Tucker, & Throckmorton, 1987).

In addition to the reasons listed in her paper, O'Sullivan (2003) offers yet another reason for why people are poor at detecting deception. Her point of departure is a well-established cognitive heuristic: the fundamental attribution error (Ross & Nisbett, 1991). This is the tendency, when forming impressions about others, to overestimate the importance of trait-dispositional factors (e.g., sociability) and to underestimate the importance of the situation in which the judged person is placed (e.g., a police interrogation). O'Sullivan shows that lie catchers who attributed positive trait characteristics (dispositional) to the person they were judging also tended to judge this person as truthful in a given situation (state). Conversely, persons who received negative ratings in terms of trait (trustworthiness) were often judged as liars. In sum, the fundamental attribution error was found to significantly undermine the lie-catcher's ability to detect truth and deception. For future research it might be fruitful to focus further on trait–state consistencies and inconsistencies.

OBJECTIVE INDICATORS OF DECEPTION AND TRUTH

One of the reasons why accuracy rates in lie detection are never perfect (100%) is that no single behavioral pattern, verbal response, or physiological response is uniquely related to deception. In other words, there is no giveaway cue, like Pinocchio's growing nose. However, the accuracy scores are typically above the level of chance, implying that *something* noticeable must occur in liars that gives away their lies. Indeed, it has been found that some responses are more likely to occur during deception than others. This selection probably depends on three processes that a liar may experience: emotion, content complexity, and attempted control (DePaulo, Stone, & Lassiter, 1985a; Vrij, 2000a; Zuckerman et al., 1981). Each of these processes may influence a person's response (Vrij, 2000a). In other words, a liar's behavior, voice, or speech might be affected not because he or she is lying but because, for example, he or she experiences certain emotions when lying. Each process emphasizes a different aspect of deception and deceptive responses; however, the distinction between these aspects is artificial. Lies may well feature all three aspects, and the three processes should not be considered as exclusive camps. Zuckerman and colleagues (1981), who introduced these three factors, also included a fourth factor in their theoretical model: arousal. We do not include this factor because, in our view, it overlaps the emotion factor. Zuckerman et al. suggested this overlap by concluding their paragraph on the arousal factor with the following statement: "It is possible, however, that the general autonomic responsivity to deception reflects specific emotions. If so, cues to deception may be accounted for by the particular affects that are involved rather than by general arousal" (p. 9). Other theoretical models for explaining nonverbal cues to deception are described in the deception literature (Buller & Burgoon, 1996; Ekman, 2001; Ekman & Friesen, 1969; for a description of each of these theoretical models, see DePaulo et al., 2003.)

Three Processes That Influence Lying

The three most common types of emotion associated with deception are guilt, fear, and excitement (Ekman, 2001). A liar might feel guilty because he or she is lying, might be afraid of getting caught, or might be excited about having the opportunity to fool someone. The strength of these emotions depends on the personality of the liar and on the circumstances under which the lie takes place (Ekman, 2001).

Sometimes liars find it difficult to lie (content complexity), because they have to think of plausible answers, avoid contradicting themselves, and tell a lie that is consistent with everything the observer knows or might find out, while avoiding slips of the tongue. Moreover, liars have to remember what they have said so that they can say the same things again when asked to repeat their story (Burgoon, Buller, & Guerrero, 1995; Vrij, 2000a).

The process of attempted control refers to liars' attempts to suppress any cues that would reveal their lies; they engage in impression management in order to avoid getting caught (Buller & Burgoon, 1996; Krauss, 1981). This management requires liars to suppress their nervousness effectively, mask evidence that they have to think hard, know how they normally respond in order to convey an honest and convincing impression, and show only the responses they want to show. It may well be the case that when controlling their body language, liars may overcontrol their behavior, possibly exhibiting body language that appears planned, rehearsed—and lacking in all spontaneity. For example, liars may believe that movements will give away their lies (Hocking & Leathers, 1980; Vrij & Semin, 1996) and so move very deliberately, avoiding any movements that are not strictly essential. This attempt would result in an unusual degree of rigidity and inhibition, because people do normally make movements that are not essential (DePaulo & Kirkendol, 1989). Liars may also be reluctant to say certain things (e.g., they might be reluctant to spontaneously admit that what they said previously was incorrect) because they will fear that this retraction will make their stories appear less convincing. Another possible cue that may result from impression management is a "flat" performance due to a lack of spontaneous (*un*-premeditated) involvement (Burgoon & Buller, 1994; DePaulo et al., 2003). Charles Ingram, who was found guilty in the United Kingdom of trying to cheat his way to the top prize in the popular TV quiz *Who Wants to Be a Millionaire?* might have experienced this giveaway. Staff working for the TV program became suspicious when Ingram and his wife, after winning the top prize of £1,000,000, "had not appeared as jubilant as the newly rich might" (*The Independent*, 8 April 2003, p. 9).

All three processes may occur at the same time. That is, liars could be nervous, having to think hard, and trying to control themselves all simultaneously. Which of these processes is most prevalent depends on the type of lie. Liars are more nervous when the stakes (i.e., negative consequences of getting caught and positive consequences of succeeding) are high; hence, nervous responses are more likely to accompany high-stake lies. Liars have to think harder when the lie is complicated; therefore, indicators of increased cognitive load are more likely to occur with complicated lies than easy lies. Liars who are motivated to avoid getting caught may try harder to make an honest impression than those who are less motivated. Therefore, attempts to control behavior, voice, and speech may be more likely to occur in motivated liars.

Before discussing the outcomes of reviews about how liars respond, it should be emphasized that the approaches only suggest that the presence of signs of emotions, content complexity, and impression management may be indicative of deception. None of these approaches claims that the presence of these signs *necessarily* indicates deception. Truth tellers might experience exactly the same processes. For example, innocent (truthful) suspects might also be anxious if they worry that they will not be believed by a police officer (Ofshe & Leo, 1997). Because of that fear, they may show the same nervous reactions as guilty liars who are afraid of being caught (Bond & Fahey, 1987). This crossover of cues puts the lie detector in a difficult position. Should the signs of fear be interpreted as indicators of guilt or of innocence? The behavior does not provide the answer. Ekman (2001) labeled the false accusation of a truth teller on the basis of the emotional reactions he or she displays the "Othello error," after Shakespeare's character. Othello falsely accuses Desdemona (his wife) of betrayal. He tells her that she may as well confess, because he is going to kill her for her treachery. Desdemona asks Cassio (her alleged lover) to be called so that he can testify to her innocence. Othello tells her that he has already murdered Cassio. Realizing that she cannot prove her innocence, Desdemona reacts with an emotional outburst. Othello misinterprets this outburst as a sign of her infidelity.

Diagnostic Cues to Deception

Here we briefly summarize the main findings of several reviews of verbal and nonverbal cues to deception (DePaulo et al., 2003; Vrij, 2000a, in press). An overview of these cues is also presented in Table 3.2. Several of these cues are part of the CBCA and Reality Monitoring instruments (indicated in Table 3.2). Not included in the present review are the cues listed by DePaulo et al. (2003, Appendix B), which were based on a small number of estimates (with the exception of the facial micro-expressions that we discuss later). In addition to the cues mentioned in the present section, DePaulo et al.'s (2003) review discussed additional cues that cannot be easily classified as verbal or nonverbal behaviors, for example, pressed lips, facial pleasantness, and nervous appearance.

Liars tend to speak with a higher-pitched voice that might be the result of

TABLE 3.2. Overview of Diagnostic Verbal and Nonverbal Cues of Deception

Nonverbal cues		Verbal cues	
High-pitched voice	>	Story sounds plausible	<
Voice sounds tense	>	Person sounds ambivalent	>
Speech errors	</>	Unstructured production (CBCA)	<
Speech hesitations	</>	Speech length	<
Illustrators	<	Number of details (CBCA)	<
Hand and finger movements	<	Visual details (Reality Monitoring)	<
		Auditory details (Reality Monitoring)	<
		Quotes (CBCA)	<
		Spatial details (Reality Monitoring)	<
		Temporal details (Reality Monitoring)[a]	<
		Person sounds expressive	<
		Person sounds passive	>
		Person sounds uncertain	>
		Person sounds involved	<
		Person is cooperative	<
		Negative statements	>

Note. >, more during deception; <, less during deception.
[a]Contextual embeddings (a CBCA criterion) is a combination of auditory and temporal details.

arousal (Ekman, Friesen, & Scherer, 1976). However, differences in pitch between liars and truth tellers are usually very small and only detectable with sophisticated equipment. Also, sometimes liars' voices sound tenser than truth tellers' voices—another concomitant of arousal. The results concerning speech errors (e.g., word or sentence repetition, sentence change, sentence incompletions, slips of the tongue) and speech hesitations (e.g., use of speech fillers such as "ah," "um," "er") show a conflicting pattern. In most studies an increase in such errors (particularly word and phrase repetitions) and in hesitations during deception have been found. These behaviors might have been the result of the need for the liars to think hard about their answers. Alternatively, the increased behaviors might be the result of nervousness. In some studies, however, a decrease in speech errors and hesitations occurred. There is some evidence that variations in lie complexity are responsible for these conflicting findings (Vrij & Heaven, 1999). Lies that are difficult to tell are associated with in an increase in speech errors and hesitations (in line with the content complexity explanation), whereas lies that are easy to tell are associated with a decrease in speech hesitations and speech errors (in line with the attempted control explanation).

Liars tend to make fewer illustrators (i.e., hand and arm gestures designed to modify, emphasize, or supplement what is being said verbally) and fewer hand and finger movements (nonfunctional movements of hands and fingers that do not involve arm movements) than truth tellers. The decrease in these movements might be the result of lie complexity, the increased cognitive load of which results in a neglect of body language, thereby reducing overall animation (Ekman & Friesen, 1972). The decrease in movements might also be the result of an overcontrol of behavior. Finally, the decrease in movements might be the result of a lack of emotional involvement analogous to the Charles Ingram example mentioned above.

Compared to stories told by truth tellers, liars' stories sound less plausible and more ambivalent—possibly the result of the difficulties liars face when they tell their stories. Another verbal indicator of lies is structured production: Liars tend to tell their stories in chronological order (this happened first, and then this, and then that, and so on), whereas truth tellers sometimes tend to give their account in unstructured ways, particularly when they talk about emotional events. When a person is clearly upset, he or she may report what has happened in a chaotic and incomprehensible way. In fact, the story can be so incomprehensible that the listener has to ask the person to sit down for a while, to calm down, and repeat exactly what has happened, beginning with the start of the event. This unstructured production effect disappears when the person has already told the story a couple of times or frequently thought about the event, rehearsing it in his or her head, because this repetition produces a more chronological order in the story telling (Vrij, 2000a). Liars tend to tell their stories in a logical time sequence (Zaparniuk, Yuille, & Taylor, 1995), perhaps because this is easier to do.

Truth tellers tend to speak for longer time periods than liars do, probably because they include more details in their statements than liars (Vrij, in press). In particular, truth tellers include more visual details (they describe things they saw) and more auditory details (they describe things they heard) into their accounts. They also tend to literally repeat what has been said more frequently (e.g., "Then he asked, 'Could you please pass me the salt?' " whereas liars would be more inclined to say, "Then he asked me to give him the salt"). Moreover, truth tellers mention more spatial details (e.g., "He walked behind us," "The chair was under the window," "We were in his bedroom") and more temporal details (e.g., "He let the cat out before he put the kettle on," "Approximately 15 minutes later the phone rang again," "He stayed with me for about 3 hours"). There are several reasons for these differences between liars and truth tellers (Vrij, 2000a). Liars sometimes do not have enough imagination to invent such details, or the details may be too difficult to fabricate. Moreover, liars may not want to provide many different details, because they are afraid that they will forget what they have said and will not be able to repeat these details when asked to do so. Finally, differences might occur because memories of *experienced* events differ in quality from memories of *imagined* events (Johnson & Raye, 1981, 1998). Unlike memories of imagined events, memories of real experiences are obtained through perceptual processes and are therefore more likely to contain perceptual information when relayed (i.e., information about what someone saw, heard, said, and so on).

Compared to truth tellers, liars tend to sound less vocally expressive, more passive, and more uncertain. These characteristics might be the result of an attempt to overcontrol behavior. Liars also sound less involved, come across as less cooperative, and tend to make more negative statements (which might be caused by a negative emotion felt by the liar).

Perhaps the most remarkable outcome of the literature reviews is that several signs of nervousness, such as gaze aversion and fidgeting, are *unrelated* to deception. Many people (both laypersons and professional lie catchers) believe that those behaviors are associated with deception (Akehurst et al., 1996; Mann et al., 2004; Strömwall & Granhag, 2003; Strömwall, Granhag, & Hartwig, 2004; Taylor & Vrij, 2000; Vrij & Semin, 1996; Vrij & Taylor, 2003). One reason why cues of nervousness do not seem to be related to deception is that truth tellers also may be nervous (see the Othello error above). Secondly, the absence of cues of nervousness might be the result of an artifact. As discussed before, most deception studies are conducted in a laboratory, in which people are requested to lie or tell the truth for the sake of the experiment. In such studies liars might not be worried enough to show cues of nervousness. Different outcomes may therefore emerge when researchers investigate the reactions of liars in high-stake situations.

Vrij and Mann (2001) and Mann, Vrij, and Bull (2002) are among the very few researchers who have investigated liars' behavioral responses in high-stake situations. For example, Mann et al. (2002) examined the behavioral responses of 16 suspects during their police interviews. The police interviews were videotaped and the tapes were made available to the researchers for detailed scoring of the suspects' behavioral responses. All interviews were clear high-stake situations. The suspects were interviewed in connection with serious crimes such as murder, rape and arson, and were facing long prison sentences if found guilty. Results revealed that the suspects in these high-stake situations did not show the nervous behaviors typically believed to be associated with lying, such as gaze aversion and fidgeting. In fact, they exhibited an increase in pauses, a decrease in eye blinks, and (male suspects) a decrease in finger, hand, and arm movements. These characteristics are more in line with the content complexity and attempted control explanations than with the emotional explanations. The strongest evidence that content complexity affected suspects' behavior more than nervousness was the finding that liars made fewer eye blinks. Research has shown that nervousness results in an increase in eye blinking (Harrigan & O'Connell, 1996), whereas increased cognitive load results in a decrease in eye blinking (Wallbott & Scherer, 1991).

The apparent predominance of cognitive processes compared to emotional processes in those suspects is perhaps not surprising. Many of the suspects included in Mann et al.'s (2002) study have had regular contact with the police. Therefore, they were probably familiar with police interviews—a familiarity that might decrease their nervousness. However, suspects in police interviews are often less intelligent than the average person (Gudjonsson, 1992), and there is evidence that less intelligent people have more difficulty in inventing plausible and convincing stories (Ekman & Frank, 1993).

The review revealed more verbal cues to deception than nonverbal cues. This finding contradicts the information found in most police manuals, which typically emphasizes nonverbal cues to deception. Researchers have concentrated on nonverbal cues to deception up until the late 1980s (DePaulo & Kirkendol, 1989; Ekman, 2001). Ekman's work (2001) has revealed that observing emotional micro-expressions in the face might reveal valuable information about deception. Strongly felt emotions almost automatically activate muscle actions in the face. Anger, for example, results in a narrowing of the lips and lowering of the eyebrows. Eyebrows that are simultaneously raised and pulled together; a raised upper eyelid and tensed lower eyelid typically denote fear. If a person denies an emotional state that is actually being felt, he or she will have to suppress these facial expressions to be credible. Thus, a scared person claiming to be unafraid has to suppress the facial micro-expressions that typically indicate fear. This suppression is difficult to manage, especially because these emotions may arise unexpectedly and autonomically. For instance, people do not usually deliberately choose to become frightened; this response happens automatically, in response to a particular event that took place or a particular thought. The moment fright occurs, a fearful facial expression may appear that gives away the lie. People are usually able to suppress these expressions within $\frac{1}{25}$ of a second after they begin to appear (Ekman, 2001).

The opposite can occur as well. A person can pretend to experience a particular emotion, whereas in fact this emotion is not felt. A person can pretend to be angry, whereas in reality he or she is not angry at all. In order to be convincing, the liar should produce an angry facial expression; that is, he or she should try to narrow the lips and so on. However, these muscle actions are very difficult for most people to make voluntarily (Ekman, 2001). It is also difficult to fake an emotion other than the one that is actually felt. For example, a potential hijacker may become scared during a conversation with security personnel when he realizes that they might discover his plans. He can decide to mask this emotional state by pretending to be angry with the security personnel because they are checking on him so thoroughly and apparently do not trust him. In order to be convincing, he has to suppress his fearful facial expression and replace it with an angry facial expression. This switch is difficult to achieve: He has to lower his eyebrows (sign of anger), whereas his eyebrows tend to raise (sign of fear; Ekman, 2001).

Ekman's observations could well be of value. For example, in one of our studies (Vrij & Mann, 2001) we included a person who held a televized press conference to ask for information about his missing girlfriend. Later it turned out that he himself had killed his girlfriend. A detailed analysis of the video clip revealed that he showed a micro-expression of a (suppressed) smile during that press conference. His smile was interesting, given the context. Why did the man smile? And why did he attempt to suppress that smile? Although his smiling at a press conference cannot be interpreted as a definite indication of deceit, at least, it made the man appear suspicious. Unfortunately, no empirical test of the frequency of emotional micro-expressions during lying and truth telling has been published in peer-reviewed journals—which is also the reason why these micro-expressions did not emerge as cues to deception in the literature reviews we cited.

Ekman and colleagues also discovered that smiles are related to deception only when a distinction is made between felt and false smiles (Ekman, Friesen, & O'Sullivan, 1988). They found that truth tellers showed more felt smiles and liars more false smiles. Felt smiles include all smiles in which the person actually experiences a positive emotion and presumably would report that positive emotion. False smiles are deliberately made to convince another person that a positive emotion is felt, whereas, in fact, it is not. Felt and false smiles produce slightly different facial muscular actions, and the skilled observer is able to spot these differences (Ekman, 2001).

We believe that one explanation for an emphasis on nonverbal cues to deception has been that researchers did not know to which verbal cues they should attend. The introduction of CBCA in the late 1980s and Reality Monitoring in the 1990s provided researchers with a framework to use in analyzing speech content. Several of the cues included in these instruments have been found to discriminate between truths and lies.

LIARS' AND TRUTH TELLERS' STRATEGIES

In contrast to extensively researched topics such as nonverbal cues to deception and deception-detection abilities, liars' and truth tellers' strategies have been investigated to a very limited extent (DePaulo et al., 2003). This paucity is unfortunate, because reflecting on strategies and their consequences might help us understand both the (apparent lack of) differences between liars' and truth tellers' nonverbal behavior and the poor deception-detection performance commonly found. Just as lie catchers' beliefs guide their deception-detection strategies, it is reasonable to believe that suspects' strategies will guide their behavior, irrespective of whether they are telling the truth or lying. In the few instances where strategies have been highlighted, there is a tendency to overlook the fact that truth tellers employ strategies to convince the people to whom they are talking (DePaulo et al., 2003). DePaulo et al. (2003) suggested that both liars' and truth tellers' behaviors can be seen from a self-presentational perspective, in which all self-presentations (even truthful ones) are edited.

At the most basic level, distinctions can be made between strategies pertaining to (1) the theme of the statement (e.g., story line, plausibility), (2) how the statement should be presented (e.g., level of details, order of events), and (3) how to act in terms of nonverbal behavior (e.g., eye contact, body language). First we briefly touch upon the issue of credible stories, then close in on verbal and nonverbal strategies as the stakes rise, and lastly, address verbal strategies and their consequences when suspects are interrogated repeatedly. Because systematic knowledge on this topic is meager, in addition to studies on liars' and truth tellers' self-reported strategies, we need to learn from studies that have examined what people believe characterizes credible stories, as well as offer some speculations on how liars and truth tellers may reason in terms of strategies.

The Hallmarks of a Credible Story

What constitutes a plausible story? Several researchers have suggested rules to which plausible stories must conform: so-called story grammars (e.g., Robinson, 1981). Bennett and Feldman (1981) imported this line of reasoning into a forensic context by asking students to tell true and false stories. In the next phase, they found that those asked to assess these stories had a difficult time, but that stories assessed as truthful shared some properties that stories assessed as deceptive lacked. Stories assessed as truthful were characterized by a clear-cut central action to which all other elements connected, and a context that explained the different actors' behavior. Importantly, a credible story is free from ambiguities, such as contradictions and missing elements. For a more detailed discussion of story plausibility and construction, see the work by Pennington and Hastie (1986) and the theory of anchored narratives by Wagenaar, van Koppen, and Crombag (1993).

There is a link between what people think constitutes a plausible story and the strategies that liars use. In one of the very few studies on liars' strategies, Malone et al. (1997, as cited in DePaulo et al., 2003) asked liars about how they created their lies; as many as half of them said that they based their lies on experiences from their own lives, but altered critical details. In line with this finding, Granhag, Strömwall, and Jonsson (2003) speculate that placing oneself in a familiar environment and performing highly scripted activities is probably a wise route to choose when, for example, fabricating an alibi. In addition, preliminary data from a study by Strömwall, Granhag, and Landström (2004) indicate that children (ages 11–13), when asked to deceive, placed themselves in a scenario that they had heard about but not actually participated in, as one of their major deceptive strategies. In brief, it seems that skillful liars use real episodes as raw material for their lies.

Suspects' Strategies as the Stakes Rise

In a study by Strömwall, Granhag, and Hartwig (in press), 30 students were interrogated by experienced police officers about a mock crime (half lied and half told the truth). After the interrogations the suspects were asked about the strategies they had used to make (1) a credible impression (nonverbal strategies), and (2) their statements appear reliable (verbal strategies). The most common nonverbal strategy cited by both truth tellers and liars was to refrain from making any excess movements (about 50% of the liars and truth tellers reported using this strategy); the second most common strategy was to try to maintain eye contact (approximately 25% of the liars and the truth tellers reported using this strategy). In sum, both liars and truth tellers decided on a plan of attempted control, and the results showed that they managed to follow this plan to the same extent (i.e., there were no significant differences between liars and truth tellers in terms of nonverbal behavior).

The most common verbal strategy for truth tellers was to "keep it real" (about 50% of the truth tellers reported using this strategy), whereas the most common verbal strategy for liars was to "keep it simple" (about 40% of the liars reported using this strategy). The finding that the liars decided to keep their story simple and to not add details is supported in previous research (Granhag & Strömwall, 2002). Interestingly, as many as 30% of the truth tellers reported that they had lacked a verbal strategy, whereas the corresponding figure for liars was only about 10%.

Strömwall et al. (in press) speculate that their findings might speak against the idea that a more realistic setting (e.g., as the stakes get higher) will produce more salient differences between liars' and truth tellers' nonverbal behavior (which, in turn, would facilitate the detection of lies). Strömwall et al. raise three arguments in support of their skepticism. First, in high-stake situations the pressure increases for both liars and truth tellers. Second, as the pressure increases, both liars and truth tellers will try harder to appear credible; thus, their awareness of self-presentational strategies will increase, as will their effort in adhering to these strategies. Finally, because the nonverbal strategies used by liars and truth tellers seem to be very similar, guilty and innocent suspects will be very difficult to separate in terms of their nonverbal behavior. However, these conclusions do not rule out that there is *something* that gives away lies, particularly when the stakes are higher. In a series of experiments in which the stakes were manipulated (although the stakes were never really high), it was found that high-stakes lies were easier to detect than low-stakes lies (DePaulo, Kirkendol, Tang, & O'Brien, 1988; DePaulo, Lanier, & Davis, 1983; DePaulo, LeMay, & Epstein, 1991; DePaulo et al., 1985b; Lane & DePaulo, 1999; Vrij, 2000b; Vrij, Harden, Terry, Edward, & Bull, 2001).

Suspects' Strategies When Interrogated Repeatedly

In order to explain the processes at play during repeated interrogations, Granhag and Strömwall (1999) formulated a "repeat-versus-reconstruct" hypothesis that rests on two premises. First, liars know that in order to avoid detection, they must remember what they have stated in previous interrogations. Second, it is a well-established finding that human memory is malleable in its nature (Baddeley, 1990), and that truth tellers therefore can be expected to both gain, lose, and change information over time. In brief, liars will try to repeat what they have said in previous interrogations, whereas truth tellers will try to reconstruct what they have experienced and be less concerned with what they have said in previous interrogations. Granhag and Strömwall (1999) argue that the strategy of repetition used by liars will promote consistency, whereas the truth tellers' more recollective memory processes may, undermine consistency, to some extent.

If the repeat-versus-reconstruct hypothesis holds, what are the consequences in terms of liars' and truth tellers' consecutive statements? Analyzing consistency within single suspects who had been interrogated twice, Granhag et al. (2003) found no significant differences between truthful and deceptive statements in terms of repeated themes, omissions, and contradictions. However, during the second interrogation session, truth tellers were found to add significantly more new themes to their initial story than did liars. That is, there was a stronger reminiscence effect for truthful than for deceptive statements. This finding supports the idea that asking a person to elaborate on a previously reported story is less likely to result in the addition of information if the story is fabricated than if the story is truthful (e.g., Soppe, 1995 as cited in Vrij, 2000a). Shuy (1998) argued, without any qualifications, that a memory that improves over time belongs to a liar. Empirical data suggest that this idea is wrong.

We are not suggesting that lie catchers would be better off ignoring whether consecutive statements are consistent or inconsistent. A suspect who flagrantly contradicts him- or herself should obviously evoke suspicion and merit further investigation. What we are suggesting, however, is that lie catchers should be careful interpreting what could be "natural inconsistency" (e.g., omission and commission errors) as an indication of deception, and to be equally careful in crediting consecutive statements that are "over the top" in terms of consistency.

In this section we stress the strong need for more research on liars' and truth tellers' strategies. The meager amount of research conducted shows that there are some similarities between liars' and truth tellers' strategies (e.g., regarding some nonverbal behaviors), but that differences also exist (e.g., regarding some verbal behaviors). By carefully examining liars' and truth tellers' strategies and the factors that moderate them, we will increase our understanding of deceptive behaviors and perhaps avoid some of the pitfalls that impede the deception-detection process.

MEMORY AS A FACTOR IN DECEPTION

Memory is an important but probably underestimated factor in deception. For example, there is a very close link between memory and the formation of beliefs about cues to deception; theories and research on human memory are the basis for reliability assessment techniques such as the SVA and Reality Monitoring; and human memory holds the raw material of which lies are made. Furthermore, individuals' notions of memory performance and failure are frequently translated into explicit lie-detection strategies, and, as is discussed below, turning lie catchers' attention to whether or not suspects have to think hard in order to remember might work as an implicit lie-detection technique. Here we discuss two additional areas in which research on memory and deception overlap: simulated amnesia, and why deceptive and truthful statements are remembered differently.

The Detection of Simulated Amnesia

In order to avoid punishment, some guilty suspects claim to be amnesic. They conceal the truth (i.e., they lie) by claiming that they cannot remember what took place ("malingered amnesia"). According to different surveys, it is far from rare that suspects claim to be amnesic (e.g., Christianson, Bylin, & Holmberg, 2003; Gudjonsson, Petursson, Skulason, & Sigurdardottir, 1989); indeed, a rule of thumb suggested by Christanson and Merkelbach (2004) is that 20–30% of the perpetrators of violent crimes claim amnesia. In some of these cases the amnesia is real, caused, for example, by neurological defects (Kopelman, 1995), but in other cases there are reasons to believe that the amnesia is feigned.

To distinguish between simulated and genuine amnesia is far from an easy task. A good starting point, though, might be to match the characteristics typical for non-crime-related amnesia (data from clinical settings) against the characteristics typical for crime-related amnesia (Christianson & Merkelbach, 2004). First, victims of non-crime-related amnesia tend to have fragments or islands of memories from the amnesic part of the event, whereas crime-related amnesia tends to be characterized by a total memory loss (e.g., "Everything is black"). Second, in contrast to non-crime-related amnesia, crime-related amnesia typically tends to be described as having a distinct and sharp beginning and end (e.g., "From the moment I arrived at her mobile home to when I woke up the morning after, everything is lost"). Third, those claiming crime-related amnesia tend to be more dogmatic about their amnesia ("Ask me as much as you want, I will *never* remember"), whereas victims of non-crime-related amnesia are more willing to try different memory-enhancing techniques.

In their state-of-the-art paper, Christianson and Merkelbach (2004) suggest that mental health professionals and others who appear as expert witnesses in cases on crime-related amnesia should avoid giving testimony solely on the basis of interviews. They argue that a valid diagnostic differentiation between different types of amnesia demands knowledge about typical malingering behavior as well as knowledge about how to administer and evaluate tests designed to detect malingering. Boldly, Christianson and Merkelbach state that most suspects who claim amnesia are, in fact, liars.

Memory of Deceptive and Truthful Statements

In a study by Landström, Granhag, and Hartwig (2004), undergraduate students witnessed a staged car–bicycle accident caused by the driver of the car.

Half of the witnesses were asked to lie about the event (i.e., they blamed the cyclist), and the other half were asked to tell the truth (i.e., they blamed the driver of the car). Later these witnesses were interviewed in a mock-trial setting, and their testimonies were assessed by a large number of judges (law students). In line with the findings from previous research, the judges had a difficult time distinguishing between liars and truth tellers (their accuracy was not far from chance level). In addition to assessing veracity, each judge was asked to try to remember the statement he or she had heard "in court" (each judge only saw and assessed one witness).

The results of the memory test showed that the judges who had observed truthful witnesses showed a significantly better memory performance compared to those judges who had observed lying witnesses (i.e., they reported more correct and less incorrect details). To explain this finding, it is important to recall that the meta-analysis on objective cues to deception conducted by DePaulo et al. (2003) showed that deceptive statements tend to be less plausible, less structured in a logical and sensible way, and more internally discrepant, compared to truthful statements. In brief, liars' stories seem to make less sense than truth tellers' stories. The fact that memory performance is dependent on the organization and structure of the material (Baddeley, 1990) and the schemas and scripts formed for events, persons, and objects (Schank & Abelson, 1977) may explain why memory for truthful statements was found to be better than memory for deceptive statements. In sum, in order to gain valid information about the actual veracity of the witnesses, we would, for the Landström et al. (2004) study, be better off analyzing the judges' memory performance than their explicit assessments of veracity (for which they used a dichotomous scale). This result is pertinent to the issue of implicit lie detection, which is discussed in a subsequent section.

IMPROVING THE ABILITY TO DETECT DECEPTION

In this section we first briefly review different attempts made to train people to detect deception based on nonverbal cues, then give examples of different types of training programs and their effectiveness, and conclude by focusing on some new and promising techniques for detecting deception.

Training to Detect Deception

In one of the first training studies, Zuckerman, Koestner, and Alton (1984) investigated the effect of feedback on lie-detection accuracy and showed that the more information the participants received about the veracity of the targets, the more accurate they were in detecting deception in these targets. However, this increase in accuracy did not generalize to other targets, indicating that a target-specific lie-detection ability had evolved due to the provision of feedback.

In 1989 Ray Bull wrote one of the first chapters on deception-detection training. After reviewing both the advice found in police manuals and the results of the few scientific training studies that had been conducted in the 1980s, he concluded that "until a number of publications in refereed journals appear demonstrating that training enhances the detection of deception, it seems that some police recruitment advertisements and police training books are deceiving their readers" (p. 97).

Fifteen years later, Bull (2004) presents a new chapter on the same topic, and reviews a number of studies conducted in the 1990s. The results from these studies are somewhat mixed. For example, a study by DeTurck, Harszlak, Bodhorn, & Texter (1990) found that student observers who received training involving practice and feedback with regard to six visual and vocal cues (adaptors, hand gestures, pauses, response latency, speech errors, and message duration) were able to slightly improve their deception-detection accuracy. This result was supported by the findings of DeTurck (1991) and DeTurck and Miller (1990). In addition, DeTurck, Feeley, and Roman (1997) reported that observers who were trained in detecting both vocal cues (speech errors, pauses, response latency, message duration) and visual cues (adaptors, hand gestures, head movements, hand shaking) or visual cues alone, performed better than those observers who received no training or training involving only vocal cues. In the same vein, Fiedler and Walka (1993) found better deception-detection performance for those observers who had been informed about the seven most frequent concomitants of lying, compared to a control group to which no such information was given. In a study by Vrij (1994), the participants were instructed to focus on the suspect's hand movements. Specifically, he informed police detectives that research tells us that that deception is associated with a decrease in subtle hand and finger movements. He found that deception-detection performance was significantly improved for those detectives who received this information and who saw videotapes in which the suspect's hands were visible but the sound was turned off.

More recently, a test of the effect of feedback and cue information on parole officers' deception-detection ability was conducted by Porter et al. (2000). Results from this study showed that receiving immediate and reliable outcome feedback had a positive effect on lie-detection accuracy, even if no information about reliable cues to deception was available. A possible interpretation of this finding is that even though no information about valid cues to deception was provided, feedback helped the lie catchers gradually learn reliable cues to deception.

Frank and Feeley (2003) presented a meta-analysis on the effects of lie-detection training. The analysis was based on 20 paired comparisons (training vs. no training) extracted from 11 published studies. Frank and Feeley highlighted two conclusions: First, a small but significant gain in detection accuracy (4%) was found with training; second, the positive effects found might, in fact, be an underestimation of the true effects of training. The latter conclusion was drawn because the methodology used in the studies included in their meta-analysis did not meet the suggested standards for deception-detection research (e.g., high-stake situations and proper training).

Techniques to Enhance Lie Detection

We believe it is fair to say that the different attempts made to train observers in the detection of nonverbal cues to improve their deception-detection ability have shown some, but rather limited, success. The studies showing an improvement usually report a small degree of it. Nevertheless, we are not without hope for the future. Below we discuss three alternative ways to detect deceit. First we review research on the effects of combining verbal and nonverbal cues. We then turn to the thought-provoking topic of implicit lie detection. We close the section with a brief discussion on the relation between deception detection and strategic disclosure of evidence.

Combining Verbal and Nonverbal Cues

When reviewing the deception-detection research a striking observation is that this type of research is very much divided into camps. Some researchers examine nonverbal responses, others, verbal responses, and a third group focuses on physiological responses (Vrij, 2000a). Research that combines these approaches is rare. Recently it was argued, and demonstrated, that examining verbal and nonverbal cues simultaneously results in more accurate truth and lie classifications than examining verbal and nonverbal responses separately (Vrij & Mann, 2004; Vrij et al., 2000, 2004a). The accuracy rates (up to 88%) obtained in these studies by considering a combination of verbal and nonverbal cues were among the highest ever reported in deception research.

Implicit Lie Detection

Another possible way to improve the ability to detect deceit is by using implicit or indirect lie-detection methods. Here we take a closer look at such methods. In a novel study Hurd and Noller (1988) asked their participants to think aloud as they made their veracity judgments. In line with previous findings, the participants' deception-detection accuracy was modest. However, a closer analysis of the transcribed think-aloud protocols revealed something interesting: When the participants had heard a deceptive statement, they were more open to the possibility that the message was a lie than when they had just heard a truthful statement. That is, they were heading for the correct assessment. But when it was time to commit to the actual veracity assessment, they did not always listen to their own intuitions—intuitions that turned out to be more correct than their explicit assessments of veracity.

In several preceding studies on the same theme, participants, after watching a truthful or deceptive story, were asked to detect deception both in an explicit way (e.g., "Is the person lying?") and in an implicit way (e.g., "Does the speaker sincerely like the person [he or she] just described?"). All studies found greater accuracy with use of the implicit measures, and the observers in some studies were able to detect deception above the level of chance only via the implicit method (for reviews of implicit lie-detection studies, see DePaulo, 1994; Vrij, 2001). This finding may be the result of conversation rules that regulate polite behavior. Observers are often unsure as to whether someone is lying to them. In such instances it would be impolite, or for other reasons undesirable, to accuse someone of being a liar, but it might be possible to challenge the words of a speaker more subtly. In other words, it is more difficult to say "I do not believe you!" than to say "Do you really like so and so that much?" Alternatively, people might consider more diagnostic cues when detecting lies implicitly.

In a study by Vrij et al. (2001a), police officers watched videotapes of truth tellers and liars. Some participants were asked whether each of the people was lying (direct lie-detection method), and others were asked to indicate whether each person "had to think hard" (indirect lie-detection method; they were not informed that some people were actually lying). The police officers' responses distinguished between truths and lies, but only when using the indirect method. When detecting deceit directly, police officers' judgments about deceit were significantly correlated with increases in gaze aversion and movements shown by the people on the videotape. In the indirect method, however, police officers' decisions were significantly correlated with a decrease in hand and finger movements. A decrease in hand and finger movements is a more diagnostic cue to deception than, for example, gaze aversion (DePaulo et al., 2003; Vrij, 2000a).

In the same vein, Vrij, Evans, Akehurst, and Mann (2004) taught observers (college students with no previous training in lie detection) how to make rapid (instant) assessments of the frequency of occurrence of several verbal and nonverbal cues, which had been identified as diagnostic cues to deception in previous research. Participants were then shown videotaped clips of liars and truth tellers and asked to estimate the frequency of occurrence of each of these diagnostic cues, and to write down these estimates. Lastly, they were asked to indicate whether or not each person was lying on the basis of their estimates. An overall accuracy rate of 74% was found, considerably higher than the 57% typically found in lie-detection research.

Finally, the previously discussed meta-analysis on the relation between subjective confidence and deception-detection accuracy (DePaulo et al., 1997) offers an interesting finding that is relevant to the issue of implicit lie detection: namely, people tend to express higher confidence levels when assessing a truthful statement than when assessing a deceptive statement, independently of whether they are assessing the statement as truthful or deceptive. This finding shows that the judges' subjective feelings of confidence can sometimes distinguish the lies from the truths, even when the explicit assessments of veracity are not discriminating.

Strategic Disclosure of Evidence

Most real-life police investigations, and other forensic investigations, generate case-specific facts. Such facts and evidence can, if used properly by the interrogators, be of great importance in assessing the veracity of suspects. However, the scientifically based literature offers no explicit guidelines on the strategic disclosure of facts and evidence. What we do know from archival analysis is that police officers often start the interrogation by confronting the suspect (Leo, 1996, 2001), a tactic that often also includes disclosure of evidence.

Hartwig, Granhag, Strömwall, and Vrij (2004a) investigated the link between strategic disclosure of evidence and deception-detection performance. The "suspects" in the study were 58 undergraduates, half of whom had committed a mock crime (stealing a wallet from a briefcase in a shop) and later denied this (liars), and half of whom had committed no such crime but who had touched the briefcase while visiting the same shop (truth tellers). For half of the liars and half of the truth tellers, the interrogators began by confronting them with the case-specific evidence against them (two witness testimonies and the fact that their fingerprints had been found on the briefcase). The remaining two halves had the same case-specific evidence presented to them at the end of the interrogation session. All interrogations were videotaped. In the next phase these interrogations were shown to 112 observers (again, undergraduates) who were asked to assess veracity. The results showed that those observers who were shown videotapes in which the case-specific evidence against the suspect was disclosed late in the interrogation achieved a significantly higher deception-detection accuracy (61.7%) compared to observers who were shown videotapes in which the (exact same) evidence was disclosed early in the interrogation (42.8%). Furthermore, the observers in the late-evidence condition reported having relied more on verbal cues when assessing veracity, compared to the observers in the early-evidence condition.

The fact that this rather crude manipulation—in terms of disclosure of evidence (early vs. late)—had a significant effect on deception-detection accuracy demonstrates that it might be meaningful to investigate how more sophisticated ways of disclosing evidence (e.g., different "drip-feeding" procedures) may moderate deception-detection performance.

We believe that all three techniques discussed above have clear potential for lie detection. Although the results are promising, however, much more research is needed on each of these techniques.

SUMMARY AND FUTURE CHALLENGES

In the present chapter we have explored what scientific psychology can tell us about deception detection in forensic contexts. Here we summarize the most important findings and highlight future challenges. Our investigation departed from the finding that both presumed experts and laypeople tend to hold wrongful beliefs about how liars actually behave: That is, both groups seem to advocate reliance on cues that are indicative of nervousness. We highlighted one major reason for this misconception: When feedback about deception-detection success and failure is lacking (and in field situations, it often is), people will have a difficult time learning the right lesson from each of their detection experiences. We also warned about some of the claims regarding deceptive behavior found in police interrogation manuals. Many of these claims lack empirical support, and researchers within the deception-detection domain have an important job of debunking the nonsense found in such manuals.

We then reviewed the accuracy of different lie-detection methods used in criminal investigations. A closer look at the SVA, the most popular technique for analyzing speech, showed an accuracy rate that is clearly above chance, but also revealed that reliable data regarding the accuracy of the technique when applied to real-life cases is lacking. We also acknowledged the encouraging results for an alternative technique of analyzing speech content, the Reality Monitoring technique. However, in line with Davies (2001), we want to stress that although the techniques focusing on the verbal content of a testimony are widely used (particularly, SVA), the scientific evaluation of these techniques is still in an initial stage. In addition, the scientific evaluation of polygraph testing is far from perfect; there are very few well-conducted polygraph studies using real-life cases. Research concerning the most popular polygraph test, the CQT, suggests that incorrect judgments are made particularly in regard to innocent suspects. Reviews of CQT testing showed that between 53 and 78% of innocent suspects were incorrectly classified as guilty. Furthermore, research shows that deception detection on the basis of nonverbal behavior is a very difficult task. Specifically, the studies conducted show an average "hit rate" just above the level of chance, both for laypersons and presumed experts. Although our review also included a few studies that reported a somewhat higher hit rate, such results are exceptions. Many explanations for the poor levels of deception-detection accuracy have been suggested, and we listed six such explanations that are relevant in forensic contexts.

Turning to objective indicators of deception and truth, we first acknowledged the ideas presented on the three major emotional states that are associated with deception (guilt, fear, and excitement) and noted how these internal states might translate into certain verbal and nonverbal behaviors. A review of the literature on diagnostic cues to deception shows that there is no single behavioral, verbal, or physiological response that is uniquely related to deception. In fact, a careful look at the research literature shows that very few objective cues are systematically related to deception. In terms of nonverbal behavior, it has been found that liars tend to speak with a higher-pitched voice and make fewer illustrators and hand and finger movements. The list of diagnostic verbal cues is somewhat longer: For example, liars' stories tend to sound less plausible, and the lies tend to include less details (particularly visual, auditory, spatial, and temporal details) than truthful stories. In essence, very few behaviors are systematically related to deception, and when such a systematic link is found, it is usually rather weak. We also need to keep in mind (1) that the behaviors that indicate deception do so only probabilistically, and (2) that these cues also can be indicative of states and processes other than deception. In an attempt to learn more about why there exists so few and such small behavioral differences between liars and truth tellers, we summarized the scarce research conducted on liars' and truth tellers' strategies.

We also discussed ways of improving the ability to detect deception. A review of the literature shows that the attempts made to train people to detect deception based on nonverbal behavior have been met with limited success. We closed this section on a somewhat more positive note, however, by discussing the encouraging results found for three new avenues for detecting deception: (1) combining verbal and nonverbal cues, (2) using implicit lie-detection methods, and (3) disclosing evidence in a strategic manner. These techniques for detecting deception are promising, though still in a very early stage in terms of scientific evaluation.

In spite of the increased interest in deception and the growing body of research literature on this topic, significant future challenges remain. Much of the research within the field has been focused on determining how accurate people are at detecting deception. The studies conducted on deception-detection performance differ in many aspects: for example, the lie catcher's background and motivation, the length of the interrogation, the number of interrogations conducted with the same suspect, the number of suspects, and the suspect's motivation. However, the studies have one important feature in common: The lie catcher is placed in a situation in which his or her action is restricted to a belief-driven processing of the information presented (Strömwall, Granhag, & Hartwig, 2004). For example, in many studies the lie catcher is forced to match his or her beliefs about nonverbal cues to deception against perceptions of the suspect's nonverbal behavior. The lie catcher has no background information about the suspect, no case-specific evidence, and no opportunity to affect how the suspect is questioned. It is reasonable to argue that this limitation has particular relevance to studies that investigate presumed experts. Placing an expert in an unusual context (e.g., where he or she must resort to a belief-driven strategy in order to assess veracity) might conceal structures with which the expert is actually quite familiar (e.g., strategic disclosure of case-specific evidence). In brief, for a better understanding of presumed experts' lie-detection performance, tests must be conducted in contexts that allow for both knowledge-driven and belief-driven information processing. To test lie catchers in situations that allow for—and even encourage—knowledge-driven information processing might be an important step toward the creation of a more ecologically valid research agenda.

In the same vein, it is currently possible to note a shift in research focus from studies mapping people's ability to detect deception to studies investigating how people's deception-detection performance can be enhanced. We predict that future research within the field will pay much more attention to how different interrogation strategies and techniques affect deception-detection performance. Hopefully, such a paradigmatic shift in research focus might contribute to the cultivation of different interrogation techniques.

Finally, research on deception is dominated by practical perspectives and driven by theory to a rather low extent (Granhag & Strömwall, 2004b). For future work, a much more developed theoretical framework is needed in order to be able to generalize the existing body of knowledge to situations and conditions not yet addressed.

REFERENCES

Akehurst, L., Köhnken, G., Vrij, A., & Bull, R. (1996). Lay persons' and police officers' beliefs regarding deceptive behaviour. *Applied Cognitive Psychology, 10,* 461–473.

Allwood, C. M., & Granhag, P. A. (1999). Feelings of confidence and the realism of confidence judgments in everyday life. In P. Juslin & H. Montgomery (Eds.), *Judgment and decision making: Neo-Brunswikian and process-tracing approaches* (pp. 123–146). Mahwah, NJ: Erlbaum.

Alonso-Quecuty, M. L. (1992). Deception detection and Reality Monitoring: A new answer to an old question? In F. Lösel, D. Bender, & T. Bliesener (Eds.), *Psychology and law: International perspectives* (pp. 328–332). Berlin: de Gruyter.

Alonso-Quecuty, M. L., Hernandez-Fernaud, E., & Campos, L. (1997). Child witnesses: Lying about something heard. In S. Redondo, V. Garrido, J. Perez, & R. Barbaret (Eds.), *Advances in psychology and law* (pp. 129–135). Berlin: de Gruyter.

Baddeley, A. (1990). *Human memory: Theory and practice.* Hove, UK: Erlbaum.

Bennett, W. L., & Feldman, M. S. (1981). *Reconstructing reality in the courtroom.* London: Tavistock.

Ben-Shakhar, G., & Elaad, E. (2003). The validity of psychophysiological detection of information with the Guilty Knowledge Test: A meta-analytic review. *Journal of Applied Psychology, 88,* 131–151.

Bond, C. F., & Fahey, W. E. (1987). False suspicion and the misperception of deceit. *British Journal of Social Psychology, 26,* 41–46.

Bond, C. F., Omar, A., Pitre, U., & Lashley, B. R. (1992). Fishy-looking liars: Deception judgment from expectancy violation. *Journal of Personality and Social Psychology, 63,* 969–977.

Buck, J. A., Warren, A. R., Betman, S., & Brigham, J. C. (2002). Age differences in Criteria-Based Content Analysis scores in typical child sexual abuse interviews. *Applied Developmental Psychology, 23,* 267–283.

Bull, R. (1988). What is the lie-detection test? In A. Gale (Ed.), *The polygraph test: Lies, truth and science* (pp. 10–19). London: Sage.

Bull, R. (1989). Can training enhance the detection of deception? In J. Yuille (Ed.), *Credibility assessment* (pp. 83–100). Deventer, The Netherlands: Kluwer.

Bull, R. (2004). Training to detect deception from behavioural cues: Attempts and problems. In P. A. Granhag & L. A. Strömwall (Eds.), *The detection of deception in forensic contexts* (pp. 251–268). Cambridge, UK: Cambridge University Press.

Bull, R., & Vine, M. (2003, July). *Attractive people tell the truth: Can you believe it?*

Poster presented at the annual conference of the European Association of Psychology and Law, Edinburgh.

Buller, D. B., & Burgoon, J. K. (1996). Interpersonal deception theory. *Communication Theory, 6*, 203–242.

Buller, D. B., Strzyzewski, K. D., & Hunsaker, F. G. (1991). Interpersonal deception: II. The inferiority of conversational partners as deception detectors. *Communication Monographs, 58*, 25–40.

Burgoon, J. K., & Buller, D. B. (1994). Interpersonal deception: III. Effects of deceit on perceived communication and nonverbal behavior dynamics. *Journal of Nonverbal Behavior, 18*, 155–184.

Burgoon, J. K., Buller, D. B., & Guerrero, L. K. (1995). Interpersonal deception IX: Effects of social skill and nonverbal communication on deception success and detection accuracy. *Journal of Language and Social Psychology, 14*, 289–311.

Ceci, S. J., & Bruck, M. (1995). *Jeopardy in the courtroom.* Washington, DC: American Psychological Association.

Christianson, S. Å., Bylin, S., & Holmberg, U. (2003). *Homicide and sexual offenders' view of crime-related amnesia.* Manuscript in preparation.

Christianson, S. Å., & Merckelbach, H. (2004). Crime related amnesia as a form of deception. In P. A. Granhag & L. A. Strömwall (Eds.), *The detection of deception in forensic contexts* (pp. 195–225). Cambridge, UK: Cambridge University Press.

Committee to Review the Scientific Evidence on the Polygraph. (2003). *The polygraph and lie detection.* Washington, DC: National Academic Press.

Davies, G. M. (2001). Is it possible to discriminate true from false memories? In G. M. Davies & T. Dalgleish (Eds.), *Recovered memories: Seeking the middle ground* (pp. 153–176). Chichester, UK: John Wiley.

Davies, G. M., Westcott, H. L., & Horan, N. (2000). The impact of questioning style on the content of investigative interviews with suspected child sexual abuse victims. *Psychology, Crime, and Law, 6*, 81–97.

DePaulo, B. M. (1994). Spotting lies: Can humans learn to do better? *Current Directions in Psychological Science, 3*, 83–86.

DePaulo, B. M., & Bell, K. L. (1996). Truth and investment: Lies are told to those who care. *Journal of Personality and Social Psychology, 71*, 703–716.

DePaulo, B. M., Charlton, K., Cooper, H., Lindsay, J. L., & Muhlenbruck, L. (1997). The accuracy–confidence relation in the detection of deception. *Personality and Social Psychology Review, 1*, 346–357.

DePaulo, B. M., Kashy, D. A., Kirkendol, S. E., Wyer, M. M., & Epstein, J. A. (1996). Lying in everyday life. *Journal of Personality and Social Psychology, 70*, 979–995.

DePaulo, B. M., & Kirkendol, S. E. (1989). The motivational impairment effect in the communication of deception. In J. C. Yuille (Ed.), *Credibility assessment* (pp. 51–70). Dordrecht, The Netherlands: Kluwer.

DePaulo, B. M., Kirkendol, S. E., Tang, J., & O'Brien, T. P. (1988). The motivational impairment effect in the communication of deception: Replications and extensions. *Journal of Nonverbal Behavior, 12*, 177–201.

DePaulo, B. M., Lanier, K., & Davis, T. (1983). Detecting the deceit of the motivated liar. *Journal of Personality and Social Psychology, 45*, 1096–1103.

DePaulo, B. M., LeMay, C. S., & Epstein, J. A. (1991). Effects of importance of success and expectations for success on effectiveness at deceiving. *Personality and Social Psychology Bulletin, 17*, 14–24.

DePaulo, B. M., Lindsay, J. J., Malone, B. E., Muhlenbruck, L., Charlton, K., & Cooper, H. (2003). Cues to deception. *Psychological Bulletin, 129,* 74–118.

DePaulo, B. M., & Pfeifer, R. L. (1986). On-the-job experience and skill at detecting deception. *Journal of Applied Social Psychology, 16,* 249–267.

DePaulo, B. M., Rosenthal, R., Rosenkrantz, J., & Green, C. R. (1982). Actual and perceived cues to deception: A closer look at speech. *Basic and Applied Social Psychology, 19,* 1552–1577.

DePaulo, B. M., Stone, J. L., & Lassiter, G. D. (1985a). Deceiving and detecting deceit. In B. R. Schenkler (Ed.), *The self and social life* (pp. 323–370). New York: McGraw-Hill.

DePaulo, B. M., Stone, J. I., & Lassiter, G. D. (1985b). Telling ingratiating lies: Effects of target sex and target attractiveness on verbal and nonverbal deceptive success. *Journal of Personality and Social Psychology, 48,* 1191–1203.

DeTurck, M. (1991). Training observers to detect spontaneous deception: Effects of gender. *Communication Reports, 4,* 81–89.

DeTurck, M., Feeley, T., & Roman, L. (1997). Vocal and visual training in behavioral lie detection. *Communication Research Reports, 14,* 249–259.

DeTurck, M., Harszlak, J., Bodhorn, D., & Texter, L. (1990). The effects of training social perceivers to detect deception from behavioral cues. *Communication Quarterly, 38,* 189–199.

DeTurck, M., & Miller, G. (1990). Training observers to detect deception: Effects of self-monitoring and rehearsal. *Human Communication Research, 16,* 603–620.

Einhorn, H. J. (1982). Learning from experience and suboptimal rules in decision making. In D. Kahneman, P. Slovic, & A. Tversky (Eds.), *Judgment under uncertainty: Heuristics and biases* (pp. 268–283). Cambridge, UK: Cambridge University Press.

Ekman, P. (2001). *Telling lies.* New York: Norton.

Ekman, P., & Frank, M. G. (1993). Lies that fail. In M. Lewis & C. Saarni (Eds.), *Lying and deception in everyday life* (pp. 184–201). New York: Guilford Press.

Ekman, P., & Friesen, W. V. (1969). Nonverbal leakage and clues to deception. *Psychiatry, 32,* 88–106.

Ekman, P., & Friesen, W. V. (1972). Hand movements. *Journal of Communication, 22,* 353–374.

Ekman, P., Friesen, W. V., & O'Sullivan, M. (1988). Smiles when lying. *Journal of Personality and Social Psychology, 54,* 414–420.

Ekman, P., Friesen, W. V., & Scherer, K. R. (1976). Body movement and voice pitch in deceptive interaction. *Semiotica, 16,* 23–27.

Ekman, P., & O'Sullivan, M. (1991). Who can catch a liar? *American Psychologist, 46,* 913–920.

Ekman, P., O'Sullivan, M., & Frank, M. G. (1999). A few can catch a liar. *Psychological Science, 10,* 263–266.

Ekman, P., O'Sullivan, M., Friesen, W. V., & Scherer, K. (1991). Face, voice, and body in detecting deceit. *Journal of Nonverbal Behavior, 15,* 125–135.

Feeley, T. H., & deTurck, M. A. (1997). *Perceptions of communications as seen by the actor and as seen by the observer: The case of lie detection.* Paper presented at the International Communication Association annual conference, Montreal.

Fiedler, K., Schmid, J., & Stahl, T. (2002). What is the current truth about polygraph lie detection? *Basic and Applied Social Psychology, 24,* 313–324.

Fiedler, K., & Walka, I. (1993). Training lie detectors to use nonverbal cues instead of global heuristics. *Human Communication Research, 20,* 199–223.

Frank, M. G., & Ekman, P. (1997). The ability to detect deceit generalizes across different types of high-stake lies. *Journal of Personality and Social Psychology, 72*, 1429–1439.

Frank, M. G., & Feeley, T. H. (2003). To catch a liar: Challenges for research in lie detection training. *Journal of Applied Communication Research, 31*, 58–75.

Garrido, E., & Masip, J. (1999). How good are police officers at spotting lies? *Forensic Update, 58*, 14–21.

Granhag, P. A., Andersson, L. O., Strömwall, L. A., & Hartwig, M. (2004). Imprisoned knowledge: Criminals' beliefs about deception. *Legal and Criminological Psychology, 9*, 103–119.

Granhag, P. A., & Strömwall, L. A. (1999). Repeated interrogations: Stretching the deception detection paradigm. *Expert Evidence: The International Journal of Behavioural Sciences in Legal Context, 7*, 163–174.

Granhag, P. A., & Strömwall, L. A. (2000). The effects of preconceptions on deception detection and new answers to why lie-catchers often fail. *Psychology, Crime, and Law, 6*, 197–218.

Granhag, P. A., & Strömwall, L. A. (2001a). Deception detection based on repeated interrogations. *Legal and Criminological Psychology, 6*, 85–101.

Granhag, P. A., & Strömwall, L. A. (2001b). Deception detection: Interrogators' and observers' decoding of repeated interrogations. *Journal of Psychology: Interdisciplinary and Applied, 6*, 603–620.

Granhag, P. A., & Strömwall, L. A. (2002). Repeated interrogations: Verbal and nonverbal cues to deception. *Applied Cognitive Psychology, 16*, 243–257.

Granhag, P. A., & Strömwall, L. A. (Eds.). (2004a). *The detection of deception in forensic contexts.* Cambridge, UK: Cambridge University Press.

Granhag, P. A., & Strömwall, L. A. (2004b). Deception detection in forensic contexts: Intersections and future challenges. In P. A. Granhag & L. A. Strömwall (Eds.), *The detection of deception in forensic contexts* (pp. 317–330). Cambridge, UK: Cambridge University Press.

Granhag, P. A., Strömwall, L. A., & Hartwig, M. (in press). Granting asylum or not?: Migration Board personnel's beliefs on deception. *Journal of Ethnic and Migration Studies.*

Granhag, P. A., Strömwall, L. A., & Jonsson, A.C. (2003). Partners in crime: How liars in collusion betray themselves. *Journal of Applied Social Psychology, 4*, 848–867.

Gudjonsson, G. H. (1992). *The psychology of interrogations, confessions and testimony.* Chichester, UK: Wiley.

Gudjonsson, G. H., Petursson, H., Skulason, S., & Sigurdardottir, H. (1989). Psychiatric evidence: A study of psychological issues. *Acta Psychiatrica Scandinavia, 80*, 165–169.

Harrigan, J. A., & O'Connell, D. M. (1996). Facial movements during anxiety states. *Personality and Individual Differences, 21*, 205–212.

Hartwig, M., Granhag, P. A., Strömwall, L. A., & Andersson, L. O. (2004). Suspicious minds: Criminals' ability to detect deception. *Psychology, Crime, and Law, 10*, 83–95.

Hartwig, M., Granhag, P. A., Strömwall, L. A., & Vrij, A. (2004a). *Deception detection via strategic disclosure of evidence.* Manuscript submitted for publication.

Hartwig, M., Granhag, P. A., Strömwall, L. A., & Vrij, A. (2004b). Police officers' lie detection accuracy: Interrogating freely versus observing video. *Police Quarterly, 7*, 429–456.

Hocking, J. E., & Leathers, D. G. (1980). Nonverbal indicators of deception: A new theoretical perspective. *Communication Monographs, 47,* 119–131.

Höfer, E., Akehurst, L., & Metzger, G. (1996, August). *Reality Monitoring: A chance for further development of CBCA?* Paper presented at the annual meeting of the European Association on Psychology and Law, Siena, Italy.

Hogarth, R. M. (2001). *Educating intuition.* Chicago: University of Chicago Press.

Hurd, K., & Noller, P. (1988). Decoding deception: A look at the process. *Journal of Nonverbal Behavior, 12,* 217–233.

Iacono, W. G., & Patrick, C. J. (1997). Polygraphy and integrity testing. In R. Rogers (Eds.), *Clinical assessment of malingering and deception* (pp. 252–281). New York: Guilford Press.

Inbau, F. E., Reid, J. E., & Buckley, J. P. (1986). *Criminal interrogation and confessions.* Baltimore: Williams & Wilkins.

Inbau, F. E., Reid, J. E., Buckley, J. P., & Jayne, B. C. (2001). *Criminal interrogation and confessions.* Gaithersburg, MD: Aspen Publishers.

Johnson, M. K., Hashtroudi, S., & Lindsay, D. S. (1993). Source monitoring. *Psychological Bulletin, 114,* 3–29.

Johnson, M. K., & Raye, C. L. (1981). Reality Monitoring. *Psychological Review, 88,* 67–85.

Johnson, M. K., & Raye, C. L. (1998). False memories and confabulation. *Trends in Cognitive Sciences, 2,* 137–145.

Kassin, S. M., & Fong, C. T. (1999). "I'm innocent": Effects of training on judgments of truth and deception in the interrogation room. *Law and Human Behavior, 23,* 499–516.

Kleiner, M. (Ed.). (2002). *Handbook of polygraph testing.* London, UK: Academic Press.

Kleinmuntz, B., & Szucko, J. J. (1984). Lie detection in ancient and modern times: A call for contemporary scientific study. *American Psychologist, 39,* 766–776.

Köhnken, G., Schimossek, E., Aschermann, E., & Höfer, E. (1995). The cognitive interview and the assessment of the credibility of adult's statements. *Journal of Applied Psychology, 80,* 671–684.

Kopelman, M. D. (1995). The assessment of psychogenic amnesia. In A. D. Baddeley, B. A. Wilson, & F. N. Watts (Eds.), *Handbook of memory disorders* (pp. 427–448). New York: Wiley.

Krauss, R. M. (1981). Impression formation, impression management, and nonverbal behaviors. In E. T. Higgins, C. P. Herman, & M. P. Zanna (Eds.), *Social cognition: The Ontario Symposium* (Vol. 1, pp. 323–341). Hillsdale, NJ: Erlbaum.

Landström, S., Granhag, P. A., & Hartwig, M. (2004). *Witnesses appearing live vs. on video: How presentation format affects observers' perception, assessment and memory.* Manuscript submitted for publication.

Lane, J. D., & DePaulo, B. M. (1999). Completing Coyne's cycle: Dysphorics' ability to detect deception. *Journal of Research in Personality, 33,* 311–329.

Leo, R. A. (1996). Inside the interrogation room. *Journal of Criminal Law and Criminology, 86,* 266–303.

Leo, R. A. (2001). False confessions: Causes, consequences, and solutions. In S. D. Westervelt & J. A. Humphrey (Eds.), *Wrongly convicted: Perspectives on failed justice* (pp. 36–54). New Brunswick, NJ: Rutgers University Press.

Levine, T. R., Sun Park, H., & McCornack, S. A. (1999). Accuracy in detecting truths and lies: Documenting the "Veracity Effect." *Communication Monographs, 66,* 125–144.

Lykken, D. T. (1998). *A tremor in the blood: Uses and abuses of the lie detector.* New York: Plenum Press.

MacLaren, V. V. (2001). A qualitative review of the Guilty Knowledge Test. *Journal of Applied Psychology, 86,* 674–683.

Mann, S., Vrij, A., & Bull, R. (2002). Suspects, lies and videotape: An analysis of authentic high-stakes liars. *Law and Human Behavior, 26,* 365–376.

Mann, S., Vrij, A., & Bull, R. (2004). Detecting true lies: Police officers' ability to detect deceit. *Journal of Applied Psychology, 89,* 137–149.

Manzanero, A. L., & Diges, M. (1996). Effects of preparation on internal and external memories. In G. Davies, S. Lloyd-Bostock, M. McMurran, & C. Wilson (Eds.), *Psychology, law, and criminal justice: International developments in research and practice* (pp. 56–63). Berlin: de Gruyter.

Meissner, C. A., & Kassin, S. M. (2002). "He's guilty!": Investigator bias in judgments of truth and deception. *Law and Human Behavior, 26,* 469–480.

Memon, A., Vrij, A., & Bull, R. (2003). *Psychology and law: Truthfulness, accuracy and credibility* (2nd ed.). Chichester, UK: Wiley.

Milne, R., & Bull, R. (1999). *Investigative interviewing: Psychology and practice.* Chichester, UK: Wiley.

Norwick, R. J., Kassin, S. M., Meissner, C. A., & Malpass, R. A. (2002, March). *"I'd know a false confession if I saw one": A comparative study of college students and police investigators.* Paper presented at the biennial meeting of the American Psychology–Law Society, Austin, TX.

Ofshe, R. J., & Leo, R. A. (1997). The decision to confess falsely: Rational choice and irrational action. *Denver University Law Review, 74,* 979–1112.

O'Sullivan, M. (2003). The fundamental attribution error in detecting deception: The boy-who-cried-wolf effect. *Personality and Social Psychology Bulletin, 29,* 1316–1326.

Pennington, N., & Hastie, R. (1986). Evidence evaluation in complex decision making. *Journal of Personality and Social Psychology, 51,* 242–258.

Porter, S., Woodworth, M., & Birt, A. R. (2000). Truth, lies and videotape: An investigation of the ability of federal parole officers to detect deception. *Law and Human Behavior, 24,* 643–658.

Raskin, D. C., & Esplin, P. W. (1991). Statement Validity Assessment: Interview procedures and content analysis of children's statements of sexual abuse. *Behavioral Assessment, 13,* 265–291.

Raskin, D. C., & Honts, C. R. (2002). The Comparison Question Test. In M. Kleiner (Ed.), *Handbook of polygraph testing* (pp. 1–48). London: Academic Press.

Riggio, R. E., Tucker, J., & Throckmorton, B. (1987). Social skills and deception ability. *Personality and Social Psychology Bulletin, 13,* 568–577.

Roberts, K. P., Lamb, M. E., Zale, J. L., & Randall, D. W. (1998, March). *Qualitative differences in children's accounts of confirmed and unconfirmed incidents of sexual abuse.* Paper presented at the biennial meeting of the American Psychology–Law Society, Redondo Beach, CA.

Robinson, J. A. (1981). Personal narratives reconsidered. *Journal of American Folklore, 94,* 58–85.

Ross, L., Greene, D., House, P. (1977). The false consensus phenomenon: An attributional bias in self-perception and social-perception processes. *Journal of Experimental Social Psychology, 13,* 279–301.

Ross, L., & Nisbett, R. E. (1991). *The person and the situation: Perspectives of social psychology.* New York: McGraw-Hill.

Ruby, C. L., & Brigham, J. C. (1997). The usefulness of the criteria-based content analysis technique in distinguishing between truthful and fabricated allegations. *Psychology, Public Policy, and Law, 3*, 705–737.

Saxe, L. (1991). Science and the GKT polygraph: A theoretical critique. *Integrative Physiological and Behavioral Science, 26*, 223–231.

Saxe, L., Dougherty, D., & Cross, T. (1985). The validity of polygraph testing: Scientific analysis and public controversy. *American Psychologist, 40*, 355–366.

Schank, R. C., & Abelson, R. (1977). *Scripts, plans, goals, and understanding.* Hillsdale, NJ: Erlbaum.

Shuy, R. W. (1998). *The language of confession, interrogation, and deception.* Thousand Oaks, CA: Sage.

Sporer, S. L. (1997). The less travelled road to truth: Verbal cues in deception detection in accounts of fabricated and self-experienced events. *Applied Cognitive Psychology, 11*, 373–397.

Steller, M. (1989). Recent developments in statement analysis. In J. C. Yuille (Ed.), *Credibility assessment* (pp. 135–154). Deventer, The Netherlands: Kluwer.

Steller, M., & Köhnken, G. (1989). Criteria-Based Content Analysis. In D. C. Raskin (Ed.), *Psychological methods in criminal investigation and evidence* (pp. 217–245). New York: Springer-Verlag.

Sternberg, K. J., Lamb, M. E., Esplin, P. W., Orbach, Y., & Hershkowitz, I. (2002). Using a structured interview protocol to improve the quality of investigative interviews. In M. L. Eisen, J. A. Quas, & G. S. Goodman (Eds.), *Memory and suggestibility in the forensic interview* (pp. 409–436). Mahwah, NJ: Erlbaum.

Strömwall, L. A., Bengtsson, L., Leander, L., & Granhag, P. A. (2004). Assessing children's statements: The impact of a repeated experience on CBCA and RM ratings. *Applied Cognitive Psychology, 18*, 653–668.

Strömwall, L. A., & Granhag, P. A. (2003). How to detect deception? Arresting the beliefs of police officers, prosecutors and judges. *Psychology, Crime, and Law, 9*, 19–36.

Strömwall, L. A., Granhag, P. A., & Hartwig, M. (in press). To act truthfully: Nonverbal behaviour and strategies during a police interrogation. *Psychology, Crime, and Law.*

Strömwall, L. A., Granhag, P. A., & Hartwig, M. (2004). Professionals' beliefs about deception. In P. A. Granhag & L. A. Strömwall (Eds.), *The detection of deception in forensic contexts* (pp. 229–250). Cambridge, UK: Cambridge University Press.

Strömwall, L. A., Granhag, P. A., & Jonsson, A. C. (2003). Deception among pairs: "Let's say we had lunch and hope they swallow it!" *Psychology, Crime, and Law, 9*, 109–124.

Strömwall, L., Granhag, P. A., & Landström, S. (2004). *Deception in children: Adult's ability to discriminate between lies and truths.* Manuscript in preparation.

Taylor, R., & Vrij, A. (2000). The effects of varying stake and cognitive complexity on beliefs about the cues to deception. *International Journal of Police Science and Management, 3*, 111–124.

Undeutsch, U. (1967). *Beurteilung der Glaubhaftigkeit von Aussagen* [*Credibility judgements on the basis of verbal statements*]. In U. Undeutsch (Ed.), *Handbuch der Psychologie: Forensische Psychologie* (Vol. 11, pp. 26–181). Göttingen, Germany: Hogrefe.

Undeutsch, U. (1982). Statement reality analysis. In A. Trankell (Ed.), *Reconstructing the past: The role of psychologists in criminal trials* (pp. 27–56). Deventer, The Netherlands: Kluwer.

Vrij, A. (1994). The impact of information and setting on detection of deception by police detectives. *Journal of Nonverbal Behavior, 18*, 117–137.

Vrij, A. (2000a). *Detecting lies and deceit: The psychology of lying and the implications for professional practice.* Chichester, UK: Wiley.

Vrij, A. (2000b). Telling and detecting lies as a function of raising the stakes. In C. M. Breur, M. M. Kommer, J. F. Nijboer, & J. M. Reintjes (Eds.), *New trends in criminal investigation and evidence* (Vol. 2, pp. 699–709). Antwerpen, Belgium: Intersentia.

Vrij, A. (2001). Detecting the liars. *Psychologist, 14*, 596–598.

Vrij, A. (2002). Deception in children: A literature review and implications for children's testimony. In H. L. Westcott, G. M. Davies, & R. H. C. Bull (Eds.), *Children's testimony* (pp. 175–194). Chichester, UK: Wiley.

Vrij, A. (2003). "We will protect your wife and child, but only if you confess." In P. J. van Koppen & S. D. Penrod (Eds.), *Adversarial versus inquisitorial justice: Psychological perspectives on criminal justice systems* (pp. 55–79). New York: Kluwer Academic.

Vrij, A. (in press). Criteria-Based Content Analysis: The first 37 studies. *Psychology, Public Policy, and Law.*

Vrij, A., Akehurst, L., Soukara, S., & Bull, R. (2004a). Detecting deceit via analyses of verbal and nonverbal behavior in children and adults. *Human Communication Research, 30*, 8–41.

Vrij, A., Akehurst, L., Soukara, S., & Bull, R. (2004b). "Let me inform you how to tell a convincing story": CBCA and reality monitoring scores as a function of age, coaching, and deception. *Canadian Journal of Behavioural Science, 36*, 113–126.

Vrij, A., Edward, K., & Bull, R. (2001a). Police officers' ability to detect deceit: The benefit of indirect deception measures. *Legal and Criminological Psychology, 6*, 185–196.

Vrij, A., Edward, K., & Bull, R. (2001b). Stereotypical verbal and nonverbal responses while deceiving others. *Personality and Social Psychology Bulletin, 27*, 899–909.

Vrij, A., Edward, K., Roberts, K. P., & Bull, R. (2000). Detecting deceit via analysis of verbal and nonverbal behavior. *Journal of Nonverbal Behavior, 24*, 239–263.

Vrij, A., Evans, H., Akehurst, L., & Mann, S. (2004). Rapid judgements in assessing verbal and nonverbal cues: Their potential for deception researchers and lie detection. *Applied Cognitive Psychology, 18*, 283–296.

Vrij, A., Harden, F., Terry, J., Edward, K., & Bull, R. (2001). The influence of personal characteristics, stakes and lie complexity on the accuracy and confidence to detect deceit. In R. Roesch, R. R. Corrado, & R. J. Dempster (Eds.), *Psychology in the courts: International advances in knowledge* (pp. 289–304). London: Routledge.

Vrij, A., & Heaven, S. (1999). Vocal and verbal indicators of deception as a function of lie complexity. *Psychology, Crime, and Law, 4*, 401–413.

Vrij, A., & Mann, S. (2001). Telling and detecting lies in a high-stake situation: The case of a convicted murderer. *Applied Cognitive Psychology, 15*, 187–203.

Vrij, A., & Mann, S. (2003). Deceptive responses and detecting deceit. In P. W. Halligan, C. Bass, & D. Oakley (Eds.), *Malingering and illness deception: Clinical and theoretical perspectives* (pp. 347–361). Oxford, UK: Oxford University Press.

Vrij, A., & Mann, S. (2004). Detecting deception: The benefit of looking at a combination of behavioral, auditory and speech content related cues in a systematic manner. *Group Decision and Negotiations, 13*, 61–79.

Vrij, A., & Semin, G. R. (1996). Lie experts' beliefs about nonverbal indicators of deception. *Journal of Nonverbal Behavior, 20*, 65–80.

Vrij, A., & Taylor, R. (2003). Police officers' and students' beliefs about telling and detecting little and serious lies. *International Journal of Police Science and Management, 5,* 1–9.

Wagenaar, W. A., van Koppen, P. J., & Crombag, H. F. M. (1993). *Anchored narratives: The psychology of criminal evidence.* New York: Harvester Wheatsheaf.

Wallbott, H. G., & Scherer, K. R. (1991). Stress specifics: Differential effects of coping style, gender, and type of stressor on automatic arousal, facial expression, and subjective feeling. *Journal of Personality and Social Psychology, 61,* 147–156.

Yzerbyt, V. Y., Dardenne, B., & Leyens, J. P. (1998). Social judgeability concerns in impression formation. In V. Y. Yzerbyt, G. Lories, & B. Dardenne (Eds.), *Metacognition: Cognitive and social dimensions* (pp. 126–156). London: Sage.

Zaparniuk, J., Yuille, J. C., & Taylor, S. (1995). Assessing the credibility of true and false statements. *International Journal of Law and Psychiatry, 18,* 343–352.

Zuckerman, M., DePaulo, B. M., & Rosenthal, R. (1981). Verbal and nonverbal communication of deception. In L. Berkowitz (Ed.), *Advances in experimental social psychology* (Vol. 14, pp. 1–57). New York: Academic Press.

Zuckerman, M., Koestner, R., & Alton, A. (1984). Learning to detect deception. *Journal of Personality and Social Psychology, 46,* 519–528.

Zulawski, D. E., & Wicklander, D. E. (1993). *Practical aspects of interview and interrogation.* Boca Raton, FL: CRC Press.

CHAPTER FOUR

Eyewitness Recall and Testimony

AINAT PANSKY
ASHER KORIAT
MORRIS GOLDSMITH

THE *RASHOMON* DILEMMA:
THE COMPLEXITY OF EYEWITNESS RECALL

In Akira Kurosawa's classic film *Rashomon*, four eyewitnesses recount different versions of an event involving a man's murder and the rape of his wife. The four highly discrepant recollections of the same event suggest that not only are many details forgotten, but that much of the information that is "remembered" may be distorted or fabricated, or is at the very least, inherently subjective. The film highlights the intricacies of eyewitness recall and testimony in real-life situations, forcefully conveying the fact that memory does not operate like a video recorder. Identifying the factors and memory processes that may account for such discrepancies between different recollections of the same event poses an important challenge for memory researchers. It also raises difficult questions concerning "truth" and "accuracy."

What causes one person's recollection to differ from another's and from the observed event? Following the classic work of Ebbinghaus (1895/1964), the traditional experimental approach in memory research has focused almost exclusively on memory *quantity*; that is, on the amount of information that is retained or can be reproduced (Koriat & Goldsmith, 1996a, 1996b). This line of research has identified various factors that determine the strength of the memory "trace," thereby affecting the amount of event-related information that is remembered. First, people's original encoding of events may vary as a result of differences in such factors as perceptual conditions (e.g., lighting, vantage point, quality of the physical stimuli), the distinctiveness and impor-

tance of the event, the amount of attention allocated, and the degree of elaboration. Second, in terms of storage, different witnesses may suffer differential
weakening of memory representations with the passage of time, and differential amounts of interference from newly encoded memories, resulting in varying degrees of forgetting of the original details. Finally, the strength of retrieval cues and the degree of match between their properties and those
encoded may also affect the quantity of information that is recollected.

A separate body of research that focuses on memory distortions rather
than on mere forgetting has identified many ways in which memory can go
wrong (see Koriat, Goldsmith, & Pansky, 2000; Schacter, 1999). This focus,
catalyzed in part by the recent wave of naturalistic, "everyday memory" research, has disclosed an unparalleled preoccupation with the *accuracy* of
memory—that is, with the extent to which memory can be trusted. For example: To what extent can we trust the memory of a courtroom witness? How
authentic is a person's memory of a childhood traumatic event that is "recovered" years later in the course of psychotherapy? These questions are concerned with the accuracy of what one remembers rather than the amount.

Much of the contemporary research on memory accuracy and distortion
owes its inspiration to the seminal work of Bartlett (1932), who viewed remembering as a dynamic, goal-directed "effort after meaning." Bartlett's reconstructive approach, gaining impetus from Neisser (1967), holds that what
is remembered is not simply a reproduction of the original input but, rather,
an active construction or reconstruction based on inference and interpretation
processes that are guided by each person's general knowledge and expectations about the world (i.e., schemas; for reviews, see Alba & Hasher, 1983;
Brewer & Nakamura, 1984; Roediger, 1996). These processes are applied to
that input—first, when the information is initially encoded, and then again
when the stored information is later retrieved. For example, when recalling
which objects were present in an office that they have briefly visited, people
tend to recall objects that are normally found in such an office, including typical objects that were *not* present in that particular office (Brewer & Treyens,
1981). Such schema-based intrusions reflect a confusion between what we expect and what we actually experience. Thus, people's individual perspectives,
goals, and motivations have been found to bias their memory reports, even
when they believe that they are recollecting what "really" happened (e.g.,
Bahrick, Hall, & Berger, 1996; Tversky & Marsh, 2000).

Finally, memory performance has been shown to depend not only on the
information that people retrieve or reconstruct, but also on "metamemory"
processes used in the strategic regulation of memory reporting. In this context,
metamemory refers to what people know about their own memories and how
that knowledge is put to use in regulating what they report. To illustrate, consider a witness in the *Rashomon* film attempting to tell "the whole truth and
nothing but the truth" about the target event. To fulfill that goal, witnesses
must try to distinguish between correct and incorrect information that comes
to mind and report only (and all of) the correct information. However, the

metamemory processes of these witnesses may fail in one of two opposite ways. First, they may omit or "forget" event information, not because the information fails to come to mind but because they judge that the retrieved information is in fact "not correct." Worse still, perhaps, they may report incorrect information, falsely judging it to be correct.

Assessing the Quality of an Eyewitness Recollection

How can we determine the quality of a witness's recollection? Without an external criterion against which we can compare the eyewitness accounts, this determination is virtually impossible to make. Indeed, in the case of the *Rashomon* story, we cannot determine which of the different accounts is better because the details of the original event are not known to us (of course, this is true of most real-world eyewitness situations as well). But suppose we had been given access to the initial event: How would we evaluate the quality of one account compared to another?

In attempting to answer this question, we must distinguish between two different properties of memory: its quantity and its accuracy (see Koriat & Goldsmith, 1996a, 1996b). As mentioned before, these two properties have received rather different emphases in contemporary approaches to memory: On the one hand, traditional memory research has been guided by a storehouse conception (Roediger, 1980), evaluating memory primarily in terms of the number of (stored) items that can be recovered. On the other hand, the more recent wave of naturalistic, "everyday memory" research (see Cohen, 1989; Neisser, 1978) has inclined more toward a correspondence conception (Bartlett, 1932; Koriat & Goldsmith, 1996a, 1996b), in which there is a greater concern for the accuracy or faithfulness of memory in representing past events. Here the focus is on the extent to which memory reports can be relied upon to provide accurate information. Indeed, we would not expect an eyewitness in *Rashomon* to remember everything that had taken place. We do, however, want to be able to depend on the correctness of the information that he or she does report.

In the context of the storehouse metaphor, percent recall and percent recognition have been useful as standard all-purpose measures of memory quantity. These measures have been used to investigate a multitude of questions about memory, to derive "forgetting curves," and to examine the general effects of such variables as study time, divided attention, level of processing, and so forth.

It is more difficult to derive all-purpose measures of memory correspondence that would allow a similar study of factors affecting the overall faithfulness of memory (Koriat & Goldsmith, 1996a, 1996b; Koriat et al., 2000). In the context of traditional item-based assessment, overall measures of memory quantity and accuracy can be derived from the input-bound and output-bound proportion correct, respectively. The input-bound quantity measure (e.g., percent recall) traditionally used to tap the amount of studied information that can be recovered, reflects the likelihood that each input item is correctly recalled or recognized. The output-bound accuracy measure (e.g., percent of recalled items that is correct), in contrast, reflects the likelihood that each reported item is, in fact, correct. Hence, it uniquely evaluates the dependability of memory—the extent to which remembered information can be trusted to be correct. Suppose, for example, that the information in a crime scene could be segmented into 20 items. An eyewitness manages to recall 10 of these items and recalls two additional items that were not part of the original scene. This witness's input-bound quantity is $10/20 = 50\%$, whereas her output-bound accuracy is much higher: $10/12 = 83\%$. Essentially, whereas the input-bound measure holds the person responsible for what he or she fails to report, the output-bound measure holds the person accountable only for what he or she does report.

Note that when memory is tested through a forced-report procedure, memory quantity and accuracy measures are necessarily equivalent, because the likelihood of remembering each input item (quantity) is equal to the likelihood that each reported item is correct (accuracy). Accuracy and quantity measures can differ substantially, however, under free-report conditions, in which subjects are implicitly or explicitly given the option either to volunteer a piece of information or to abstain. Most everyday situations are of this sort. In the laboratory, the most typical example is the standard free-recall task, in which reporting is essentially controlled by the participant. Because the number of volunteered answers is generally smaller than the number of input items, the output-bound (accuracy) and input-bound (quantity) memory measures can vary substantially.

THE STRATEGIC REGULATION OF MEMORY REPORTING

Koriat and Goldsmith (1994, 1996c; Goldsmith & Koriat, 1999; Goldsmith, Koriat, & Weinberg-Eliezer, 2002) have developed a theoretical framework that specifies the critical role of metacognitive monitoring and control processes in strategically regulating memory performance. Our work is based on the assumption that in recounting past events, people do not simply report everything that comes to mind, but attempt to control their memory reporting in accordance with a variety of personal and situational goals, whether these involve aiding a criminal investigation or impressing their friends. Thus, people make strategic choices about which aspects of the event to relate and which to ignore, what perspective to adopt, what degree of generality or detail to use, and so forth. Such strategic control has been shown to have a substantial impact on the quality of memory reports.

Our framework focuses on two types of control by which rememberers can enhance the accuracy of what they report in real-life situations. The first, *report option*, involves choosing either to volunteer or to withhold particular items of information (i.e., to respond "I don't know" or "I don't remember";

Koriat & Goldsmith, 1994, 1996c; Koriat, Goldsmith, Schneider, & Nakash-Dura, 2001). The second type of control, *control over grain size*, involves choosing the level of detail (precision) or generality (coarseness) at which to report remembered information (Goldsmith & Koriat, 1999; Goldsmith, Koriat, & Pansky, in press; Goldsmith et al., 2002).

Figure 4.1 depicts a rough scheme for conceptualizing and distinguishing various basic components that underlie overt memory (recall) performance. Within this framework, the encoding, representation, and retrieval/reconstruction of information at different grain levels (e.g., gist vs. details) contribute the raw materials from which memory reports are ultimately produced, and the quality of this contribution, of course, substantially constrains the quality of the final product. Nevertheless, both the accuracy and the informativeness of what people report from memory also depend on strategic regulatory processes that operate in the service of personal and situational goals. These processes intervene in converting the retained information into actual memory responses (cf. conversion processes in Tulving, 1983). Thus, between the retrieval (or reconstruction) of information, on the one hand, and overt memory performance, on the other hand, lie metacognitive processes of monitoring and control. The monitoring mechanism subjectively assesses the correctness and informativeness of potential memory responses, whereas the control mechanism determines whether or not to volunteer the best available candi-

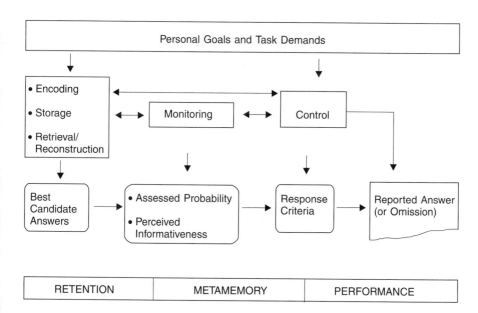

FIGURE 4.1. A scheme for conceptualizing and distinguishing cognitive and metacognitive components underlying recall memory performance, focusing on the strategic regulation of report option and grain size. Adapted from Goldsmith, Koriat, and Weinberg-Eliezer (2002).

date answer. The control mechanism operates by setting a report criterion on the monitoring output: A specific answer will be volunteered only if its assessed probability of being correct passes the criterion. Otherwise, either a more coarsely grained answer will be provided (control of grain size) or the answer will be withheld entirely (control of report option). The report criterion is set on the basis of implicit or explicit payoffs; that is, the gain for providing correct information relative to the cost of providing incorrect information.

The scheme is certainly oversimplified, and there is more overlap, undoubtedly, between the memory, monitoring, and control processes than is apparent in the figure (cf. Norman & Schacter, 1996). Nonetheless, for heuristic and organizational purposes, we separately address the three components of retention, monitoring, and control, noting how each of these is affected by various factors that determine both the quantity and accuracy of the information reported from memory. Our review of the literature is not confined to eyewitness research but also (primarily) includes an examination of theoretically oriented experimental studies, as they pertain to issues of memory quantity and memory accuracy.

THREE COMPONENTS CONTRIBUTING TO MEMORY PERFORMANCE: RETENTION, MONITORING, AND CONTROL

Retention

In terms of the scheme presented in Figure 4.1, most memory research has focused on elements contained in the left-hand box, investigating processes of encoding, storage, and retrieval that are generally considered to concern retention or memory, per se. These studies have employed a wide range of paradigms that vary in the degree to which they pertain to real-life situations. In some cases, the target stimuli are presented in naturalistic settings; more often, they are embedded in a filmed or narrated event; most often, perhaps, they are presented in a list.

A very productive list-learning paradigm that has been used extensively in recent years is the Deese–Roediger–McDermott (DRM) paradigm (see Roediger & McDermott, 1995). In the first phase of this paradigm, participants are presented with to-be-remembered lists of words (e.g., *THREAD, PIN, EYE, SEW*) that are associated with a common, critical theme word (e.g., *NEEDLE*) that is *not* presented. Typically, in the consequent memory test, participants tend to falsely recall and/or recognize the critical lures (theme words) as having been presented in the study list (for a review, see Roediger, McDermott, & Robinson, 1998). Manipulations involving this paradigm have yielded a wealth of findings on both true and false recall, some of which are reported below.

Contributions to Memory Quantity and Accuracy

Memory quantity and accuracy often go hand in hand (e.g., Roediger, Watson, McDermott, & Gallo, 2001). For example, both measures are impaired by divided attention at encoding (e.g., Kelley & Sahakyan, 2003) and by longer retention intervals (Belli, Windschitl, McCarthy, & Winfrey, 1992; Hanawalt & Demarest, 1939; Hirt, McDonald, & Erickson, 1995). In general, the weaker the memory trace, the more memory is prone to reconstructive processes that may lead to distortion (e.g., Hanawalt & Demarest, 1939; for a review, see Brewer & Nakamura, 1984).

On the other hand, there are factors that enhance quantity but impair accuracy at the same time (e.g., Goff & Roediger, 1998; Toglia, Neuschatz, & Goodwin, 1999). For example, using the DRM paradigm, Toglia et al. (1999) demonstrated a "more is less" effect by which deep processing at encoding increased the recall of true items (i.e., quantity) but also increased false recall, resulting in less accurate recall overall. Similarly, the act of imagining both true and false events has been found to increase the tendency to recall these events, thereby increasing quantity but decreasing accuracy (e.g., Goff & Roediger, 1998), and the recall of both true and false childhood events has been found to increase with repeated interviewing (e.g., Hyman & Pentland, 1996). Such findings support the idea that under certain conditions, "ironically, the techniques that are effective in aiding recall are the very ones that can distort memory" (Pennebaker & Memon, 1996, p. 383).

Consequently, in assessing the contribution of various factors to memory performance, it is important to consider separately the effects on memory quantity and on memory accuracy. Unfortunately, the necessary data are not always reported. Because most research does not separate retention from other influences on performance, we too initially treat memory quantity and accuracy performance as reflecting (primarily) retention. In later sections, we discuss how metacognitive monitoring and control processes may add to, or interact with, the level of retention in determining memory performance. Again, mainly for heuristic convenience, our examination of the factors that influence retention is partitioned according to three overlapping and interacting stages: (1) the initial encoding of information, (2) the storage or maintenance of information over time, and (3) the retrieval or reconstruction of the stored information.

Factors Affecting Retention: Encoding Factors

The Perceptual Quality of the Target Event

Not surprisingly, factors that improve the perceptual quality of the target event tend to improve its encoding, consequently improving event recall (for reviews, see Davies, 1993; Deffenbacher, 1991). For example, Shapiro and Penrod's (1986) meta-analysis of eight eyewitness lineup studies indicates that shorter exposure durations result in lower correct face identification rates and higher false identification rates. Thus, both quantity and accuracy measures are affected (see also Read, Lindsay, & Nicholls, 1998). Other studies have shown that eyewitness memory varies as a function of illumination conditions, with better memory quantity occurring in daylight and early evening viewing than in nighttime viewing (Yarmey, 1986). Thus, all else equal, it appears that we should, in fact, tend to trust the account of the eyewitness who had the better view.

Distinctiveness: The Importance or Salience of the Event

Distinctiveness is a complex theoretical concept with many definitions (e.g., Hunt & McDaniel, 1993; Schmidt, 1991). Common to all of these is the general idea that distinctive encoding improves memory performance. In this section, we focus on one form of distinctiveness: the importance or salience of the target event. One of the most extensively studied phenomena in this context is "flashbulb memory," a term used to label vivid and detailed recollection of the circumstances in which people hear about an important, surprising, and emotionally arousing event (e.g., the Columbia space shuttle disaster, the destruction of the "Twin Towers" on September 11, 2001). Initially, it was suggested that flashbulb memories are more accurate and durable than ordinary memories (Brown & Kulik, 1977).

However, despite the relative vividness and elaborateness of flashbulb memories, their accuracy is less than compelling, with many observed inconsistencies between the details reported after long retention intervals and those reported initially (e.g., McCloskey, Wible, & Cohen, 1988; Neisser & Harsch, 1992; Schmolck, Buffalo, & Squire, 2000; Talarico & Rubin, 2003). Some of the variance in the quantity and accuracy of flashbulb memories appears to be due to differences in the personal importance of the target event (e.g., Conway et al., 1994; Rubin & Kozin, 1984). Indeed, several researchers have pointed out that "ordinary" memories are also relatively accurate and long-lasting when they relate to highly distinctive and personally significant events (e.g., McCloskey et al., 1988; Weaver, 1993). Thus, for instance, a soccer fan attending his or her first live match is more likely to recollect the details of a fight that broke out in the stands than a fan who has attended dozens of soccer matches (and perhaps witnessed many such fights).

Amount of Allocated Attention

The role of attention as the key to successful encoding was highlighted in the multistore or modal model of memory (Atkinson & Shiffrin, 1968). Conscious attention to the incoming information was considered a necessary condition for the encoding or transfer of that information into long-term memory. More recent proposals have emphasized the role of attention in facilitating strategic/effortful and deep semantic processing (e.g., Craik, Govoni, Naveh-

Benjamin, & Anderson, 1996; Hasher & Zacks, 1979; Naveh-Benjamin, Craik, Gavrilescu, & Anderson, 2000) and in the binding of various pieces of information or features into one cohesive event (Naveh-Benjamin, 2002).

Whatever the particular mechanisms involved, many studies support the idea that eyewitnesses whose attention is overloaded or distracted during the original event will later remember fewer details from that event and also remember them less accurately. For example, increasing the attentional load in the original scene, by increasing the number of perpetrators simultaneously present, has been found to reduce memory quantity (Clifford & Hollin, 1981), as has dividing attention by having participants perform a simultaneous distraction task (e.g., counting backward by 3; Craik et al., 1996; for a review, see Naveh-Benjamin, 2002). Divided attention at encoding has also been shown to impair memory accuracy (e.g., Kelley & Sahakyan, 2003; Naveh-Benjamin, 1987; Perez-Mata, Read, & Diges, 2002; Seamon et al., 2003). Thus, the evidence suggests that an eyewitness who was fully attending to the target event is likely to remember the event more completely and more accurately than an eyewitness whose attention was distracted or overloaded.

Incidental versus Intentional Encoding

Another attention-related factor that may affect memory performance is whether encoding is incidental or intentional (e.g., Lampinen, Copeland, & Neuschatz, 2001). In a typical memory experiment, subjects intentionally study the target stimuli or event for a subsequent memory test. By contrast, in most real-life memory situations, particularly those of forensic interest, the witnessed events were not intentionally memorized. Rather, they were experienced *incidentally* and later recollected when the need arose. Thus, on the face of it, it would seem that incidental encoding is a more ecologically valid approach for eyewitness research.

Do empirical studies indicate a difference in memory quantity and accuracy for incidental compared with intentional encoding? In an early accuracy-focused study, Herman, Lawless, and Marshall (1957), adapting a paradigm developed by Carmichael, Hogan, and Walter (1932), presented participants with ambiguous figures (e.g., a pair of circles with a small adjoining line) along with one of two alternate labels (*EYEGLASSES, DUMBELLS*). Participants who were told that they would be asked to reproduce the figures from memory (i.e., intentional learning) produced more accurate reproductions than those who were not (i.e., incidental learning). The reproduced drawings based on incidental learning were biased more by the semantic labels present at encoding, apparently because the intentional-learning participants paid more attention to the exact details of the figures.

More recent studies have shown that memory quantity performance is also superior following intentional rather than incidental learning (e.g., Lampinen et al., 2001; Migueles & Garcia-Bajos, 1999; Naveh-Benjamin, 2002; Pezdek, Whetstone, Reynolds, Askari, & Dougherty, 1989). Particularly interesting are findings suggesting that the binding of contextual information with item information is partly dependent on intentional encoding. Compared to intentional encoding, incidental encoding was found to yield inferior memory for spatial location (Naveh-Benjamin, 1987) and for the joint (bound) combinations of item and color (Chalfonte & Johnson, 1996). This disadvantage of incidental encoding (and divided attention, e.g., Reinitz, Morrissey, & Demb, 1994, Experiment 2) may be particularly harmful to witness memory because of the role of feature binding in attributing memories to their proper source (i.e., *source monitoring*; see section on monitoring).

Depth of Processing (Elaboration)

Other research, however, has shown that the processes that are applied to the originally presented stimuli are more influential on subsequent recollection than is the intent to learn (Bernstein, Beig, Siegenthaler, & Grady, 2002; Craik & Lockhart, 1972; Hyde & Jenkins, 1973). According to Craik and Lockhart's (1972) landmark levels-of-processing (LOP) approach, memory is a by-product of perceptual and cognitive processes that are applied to the incoming information: The more deeply or meaningfully the incoming information is processed, the better it is retained, regardless of the intention to learn (see Lockhart & Craik, 1990). In Craik and Tulving's (1975) classic study, for example, the proportion of words recognized under incidental learning was higher when the encoding task required semantic processing than when it merely required the processing of either phonemic or orthographic features. This pattern was virtually the same whether learning was intentional or incidental. Although the mechanisms underlying LOP effects are not completely clear, the beneficial effect of deep semantic processing is generally attributed to more *elaborative* encoding, which in turn yields greater distinctiveness or differentiation of the richly elaborated trace from other memory traces, and enhanced connectivity and integration of the target information with other stored information (see Craik, 2002).

Interestingly, whereas elaborative or deep semantic processing generally has a beneficial effect on memory quantity, it may, at the same time, impair memory accuracy. Relative to nonsemantic processing, semantic processing has been found not only to increase true memory for the target items but also false memory for semantically related stimuli that were not part of the target event (e.g., Barclay, Toglia, & Chevalier, 1984; Rhodes & Anastasi, 2000; Thapar & McDermott, 2001; Toglia et al., 1999; but see Read, 1996; Tussing & Greene, 1997). Perhaps, then, an eyewitness will remember more information regarding events that have been processed more deeply, yet be less able to distinguish between the witnessed information, per se, and related information generated or activated in the process of understanding the events. This pattern resembles the one that emerges as a result of constructive processing, discussed next.

Constructive Processes

In general, the effects of prior knowledge, expertise, and interest on recall can be both positive and negative (for reviews, see Alba & Hasher, 1983; Davies, 1993). On the one hand, the assimilation of newly acquired information into preexisting knowledge or schemas increases the likelihood that the information will be recalled later. For example, skilled chess players perform better than novices when reconstructing from memory the locations of chess pieces from a real game, but not when the locations are random (Chase & Simon, 1973; de Groot, 1965). Similarly, baseball experts have been found to recall more details than low-knowledge participants from a narrative depicting baseball scenes (Chiesi, Spilich, & Voss, 1979). Powers, Andriks, and Loftus (1979) found differential patterns of memory performance between males and females for certain event details, consistent with typical gender interests: Whereas overall memory performance was comparable for the two gender groups, males showed superior memory quantity and more resistance to suggestion for typical male-oriented details (e.g., details of the purse snatcher), and females showed superior memory for typical female-oriented details (e.g., the victim's clothing).

On the other hand, however, prior knowledge, schemas, and attitudes may often impair accuracy. For example, Bartlett's (1932) classic study demonstrated how background and social–cultural schemas can distort memory to conform to these schemas. In that study, British college students who recalled the Native American folktale "The War of the Ghosts" tended to distort names, phrases, and events to more familiar Western forms. Explanations were often added in the story recollections, in attempts to make sense of ambiguous or incomprehensible sequences of events in terms of Western schemas. Recently, Tuckey and Brewer (2003) showed that eyewitnesses use schemas to interpret ambiguous scenes. They found less correct recall (i.e., reduced quantity) and more schema-based intrusions (i.e., reduced accuracy) in the recall of a videotaped bank robbery containing ambiguous scenes than for the unambiguous version of the event.

Owens, Bower, and Black (1979) showed that providing participants with information regarding the motivation behind a character's actions biased later recall of the events to be more motive related. Attitudes have also been shown to bias memory. For example, Echabe and Paez-Rovira (1989) showed that memory for technical information about AIDS was distorted to support the rememberers' preexisting views regarding the causes of AIDS (i.e., a conservative-blaming or liberal approach). Following Hastorf and Cantril's (1954) classic experiment, Boon and Davies (1996) showed that football fans' perceptions of a football game (e.g., estimated number of infractions of each team, degree of roughness) were systematically distorted in favor of their preferred teams.

Clearly, many witnessed events in real life involve aspects that evoke prior knowledge, dispositions, and expectancies that can either enhance or impair later recall. The type of effect will generally depend on the strength of the preexisting schemas, the degree of match between these schemas and the target information, and on whether memory accuracy or memory quantity is of primary concern (see Fiske, 1993).

Factors Affecting Retention: Storage Factors

Although the manner in which a target event is encoded strongly influences the quality of subsequent recollection, events occurring after encoding are also critical. In this section, we relate several factors that may operate between the encoding of the target event and its subsequent retrieval, and examine their potential effects on the memory quantity and accuracy of that recollection.

Passage of Time (Retention Interval)

Perhaps no phenomenon is as intrinsic to the notion of memory as the forgetting of information over time. Following Ebbinghaus's (1895/1964) classic work on the forgetting curve, many studies have shown a gradual reduction in memory quantity with increasing retention interval (Schacter, 1999). Initially, forgetting was viewed as a spontaneous decay or weakening of memory traces: These traces were assumed to be strengthened through "usage" (i.e., retrieval) but to fade away with disuse (for a short review on strength theory, see Roediger & Meade, 2000). An alternative to this view was first put forward by McGeoch (1932), who proposed that it is not the passage of time, per se, that impairs memory quantity but rather interference from other material that accumulates during that time. Supporting this idea was Brown's (1923) finding that items that could not be recalled at one point in time could be recalled on subsequent memory tests without additional study. Thus, the memory traces of these items were not lost (i.e., unavailable) but merely inaccessible during particular retrieval attempts. Many experiments have since replicated this phenomenon, often termed *reminiscence* (for a recent review, see Roediger, McDermott, & Goff, 1997). It is experienced, for example, by witnesses who cannot recall certain information when questioned about it, but then spontaneously recall that information after the questioning is over. Similarly, temporary inaccessibility is also evident in the "tip-of-the-tongue" (TOT) phenomenon, in which a person has a strong feeling that he or she knows the answer to a question (e.g., "Who was the lead actor in [a certain] movie?") but is temporarily unable to retrieve it. Often, the sought-for information suddenly pops up at a later time (for a review, see Brown, 1991). Such insights eventually led to a fundamental change in the conception of forgetting, catalyzed by Tulving and Pearlstone's (1966) influential distinction between *availability* and *accessibility*, which holds that much more information is available in memory than is accessible at any moment. In fact, it is now commonly believed that the primary cause of forgetting is loss of access to stored information rather than loss of the information itself (Tulving, 1983).

Although the decrease in memory quantity over time is a very robust finding, interestingly, the findings regarding memory accuracy are quite mixed. Although some studies have observed a decrease in output-bound accuracy that parallels the decrease in memory quantity (e.g., Bahrick, Hall, & Dunlosky, 1993; Koriat et al., 2001), other studies have suggested that output-bound accuracy may be relatively stable across long retention intervals. For example, Ebbesen and Rienick (1998) found that the number of correct statements reported about a past event decreased dramatically over a 4-week period (15 after 1 day; 10.3 after 1 week; 5.5 after 4 weeks). At the same time, however, output-bound accuracy remained relatively stable (.89, .92, and .84, respectively). Similarly, McCauley and Fisher (1995), and Brock, Fisher, and Cutler (1999) found no reduction in output-bound accuracy from an immediate test (within 5 minutes) to a test given 1 or 2 weeks later. Even more impressive is the finding of Poole and White (1993): Accuracy rates for statements about a staged event remained constant over a 2-year period, averaging 95% after 1 week and 93% after 2 years! Such results led Ebbesen and Reinick (1998, p. 757) to note:

> It seems obvious that the key issue in the real world is not how many facts a witness can recall from all those available to recall but the accuracy of the facts that are recalled. . . . Thus, if the legal system is concerned with the accuracy of the information that witnesses supply rather than the amount of information that can be remembered, it seems reasonable to question whether the "generally accepted" expert opinion that the rapid drop and then leveling-off result [assumed to describe the time course of forgetting] is reliable enough to testify about in court.

The ability of rememberers to maintain a constant level of (output-bound) memory accuracy over time, despite a reduction in (input-bound) memory quantity, may be due to the operation of metacognitive monitoring and control processes used to regulate memory accuracy (see sections on monitoring and control, below). If so, however, why is accuracy sometimes stable, but in other cases declines over time? Ongoing work suggests that part of the answer may be found in differences in the control over memory reporting that participants are allowed and the perceived incentives for complete-versus-accurate reporting (Koriat & Goldsmith, 2004).

Hierarchical Storage

Certain types of information appear to be more likely than others to remain accessible over time. In particular, a large amount of work has shown that the general meaning or "gist" of encoded material remains more accessible than does more detailed information, such as the surface form or verbatim form of that material (e.g., Begg & Wickelgren, 1974; Kintsch, Welsch, Schmalhofer, & Zimny, 1990; Posner & Keele, 1970). Much of that research has examined gist-versus-verbatim memory of linguistic-textual information. For example, Kintsch et al. (1990) found differential forgetting rates for three different levels of textual information, with (1) surface information (i.e., verbatim memory) becoming inaccessible within 4 days, (2) memory for the semantic content (i.e., gist) declining at a slower rate, and (3) judgments based on situational memory (i.e., inferences from a relevant knowledge schema) showing highly stable memory quantity over time. Studies of story recall have also reported superior memory quantity over time for higher-level (thematic or superordinate) propositions than lower-level (subordinate) propositions, as well as diminished memory accuracy over time due to a large amount of intrusions (e.g., Kintsch, Kozminsky, Streby, McKoon, & Keenan, 1975). Similarly, in testing memory for university course content, Conway, Cohen, and Stanhope (1991) found little forgetting of general principles and concepts over a 12-year retention period, whereas memory of specific details had declined sharply.

A shallower rate of forgetting has also been observed for categorical than for item information. For example, Dorfman and Mandler (1994) presented participants with items from various categories (e.g., SPARROW). Item memory declined over a 1-week interval, so that participants failed to discriminate between items (e.g., SPARROW) and related distractors (e.g., CANARY). However, they were able to discriminate between same-category and different-category distractors, suggesting that category information remained accessible over time, despite the loss of item information. Recently, Pansky and Koriat (2004) have shown an advantage in accessibility over time for an intermediate hierarchical level—the basic level (Rosch, Mervis, Gray, Johnson, & Boyes-Braem, 1976). They presented participants with a story containing target items, each of which could appear at one of three hierarchical levels: subordinate (e.g., SPORTS CAR), basic level (e.g., CAR), or superordinate (e.g., VEHICLE). Irrespective of the original level at which an item was presented, the participants tended to falsely recall it at the basic level. In other words, bidirectional shifts from both subordinate and superordinate levels were found, with the retained information converging at the basic level. The basic-level convergence effect was obtained at immediate testing, but it was especially pronounced following a 1-week retention interval, resulting in both reduced memory quantity (i.e., less correct recall) and reduced memory accuracy (i.e., more shifts to the basic level) over time. These results suggest that the basic level, which has been shown to be the cognitively optimal level for perception and categorization (e.g., Rosch et al., 1976), is also the preferred level for retaining episodic information over time.

The differential forgetting rates that occur at various hierarchical levels of information support the view that memory and forgetting are not all-or-nothing processes (e.g., Brainerd, Reyna, Howe, & Kingma, 1990). Rather, concepts and episodes may be represented in memory as bundles of features or attributes that are bound together to different degrees and are accessible or inaccessible with relative independence from one another (e.g., Brainerd et al., 1990; Chalfonte & Johnson, 1996; Lindsay & Johnson, 2000; Reyna & Titcomb, 1997). If so, when some of the features of an item are lost, or when the cohesion between these features weakens, item recall might fail and yet access to some individual features—those supporting recall or recognition at the categorical or gist level—may be preserved (see also Cowan, 1998; Koriat, Levy-Sadot, Edry, & de Marcas, 2003). Thus, particularly after a long time has passed since the witnessed event, it is much more likely that a witness's testimony will correctly reflect the gist or general characteristics of what occurred than the specific verbatim details (for a well-known example, see Neisser's [1981] analysis of John Dean's memory of conversations concerning the Watergate cover-up).

Interpolated Testing/Retelling

As discussed earlier, although the mere passage of time may affect the representation of events in memory, it is clear that more active processes also influence these representations. People frequently reflect upon what they saw or heard, recalling past events either to themselves or to others on different occasions following their occurrence. It has long been realized that the process of retrieving information does not merely test retention but also modifies the memory representation of that information and, consequently, its later retrieval (e.g., Bjork, 1975; Schooler, Foster, & Loftus, 1988). Early research focused mainly on the positive outcomes of retrieval "practice" on the subsequent recollection of the same information or event. Often referred to as the *testing effect*, an enhancement of memory quantity for recalled information following the interpolated testing of that information was demonstrated in word-list experiments (e.g., Allen, Mahler, & Estes, 1969; Carrier & Pashler, 1992; Wheeler, Ewers, & Buonanno, 2003), in eyewitness memory studies (Bornstein, Liebel, & Scarberry, 1998; Dent & Stephenson, 1979; Dunning & Stern, 1992; Eugenio, Buckhout, Kostes, & Ellison, 1982; Scrivner & Safer, 1988), and in autobiographical memory research (Linton, 1975). Some of these studies have shown that the benefit in memory quantity that results from interpolated recall of the target material exceeds that gained from additional study of the target materials (e.g., Carrier & Pashler, 1992; Cull, 2000; Kuo & Hirshman, 1996). In fact, memory testing was suggested as an effective inoculator against forgetting (e.g., Brainerd et al., 1990).

Nonetheless, interpolated reviewing of events can also have negative effects on recollection, some of which derive from the fact that such reviewing is usually selective. For example, Wenger, Thompson, and Bartling (1980) showed that the advantage of repeated testing over repeated study was reversed when the interpolated recall test was selective (i.e., only a few items were recalled). More recent research on a phenomenon known as retrieval-induced forgetting (RIF) has shown opposite effects on memory quantity for those items or pieces of information that were selected for review and those that were not: Whereas memory quantity for the reviewed items is enhanced, memory quantity for related, nonreviewed, items is reduced (see Anderson, Bjork, & Bjork, 1994; Levy & Anderson, 2002). RIF was first demonstrated for exemplars of semantic categories (Anderson et al., 1994), but has since been generalized to a wide range of stimuli and domains, such as visuospatial memory (Ciranni & Shimamura, 1999), action memory (Koutstaal, Schacter, Johnson, & Galluccio, 1999, Experiment 1), and social cognition (e.g., Dunn & Spellman, 2003; Macrae & MacLeod, 1999).

RIF is highly relevant to eyewitness memory. After viewing a typical crime scene, repeated questions relating to a subset of some of its details were found to increase memory quantity for the questioned details but to reduce memory quantity for details that were omitted from the interrogation (MacLeod, 2002; Shaw, Bjork, & Handal, 1995). In real life, witnesses to crimes are repeatedly questioned about the witnessed event by the police, legal representatives, family members, and others. These questions may often be limited to specific aspects of the incident, thus constituting selective retrieval tasks. Based on the RIF literature, those details that were not the subject of initial retrieval practice may be poorly recalled in a subsequent retrieval attempt (e.g., during a trial), resulting in an impairment in memory quantity for what might be critical aspects for a case (see Shaw et al., 1995).

Memory testing may also have negative consequences on memory accuracy. As previously reported, Bartlett (1932) found distortions in participants' recollections of the Native American folktale, "The War of the Ghosts." Testing the same participants repeatedly, following various retention intervals, he found both more forgetting (i.e., lower memory quantity) and more pronounced distortions (i.e., lower memory accuracy) over the repeated reproductions. Bergman and Roediger (1999) replicated these findings and also included a control group that was not tested immediately. Interestingly, delayed recall tests (after 1 week and after 6 months) revealed fewer distortions for the control participants than for those who were tested previously. Thus, immediate testing may preserve not only true memory but also false memory, resulting in enhanced memory quantity but reduced memory accuracy (see Bergman & Roediger, 1999; Brainerd & Reyna, 2002). These findings are consistent with findings obtained in the DRM paradigm, which showed an increase in false recall of the critical lure following prior recall of the list (e.g., McDermott, 1996; Payne, Elie, Blackwell, & Neuschatz, 1996).

Other findings suggest that merely asking subjects about events that never occurred increases the probability that on a later occasion they will remember the event as having occurred (the "mere memory testing effect"; see Brainerd & Mojardin, 1998; Reyna, 1998). Boon and Davies (1988) presented participants with a series of slides depicting a subway, one of which depicted a white man pulling a knife on a black man. When recalling this slide, participants wrote accurate accounts of the scene. However, when the recall test was preceded by a recognition test that presented a racially prejudiced and false alternative (that it was the black man holding the knife), both recognition and subsequent recall were significantly distorted. Thus, merely presenting the false stereotype-consistent version in an interpolated recognition test impaired the accuracy of subsequent recall. Similarly, Fiedler, Walther, Armbruster, Fay, and Naumann (1996) demonstrated that merely considering false propositions increased the tendency to remember them later as true. In fact, even when these propositions were initially (correctly) rejected as false, they nonetheless intruded on subsequent memory reports, particularly following longer retention intervals between questioning and memory testing.

Other studies have shown that particular types of review or reflection are especially likely to impair memory accuracy (see Roediger et al., 1997). For example, Mather and Johnson (2003) found that following a review that focused on feelings and reactions to the target event, subsequent recall and recognition of event details were more prone to schema-based intrusions than following a review of the event details or no review at all. Tversky and Marsh (2000) demonstrated the influence of biased retellings of events on subsequent memory for these events. For example, in Experiment 3 of their study, participants were presented with a story of a murder that suggested two possible suspects. Afterward, participants in the biased retelling condition were asked to write a prosecuting summation accusing one of the suspects. In a subsequent recall test, participants in the biased retelling condition, but not those in a neutral retelling condition, recalled more incriminating items and made more incriminating errors for the suspect they wrote about than for the other suspect. Tversky and Marsh (2000) explain the role of the retelling perspective as a schema that guides the elaboration and reorganization of the event details, resulting in enhanced recall of both true and false information that is consistent with this schema.

To summarize, reflection on events, a frequent human activity, can enhance memory quantity for the reviewed details. At the same time, it may reduce memory quantity for those details that were not reviewed. Worse yet, any biases or schema-based intrusions that taint such a review may become even more pronounced in the subsequent recollection of the event, thus impairing memory accuracy. Although an attempt can be made to minimize selectivity and bias in review that is elicited by official questioning, clearly many opportunities for such review and reflection exist that are beyond the control of the legal system.

Misleading Postevent Information

If nonsuggestive review or reflection on an event can sometimes impair the quantity and accuracy of subsequent recollections, how much more impairment occurs when that review involves misleading suggestions. Classic studies by Elizabeth Loftus in the 1970s demonstrated the powerful effect of (mis)leading questions on memory of the target event (for a review, see Loftus,

1979). For example, Loftus and Palmer (1974) tested subjects' memory of a film depicting a car accident. They found that the question "How fast were the cars going when they *smashed* into each other?" yielded higher speed estimates than a more neutral question that used the verb *hit*. Furthermore, the "smashed" question later led more people to falsely claim that they had seen broken glass, resulting in reduced memory accuracy. Other studies have shown that simply using a definite article when questioning a person about an object that was not part of the original event (e.g., "Did you see *the* broken headlight?") rather than an indefinite article ("Did you see *a* broken headlight?") can bias witnesses into falsely remembering the specified object (e.g., Loftus, 1975; Loftus & Zanni, 1975; see also Fiedler et al., 1996). Apparently, false information presupposed in the formulation of a question is often accepted by the witness as true.

Subsequent work by Loftus and her colleagues highlighted the contaminating effect of less subtle forms of misleading postevent information on eyewitness testimony (e.g., Loftus, Miller, & Burns, 1978; see Gerrie, Garry, & Loftus, Chapter 7, this volume). This research stimulated a great number of subsequent studies that have replicated the basic finding that exposure to misleading information, presented after an event, can distort the memory for that event by what is known as the "misinformation effect."

In a prototypical misinformation experiment, participants who are exposed to an event are later misinformed about some details, then finally tested for their memory of the original details. For example, Loftus et al. (1978) presented participants with a film depicting a car accident and later asked them a series of questions about the events in the slides. Embedded in one of these questions was the misleading presupposition that the car stopped at a *yield* sign, although the film had shown a *stop* sign. In the final stage of the experiment, memory for the information seen in the film was tested using a two-alternative recognition test containing both the original and the misled item. The findings showed that participants who received the misleading question were less likely to report having seen the original stop sign and more likely to report having seen a yield sign than were the participants who received correct information (i.e., stop sign) or neutral information (i.e., intersection). Note that when using this testing procedure, a reduction in memory accuracy as a result of exposure to misinformation necessarily entails a corresponding reduction in memory quantity as well, because falsely selecting the misleading item comes at the expense of not selecting the original item. To better distinguish these effects, in this section we focus on studies that used a recall test or a yes/no recognition test, either of which allows an independent assessment of memory quantity and accuracy.

It is interesting that, in contrast to most of the factors we have reviewed so far, the introduction of misleading postevent information has been found to affect memory accuracy more strongly than memory quantity. Virtually all the studies have shown a decline in memory accuracy, evident in a larger tendency in the misled than in the control condition to falsely remember the misleading item as having appeared in the original event (henceforth, "suggestibility"). However, reduced memory quantity for the original item in the misled condition than in the control condition (henceforth, "memory impairment") has only been obtained under certain circumstances.

First, memory impairment appears to depend on the relative accessibility of the original memory representation. Once memory for the original information exceeds chance levels (see Belli, 1989; Frost, 2000), stronger memory impairment effects are more likely to be found for weaker representations of the original information (see Pezdek & Roe, 1995; Reyna & Titcomb, 1997; Titcomb & Reyna, 1995).

Second, it has been suggested that the postevent information must be believed to be redundant or the same as old information in order for memory impairment to occur (Windschitl, 1996). Consistent with this hypothesis, memory impairment was found on a recall test when the misleading items were more conceptually similar to the original items (i.e., belonged to the same category; e.g., Eakin, Schreiber, & Sergent-Marshall, 2003; Lindsay, 1990) but not when they were less conceptually similar (e.g., Zaragoza, McCloskey, & Jamis, 1987). A recent study (Pansky & Bar, 2004) specifically manipulated conceptual similarity and found memory impairment when the misleading information (e.g., *GOLD RING*) shared the same basic level with the original information (e.g., *SILVER RING*), but not when the misleading item belonged to a different basic level (e.g., *GOLD EARRING*).

There are several possible accounts for the joint reduction in memory accuracy and quantity that results from the introduction of misleading postevent information. Initially, these effects were attributed to a storage-based impairment by which the postevent information replaces or overwrites the stored memory traces for the original information, rendering the original traces unavailable for consequent retrieval (e.g., Loftus, 1979; Loftus & Loftus, 1980). However, subsequent studies have convincingly shown that the effects of misinformation can be temporary (e.g., Chandler, 1989, 1991; Christiaansen & Ochalek, 1983) or reduced by using retrieval manipulations (e.g., Bekerian & Bowers, 1983), suggesting that the postevent information does not impair the stored representation of the original information but rather impairs its accessibility relative to that of the misleading information (see also Eakin et al., 2003). Alternatively, moderate storage-based accounts have proposed a partial degradation hypothesis, according to which misleading suggestions weaken or disintegrate original memories (see Belli, Lindsay, Gales, & McCarthy, 1994; Belli & Loftus, 1996; Belli et al., 1992). A similar compromise between the storage-based and accessibility-based accounts has been suggested in terms of fuzzy-trace theory, in which memory impairment depends on the relative accessibility of verbatim and gist representations of the original information and the verbatim representation of the misleading information (see Brainerd & Reyna, 1998; Reyna & Titcomb, 1997; Titcomb & Reyna, 1995). Nonimpairment accounts of suggestibility (i.e., reduced accuracy) attribute it to (1) response biases or strategic effects that occur when no memory for the original event details exists (McCloskey & Zaragoza, 1985; Zaragoza & Koshmider, 1989), or to (2) an error in source monitoring that wrongly attributes the mis-led item to the original event (e.g., Johnson, Hashtroudi, & Lindsay, 1993; Lindsay & Johnson, 1989).

Memory Implantation

A more extreme case of misleading postevent information is the suggestion of entire episodes that did not occur, as induced in memory implantation studies (e.g., Hyman, Husband, & Billings, 1995; Loftus & Pickrell, 1995). Inspired by the heated debate over the authenticity of memories of childhood sexual abuse that are recovered in adulthood (often through psychotherapy), such studies are designed to test whether, and under which conditions, people can "remember" entire events that did not occur (see Gerrie et al., Chapter 7, this volume). In a typical experiment, young adults are asked to try to remember childhood events that were allegedly reported by a relative. These include several true events that had actually occurred in the participant's childhood and one false event that had not occurred (e.g., getting lost in a shopping mall). Studies using this procedure have shown that, under certain conditions, people can be induced to confidently and vividly recall entire events that did not occur in reality, and to provide a detailed account of them. Recollection of the false event, resulting in a reduction in memory accuracy, was found to be especially likely to occur following (1) repeated interviews or suggestions (Hyman et al., 1995; Hyman & Pentland, 1996; Wade, Garry, Read, & Lindsay, 2002), (2) instructions to imagine the false event (Hyman & Billings, 1998; Hyman & Pentland, 1996), and (3) when the false event is plausible (Pezdek, Finger, & Hodge, 1997).

On the basis of these findings and consistent with the source-monitoring framework (Johnson et al., 1993), Hyman and associates (Hyman, 1999; Hyman & Loftus, 1998) have suggested three interactive processes that underlie the implantation of false personal memories, each of which may be affected by situational demands. The first process is the acceptance of the plausibility of the suggested event. The second process is the creation of contextual information for the event, such as an image or a narrative, often by tying the false event with self-knowledge and other schematic knowledge that comes to mind. The final process is the commission of a source-monitoring error, in which the person wrongly attributes the created image to a past personal experience.

Factors Affecting Retention: Retrieval Factors

The encoding and storing of information is not sufficient for its subsequent recollection. Perhaps the first to put forward this idea was Semon (1921), who referred to a memory process he called "ecphory" as "the influences which awaken the mnemic trace or engram out of its latent state into one of manifested activity" (p. 12). However, this process, and the factors affecting it, only became the object of empirical study from the mid-1960s (see Roediger & Gallo, 2002; Roediger & Guynn, 1996; Tulving, 1983). Since then, numerous studies have shown that memory performance is highly dependent on the conditions of testing (e.g., Tulving & Pearlstone, 1966; Tulving & Thomson, 1973).

In addition to its theoretical importance, the study of retrieval factors has important practical implications because, compared to encoding factors and many storage factors, retrieval factors are more often under the control of the interviewer (e.g., see Wells, 1978, for a discussion of system, as opposed to estimator, variables). In our analysis of factors affecting retrieval, we separate those that play a role in forced reporting from metacognitive factors that play a role in free reporting (cf. the distinction between *ecphory* and *conversion* processes in Tulving, 1983; see subsequent sections on monitoring and control).

Retrieval Cues

Retrieval cues can be thought of as those aspects of the rememberer's physical and cognitive environment that drive the retrieval process (Tulving, 1983), whether they are explicitly presented as part of the memory query, self-generated, or simply part of the general retrieval context. All else equal, memory tests that provide more, or more effective, cues have generally been found to yield superior memory quantity than tests that provide fewer, or less effective, cues: Cued recall generally yields superior memory quantity than free recall (Lewis, 1971; Tulving & Pearlstone, 1966), and recognition testing generally yields superior memory quantity than cued recall (Brown, 1976). Additionally, providing more recall cues yields superior memory quantity than providing fewer recall cues (e.g., Mäntylä, 1986).

According to the well-known "encoding specificity principle" (Tulving, 1983), the effectiveness of retrieval cues in enhancing memory quantity depends on the degree of match between the features they provide and the encoded features (Thomson & Tulving, 1970; Tulving & Osler, 1968; Tulving & Thomson, 1973). There is a wealth of evidence supporting this principle. For example, Barclay, Bransford, Franks, McCarrell, and Nitsch (1974) presented participants with sentences containing target words (e.g., *PIANO*), in one of two possible contexts (e.g., "The man lifted the piano" or "The man tuned the piano"). On a subsequent recall test, the target word was more likely to be recalled when the recall cue was congruent with the context in which the word was presented initially (e.g., "something heavy" for the first sentence, and "something with a nice sound" for the second sentence) than when it was incongruent. Thus, cues that tap the features that were encoded are more effective cues in terms of memory quantity. Much less is known about the effect of encoding specificity on output-bound memory accuracy. In an adaptation of Thomson and Tulving's (1970) classic study, Higham (2002) found that strong-associate retrieval cues not presented in the study phase were inferior to weak-associate retrieval cues presented during study, both in terms of memory quantity (fewer correct recalls) and in terms of memory accuracy (more commission errors). However, in an adaptation of Tulving and Osler's (1968) study (comparing two sets of weak-associate cues), Rosenbluth-Mor (2001) found that presenting the same weak-associate cue both during retrieval and during study increased memory quantity compared to no retrieval cue, but did not improve memory accuracy. In contrast, presenting a different weak-associate retrieval cue than the one presented in the study phase impaired both memory quantity and memory accuracy compared to the neutral (no-cue) condition. This finding suggests that it is not the match between retrieval and study cues that enhances accuracy but, rather, the mismatch between these cues that impairs accuracy. It also suggests that we should be wary of providing external retrieval cues to witnesses when output-bound accuracy is of primary concern—there may be little to be gained (in terms of accuracy) from providing compatible cues and much to be lost by providing incompatible cues.

It has been proposed that encoding specificity, or trace–cue compatibility, is one (important) instance of a more general factor that promotes memory quantity: "cue distinctiveness" (Mäntylä & Nilsson, 1988; Nairne, 2002). In general, recall improves to the extent that the information that is provided by the cue is diagnostic of the target (for a review, see Schmidt, 1991). According to the "cue overload principle," the probability of recalling an item declines with the number of items associated with its retrieval cue (e.g., Watkins & Watkins, 1975). Thus, for example, an eyewitness may have difficulty accessing the details of a particular doctor's visit due to interference from many other visits with the same doctor. Also consistent with this principle is the "category size effect" (Roediger, 1973), in which the likelihood of remembering any particular category exemplar decreases as the size (number of exemplars) of the category increases. Thus, for example, all else equal, a witness recounting a meeting attended by six men and three women would be more likely to forget one of the men than one of the women. Nondistinctive retrieval cues may also impair memory accuracy, if they access competing alternatives more easily than they access the solicited information (e.g., Kato, 1985; Kelley & Sahakyan, 2003; cf. the potentially harmful effect of encoding–retrieval incompatibility, mentioned earlier).

Context Reinstatement

Effective retrieval cues can sometimes be tied to entire events rather than to particular items. For example, reinstatement of the physical study environment (e.g., the room) can provide effective retrieval cues that enhance memory quantity (Godden & Baddeley, 1975; Smith, Glenberg, & Bjork, 1978). This type of context reinstatement is frequently exploited by police authorities, who attempt to enhance the memory of eyewitnesses by having them return to the crime scene, or if this is not possible, by having the witness mentally imagine the original context (see Powell, Fisher, & Wright, Chapter 2, this volume). Similarly, reexperiencing the same state of mind or mood at retrieval that the person was in at encoding has also been found to enhance memory quantity, in what is known as "state-dependent retrieval" (e.g., Bower, 1981; Eich, 1980; Goodwin, Powell, Bremer, Hoine, & Stern, 1969). For example, participants who were intoxicated during the study session were better able to recall the studied information if they were also intoxicated in the test session than if they were not (Goodwin et al., 1969; for similar affects with marijuana, see Eich, Weingartner, Stillman, & Gillin, 1975).

However, subsequent research has shown that the beneficial effects of physical and mental reinstatement may be limited to situations in which more effective cues are unavailable (see Roediger & Guynn, 1996; Smith, 1988). Thus, physical aspects of the environment can serve as retrieval cues, but their effect is likely to be overshadowed if encoding strategies were rich enough for rememberers to supply their own, more effective retrieval cues (e.g., Eich, 1985; McDaniel, Anderson, Einstein, & O'Halloran, 1989). Similarly, state-dependent memory was found in free-recall tests but not in cued-recall tests (Eich, 1980, 1989), suggesting that the enhancing effect of the reinstatement of mental state is likely to be overshadowed if more powerful retrieval cues are available (e.g., category names).

Reconstructive Processes

In addition to the effects of constructive processes at the time of encoding, reviewed earlier, there is accumulating evidence that people's beliefs, knowledge, perspectives, and expectations at the time of retrieval also influence which information they retrieve from memory and how they interpret that information, affecting both memory quantity and memory accuracy (see Hirt, Lynn, Payne, Krackow, & McCrea, 1999). For example, Anderson and Pichert (1978) have shown that a person's perspective at retrieval (e.g., the perspective of a burglar vs. a potential home buyer) can enhance memory quantity for information that is relevant to that perspective (e.g., a rare coin collection for the burglar; a leaky roof for the home buyer) and an impairment of memory quantity for information that is irrelevant to that perspective (e.g., a leaky roof for the burglar; a rare coin collection for the home buyer). The authors interpreted their findings as suggesting that each retrieval perspective invoked a different schema that provided implicit cues for the recall of different information from the story.

Reconstructive processes operating at retrieval have also been shown to impair memory accuracy. Michael Ross and his colleagues (e.g., Conway & Ross, 1984; Ross, 1989) have shown that people's personal memories are biased by expectancies derived from implicit theories of stability and change. For example, people's belief that their attitudes are stable over time tends to bias recall of their earlier attitudes in the direction of greater consistency with their current attitudes (e.g., McFarland & Ross, 1987; Ross, McFarland, & Fletcher, 1981). On the other hand, people's expectancy that an attribute should change over time can also bias recall: Students led to believe in the effectiveness of a study skills course remembered their initial self-evaluated study skills as being lower and their subsequent test grades as being higher, than did students in a control condition (Conway & Ross, 1984; for similar results in a laboratory study, see Hirt, 1990). Bahrick et al. (1996) have demonstrated what appear to be motivational reconstructive errors. They tested college students for memory of their high school grades. Accuracy of recall declined monotonically with letter grade, ranging between 89% for A's and 29% for D's. The majority of the participants inflated their grades, resulting in an asymmetry of errors. These distortions were attributed to reconstructive inferences that biased recall in a positive, emotionally gratifying direction.

The research reviewed in this section and the earlier section on constructive encoding processes suggests that an eyewitness's knowledge, expectancies, and motivations can shape his or her memory of past events. Information that is consistent with schemas or implicit theories is selectively recalled or erroneously added, whereas inconsistent information is distorted to become more consistent. In fact, (re)constructive memory errors are so ubiquitous that some researchers have espoused a strong reconstructive view, arguing that reconstructive recall is the rule rather than the exception (e.g., Barclay, 1988; Neisser, 1984).

MONITORING

All of the stages of information processing reviewed in the previous sections (i.e., encoding, storage, retrieval) generally involve subjective monitoring (see, e.g., Barnes, Nelson, Dunlosky, Mazzoni, & Narens, 1999). In this section, we focus on processes of monitoring (and control) that operate during memory reporting. As we stated earlier, these processes mediate between retention and actual memory performance. Thus, for example, in order to tell "the whole truth and nothing but the truth," courtroom witnesses must differentiate between correct and incorrect information, volunteering the former but withholding the latter. Their ability to monitor their knowledge and to regulate their memory reporting accordingly will be critical in determining their memory performance. In fact, reporting inaccurate information reflects not only a failure of memory processes, per se, but also a failure of the monitoring process to "realize" that the information that comes to mind is faulty. Conversely, omission of event details from the memory report may result not only from failures in encoding, storing, or retrieving the solicited pieces of information, but, alternatively from a failure of the monitoring process to "realize" that certain accessible pieces of information are, in fact, correct. Hence, it is important to attempt to identify the contributions of memory monitoring to memory performance, as well as the factors that affect the accuracy of that monitoring.

Contributions to Memory Quantity and Accuracy

Many memory failures, which can reduce both quantity and accuracy, seem to stem from source-monitoring errors—that is, failures to attribute the retrieved information to its proper source (Johnson et al., 1993). For example, we may remember having called the doctor to cancel an appointment, but in fact we only thought about doing so. Reality monitoring—the ability to distinguish actual events from imaginings—is a special case of source monitoring. Source-monitoring errors can result in confusion in differentiating details of events that were experienced in one situation from those that pertain to another. A dramatic example is an incident that ironically involved a well-known memory researcher, Donald Thomson, who was wrongly identified by a rape victim as the rapist. Thomson's alibi both exonerated him immediately and helped explain the false accusation: He was giving a live television interview at the time of the rape. Apparently, the victim had been watching the interview just before she was raped, and she confused the memory of his image with that of the rapist. Thus, source-monitoring failures can often be more harmful than retrieval failures: Fragments of real experience are accurately and vividly recalled but mistakenly attributed to the wrong person, location, or time, resulting in false memory.

According to the source-monitoring framework (for a review, see Mitchell & Johnson, 2000), in discriminating the origin of information, participants usually engage a rapid heuristic process that takes advantage of the fact that mental experiences from different sources (e.g., perception vs. imagination) typically differ on various dimensions (e.g., visual clarity and contextual details). Thus, for example, memories of witnessed events tend to include more vivid sensory, temporal, and spatial information than imagined events. However, in some cases, representations of imagined events might be highly detailed and perceptually vivid, whereas representations of perceived events may be poor in perceptual detail, resulting in source confusions. The source-monitoring framework also posits a more strategic, deliberative process that is engaged under special circumstances (e.g., when trying to recall the particular conversation in which an incriminating statement was heard) and involves the retrieval of additional information and the application of conscious reasoning processes.

A number of factors have been found to promote source-monitoring errors that lead to memory distortions (see Mitchell & Johnson, 2000). These include, among others, a high degree of perceptual or semantic similarity between sources (e.g., Lindsay, Johnson, & Kwon, 1991) and the use of less thorough evaluative processes (e.g., Dodson & Johnson, 1993). Source-monitoring errors may explain many false-memory phenomena. For example, suggestibility to misleading postevent information (see earlier section) has often been attributed, in part at least, to deficient source monitoring, by which the postevent misinformation is wrongly attributed to the witnessed event (see Lindsay, 1994; Mitchell & Johnson, 2000). Consistent with this approach, suggestibility was reduced when the two sources (i.e., the witnessed event and the misleading post-event information) were more discriminable (e.g., Lindsay, 1990), and when the test format led rememberers to consider more detailed information (e.g., Lindsay & Johnson, 1989; Zaragoza & Koshmider, 1989; Zaragoza & Lane, 1994).

A more extreme case of faulty reality monitoring has been proposed to underlie memory implantation, which causes a person to remember an entire childhood episode that did not occur but was merely suggested (e.g., Hyman, 1999; Hyman & Loftus, 1998; and see earlier section). Memory implantation is particularly likely to occur if a person is encouraged to engage in mental imagery of the suggested event (Garry, Manning, Loftus, & Sherman, 1996; Hyman & Pentland, 1996), perhaps creating vivid visual images that are later difficult to distinguish from real memories, and are consequently misattributed to reality.

Closely related to the source-monitoring framework is the attributional approach to memory (e.g., Jacoby, Kelley, & Dywan, 1989; for a recent review, see Kelley & Rhodes, 2002). According to this approach, the subjective experience of familiarity does not derive directly from the retrieval of a memory trace but from the unconscious attribution of fluent processing to the past (e.g., Jacoby & Dallas, 1981; Johnston, Dark, & Jacoby, 1985). Fluent processing of a stimulus is enhanced by its previous presentation, and when such fluency is attributed to the past, it gives rise to a veridical memory. However, fluent processing can also be produced by other factors. In that case, an illusion of familiarity may ensue if such fluency is misattributed to the past. For example, Whittlesea (1993) manipulated fluency by priming the target words with predictive or nonpredictive sentences before they appeared in the recognition test. Words primed with predictive sentences were more likely to be falsely recognized than nonprimed words, presumably due to the higher conceptual fluency. Fluency can also be enhanced by perceptual manipulations: Showing a brief preview of a test word immediately prior to presenting the word in full view for a recognition memory test increases the likelihood that new (as well as old) words will be judged "old" (Jacoby & Whitehouse, 1989). The tendency to judge both unpresented and presented items as old is also greater with increased visual clarity (Whittlesea, Jacoby, & Girard, 1990) and auditory clarity (Goldinger, Kleider, & Shelley, 1999) of the test words. Within the context of Whittlesea's (2002, 2004) Selective Construction and Preservation of Experience (SCAPE) framework, remembering is based not only on the actual properties of the stimuli but also on the relationship between these stimuli and the rememberer's expectations. For example, if a novel stimulus violates the person's expectations in a surprising way that is not obvious to him or her (e.g., surprising fluency), a perception of discrepancy may ensue, creating an illusion of familiarity (e.g., Whittlesea & Williams, 2001a, 2001b). However, if the source of the expectation violation is obvious to the person, the same stimulus can elicit a perception of incongruity that can sometimes assist the rememberer in correctly and confidently rejecting this stimulus as not having been presented before (Whittlesea, 2002).

Other heuristics have also been proposed as mechanisms that can be used to screen out false memories. For example, Strack and Bless (1994) showed that if an event is judged to be memorable (salient) but elicits no clear recollection, it can accurately and confidently be rejected as not having occurred via a metacognitive strategy (e.g., "If such a salient event had occurred, I certainly would have some recollection of it"). In their study, false alarms were found for nonsalient distractors (belonging to the same category as the majority of studied items) but not for salient distractors (belonging to different categories than the majority of studied items), and participants were more confident in their responses to salient than to nonsalient distractors.

A similar mechanism by which rememberers may avoid false memories is the distinctiveness heuristic (Dodson & Schacter, 2001, 2002; Schacter, Cendan, Dodson, & Clifford, 2001). This inferential mechanism takes the absence of memory for expected distinctive information as evidence that a target item was not previously experienced. For example, false recognition of semantically related lures was reduced when the studied words were accompanied by pictures (Schacter, Israel, & Racine, 1999) or when they were read aloud by the participants (Dodson & Schacter, 2001), compared to a word-only encoding condition. These findings were attributed to participants' metamemorial belief in the first two conditions: that if a word had, in fact, been presented in the study phase, they ought to remember the distinctive pictorial information (or having said the word aloud). Absence of memory for this distinctive information could be taken to indicate that an item was not previously encountered, thereby facilitating the rejection of nonpresented distractors.

Brainerd, Reyna, Wright, and Mojardin (2003) have suggested another mechanism whereby false events are edited out of memory. Recollection rejection is a mechanism that, either deliberately or not, suppresses the reporting of false but gist consistent information when verbatim traces of the target are available. Thus, even if a semantically related distractor (e.g., PHOENIX) seems familiar because its gist (Southwest U.S. city) is consistent with that of a studied item (e.g., HOUSTON), it may be rejected if its familiarity can be satisfactorily accounted for by the recollection of the verbatim representation of the target (e.g., "No, it wasn't PHOENIX, it was HOUSTON I heard").

Of course, common to all of these memory editing–rejection mechanisms is the risk that true events may also be screened out of eyewitness reports, resulting in the omission of information that may be vital (i.e., a reduction in memory quantity; see later section on control).

Factors Affecting Monitoring and Its Accuracy

How do witnesses monitor whether certain information that comes to mind is correct or incorrect? Research indicates that monitoring the correctness of the retrieved information is based on a number of inferential heuristics that are usually (but not always) valid (see Benjamin & Bjork, 1996; Koriat & Levy-Sadot, 1999). In what follows, we examine some of the clues that serve as a basis for metacognitive monitoring of the correctness of a piece of information that comes to mind. We assume that the output of this monitoring process is a subjective assessment of the likelihood that a particular answer is correct—an assessment process that can be tapped by confidence ratings.

Koriat and Levy-Sadot (1999) have proposed a dual-process framework for the analysis of metacognitive monitoring that distinguishes between *metacognitive feelings* that are based on nonanalytic inferences and *metacognitive judgments* that are based on analytic inferences. Analytic–inferential bases entail the conscious, deliberate utilization of specific beliefs and information to form an educated guess about various aspects of one's own knowledge. Nonanalytic bases, in contrast, entail the implicit application of global, general-purpose heuristics to reach a metacognitive judgment. We examine analytic cues and nonanalytic cues in turn.

Memory Content

One prominent analytic cue on which people surely base their confidence is the content of pertinent information retrieved from memory. Surprisingly, however, not much empirical work has been conducted on this topic. In an early study, Koriat, Lichtenstein, and Fischhoff (1980) presented participants with two alternative questions, requiring them to provide reasons for and against each of the alternatives before choosing an answer, and finally to rate their confidence in the chosen answer. Correlational analyses of the data suggested that their confidence depended on the amount and strength of the information retrieved from memory that supported the chosen answer. However, the results also indicated that the subjective assessment of correctness was biased by attempts to justify the decision: Once a decision was made, the evidence was reviewed to assess the likelihood that the answer was correct. This retrospective review tended to be biased by the decision already reached: It tended to focus on evidence that was consistent with that decision and to disregard evidence contradicting it, thereby resulting in overconfidence in the decision.

A similar view appears to underlie the theoretical framework proposed by Gigerenzer, Hoffrage, and Kleinbölting (1991). In this framework, confidence judgments represent the outcome of a well-structured inductive inference. For example, when people consider a question such as "Which city has more inhabitants, Heidelberg or Bonn?" they are completely (100%) confident in their answer only if they can retrieve the number of inhabitants in each city. Otherwise, they must form a probabilistic mental model (PMM) that puts the specific question into a larger context and enables its solution by inductive inference. The PMM contains a reference class ("all cities in Germany"), a target variable ("number of inhabitants"), and several probability cues with their respective cue validities (e.g., the perceived probability that one city has more inhabitants than the other, given that it, but not the other, has a soccer team in the German Bundesliga). People's answers, the researchers propose, are based on the relevant probability cues, and confidence in the answer is based on the respective cue validities.

In contrast to the view of confidence judgments as determined by information-based inferences, other work emphasizes the contribution of mnemonic-experiential cues such as perceptual fluency and retrieval fluency.

Perceptual Fluency

Busey, Tunnicliff, Loftus, and Loftus (2000) presented participants with a series of faces in five different luminance conditions and tested them in either a bright or a dim condition. A face that was studied under low luminance was recognized more poorly, but more confidently, under bright than under dim testing. Fluent perceptual processing of the faces in the bright testing condition may have inflated participants' confidence judgments. As mentioned earlier, perceptual fluency has been repeatedly found to enhance the tendency to "remember" both items that were part of the original event and those that were not (Goldinger et al., 1999; Jacoby & Whitehouse, 1989; Whittlesea et al., 1990). Thus, for example, presenting a suspect in enhanced viewing conditions in a lineup may increase the tendency for a positive identification accompanied by high confidence, whether or not he or she had committed the crime.

Retrieval Fluency

Retrieval fluency usually refers to the ease with which an item, idea, or contextual information comes to mind during an attempt to retrieve it. Nelson and Narens (1990) found that people expressed stronger confidence in the answers that they retrieved more quickly, whether those answers were correct or incorrect. Kelley and Lindsay (1993) demonstrated a similar effect of retrieval fluency on confidence and, ultimately, on memory accuracy. Participants were asked to answer general-information questions and to express their confidence in the correctness of their answers. Prior to this task, participants were asked to read a series of words, some of which were correct answers to the later questions, whereas others were plausible but incorrect answers to the questions. This prior exposure was found to increase the speed and probability with which the (primed) answers were provided in the recall test, and in parallel, to enhance the confidence in the correctness of these answers. Importantly, these effects were observed for both correct and incorrect answers. Postevent questioning, in which participants were asked to think about each of their responses on a memory test, was also found to increase subsequent confidence ratings for these responses, whether they were correct or incorrect (Shaw, 1996). The findings from these studies support the view that retrospective confidence is based on a simple heuristic: Answers that come to mind easily are more likely to be correct than those that take longer to retrieve. This heuristic is generally—but not always—valid.

Retrieval fluency may also underlie the imagination-inflation phenomenon: that is, the finding that the mere act of imagining a past event increases a person's confidence that the event actually happened in the past. Garry et al. (1996) pretested their participants on how confident they were that a number of childhood events had happened, asked them to imagine some of those events, and then gathered new confidence judgments. Imagination instructions inflated confidence that the event had occurred in childhood. Moreover, merely being asked about the event twice (on pretest and posttest) without imagining it led to an increase in subjective confidence, although not as large as the one produced by the act of imagination. A plausible account of these findings is that imagination of an event, and even the mere attempt to recall it, increases its retrieval fluency, which in turn contributes to the confidence that the event has occurred. Hastie, Landsman, and Loftus (1978) also found that repeated questioning about an imagined detail of a story increased confidence in that detail, and Turtle and Yuille (1994, Experiment 1) observed an increase in subjective confidence from one to two recall occasions (but see Ryan & Geiselman, 1991).

The metacognitive illusions outlined above support the view of monitoring as an error-prone heuristic process. Nonetheless, such monitoring illusions seem to be the exception rather than the rule. Although people are generally overconfident of the correctness of their answers (Keren, 1991; Lichtenstein, Fischhoff, & Phillips, 1982; McClelland & Bolger, 1994), by and large, they are successful in monitoring the correctness of their memories. Indeed, within-subject correlations between confidence and accuracy are typically moderate to high (e.g., Bornstein & Zickafoose, 1999; Kelley & Sahakyan, 2003; Koriat & Goldsmith 1996c). Thus, both the witnesses themselves and investigators, judges, and jurors are justified in placing more faith in details the witness is sure about than in details about which he or she is unsure (see also Roberts & Higham, 2002). This level of monitoring effectiveness, however, should be distinguished from the generally weak confidence–accuracy relation observed using between-subjects designs in eyewitness research (see Gruneberg & Sykes, 1993; Perfect, Watson, & Wagstaff, 1993). Based on this latter relation, there may be little or no justification for trusting the account of a confident witness more than the account of a witness with little or no confidence—although, quite naturally, both judges and jurors are prone to do so (e.g., Penrod & Cutler, 1995).

CONTROL

The preceding section presented evidence concerning the contribution of memory monitoring to memory performance—to some extent its quantity, but primarily its accuracy. However, the effect of monitoring on the amount and accuracy of reported information is realized via control: Whereas the monitoring mechanism provides an assessment of the source and ultimately the correctness of the information that comes to mind, it is the control mechanism that determines what to do with that assessment—for example, whether to provide an answer or to respond "I don't know."

Earlier, we used the *Rashomon* example to illustrate the great flexibility that people generally have in controlling their memory reporting, and the potential impact of such control on memory performance. Yet, in general, experimental psychologists have shied away from the systematic study of such control, treating it instead as a mere methodological nuisance (Nelson & Narens, 1994). Thus, in dealing with the "problem," the approach has been either to take control away from the rememberer, for instance, by using forced-report testing techniques (Erdelyi, 1996; Erdelyi & Becker, 1974), or to apply some sort of "correction" technique (Banks, 1970; Budescu & Bar-Hillel, 1993; Erdelyi, 1996).

There has been more intrinsic interest in the control of memory reporting in naturalistic memory research, perhaps because not only is such control ubiquitous in real-life remembering, but also because it clearly has a substantial impact on memory accuracy. For example, it is established wisdom in eyewitness research that witnesses should first be allowed to tell their story in their own words (i.e., in a free-narrative format) before being subjected to more directed questioning, and that even then, greater faith should be placed in the accuracy of the former type of testimony (e.g., Hilgard & Loftus, 1979; Neisser, 1988). This wisdom has been incorporated, for instance, into the Cognitive Interview technique (Fisher & Geiselman, 1992; see Powell, Fisher, & Wright, Chapter 2, this volume), and also into various government documents concerning the proper way to interview witnesses (see Memon & Stevenage, 1996). Nevertheless, the mechanisms and performance consequences of such control are far from clear (Goldsmith & Koriat, 1999; Memon & Higham, 1999).

As mentioned earlier, recall questioning offers rememberers at least two means by which they can enhance the accuracy of what they report. The first, report option, involves choosing either to volunteer or to withhold particular items of information (i.e., to respond "don't know" or "don't remember"). The second, control over grain size, involves choosing the level of detail (precision) or generality (coarseness) at which to report remembered information. Both of these are intrinsic aspects of real-life remembering. Thus, as we have argued previously (Goldsmith & Koriat, 1999; Koriat & Goldsmith, 1996c), rather than constituting a mere methodological nuisance that should be eliminated or corrected for, both report option and control over grain size constitute important topics of study in their own right, with underlying dynamics and performance consequences that deserve systematic investigation, particularly in the domain of eyewitness testimony.

Contributions to Memory Quantity and Memory Accuracy

Control of Report Option

The distinction between memory quantity and memory accuracy is particularly crucial with regard to the performance effects of personal control of memory reporting. This is because these effects are typically characterized by a quantity-accuracy trade-off (Klatzky & Erdelyi, 1985; Koriat & Goldsmith, 1996c): The accuracy of what one reports can be enhanced by the selective screening of one's answers, but this generally comes at the expense of a reduction in the quantity of correct information that is provided.

Koriat and Goldsmith (1994, Experiment 1) conducted a study in which participants answered general-knowledge questions using either a recall or recognition test format. In addition, report option was orthogonally manipulated: Under forced-report instructions, the participants were required to answer every question, whereas under free-report instructions they were allowed to refrain from answering questions about which they were unsure. A payoff schedule provided all subjects with a common performance incentive, essentially rewarding them for each correct answer but penalizing them by an equal amount for each incorrect answer. Performance on all conditions was scored for both input-bound quantity and output-bound accuracy. The results indicated that, for both recall and recognition, participants were able to utilize the option of free report to increase their accuracy substantially compared to forced report, with only a negligible reduction in performance quantity (for similar findings, see Erdelyi, Finks, & Feigin-Pfau, 1989; Roediger & Payne, 1985; Roediger, Srinivas, & Waddill, 1989).

In addition, however, the accuracy of memory reporting was found to be under strategic control: In a high accuracy-incentive condition (Koriat & Goldsmith, 1994, Experiment 3) participants received the same monetary bonus for each correct answer, as in the first experiment, but forfeited all winnings if even a single incorrect answer was volunteered. These subjects achieved substantially better accuracy for both recall and recognition compared to subjects performing under the more moderate (1:1) penalty-to-bonus ratio. In fact, fully one-fourth of the high-incentive subjects succeeded in achieving 100% accuracy. Thus, the participants were able to adjust their memory accuracy in accordance with the operative level of accuracy incentive. Now, however, the improved accuracy was accompanied by a rather large reduction in quantity performance. That is, the participants traded quantity for accuracy in attempting to maximize their bonus in the high-incentive condition (for similar results, see Barnes et al., 1999; Kelley & Sahakyan, 2003; Koriat & Goldsmith, 1996c; Koriat et al., 2001).

In a subsequent study (Koriat & Goldsmith, 1996c), confidence judgments regarding the best answer that came to mind (assessed probability of correctness) were also elicited during a forced-report phase (report option manipulated within participants), shedding light on the monitoring and control mechanisms assumed to mediate the effects of report option and accuracy incentive on memory accuracy and quantity performance (see Figure 4.1, p. 97). First, participants were fairly successful in monitoring the correctness of their answers, and they appeared to base their decision to volunteer or withhold each answer almost entirely on their confidence (within-participant gamma correlations between confidence and volunteering averaged about .95!). Second, the participants' control policies were sensitive to the specific level of accuracy incentive: Participants who were given a high accuracy incentive (10:1 penalty-to-bonus ratio) were more selective in their reporting, adopting a stricter confidence criterion for volunteering an answer than those given a more moderate (1:1) incentive.

Importantly, the rate of the quantity–accuracy trade-off was shown to depend both on accuracy incentive and monitoring effectiveness. First, simulation analyses indicated that, under typical (moderate) levels of monitoring effectiveness, the rate of the trade-off tended to increase as the report criterion was raised, so that simply providing the option of free report should allow relatively large gains in accuracy to be achieved at relatively small quantity costs, compared to forced report, but additional gains in accuracy in response to higher accuracy incentives should involve disproportionately larger quantity costs. This pattern was confirmed by Koriat and Goldsmith's (1996c, Experiment 1) empirical results, and was shown to be consistent with the general pattern observed across several other studies (for a discussion, see Koriat & Goldsmith, 1996c).

The second factor affecting the rate of the trade-off is monitoring effectiveness: As monitoring effectiveness improves, the option of selective reporting allows larger increases in accuracy to be achieved at smaller costs in quantity. At the extreme, when monitoring resolution (i.e., discrimination between correct and incorrect answers) is perfect, the simple option of free report allows 100% accuracy to be achieved without any cost in quantity. On the other hand, when monitoring resolution is poor, selective reporting hardly improves accuracy at all, and the quantity cost of withholding answers is relatively high (see Koriat & Goldsmith, 1996c, Experiment 2, and simulation analyses).

The implications of this research in regard to the quantity and accuracy of eyewitness testimony can be gauged with respect to Figure 4.1 (p. 97). Above and beyond whatever can be done to improve the quality (i.e., quantity and accuracy) of the information that people retrieve (see earlier section on retention), people can further regulate the quality of what they report by the selective screening of candidate answers. Because monitoring one's answers is generally imperfect (see earlier section on monitoring), the enhancement of memory accuracy can be achieved only at the risk of reduced memory quantity. Thus, witnesses must weigh the relative incentives for providing more accurate versus more complete memory reports when deciding upon the most effective control policy for the situation at hand. This trade-off dynamic requires experimenters to take these incentives into account as well as the level of monitoring effectiveness, and to consider both accuracy and quantity in tandem when evaluating free-report memory performance (Klatzky & Erdelyi, 1985; Koriat & Goldsmith, 1996b, 1996c). In practical terms, it also means that investigators and other agents of the law-enforcement and judiciary systems should be able to manipulate witness's control policy—and, ultimately, the quality of their testimony—depending on whether they want to flesh out every possible lead or glean only information that is highly likely to be correct (see Fisher, 1995).

Control over Grain Size

The potential contributions of monitoring and control processes to memory quantity and accuracy are complicated even further when a second means of control is considered: control over the level of precision or "grain" of the information that is reported (e.g., reporting that the assailant's height was "5 feet, 11 inches" "around 6 feet," or "fairly tall"). Neisser (1988), in attempting to make sense of results indicating the superior accuracy of open-ended recall over forced-choice recognition testing, noted that unlike the recognition participants, the recall participants tended to provide answers at "a level of generality at which they were not mistaken" (p. 553). Furthermore Fisher (1996), in assessing participants' freely reported recollections of a filmed robbery, was surprised to find that the accuracy of people's reports after 40 days was no lower than on immediate testing, even though the same number of propositions was volunteered. The anomaly was resolved by considering the grain size of the reported information: Propositions volunteered after 40 days were as likely to be correct as those provided soon after the event (about 90% accuracy in both cases), but this equivalence was achieved by rememberers providing information that was more coarse (as rated by two independent judges) at the later testing than that contained in the earlier reports.

Goldsmith and Koriat (1999) and Goldsmith et al. (2002) proposed that both the mechanisms (monitoring and control) and the performance consequences of the control of grain size in memory reporting are similar to, though perhaps more complex than, those underlying the exercise of report option. Once again, consider a witness who would like to fulfill her vow to "tell the whole truth and nothing but the truth." How should she proceed? On the one hand, a very coarsely grained response (e.g., "between noon and midnight") will always be the wiser choice if accuracy (i.e., the probability of including the true value—telling nothing but the truth) is the sole consideration. However, such a response may not be very informative, falling short of the goal to tell the whole truth. On the other hand, although a very fine-grained answer (e.g., 6:22 P.M.) is much more informative, it is also much more likely to be wrong. Thus, the control over grain size would seem to involve an accuracy–informativeness trade-off similar to the accuracy–quantity trade-off observed with regard to the control of report option; here, too, witnesses will have to aim for a compromise between accuracy and informativeness in choosing a grain size for their answers (see also Yaniv & Foster, 1995, 1997).

Goldsmith et al. (2002) examined this idea in relation to the recall of quantitative semantic information, using a two-phase paradigm similar to the one used for report option (e.g., Koriat & Goldsmith, 1996c). In the first, forced-report phase, participants were presented with a set of 40 questions and required to answer each of them at two different grain levels, as specified by the experimenter. For example, "When did Boris Becker last win the Wimbledon men's tennis finals? (a) Provide a 3-year interval; (b) Provide a 10-year interval." In the second, free-choice phase, the participants were asked to go over their answers, and for each item, to indicate which of the two answers (i.e., which grain size) they would prefer to provide, assuming that they were "an expert witness testifying before a government committee." To shed light on the monitoring and control processes underlying the choice of grain size, in some experiments participants also provided confidence judgments, and accuracy–informativeness incentives were manipulated.

The results indicated that people trade off accuracy and informativeness in reporting information from memory. Participants tended to report coarse-grained answers when a more precise answer was likely to be wrong, thereby enhancing output-bound accuracy. Their choices of when to provide a fine-grained answer and when to report a coarse-grained answer were both systematic (dependent on confidence and incentives) and fairly efficient. Two models of the control process were compared: A "satisficing" model (cf. Simon, 1956), in which people report as finely grained (i.e., precise) an answer as possible, as long as its assessed probability of being correct passes some adjustable criterion, versus an "expected subjective utility" model, in which participants choose the grain size that they believe will maximize the utility of their answer in terms of both accuracy and informativeness. The results strongly supported the "satisficing" model, and this was so even when they were given differential monetary incentives for correct answers at the two grain sizes (Goldsmith et al., 2002, Experiment 3).

A similar pattern was observed in the regulation of memory grain size over time (Goldsmith et al., in press). In this study, Goldsmith et al.'s (2002) two-phase paradigm was adapted for use with episodic information contained in a short story read by the participants. Consistent with previous findings (e.g., Fisher, 1996), there was a tendency to report more coarse-grained answers at longer retention intervals (1 week vs. 1 day vs. immediate testing), and, again, the choice of grain size was sensitive both to participants' level of confidence and to the particular level of accuracy–informativeness incentive. However, control over grain size alone was not sufficient to prevent a reduction in output-bound accuracy over the 1-week interval. Perhaps when participants are allowed the freedom to choose a grain size for their answers *and* to withhold the answer entirely if necessary (as is the case, for instance, in open-ended free-narrative memory reporting), they will utilize this freedom to maintain a stable level of accuracy over time. Work in progress is examining this issue and other aspects of the joint control of grain size and report option in memory reporting.

Factors Affecting Control

Clearly, the most basic factor affecting the control of memory reporting is whether or not the rememberer is allowed to exercise such control. Under conditions of forced reporting, control over whether or not to provide an answer is taken away from the rememberer (e.g., Erdelyi, 1996), though in recall testing there may still be some limited control over grain size, and in recognition testing, the rememberer may have control over the placement of the yes/no (old/new) response criterion (not to be confused with the report criterion being addressed here; for discussions, see Higham, 2002; Koriat & Goldsmith, 1996a, 1996c). Conversely, under conditions of free report, control of grain size can be limited by using a recognition test format, or, in recall testing, by using word-list stimuli or other materials that require single-word answers (e.g., Koriat & Goldsmith, 1994, 1996c).

When control of report option or grain size is given to the rememberer, whether and how he or she will exercise that control is undoubtedly influenced by a constellation of factors, several of which are reviewed here.

Accuracy Motivation, Communication Factors, and Personal–Social Goals

Koriat and Goldsmith's (1994, 1996c) work, described earlier, highlights the importance of accuracy motivation: When people are more highly motivated to be accurate, they tend to employ a more conservative control policy (i.e., a higher report criterion). Conversely, when the quantity of information is stressed (e.g., "uninhibited retrieval" instructions in Bousfield & Rosner, 1970; Fisher, 1999), a more liberal policy is employed. Fisher (1999) explains that the use of uninhibited retrieval instructions in the Cognitive Interview is designed to elicit details edited out by witnesses in their spontaneous reporting, but which may be forensically important. He reports not only an increase in the number of correct propositions elicited with the Cognitive Interview, but also an increase in their average precision (i.e., the grain size of the responses). Interestingly, this improvement is not accompanied by a decrease in output-bound accuracy, suggesting that memory monitoring may be improved as well (perhaps by other components of the interview; see Memon & Higham, 1999). Other "communication" factors that are also utilized in standard interviewing techniques, such as rapport building and transfer of control from the interviewer to the witness (Memon & Stevenage, 1996), may also exert their effect via changes in report criteria.

Opposing concerns have generally been expressed with regard to the questioning of child witnesses; here increasing the output-bound accuracy of children's testimony has been emphasized (see Koriat et al., 2001). Findings from several studies suggest that children are particularly reluctant to say "I don't know" in response to memory questions (e.g., Cassel, Roebers, & Bjorklund, 1996; Mulder & Vrij, 1996; Roebers & Fernandez, 2002). Thus, children may be less able or less willing than adults to control their memory reporting on the basis of their subjective monitoring. One approach to correcting this problem is to explicitly instruct children in the "rules" of memory reporting. Mulder and Vrij (1996), for example, found that explicitly instructing children, ages 4–10, that "I don't know" is an acceptable answer significantly reduced the number of incorrect responses to misleading questions (i.e., questions about events that had not, in fact, occurred). Moston (1987) also found that such instructions induced children, ages 6–10, to make more "I don't know" responses, but in that study this instruction had no effect on the overall proportion of correct responses. On the other hand, Cassel et al. (1996) found that children (kindergartners, second graders, and fourth graders) exhibit a developmental trend and a greater tendency than adults to provide wrong answers to leading questions, even when they are reminded that they have the option to say "I don't know" (see also Roebers & Fernandez, 2002). Similarly, Koriat et al. (2001) found that although even 6- to 7-year-old children were able to utilize the option of free report to boost the accuracy of their reporting (increasing accuracy even further under a strong accuracy incentive), they were nevertheless less accurate in their reporting than 8- to 9-year-olds. This developmental trend could be due to monitoring effectiveness, report criterion, or both, and was found despite the use of explicit accuracy incentives.

Of course, in most cases the incentives for accuracy or quantity/informativeness are not explicit; rather, they are implicit in the personal–social context of remembering (Pasupathi, 2001). For example, picking up on social cues, people convey more detailed information to attentive than to inattentive listeners (Pasupathi, Stallworth, & Murdoch, 1998), and, in line with Grice's (1975) maxim of quantity, adjust the detail of their reporting to the perceived needs of the listener (Vandierendonck & Van Damme, 1988). Even young children have been shown to provide more details about experiences that were shared with the listener than about unshared experiences (Reese & Brown, 2000). Differential editing of memory reporting may be both quantitative and qualitative. For example, Hyman (1994) found that recalling a story to a peer yielded more opinions, evaluations, and world knowledge than did recalling it to an experimenter, which elicited a greater focus on story details and narrative structure. In many contexts, the goals of accuracy and completeness are subservient to other goals, such as goals to amuse, entertain, convince, and impress (e.g., Neisser, 1988; Sedikides, 1990; Tversky & Marsh, 2000; Wade & Clark, 1993; Winograd, 1994). Such insights have begun to be taken into account in the questioning of witnesses as well (Fisher, 1995, 1999).

Test Format

Test format refers to whether the rememberer produces his or her own answers (production or recall format) or must choose a response from a limited set provided by the questioner (selection or recognition format). This variable is also implicated in the belief that directed questioning or recognition testing can have contaminating effects on memory (e.g., Brown, Deffenbacher, & Sturgill, 1977; Gorenstein & Ellsworth, 1980; Lipton, 1977). Test format is also implicated in the "established wisdom" mentioned earlier, that witnesses should first be allowed to tell their story in their own words (i.e., in a free-narrative format) before being subjected to directed or recognition questioning, because of the harmful effects of the latter formats on memory accuracy (e.g., Hilgard & Loftus, 1979; Neisser, 1988). However, it is not clear to what extent the harmful effects of selection-format testing are mediated by memory contamination (e.g., due to misinformation contained in the question) or are due instead to a lowering of the report criterion. Both aspects are often implied in discussions in the literature (e.g., Hilgard & Loftus, 1979; Lipton, 1977).

Answering this question is made difficult by the general confounding of test format and report option that occurs in memory testing: In free-narrative and recall testing, people both produce their own answers (production format) and report only what they feel they actually remember (free report), whereas in directed questioning and recognition testing, people are not only confined to choosing between the alternatives presented by the interrogator (selection format), but are generally exposed to either implicit or explicit demands to answer each and every question (forced report). Conceivably, then, either variable could be responsible for the general superiority of production over selection testing in terms of memory accuracy (or, in fact, for the reverse pattern with regard to memory quantity; see Brown, 1976).

Koriat and Goldsmith (1994) called this confounded pattern the recall–recognition paradox. In order to unravel this paradox and separate the contributing effects of report option and test format, they conducted several experiments (described earlier) in which report option (free vs. forced), test format (recall vs. recognition) and memory property (accuracy vs. quantity) were orthogonally manipulated. That is, in addition to the standard tests of free recall and forced-choice recognition (five alternatives), two relatively uncommon procedures were added: forced recall (requiring subjects to respond to all questions) and free recognition (permitting subjects to skip items). The important result in this context is that report option, not test format, was found to be the critical variable affecting memory accuracy. In fact, under free-report conditions, test format had no effect at all on memory accuracy: Given equal opportunity to screen out wrong answers, the recall and recognition participants achieved virtually identical accuracy scores. Although these results were obtained using general-knowledge questions (see also Koriat & Goldsmith, 1996c), the same pattern was observed using a standard list-learning paradigm (Koriat & Goldsmith, 1994, Experiment 2) and using more naturalistic episodic stimuli (Koriat et al., 2001).

Based on their results, Koriat and Goldsmith (1994, 1996c) concluded that free selection may be a generally superior testing procedure to free production, because it elicits better quantity performance with no reduction in accuracy. This outcome, however, assumes that the option to withhold answers is emphasized by the questioner and clearly understood by the rememberer (see earlier discussion of communication factors). In many cases, there may be implicit pressures to respond to directed or recognition queries that cause witnesses to lower their report criterion, even though ostensibly they are given the option to respond "I don't know."

State of Mind

The witness's "state of mind" at the time of reporting may also affect the control of memory reporting. An interesting case is hypnosis, which is often used as a mnemonic enhancement technique (Pettinatti, 1988). Although memory testing under hypnosis has generally been shown to yield more correct recalls than without hypnosis, it yields more incorrect recalls as well (Dywan & Bowers, 1983), consistent with the idea that the effects of hypnosis are mediated by a lowering of the report criterion (Klatzky & Erdelyi, 1985). Indeed, when response selectivity is controlled by using a forced-recall procedure, the advantage of hypnosis compared to nonhypnotic retrieval is eliminated (Dinges et al., 1992; Whitehouse, Dinges, Orne, & Orne, 1988). It is not clear, however, whether the effect of hypnosis is simply a matter of inflating confidence in one's answers (Krass, Kinoshita, & McConkey, 1989), a lowering of the report criterion, or both. Interestingly, intoxication by alcohol does *not* appear to affect the control of memory reporting. Nelson et al. (1998; see also Nelson, McSpadden, Fromme, & Marlatt, 1986) found that although alcohol consumption impaired memory for lists of paired associates, compared to sober controls, confidence levels were reduced correspondingly, and there was no difference between the groups in the proportion of commission errors conditioned on recall failure (an indirect measure of output-bound accuracy). By contrast, other drugs such as marijuana (Darley, Tinklenberg, Roth, Vernon, & Kopelt, 1977) and lithium (Weingartner, Rudorfer, & Linnoila, 1985) do yield increased commission-error rates, suggesting that those drugs make people less conservative in withholding potential answers during retrieval.

Control Sensitivity

Other factors that affect control may do so by influencing the relationship between control and memory monitoring (what Koriat & Goldsmith, 1996c, termed "control sensitivity"). Koriat and Goldsmith (1996c) found an exceedingly high correlation between the decision to volunteer an answer and confidence in that answer (averaging about .95 for both recall and recognition!) with undergraduate participants. More recent work, however, has found lower correlations with elderly subjects (Pansky, Koriat, Goldsmith, & Pearlman-Avnion, 2002; but see Kelley and Sahakyan, 2003) and with clinical populations (Danion, Gokalsing, Robert, Massin-Krauss, & Bacon, 2001; Koren et al., 2004). Interestingly, relatively high correlations between control sensitivity and measures of executive functioning (e.g., rate of perseverance errors on the

Wisconsin card sorting task; Pansky et al., 2002) and measures of clinical awareness (Koren et al., 2004) were found, suggesting a link between control sensitivity and overall level of metacognitive and executive functioning. Conceivably, situational factors at retrieval, such as divided attention, time pressure, and drugs or intoxication might affect control sensitivity as well, though this possibility remains a topic for future research.

CONCLUSION: SOME METATHEORETICAL IMPLICATIONS FOR EYEWITNESS (MEMORY) RESEARCH

In this chapter, we have taken a somewhat unorthodox approach to the topic of eyewitness recall. First, we emphasized the basic distinction between two properties of memory—quantity and accuracy—and examined the factors affecting memory in terms of both properties. Second, we highlighted the contribution of metacognitive monitoring and control processes to memory performance and gave these contributions great weight in our presentation.

In assessing eyewitness recollections, the quantity of the target information that is recalled has received considerable attention in both traditional and eyewitness memory research. However, in real-life situations, and particularly in the courtroom, output-bound accuracy is no less important. In fact, errors made by eyewitnesses have been found to be the most common cause of the false conviction of innocent people (Huff, Rattner, & Sagarin, 1996).

As we have argued elsewhere (Koriat & Goldsmith, 1994, 1996b), the distinction between memory quantity and its accuracy is not just a distinction between two properties or measures of memory but, rather, is associated with two quite different approaches to the study of memory. Each approach has its own distinct focus, its unique paradigms and methodologies, and even its own underlying metaphor of memory (Koriat & Goldsmith, 1996b). Unfortunately, due to these differences in underlying conception and methodology, there has been relatively little cross-talk between researchers in the two approaches (Winograd, 1988), though recent years have brought some improvement (Koriat et al., 2000). One goal of the present chapter, then, is to bring findings from the two approaches together and attempt to integrate them into a common "coordinate system" (cf. Koriat & Goldsmith, 1994, Figure 1). Such integration would seem to be a necessary first step toward the development of a theoretical framework that could provide a comprehensive understanding of the different aspects of memory—including eyewitness memory—and engender a unified research approach. The benefits of such a framework would be immense. It would allow researchers, for instance, to apply the broad base of knowledge regarding the factors affecting memory quantity performance toward an understanding of memory accuracy performance, and vice versa.

Consider, for example, many of the classic memory principles and findings, such as levels of processing, encoding specificity, subjective organization, and so forth. What is the relevance of these principles for memory accuracy, which is so crucial in evaluating eyewitness testimony? Although some scattered studies have been conducted (some reviewed above), the general answer is that we simply do not know. In fact, accuracy was of such little concern in traditional, quantity-oriented memory research, that accuracy rates (false alarms or commission errors) were not even reported in many classic studies (see, e.g., Craik & Tulving, 1975; Thomson & Tulving, 1970; Tulving & Osler, 1968)!

The second unique feature of this chapter is the attention devoted to the metacognitive processes of monitoring and control at the reporting stage, as they mediate both memory quantity and accuracy. Actually, this feature is closely tied to the first. Although such processes certainly have an effect on memory quantity, they are particularly crucial in affecting memory accuracy, because output-bound memory accuracy is much more under the control of the rememberer than is input-bound memory quantity (Koriat & Goldsmith, 1996b, 1996c). In fact, these processes seem to be employed specifically in the service of enhancing memory accuracy, either by screening out incorrect answers (i.e., control of report option) or by "hedging" an answer by choosing a level of generality that makes it more likely to be correct (i.e., control of grain size). Nevertheless, because of the fundamental dynamic of the accuracy–quantity (or accuracy–informativeness) trade-off, the metacognitive regulation of memory reporting can have a substantial impact on both accuracy and quantity performance.

The joint consideration of cognitive and metacognitive components of memory performance has important theoretical and practical implications. On a theoretical level, this perspective implies that factors thought to affect retention might, in fact, exert their influence via an effect on monitoring or control (e.g., see Higham, 2002; Memon & Higham, 1999). In addition, differential effects on memory quantity and accuracy performance are to be expected when different underlying components are affected in different ways (e.g., the comparison of recall vs. recognition testing in Koriat & Goldsmith, 1996c). Teasing apart the separate contributions of retention, monitoring, and control to many other manipulations could be of great theoretical importance, and could also enhance the understanding of individual and group differences in memory performance (e.g., Kelley & Sahakyan, 2003; Koren et al., 2004; Koriat et al, 2001; Pansky et al., 2002; Roebers, 2002). At a practical level, methods for improving memory performance or safeguarding against error (e.g., in witness questioning techniques) could be targeted toward improving monitoring and control, in addition to the traditional focus on encoding and retrieval processes that improve retention.

Of course, the metacognitive regulatory processes that guide memory performance in real-life eyewitness situations are certainly more varied and complex than those addressed in this chapter, as are the goals and considerations of the witness in utilizing those processes. Providing a complete or accurate account of an event may not be the only or even primary aim of an eyewitness.

Therefore, the evaluation of memory performance in terms of memory quantity and memory accuracy may not always be appropriate—at least not from the witness's perspective. Memory does not operate in a vacuum, and hence memory performance, and the cognitive and metacognitive processes that mediate such performance, need to be analyzed in the context of the personal and social goals of the rememberer (e.g., Neisser, 1996; Pasupathi, 2001; Winograd, 1994). Taking this point seriously will require even more attention to the role of strategic regulatory processes as well as to the complexities involved in the evaluation of eyewitness memory performance.

ACKNOWLEDGMENTS

The preparation of this chapter was supported by the German Federal Ministry of Education and Research (BMBF) within the framework of German–Israeli Project Cooperation (DIP). We thank the BMBF for their support. We also thank Liat Levy-Bushusha for her help in the preparation of this chapter.

REFERENCES

Alba, J. W., & Hasher, L. (1983). Is memory schematic? *Psychological Bulletin, 93*, 203–231.

Allen, G. A., Mahler, W. A., & Estes, W. K. (1969). Effects of recall tests on long-term retention of paired associates. *Journal of Verbal Learning and Verbal Behavior, 8,* 463–470.

Anderson, M. C., Bjork, R. A., & Bjork, E. L. (1994). Remembering can cause forgetting: Retrieval dynamics in long-term memory. *Journal of Experimental Psychology: Learning, Memory, and Cognition, 20*, 1063–1087.

Anderson, R. C., & Pichert, J. W. (1978). Recall of previously unrecallable information following a shift in perspective. *Journal of Verbal Learning and Verbal Behavior, 17*, 1–12.

Atkinson, R. C., & Shiffrin, R. M. (1968). Human memory: A proposed system and its control processes. In K. W. Spence & J. T. Spence (Eds.), *The psychology of learning and motivation: Advances in research and theory* (Vol. 2, pp. 89–195). New York: Academic Press.

Bahrick, H. P., Hall, L. K., & Berger, S. A. (1996). Accuracy and distortion in memory for high school grades. *Psychological Science, 7*, 265–271.

Bahrick, H. P., Hall, L. K., & Dunlosky, J. (1993). Reconstructive processing of memory content for high versus low test scores and grades. *Applied Cognitive Psychology, 7*, 1–10.

Banks, W. P. (1970). Signal detection theory and human memory. *Psychological Bulletin, 74*, 81–99.

Barclay, C. R. (1988). Truth and accuracy in autobiographical memory. In M. M. Gruneberg & P. E. Morris (Eds.), *Practical aspects of memory: Current research and issues* (Vol. 1, pp. 289–294). New York: Wiley.

Barclay, C. R., Toglia, M. P., & Chevalier, D. S. (1984). Pragmatic inference and type of processing. *American Journal of Psychology, 97*, 285–296.

Barclay, J. R., Bransford, J. D., Franks, J. J., McCarrell, N. S., & Nitsch, K. (1974). Comprehension and semantic flexibility. *Journal of Verbal Learning and Verbal Behavior, 13*, 471–481.

Barnes, A. E., Nelson, T. O., Dunlosky, J., Mazzoni, G., & Narens, L. (1999). An intergrative system of metamemory components involved in retrieval. In D. Gopher & A. Koriat (Eds.), *Attention and performance XVII—cognitive regulation of performance: Interaction of theory and application* (pp. 287–313). Cambridge, MA: MIT Press.

Bartlett, F. C. (1932). *Remembering: A study in experimental and social psychology.* New York: Cambridge University Press.

Begg, I., & Wickelgren, W. A. (1974). Retention functions for syntactic and lexical vs. semantic information in sentence recognition memory. *Memory and Cognition, 2,* 353–359.

Bekerian, D. A., & Bowers, J. M. (1983). Eyewitness testimony: Were we misled? *Journal of Experimental Psychology: Learning, Memory, and Cognition, 9,* 139–145.

Belli, R. F. (1989). Influences of misleading postevent information: Misinformation interference and acceptance. *Journal of Experimental Psychology: General, 118,* 72–85.

Belli, R. F., Lindsay, D. S., Gales, M. S., & McCarthy, T. T. (1994). Memory impairment and source misattribution in postevent misinformation experiments with short retention intervals. *Memory and Cognition, 22,* 40–54.

Belli, R. F., & Loftus, E. F. (1996). The pliability of autobiographical memory: Misinformation and the false memory problem. In D. C. Rubin (Ed.), *Remembering our past: Studies in autobiographical memory* (pp. 157–179). New York: Cambridge University Press.

Belli, R. F., Windschitl, P. D., McCarthy, T. T., & Winfrey, S. E. (1992). Detecting memory impairment with a modified test procedure: Manipulating retention interval with centrally presented event items. *Journal of Experimental Psychology: Learning, Memory, and Cognition, 18,* 356–367.

Benjamin, A. S., & Bjork, R. A. (1996). Retrieval fluency as a metacognitive index. In L. M. Reder (Ed.), *Implicit memory and metacognition* (pp. 309–338). Hillsdale, NJ: Erlbaum.

Bergman, E. T., & Roediger, H. L. (1999). Can Bartlett's repeated reproduction experiments be replicated? *Memory and Cognition, 27,* 937–947.

Bernstein, L. J., Beig, S., Siegenthaler, A. L., & Grady, C. L. (2002). The effect of encoding strategy on the neural correlates of memory for faces. *Neuropsychologia, 40,* 86–98.

Bjork, R. A. (1975). Retrieval as a memory modifier: An interpretation of negative recency and related phenomena. In R. C. Solso (Ed.), *Information processing and cognition* (pp. 123–144). New York: Wiley.

Boon, J. W. C., & Davies, G. (1988). Attitudinal influences on witness memory: Fact and fiction. In M. M. Gruneberg (Ed.), *Practical aspects of memory: Current research and issues* (Vol. 1, pp. 53–58). Oxford, UK: Wiley.

Boon, J. W. C., & Davies, G. (1996). Extra-stimulus influences on eyewitness perception and recall: Hastorf and Cantril revisited. *Legal and Criminological Psychology, 1*(Part 2), 155–164.

Bornstein, B. H., Liebel, L. M., & Scarberry, N. C. (1998). Repeated testing in eyewitness memory: A means to improve recall of a negative emotional event. *Applied Cognitive Psychology, 12,* 119–131.

Bornstein, B. H., & Zickafoose, D. J. (1999). "I know I know it, I know I saw it": The stability of the confidence–accuracy relationship across domains. *Journal of Experimental Psychology: Applied, 5*, 76–88.

Bousfield, W. A., & Rosner, S. R. (1970). Free vs. uninhibited recall. *Psychonomic Science, 20*, 75–76.

Bower, G. H. (1981). Mood and memory. *American Psychologist, 36*, 129–148.

Brainerd, C. J., & Mojardin, A. H. (1998). Children's and adults' spontaneous false memories: Long-term persistence and mere-testing effects. *Child Development, 69*, 1361–1377.

Brainerd, C. J., & Reyna, V. F. (1998). When things that were never experienced are easier to "remember" than things that were. *Psychological Science, 9*, 484–489.

Brainerd, C. J., & Reyna, V. F. (2002). Fuzzy-trace theory and false memory. *Current Directions in Psychological Science, 11*, 164–169.

Brainerd, C. J., Reyna, V. F., Howe, M. L., & Kingma, J. (1990). The development of forgetting and reminiscence. *Monographs of the Society for Research in Child Development, 55*(3–4), v–93.

Brainerd, C. J., Reyna, V. F., Wright, R., & Mojardin, A. H. (2003). Recollection rejection: False-memory editing in children and adults. *Psychological Review, 110*, 762–784.

Brewer, W. F., & Nakamura, G. V. (1984). The nature and functions of schemas. In R. S. Wyer, Jr. & T. K. Srull (Eds.), *Handbook of social cognition* (Vol. 1, pp. 119–160). Hillsdale, NJ: Erlbaum.

Brewer, W. F., & Treyens, J. C. (1981). Role of schemata in memory for places. *Cognitive Psychology, 13*, 207–230.

Brock, P., Fisher, R. P., & Cutler, B. L. (1999). Examining the cognitive interview in a double-test paradigm. *Psychology, Crime, and Law, 5*(1–2), 29–45.

Brown, A. S. (1991). A review of the tip-of-the-tongue experience. *Psychological Bulletin, 109*, 204–223.

Brown, E., Deffenbacher, K., & Sturgill, W. (1977). Memory for faces and the circumstances of encounter. *Journal of Applied Psychology, 62*, 311–318.

Brown, J. (Ed.). (1976). *Recall and recognition.* Oxford, UK: Wiley.

Brown, R., & Kulik, J. (1977). Flashbulb memories. *Cognition, 5*, 73–99.

Brown, W. (1923). To what extent is memory measured by a single recall? *Journal of Experimental Psychology, 6*, 377–382.

Budescu, D., & Bar-Hillel, M. (1993). To guess or not to guess: A decision-theoretic view of formula scoring. *Journal of Educational Measurement, 30*, 277–291.

Busey, T. A., Tunnicliff, J., Loftus, G. R., & Loftus, E. F. (2000). Accounts of the confidence–accuracy relation in recognition memory. *Psychonomic Bulletin and Review, 7*, 26–48.

Carmichael, L., Hogan, H. P., & Walter, A. A. (1932). An experimental study of the effect of language on the reproduction of visually perceived form. *Journal of Experimental Psychology, 15*, 73–86.

Carrier, M., & Pashler, H. (1992). The influence of retrieval on retention. *Memory and Cognition, 20*, 633–642.

Cassel, W. S., Roebers, C. M., & Bjorklund, D. F. (1996). Developmental patterns of eyewitness responses to repeated and increasingly suggestive questions. *Journal of Experimental Child Psychology, 61*, 116–133.

Chalfonte, B. L., & Johnson, M. K. (1996). Feature memory and binding in young and older adults. *Memory and Cognition, 24*, 403–416.

Chandler, C. C. (1989). Specific retroactive interference in modified recognition tests: Evidence for an unknown cause of interference. *Journal of Experimental Psychology: Learning, Memory, and Cognition, 15,* 256–265.

Chandler, C. C. (1991). How memory for an event is influenced by related events: Interference in modified recognition tests. *Journal of Experimental Psychology: Learning, Memory, and Cognition, 17,* 115–125.

Chase, W. G., & Simon, H. A. (1973). Perception in chess. *Cognitive Psychology, 4,* 55–81.

Chiesi, H. L., Spilich, G. J., & Voss, J. F. (1979). Acquisition of domain-related information in relation to high and low domain knowledge. *Journal of Verbal Learning and Verbal Behavior, 18,* 257–273.

Christiaansen, R. E., & Ochalek, K. (1983). Editing misleading information from memory: Evidence for the coexistence of original and postevent information. *Memory and Cognition, 11,* 467–475.

Ciranni, M. A., & Shimamura, A. P. (1999). Retrieval-induced forgetting in episodic memory. *Journal of Experimental Psychology: Learning, Memory, and Cognition, 25,* 1403–1414.

Clifford, B. R., & Hollin, C. R. (1981). Effects of the type of incident and the number of perpetrators on eyewitness memory. *Journal of Applied Psychology, 66,* 364–370.

Cohen, G. (1989). *Memory in the real world.* Hillsdale, NJ: Erlbaum.

Conway, M., & Ross, M. (1984). Getting what you want by revising what you had. *Journal of Personality and Social Psychology, 47,* 738–748.

Conway, M. A., Anderson, S. J., Larsen, S. F., Donnelly, C. M., McDaniel, M. A., McClelland, A. G. R., Rawless, R. E., & Logie, R. H. (1994). The formation of flashbulb memories. *Memory and Cognition, 22,* 326–343.

Conway, M. A., Cohen, G., & Stanhope, N. (1991). On the very long-term retention of knowledge acquired through formal education: Twelve years of cognitive psychology. *Journal of Experimental Psychology: General, 120,* 395–409.

Cowan, N. (1998). Children's memories according to fuzzy-trace theory: An endorsement of the theory's purpose and some suggestions to improve its application. *Journal of Experimental Child Psychology, 71,* 144–154.

Craik, F. I. M. (2002). Levels of processing: Past, present . . . and future? *Memory, 10*(5–6), 305–318.

Craik, F. I. M., Govoni, R., Naveh-Benjamin, M., & Anderson, N. D. (1996). The effects of divided attention on encoding and retrieval processes in human memory. *Journal of Experimental Psychology: General, 125,* 159–180.

Craik, F. I. M., & Lockhart, R. S. (1972). Levels of processing: A framework for memory research. *Journal of Verbal Learning and Verbal Behavior, 11,* 671–684.

Craik, F. I. M., & Tulving, E. (1975). Depth of processing and the retention of words in episodic memory. *Journal of Experimental Psychology: General, 104,* 268–294.

Cull, W. L. (2000). Untangling the benefits of multiple study opportunities and repeated testing for cued recall. *Applied Cognitive Psychology, 14,* 215–235.

Danion, J. M., Gokalsing, E., Robert, P., Massin-Krauss, M., & Bacon, E. (2001). Defective relationship between subjective experience and behavior in schizophrenia. *American Journal of Psychiatry, 158,* 2064–2066.

Darley, C. F., Tinklenberg, J. R., Roth, W. T., Vernon, S., & Kopelt, B. S. (1977). Marijuauna effects on long-term memory assessment and retrieval. *Psychopharmacology, 52,* 239–241.

Davies, G. M. (1993). Witnessing events. In G. M. Davies & R. H. Logie (Eds.), *Memory in everyday life* (pp. 367–401). Amsterdam: North-Holland/Elsevier.

Deffenbacher, K. A. (1991). A maturing of research on the behavior of eyewitnesses. *Applied Cognitive Psychology, 5,* 377–402.

de Groot, A. D. (1965). *Thought and choice in chess.* The Hague, The Netherlands: Mouton.

Dent, H. R., & Stephenson, G. M. (1979). An experimental study of the effectiveness of different techniques of questioning child witnesses. *British Journal of Social and Clinical Psychology, 18,* 41–51.

Dinges, D. F., Whitehouse, W. G., Orne, E. C., Powell, J. W., Orne, M. T., & Erdelyi, M. H. (1992). Evaluating hypnotic memory enhancement (hypermnesia and reminiscence) using multitrial forced recall. *Journal of Experimental Psychology: Learning, Memory, and Cognition, 18,* 1139–1147.

Dodson, C. S., & Johnson, M. K. (1993). Rate of false source attributions depends on how questions are asked. *American Journal of Psychology, 106,* 541–557.

Dodson, C. S., & Schacter, D. L. (2001). "If I had said it I would have remembered it": Reducing false memories with a distinctiveness heuristic. *Psychonomic Bulletin and Review, 8,* 155–161.

Dodson, C. S., & Schacter, D. L. (2002). When false recognition meets metacognition: The distinctiveness heuristic. *Journal of Memory and Language, 46,* 782–803.

Dorfman, J., & Mandler, G. (1994). Implicit and explicit forgetting: When is gist remembered? *Quarterly Journal of Experimental Psychology: Human Experimental Psychology, 47a,* 651–672.

Dunn, E. W., & Spellman, B. A. (2003). Forgetting by remembering: Stereotype inhibition through rehearsal of alternative aspects of identity. *Journal of Experimental Social Psychology, 39,* 420–433.

Dunning, D., & Stern, L. B. (1992). Examining the generality of eyewitness hypermnesia: A close look at time delay and question type. *Applied Cognitive Psychology, 6,* 643–657.

Dywan, J., & Bowers, K. (1983). The use of hypnosis to enhance recall. *Science, 222,* 184–185.

Eakin, D. K., Schreiber, T. A., & Sergent-Marshall, S. (2003). Misinformation effects in eyewitness memory: The presence and absence of memory impairment as a function of warning and misinformation accessibility. *Journal of Experimental Psychology: Learning, Memory, and Cognition, 29,* 813–825.

Ebbesen, E. B., & Rienick, C. B. (1998). Retention interval and eyewitness memory for events and personal identifying attributes. *Journal of Applied Psychology, 83,* 745–762.

Ebbinghaus, H. (1964). *Memory: A contribution to experimental psychology.* New York: Dover. (Original work published 1895)

Echabe, A. E., & Paez-Rovira, D. (1989). Social representations and memory: The case of AIDS. *European Journal of Social Psychology, 19,* 543–551.

Eich, E. (1985). Context, memory, and integrated item/context imagery. *Journal of Experimental Psychology: Learning, Memory, and Cognition, 11,* 764–770.

Eich, E. (1989). Theoretical issues in state dependent memory. In H. L. Roediger, III & F. I. M. Craik (Eds.), *Varieties of memory and consciousness: Essays in honor of Endel Tulving* (pp. 331–354). Hillsdale, NJ: Erlbaum.

Eich, J. E. (1980). The cue-dependent nature of state-dependent retrieval. *Memory and Cognition, 8,* 157–173.

Eich, J. E., Weingartner, H., Stillman, R. C., & Gillin, J. C. (1975). State-dependent accessibility of retrieval cues in the retention of a categorized list. *Journal of Verbal Learning and Verbal Behavior, 14,* 408–417.

Erdelyi, M. H. (1996). *The recovery of unconscious memories: Hypermnesia and reminiscence.* Chicago: University of Chicago Press.

Erdelyi, M. H., & Becker, J. (1974). Hypermnesia for pictures: Incremental memory for pictures but not words in multiple recall trials. *Cognitive Psychology, 6,* 159–171.

Erdelyi, M. H., Finks, J., & Feigin-Pfau, M. B. (1989). The effect of response bias on recall performance, with some observations on processing bias. *Journal of Experimental Psychology: General, 118,* 245–254.

Eugenio, P., Buckhout, R., Kostes, S., & Ellison, K. W. (1982). Hypermnesia in the eyewitness to a crime. *Bulletin of the Psychonomic Society, 19,* 83–86.

Fiedler, K., Walther, E., Armbruster, T., Fay, D., & Naumann, U. (1996). Do you really know what you have seen? Intrusion errors and presuppositions effects on constructive memory. *Journal of Experimental Social Psychology, 32,* 484–511.

Fisher, R. P. (1995). Interviewing victims and witnesses of crime. *Psychology, Public Policy, and Law, 1,* 732–764.

Fisher, R. P. (1996). Implications of output-bound measures for laboratory and field research in memory. *Behavioral and Brain Sciences, 19,* 197.

Fisher, R. P. (1999). Probing knowledge structures. In D. Gopher & A. Koriat (Eds.), *Attention and performance XVII—cognitive regulation of performance: Interaction of theory and application* (pp. 537–556). Cambridge, MA: MIT Press.

Fisher, R. P., & Geiselman, R. E. (1992). *Memory-enhancing techniques for investigative interviewing: The cognitive interview.* Springfield, IL: Thomas.

Fiske, S. T. (1993). Social cognition and social perception. *Annual Review of Psychology, 44,* 155–194.

Frost, P. (2000). The quality of false memory over time: Is memory for misinformation "remembered" or "known"? *Psychonomic Bulletin and Review, 7,* 531–536.

Garry, M., Manning, C. G., Loftus, E. F., & Sherman, S. J. (1996). Imagination inflation: Imagining a childhood event inflates confidence that it occurred. *Psychonomic Bulletin and Review, 3,* 208–214.

Gigerenzer, G., Hoffrage, U., & Kleinbölting, H. (1991). Probabilistic mental models: A Brunswikian theory of confidence. *Psychological Review, 98,* 506–528.

Godden, D. R., & Baddeley, A. D. (1975). Context-dependent memory in two natural environments: On land and underwater. *British Journal of Psychology, 66,* 325–331.

Goff, L. M., & Roediger, H. L. (1998). Imagination inflation for action events: Repeated imaginings lead to illusory recollections. *Memory and Cognition, 26,* 20–33.

Goldinger, S. D., Kleider, H. M., & Shelley, E. (1999). The marriage of perception and memory: Creating two-way illusions with words and voices. *Memory and Cognition, 27,* 328–338.

Goldsmith, M., & Koriat, A. (1999). The strategic regulation of memory reporting: Mechanisms and performance consequences. In D. Gopher & A. Koriat (Eds.), *Attention and performance XVII—cognitive regulation of performance: Interaction of theory and application* (pp. 373–400). Cambridge, MA: MIT Press.

Goldsmith, M., Koriat, A., & Pansky, A. (in press). Strategic regulation of grain size in memory reporting over time. *Journal of Memory and Language.*

Goldsmith, M., Koriat, A., & Weinberg-Eliezer, A. (2002). Strategic regulation of grain size memory reporting. *Journal of Experimental Psychology: General, 131,* 73–95.

Goodwin, D. W., Powell, B., Bremer, D., Hoine, H., & Stern, J. (1969). Alcohol and recall: State-dependent effects in man. *Science, 163,* 1358–1360.

Gorenstein, G. W., & Ellsworth, P. C. (1980). Effect of choosing an incorrect photograph on a later identification by an eyewitness. *Journal of Applied Psychology, 65,* 616–622.

Grice, H. P. (1975). Logic and conversation. In P. Cole & J. L. Morgan (Eds.), *Syntax and semantics: Speech acts* (Vol. 3, pp. 41–58). New York: Academic Press.

Gruneberg, M. M., & Sykes, R. N. (1993). The generalizability of confidence–accuracy studies in eyewitnessing. *Memory, 1,* 185–189.

Hanawalt, N. G., & Demarest, I. H. (1939). The effect of verbal suggestion upon the reproduction of visually perceived forms. *Journal of Experimental Psychology, 25,* 159–174.

Hasher, L., & Zacks, R. T. (1979). Automatic and effortful processes in memory. *Journal of Experimental Psychology: General, 108,* 356–388.

Hastie, R., Landsman, R., & Loftus, E. F. (1978). Eyewitness testimony: The dangers of guessing. *Jurimetrics Journal, 19,* 1–8.

Hastorf, A. H., & Cantril, H. (1954). They saw a game: A case study. *Journal of Abnormal and Social Psychology, 49,* 129–134.

Herman, D. T., Lawless, R. H., & Marshall, R. W. (1957). Variables in the effect of language on the reproduction of visually perceived forms. *Perceptual and Motor Skills, 7,* 171–186.

Higham, P. A. (2002). Strong cues are not necessarily weak: Thomson and Tulving (1970) and the encoding specificity principle revisited. *Memory and Cognition, 30,* 67–80.

Hilgard, E. R., & Loftus, E. F. (1979). Effective interrogation of the eyewitness. *International Journal of Clinical and Experimental Hypnosis, 27,* 342–357.

Hirt, E. R. (1990). Do I see only what I expect? Evidence for an expectancy-guided retrieval model. *Journal of Personality and Social Psychology, 58,* 937–951.

Hirt, E. R., Lynn, S. J., Payne, D. G., Krackow, E., & McCrea, S. M. (1999). Expectancies and memory: Inferring the past from what must have been. In I. Kirsch (Ed.), *How expectancies shape experience* (pp. 93–124). Washington, DC: American Psychological Association.

Hirt, E. R., McDonald, H. E., & Erikson, G. A. (1995). How do I remember thee? The role of encoding set and delay in reconstructive memory processes. *Journal of Experimental Social Psychology, 31,* 379–409.

Huff, C. R., Rattner, A., & Sagarin, E. (1996). *Convicted but innocent: Wrongful conviction and public policy.* London: Sage.

Hunt, R. R., & McDaniel, M. A. (1993). The enigma of organization and distinctiveness. *Journal of Memory and Language, 32,* 421–445.

Hyde, T. S., & Jenkins, J. J. (1973). Recall for words as a function of semantic, graphic, and syntactic orienting tasks. *Journal of Verbal Learning and Verbal Behavior, 12,* 471–480.

Hyman, I. E. (1994). Conversational remembering: Story recall with a peer versus for an experimenter. *Applied Cognitive Psychology, 8,* 49–66.

Hyman, I. E. (1999). Creating false autobiographical memories: Why people believe their memory errors. In E. Winograd & R. Fivush (Eds.), *Ecological approaches to cognition: Essays in honor of Ulric Neisser* (pp. 229–252). Mahwah, NJ: Erlbaum.

Hyman, I. E., & Billings, F. J. (1998). Individual differences and the creation of false childhood memories. *Memory, 6,* 1–20.

Hyman, I. E., Husband, T. H., & Billings, F. J. (1995). False memories of childhood experiences. *Applied Cognitive Psychology, 9,* 181–197.

Hyman, I. E., & Loftus, E. F. (1998). Errors in autobiographical memory. *Clinical Psychology Review, 18,* 933–947.

Hyman, I. E., & Pentland, J. (1996). The role of mental imagery in the creation of false childhood memories. *Journal of Memory and Language, 35*, 101–117.

Jacoby, L. L., & Dallas, M. (1981). On the relationship between autobiographical memory and perceptual learning. *Journal of Experimental Psychology: General, 110*, 306–340.

Jacoby, L. L., Kelley, C. M., & Dywan, J. (1989). Memory attributions. In H. L. Roediger & F. I. M. Craik (Eds.), *Varieties of memory and consciousness: Essays in honour of Endel Tulving* (pp. 391–422). Hillsdale, NJ: Erlbaum.

Jacoby, L. L., & Whitehouse, K. (1989). An illusion of memory: False recognition influenced by unconscious perception. *Journal of Experimental Psychology: General, 118*, 126–135.

Johnson, M. K., Hashtroudi, S., & Lindsay, D. S. (1993). Source monitoring. *Psychological Bulletin, 114*, 3–28.

Johnston, W. A., Dark, V. J., & Jacoby, L. L. (1985). Perceptual fluency and recognition judgments. *Journal of Experimental Psychology: Learning, Memory, and Cognition, 11*, 3–11.

Kato, T. (1985). Semantic-memory sources of episodic retrieval failure. *Memory and Cognition, 13*, 442–452.

Kelley, C. M., & Lindsay, D. S. (1993). Remembering mistaken for knowing: Ease of retrieval as a basis for confidence in answers to general knowledge questions. *Journal of Memory and Language, 32*, 1–24.

Kelley, C. M., & Rhodes, M. G. (2002). Making sense and nonsense of experience: Attributions in memory and judgment. In B. H. Ross (Ed.), *The psychology of learning and motivation: Advances in research and theory* (Vol. 41, pp. 293–320). San Diego, CA: Academic Press.

Kelley, C. M., & Sahakyan, L. (2003). Memory, monitoring, and control in the attainment of memory accuracy. *Journal of Memory and Language, 48*, 704–721.

Keren, G. (1991). Calibration and probability judgments: Conceptual and methodological issues. *Acta Psychologica, 77*, 217–273.

Kintsch, W., Kozminsky, E., Streby, W., McKoon, G., & Keenan, J. (1975). Comprehension and recall of text as a function of content variables. *Journal of Verbal Learning and Verbal Behavior, 14*, 196–214.

Kintsch, W., Welsch, D., Schmalhofer, F., & Zimny, S. (1990). Sentence memory: A theoretical analysis. *Journal of Memory and Language, 29*, 133–159.

Klatzky, R. L., & Erdelyi, M. H. (1985). The response criterion problem in tests of hypnosis and memory. *International Journal of Clinical and Experimental Hypnosis, 33*, 246–257.

Koren, D., Seidman, L. J., Poyurovsky, M., Goldsmith, M., Viksman, P., Zichel, S., et al. (2004). The neuropsychological basis of insight in first-episode schizophrenia: A pilot metacognitive study. *Schizophrenia Research, 70*(2–3), 195–202.

Koriat, A., & Goldsmith, M. (1994). Memory in naturalistic and laboratory contexts: Distinguishing the accuracy-oriented and quantity-oriented approaches to memory assessment. *Journal of Experimental Psychology: General, 123*, 297–315.

Koriat, A., & Goldsmith, M. (1996a). Memory as something that can be counted vs. memory as something that can be counted on. In D. J. Herrmann, C. McEvoy, C. Hertzog, P. Hertel, & M. K. Johnson (Eds.), *Basic and applied memory research: Practical applications* (Vol. 2, pp. 3–18). Hillsdale, NJ: Erlbaum.

Koriat, A., & Goldsmith, M. (1996b). Memory metaphors and the real-life/laboratory controversy: Correspondence versus storehouse conceptions of memory. *Behavioral and Brain Sciences, 19*, 167–228.

Koriat, A., & Goldsmith, M. (1996c). Monitoring and control processes in the strategic regulation of memory accuracy. *Psychological Review, 103*, 490–517.

Koriat, A., & Goldsmith, M. (2004). *Monitoring and control processes in the strategic regulation of memory accuracy over time.* Manuscript in preparation.

Koriat, A., Goldsmith, M., & Pansky, A. (2000). Toward a psychology of memory accuracy. *Annual Review of Psychology, 51*, 481–537.

Koriat, A., Goldsmith, M., Schneider, W., & Nakash-Dura, M. (2001). The credibility of children's testimony: Can children control the accuracy of their memory reports? *Journal of Experimental Child Psychology, 79*, 405–437.

Koriat, A., & Levy-Sadot, R. (1999). Processes underlying metacognitive judgments: Information-based and experience-based monitoring of one's own knowledge. In S. Chaiken & Y. Trope (Eds.), *Dual-process theories in social psychology* (pp. 483–502). New York: Guilford Press.

Koriat, A., Levy-Sadot, R., Edry, E., & de Marcas, S. (2003). What do we know about what we cannot remember? Accessing the semantic attributes of words that cannot be recalled. *Journal of Experimental Psychology: Learning, Memory, and Cognition, 29*, 1095–1105.

Koriat, A., Lichtenstein, S., & Fischhoff, B. (1980). Reasons for confidence. *Journal of Experimental Psychology: Human Learning and Memory, 6*, 107–118.

Koutstaal, W., Schacter, D. L., Johnson, M. K., & Galluccio, L. (1999). Facilitation and impairment of event memory produced by photograph review. *Memory and Cognition, 27*, 478–493.

Krass, J., Kinoshita, S., & McConkey, K. M. (1989). Hypnotic memory and confident reporting. *Applied Cognitive Psychology, 3*, 35–51.

Kuo, T. M., & Hirshman, E. (1996). Investigations of the testing effect. *American Journal of Psychology, 109*, 451–464.

Lampinen, J. M., Copeland, S. M., & Neuschatz, J. S. (2001). Recollections of things schematic: Room schemas revisited. *Journal of Experimental Psychology: Learning, Memory, and Cognition, 27*, 1211–1222.

Levy, B. J., & Anderson, M. C. (2002). Inhabituation processes and the control of memory retrieval. *Trends in Cognitive Sciences, 6*, 299–305.

Lewis, M. Q. (1971). Categorized lists and cued recall. *Journal of Experimental Psychology, 87*, 129–131.

Lichtenstein, S., Fischhoff, B., & Phillips, L. D. (1982). Calibration of probabilities: The state of the art to 1980. In D. Kahneman, P. Slovic, & A. Tversky (Eds.), *Judgment under uncertainty: Heuristics and biases* (pp. 306–334). Cambridge, UK: Cambridge University Press.

Lindsay, D. S. (1990). Misleading suggestions can impair eyewitnesses' ability to remember event details. *Journal of Experimental Psychology: Learning, Memory, and Cognition, 16*, 1077–1083.

Lindsay, D. S. (1994). Memory source monitoring and eyewitness testimony. In D. F. Ross, J. D. Read, & M. P. Toglia (Eds.), *Adult eyewitness testimony: Current trends and developments* (pp. 27–55). New York: Cambridge University Press.

Lindsay, D. S., & Johnson, M. K. (1989). The eyewitness suggestibility effect and memory for source. *Memory and Cognition, 17*, 349–358.

Lindsay, D. S., & Johnson, M. K. (2000). False memories and the source monitoring framework: Reply to Reyna and Lloyd (1997). *Learning and Individual Differences, 12*, 145–161.

Lindsay, D. S., Johnson, M. K., & Kwon, P. (1991). Developmental changes in memory source monitoring. *Journal of Experimental Child Psychology, 52,* 297–318.

Linton, M. (1975). Memory for real-world events. In D. A. Norman & D. E. Rumelhart (Eds.), *Explorations in cognition* (pp. 376–404). San Francisco: Freeman.

Lipton, J. P. (1977). On the psychology of eyewitness testimony. *Journal of Applied Psychology, 62,* 90–95.

Lockhart, R. S., & Craik, F. I. M. (1990). Levels of processing: A retrospective commentary on a framework for memory research. *Canadian Journal of Psychology, 44,* 87–112.

Loftus, E. F. (1975). Leading questions and the eyewitness report. *Cognitive Psychology, 7,* 560–572.

Loftus, E. F. (1979). *Eyewitness testimony.* Cambridge, MA: Harvard University Press.

Loftus, E. F., & Loftus, G. R. (1980). On the permanence of stored information in the human brain. *American Psychologist, 35,* 409–420.

Loftus, E. F., Miller, D. G., & Burns, H. J. (1978). Semantic integration of verbal information into a visual memory. *Journal of Experimental Psychology: Human Learning and Memory, 4,* 19–31.

Loftus, E. F., & Palmer, J. C. (1974). Reconstruction of automobile destruction: An example of the interaction between language and memory. *Journal of Verbal Learning and Verbal Behavior, 13,* 585–589.

Loftus, E. F., & Pickrell, J. E. (1995). The formation of false memories. *Psychiatric Annals, 25,* 720–725.

Loftus, E. F., & Zanni, G. (1975). Eyewitness testimony: The influence of the wording of a question. *Bulletin of the Psychonomic Society, 5,* 86–88.

MacLeod, M. (2002). Retrieval-induced forgetting in eyewitness memory: Forgetting as a consequence of remembering. *Applied Cognitive Psychology, 16,* 135–149.

Macrae, C. N., & MacLeod, M. D. (1999). On recollections lost: When practice makes imperfect. *Journal of Personality and Social Psychology, 77,* 463–473.

Mäntyla, T. (1986). Optimizing cue effectiveness: Recall of 500 and 600 incidentally learned words. *Journal of Experimental Psychology: Learning, Memory, and Cognition, 12,* 66–71.

Mäntyla, T., & Nilsson, L. G. (1988). Cue distinctiveness and forgetting: Effectiveness of self-generated retrieval cues in delayed recall. *Journal of Experimental Psychology: Learning, Memory, and Cognition, 14,* 502–509.

Mather, M., & Johnson, M. K. (2003). Affective review and schema reliance in memory in older and younger adults. *American Journal of Psychology, 116,* 169–189.

McCauley, M. R., & Fisher, R. P. (1995). Facilitating children's eyewitness recall with the revised cognitive interview. *Journal of Applied Psychology, 80,* 510–516.

McClelland, A. G. R., & Bolger, F. (1994). The calibration of subjective probability: Theories and models 1980–94. In G. Wright (Ed.), *Subjective probability* (pp. 453–482). Oxford, UK: Wiley.

McCloskey, M., Wible, C. G., & Cohen, N. J. (1988). Is there a special flashbulb-memory mechanism? *Journal of Experimental Psychology: General, 117,* 171–181.

McCloskey, M., & Zaragoza, M. (1985). Misleading postevent information and memory for events: Arguments and evidence against memory impairment hypotheses. *Journal of Experimental Psychology: General, 114,* 1–16.

McDaniel, M. A., Anderson, D. C., Einstein, G. O., & O'Halloran, C. M. (1989). Modulation of environmental reinstatement effects through encoding strategies. *American Journal of Psychology, 102,* 523–548.

McDermott, K. B. (1996). The persistence of false memories in list recall. *Journal of Memory and Language, 35*, 212–230.

McFarland, C., & Ross, M. (1987). The relation between current impressions and memories of self and dating partners. *Personality and Social Psychology Bulletin, 13*, 228–238.

McGeoch, J. A. (1932). Forgetting and the law of disuse. *Psychological Review, 39*, 352–370.

Memon, A., & Higham, P. A. (1999). A review of the cognitive interview. *Psychology, Crime, and Law, 5*(1–2), 177–196.

Memon, A., & Stevenage, V. S. (1996). Interviewing witnesses: What works and what doesn't? *Psycholoquy, 7*. Retrieved from *www.cogsci.ecs.soton.ac.uk/psycoloquy/raw/1996.volume.7/psyc.96.7.06.witness-memory.1.memon*.

Migueles, M., & Garcia-Bajos, E. (1999). Recall, recognition, and confidence patterns in eyewitness testimony. *Applied Cognitive Psychology, 13*, 257–268.

Mitchell, K. J., & Johnson, M. K. (2000). Source monitoring: Attributing mental experiences. In E. Tulving (Ed.), *The Oxford handbook of memory* (pp. 179–195). New York: Oxford University Press.

Moston, S. (1987). The suggestibility of children in interview studies. *First Language, 7*(19, Pt. 1), 67–78.

Mulder, M. R., & Vrij, A. (1996). Explaining conversation rules to children: An intervention study to facilitate children's accurate responses. *Child Abuse and Neglect, 20*, 623–631.

Nairne, J. S. (2002). The myth of the encoding-retrieval match. *Memory, 10*(5–6), 389–395.

Naveh-Benjamin, M. (1987). Coding of spatial location information: An automatic process? *Journal of Experimental Psychology: Learning, Memory, and Cognition, 13*, 595–605.

Naveh-Benjamin, M. (2002). The effects of divided attention on encoding processes: Underlying mechanisms. In M. Naveh-Benjamin, M. Moscovitch, & H. L. Roediger (Eds.), *Perspectives on human memory and cognitive aging: Essays in honor of Fergus Craik* (pp. 193–207). Philadelphia: Psychology Press.

Naveh-Benjamin, M., Craik, F. I. M., Gavrilescu, D., & Anderson, N. D. (2000). Asymmetry between encoding and retrieval processes: Evidence from divided attention and a calibration analysis. *Memory and Cognition, 28*, 965–976.

Neisser, U. (1967). *Cognitive psychology.* New York: Appleton-Century-Crofts.

Neisser, U. (1978). Memory: What are the important questions? In M. M. Gruneberg & P. E. Morris (Eds.), *Practical aspects of memory* (pp. 3–24). New York: Academic Press.

Neisser, U. (1981). John Dean's memory: A case study. *Cognition, 9*, 1–22.

Neisser, U. (1984). Interpreting Harry Bahrick's discovery: What confers immunity against forgetting? *Journal of Experimental Psychology: General, 113*, 32–35.

Neisser, U. (1988). Time present and time past. In M. M. Gruneberg, P. E. Morris, & R. N. Sykes (Eds.), *Practical aspects of memory: Current research and issues* (Vol. 2, pp. 545–560). Chichester, UK: Wiley.

Neisser, U. (1996). Remembering as doing. *Behavioral and Brain Sciences, 19*, 203–204.

Neisser, U., & Harsch, N. (1992). Phantom flashbulbs: False recollections of hearing the news about Challenger. In E. Winograd & U. Neisser (Eds.), *Affect and accuracy in recall: Studies of "flashbulb memories"* (pp. 9–31). Cambridge, UK: Cambridge University Press.

Nelson, T. O., Graf, A., Dunlosky, J., Marlatt, A., Walker, D., & Luce, K. (1998). Effect of acute alcohol intoxication on recall and on judgments of learning during the acquisition of new information. In G. Mazzoni & T. O. Nelson (Eds.), *Metacognition and cognitive neuropsychology: Monitoring and control processes* (pp. 161–180). Mahwah, NJ: Erlbaum.

Nelson, T. O., McSpadden, M., Fromme, K., & Marlatt, G. A. (1986). Effects of alcohol intoxication on metamemory and on retrieval from long-term memory. *Journal of Experimental Psychology: General, 115,* 247–254.

Nelson, T. O., & Narens, L. (1990). Metamemory: A theoretical framework and new findings. In G. H. Bower (Ed.), *The psychology of learning and motivation: Advances in research and theory* (Vol. 26, pp. 125–123). San Diego, CA: Academic Press.

Nelson, T. O., & Narens, L. (1994). Why investigate metacognition? In J. Metcalfe & A. P. Shimamura (Eds.), *Metacognition: Knowing about knowing* (pp. 1–25). Cambridge, MA: MIT Press.

Norman, K. A., & Schacter, D. L. (1996). Implicit memory, explicit memory, and false recollection: A cognitive neuroscience perspective. In L. M. Reder (Ed.), *Implicit memory and metacognition* (pp. 229–257). Hillsdale, NJ: Erlbaum.

Owens, J., Bower, G. H., & Black, J. B. (1979). The "soap opera" effect in story recall. *Memory and Cognition, 7,* 185–191.

Pansky, A., & Bar, S. K. (2004). *The role of basic level convergence in accounting for the misinformation effect.* Manuscript in preparation.

Pansky, A., & Koriat, A. (2004). The basic level convergence effect in memory distortions. *Psychological Science, 15,* 52–59.

Pansky, A., Koriat, A., Goldsmith, M., & Pearlman-Avnion, S. (2002). *Memory accuracy and distortion in old age: Cognitive, metacognitive, and neurocognitive determinants.* Poster session presented at the 30th anniversary conference of the National Institute for Psychobiology in Israel, Jerusalem.

Pasupathi, M. (2001). The social construction of the personal past and its implications for adult development. *Psychological Bulletin, 127,* 651–672.

Pasupathi, M., Stallworth, L. M., & Murdoch, K. (1998). How what we tell becomes what we know: Listener effects on speakers' long-term memory for events. *Discourse Processes, 26,* 1–25.

Payne, D. G., Elie, C. J., Blackwell, J. M., & Neuschatz, J. S. (1996). Memory illusions: Recalling, recognizing, and recollecting events that never occurred. *Journal of Memory and Language, 35,* 261–285.

Pennebaker, J. W., & Memon, A. (1996). Recovered memories in context: Thoughts and elaborations on Bowers and Farvolden (1996). *Psychological Bulletin, 119,* 381–385.

Penrod, S., & Cutler, B. (1995). Witness confidence and witness accuracy: Assessing their forensic relation. *Psychology, Public Policy, and Law, 1,* 817–845.

Perez-Mata, M. N., Read, J. D., & Diges, M. (2002). Effects of divided attention and word concreteness on correct recall and false memory reports. *Memory, 10,* 161–177.

Perfect, T. J., Watson, E. L., & Wagstaff, G. F. (1993). Accuracy of confidence ratings associated with general knowledge and eyewitness memory. *Journal of Applied Psychology, 78,* 144–147.

Pettinati, H. M. (Ed.). (1988). *Hypnosis and memory.* New York: Guilford Press.

Pezdek, K., Finger, K., & Hodge, D. (1997). Planting false childhood memories: The role of event plausibility. *Psychological Science, 8,* 437–441.

Pezdek, K., & Roe, C. (1995). The effect of memory trace strength on suggestibility. *Journal of Experimental Child Psychology, 60,* 116–128.

Pezdek, K., Whetstone, T., Reynolds, K., Askari, N., & Dougherty, T. (1989). Memory for real-world scenes: The role of consistency with schema expectation. *Journal of Experimental Psychology: Learning, Memory, and Cognition, 15,* 587–595.

Poole, D. A., & White, L. T. (1993). Two years later: Effect of question repetition and retention interval on the eyewitness testimony of children and adults. *Developmental Psychology, 29,* 844–853.

Posner, M. I., & Keele, S. W. (1970). Retention of abstract ideas. *Journal of Experimental Psychology, 83*(2, Pt. 1), 304–308.

Powers, P. A., Andriks, J. L., & Loftus, E. F. (1979). Eyewitness accounts of females and males. *Journal of Applied Psychology, 64,* 339–347.

Read, J. D. (1996). From a passing thought to a false memory in 2 minutes: Confusing real and illusory events. *Psychonomic Bulletin and Review, 3,* 105–111.

Read, J. D., Lindsay, D. S., & Nicholls, T. (1998). The relation between confidence and accuracy in eyewitness identification studies: Is the conclusion changing? In C. P. Thompson & D. J. Herrmann (Eds.), *Eyewitness memory: Theoretical and applied perspectives* (pp. 107–130). Mahwah, NJ: Erlbaum.

Reese, E., & Brown, N. (2000). Reminiscing and recounting in the preschool years. *Applied Cognitive Psychology, 14,* 1–17.

Reinitz, M. T., Morrissey, J., & Demb, J. (1994). Role of attention in face encoding. *Journal of Experimental Psychology: Learning, Memory, and Cognition, 20,* 161–168.

Reyna, V. F. (1998). Fuzzy-trace theory and false memory. In M. J. Intons-Peterson & D. L. Best (Eds.), *Memory distortions and their prevention* (pp. 15–27). Mahwah, NJ: Erlbaum.

Reyna, V. F., & Titcomb, A. L. (1997). Constraints on the suggestibility of eyewitness testimony: A fuzzy-trace theory analysis. In D. G. Payne & F. G. Conrad (Eds.), *A synthesis of basic and applied approaches to human memory* (pp. 157–174). Hillsdale, NJ: Erlbaum.

Rhodes, M. G., & Anastasi, J. S. (2000). The effects of a levels-of-processing manipulation on false recall. *Psychonomic Bulletin and Review, 7,* 158–162.

Roberts, W. T., & Higham, P. A. (2002). Selecting accurate statements from the cognitive interview using confidence ratings. *Journal of Experimental Psychology: Applied, 8,* 33–43.

Roebers, C. M. (2002). Confidence judgments in children's and adult's event recall and suggestibility. *Developmental Psychology, 38,* 1052–1067.

Roebers, C. M., & Fernandez, O. (2002). The effects of accuracy motivation and children's and adults' event recall, suggestibility, and their answers to unanswerable questions. *Journal of Cognition and Development, 3,* 415–443.

Roediger, H. L. (1973). Inhibition in recall from cueing with recall targets. *Journal of Verbal Learning and Verbal Behavior, 12,* 644–657.

Roediger, H. L. (1980). Memory metaphors in cognitive psychology. *Memory and Cognition, 8,* 231–246.

Roediger, H. L. (1996). Memory illusions. *Journal of Memory and Language, 35,* 76–100.

Roediger, H. L., & Gallo, D. A. (2002). Processes affecting accuracy and distortion in memory: An overview. In M. L. Eisen, J. A. Quas, & G. S. Goodman (Eds.), *Memory and suggestibility in the forensic interview* (pp. 3–28). Mahwah, NJ: Erlbaum.

Roediger, H. L., & Guynn, M. J. (1996). Retrieval processes. In E. L. Bjork & R. A. Bjork

(Eds.), *Memory: Handbook of perception and cognition* (2nd ed., pp. 197–236). San Diego, CA: Academic Press.

Roediger, H. L., & McDermott, K. B. (1995). Creating false memories: Remembering words not presented in lists. *Journal of Experimental Psychology: Learning, Memory, and Cognition, 21,* 803–814.

Roediger, H. L., McDermott, K. B., & Goff, L. M. (1997). Recovery of true and false memories: Paradoxical effects of repeated testing. In M. A. Conway (Ed.), *Recovered memories and false memories* (pp. 118–149). Oxford, UK: Oxford University Press.

Roediger, H. L., McDermott, K. B., & Robinson, K. J. (1998). The role of associative processes in creating false memories. In M. A. Conway, S. E. Gathercole, & C. Cornoldi (Eds.), *Theories of memory* (Vol. 2, pp. 187–245). Hove, UK: Psychological Press.

Roediger, H. L., & Meade, M. L. (2000). Memory processes. In K. Pawlik & M. R. Rosenzweig (Eds.), *International handbook of psychology* (pp. 117–135). London: Sage.

Roediger, H. L., & Payne, D. G. (1985). Recall criterion does not affect recall level or hypermnesia: A puzzle for generate/recognize theories. *Memory and Cognition, 13,* 1–7.

Roediger, H. L., Srinivas, K., & Waddill, P. (1989). How much does guessing influence recall? Comment on Erdelyi, Finks, and Feigin-Pfau. *Journal of Experimental Psychology: General, 118,* 255–257.

Roediger, H. L., Watson, J. M., McDermott, K. B., & Gallo, D. A. (2001). Factors that determine false recall: A multiple regression analysis. *Psychonomic Bulletin and Review, 8,* 385–407.

Rosch, E., Mervis, C. B., Gray, W. D., Johnson, D. M., & Boyes-Braem, P. (1976). Basic objects in natural categories. *Cognitive Psychology, 8,* 382–439.

Rosenbluth-Mor, M. (2001). *Accuracy and quantity in memory reports: The effects of context reinstatement.* Unpublished master's thesis, University of Haifa, Haifa, Israel.

Ross, M. (1989). Relation of implicit theories to the construction of personal histories. *Psychological Review, 96,* 341–357.

Ross, M., McFarland, C., & Fletcher, G. J. (1981). The effect of attitude on the recall of personal histories. *Journal of Personality and Social Psychology, 40,* 627–634.

Rubin, D. C., & Kozin, M. (1984). Vivid memories. *Cognition, 16,* 81–95.

Ryan, R. H., & Geiselman, R. E. (1991). Effects of biased information on the relationship between eyewitness confidence and accuracy. *Bulletin of the Psychonomic Society, 29,* 7–9.

Schacter, D. L. (1999). The seven sins of memory. *American Psychologist, 54,* 182–203.

Schacter, D. L., Cendan, D. L., Dodson, C. S., & Clifford, E. R. (2001). Retrieval conditions and false recognition: Testing the distinctiveness heuristic. *Psychonomic Bulletin and Review, 8,* 827–833.

Schacter, D. L., Israel, L., & Racine, C. (1999). Suppressing false recognition in younger and older adults: The distinctiveness heuristic. *Journal of Memory and Language, 40,* 1–24.

Schmidt, S. R. (1991). Can we have a distinctive theory of memory? *Memory and Cognition, 19,* 523–542.

Schmolck, H., Buffalo, E. A., & Squire, L. R. (2000). Memory distortions develop over time: Recollections of the O. J. Simpson trial verdict after 15 and 32 months. *Psychological Science, 11,* 39–45.

Schooler, J. W., Foster, R. A., & Loftus, E. F. (1988). Some deleterious consequences of the act of recollection. *Memory and Cognition, 16,* 243–251.

Scrivner, E., & Safer, M. A. (1988). Eyewitnesses show hypermnesia for details about a violent event. *Journal of Applied Psychology, 73,* 371–377.

Seamon, J. G., Goodkind, M. S., Dumey, A. D., Dick, E., Aufseeser, M. S., Strickland, S. E., Woulfin, J. R., & Fung, N. S. (2003). "If I didn't write it, why would I remember it?" Effects of encoding, attention, and practice on accurate and false memory. *Memory and Cognition, 31,* 445–457.

Sedikides, C. (1990). Effects of fortuitously activated constructs versus activated communication goals on person impressions. *Journal of Personality and Social Psychology, 58,* 397–408.

Semon, R. (1921). *The mneme.* London: Allen & Unwin.

Shapiro, P. N., & Penrod, S. (1986). Meta-analysis of facial identification studies. *Psychological Bulletin, 100,* 139–156.

Shaw, J. S. (1996). Increases in eyewitness confidence resulting from postevent questioning. *Journal of Experimental Psychology: Applied, 2,* 126–146.

Shaw, J. S., Bjork, R. A., & Handal, A. (1995). Retrieval-induced forgetting in an eyewitness-memory paradigm. *Psychonomic Bulletin and Review, 2,* 249–253.

Simon, H. A. (1956). Rational choice and the structure of environments. *Psychological Review, 63,* 129–138.

Smith, S. M. (1988). Environmental context-dependent memory. In G. M. Davies & D. M. Thomson (Eds.), *Memory in context: Context in memory* (pp. 13–34). Chichester, UK: Wiley.

Smith, S. M., Glenberg, A., & Bjork, R. A. (1978). Environmental context and human memory. *Memory and Cognition, 6,* 342–353.

Strack, F., & Bless, H. (1994). Memory for nonoccurrences: Metacognitive and presuppositional strategies. *Journal of Memory and Language, 33,* 203–217.

Talarico, J. M., & Rubin, D. C. (2003). Confidence, not consistency, characterizes flashbulb memories. *Psychological Science, 14,* 455–461.

Thapar, A., & McDermott, K. B. (2001). False recall and false recognition induced by presentation of associated words: Effects of retention interval and level of processing. *Memory and Cognition, 29,* 424–432.

Thomson, D. M., & Tulving, E. (1970). Associative encoding and retrieval: Weak and strong cues. *Journal of Experimental Psychology, 86,* 255–262.

Titcomb, A. L., & Reyna, V. F. (1995). Memory interference and misinformation effects. In F. N. Dempster & C. J. Brainerd (Eds.), *Interference and inhibition in cognition* (pp. 263–294). San Diego, CA: Academic Press.

Toglia, M. P., Neuschatz, J. S., & Goodwin, K. A. (1999). Recall accuracy and illusory memories: When more is less. *Memory, 7,* 233–256.

Tuckey, M. R., & Brewer, N. (2003). The influence of schemas, stimulus ambiguity, and interview schedule on eyewitness memory over time. *Journal of Experimental Psychology: Applied, 9,* 101–118.

Tulving, E. (1983). *Elements of episodic memory.* Oxford, UK: Clarendon.

Tulving, E., & Osler, S. (1968). Effectiveness of retrieval cues in memory for words. *Journal of Experimental Psychology, 77,* 593–601.

Tulving, E., & Pearlstone, Z. (1966). Availability versus accessibility of information in memory for words. *Journal of Verbal Learning and Verbal Behavior, 5,* 381–391.

Tulving, E., & Thomson, D. M. (1973). Encoding specificity and retrieval processes in episodic memory. *Psychological Review, 80,* 359–380.

Turtle, J. W., & Yuille, J. C. (1994). Lost but not forgotten details: Repeated eyewitness recall leads to reminiscence but not hypermnesia. *Journal of Applied Psychology, 79*, 260–271.

Tussing, A. A., & Greene, R. L. (1997). False recognition of associates: How robust is the effect? *Psychonomic Bulletin and Review, 4*, 572–576.

Tversky, B., & Marsh, E. J. (2000). Biased retellings of events yield biased memories. *Cognitive Psychology, 40*, 1–38.

Vandierendonck, A., & Van Damme, R. (1988). Schema anticipation in recall: Memory process or report strategy? *Psychological Research, 50*, 116–122.

Wade, E., & Clark, H. H. (1993). Reproduction and demonstration in quotations. *Journal of Memory and Language, 32*, 805–819.

Wade, K. A., Garry, M., Read, J. D., & Lindsay, S. (2002). A picture is worth a thousand lies: Using false photographs to create false childhood memories. *Psychonomic Bulletin and Review, 9*, 597–603.

Watkins, O. C., & Watkins, M. J. (1975). Buildup of proactive inhibition as a cue-overload effect. *Journal of Experimental Psychology: Human Learning and Memory, 1*, 442–452.

Weaver, C. A. (1993). Do you need a "flash" to form a flashbulb memory? *Journal of Experimental Psychology: General, 122*, 39–46.

Weingartner, H., Rudorfer, M. V., & Linnoila, M. (1985). Cognitive effects of lithium treatment in normal volunteers. *Psychopharmacology, 86*, 472–474.

Wells, G. L. (1978). Applied eyewitness-testimony research: System variables and estimator variables. *Journal of Personality and Social Psychology, 36*, 1546–1557.

Wenger, S. K., Thompson, C. P., & Bartling, C. A. (1980). Recall facilitates subsequent recognition. *Journal of Experimental Psychology: Human Learning and Memory, 6*, 135–144.

Wheeler, M. A., Ewers, M., & Buonanno, J. F. (2003). Different rates of forgetting following study versus test trials. *Memory, 11*, 571–580.

Whitehouse, W. G., Dinges, D. F., Orne, E. C., & Orne, M. T. (1988). Hypnotic hypermnesia: Enhanced memory accessibility or report bias? *Journal of Abnormal Psychology, 97*, 289–295.

Whittlesea, B. W. A. (1993). Illusions of familiarity. *Journal of Experimental Psychology: Learning, Memory, and Cognition, 19*, 1235–1253.

Whittlesea, B. W. A. (2002). Two routes to remembering (and another to remembering not). *Journal of Experimental Psychology: General, 131*, 325–348.

Whittlesea, B. W. A. (2004). The perception of integrality: Remembering through the validation of expectation. *Journal of Experimental Psychology: Learning, Memory, and Cognition, 30*, 891–908.

Whittlesea, B. W. A., Jacoby, L. L., & Girard, K. (1990). Illusions of immediate memory: Evidence of an attributional basis for feelings of familiarity and perceptual quality. *Journal of Memory and Language, 29*, 716–732.

Whittlesea, B. W. A., & Williams, L. D. (2001a). The discrepancy-attribution hypothesis: I. The heuristic basis of feelings and familiarity. *Journal of Experimental Psychology: Learning, Memory, and Cognition, 27*, 3–13.

Whittlesea, B. W. A., & Williams, L. D. (2001b). The discrepancy-attribution hypothesis: II. Expectation, uncertainty, surprise, and feelings of familiarity. *Journal of Experimental Psychology: Learning, Memory, and Cognition, 27*, 14–33.

Windschitl, P. D. (1996). Memory for faces: Evidence of retrieval-based impairment.

Journal of Experimental Psychology: Learning, Memory, and Cognition, 22, 1101–1122.

Winograd, E. (1988). Continuities between ecological and laboratory approaches to memory. In U. Neisser & E. Winograd (Eds.), *Remembering reconsidered: Ecological and traditional approaches to the study of memory* (pp. 11–20). Cambridge, UK: Cambridge University Press.

Winograd, E. (1994). The authenticity and utility of memories. In U. Neisser & R. Fivush (Eds.), *The remembering self: Construction and accuracy in the self narrative* (pp. 243–251). New York: Cambridge University Press.

Yaniv, I., & Foster, D. P. (1995). Graininess of judgment under uncertainty: An accuracy–informativeness trade-off. *Journal of Experimental Psychology: General, 124,* 424–432.

Yaniv, I., & Foster, D. P. (1997). Precision and accuracy of judgmental estimation. *Journal of Behavioral Decision Making, 10,* 21–32.

Yarmey, A. D. (1986). Verbal, visual, and voice identification of a rape suspect under different levels of illumination. *Journal of Applied Psychology, 71,* 363–370.

Zaragoza, M. S., & Koshmider, J. W. (1989). Misled subjects may know more than their performance implies. *Journal of Experimental Psychology: Learning, Memory, and Cognition, 15,* 246–255.

Zaragoza, M. S., & Lane, S. M. (1994). Source misattributions and the suggestibility of eyewitness memory. *Journal of Experimental Psychology: Learning, Memory, and Cognition, 20,* 934–945.

Zaragoza, M. S., McCloskey, M., & Jamis, M. (1987). Misleading postevent information and recall of the original event: Further evidence against the memory impairment hypothesis. *Journal of Experimental Psychology: Learning, Memory, and Cognition, 13,* 36–44.

CHAPTER FIVE

Children's Recall and Testimony

JASON J. DICKINSON
DEBRA A. POOLE
RACHEL L. LAIMON

Beginning in the 1980s, a number of legal and sociopolitical movements thrust children onto the center stage of the legal arena, fostering unprecedented interest in their ability to recall autobiographical events. In today's courtrooms, children's reports are considered when rendering judgments about custody, relied upon to make prosecutorial decisions regarding suspected sexual abuse, and elicited to flesh out evidence in product liability and personal injury lawsuits. But regardless of how children come to play a role in forensic investigations, the legal arena is fundamentally a forum for resolving disputes, and therefore their reports are frequently challenged. In the midst of contentious and high-stake battles, legal and social service professionals often turn to memory researchers for information about the strengths and limitations of children's testimony.

Academicians who stray into the world of courtroom drama invariably find themselves in an uncomfortable situation. Whether they are on the witness stand or writing policy papers, researchers are typically asked to advance brief, straightforward conclusions about recall and testimony, even when there are numerous exceptions to their findings. As the resulting aphorisms gain momentum, people begin to apply them so broadly that misunderstandings arise. This chapter focuses on conclusions about children's reports that are sometimes given so much weight—regardless of the circumstances—that it may be time to abandon them altogether.

Many misunderstandings about children's testimony arose when findings from studies that did not involve memory contamination were generalized to situations involving suggestive influences. To prevent further confusion, this review separates children's performance under these two conditions, first discussing recall for experienced events when contaminating influences are not present, then focusing on reports from children who have been exposed to misinformation. The historical focus on preschool children's suggestibility has also propagated inappropriate conclusions. For example, some professionals have learned that preschool children are especially suggestible, so they assume that suggestive influences are irrelevant in cases involving school-age children. Now that studies have included children from a wider age range, however, it is possible to describe memory development during the early school years in more accurate terms.

Our approach to the topic of children's recall and testimony is guided by the questions professionals ask when they are trying to make sense of children's reports. Typically, evaluators highlight specific features of a child's narrative (e.g., the amount of detail, consistency of details, or the presence of "silly talk" in the middle of a narrative) and ask the memory researcher, "Is this feature characteristic of children who have experienced this type of event?" Our answers are guided by a body of literature on children's autobiographical recall and a unique experience: the opportunity to read hundreds of transcripts from children who enrolled in memory studies—transcripts that reveal how they describe events, what they do when their vocabulary fails them, and how their narratives evolve over time. To convey what we have learned from this experience, we selected transcripts from one study (Poole & Lindsay, 2001) to use as a sample project in this review, sometimes citing from the published report and other times relying on an archived report or new analyses.[1] We supplemented these data with findings from other investigators to illuminate the mechanisms that underlie trends, provide further support for our findings, and contribute information that cannot be mined from the sample project.

CHILDREN'S TESTIMONY FREE
OF CONTAMINATING INFLUENCES

The assumption that very young children cannot recall past events has a long history (Bauer, Burch, & Kleinknecht, 2002). In 1905, Sigmund Freud coined the term "infantile amnesia" to label the fact that people have few memories for their earliest years of life. For many decades, Piaget's (1952) explanation for this phenomenon continued to discourage research on early autobiographical memories: Young children, Piaget explained, lack the ability to internally represent events in ways that support later recall. As research on infants and preschoolers gradually chipped away at Piaget's pessimistic predictions, developmentalists found a new reason to believe that young preschoolers would be unreliable witnesses: The brain regions that support recall, some argued, were late to develop. In the 1980s, expectations for children's ability to recall the past were so modest that it was noteworthy when a 3-year-old gave accurate information about her abduction and attempted murder (Jones & Krugman, 1986).

Since the late 1980s, research on infant and toddler memory has clarified how basic memory architecture develops. It is now accepted that the capacity to recall an ordered sequence of events after several weeks begins to emerge around 9 months of age, with rapid articulation of brain networks that support event recall occurring during the second year of life (Bauer, Wenner, Dropik, & Wewerka, 2000; Bauer, Wiebe, Carver, Waters, & Nelson, 2003; Bauer, Wiebe, Waters, & Bangston, 2001). Consequently, the lower limit on when children can provide meaningful testimony is determined more by their linguistic repertoire and their willingness to talk than by fundamental limitations of their memory systems.

Although the functional capacities that support event memories emerge early in development, dramatic changes occur in the quality of event reports during the preschool and early elementary school years. Unqualified conclusions are impossible, however, because the quantity and quality of information from witnesses is influenced by the methods interviewers use to elicit reports. For this reason, it is necessary to discuss children's responses to open-ended questions separately from their responses to specific questions.

Age Trends in Event Recall: Responses to Open-Ended Questions

Investigators have studied children's memories for experienced events in a number of ways. Typically, interviewers ask children to reenact sequences of actions or to answer open-ended questions about staged events, naturally occurring but pleasurable events (e.g., family outings or school activities), or various types of unpleasant events (e.g., pediatric checkups, traumatic injuries, painful medical procedures). Results have been strikingly similar despite the range of procedures and the diverse nature of these target events.

First, although children as young as 2 years often talk about the past, younger children are less likely than older children to provide information about specific events selected by the interviewer. For example, Fivush and Shukat (1995) summarized reports from children who were interviewed about events (e.g., zoo and amusement park trips) when they were 3 years, 4 months of age and again at 3 years, 10 months. Children who had something to say gave remarkably coherent and informative narratives, as illustrated by the following transcript from a 3-year-old:

> (Unintelligible) in downtown. It was in winter. There were all sorts of things going. And first they had wheels! And an old car that they used in the olden days . . . Clowns with all different colors of hair . . . They gave me little bags. You could put anything you like in those bags. (p. 15)

The existence of coherent narratives should not be misconstrued to mean that young children *usually* talk about experienced events, however. In Fivush and Shukat's study (1995), only about half of the children who were asked to recall a previously recounted event recalled any information at all. One reason for this finding is that young children forget rapidly, which many memory studies have documented (Brainerd, Reyna, Howe, & Kingma, 1990; Howe, 1991). But forgetting does not tell the whole story; age trends in volunteering information are sometimes as pronounced immediately after events as they are after several months. In our sample study, for example, children were interviewed immediately after participating in four science demonstrations, then again 3 and 4 months later. As shown in Table 5.1, the majority of 3- and 4-year-olds said nothing about the demonstrations when they were prompted by five open-ended questions/invitations only minutes after the experience. (The term *invitations* includes prompts such as, "Tell me everything you can about what you did in the science room.") Both immediately and 3 months later, the 3-year-olds described only about 9% of the science demonstrations, although a noticeable improvement occurred by 4 years. The 3- and 4-year-olds who *did* talk, however, performed similarly to the 5-year-olds, remarking on about 44% and 59% of the demonstrations, respectively. We know that disappointing performance was not due to lack of memories, because the 3- and 4-year-olds described 49% of the events they experienced (but never heard discussed) when interviewers prompted them with specific questions 3 months later.

There are many reasons why children who remember an event might nonetheless say nothing at all about it. Some youngsters are shy about talking to unfamiliar adults, and others avoid discussing topics when they lack the words to describe target objects or events. But two other mechanisms probably contribute to the fact that young witnesses are often disappointing informants. First, young children sometimes fail to grasp the topic of the conversation. In our study, for example, some children talked about unrelated information before realizing what the topic was, even after they had just finished playing in the science room (e.g., Child: "What science room?" Interviewer: "Today when you were playing with Mr. Science." Child: "Played with silly putty.") Another reason for silence is simple retrieval failure, which

TABLE 5.1. Children's Immediate Recall of Four Science Demonstrations

Age (years)	Proportion of children who described no science demonstrations	Mean proportion of science demonstrations described[a]
3	.79	.09
4	.58	.25
5	.17	.51
6	.00	.71
7	.11	.68
8	.00	.74

Note. From transcripts described in Poole and Lindsay (2001).
[a]Means include children who reported no science demonstrations in response to the five open-ended prompts.

is a problem that plagues us throughout our lives. In one study, over one-quarter of the adults interviewed failed to immediately recall an automobile accident that had occurred during the last 12 months, even though the events were serious enough to have injured someone in the car (Cash & Moss, 1972; for other striking examples of retrieval failure, see Loftus, Garry, & Feldman, 1994). Because the brain networks that play an important role in planful activities mature slowly, it is not surprising that children are even less successful than adults at searching for and retrieving specific event memories.

Young children are also less likely than older children to produce long, informative narratives. It is typical for preschoolers to provide little information in response to individual questions, even though they are often willing to say more when interviewers prompt them. In our sample study, the 3-year-olds who started talking in response to the first prompt averaged only 12 units of information (counting utterances such as "the table" or "on the hook" as a single unit of information), whereas 8-year-olds averaged 56 units of information. Nonetheless, as shown in Table 5.2, prompting with additional open-ended invitations yielded more information from all age groups.

Just as it is common for children to misread what interviewers want them to talk about at the start of a conversation, it is also common for them to drift off topic—especially when interviewers fail to remind them of the topic. Children are notoriously bad at keeping an idea, rule, or instruction in mind, and this is true even when they have been successfully sharing relevant information for several minutes or more. In our study, we looked for children who strayed off topic during initial rapport building or during a final open-ended invitation that did not specifically mention the science demonstrations ("Think about what you told me. Is there something you didn't tell me that you can tell me now?"). Regarding the final invitation, many children erroneously assumed that this prompt was unrelated to the events they had discussed in response to four previous prompts. As shown in Table 5.3, over half of the 3-

TABLE 5.2. Proportion of Children Who Reported Any New Accurate Information in Response to Each Open-Ended Prompt

Prompt	Age (years)					
	3	4	5	6	7	8
1. *Tell*	.21	.58	.83	1.00	.89	.96
2. *More*	.26	.26	.44	.50	.72	.73
3. *Looked* or *heard*	.37	.37	.78	.78	.78	.82
4. *Heard* or *looked*	.26	.53	.56	.83	.67	.96
5. *Think*	.11	.11	.22	.22	.28	.27

Note. From the supplementary report for Poole and Lindsay (2001). Interviewers asked children to *tell* what happened in the science room, tell *more*, tell how everything *looked*, tell everything they *heard* (with the order of the *looked* and *heard* prompts counterbalanced), and *think* about what they had already said and tell if there was something they had not said that they could say now.

TABLE 5.3. Children's Tendency to Stray Off Topic during Open-Ended Questioning in Three Interviews

Age (years)	Proportion of children who were off topic during any rapport-building session	Proportion of children who were off topic during any final open-ended prompt	Mean proportion of details that were intrusion errors		
			Immediately after the events	3 months after the events	4 months after the events
3	.37	.53	.10	.05	.00
4	.47	.32	.02	.00	.01
5	.22	.22	.05	.00	.01
6	.11	.17	.00	.00	.00
7	.22	.11	.00	.00	.00
8	.14	.05	.00	.00	.00

Note. From transcripts and data described in Poole and Lindsay (2001).

year-olds drifted off topic at least once during the three interviews, compared to only 5% of the 8-year-olds. Moreover, many of their off-topic comments would have confused interviewers who did not know what actually had transpired (e.g., "Yes, my dad, my daddy eat food" from a child whose father was not present during the target events).

How accurate are children's free-recall narratives? Does accuracy decline when interviewers continue to prompt for more information? In our sample study, information was coded as a "detail" error if it misrepresented a target event, and an "intrusion" error if it was off-topic information that was potentially confusing (i.e., information that would not be recognized as off topic by someone who did not know what actually had happened). Regardless of age, very little information provided by the children in response to open-ended questions was coded as a detail error. Errors that did occur were mostly minor confusions, such as calling a *tomato* a *potato* or misreporting the order of events. Under our interviewing conditions (i.e., the target events actually occurred and responses were elicited with open-ended prompts), only 1–2% of the information provided by 3- to 8-years-olds was inaccurate, even 3 and 4 months after the events. Errors due to potentially confusing off-topic conversation also constituted a small proportion of the total information provided, especially as the children became accustomed to being interviewed. By the third interview, for example, only 4- and 5-year-olds reported any potentially confusing off-topic remarks, and these comments accounted for only 1% of their total information (see Table 5.3). Moreover, there was no evidence that children's accuracy declined across five open-ended prompts. These data suggest that there is little danger from encouraging children to talk as long as interviewers use nonsuggestive prompts, even with long delays between target events and interviews.

Because free-recall accuracy is generally high (with error rates typically ranging from 1–7%; e.g., Gee & Pipe, 1995; Rudy & Goodman, 1991), many professionals believe they can take children's event descriptions at face value. Close reading of the transcripts from our study reveals that this strategy would be a mistake, however, because many of the children's errors could throw an investigation off course. For example, one child said that he was told to keep the events secret (although Mr. Science said no such thing), and some children substituted what was familiar to them for what they actually saw. The following example, from an enthusiastic 8-year-old boy, illustrates why it is naive to assume that children who report many details must be reliable informants:

> "Oh sure, it was, the tops were round, they were kind of like miniature tops, cheap kind, like plastic, the cheapest kind, I mean, they were plastic. If you split one in half it would look like an arrow with background, and then there was like a cardboard-like design—cardboard, that was part of the top that I was most interested in that had like a swirly design that would cover up part of the plastic. The bowl was shiny. It was silverish-grey. There was kind of like a green portable wall. And there was, the lights were kind of like in the ceiling, there was kind of like panels—I mean, tall tiles and a rectangle. And there was kind of like a checkered pattern of lights and tiles like certain rows where there were much more regular tiles, so the tiles in the room where, in the ceiling were 25% or a quarter of them were lights and 75% or three-quarters were regular tiles, Styrofoam or cardboard. The closet was kind of like beige, pale beige, and it had a white knob. The side of the wall where there was a window there was cinderblock painted white or whitewash. And then there was also plaster walls on the other areas."

This boy was a very good witness, with one exception: The room the events occurred in did not have cinderblock walls or the "drop ceiling" that is often found in elementary school classrooms. Apparently, this child's preconception of how a commercial building looks intruded into his narrative about our "school" building. In a criminal trial, description errors such as these could be used to argue that the prosecution misplaced the location of the crime. For this reason, forensic interviewers are trained not to press children for unnecessary descriptions that could be used to discredit them.

Robyn Fivush and her associates identified another feature of event narratives that might lead adults to question the reliability of children's reports: Children who discuss an event on several occasions often talk about different information during each interview. In one study, for example, only 20% of the information 2-year-olds reported during interviews conducted 6 weeks apart was repeated information (Fivush, Hamond, Harsch, Singer, & Wolf, 1991). Similarly, in a study of children who recalled events when they were between 3 and 5 years of age, less than 10% of the information from any two interviews overlapped (Fivush & Shukat, 1995).

In sum, detailed analyses of interview transcripts paint a clear picture of what adults can expect when they ask children to recall experienced events under optimal conditions—that is, when reports have not been contaminated by suggestive information and interviewers elicit information with open-ended questions:

- It is not uncommon for the majority of 3- to 4-year-olds to say nothing about target events, even immediately after those events have occurred. However, the proportion of children who provide useful information increases with age.
- During the preschool years, there is a large increase in the amount of information children volunteer, and children of all ages benefit from repeated prompting with open-ended questions/invitations.
- Younger children have more difficulty than older children staying on topic, so a higher proportion of the information they report is confusing, off-topic information. However, even elementary school children sometimes drift off topic when interviewers ask questions that do not explicitly mention the topic of the conversation.
- Children of all ages have approximately the same low rate of detail errors (1–7% of their total information), and there is no evidence that this rate increases across a series of nonsuggestive prompts. Nonetheless, it is not uncommon for transcripts to contain errors that might mislead investigators.
- Event reports that are elicited on multiple occasions often contain little overlapping information, especially when the witnesses are preschoolers.

These findings are valuable evidence that counteracts the tendency to infer complicated emotional or social reasons for verbal behavior that is developmentally normative. For example, we have heard adults say that a child's reticence is clear evidence of trauma, that the lack of detail in a 5-year-old's narrative is evidence he was coached to report fictitious events, and that a child who strayed off topic must have been evasive due to embarrassment. In fact, all of these observations describe how some children act when adults ask them to report engaging, enjoyable activities.

Age Trends in Event Recall: Responses to Specific Questions

Children's accuracy declines markedly when interviewers move from open-ended prompts to specific questions. It is common to code accuracy separately for two types of questions: *wh*-questions (e.g., "Who was with you?") and yes/no-format questions (e.g., "Did Mr. Science push your tummy?"). Although children sometimes answer these types of questions accurately (depending on their ages, the nature of the event, and the information they are asked to report), it is typical for accuracy to decline somewhat for specific questions and dramatically for yes/no questions. Moreover, this generalization holds even when children are talking about highly meaningful events. For example, a quarter of the preschool children interviewed about an emergency room visit could not accurately describe the person who first responded to their injury, when interviewers questioned them about these experiences only days later (Peterson, 1996). Young children are especially poor at providing information about specific details. For example, a quarter of the information provided in response to specific questions by children who were 26–34 months of age at the time of the events was wrong in one study, and their performance on yes/no questions was not above chance (Peterson & Rideout, 1998). Difficulty responding to specific questions is not restricted to very young children, however. For example, in another study 6-year-olds were correct only 64% of the time in response to unbiased questions about a pair of videos (Roebers & Schneider, 2002; for a review of children's long-term autobiographical recall, see Peterson, 2002).

Why does accuracy decline so sharply when interviewers shift to specific questions? One reason is that specific questions are more likely than general prompts to ask children about details they never encoded to begin with or have already forgotten. It is risky to assume that specific questions are safe for "central" details, however, because adults' opinions about what information is central do not always predict differences in children's accuracy across questions (Brady, Poole, Warren, & Jones, 1999). Another reason for poor accuracy is that children sometimes respond to questions they do not understand or cannot factually answer in an effort to be cooperative conversational partners (Waterman, Blades, & Spencer, 2001).

Are children unreliable witnesses when interviewers ask specific questions about the gist of salient events? The answer depends on the children's experiences and the nature of the questions. In our study, interviewers asked children a series of yes/no questions 3 months after they had participated in the science demonstrations. Among other questions, each child responded to two questions about experienced demonstrations that were not discussed afterward, two questions about novel science demonstrations (not experienced or suggested), and one question about a novel event involving touching by "Mr. Science." As shown in Table 5.4, the younger children denied the experienced events more often than the older children did, but they falsely assented to more questions about novel science demonstrations. Errors rates were low at all ages for questions about novel touching events, probably because these questions conflicted with the gist of what *was* experienced. When interviewers repeated the questions a month later, however, false assents to touching events increased, possibly because the gist of these events was now familiar due to earlier questioning. Thus, children are sometimes highly accurate (i.e., when the questions concern distinctive events that deviate from what they expect to discuss), but they can also be susceptible to effects of repeated interviewing.

TABLE 5.4. Mean Proportion of "Yes" Responses to Direct Questions about Nonsuggested Events after a 3-Month Delay

Age (years)	Event condition		
	Experienced science demonstrations	Novel science demonstrations	Novel touching events
3	.58	.21	.00
4	.84	.26	.16
5	.67	.11	.00
6	.83	.14	.00
7	.81	.06	.00
8	.93	.09	.00

Note. From data described in Poole and Lindsay (2001).

Children's Memory for Repeated Events

Research on children's memory for repeated events is motivated by two features that are common to investigations of child sexual abuse. First, a substantial number of abused children suffer repeated victimization. Second, prosecutors who wish to file multiple charges are often required to extricate the circumstances of each allegation they make, by providing evidence that sufficiently reflects the critical details of those charges. In some jurisdictions, this stipulation is known as "particularization" (Pearse, Powell, & Thomson, 2003). Because child sexual abuse is a secretive crime—often leaving little, if any, physical evidence—justice may hinge on a child's ability to provide accurate details about multiple abuse experiences. Concern over children's abilities to discriminate between such memories has launched a small but growing line of research aimed at mapping (and improving) children's ability to recall information from repeated events. (For a review, see Roberts, 2002.)

Past research has found that when events are highly similar, children (and adults) develop general event representations, or scripts, for those events (Farrar & Boyer-Pennington, 1999). Because scripts provide an efficient way of organizing and retrieving information common to event episodes, memory is strengthened when events are highly similar to one another (e.g., Hudson, Fivush, & Kuebli, 1992). However, source-monitoring errors may occur when children attempt to recall information that is inconsistent with the script for a given event. Under these conditions, children tend to recall information from similar events as having occurred in the episode in question (Roberts & Blades, 2000). Unfortunately, abused children are likely to experience recurring transgressions that are similar in nature (e.g., the events involved fondling) but different in contextual detail (e.g., the location of particular fondling events varied). When events are experienced once, or when repeated events contain details that are consistent across episodes, children only need to recall the "content" details of those events (e.g., *what* happened). However, when repeated events contain details that are inconsistent across episodes, children must also make "temporal-source" discriminations among event details (e.g., *when* it happened). The standard paradigm used to capture this dynamic exposes children to a series of similar events containing fixed details that remain constant across episodes (e.g., children read the same story each time) and/or variable details that differ across episodes (e.g., children read a different story each time) (Connolly & Lindsay, 2002; Powell & Roberts, 2002; Powell & Thomson, 1996; Powell, Roberts, Ceci, & Hembrooke, 1999).

Consistent with previous research on children's memory and source-monitoring capabilities (see Ceci & Bruck, 1995; Roberts & Blades, 2000), memory for repeated events generally improves as children grow older but declines with the passage of time for all age groups. In addition to standard effects of age and delay, research has produced several reliable findings. Most significant is that exposure to recurring events is a double-edged sword, capable of augmenting or abating memory depending on the degree of similarity among those events. As mentioned, when similar events are repeatedly experienced, children display greater recall for details that are consistent (i.e., fixed) across events, compared to details experienced once or to a lesser extent. However, when repeated events contain inconsistent (i.e., variable) details, children's ability to recall those details and match them to the respective episode is relatively poor (e.g., Connolly & Lindsay, 2001; McNichol, Shute, & Tucker, 1999; Powell et al., 1999; Powell & Thomson, 1996).

The most common errors made when children discuss repeated events are internal intrusion errors; that is, they tend to recall details from nontarget episodes when questioned about the target event. However, children exposed to repeated events make fewer external intrusion errors, meaning they are less likely to import non-event-related information into their reports. As discussed previously, this pattern of recall errors is attributed to the cognitive demands inherent in recalling details from events experienced once versus multiple times (Roberts & Powell, 2001). To illustrate, suppose an investigator wanted to know what color shirt a perpetrator was wearing when a child was molested. To provide this information, a child molested on a single occasion would have to merely recall the shirt color, whereas the child molested multiple times would have to further discriminate shirt colors from multiple abuse episodes. Thus, describing a single event requires children to recall details of that event, whereas describing one episode from a series of events further demands that children make source discriminations among similar details.

In sum, children's memory for repeated events is generally better when details are consistent rather than inconsistent across event episodes. In the latter case, children tend to make source confusions among inter-event details and consequently report nontarget details as having occurred in the target event.

CHILDREN'S SUGGESTIBILITY

Intense interest in children's suggestibility has been matched by a proliferation of review articles on the topic. We now know that a variety of influences can contaminate children's testimonies, including false information and negative stereotypes conveyed outside the interviewing context, misleading questions during interviews, social reinforcement for particular types of answers, and instructions to visualize or speculate about nonexperienced events. Rates of false reports generally increase as the strength and number of suggestibility manipulations increases, so that higher rates of false reports are found when multiple techniques are imposed across a number of sessions (e.g., Bruck & Ceci, 1999; Bruck, Ceci, & Hembrooke, 2002; Ceci, Loftus, Leichtman, & Bruck, 1994; Poole & Lindsay, 1998).

Here we focus on conclusions we have read or heard that *cannot* be justified by the weight of current evidence. Specifically, children's answers to open-ended questions do not support the assumption that information reported in free recall is highly accurate, that older children are always more resistant to suggestion than younger children, that suggestibility procedures must be intense to produce high degrees of false information, or that touching experiences enjoy special resistance to suggestion. Moreover, analyses of responses to specific questions have challenged the assumption that adults can judge which events occurred by looking at structural features of children's narratives.

Age Trends in Suggestibility: Reports Elicited with Open-Ended Questions

The recent wave of interest in children's suggestibility emerged from high-profile day-care cases in which interviewers elicited abuse disclosures by using highly suggestive techniques. (For descriptions of these techniques and their consequences, see Garven, Wood, & Malpass, 2000; Garven, Wood, Malpass, & Shaw, 1998.) The research that followed produced many positive changes, including improved understanding of how interviewers can elicit accurate event reports and the consolidation of findings into interviewing protocols (e.g., Orbach, Hershkowitz, Lamb, Esplin, & Horowitz, 2000; Poole & Lamb, 1998; State of Michigan Governor's Task Force on Children's Justice and Family Independence Agency, 1998).

One downside to the emphasis on interviewing techniques is a false confidence that good interviewing reliably elicits accurate reports. In fact, it does not take suggestive interviewing to elicit false information when children's reports have already been contaminated by information presented outside the interview setting or by prior interviews. Our study is a case in point. Three months after participating in the science demonstrations, each family received a small book that described two science demonstrations the child had experienced, two suggested science demonstrations, and a suggestion about bodily touch. After a parent had read the book three times, research assistants established rapport with the child and explained the ground rules (e.g., "Don't guess or make anything up—just tell me what you saw or heard or did the time you played in the science room with Mr. Science") before delivering the same open-ended prompts the child had answered 3 months earlier.

To our surprise, (1) many children reported nonexperienced events in free recall, and (2) there was no tendency for the younger children to report more false information than the older children. (From ages 3 through 8, the proportion of children who reported one or more suggested events was .26, .53, .17, .39, .39, and .36, respectively.) The figures listed in Table 5.5 show that the children were both highly accurate (when adults had not contaminated their reports) and highly inaccurate (when adults had exposed them to false information). Several points deserve emphasis. First, the suggestibility manipulation in this study was not particularly strong: The misleading book took only 1.5–2 minutes to read, so the entire manipulation took no more than 6 minutes. Moreover, the children were not told that the fictitious events actually took place (i.e., these events were merely described in the book). Second, the children reported comparable rates of false events regardless of whether or not the events involved touching, demonstrating that touching events are not always especially salient or distinctive. Finally, a procedure at the end of the interview to determine whether children would report the source of their knowledge proved that the older children often knew that the suggested events had not actually happened. Still, even 8-year-old children often reported any information they knew in response to open-ended questions, regardless of its source. This lack of an age trend in the reporting of false information in free recall reflects the fact that older children are more motivated than younger

TABLE 5.5. Mean Proportion of Nonexperienced Events Reported in Response to Open-Ended Prompts after a 3-Month Delay

Age (years)	Event condition			
	Suggested science demonstration	Novel science demonstration	Suggested touching event	Novel touching event
3	.16	.00	.11	.00
4	.29	.00	.32	.00
5	.08	.00	.00	.00
6	.19	.00	.11	.00
7	.17	.00	.28	.00
8	.18	.00	.09	.00

Note. From data described in Poole and Lindsay (2001).

children to impress interviewers, and they are better at describing what they know. In fact, flat or reversed age trends often appear when older participants have skills and knowledge that foster false reports. For example, adults in one study were more likely than children to speculate about the occupation of a research assistant, largely because they had knowledge that allowed them to make a reasonable guess (Poole & White, 1991).

Age Trends in Suggestibility: Reports Elicited with Specific Questions

Suggestibility is more pronounced when interviewers ask specific questions. For example, it is amazingly easy to elicit false information with yes/no questions, even when children are 7 or 8 years old. In our study, 3- and 4-year-olds had the highest rate of erroneous "yes" responses to questions that referred to suggested science demonstrations (63%), but the 7- and 8-year-olds also erred on many of these questions (35%). Furthermore, rates were not dramatically different across age groups for questions about suggested touching (40% and 35%, respectively).

One of our most surprising findings reflected what occurred when interviewers prompted children to describe events, regardless of whether they had answered "yes" or "no." (In the case of "no" responses, interviewers asked questions such as, "Can you tell me about the machine?") As Table 5.6 reports, many children provided narratives after "yes" responses, but many also provided narratives after "no" responses. Poole and Lindsay (2001) computed how accurate investigators would be if they based decisions on "yes" or "no" responses only, then compared that value to what decision accuracy would be if investigators ignored initial answers and assumed that events occurred only if children described them. Counter to what many professionals might predict, initial yes/no responses discriminated between true and false events better than the presence of narrative descriptions.

A recent study by Principe and Ceci (2002) drives home the message that (1) subtle influences outside interview settings can contaminate children's reports, even when reports are elicited with open-ended questions; and (2) suggestive questioning dramatically increases the rate of false reporting. These investigators arranged for preschoolers to witness one of three archeological digs: one group witnessed two target events (ruining a treasure map or breaking a rock with a secret message); one group consisted of classmates of the children who witnessed the target events; and one group did not experience the target events or share a classroom with children who had. During three subsequent sessions, interviewers asked neutral or suggestive questions (e.g., "What did Dr. Diggs spill on the treasure map? Did he [she] spill a cup of coffee or a cup of juice?"). A final interview tracked the infiltration of target events into responses to open-ended, specific, and source-monitoring questions. Astoundingly, children who were merely exposed to informed classmates falsely reported an average of 16% of the target events in response to

TABLE 5.6. Proportion of Children Who Provided Narrative Information after "No"and "Yes" Responses 3 Months after the Events

Age (years)	No		Yes	
	N	Proportion narrative	N	Proportion narrative
Experienced science demonstrations				
3–4	22	.14	54	.63
5–6	18	.22	54	.93
7–8	10	.20	70	.90
Experienced science demonstrations also described in the book				
3–4	10	.00	66	.70
5–6	0	—	72	.89
7–8	4	.50	76	.92
Suggested science demonstrations				
3–4	28	.14	48	.58
5–6	35	.31	37	.89
7–8	52	.13	28	.89
Novel science demonstrations				
3–4	58	.19	18	.28
5–6	63	.16	9	.78
7–8	74	.05	6	1.00
Suggested touching events				
3–4	23	.43	15	.73
5–6	23	.22	13	.92
7–8	26	.19	14	.93
Novel touching events				
3–4	35	.11	3	1.00
5–6	36	.17	0	—
7–8	40	.03	0	—

Note. From the supplementary report for Poole and Lindsay (2001). *N* refers to the number of questions answered "no" or "yes."

open-ended questions, and that figure jumped to 50% for children who had a history of suggestive interviewing. After specific questioning, those averages jumped to 31% and 86%, respectively. Importantly, children exposed to informed classmates and suggestive interviewing reported as many target events as those who had actually experienced the events.[2]

The difficulty of ferreting out who did and did not experience an event is illustrated by fine-grain analyses of the narrative length and structure of true and false reports. In our sample study, children who reported a false event from the misleading book produced descriptions that were as long as those from children who actually experienced the events. In Principe and Ceci's (2002) study, suggested events generated *more* elaborate narratives than actual events did. Similarly, in a thorough analysis of true and false narratives,

Bruck et al. (2002) found that children's narratives for false events contained more details, more spontaneous utterances, and more markers of narrative coherence, temporal markers, and elaborations than true narratives did.

Children's Memory for Repeated Events

Studies of the effects of misinformation on reports of repeated events also illustrate how difficult it is to summarize patterns of eyewitness accuracy without making numerous qualifications. In a study by Connolly and Lindsay (2001), children took part in an event one or four times (containing fixed and variable details) and then answered yes/no recognition questions about final-event details that probed for suggested and true information. Four days after the first/last event, participants were interviewed about final-event details with misleading (e.g., "Was the wand silver?" when it was actually yellow) and non-misleading questions. Relative to children in the single-event condition, children who took part in repeated events made fewer errors regarding fixed details but more errors regarding variable details. In other words, repeated experience both decreased and increased susceptibility, depending on the degree of detail stability across the repeated events.

Using a similar design, Powell et al. (1999) also found that suggestibility was reduced for fixed details of repeated events. However, unlike Connolly and Lindsay's (2001) results, error rates were not higher for variable details than for details that were experienced in only a single event. Powell and Roberts (2002) argued that this discrepancy could be attributed to question format: Connolly and Lindsay (2001) used yes/no recognition questions to elicit information (which promotes answering without initiating a comprehensive memory search), whereas Powell et al. (1999) used cued recall. To address the discrepancy, Powell and Roberts (2002) replicated the study by Powell et al. (1999) but included question format (cued recall vs. yes/no recognition) as a between-subjects factor. Their central finding was that, after exposure to misinformation, children exposed to repeated events made more errors regarding variable details compared to children exposed to a single event, but only when they were responding to yes/no questions. When interviewers asked cued-recall questions, the pattern of recall errors for variable details was similar to that reported by Powell et al. (1999). In short, the collective results of these studies illustrate why conclusions about susceptibility to suggestion cannot go unqualified.

CHILDREN'S TESTIMONIES AND COGNITIVE DEVELOPMENT

Suggestibility research has increasingly focused on two questions: What can interviewers do to improve children's accuracy (besides relying on open-ended questions)? Can the cognitive maturity of individual children help decision makers judge the reliability of their testimonies?

Unfortunately, the standards experimenters use to judge the success of a procedure are different than the standards investigators need to use. For example, researchers sometimes report that "do not guess" instructions significantly improve children's accuracy; this finding elucidates our understanding of the age at which children begin to monitor and edit their reports. However, imagine a case in which instructions reduce guessing from 40% of unanswerable questions to 30%. If these results generalized to front-line interviews, investigators would still need to be highly doubtful about answers to specific questions, even from children who received instructions not to guess. In the field, the issue is not whether an interviewing innovation or marker of reliability is significant statistically but, rather, whether it is sufficiently powerful to alter how professionals evaluate evidence.

Researchers who search for powerful techniques to quell false reports are faced with an enormous challenge: the realities of cognitive development. Four principles help explain why data on children's testimony that is theoretically exciting may nonetheless have limited value for practitioners who evaluate complicated cases (i.e., cases involving numerous interviews, possible exposure to misinformation, and conflicting or questionable details). After addressing each principle in turn, we discuss the collective implications of all four for cases involving child witnesses.

Children Have Difficulty Using Rules to Guide Their Behavior

One set of interviewing strategies involves instructions that motivate children to report completely and accurately. For example, forensic interviewers deliver ground rules to inform children that it is appropriate to say "I don't know" rather than to guess, to ask the interviewer to clarify questions, and to correct the interviewer if he or she says something that is incorrect (Poole & Lamb, 1998). These instructions are intended to ameliorate the fact that young children rarely say "I don't know" or correct interviewers who distort what they say (Roberts & Lamb, 1999). However, these efforts might have limited value with young children who have difficulty using rules to direct their behavior.

In a compelling demonstration of this problem, Zelazo and Reznick (1991) taught children (from 31 to 37 months of age) to sort picture cards into two categories, such as "tools—something you work with" versus "clothes—something you wear." For the "sorting" task, assistants first named each item (e.g., "This is a saw—where does it go?") before encouraging the child to place the card in one of two bins that had clearly visible examples of the categories. For the "knowledge" task, assistants named each card before asking an explicit category question (e.g., "Is this something you work with or something you can wear?"). Although the children knew the correct categories, many were incapable of using rules to guide their sorting behavior, and performance was no better when assistants frequently reminded them of the rule.

One reason children fail to follow rules is that they have difficulty with behavioral inhibition; that is, difficulty blocking a strong or desirable response in order to substitute another response. Interesting cognitive implications come with the fact that brain areas responsible for inhibitory processes show a protracted period of development. For example, young children have more difficulty than older children keeping task-irrelevant information out of working memory, so their recall protocols tend to include more intrusions. Moreover, elementary school children tend to report intrusions that are related to target material, whereas the intrusions of kindergarten children are often unrelated to the task (Bjorklund & Harnishfeger, 1995).

How much do child witnesses benefit from ground rules that instruct them to inhibit their tendency to answer every question? In their review, Poole and Lamb (1998) found that "I don't know" instructions had neither large nor uniformly positive results. In general, studies that have found benefits tested children over 6 years of age, whereas studies involving younger children generally have proven more disappointing (see also Geddie, Beer, Bartosik, & Wuensch, 2001). Furthermore, studies that successfully improved preschoolers' accuracy via discussion of ground rules tended either to have short interviews with target questions that contained explicitly false information (Mulder & Vrij, 1996) or instructions that were inappropriate for forensic interviews. For example, Nesbitt and Markham (1999) successfully increased the number of "I don't know" responses volunteered by 4-year-olds, but they trained them with a scenario in which an error could "put the wrong person in jail" and transferred training to the target interview using examples from the target event. Even with these explicit instructions, the proportion of correct responses to yes/no recognition questions was only 61% for trained children versus 58% for untrained children.

Studies of rule use and inhibition help explain why interviewing interventions that require children to maintain instructional sets may not dramatically improve reporting accuracy. Relying on children to edit their reports is likely to be least effective when children are young or when interviews are so long that children lose sight of initial instructions.

Children Often Perform Poorly When Instructions Are Abstract and Not Explicitly Connected to the Task

Cases involving children often hinge on whether young witnesses actually experienced alleged events or whether reports stemmed from other sources (e.g., misinformation from a parent or peer). Consequently, there has been a great deal of interest in discovering innovations that improve children's source-monitoring ability. Studies in our laboratory (Poole & Lindsay, 2001, 2002) suggest optimism or despair, depending on the cognitive demands placed on children. In the sample study, children recalled the content of the misleading story, received practice saying "no" when appropriate, and were told that some events mentioned in the story might not have happened. Finally, interviewers asked if each of 10 events in the study design had really happened.

With these explicit instructions, 7- and 8-year-olds rejected an average of 65% of the false touching events they had previously reported in response to direct questioning. In contrast, the 3- and 4-year-olds were incapable of making source discriminations: They continued to affirm 100% of their previous errors. The 5- and 6-year-olds constituted an intermediate group that rejected 56% of their previous false reports.

Results from a second study were less encouraging (Poole & Lindsay, 2002). Because interviewers would be accused of suggestive tactics if they mentioned possible alternative sources, the goal of this project was to test whether source-monitoring training that was unrelated to target events would generalize to discussions about target events. Two findings deserve emphasis. First, only the 7- and 8-year-olds benefited from training that gave them practice reporting only experienced events. Second, 7- and 8-year-olds who were interviewed once *before* training rejected few of their false reports when interviewers asked them to reconsider previous responses.

Coupled with other studies that have tested the efficacy of instructions to improve accuracy, these studies illustrate that success with one training procedure does not necessarily generalize to other training procedures. Even children as young as 5 or 6 years of age sometimes benefit from explicit instructions that do not tax their ability to maintain attention, but often fail to benefit from abstract instructions that require them to generalize training to new situations. Furthermore, even older children may not benefit from accuracy instructions if they experienced a prior interview, perhaps because they then answer based on prior responses rather than approaching the task with a new "mind set." Other laboratories that have successfully trained young children to monitor the source of their memories have done so within these parameters; that is, (1) source-monitoring training and target items were drawn from the same target events, (2) consistent question types were used for training and testing, and (3) there were no intermediate interviews (e.g., Thierry & Spence, 2002). Because actual investigative interviews often fail to reproduce such optimal conditions, the advantage of source-monitoring training in the field could be much less than has been documented in experimental settings.

Children Display Mental Abilities before They Acquire the Ability to Reflect upon Their Mental Processes

Another line of source-monitoring research reveals a third developmental principle. Robinson and Whitcombe (2003) tested whether preschoolers would rely on their own knowledge or an experimenter's knowledge to answer a question. On some trials, the child was the better informed of the two (e.g., could see the color of a toy), whereas on other trials the experimenter was better informed. The children tended to base their decisions on information from the better-informed source (i.e., implicit source monitoring) but had difficulty reporting what information they had used to make their decisions (i.e., explicit source monitoring). Studies such as this one document that children often reveal competence in tasks that do not require them to actively reflect on their knowledge before they are competent in tasks that require more explicit processes. As Robinson (2000, pp. 72–73) summarized, "Children may be able to monitor sources when the decision processes are automatic and require no effortful reflection but may nevertheless have difficulty when they are required to engage in more deliberate and strategic decision making."

Children's limited ability to reflect on the process of witnessing and testifying is also illustrated by a recent study of metasuggestibility. London, Bruck, and Poole (2003) showed a videotape to 6- to 9-year-old children in which an adult encouraged a boy to say that a fireman had hit him. Despite the fact that the children had excellent recall for the facts of the video, only 16% of the 6-year-olds and 63% of the 9-year-olds gave responses that mentioned adult influence, when interviewers asked them why the boy had changed his mind. Along with other studies that show that children have difficulty articulating their own or other people's mental processes, this study suggests that efforts to question child witnesses about why their stories changed might be unsatisfying.

Children's Performance Is Highly Variable, So It Is Difficult to Judge Which Children Are Reliable Witnesses

How can decision makers decide which children are mature enough to say "I don't know," to resist the tendency to answer yes/no questions in the absence of knowledge, and to accurately answer source-monitoring questions? One approach is to look at how they respond to similar questions about other events. It makes intuitive sense that children who decline to answer unanswerable questions, or resist the lead of an interviewer, might be more accurate informants than children who fail these "suggestibility check" questions. Is this approach fruitful?

The answer, unfortunately, is "probably not." In a study of 3- to 7-year-olds, for example, Brady et al. (1999) tried to predict accuracy on yes/no questions by examining how children performed on three tasks: two suggestibility check questions (i.e., whether they ventured a guess when asked the name of the interviewer's dog, and whether they went along with a misleading question about a pair of dog pictures) and consistency across two repetitions of yes/no questions about a videotaped interaction. Even though many children erred on the suggestibility check questions (e.g., 36% falsely agreed that the smaller dog was bigger), age was a better predictor of accuracy on a target question about the videotape. Furthermore, there was no significant correlation between consistency and accuracy. Brady et al. concluded (p. 55):

> Children err on questions for a variety of reasons, and those who err on one type of question may not err on another type. For example, many older children in our sample acquiesced to the misleading suggestibility question,

"This is the biggest dog, isn't it?", yet this group was very accurate on a simple yes-no question about the central theme of the video. For these children, responses to explicitly misleading questions would underestimate their ability to answer accurately about a recent event they had experienced. Similarly, many younger children resisted suggestion, yet nonetheless were inaccurate on many questions about the target, most likely due to poorer memories or poorer memory monitoring during questioning. Clearly, arguments about a specific child's deficiencies must be linked to data that target specific social or cognitive processes. Although it is not practical (or justified by the data) to argue that yes-no questions should be prohibited, factors outside the interview environment—such as witness age, event recency and intensity, and the presence of corroborating evidence—will remain important considerations whenever forensic information from young children hinges predominantly on their responses to yes-no questions.

Brady et al.'s (1999) data are not atypical. Instead, counterintuitive results are common in studies of children's eyewitness testimony. For example, when Ridley, Clifford, and Keogh (2002) misled 9- and 10-year-olds about a videotaped car accident, they found no relationship between children's accuracy on non-misled items and suggestibility. Even more surprising, path analyses from our sample project revealed *positive* path coefficients between the amount of information recalled about target events and suggestibility. To try to make sense of this finding, consider the fact that children who remembered a lot about the target events probably also remembered a lot about the misleading story. Because the story added events to memory (rather than substituting details), the trace strength of individual experienced events did not predict reduced intrusions from the story.[3]

Unfortunately, researchers have not fared better by considering an array of individual difference variables. In many studies, relationships that do emerge between various characteristics and suggestibility are weak or have no practical value in forensic settings (for reviews, see Pipe & Salmon, 2002; Quas, Qin, Schaaf, & Goodman, 1997). Often, individual difference variables simply fail to predict the quality of children's testimony. As one research team recently noted, "None of the individual-difference variables examined would allow us, with any confidence, to make predictions about the individual child in terms of his or her reliability or accuracy" (Pipe & Salmon, 2002, p. 255).

IMPLICATIONS FOR CASE ANALYSES AND FUTURE RESEARCH

Cases that cross the desks of child witness researchers fall along a continuum. On one side are those that make it easy to advocate for the accuracy of children's reports. Consider a young preschooler who is the only witness to an accident that injures her father. When adults arrive on the scene immediately afterward, the child's brief but clear description of the incident contains words that are unambiguous and obviously part of her vocabulary, and there is no motivation for anyone to misreport what the child said. On the other side are complicated cases involving adults with multiple and conflicting interests in the child's reports, a long history of possible influences, and a story that has evolved over time to contain implausible information.

Unfortunately, there appears to be no magic bullet for resolving the difficult cases: (1) An open-ended interview may not overcome the damage done by prior suggestive influences; (2) even school-age children sometimes have difficulty distinguishing information from several sources; (3) there are no known markers of reliability in the structure of event narratives that work well enough to remove uncertainty in individual cases; and (4) children often lack the insight to reflect upon and discuss the evolution of their reports. Furthermore, evidence of family conflict, silly talk from children, and details that cannot be corroborated may be present in the transcripts of children who *have* experienced target events as well as the transcripts of children who have not, so sweeping disbelief is not the answer.

Given this state of affairs, do developmental psychologists bring anything to the task of analyzing cases? Yes. They understand how children use language, so they can suggest alternative interpretations of children's reports and point out statements that lend themselves to independent corroboration. They can spot statements that are better ignored because they sound off-topic or were elicited by unintelligible questions. Most importantly, they can shift focus away from a single hypothesis and help set children's reports in a broader temporal and social context. Still, given our current knowledge, children's reports are only one line of evidence in a complicated case, and they may not always be the most important evidence. Therefore, it is as important for researchers to convey the limitations of the knowledge base as it is for them to share what is known.

In a special issue devoted to child testimony, Bruck and Poole (2002) proposed the term "forensic developmental psychology" for the field that applies developmental knowledge to the problems that arise when children intersect with the legal system. Increasingly, it has become apparent that child testimony is not just about language, memory, and social development, but also about cognitive development in the broadest sense. The line between disappointing and excellent performance is thin and often hinges on minor differences in procedures. Seemingly small changes can interfere dramatically with children's ability to coordinate the tasks of maintaining instructional sets, executing memory retrieval, editing memories, and producing the language to respond. (For example, consider the excellent performance of 7- and 8-year-olds in Poole and Lindsay, 2002, when children received source-monitoring training before an interview, but their disappointing performance when they were trained after one interview.) Understanding the boundary conditions for accuracy when children are faced with the types of challenges that exist in complicated cases is one of the remaining frontiers for forensic developmental psychology.

NOTES

1. Interview transcripts, data files, and the supplementary report from this study are archived at the National Data Archive on Child Abuse and Neglect, Cornell University, FLDC-MVR Hall, Ithaca, NY 14853. The study was supported by the National Science Foundation under Grant No. SBR-9409231 to Debra Poole and Stephen Lindsay. Rachel (Johnson) Laimon was an interviewer for this project and a subsequent replication and extension (Poole & Lindsay, 2002); Jason Dickinson and Rachel Laimon were laboratory managers for the 2002 study. Any opinions, findings, and conclusions or recommendations expressed in this material are those of the authors and do not necessarily reflect the views of the National Science Foundation.
2. Principe and Ceci's (2002) results indicated that reports of "control" events (i.e., events that are not experienced and not suggested) might be elevated when experimenters counterbalance events across conditions and test children within the same classroom. Poole and Lindsay (2001) minimized this problem by recruiting children by flyers and newspaper advertisements, restricting participation to one child per family, and testing children from 14 small towns within a 30-mile (48-kilometer) radius.
3. The lack of a relationship between accuracy and suggestibility (or a positive relationship) does not contradict evidence that greater trace strength reduces suggestibility. Accuracy–suggestibility correlations are calculated by aggregating data across details, whereas trace-strength studies manipulate memory strength for specific items and measure suggestibility regarding those individual items.

REFERENCES

Bauer, P. J., Burch, M. M., & Kleinknecht, E. E. (2002). Developments in early recall memory: Normative trends and individual differences. *Advances in Child Development and Behavior, 30,* 103–152.

Bauer, P. J., Wenner, J. A., Dropik, P. L., & Wewerka, S. S. (2000). Parameters of remembering and forgetting in the transition from infancy to early childhood. *Monographs of the Society for Research in Child Development, 65*(4, Serial No. 263).

Bauer, P. J., Wiebe, S. A., Carver, L. J., Waters, J. M., & Nelson, C. A. (2003). Developments in long-term explicit memory late in the first year of life: Behavioral and electrophysiological indices. *Psychological Science, 14,* 629–635.

Bauer, P. J., Wiebe, S. A., Waters, J. M., & Bangston, S. K. (2001). Reexposure breeds recall: Effects of experience on 9-month-olds' ordered recall. *Journal of Experimental Child Psychology, 80,* 174–200.

Bjorklund, D. F., & Harnishfeger, K. K. (1995). The evolution of inhibition mechanisms and their role in human cognition and behavior. In F. N. Dempster & C. J. Brainerd (Eds.), *Interference and inhibition in cognition* (pp. 141–173). New York: Academic Press.

Brady, M. S., Poole, D. A., Warren, A. R., & Jones, H. R. (1999). Young children's responses to yes-no questions: Patterns and problems. *Applied Developmental Science, 3,* 47–57.

Brainerd, C. J., Reyna, V. F., Howe, M. L., & Kingma, J. (1990). The development of forgetting and reminiscence. *Monographs of the Society for Research in Child Development, 55*(3–4, Serial No. 222).

Bruck, M., & Ceci, S. J. (1999). The suggestibility of children's memory. *Annual Review of Psychology, 50,* 419–439.

Bruck, M., Ceci, S. J., & Hembrooke, H. (2002). The nature of children's true and false narratives. *Developmental Review, 22,* 520–554.

Bruck, M., & Poole, D. A. (2002). Introduction to the special issue on forensic developmental psychology. *Developmental Review, 22,* 331–333.

Cash, W. S., & Moss, A. J. (1972, April). *Optimum recall period for reporting persons injured in motor vehicle accidents.* National Center for Health Statistics, Series 2, No. 50. DHEW Publication No. HSM 72-1050. Washington, DC: U.S. Government Printing Office.

Ceci, S. J., & Bruck, M. (1995). *Jeopardy in the courtroom: A scientific analysis of children's testimony.* Washington, DC: American Psychological Association.

Ceci, S. J., Loftus, E. F., Leichtman, M. D., & Bruck, M. (1994). The possible role of source misattributions in the creation of false beliefs among preschoolers. *International Journal of Clinical and Experimental Hypnosis, 42,* 304–320.

Connolly, D. A., & Lindsay, D. S. (2001). The influence of suggestions on children's reports of a unique experience versus an instance of a repeated experience. *Applied Cognitive Psychology, 15,* 205–223.

Farrar, M. J., & Boyer-Pennington, M. E. (1999). Remembering specific episodes of a scripted event. *Journal of Experimental Child Psychology, 73,* 266–288.

Fivush, R., Hamond, N. R., Harsch, M., Singer, N., & Wolf, A. (1991). Content and consistency in young children's autobiographical recall. *Discourse Processes, 14,* 373–388.

Fivush, R., & Shukat, J. R. (1995). Content, consistency, and coherence of early autobiographical recall. In M. S. Zaragoza, J. R. Graham, G. C. N. Hall, R. Hirschman, & Y. S. Ben-Porath (Eds.), *Memory and testimony in the child witness* (pp. 5–23). Thousand Oaks, CA: Sage.

Garven, S., Wood, J. M., & Malpass, R. S. (2000). Allegations of wrongdoing: The effects of reinforcement on children's mundane and fantastic claims. *Journal of Applied Psychology, 85,* 38–49.

Garven, S., Wood, J. M., Malpass, R. S., & Shaw, J. S. III (1998). More than suggestion: The effect of interviewing techniques from the McMartin Preschool case. *Journal of Applied Psychology, 83,* 347–359.

Geddie, L. F., Beer, J., Bartosik, S., & Wuensch, K. L. (2001). The relationship between interview characteristics and accuracy of recall in young children: Do individual differences matter? *Child Maltreatment, 6,* 59–68.

Gee, S., & Pipe, M-E. (1995). Helping children to remember: The influence of object cues on children's accounts of a real event. *Developmental Psychology, 31,* 746–758.

Howe, M. L. (1991). Misleading children's story recall: Forgetting and reminiscence of the facts. *Developmental Psychology, 27,* 746–762.

Hudson, J. A., Fivush, R., & Kuebli, J. (1992). Scripts and episodes: The development of event memory. *Applied Cognitive Psychology, 6,* 483–505.

Jones, D. P., & Krugman, R. D. (1986). Can a three-year-old child bear witness to her sexual assault and attempted murder? *Child Abuse and Neglect, 10,* 253–258.

Loftus, E. F., Garry, M., & Feldman, J. (1994). Forgetting sexual trauma: What does it mean when 38% forget? *Journal of Consulting and Clinical Psychology, 62,* 1177–1181.

London, K., Bruck, M., & Poole, D. A. (2003, August). *Children's causal explanations for false reports induced by interrogative suggestibility.* Paper presented at the annual meeting of the American Psychological Association, Toronto.

McNichol, S., Shute, R., & Tucker, A. (1999). Children's eyewitness memory for a repeated event. *Child Abuse and Neglect, 23,* 1127–1139.

Mulder, M. R., & Vrij, A. (1996). Explaining conversation rules to children: An intervention study to facilitate children's accurate responses. *Child Abuse and Neglect, 20,* 623–631.

Nesbitt, M., & Markham, R. (1999). Improving young children's accuracy of recall for an eyewitness event. *Journal of Applied Developmental Psychology, 20,* 449–459.

Orbach, Y., Hershkowitz, I., Lamb, M. E., Esplin, P. W., & Horowitz, D. (2000). Assessing the value of structured protocols for forensic interviews of alleged child abuse victims. *Child Abuse and Neglect, 24,* 733–752.

Pearse, S. L., Powell, M. B., & Thomson, D. M. (2003). The effect of contextual cues on children's ability to remember an occurrence of a repeated event. *Legal and Criminological Psychology, 8,* 39–50.

Peterson, C. (1996). The preschool child witness: Errors in accounts of traumatic injury. *Canadian Journal of Behavioural Science, 28,* 36–42.

Peterson, C. (2002). Children's long-term memory for autobiographical events. *Developmental Review, 22,* 370–402.

Peterson, C., & Rideout, R. (1998). Memory for medical emergencies by 1- and 2-year-olds. *Developmental Psychology, 34,* 1059–1072.

Piaget, J. (1952). *The origins of intelligence in children.* New York: International Universities Press.

Pipe, M-E., & Salmon, K. (2002). What children bring to the interview context: Individual differences in children's event reports. In M. L. Eisen, J. A. Quas, & G. S. Goodman (Eds.), *Personality and clinical psychology series: Memory and suggestibility in the forensic interview* (pp. 235–261). Mahwah, NJ: Erlbaum.

Poole, D. A., & Lamb, M. E. (1998). *Investigative interviews of children: A guide for helping professionals.* Washington, DC: American Psychological Association.

Poole, D. A., & Lindsay, D. S. (1998). Assessing the accuracy of young children's reports: Lessons from the investigation of child sexual abuse. *Applied and Preventive Psychology, 7,* 1–26.

Poole, D. A., & Lindsay, D. S. (2001). Children's eyewitness reports after exposure to misinformation from parents. *Journal of Experimental Psychology: Applied, 7,* 27–50.

Poole, D. A., & Lindsay, D. S. (2002). Reducing child witnesses' false reports of misinformation from parents. *Journal of Experimental Child Psychology, 81,* 117–140.

Poole, D. A., & White, L. T. (1991). Effects of question repetition on the eyewitness testimony of children and adults. *Developmental Psychology, 27,* 975–986.

Powell, M. B., & Roberts, K. P. (2002). The effect of repeated experience on children's suggestibility across two question types. *Applied Cognitive Psychology, 16,* 367–386.

Powell, M. B., Roberts, K. P., Ceci, S. J., & Hembrooke, H. (1999). The effects of repeated experience on children's suggestibility. *Developmental Psychology, 35,* 1462–1477.

Powell, M. B., & Thomson, D. M. (1996). Children's memory of an occurrence of a repeated event: Effects of age, repetition, and retention interval across three question types. *Child Development, 67,* 1988–2004.

Principe, G. F., & Ceci, S. J. (2002). "I saw it with my own ears": The effects of peer conversations on preschoolers' reports of nonexperienced events. *Journal of Experimental Child Psychology, 83,* 1–25.

Quas, J. A., Qin, J., Schaaf, J. M., & Goodman, G. S. (1997). Individual differences in children's and adults' suggestibility and false event memory. *Learning and Individual Differences*, 9, 359–390.

Ridley, A. M., Clifford, B. R., & Keogh, E. (2002). The effects of state anxiety on the suggestibility and accuracy of child eyewitnesses. *Applied Cognitive Psychology*, 16, 547–558.

Roberts, K. P. (2002). Children's ability to distinguish between memories from multiple sources: Implications for the quality and accuracy of eyewitness statements. *Developmental Review*, 22, 403–435.

Roberts, K. P., & Blades, M. (Eds.). (2000). *Children's source monitoring*. Mahwah, NJ: Erlbaum.

Roberts, K. P., & Lamb, M. E. (1999). Children's responses when interviewers distort details during investigative interviews. *Legal and Criminological Psychology*, 4, 23–31.

Roberts, K. P., & Powell, M. B. (2001). Describing individual incidents of sexual abuse: A review of research on the effects of multiple sources of information on children's reports. *Child Abuse and Neglect*, 25, 1643–1659.

Robinson, E. J. (2000). Belief and disbelief: Children's assessment of the reliability of sources of knowledge about the world. In K. P. Roberts & M. Blades (Eds.), *Children's source monitoring* (pp. 59–83). Mahwah, NJ: Erlbaum.

Robinson, E. J., & Whitcombe, E. L. (2003). Children's suggestibility in relation to their understanding about sources of knowledge. *Child Development*, 74, 48–62.

Roebers, C. M., & Schneider, W. (2002). Stability and consistency of children's event recall. *Cognitive Development*, 17, 1085–1103.

Rudy, L., & Goodman, G. S. (1991). Effects of participation on children's reports: Implications for children's testimony. *Developmental Psychology*, 27, 527–538.

State of Michigan Governor's Task Force on Children's Justice and Family Independence Agency. (1998). *Forensic interviewing protocol*. Lansing, MI: Family Independence Agency.

Thierry, K. L., & Spence, M. J. (2002). Source-monitoring training facilitates preschoolers' eyewitness memory performance. *Developmental Psychology*, 38, 428–437.

Waterman, A. H., Blades, M., & Spencer, C. (2001). Interviewing children and adults: The effect of question format on the tendency to speculate. *Applied Cognitive Psychology*, 15, 521–531.

Zelazo, P. D., & Reznick, J. S. (1991). Age-related asynchrony of knowledge and action. *Child Development*, 62, 719–735.

CHAPTER SIX

Eyewitness Identification

NEIL BREWER
NATHAN WEBER
CAROLYN SEMMLER

In many criminal investigations police may, at some stage, ask an eyewitness to view either a live or photo-spread lineup to see if a positive identification of a suspect can be made. The witness's response on such an identification test can have a number of different consequences. If the witness makes a positive identification of the police suspect, the likelihood of the suspect being prosecuted will increase. A positive identification is also likely to make the prosecution case more persuasive to a jury, thereby increasing the chances of a guilty verdict. If, however, the witness rejects the lineup, either because he or she is too unsure to make an identification or believes that the offender is not present, the police may revise their theories about the identity of the offender and search for a new suspect. Or they may simply form the view that the witness is not reliable and seek alternative evidence to support their hypothesis about the offender's identity. Either way the witness's behavior at the identification test is likely to exert an important influence on the direction of the police investigations and, indeed, on the outcome of any trial that results.

There are probably two main reasons why the performance of witnesses at identification tests has attracted the interest of researchers. First, the study of eyewitness identification and other eyewitness memory issues provides a real-world context in which to explore, test, and refine theories of the operation of memory processes. The second and probably much more influential reason is the practical import of the now overwhelming body of evidence that demonstrates the fallibility of eyewitnesses when confronted with an identification test. Numerous laboratory and field experiments attest to the often poor performance of eyewitnesses in identification tests—a matter that becomes of particular concern when it is appreciated that, in many cases, the only evidence against a suspect is an identification made by an eyewitness.

Although eyewitnesses frequently do make accurate identifications, identification performance is also characterized by (1) false or mistaken identifications of innocent members of culprit- or target-absent lineups, (2) incorrect identifications of known-innocent lineup foils or fillers, and (3) incorrect rejections of culprit- or target-present lineups (see, for example, Cutler & Penrod, 1995). The prevalence of these response patterns will vary, of course, depending on factors such as the characteristics of the stimulus event, the lineup, the intervening events, and the interactions between these factors. Still, it is important to note here that the available evidence provides cause for considerable concern about the reliability of eyewitness identification evidence (Huff, 1987; Wells et al., 1998). Such concerns have escalated in recent years with the proliferation and high public profile of cases in which forensic DNA evidence has led to the exoneration of people convicted, sentenced, and often imprisoned for lengthy periods of time on the basis of eyewitness identification evidence (Innocence Project, 2004; Wells et al., 1998).

Given (1) the repeated and compelling demonstrations of eyewitness unreliability, (2) the significant consequences that can flow from a mistaken identification of an innocent suspect or from the failure to identify the actual offender, and (3) the relative ease of simulating a crime and an identification test in the laboratory, it is not very surprising that researchers embraced the now well-known eyewitness identification paradigm. This involves mock witnesses viewing a live or videotaped enactment of a crime, going away and doing something else for some period of time (i.e., a filler activity), and then viewing a lineup (either live or photo array). Because much of the eyewitness identification research has developed in a way that allows it to parallel actual practices, the degree of correspondence between identification research and actual practices tends to be relatively high. Although ecological validity is seldom perfect, the laboratory–real-world correspondence is typically much higher than found in many areas of experimental research. Furthermore, many of the variations introduced into the experimental paradigm have been stimulated by researchers' attempts to mirror real-world fluctuations in variables such as length of exposure to the offender, retention interval between exposure and test, and the composition of test stimuli.

As research in this area has progressed over the years, a striking characteristic of it has been the degree of adherence to this kind of approach, with methodologies or paradigms seldom departing very far from the real-world scenario. Clearly there is nothing inherently bad about this; indeed, it is a positive feature. But it also may reflect a belief that nothing useful or potentially applicable can be discovered if the research paradigm departs in any way from the highest level of ecological validity. And perhaps this adherence to (or preoccupation with) ecological validity has, in part, contributed to a tendency to neglect the contributions that sound theorizing (and the associated basic research) might make to answering important research questions and developing appropriate practical recommendations. This is not to say that the field has completely neglected theorizing; but often researchers have proceeded in a way that suggests a belief that more basic research in a number of domains has little to offer in terms of either theory or empirical results. For example, in eyewitness identification research we have seen relatively little systematic exploitation of more basic and potentially informative research from areas such as perceptual discrimination, recognition memory, confidence calibration, social comparison theory, and the like. Even if eyewitness identification researchers do not explicitly state that theory and research from these or other areas is irrelevant to the pursuit of their objectives, the neglect of such work suggests that there seems to be an implicit acceptance of the fact that the research cause cannot be advanced by such work. Perhaps our view here paints a black-and-white picture of what has transpired, and not all research in the area can be characterized in this way—but we suspect that most serious researchers in this field would be forced to concede that there is at least some validity to this perspective.

OUR FOCUS

The approach we take here is to organize our analysis of research in a manner that roughly parallels the sequence in which events are likely to unfold in the real world. So we begin by considering the issues surrounding the witnessed event or crime (e.g., witness, offender, and situational variables). We then consider variables that intervene between the event and the identification test (e.g., the retention interval and some of the key events that can occur therein). Next we examine the identification test itself in some detail (e.g., the presentation of the lineup, lineup composition, and characteristics of the identification decision). Finally we examine events that occur following the identification test (e.g., the effects of postidentification information). While we proceed through these stages, we hope to demonstrate that there are important interactions between events that occur at these different stages, and that real progress in this area requires recognition and understanding of those interactions. Thus, for example, variations in the quality of encoding may manifest themselves differently depending on the structure of the lineup. For each stage we examine the major findings, consider how theory could be useful (or where it could have been useful), and where future work might profitably take us. From the outset, however, we stress that our primary concern is not to comprehensively review (or even touch on) all issues covered in prior research,[1] but rather to highlight what seem to us to be the current salient issues and questions.

GENERAL METHODOLOGICAL CONSIDERATIONS

First, however, we briefly canvass some general methodological considerations, making no attempt to provide a comprehensive coverage of all possible methodological issues. Rather, we consider three broad categories of issues: generalizability from laboratory experiments, statistical power, and target-absent base rates.

Generalizability from Laboratory Experiments

Here we are concerned with the sorts of issues that are typically raised regarding the generality or external validity of research findings. For example, are findings from identification experiments that use university students as witnesses generalizable? Does it make a difference that laboratory witnesses might expect to observe a crime whereas "real" witnesses often have no prior warning that a crime is about to occur, or perhaps do not realize that a crime has occurred until afterward? In the real world, crimes are often characterized by levels of violence that may produce a heightened degree of arousal in the witness; can we reasonably expect the results of laboratory eyewitness identification experiments, which evoke relatively low levels of arousal and involve a much more constrained sequence of events, to be generalizable? Or, in the real world, unlike in the laboratory, the consequences of a positive or negative identification are significant and most likely obvious to a witness, raising the question of whether such consequences are likely to affect identification performance.

Our perspective on this first broad set of issues is that we cannot answer any of these questions with confidence, a not-dissimilar conclusion to that presented in Cutler and Penrod's (1995) major review. Although it is easy to say that things are certain to be quite different in the real world than in the laboratory, we are not aware of any more recent data sets that are sufficiently robust or comprehensive to allow a decisive answer to any of these questions. Furthermore, what should be of most interest to researchers is evidence that indicates qualitative differences in the processes underpinning identification performance in the laboratory versus real-world contexts, not quantitative differences in, say, proportions of correct or false identifications that could easily emerge from uncontrolled differences in the levels of key variables. Consequently, given that we do not yet have much firm evidence that sheds light on identification processes, we will not pursue these issues further, though we do commend to readers the broad discussion of a related set of issues for the jury decision-making literature that can be found in Chapter 10 of this volume.

One generalizability issue that we believe does warrant special attention at this stage of this research field's development concerns what might be termed the breadth of sampling of eyewitness performance. A substantial proportion of eyewitness identification studies involves a witness viewing a single crime, an identification test involving presentation of a single lineup, and the consequent collection of one data point per witness—a situation that, of course, closely resembles a typical real-world scenario. To what extent, though, might experimental findings and conclusions not apply beyond that particular set of stimulus and test conditions? We cannot know for sure, at least until we have data encompassing different stimulus and test materials. But we do know that individual studies could be characterized by quirky encoding conditions (e.g., particularly clear vs. obscure) and stimulus targets (distinctive vs. typical looking), variable degrees of match between the encoding and test stimulus, lineups that vary considerably in terms of discriminability of target from foils, and so on. Moreover, variations along any of these dimensions are seldom specified in quantitative terms. In other words, there are potentially many unknown influences operating on identification performance, some of which may simply produce quantitative differences in lineup performance, but others may affect the processes underlying identification decisions. Given our current state of knowledge, all we can say at this stage is that these issues suggest that researchers should be thinking about new (or at least not commonly used) methodological approaches, such as using a variety of encoding and test stimuli within a study, within-subjects or multiple-identification designs that gather multiple data points from each participant, and systematic replications across stimuli.

Statistical Power

A second issue—and the one that we think has been, and remains, the most significant methodological issue in this field—is that of statistical power, an issue that plagues many areas. Although many identification studies may appear, to the casual observer, to have relatively large overall sample sizes when compared with some areas of experimental research, the combination of many experimental conditions and the effective reduction in data points that can occur as a result of participants rejecting the lineup (i.e., not choosing) often means that contrasts of identification performance across conditions for choosers, nonchoosers or both are, in fact, based on relatively small sample sizes. Close inspection of the data patterns, coupled with a simple chi-square calculation, often suggest that if another 5–10 data points were added to each condition, and most of these points went in the same direction (and it is certainly not uncommon in any identification experiment to get runs of responses like this), then the conclusions would be quite different. To highlight the importance of this point, we present some summary statistics taken from a data set of Brewer and Wells (2004). In this study a between-subjects design was used to manipulate two levels of instructional bias and foil similarity for target-present and target-absent lineups (for two separate targets), with 150 participants in each cell (i.e., $N = 1,200$). Table 6.1 presents the chi-square and associated p values for the accuracy data (for the target-present condition, for one target only) for each of six consecutive cohorts of 25 participants who completed the experiment. Note that, despite overall significant effects for each variable on identification accuracy, less than half of the cohorts displayed significant effects for the respective independent variables.

TABLE 6.1. Chi-Square and Associated p Values for Identification Accuracy for Consecutive Cohorts within a Large Sample

Participant numbers	Instructional bias		Foil similarity	
	χ^2	p	χ^2	p
1–25	8.03	.02	0.59	.74
26–50	0.98	.61	1.55	.46
51–75	1.46	.48	0.54	.76
76–100	7.31	.03	1.40	.50
101–125	0.39	.82	0.39	.82
126–150	5.54	.06	6.32	.04
Overall	11.64	.00	7.45	.02

Target-Absent Base Rates

Eyewitness identification experiments typically use some combination of target-present and target-absent lineup conditions, so that effects of experimental variables are clarified under both of these possible states. Of course, there may be exceptions to this design: for example, studies that are interested only in some aspect of mistaken identifications may use target-absent lineups only. The proportions of each lineup condition used in experiments vary, although a 50:50 split is now a common practice. Unfortunately, the "real-world" proportions of each (or the target-absent base rate) are unknown and almost certainly will vary across police jurisdictions, depending on idiosyncratic practices. Although many police and prosecutors are likely to argue that it would be an extremely rare occurrence for a witness to be presented with a lineup containing an innocent suspect, we know from the DNA exoneration cases that it can and has occurred. It seems unlikely that the police would get things wrong so often that the target-absent base rate would approach the 50% often used in experiments, but whether the target-absent base rate lies closer to 0% or 50% is unknown.

For some experimental purposes, such as the examination of how a particular variable affects identification accuracy, the respective proportions of the two types of lineups may appear to be of little importance, provided adequate statistical power is achieved under both lineup conditions. However, it is quite likely that witnesses' expectations about the likelihood of their being shown a target-absent lineup, as distinct from the actual base rate, will affect their choosing behavior, which can shape the patterns of identification responses obtained. Thus, for example, low target-absent base-rate expectations are likely to lead to high rates of choosing, which, given a relatively high target-absent base rate, will produce more mistaken identifications. A later section of this chapter discusses the fact that indirect influences on witnesses' expectations (e.g., via warnings about the possible absence of the offender from the lineup) demonstrate robust effects on choosing behavior.

Another important impact of the target-absent base rate is on decisions about the overall accuracy of lineup procedures, which differ in their impact on target-present and -absent accuracy rates. Specifically, the sequential lineup procedure—when compared to the simultaneous procedure—reduces both false alarms (i.e., incorrect decisions) from target-absent lineups and hits (i.e., correct decisions) from target-present lineups. Thus, when considering overall accuracy, the superior lineup procedure will vary with base rate, such that a higher base rate will favor the sequential procedure and a lower base rate, the simultaneous procedure. Nevertheless, we are not aware of any attempts to directly investigate the impact of witnesses' base-rate expectations on choosing behavior. Elsewhere in this chapter we review evidence that highlights the significance of the target-absent base rate and discuss how informative it would be to have some reasonable real-world estimates of target-absent base rates. For example, base rates are a major determinant of the veridicality of witnesses' postdecisional confidence judgments and, consequently, of the relationship between eyewitness confidence and accuracy.

IDENTIFICATION PERFORMANCE

The following sections examine the evidence of the impact of an array of variables on identification performance and behavior. This review necessarily focuses on identification accuracy; that is, whether a person has made a correct or incorrect (i.e., foil) identification from a target-present lineup, a mistaken identification from a target-absent lineup, and so on. We think it is important, at this stage, to draw attention to the fact that the distinction between making a choice and the accuracy of that choice has often been ignored in the literature. Attention to these issues as distinct concepts is, we believe, likely to benefit our understanding of the identification process. A consideration of choosing, as distinct from accuracy, has already benefited identification research in such areas as examination of the impact of lineup instructions, the difference between absolute and relative judgments, and the confidence–accuracy relationship. A more careful delineation between choosing and accuracy in all areas of identification research may well provide similar gains. At different stages throughout this chapter, we attempt to highlight where pursuing this distinction is likely to be valuable.

The Event

In this main section we have several different foci: characteristics of the offender, characteristics of the witness, and characteristics of the situation/event/crime. The variables that we consider here help us to understand why or when witnesses might be accurate or inaccurate in their identification or why they might choose, or not choose, during the identification test. But while consideration of these variables can certainly contribute to our understanding of identification performance and the process of making an identification decision, it is important to remember that these variables are outside our control. Consequently, the related research does not translate into direct implications for the practical conduct of identification tests, although any significant advances in our understanding of identification decision processes should ultimately lead to important practical advances.

To guide our considerations, let us consider the psychological processes involved in an identification decision. A person observes the event and forms a memorial representation of it. Two broad aspects of this memory are important for eyewitness identification. First, the quality and accuracy of the visual image of the offender encoded in memory should influence the accuracy with which an identification decision is made. Second, some aspects of the memory may influence the predecisional (or preidentification test) confidence of the witness that he or she will be able to accurately identify the offender. Thus, the propensity of the witness to make a positive identification may be affected: For example, if a person is very close to the scene of the crime or other event, the event lasts for a long time and includes no distracting elements, then regardless of the witness's memorial representation, he or she may well believe that he or she can pick out this person. So when we look at the contributions of offender, witness, and situational characteristics, it may be useful to consider their impact in both of these areas.

Offender Variables

We focus here on the two variables that seem to be the most important: the effects of changing appearance, and the distinctiveness of the offender. Later in the chapter we also address the issue of offender race, but do so in the context of the interaction between the race of the offender and the race of the witness.

Changed Appearance and Disguises. There are two main scenarios to consider here. The first involves the case in which, after the event, the offender's appearance either changes "naturally" with time (e.g., changes in face or build with age, changes in complexion) or is deliberately changed in a natural way (e.g., shaving a beard off, wearing a mustache, wearing glasses). In other words, regardless of original encoding, the test stimulus will not match well with the encoded stimulus. The consequence of this variable is that witnesses should either choose less from a lineup or choose incorrectly (either choosing a known-innocent foil in a target-present or absent- lineup or an innocent suspect in a target-absent lineup) more often than in situations in which the appearance has not changed. Yes/no face recognition experiments demonstrate that when faces change in appearance from study to test, they are correctly recognized less often (Patterson & Baddeley, 1977; Read, Vokey, & Hammersley, 1990). A meta-analysis of facial identification studies (i.e., face recognition and eyewitness identification paradigms) has confirmed this pattern (Shapiro & Penrod, 1986). Likewise, Read (1995) demonstrated reduced lineup identification accuracy when the target's appearance was altered by changes to hair style or facial hair and the presence or absence of glasses.

The second scenario involves the offender, at the time of the event, concealing or unrealistically distorting his or her appearance (e.g., by wearing a beanie, balaclava, or stocking on their head). In this case two issues emerge. First, the witness is not able to encode the entire stimulus (face), thus producing a mismatch between the encoding and test stimuli. Second, it is also quite possible that the witness will perceive the subsequent identification task to be more difficult, thus reducing predecisional confidence and potentially influencing choosing behavior. Surprisingly little eyewitness identification research has addressed the issue of disguise, and a clear picture has not emerged. Some studies found reduced identification accuracy when the offender was disguised (Cutler, Penrod, Martens, 1987a, 1987b), but another found no effect of disguise on accuracy (O'Rourke, Penrod, Cutler, & Stuve, 1989). Similarly, a consistent effect of disguise on choosing has not emerged. Cutler and colleagues identified reduced choosing in the disguise condition in one study (1987b) but no effect in another (1987a).

Distinctiveness. By dint of a particular feature, features, or configuration of features, a distinctive face lies outside the domain of typical faces. Variations in distinctiveness of the offender may exert important influences at the levels of encoding, retrieval, and metacognition. Consider how encoding may differ for distinctive and typical faces. Two things are likely to happen with a distinctive stimulus: (1) It will attract greater attention and produce stronger encoding, and (2) the specific distinctive element is more likely than a typical element to be clearly represented in memory. The net effect should be a stronger trace against which the test stimulus can be matched, thus increasing the likelihood of a correct selection or rejection. Furthermore, the combination of closer attention and the particular distinctive feature(s) has been shown to increase the likelihood of "remember" judgments (i.e., qualitative or contextual aspects of the event recalled) relative to "know" judgments (i.e., no qualitative or contextual aspects recalled), thereby pointing to what are known as recollection-based, rather than familiarity-based, judgments (Brandt, Macrae, Schloerscheidt, & Milne, 2003). From a retrieval perspective, an item in memory that is clearly tagged with a distinctive feature might be more readily retrieved than a more typical item when the witness is presented with the distinctive cue. In contrast, retrieving a typical item is likely to identify more candidates than a distinctive item, leading to mismatch and more false alarms (Valentine & Ferrara, 1991). At the metacognitive level, it is likely that a witness will think that a distinctive face is easy to remember (Vokey & Read, 1992) and perhaps believe that he or she can pick the offender from the lineup. Evidence from other domains shows that individuals use distinctiveness as a basis for inferring the accuracy of their memory (Dodson & Schacter, 2001). Such beliefs could have one of two consequences. A witness could be so sure that he or she could make a correct identification that he or she may require less evidence to make a choice—in other words, the witness lowers his or her decision criterion. Alternatively, the decision criterion could be raised because the witness believes that the highly distinctive face should evoke a strong feeling of memorability, and thus, unless one of the test stimuli does the same thing, he or she will not be willing to make a positive identification. Apparent from this discussion is the important notion, already canvassed in the previous section, that the precise effects of a distinctive target on identification performance are almost certainly moderated by lineup parameters.

Before we expand on what the actual data show us in this area, it is important to make one key point. The "distinctiveness" construct described in Shapiro and Penrod's (1986) meta-analysis, and sometimes used in the literature to characterize the effects of distinctiveness, appears to be operationalized as the degree of similarity between the target and the decoys (see p. 141), although it would not be surprising if this actually varied across the studies included. Such a manipulation is much more akin to the notions typically referred to as "functional size" or "discriminability" (discussed in a later section on identification test variables) than it is to the notions of distinctiveness that we have been talking about here. What, then, do we know about distinctiveness as operationalized here? First, recognition performance for distinctive and typical faces differs, with correct recognitions more prevalent and false recognitions less prevalent for distinctive stimuli (Light, Kayra-Stuart, & Hollander, 1979). Additionally, distinctive faces—and distinctiveness of encoding—produce a higher proportion of remember (recollection-based) relative to know (familiarity-based) judgments than do typical faces (Brandt et al., 2003; Mäntylä, 1997; Mäntylä & Cornoldi, 2002). However, based on these data, we are not able to distinguish whether encoding or retrieval processes (or, indeed, both) comprise the underlying mechanism. Furthermore, although the remember/know data are consistent with the notion that distinctiveness affects witnesses' phenomenological experience of the event, these studies do not clarify the precise role of metacognition in these judgments.

In sum, we have a number of different ideas about how distinctiveness might affect identification performance, but, to the best of our knowledge, these ideas remain without direct empirical support. Understanding the mechanisms underlying the effect of distinctiveness on identification performance is crucial if we are to integrate its influence with those of lineup characteristics that are likely to interact with the data provided by the encoding and retrieval processes.

Witness Variables

It is clear that age is, by far, the most important witness variable. Much more systematic investigation has been undertaken in this area than in relation to any other witness variable, and the findings are more clear-cut.

Young Children. Perhaps the major issue to consider is the converging results from children's studies indicating a greater propensity to choose when confronted with a target-absent lineup and, hence, the increased likelihood of a false identification (Pozzulo & Lindsay, 1998). For example, Lindsay, Pozzulo, Craig, Lee, and Corber (1997) showed that the tendency to choose greatly reduced the accuracy of both preschool children (33–72 months of age) and older children (8–15 years) from target-absent showups, sequential lineups, and simultaneous lineups. Young children (preschool age) also showed a tendency to select multiple individuals from a sequential lineup. Overall, children (both younger and older) showed a greater tendency to choose than adults, irrespective of the type of lineup format employed.

The second finding concerns the behavior of child witnesses confronted with a target-present lineup. There has been a tendency to conclude that young children (except, perhaps, the very young, that is, preschoolers) do no worse than adults when confronted with a target-present lineup. Because many of the relevant studies, however, have relatively small sample sizes, caution should be exercised in drawing such conclusions, a view also expressed by Pozzulo and Lindsay (1998) in their meta-analysis. A recent study (Keast, Brewer, & Wells, 2005), with a very large sample ($N = 656$), found mixed results. For one target or stimulus, children whose ages ranged from 9 years, 0 months to 13 years, 11 months ($M = 11$ years, 8 months) recorded higher choosing rates than adults with a target-present lineup, translating into a significantly lower proportion of correct identifications and a higher proportion of incorrect (i.e., foil) identifications. For another target, children's and adults' choosing rates did not differ; nor were there significant differences between the two samples in accuracy rates. Keast et al.'s target-absent data were consistent with previous research: Children recorded significantly, and markedly, higher proportions of false identifications for both targets.

In sum, the evidence that young children's identification performance is characterized by a "choosing problem" is relatively strong, although the underlying mechanism is not yet clear. Perhaps children are simply more sensitive to the social, situational demands to choose and set a laxer decision criterion. They may, for example, have a less sophisticated understanding of the purposes of an identification test and the consequences of choosing or not choosing, making an incorrect choice, or even making a correct choice. In other words, their behavior may reflect a misunderstanding of the situation that leads to the application of an inappropriate decision strategy. Perhaps children are poor at monitoring their own memory and are thus particularly susceptible to the social demands to choose. Keast et al.'s (2005) study also demonstrates that children's identification performance is characterized by a marked degree of overconfidence that is consistent with poor memory monitoring. At present, we are not in a position to arbitrate on these alternatives, but resolving these issues is not only of theoretical interest but also of considerable practical importance, if we are to clarify whether these problems are inevitable or could be trained away.

Older Witnesses. Older individuals (in the 60- to 80-year-old age range) also exhibit similar patterns of choosing behavior to those shown by young children: That is, they are more likely to choose from target-absent lineups, and there is some suggestion that this pattern may also apply to target-present lineups (Memon & Gabbert, 2003; Searcy, Bartlett, & Memon, 1999; Searcy, Bartlett, Memon, & Swanson, 2001). Not all of the mechanisms advanced as possible explanations for children's performance are likely to be applicable here. For example, older people should have a clear understanding of the context in which their decisions are being made and the possible consequences of those decisions. Just as the mechanism(s) underlying children's choosing behavior is unclear, so too are the sources of old people's identification performance. An interesting pointer regarding possible mechanisms is provided by Searcy et al.'s (2001) finding that, within an elderly sample, choosing from a target-absent lineup was associated with increased memory self-efficacy and increased verbal recall of events. These findings suggest the possibility that old people's decisions to choose are shaped by metacognitive beliefs surrounding the general strength of their memory of the witnessed event. As is the case for child witnesses, clarifying the origins of old people's choosing problems is likely to have important practical implications.

Other Witness Factors. A wide range of other witness variables has been explored, including individual difference variables as diverse as field independence, trait anxiety, self-monitoring, and ability to describe faces. The number of published studies in each of these areas is generally small, the effects are typically modest in magnitude, and it is fair to say that this work has not had a significant impact on either theoretical or practical developments in the field. Although most of these studies articulated plausible grounds for detecting the sort of relationship that was being examined, often the theoretical rationale has not been well developed and, generally, the research has not been well integrated with the mainstream identification literature.

Situational Variables

Our examination of situational factors begins with a consideration of variables that operate at the time of encoding: specifically, exposure duration and viewing conditions, weapon focus, and cross- or other-race effects.

Exposure Duration and Viewing Conditions. The importance of the viewing conditions experienced by the witness (e.g., exposure duration, viewing distance, lighting conditions) has received strong emphasis in judicial guidelines (*Neil v. Biggers*, 1972; *R v. Turnbull and others*, 1976). Longer exposure durations and better viewing conditions would obviously be expected to produce a better or more readily accessible memory representation and, hence, increase the likelihood of an accurate identification. There are data from real-world lineups showing that witnesses who viewed the offender for more than a minute were more likely to pick the suspect from the lineup than those who experienced a briefer exposure (Valentine, Pickering, & Darling, 2003). Interpretation of this pattern, however, is complicated because the proportion of suspects known to be the actual offender is unknown, and therefore these suspect identifications include both correct and mistaken identifications. Experimental evidence has demonstrated superior recognition performance with longer exposure durations (Ellis, Davies, & Shepherd, 1977; MacLin, MacLin, & Malpass, 2001; Shapiro & Penrod, 1986; Weber & Brewer, 2004a), although most of the evidence comes from studies using a face recognition rather than an eyewitness identification paradigm, or report effects combined across paradigms (cf. Shapiro & Penrod's, 1986, meta-analysis). Indeed, we have been remarkably unsuccessful in locating studies that manipulate exposure duration in an eyewitness identification paradigm. One study conducted by Memon, Hope, and Bull (2003) did report markedly higher hit rates and lower false-alarm rates for a long (45 seconds) exposure compared with a short (12 seconds) exposure duration, but some features of the results raise the possibility that these results may reflect, at least in part, the characteristics of the stimulus and/or lineup: Specifically, hit rates were extremely high at the long exposure (.95), as were false alarms at the short exposure (.90).

Just as we might expect longer exposure durations to result in improved identification performance, we would also expect that, if something were to distract the witness from key features of the offender's appearance, a poorer memorial representation would most likely result. One particular example of this phenomenon is provided by what has become known as the "weapon focus effect." This term refers to the diminished identification accuracy found when an offender is brandishing a weapon (Loftus, Loftus, & Messo, 1987; Steblay, 1992).

Attempting to specify the degree to which identification performance improves with manipulations of exposure duration or other viewing condition parameters seems to us to be a futile exercise. In many witnessing situations we are unlikely to know, with any degree of precision, what the exposure time and viewing conditions were. We might know that a crime lasted only briefly or for a long time, that it was light or dark, or we might even know where the witness was standing in relation to the offender. But assessment of the levels of these variables will never be achieved with the sort of precision that would allow us to match up an actual case with some set of empirical results. Furthermore, even if we were able to specify the encoding conditions, their effect on identification performance is likely to be moderated by factors such as the lineup composition and the interaction between these two sets of variables.

Nevertheless, some particularly interesting questions arise in relation to the links between viewing conditions, metacognitive influences, and identification test performance. It may well turn out that a person who considers that he or she has had an exceptional view of an offender goes into an identification test with a relatively high degree of certainty about his or her capacity to make a correct choice, with a resultant strong disposition to make a choice. Depending on the composition of the lineup (e.g., lineup fairness), this disposition may make it more likely that the witness will make a correct choice from a target-present lineup, but it could also mean an increased likelihood of a mistaken identification from a target-absent lineup. The data patterns reported in Valentine et al.'s (2003) field study could well be explained by this type of phenomenon. Evidence consistent with such speculation about metacognitive influences comes from two separate findings reported by Read (1995). First, he found that increased exposure duration produced higher rates of choosing in target-present and, particularly, in target-absent lineups, without associated accuracy gains. (Interestingly, Shapiro and Penrod's [1986] facial identification meta-analysis reported the "anomalous" finding that exposure duration was related not only to increased hits but also false alarms.) Second, Read found that witnesses' predictions of their likely success on an identification test were influenced by cognitive events intervening between encoding and test—specifically, manipulations designed to enhance witnesses' perceptual or contextual knowledge—thereby suggesting the influence of metacognitive influences on their judgments. Although the research evidence on the influence of such factors is scarce, it does point to a promising line of enquiry.

Cross-Race Effect. One other situational variable that has attracted considerable attention in both the research and popular literatures is what has often been referred to as the cross-race or other-race effect.[2] This term refers to the poorer identification performance demonstrated by people of a particular race when attempting to identify someone from another race compared with that shown when identifying someone of their own race. The effect has been reported for various different races: for example, whites identifying blacks, blacks identifying whites, whites identifying Asians, Asians identifying whites, and so on. The basic finding is that attempts to recognize faces of the same race produce a higher proportion of hits, or correct identifications, from target-present lineups than attempts to identify faces of another race. Conversely, a lower proportion of false alarms, or false identifications, from target-absent lineups is made for same- compared with other-race face identifications (Meissner & Brigham, 2001). It is interesting to note that two recent studies have reported parallel findings for both gender and age, with better recognition for own age and gender than for other (Wright & Sladden, 2003; Wright & Stroud, 2002).

There have been several broad categories of explanation for the cross-race effect. The broadest explanation is usually referred to as the "contact hypothesis" and suggests that people will be less effective at encoding and/or discriminating faces from a racial group with which they have had less contact. More specific formulations have argued, for example, that cross-race faces are psychologically more similar to each other than same-race faces and that we lack the encoding expertise to discriminate effectively (cf. Valentine,

1991; Valentine & Endo, 1992). A similar tack is taken by Meissner and Brigham (2001), who suggest differences in the encoding of key featural or configural information. Levin (2000) brings a social–cognitive perspective to bear, arguing that we tend to code other-race faces in terms of race-specifying (i.e., stereotype-driven) attributes rather than in terms of idiosyncratic facial features. By attending to race-specifying attributes, we ignore the individuating information that allows us to recognize faces. For example, Levin found that white people who were poor at recognizing black faces were, in fact, very quick to detect their presence and also very accurate at discriminating them when they were distorted in a way that made them vary in terms of race-specifying features. Conversely, these characteristics were not shown by people who showed no recognition deficit for other-race faces.

Variables Operating between the Event and the Identification Test

Here we examine several issues: the effect of variations in retention interval; the effect of experiences such as being interviewed, looking at mug shots, or other forms of interference prior to the identification test; and context reinstatement.

Retention Interval

A number of studies have examined how identification accuracy is affected by retention interval: that is, the delay between the event and the identification test (e.g., Krafka & Penrod, 1985; Malpass & Devine, 1981; Shepherd 1983). Different studies used different retention interval manipulations, ranging from a few hours to many months. Although some evidence indicates that facial identification performance is not neatly predicted by retention interval (Shapiro & Penrod, 1986)—possibly reflecting the range of retention intervals examined—relatively long retention intervals have been implicated in poorer identification performance. Both laboratory and real-world data sets (e.g., Shepherd, 1983; Valentine et al., 2003) suggest that the most apparent performance decrement occurs after a delay of a week or so, although the evidence certainly does not point to the existence of a neat relationship between the two variables.

   An increased retention interval clearly provides increased opportunities for interference with, as well as decay of, the memory trace of the offender. Furthermore, a theoretically guided approach leads to the suggestion that identification performance should vary systematically with retention interval. For example, signal detection theory (e.g., Macmillan & Creelman, 1991) suggests that, all other things being equal, increasing retention interval and/or interference would reduce the discriminability of old from new items. In an eyewitness identification context, this principle would mean fewer correct identifications from a target-present lineup and more false identifications from a target-absent lineup. It seems to us that, having demonstrated that identifi-

cation performance is broadly consistent with these predictions, continued investigation into the impact of particular retention intervals is not interesting,
unless some new theoretical or practical issue arises. We make this statement
because we should expect the retention interval to interact with a number of
other variables to predict the time course and extent of performance decline.
Examples of the variables expected to interact with retention interval include
the characteristics of the stimuli to be encoded and the stimuli to be presented
at test, the relationships between the two, and the nature of any interference.
Without knowing the parameters on any of these variables, debates about the
specific time course and the extent of any performance decline with retention
interval are unsatisfying. This is not to say that retention interval effects are
unimportant; rather, we question whether it is particularly meaningful to try
to say much more than that identification performance is likely to decline with
retention interval.

Effects of Intervening Experiences

After witnessing a crime, a witness is likely to experience, as part of the investigation, a number of events that have the potential to influence his or her identification performance. Here we examine four different effects on identification
performance: effects of prior interviews with the witness (what is referred to as
"verbal overshadowing"), memory transference, repeated attempts by the witness to retrieve the image of the offender, and context reinstatement.

Verbal Overshadowing. The most common way in which an investigator
begins is by conducting one or more interviews with the witness. As part of
this process the witness would normally be asked to give one or more verbal
descriptions of the offender or offenders. How this process affects subsequent
identification test performance has been the focus of a large amount of research.[3] The verbal overshadowing effect was first described by Schooler and
Engstler-Schooler (1990). The term refers to the reduction in the proportion of
correct identifications observed when witnesses are asked to give a verbal description of the offender before making an identification (compared with performance of those not required to verbally describe the offender). Given the
importance in a criminal investigation of first securing a description of the
suspect, the applied implications of such an effect are obvious.

Although the verbal overshadowing effect has been replicated many times
(see the meta-analysis of Meissner & Brigham, 2001), not all experiments
(e.g., Meissner, Brigham, & Kelley, 2001) have found the effect. Meissner and
Brigham's meta-analysis suggests that there is a small (1.4% of variance explained) yet consistent effect across the literature. They also point out that, although the effect is small, witnesses required to give a verbal description of the
offender are 1.27 times more likely to "misidentify" the offender. Importantly,
the use of the term *misidentify* is potentially misleading, because the meta-
analysis does not examine false identifications and incorrect rejections, only

the proportion of correct identifications. Thus, witnesses required to give a verbal description are less likely to correctly identify the offender, but the likely type of error (i.e., incorrect identification or rejection) is not known.

Three major theoretical accounts of the verbal overshadowing effect have been proposed. Originally, the verbal overshadowing effect was attributed to verbal recoding of the original visual memory, which subsequently interfered with access to the original memory. Support for this account, known as "retrieval-based interference," is provided by some experiments that have demonstrated a negative association between the amount of incorrect information in the verbal description and identification accuracy (e.g., Finger & Pezdek, 1999; Meissner 2002; Meissner et al., 2001). The finding of Meissner and Brigham's (2001) meta-analysis that the verbal overshadowing effect is greater when participants are given elaborative instructions (i.e., those that encourage the production of as much detail as possible, leading to more incorrect information) rather than free-recall instructions also supports the retrieval-based interference account.

However, a number of results inconsistent with retrieval-based interference have been observed. First, not all studies find a relationship between description errors and identification performance (e.g., Brown & Lloyd-Jones, 2002; Kitagami, Sato, & Yoshikawa, 2002; Schooler & Engstler-Schooler, 1990). More importantly, retrieval-based interference cannot account for the finding that the verbal overshadowing effect generalizes across stimuli (Brown & Lloyd-Jones, 2002; Dodson, Johnson, & Schooler, 1997). In other words, when participants are asked to describe a face between study and test, but are tested for a different face, recognition performance is still impaired. Given that the retrieval-based interference account relies on modification of the original memory, it is not clear how describing one face could have an impact on identification of another face. Finally, Finger (2002) demonstrated that the effect can be eliminated by having participants engage in nonverbal tasks (listening to music or completing a maze in this study) between describing the offender and making the identification. Again, it is not clear how this kind of activity could influence the memory for the face and thus eliminate the retrieval-based interference. An alternative theoretical perspective that is consistent with these findings is known as "transfer inappropriate retrieval" (for full discussion, see Schooler, 2002). According to this explanation of the verbal overshadowing effect, asking participants to describe the offender encourages the use of verbal processes and inhibits the use of the nonverbal processes required for the identification decision. Thus, this theory is able to account for the observation of a verbal overshadowing effect for nondescribed faces and also for the elimination of the effect through completion of nonverbal tasks.

Clare and Lewandowsky (2004) recently suggested a third perspective. They argue that the verbal overshadowing literature has failed to adequately examine (1) the types of errors made after verbal descriptions (i.e., false identifications and incorrect rejections), and (2) the effect of verbal descriptions on performance in target-absent lineups. Examination of these areas in a series of experiments produced two results, for which neither of the earlier theories could account. First, the verbal overshadowing effect was eliminated when participants were forced to choose. Second, verbal description actually facilitated performance in target-absent lineups (i.e., a higher proportion of participants correctly rejected the lineup). Clare and Lewandowsky argued that these findings are consistent with a criterion shift explanation of the verbal overshadowing effect. Specifically, providing a verbal description causes participants to use a stricter criterion, thus reducing the likelihood that they will make a positive identification from the lineup. Obviously, if a higher proportion of participants rejects the lineup, in line with Clare and Lewandowsky's findings, the proportion of correct decisions would decrease for target-present lineups but increase for target-absent lineups. Furthermore, if the verbal overshadowing is a result of a reluctance to make a positive identification, then forcing such a decision should remove the effect. Again, their findings are consistent with this prediction. Although the criterion shift explanation appears promising, there are some data that pose a problem for it. For example, Meissner (2002) found that performance for both target-present and -absent lineups was impaired in a forced-recall condition (i.e., when participants were instructed to report a large amount of detail, even if they were guessing). Furthermore, the criterion shift account of the verbal overshadowing effect can only be considered descriptive, because it does not outline or test a mechanism underlying the change in decision criterion.

Memory Transference. A person may seem familiar at an identification test because he or she is the culprit or looks like the culprit. But other factors may underlie this familiarity. "Unconscious transference" has been described as the transfer of one individual's identity to that of another person from a different setting, time, or context (Read, Tollestrup, Hammersley, McFazden, & Christensen, 1990). In the case of eyewitness identification, a witness may identify an innocent suspect who seems familiar because he or she was encountered either at the scene of the crime (but was not involved) or afterward in a different context. For example, the witness may have seen the innocent suspect in the crime context previously (e.g., in the bank or shop) and hence mistakenly attributes the person's familiarity to his or her presence as the culprit. Or, a witness may have been shown mug shots of suspects and later misattributes the familiarity of the suspect during testing. There is mixed empirical support for these transference effects, with a number of studies failing to show an effect (e.g., Read, Tollestrup, et al., 1990). Studies that have demonstrated the effect have found that witnesses exposed to a bystander are, on average, three times more likely to mistakenly identify the bystander in a simultaneous bystander-present (target-absent) lineup than those witnesses not exposed to the bystander (Ross, Ceci, Dunning, & Toglia, 1994).

In their review Ross et al. (1994) suggested that unconscious transference is most likely to occur when the memory traces for the assailant and the bystander are of equal strength, which would thereby prevent discrimination between them on the basis of those contextual cues that were encoded when the individuals were first encountered. They suggest that the effect is due to the fact that the witness remembers having seen the perpetrator and the bystander but thinks that they are the same person (Ross et al. called this the "memory blending" account). Evidence for this account comes from post-identification reports from witnesses in transference conditions, which indicate that they thought that the bystander and the perpetrator were the same person (i.e., when asked whether there was anyone in the lineup who was in the film but was not the assailant, they responded "No"). Another piece of evidence for this interpretation of the effect is that when transference participants (i.e., those exposed to both the innocent bystander and the assailant) were told (before viewing the lineup) that the bystander and the assailant were different people, the effect of transference on lineup identification responses was eliminated. Further support for this account comes from the findings that (1) when asked about whether or not the assailant was seen anywhere else in the film, witnesses stated that the offender was seen doing what the bystander did in the film; (2) when asked to stop the videotape when they saw the same person twice, transference participants stopped the tape when the assailant appeared and indicated that they had seen the person reading to schoolchildren earlier (the activity in which the innocent bystander was engaged); and (3) participants who were in the transference condition took longer to correctly discriminate the bystander from the assailant when asked to indicate whether or not they had seen the assailant before in the film, compared to when they had to decide about nontargets in the film. Thus, it appears that the effect is due to an inference that the offender and the innocent bystander are the same person. Interestingly, when both the familiar bystander and the assailant are included in the lineup, witnesses in the transference condition were more likely to respond "not present" or "don't know" than witnesses who had not been exposed to the bystander (i.e., in the control condition), perhaps indicating their inability to discriminate between the assailant and the bystander in the lineup.

In sum, the theoretical mechanism thought to be at work in the transference effect is the formation of a composite memory, or the composite retrieval, of the offender and the bystander, which are "joined" by the contextual tag that identifies them as the same individual seen in two different places. There are, however, many unanswered questions about this effect: for example, (1) the level of similarity between the offender and the bystander required to produce the effect, (2) whether the amount of time between the exposure to the bystander and exposure to the offender would limit the effect, (3) whether the bystander would continue to be more likely to be misidentified when witnesses are exposed to more lineups with both the bystander and the assailant present, (4) whether the use of highly similar foils would protect the innocent bystander from being misidentified, and (5) whether the use of a sequential lineup presentation procedure would reduce the chances of misidentification.

Prior exposure to mug shots has also been shown to result in a higher proportion of mistaken identification decisions (Brigham & Cairns, 1988; Cutler et al., 1987b; Davies, Shepherd, & Ellis, 1979; Memon, Hope, Bartlett, & Bull, 2002). For example, a study by Dysart, Lindsay, Hammond, and Dupuis (2001) compared the identification responses of witnesses who had chosen a photo from a mug-shot book to those of witnesses who had seen the photo (but not chosen it) and witnesses who had not viewed mug shots. They found that witnesses who chose the mug shot were significantly more likely to select the photo from a six-person simultaneous lineup than witnesses who had not viewed mug shots and those who had but did not choose the suspect. They argued that this finding indicated that the effect is due to the witness committing to the photo of the suspect chosen from the mug shots rather than to transference of the memory for the suspect in the mug shot to the memory of the perpetrator in the lineup. Another study (Memon et al., 2002), however, showed that, regardless of whether or not the particular person chosen from the mug shots was in a subsequent lineup, witnesses were more likely to make a choice at the lineup if they had chosen any of the mug shots, suggesting that mug-shot choosing affected subsequent choosing during the identification test.

In sum, misidentification of innocent suspects may occur for a variety of reasons, including the inference that the offender and the bystander are the same person, and commitment to an earlier decision that was made. But misidentification clearly can arise for other reasons, including the various inferences that witnesses may make that conspire to produce a mistaken identification.

Repeated Retrieval. The previous discussions on verbal overshadowing and memory transference relate to specific examples of how intervening experiences may shape identification performance. A third type of intervening experience that, to our knowledge, has attracted little attention in the identification literature is the effect on identification performance of intervening or repeated attempts at retrieving an image of the offender. An example of this type might be any time the witness thinks about the incident and recalls the offender. This attempt at recall could be spontaneously initiated by the witness when thinking about or discussing the case, it could be triggered by questioning from others, by being invited to attempt an identification, and so on. We are making a deliberate distinction here between (1) the kind of retrieval attempt in which the witness briefly accesses the image of the offender, and (2) much more systematic attempts to reinstate the image of the offender and the context in which the offender was seen (referred to as "context reinstatement" and discussed in the next section). The former seems to us to be an extremely important phenomenon that is almost certain to characterize the behavior of all witnesses. In the absence of empirical data on the issue, we can only speculate from relevant theory as to the likely effects brief retrieval attempts may have on identification performance.

Estes's (1997) perturbation theory suggests that one effect of each retrieval attempt would be to produce an updating and subsequent re-encoding of the witness's trace. Or, as Estes puts it, the image held in memory is perturbed. The specific perturbation may result in the image more closely matching a nontarget image than the target in some stimulus area, thus leading to an erroneous response. Estes also describes how perturbations that occur over a lengthy retention interval could result in an image of a target that is actually a closer approximation of the true target, thereby increasing the probability of correct recognition. Obviously, it is not very likely that we can control when or how often a real witness accesses his or her image of an offender, but it does seem to us that it would be a worthwhile endeavor to understand this process if we are to have a detailed theory of identification performance.

There are also clear practical consequences of such a perturbation process, as illustrated by the following scenario. Imagine that a witness has an extremely strong, veridical representation of an offender, for which he or she provides a detailed description that allows the police to construct a lineup with a large number of highly plausible matches to the offender's description. Although it may be tempting to say that the good witness (i.e., the one with the strong, veridical representation) will be able to pick the offender, the perturbation theory would suggest the possibility that the witness's perturbed image will match a nontarget in the lineup. In a target-absent lineup the important consequence of this mechanism would be increased choosing and, hence, increased probability of a false identification.

Context Reinstatement. What we have discussed in the previous section could be as simple and routine as merely retrieving the image of the offender, but it could also be a spontaneous and more restricted version of what has become known as *context reinstatement.* A context reinstatement procedure attempts to improve memory performance by encouraging a witness to locate the event and the stimulus in the context in which it occurred. Witnesses may be asked to recreate their cognitive and emotional states and a mental image of the environmental characteristics associated with the target stimulus; this reinstatement may include viewing photos of, or visiting, the scene of the event. The logic is that an enriched context will increase the likelihood of an accurate retrieval (Tulving & Thomson, 1973).

Although this procedure has been carefully studied in the context of eyewitness free recall—even to the extent of being incorporated into procedures designed to enhance eyewitness recall (cf. the Cognitive Interview technique described by Fisher & McCauley, 1995)—the findings for eyewitness identification performance are less clear-cut. There is some empirical support for the utility of context reinstatement in improving identification accuracy. In their meta-analysis Shapiro and Penrod (1986) identified context reinstatement as an important predictor of recognition accuracy. They found that context reinstatement led to more correct identifications from target-present lineups but also more false identifications from target-absent lineups. This pattern is consistent with the notion that context reinstatement procedures simply increase the likelihood of participants making a positive identification from the lineup—an issue that has not yet been explored in the context reinstatement literature. Despite the support for context reinstatement, there is little consistency in the literature regarding the types of reinstatement procedure that are effective. Some studies (e.g., Smith & Vela, 1990) have found that imagined reinstatement does not influence identification accuracy, whereas others have observed significant improvements when imagined reinstatement was combined with other techniques (e.g., detailed event information, Malpass & Devine, 1981; presentation of items from the event at the scene of the event, Krafka & Penrod, 1985; and presentation of photographs of the scene, Cutler et al., 1987a). Unfortunately, much of this uncertainty stems from the small sample sizes typically employed in this area of research. Therefore, despite the existence of generally encouraging evidence for the utility of context reinstatement, little is understood about the mechanisms through which it operates and the most effective procedures by which it could be practically implemented by police.

The Identification Test

This section focuses on several important issues that relate to the conduct of the identification test: social factors, lineup instructions, lineup composition, and lineup presentation mode. Although these issues are often treated as if they were independent, there are likely to be relationships between social factors and the other aspects of the identification test that we review.

Social Factors

The social factors likely to impinge on witnesses are well documented. The following scenario has been depicted many times. Imagine that a witness is contacted by the police regarding the viewing of a lineup as part of their inquiries. Such a request from the police probably suggests to the witness that the police have a clear suspect and that the success of the investigation may well depend on the witness's selection of that person from the lineup. Most researchers are happy to assert that there are strong pressures, both external and self-imposed, on the witness to identify the suspect. There are various lines of evidence that lead people to accept this conclusion. For example, Wells (1993) showed that when we examine the pattern of choices that witnesses make from a lineup, identify the most frequently chosen individual, and then remove that person from the lineup, participants' choices are then mostly redistributed across other lineup members, apparently indicating (among other factors, as we will see in a later section) the witness's tendency to choose.

Another line of indirect evidence comes from what are known as the postidentification feedback studies, in which experimenters contrive (successfully) to produce false identifications from witnesses by (1) showing them an ambiguous stimulus, (2) leading them to expect the presence of the offender, and (3) presenting them with target-absent lineups only (e.g., Wells & Bradfield, 1998; Wells Olson, & Charman, 2003). A third indirect source—albeit problematic because it involves retrospective self-report—is provided by Memon, Gabbert, and Hope's (2004) data showing that over 90% of participants, across several identification experiments, reported that they assumed the perpetrator was in the lineup, even though all witnesses were provided with instructions cautioning that the offender may not be present. Interestingly, although we find this assertion credible, we are not aware of studies that clearly and directly (i.e., prior to any lineup exposure) illustrate those expectations. It is, of course, easy to imagine how such beliefs in witnesses could be shaped by subtle cues from police or lineup administrators.

Lineup Instructions

It has long been recognized (e.g., see Malpass & Devine, 1981) that the precise instructions received by the witness prior to, or at, the lineup exert a significant influence on identification performance and, specifically, on choosing behavior. The key element of the lineup instructions is whether the witness is clearly advised that the offender may, *or may not*, be present in the lineup. Instructions containing such a clear warning are referred to as unbiased instructions; those lacking such a warning (e.g., "See if you can pick out the offender from this lineup") are referred to as biased instructions. Unbiased instructions may vary in the extent to which they emphasize the consequences of the witness's decision, although here we focus solely on the basic (warning vs. no warning) distinction.

The most important consequence of varying this dimension of lineup instructions is an alteration in the choosing patterns of witnesses. With target-absent lineups, biased instructions increase the proportion of false identifications; for target-present lineups, such instructions result in fewer lineup rejections, with the increased choosing translating into more correct identifications, more incorrect or foil identifications, or both (Steblay, 1997). Clearly, the effect of varying the degree of bias in instructions operates through a change in the witness's decision criterion, but the specific effect of such a change on identification response patterns will depend on other factors. For example, if there are a number of very plausible, competing candidates in a lineup, an elevated rate of choosing is likely to be reflected in responses that are distributed across a number of different lineup members, thereby changing the proportions of correct to foil identifications in a target-present lineup, or the proportion of innocent suspect to foil identifications in a target-absent lineup. In contrast, in an unfair lineup (i.e., where the suspect is the only plausible choice), an elevated rate of choosing will translate into increased correct identifications or false identifications in target-present and -absent lineups, respectively.

Lineup Composition

The key issues with respect to lineup composition are the number of stimuli that should appear in the lineup and the criteria for choosing those stimuli. In different jurisdictions lineup size varies (e.g., from 6 to 12 members). The only data on the effect of nominal lineup size, of which we are aware, indicate that, as long as there were three good lineup foils, increasing lineup size did not increase the overall proportion of choosers or the proportion of choices for each innocent person in the lineup (Nosworthy & Lindsay, 1990).

However, researchers have given much more attention to the issue of the functional size of the lineup. *Functional size* refers to the number of plausible foils in the lineup: for example, when there is clearly only one plausible stimulus in the lineup, functional size is low (for a detailed discussion, see Wells, 1993). It is generally accepted that, if the police put a plausible but innocent suspect into a lineup with no plausible foils (i.e., a low functional-size lineup), the likelihood of a false identification would be high. Of course, the corollary of this pattern is that if the suspect were actually the offender, the chance of a correct identification would be high. Evidence consistent with the view that, for target-absent lineups, low functional size is a major problem can be found in Lindsay and Wells (1980) and Tredoux (2002), although functional size manipulations have not always affected identification response patterns (Gonzalez, Ellsworth, & Pembroke, 1993).

A combination of supportive empirical evidence and illustrative real-world cases seems to have led to general acceptance that low functional-size lineups are among the major causes of injustice. Despite the widespread acknowledgment of the importance of functional size, it is interesting to note that we know relatively little about how functional size interacts with other important variables, such as actual lineup size, foil similarity, viewing conditions, and so on. Furthermore, in the absence of any detailed account of the psychological processes involved in identification decisions, we can really only speculate about the effect of changing functional size for any given witnessed event and lineup. Our relatively poor theoretical understanding of identification decisions and our tendency to neglect consideration of the interactions between relevant factors are important themes in the ensuing discussion of lineup composition.

The other main lineup composition issue concerns the criteria for choosing lineup members. First, we outline the generally accepted position on the construction of a fair lineup. When the observer did not witness the crime but was, instead, given the description of the offender provided by the witness, *lineup fairness* would refer to the extent to which choices from the lineup are spread evenly across the lineup members (for discussions of lineup fairness, see Malpass, 1981; Malpass & Lindsay, 1999; Wells, Leippe, & Ostrom, 1979). The primary way of achieving a fair lineup is to ensure that all lineup members match the description of the offender provided by the witness (Shepherd, Ellis, & Davies, 1982; Wells, 1993). Consequently, no lineup member should stand out more than any other to an observer provided only with the description of the offender. This approach is also considered to be advantageous because it offers the possibility of supplementing the diagnostic information provided at recall with additional diagnostic information from a recognition test (Wells, 1993). If lineup members were not selected based on their match to the description of the offender, identification of the suspect—who is likely to be the only match to the description—will provide no new information to the police, although they may see this identification as the ultimate confirmation of their hypothesis. In contrast, it has been argued that selecting lineup members based on their similarity to the suspect (an approach that seems intuitively sensible) is considered inappropriate because (1) despite the lineup members being similar in appearance to the suspect, they may still differ on some important feature described by the witness (and thus are not a plausible alternative), and (2) it may place an unreasonable demand upon the witness's discrimination powers.

While the match-to-description approach might be the generally accepted one, we are not yet convinced that this issue is resolved. Regardless of the foil selection strategy used, the members of the lineup can be considered in terms of the extent to which they match the witness's image of the offender, and also each other, on described and nondescribed elements. In a situation in which a witness gives a scanty description and foils are selected using a match-to-description strategy, there are many undescribed dimensions on which the faces could differ in appearance. Consequently, the chance of a single face being the only plausible choice from the lineup is still, in fact, high. If the suspect is the offender, this factor is clearly not a problem. However, if the suspect is not the offender but is the closest match on the undescribed features, this factor is a major problem. The problem is exacerbated in a multiple-suspect lineup, because the chance of a suspect being the closest match to the image of the offender in the witness's memory is increased. Of course, if one of the known-innocent foils is the closest match, this again is not a problem.

Alternatively, if the foils were selected using a match-to-suspect (i.e., similarity) strategy, the likelihood that a single lineup member would be a clear match of the witness's memory of the offender is reduced. If the suspect is the offender, there are three broad possible effects of a lineup composition such as this. One is that the presence of a number of plausible alternatives in the lineup may lead to an increased rate of choosing and, given that the suspect is likely to be the best match to the witness's memory, to an increased likelihood of a correct identification. A second is that increased choosing may instead translate into a reduced likelihood of correct identifications, because the chance of a foil being the best match is higher than in a match-to-description lineup. A third possibility is that the presence of multiple alternatives in the lineup reduces the likelihood of a witness choosing and thus reduces the overall proportion of correct identifications; the ratio of correct to incorrect identifications, though, is unknown. If, however, the suspect is not the offender, these possibilities translate into different outcomes. With an increase in choosing, the likelihood of the innocent suspect being chosen increases; if choosing decreases, obviously the likelihood of identification of the innocent suspect decreases.

While people might argue about the merits of the possibilities that we have just canvassed, the unfortunate fact is that existing research simply does not allow us to arbitrate between these possibilities. What the consideration of these options tells us is that the construction of the lineup is potentially an important factor in explaining identification performance. Although the importance of lineup composition has been recognized in the research (e.g., debates about match-to-description or match-to-suspect strategies), it has not been thoroughly or systematically investigated. Thus, we are missing a detailed understanding of how the intricacies of lineup composition affect responding. For example, how do fine-grained variations in similarity of lineup members affect patterns of choosing and, in turn, the pattern of identification responses? Or how do such variations interact with other key variables, such as viewing conditions and witness and offender characteristics? So, while the generally accepted wisdom is that the match-to-description strategy is the appropriate one, we believe that a number of important underlying issues remain unresolved. Exploration of these issues will require the examination of complex interactions among many factors, and almost certainly will be most efficiently conducted with a focus on the development of a theory of the psychological processes involved in the identification task.

Lineup Presentation Mode

Perhaps one of the most prominent foci in the identification literature has been the simultaneous versus the sequential mode of lineup presentation. This interest emanated from a particular distinction highlighted by Wells (1984): the tendency for witnesses to make relative, rather than absolute, judgments when viewing a lineup. What is hoped for when conducting a lineup is that the witness will find (or not find) a lineup member who matches his or her mental representation of the offender. In other words, the witness is, ideally, making an absolute judgment about the status of each lineup member. However, it is now generally accepted that witnesses confronted with a simultaneous lineup do not necessarily proceed in this manner. Rather, researchers concur with Wells (1984) that witnesses have a strong tendency to make relative judgments. Instead of making an absolute decision about each lineup member, witnesses are considered likely to choose the person in the lineup who most closely resembles their memory of the offender. Evidence typically used to support this claim comes from the previously discussed study of Wells (1993) as well as from studies that demonstrate that, when witnesses are prevented from simultaneously viewing lineup members, they are less likely to make false identifications from target-absent lineups (Lindsay & Wells, 1985). Lindsay and Wells employed a sequential lineup procedure, the key features of which included: (1) The lineup members are presented one at a time; (2) the witness must make a final decision about each lineup member before presented with the next (i.e., any choice, whether correct or incorrect, will terminate the lineup) and is not allowed to revise that decision; and (3) the witness is unaware of the number of lineup members to be shown.

Since Lindsay and Wells's seminal study, there have been a number of demonstrations of the superiority of the sequential lineup. Typically what is claimed is a reduction in false identifications from target-absent lineups and no apparent effect on correct identifications from target-present lineups (for a recent overview, see Steblay, Dysart, Fulero, & Lindsay, 2001). Indeed, so widely accepted is this finding that formal recommendations about lineup practice place this one high on the priority list (Technical Working Group for Eyewitness Evidence, 1999). It is worth noting, however, that although there is no doubt that the procedure reduces false identifications, some studies have reported pronounced differences in correct identifications between the two presentation modes, with superior performance found in the simultaneous lineup (e.g., Memon & Gabbert, 2003; Sauer, Brewer, & Wells, 2005). Steblay et al.'s (2001) meta-analysis also detected this pattern. Although they provided a post hoc explanation in terms of the influence of moderating variables, it is premature to conclude that the sequential lineup does not also lower the rate of correct identifications.

The fact that correct identification rates can fall (possibly markedly, under some circumstances) suggests that we need to analyze further the nature of the processes that distinguish judgments made under both presentation modes. For example, one alternative theoretical perspective suggests that witnesses, when confronted with a sequential lineup, may adopt a stricter decision criterion. This criterion, it is contended, leads to a reduced rate of choosing in sequential lineups and, subsequently, a reduction in false identifications from target-absent lineups, but the pattern is also accompanied by reduced correct identifications in target-present lineups (Ebbesen & Flowe, 2004). Here, again, the importance of understanding choosing behavior comes to the fore. Clarifying the nature of the judgment processes associated with the two presentation modes is necessary to elucidate precisely those conditions that will lead to superior performance under one or the other presentation mode, particularly given the possibility that in some, potentially identifiable, circumstances the sequential lineup may lead to an unacceptably low rate of correct identifications.

Although the extant literature suggests that the sequential lineup procedure is superior with respect to preventing false identifications, it is obvious that eyewitnesses still make mistakes. One obvious focus for future work is to develop lineup procedures that will reduce the mistakes that witnesses make. A number of examples of the former approach are at the embryonic stage. One involves the use of multiple independent lineups, where witnesses view independent lineups of, for example, faces, bodies, voices, and clothes (Pryke, Lindsay, Dysart, & Dupuis, 2004). Another example involves elimination lineups—designed particularly for use with children—in which witnesses are required to successively eliminate lineup members before making an absolute judgment about the lone remaining candidate (Pozzulo & Lindsay, 1999). Both procedures show considerable promise for reducing false identifications from target-absent lineups, but it is important to note that (at least with adult witnesses) they also lower the hit rate from target-present lineups.

There are undoubtedly other lineup options that would permit witnesses to make multiple choices from extended arrays. A feature of this type of procedure is that, rather than obtaining a single judgment from a witness, they use multiple judgments in an attempt to get a broader sampling of the witness's memory. A combination of the broad sampling of a witness's memory and a good theory of how people make such judgments may well be the way forward. From other domains such as psychological testing we know full well how important broad sampling of psychological constructs is. The fact that one of the major advances in lineup technology (i.e., the sequential procedure) derived from theorizing about the nature of the underlying judgment process is testimony to the utility of a theory-driven approach. Another, and complementary, approach to improving the lineup procedures involves identifying variables that provide reliable markers of identification accuracy; this is the focus of the next section.

Characteristics of the Identification Decision

The fallibility of eyewitness identifications has spurred researchers to make concerted attempts to identify what are termed "independent markers"—or "postdictors"—of identification accuracy. The rationale underpinning this approach has been that, if there are serious question marks about the possible accuracy of an identification, knowing that there is some independent indicator of accuracy will help us assess the reliability of an identification decision. Before examining research on such markers, we wish to emphasize one general point that has attracted insufficient attention in this area of research. These markers or postdictors can do more than signal whether an identification is likely to be accurate. Importantly, they also inform us about the characteristics of the identification decision processes, which ultimately are the key to understanding the determinants of choosing behavior and, in turn, accuracy. The markers that have attracted attention are witnesses' identification latency and impressions of their decision processes, as well as identification confidence.

Identification Latency

Identification latency is considered to be one potentially informative indicator of accuracy. The rationale is that witnesses who have a strong memorial representation of the offender are able to determine if the stimuli presented during testing match their internal representation more rapidly than those with a weak representation. Although there is not a huge volume of research on this issue, the findings are consistent in showing that accurate identifications are made faster than inaccurate ones (Smith, Lindsay, & Pryke, 2000; Smith, Lindsay, Pryke, & Dysart, 2001; Sporer, 1993, 1994), with latency–accuracy correlations for choosers typically in the range of –.2 to –.4. Some studies have also reported witnesses' accounts of their decision processes (e.g., Dunning & Stern, 1994; Smith et al., 2000), noting that people who report automatic decision process are likely to be accurate. In this context, automatic processing is characterized as a generally fast, unconscious recognition and by reports such as "the face just popped out a me." In contrast, deliberative processing is considered to be slower, involving conscious comparisons of the alternative stimuli.

An interesting development in the decision-latency research has been the discovery that specific and relatively brief latencies might provide a precise marker of accuracy. For example, Smith et al. (2000) noted much higher accuracy rates for identifications with latencies less than 16 seconds (69.4%) when compared with identification decisions with latencies between 16 and 30 seconds (42.6%) and greater than 30 seconds (17.6%). Subsequently, Dunning and Perretta (2002) suggested that a specific and very short time window of 10–12 seconds may best distinguish accurate from inaccurate responses. This conclusion was based on a time boundary analysis that involved (1) identifying the number of accurate and inaccurate participants who fell inside and outside, respectively, a time boundary of 1 second, 2 seconds, 3 seconds, 4 seconds, and so on; (2) calculating, for each time boundary, a 2 (accuracy) × 2 (time boundary) chi-square statistic; and (3) identifying the time boundary at which the chi-square value peaked. Across several experiments they found that (1) accurate responses were best distinguished from inaccurate responses at a time boundary of 10–12 seconds, and (2) accuracy rates were extremely high (87.1%) within the 10-second boundary. Should research consistently demonstrate that accurate identifications are made within 10–12 seconds, the practical implications would be both obvious and significant.

Data collected in several recent studies in our laboratory, however, challenge this conclusion (Weber, Brewer, Wells, Semmler, & Keast, 2004). In several experiments with large samples, designed for other purposes, computer-recorded latencies indicated different optimum time boundaries ranging from under 5 seconds up to 29 seconds. Two other studies specifically exploring the effects of nominal lineup size and retention interval (i.e., delay between the stimulus event and the identification test) on the optimum time boundary also demonstrated that the optimum time boundary can be experimentally manipulated (Brewer, Caon, Todd, & Weber, 2004). Furthermore, it is important to note that seldom in any of these data sets did the proportion correct within the optimum time boundary approach the exceptionally high levels reported by Dunning and Perretta (2002). In light of these findings, the conclusion that an optimum time boundary of 10–12 seconds applies for all combinations of lineups and other relevant variables appears untenable and, moreover—as we (Weber et al., 2004) point out—inconsistent with relevant theory in the area of recognition memory research.

We should, however, note one promising recent finding. Although our (Weber et al., 2004) data did not support the 10- to 12-seconds rule, we did suggest useful directions to consider for possible revisions of the rule. Because our studies all had very large samples, we were able to select identifications made at any particular latency and with any particular confidence level while still maintaining a reasonable sample size. One striking finding that emerged from such analyses was that identifications made (1) within the 10-second time boundary and (2) with high confidence (90–100%) were accurate on an extremely high proportion of occasions: 88.1% correct for high confidence responses within 10 seconds versus 69.0% correct for high confidence responses beyond 10 seconds, and 53.5% correct for low confidence responses within 10 seconds versus 60.0% correct for low confidence responses beyond 10 seconds. Although it is possible that the effectiveness of the specific time boundary and confidence combination may not generalize to other contexts, this finding highlights the importance of examining the combined utility of multiple indicators of identification accuracy. It is also worth noting that dual-process models of recognition memory (for a review, see Yonelinas, 2002) would suggest that, if witnesses attempted to make a recollection-based judgment before relying on familiarity alone, an extremely strong memorial representation of the offender (that permits a recollection-based judgment) is likely to be associated with an accurate, fast, and highly confident identification.

Another approach to the use of identification latency to distinguish accurate identifications is seen in the results of Brewer, Weber, Clark, and Wells (2004). These studies were designed to examine accuracy rates in witnesses who were prepared to attempt an identification after a very brief exposure to the lineup. Specifically, accuracy rates for witnesses who were prepared to attempt an identification after 8 seconds, 16 seconds, or more than 16 seconds were contrasted with that of control participants, who were required to respond at 8 seconds, 16 seconds, or in their own time (greater than 16 seconds). The rationale underlying this approach was that witnesses who were prepared to respond after a mere 8-second exposure may be witnesses who have an extremely good representation of the offender and consequently are highly likely to make an accurate identification. Although this procedure produced higher rates of correct identifications from target-present lineups, particularly when witnesses were given biased lineup instructions, it also increased the proportion of false identifications from target-absent lineups, especially with biased instructions. It is possible, however, that more successful refinements of this general approach, particularly ones that ensure that witnesses are optimally biased toward accuracy, could emerge.

A final point on identification latency: Although research on this variable has not been plentiful, it is a variable that merits much closer attention because it is one of the few variables that is a direct measure of the decision process. It may turn out that latency does not advance our understanding of identification decision processes greatly, particularly if its examination is restricted to experiments eliciting a very small number of judgments (often only one in the identification context), where variability in the measure is a problem. However, given how valuable latency measures have proved to be in advancing our understanding in other areas of cognitive psychology, the latency category does warrant concerted investigation.

Confidence

The variable that has attracted the most attention as a marker of identification accuracy is the confidence that the witness holds in that decision. Intuitively it makes sense that there should be a meaningful relationship between the accuracy and confidence of people's judgments. Indeed, such relationships have been found in many different domains of judgment research (e.g., general knowledge, recall, recognition memory, and psychophysical discrimination). It is also the case that eyewitness identification confidence is seen as an important indicator of the likely accuracy of witness identifications by the various different sectors of the criminal justice system. For example, court rulings list identification confidence as one of the criteria that should be applied when evaluating the reliability of such evidence (*Neil v. Biggers*, 1972). Survey studies of police, lawyers, and jurors show that confidence is universally perceived as a reliable indicator of accuracy (Deffenbacher & Loftus, 1982; Potter & Brewer, 1999), and mock-jury experiments have provided a number of demonstrations of the powerful effects of witness confidence on jurors' judgments of witness credibility and, in turn, their assessments of the likely guilt of the defendant (Bradfield & Wells, 2000; Brewer & Burke, 2002; Cutler, Penrod, & Stuve, 1988; Lindsay, Wells, & Rumpel, 1981).

Does this convergence of views within the criminal justice system mean that there should be a meaningful relationship between the two variables? No, it does not, but there are, in fact, theoretical grounds for expecting such a relationship, although we can also identify a number of factors that may undermine the relationship. There are at least three broad theories of judgment for which the expectation of a meaningful confidence–accuracy (CA) relation is fundamental. For example, a basic formulation of signal detection theory (Green & Swets, 1966; Macmillan & Creelman, 1991), one of the most widely accepted theories of human judgment, is that judgmental confidence is tied to accuracy. Signal detection theory holds that binary judgments are made by comparing the amount of evidence for one response option with a criterion. In the recognition memory context, the stronger the evidence that the stimulus is old, the more likely it is to exceed the participant's threshold and be labeled old, and the more likely it is to actually be old. In signal detection theory it is this strength of evidence that is considered not only to drive accuracy but also to directly determine confidence.

Similar predictions are foreshadowed by theories of psychophysical discrimination (Baranski & Petrusic, 1994; Van Zandt, 2000; Vickers, 1979), which propose that confidence judgments are guided by the amount of evidence accumulated in favor of the chosen versus the alternative response options. Thus, when the evidence is overwhelmingly in favor of one response option compared with others, not only is accuracy likely to be high, but this evidential disparity will also lead to high confidence. Conversely, both accuracy and confidence will decline with decreasing evidential disparities. Contemporary dual-process models of recognition memory (Atkinson & Juola, 1974; Mandler, 1980; Yonelinas, 1994) also provide grounds for expecting robust CA relations. Such theories suggest that the basis of recognition judgments can be twofold: (1) the recollection of event-specific details, and (2) the familiarity of the stimulus. Any single judgment can be the result of the operation of one or both recognition processes. It has been argued that recollections are typically made with high accuracy and confidence, whereas the confidence and accuracy of familiarity-based judgments both vary with familiarity (or the strength of the memory trace). The combined operation of these processes should ensure a CA relationship.

Despite these theoretical arguments, there are reasons why confidence and accuracy may be dissociated. Some have argued, for example, that confidence is an entirely postdecisional determination and that different processes underlie the identification decision and the confidence judgment (Wells & Bradfield, 1998, 1999). We also know of specific conditions under which confidence and accuracy are dissociated. For example, it is now well documented that witnesses' confidence estimates can be significantly influenced by social factors. In the next section of the chapter we deal with such factors at some length and, particularly, the phenomenon known as the "postidentification feedback effect." Suffice it to say at this stage that postidentification confirming (or disconfirming) feedback cues from people such as police, lineup administrators, or cowitnesses can modify confidence estimates without, of course, any effect on identification accuracy.

Other researchers have shown that CA dissociation can arise when participants rely on misleading cues when assessing their confidence. For example, Busey, Tunnicliff, Loftus, and Loftus (2000) showed that, when a face was brighter at test than at encoding, confidence was elevated even though accuracy declined. They attributed this pattern to participants' reliance on the test illumination to determine confidence, when, in fact, accuracy was determined by the luminance match from study to test. Furthermore, they raised the interesting possibility that the dissociation of confidence and accuracy may be more likely when participants use the outcomes of analytical processes rather than simply relying on the direct mnemonic cues. Such a dissociation may also result when witnesses mistakenly attribute the source of familiarity invoked by the test stimulus. A particular face in a lineup may evoke a strong sense of familiarity, but this familiarity may be (mistakenly) attributed to the offender when, in fact, it may only have been seen in the context of the crime. Here, a confidence judgment based on degree of familiarity will clearly be inappropriately high. Another example of this type of dissociation has been demonstrated by Chandler (1994), who showed that viewing a target stimulus together with other similar stimuli led to an increased sense of familiarity for the target stimulus, higher confidence in the resulting judgment, but stable or decreased accuracy. It would be possible to list many other examples of how misattributing the source of familiarity may change confidence independently of accuracy. Finally, it has been suggested by CA researchers in other domains (e.g., see Soll & Klayman, 2004; Windschitl & Wells, 1996) that we may not be very good at translating internal or subjective states of confidence (which may be veridical) into external or objective confidence scales. That is, confidence–accuracy dissociation may not arise from an inability to realistically assess confidence but from an inability to express that confidence on conventional scales. We have canvassed these sorts of issues elsewhere (e.g., Brewer, Weber, & Semmler, in press), and we believe that they are worth exploring further.

For many years the evidence has been almost uniformly supportive of the view that eyewitness identification confidence and accuracy are, at best, only weakly related. Reviews and meta-analyses have consistently shown CA correlation coefficients that seldom exceed .3 (Bothwell, Deffenbacher, & Brigham, 1987; Sporer, Penrod, Read, & Cutler, 1995; Wells & Murray, 1984). There is, however, a major problem with these analyses. Specifically, the CA relation is indexed by the point–biserial correlation, which assesses the separation of the confidence distributions of accurate and inaccurate responses. A number of papers have now clearly outlined how this procedure can conceal meaningful relationships (e.g., Brewer, Keast, & Rishworth, 2002; Brewer & Wells, 2004; Juslin, Olsson, & Winman, 1996; Weber & Brewer, 2003), thereby demonstrating why discussions of this CA relation should not rely on this index. The recommended procedure for assessing the relationship is calibration, a procedure widely used in other areas of human judgment and decision making (e.g., general knowledge, psychophysics, and metacognition). Here, the proportion of accurate decisions for each level of confidence is plotted against the mean confidence for that particular level; perfect calibration occurs when all decisions at 100% confidence are correct, 90% of decisions at 90% confidence are correct, and so on. The obtained calibration function permits the detection of over- or underconfidence in witnesses and allows examination of the degree of association between confidence and proportion correct. A particular advantage in the forensic context is that knowledge of CA calibration allows confidence to provide a guide to the likely probability of identification accuracy.

Employing this procedure, a number of recent studies have detected robust CA relations using both the typical eyewitness identification paradigm (Brewer et al., 2002; Brewer & Wells, 2004; Juslin et al., 1996) and a face recognition paradigm (Olsson, Juslin, & Winman, 1998; Weber & Brewer, 2003, 2004a). Importantly, it seems to be the case that robust CA relations characterize choosers (i.e., those witnesses who make positive identifications) but not nonchoosers (i.e., those who reject the lineup; Brewer & Wells, 2004). The same pattern is observed for positive and negative recognition decisions in a face recognition paradigm (Weber & Brewer, 2004a). (The face recognition paradigm typically involves the presentation of a series of faces for study, followed by a test phase that requires participants to detect [1] whether or not a face was presented in the study, or [2] which of a set of faces was shown in the study phase.) Recent data from our laboratory (Weber & Brewer, 2004b) support the validity and generalizability of these findings to the real-world identification context. The effects of two manipulations that provide closer approximation to the real-world identification task than face recognition and many eyewitness identification experiments were examined. Neither associative nor free-decision (i.e., participants could respond "I don't know") judgments demonstrated a meaningful CA relation for negative decisions, despite doing so for positive decisions.

An important additional finding in CA calibration research is that the extent to which obtained calibration functions approximate the ideal seems to be related to the target-absent base rate (i.e., the proportion of target-absent trials). For example, the calibration functions reported by Brewer and Wells (2004) for target-absent base rates of 50% indicate a monotonic increasing relationship between confidence and accuracy, although accompanied by overconfidence. With lower target-absent base rates, specifically 25 and 15%, the calibration functions approximate the ideal much more closely. These findings have extremely important practical implications. We do not know the actual target-absent base rates in the real world, and it is certain to be the case that they will vary between jurisdictions. We do know that the target-absent base rate is not zero, but it would be surprising if it was anywhere near as high as 50%. Having some reasonable estimate of the "true" value(s) would aid in interpretation of the applied significance of results such as those reported by Brewer and Wells (2004). Also of practical significance is determining, with certainty, whether the CA calibration we have obtained for nonchoosers is reliable. Lineup rejections provide important information about the likely guilt of the suspect (Wells & Olson, 2002), but confirmation of our findings would indicate that confidence should not guide our evaluations of the veridicality of rejections.

It is too early to be able to document precisely how calibration is affected by a variety of forensically relevant variables. We do know from face recognition studies that calibration functions display the same hard–easy effect as has been reported in other areas of judgment research (e.g., Baranski & Petrusic, 1994; Lichtenstein & Fischhoff, 1977): that is, as task difficulty (e.g., briefer exposure to the stimulus) increases, so does overconfidence (Weber & Brewer, 2004b). An important focus of future research should be to elucidate those variables that affect calibration. The substantial data collection enterprise that is required to examine calibration in the eyewitness identification paradigm (e.g., see Brewer et al., 2002; Brewer & Wells, 2004) means that it would be completely impractical to explore the effects of an endless array of potentially relevant variables. We believe that the most profitable approach will involve more basic research whereby researchers strive to develop a general understanding of the origins of judgmental confidence. Once that knowledge is gained, researchers would be in a position to predict the effect of different variables on CA calibration and thus provide guidelines as to precisely when confidence is likely to be a veridical marker of identification accuracy.

The importance of obtaining such an understanding is further highlighted by recent research demonstrating how calibration can be manipulated. Brewer et al. (2002) showed substantial improvements in calibration, relative to a control group, when witnesses were exposed to relatively simple manipulations prior to finalizing their confidence assessment. In one condition witnesses were required to spend 5 minutes reflecting on their experiences at the identification test and at the time of encoding (reflection). In another condition witnesses spent the same length of time providing possible reasons as to why their identification decision may have been inaccurate (hypothesis disconfirmation). Both manipulations appeared to produce similarly good CA calibration outcomes. Thus, the calibration literature suggests that, in some circumstances, confidence and accuracy are well calibrated and that, in others, improved calibration can be produced through intervention. But again, having a detailed understanding of how confidence is determined and shaped, and precisely how manipulations such as those just described affect confidence mechanisms, seems to us to be the most economical way to clarify how optimum CA calibration can be achieved. Answers to such questions about the origins of confidence are not only important from the perspective of diagnosing identification accuracy, but they also have the potential to inform our understanding of the processes underlying the identification decision itself.

Postidentification Test Variables

Many witnesses who make an identification are asked to talk about that identification subsequently, in a courtroom. Among the things they may talk about are their recollections of the event they witnessed and their confidence in the identification. The two events, the identification and the courtroom appearance, are typically separated by long periods of time—and a lot of things can happen within that period of time that may shape witnesses' subsequent reports. Here we focus on possible influences on people's memories of their witnessing experience, their identification, and their expressed confidence in that identification.

What are some of the potentially influential events that may occur? A witness may receive some kind of feedback from the police, lawyers, cowitnesses, or even media sources. Such feedback may be explicit: For example, a cowitness may say that he or she made the same identification choice, the police may indicate that the witness picked the suspect or that he or she had failed to do so. Feedback information may also be much more subtle, for example, in the form of nonverbal cues or verbal intonation. And feedback could be in the form of cues that witnesses may interpret as confirming, such as being told that they will be called as a witness in court, that their testimony is important, and so on.

There is not a huge amount of research on these issues, and the range of variables examined is quite restricted, but the limited research that has been conducted has produced converging and clear-cut results. Several studies by Wells and colleagues have contrasted the effects of both confirming and disconfirming feedback about an identification with no feedback controls (Wells & Bradfield, 1998, Experiment 1; Wells et al., 2003). The experiments have mainly employed a paradigm designed to maximize the number of false identifications: that is, viewing conditions are typically poor, witnesses receive biased (i.e., failure to warn about the possible absence of the offender) instructions prior to viewing the lineup, and the lineup is target-absent. The typical findings demonstrate that confirming feedback inflates witnesses' confidence in false identifications, and disconfirming feedback deflates it. Effects have been reported for feedback from both the lineup administrator (Garrioch & Brimacombe, 2001; Wells & Bradfield, 1998, 1999) and cowitnesses (Luus & Wells, 1994). The effects of this feedback also extend to witnesses' recollections of the witnessing experience (e.g., how good their view of the perpetrator was), their recollections of the identification experience (e.g., the ease of the identification), and even factors such as their willingness to testify (Wells & Bradfield, 1998, 1999). Subsequent research (Semmler, Brewer, & Wells, 2004) has shown that these effects also extend to the situation wherein lineup instructions are unbiased, to target-present lineups, and all possible identification responses (i.e., correct identifications, incorrect rejections, correct rejections, incorrect identifications).

These findings have considerable forensic relevance. For example, confirming postidentification feedback seems likely to increase a witness's confidence in his or her identification, whether it was false or correct. Disconfirming feedback is likely to decrease confidence in a lineup rejection and in a correct identification. Given that witness confidence is an important determinant of how eyewitness credibility is judged, such responses to feedback can make the witness appear much more or less credible than he or she should appear. One direct consequence of these findings is that researchers have strongly advocated that any assessment of witness confidence should be taken at the time of the identification (Technical Working Group for Eyewitness Evidence, 1999). Moreover, most eyewitness researchers would agree that eyewitness expressions of confidence that emerge during a trial should be discounted.

Although the findings in this area are generally consistent, there has been little systematic exploration of the precise mechanisms underlying the effect; consequently, the boundary conditions of the effect have not been resolved. Several possible mechanisms have been suggested, including the possibility that witnesses have no access to the cognitive operations that they performed at the time of the event and later when required to make an identification decision, and so they must use the feedback information as a basis for their judgments. This mechanism draws on Bem's self-perception theory (Bem, 1972), which, in essence, proposes that individuals draw inferences about their internal states from their overt behavior. An alternative account outlined by Bradfield, Wells, and Olson (2002) suggests that feedback information is more likely to have an effect when there is a low degree of match between the individual chosen from the lineup and the memory trace of the offender (i.e., low ecphoric similarity, Tulving, 1981) and less likely to have an impact when the match between the memory trace and the individual chosen from the lineup is good. More recently there has been some suggestion that the feedback effect is another variation of the well-established hindsight bias (Bradfield & Wells, in press; Hafstad, Memon, & Logie, 2004). Although all of these accounts fit well with extant data on the effect (particularly when target-absent lineups with biased instructions are used), they offer few clues as to the boundary conditions of the effect and any possible moderators (apart from prior thought about the witnessing and test conditions, Wells & Bradfield, 1999).

One thread that seems to run through all of these suggested mechanisms is that the feedback effect is perhaps most likely when the internal cues to judgment accuracy are relatively weak, so that the witness is then more prone to draw upon the feedback information to shape his or her confidence. One focus in our research has been the testing of this idea, referred to as the "cues" hypothesis. We have worked on the assumption that the availability of information on which witnesses base their judgments may vary across witnessing and identification conditions. We have also suggested that there may be various sources of information available to witnesses when they are asked to nominate their confidence estimate. In testing the cues hypothesis, the main approach taken has been to manipulate variables associated with either the likelihood of participants correctly recognizing the target (mnemonic cues) or with expectations about the likelihood of correctly recognizing the target (metamemory cues). Findings from several studies have supported the idea that conditions that favor accurate recognition of the perpetrator (such as increased exposure duration) also reduce the degree of influence of confirming feedback. Another consistent finding has been the reduced effect of feedback (confirming and disconfirming) on confidence for recognition decisions that were made quickly (cf. slowly), suggesting that the fluency of the recognition decision may be a cue that witnesses use to determine their confidence (Semmler et al., 2004; Semmler & Brewer, 2004).

Another finding from our research (Semmler & Brewer, 2004) has been that, when confirming feedback is given when witnesses have a strong expectation that they were accurate (as indicated by either a quick response or a response to a highly distinctive face), confidence shows less inflation than when witnesses have an expectation that they were incorrect (slow response or response to a typical face). Similarly, for witnesses with a strong expectation of being correct, the receipt of disconfirming feedback produces larger confidence deflation than when they have an expectation of being incorrect. These results point to the possibility that there are situations in which witnesses may have salient expectations about the likelihood that their identification decision is correct (e.g., based on their beliefs about how their memory operates, the view they had at the crime scene, or the distinctiveness of the perpetrator), which will moderate the effect of feedback on their confidence. Further research into the impact that such expectations—or metacognitive variables— may have on the postidentification feedback effect appears to be a promising avenue.

BROAD CONCLUSIONS

Two broad conclusions emerge from the preceding discussions. First, it is clear that the available empirical research falls a long way short of providing definitive answers to many questions. In some cases (e.g., the impact of exposure duration on identification accuracy), this shortfall probably comes as quite a surprise. Despite the volume of published research on eyewitness identification, the evidence in many areas is scarce, inconclusive (often for some of the methodological reasons outlined earlier), and has not yet encompassed the examination of many potentially important interactions.

Second, much of the research has been conducted outside of some theoretical framework that would facilitate the systematic investigation of issues required to produce conclusions that would provide broad explanatory power—and, in turn, practical recommendations upon which we could rely. Not only does the lack of a clear theoretical framework restrict the likelihood of broad conclusions, but it also poses a major limitation on our capacity to integrate a diverse array of individual empirical findings. One example highlighted in previous sections (and elsewhere by the same authors, Brewer et al., in press) is the need for a theory of choosing behavior and, particularly, a theory that accommodates the complex array of likely interactions between variables. Our reference to the possible role of metacognitive factors at various points throughout this chapter is one illustration of how a search for an overarching theoretical perspective could point researchers in new empirical directions and help them understand how key variables are likely to interact.

ACKNOWLEDGMENT

This research was supported by Grant No. A00104516 from the Australian Research Council to Neil Brewer and Gary L. Wells.

NOTES

1. For reviews of a wide range of eyewitness identification topics, see Lindsay, Ross, Read, and Toglia (in press).
2. For a wide-ranging discussion of this issue, see *Psychology, Public Policy and Law* (Vol. 7, No. 1, 2001, pp. 3–262).
3. See the special issue of *Applied Cognitive Psychology* (Vol. 16, No. 8, 2002, pp. 869–997).

REFERENCES

Atkinson, R. C., & Juola, J. F. (1974). Search and decision processes in recognition memory. In D. H. Krantz, R. C. Atkinson, R. D. Luce, & P. Suppes (Eds.), *Contemporary developments in mathematical psychology: Vol. 1. Learning, memory and thinking* (pp. 243–293). San Francisco: Freeman.

Baranski, J. V., & Petrusic, W. M. (1994). The calibration and resolution of confidence in perceptual judgments. *Perception and Psychophysics, 55*, 412–428.

Bem, D. J. (1972). Self-perception theory. In L. Berkowitz (Ed.), *Advances in experimental social psychology* (Vol. 6, pp. 1–62). New York: Academic Press.

Bothwell, R. K., Deffenbacher, K. A., & Brigham, J. C. (1987). Correlation of eyewitness accuracy and confidence: Optimality hypothesis revisited. *Journal of Applied Psychology, 72*, 691–695.

Bradfield, A. L., & Wells, G. L. (2000). The perceived validity of eyewitness identification testimony: A test of the five Biggers criteria. *Law and Human Behavior, 24*, 581–594.

Bradfield, A., & Wells, G. L. (in press). Not the same old hindsight bias: Outcome information distorts a broad range of retrospective judgments. *Memory and Cognition.*

Bradfield, A. L., Wells, G. L., & Olson, E. A. (2002). The damaging effect of confirming feedback on the relation between eyewitness certainty and identification accuracy. *Journal of Applied Psychology, 87*, 112–120.

Brandt, K. R., Macrae, C., Schloerscheidt, A. M., & Milne, A. B. (2003). Remembering or knowing others? Person recognition and recollective experience. *Memory, 11*, 89–100.

Brewer, N., & Burke, A. (2002). Effects of testimonial inconsistencies and eyewitness confidence on mock-juror judgments. *Law and Human Behavior, 26*, 353–364.

Brewer, N., Caon, A., Todd, C., & Weber, N. (2004). *Eyewitness identification accuracy, response latency, and confidence.* Manuscript submitted for publication.

Brewer, N., Weber, N., Clark, A., & Wells, G. L. (2004). *Distinguishing accurate from inaccurate eyewitness identifications with an optional deadline procedure.* Manuscript submitted for publication.

Brewer, N., Keast, A., & Rishworth, A. (2002). The confidence–accuracy relationship in eyewitness identification: The effects of reflection and disconfirmation on correlation and calibration. *Journal of Experimental Psychology: Applied, 8*, 44–56.

Brewer, N., Weber, N., & Semmler, C. (in press). A role for theory in eyewitness identification research. In R. C. L. Lindsay, D. F. Ross, J. D. Read, & M. Toglia (Eds.), *Handbook of eyewitness psychology: Memory for people* (Vol. 2). Mahwah, NJ: Erlbaum.

Brewer, N., & Wells, G. L. (2004). *The confidence–accuracy relationship in eyewitness identification: Effects of lineup instructions, foil similarity and target-absent base rates.* Manuscript in preparation.

Brigham, J. C., & Cairns, D. L. (1988). The effect of mugshot inspections on eyewitness identification accuracy. *Journal of Applied Social Psychology, 18*, 1394–1410.

Brown, C., & Lloyd-Jones, T. J. (2002). Verbal overshadowing in a multiple face presentation paradigm: Effects of description instruction. *Applied Cognitive Psychology, 16*, 873–885.

Busey, T. A., Tunnicliff, J., Loftus, G. R., & Loftus, E. F. (2000). Accounts of the confidence–accuracy relation in recognition memory. *Psychonomic Bulletin and Review, 7*, 26–48.

Chandler, C. C. (1994). Studying related pictures can reduce accuracy, but increase confidence, in a modified recognition test. *Memory and Cognition, 22,* 273–280.

Clare, J., & Lewandowsky, S. (2004). Verbalizing facial memory: Criterion effects in verbal overshadowing. *Journal of Experimental Psychology: Learning, Memory, and Cognition, 30,* 739–755.

Cutler, B. L., & Penrod, S. D. (1995). *Mistaken identification: The eyewitness, psychology, and the law.* New York: Cambridge University Press.

Cutler, B. L., Penrod, S. D., & Martens, T. K. (1987a). Improving the reliability of eyewitness identification: Putting context into context. *Journal of Applied Psychology, 72,* 629–637.

Cutler, B. L., Penrod, S. D., & Martens, T. K. (1987b). The reliability of eyewitness identification: The role of system and estimator variables. *Law and Human Behavior, 11,* 233–258.

Cutler, B. L., Penrod, S. D., & Stuve, T. E. (1988). Juror decision making in eyewitness identification cases. *Law and Human Behavior, 12,* 41–55.

Davies, G. M., Shepherd, J. W., & Ellis, H. D. (1979). Effects of interpolated mugshot exposure on accuracy of eyewitness identification. *Journal of Applied Psychology, 64,* 232–237.

Deffenbacher, K. A., & Loftus, E. F. (1982). Do jurors share a common understanding concerning eyewitness behavior? *Law and Human Behavior, 6,* 15–30.

Dodson, C. S., Johnson, M. K., & Schooler, J. W. (1997). The verbal overshadowing effect: Why descriptions impair face recognition. *Memory and Cognition, 25,* 129–139.

Dodson, C. S., & Schacter, D. L. (2001). "If I had said it I would have remembered it": Reducing false memories with a distinctiveness heuristic. *Psychonomic Bulletin and Review, 8,* 155–161.

Dunning, D., & Perretta, S. (2002). Automaticity and eyewitness accuracy: A 10- to 12-second rule for distinguishing accurate from inaccurate positive identifications. *Journal of Applied Psychology, 87,* 951–962.

Dunning, D., & Stern, L. B. (1994). Distinguishing accurate from inaccurate eyewitness identifications via inquiries about decision processes. *Journal of Personality and Social Psychology, 67,* 818–835.

Dysart, J. E., Lindsay, R. C. L., Hammond, R., & Dupuis, P. (2001). Mug shot exposure prior to lineup identification: Interference, transference, and commitment effects. *Journal of Applied Psychology, 86,* 1280–1284.

Ebbesen, E. B., & Flowe, H. D. (2004). *Simultaneous v. sequential lineups: What do we really know?* Retrieved May, 1, 2004, from *http://www-psy.ucsd.edu/~eeebbesen/ SimSeq.htm#_edn1.*

Ellis, H. D., Davies, G. M., & Shepherd, J. W. (1977). Experimental studies of face identification. *Journal of Criminal Defense, 3,* 219–234.

Estes, W. (1997). Processes of memory loss, recovery, and distortion. *Psychological Review, 104,* 148–169.

Finger, K. (2002). Mazes and music: Using perceptual processing to release verbal overshadowing. *Applied Cognitive Psychology, 16,* 887–896.

Finger, K., & Pezdek, K. (1999). The effect of cognitive interview on face identification accuracy: Release from verbal overshadowing. *Journal of Applied Psychology, 84,* 340–348.

Fisher, R. P., & McCauley, M. R. (1995). Information retrieval: Interviewing witnesses. In N. Brewer & C. Wilson (Eds.), *Psychology and policing* (pp. 81–99). Hillsdale, NJ: Erlbaum.

Garrioch, L., & Brimacombe, C. (2001). Lineup administrators' expectations: Their impact on eyewitness confidence. *Law and Human Behavior, 25,* 299–314.

Gonzalez, R., Ellsworth, P. C., & Pembroke, M. (1993). Response biases in lineups and showups. *Journal of Personality and Social Psychology, 64,* 525–537.

Green, D. M., & Swets, J. A. (1966). *Signal detection theory and psychophysics.* New York: Wiley.

Hafstad, G. S., Memon, A., & Logie, R. (2004). Post-identification feedback, confidence and recollections of witnessing conditions in child witnesses. *Applied Cognitive Psychology, 18,* 901–912.

Huff, C. R. (1987). Wrongful conviction: Societal tolerance of injustice. *Research in Social Problems and Public Policy, 4,* 99–115.

Innocence Project. (2004). *Innocence Project.* Retrieved January 19, 2004, from *http://www.innocenceproject.org/about/index.php.*

Juslin, P., Olsson, N., & Winman, A. (1996). Calibration and diagnosticity of confidence in eyewitness identification: Comments on what can be inferred from the low confidence–accuracy correlation. *Journal of Experimental Psychology: Learning, Memory, and Cognition, 22,* 1304–1316.

Keast, A., Brewer, N., & Wells, G. L. (2005). *Children's eyewitness identification performance and the confidence–accuracy relation.* Manuscript in preparation.

Kitagami, S., Sato, W., & Yoshikawa, S. (2002). The influence of test-set similarity in verbal overshadowing. *Applied Cognitive Psychology, 16,* 963–972.

Krafka, C., & Penrod, S. (1985). Reinstatement of context in a field experiment on eyewitness identification. *Journal of Personality and Social Psychology, 49,* 58–69.

Levin, D. T. (2000). Race as a visual feature: Using visual search and perceptual discrimination tasks to understand face categories and the cross-race recognition deficit. *Journal of Experimental Psychology: General, 129,* 559–574.

Lichtenstein, S., & Fischhoff, B. (1977). Do those who know more also know more about how much they know? *Organizational Behavior and Human Decision Processes, 20,* 159–183.

Light, L. L., Kayra-Stuart, F., & Hollander, S. (1979). Recognition memory for typical and unusual faces. *Journal of Experimental Psychology: Human Learning and Memory, 5,* 212–228.

Lindsay, R. C. L., Pozzulo, J. D., Craig, W., Lee, K., & Corber, S. (1997). Simultaneous lineups, sequential lineups, and showups: Eyewitness identification decisions of adults and children. *Law and Human Behavior, 21,* 391–404.

Lindsay, R. C. L., Ross, D. F., Read, J. D., & Toglia, M. (Eds.). (in press). *Handbook of eyewitness psychology: Vol. 2. Memory for people.* Mahwah, NJ: Erlbaum.

Lindsay, R. C. L., & Wells, G. L. (1980). What price justice? Exploring the relationship of lineup fairness to identification accuracy. *Law and Human Behavior, 4,* 303–313.

Lindsay, R. C. L., & Wells, G. L. (1985). Improving eyewitness identifications from lineups: Simultaneous versus sequential lineup presentation. *Journal of Applied Psychology, 70,* 556–564.

Lindsay, R. C. L., Wells, G. L., & Rumpel, C. M. (1981). Can people detect eyewitness-identification accuracy within and across situations? *Journal of Applied Psychology, 66,* 79–89.

Loftus, E. F., Loftus, G. R., & Messo, J. (1987). Some facts about "weapon focus." *Law and Human Behavior, 11,* 55–62.

Luus, C., & Wells, G. L. (1994). The malleability of eyewitness confidence: Co-witness and perseverance effects. *Journal of Applied Psychology, 79,* 714–723.

MacLin, O. H., MacLin, M., & Malpass, R. S. (2001). Race, arousal, attention, exposure and delay: An examination of factors moderating face recognition. *Psychology, Public Policy, and Law, 7*, 134–152.

Macmillan, N. A., & Creelman, C. D. (1991). *Detection theory: A user's guide.* New York: Cambridge University Press.

Malpass, R. S. (1981). Effective size and defendant bias in eyewitness identification lineups. *Law and Human Behavior, 5*, 299–309.

Malpass, R. S., & Devine, P. G. (1981). Eyewitness identification: Lineup instructions and the absence of the offender. *Journal of Applied Psychology, 66*, 482–489.

Malpass, R. S., & Lindsay, R. C. L. (1999). Measuring line-up fairness. *Applied Cognitive Psychology, 13*, 1–7.

Mandler, G. (1980). Recognizing: The judgment of previous occurrence. *Psychological Review, 87*, 252–271.

Mäntylä, T. (1997). Recollections of faces: Remembering differences and knowing similarities. *Journal of Experimental Psychology: Learning, Memory, and Cognition, 23*, 1203–1216.

Mäntylä, T., & Cornoldi, C. (2002). Remembering changes: Repetition effects in face recollection. *Acta Psychologica, 109*, 95–105.

Meissner, C. A. (2002). Applied aspects of the instructional bias effect in verbal overshadowing. *Applied Cognitive Psychology, 16*, 911–928.

Meissner, C. A., & Brigham, J. C. (2001). Thirty years of investigating the own-race bias in memory for faces: A meta-analytic review. *Psychology, Public Policy, and Law, 7*, 3–35.

Meissner, C. A., Brigham, J. C., & Kelley, C. M. (2001). The influence of retrieval processes in verbal overshadowing. *Memory and Cognition, 29*, 176–186.

Memon, A., & Gabbert, F. (2003). Improving the identification accuracy of senior witnesses: Do prelineup questions and sequential testing help? *Journal of Applied Psychology, 88*, 341–347.

Memon, A., Gabbert, F., & Hope, L. (2004). The ageing eyewitness. In J. Adler (Ed.), *Forensic psychology: Debates, concepts and practice.* Devon, UK: Willan.

Memon, A., Hope, L., Bartlett, J., & Bull, R. (2002). Eyewitness recognition errors: The effects of mugshot viewing and choosing in young and old adults. *Memory and Cognition, 30*, 1219–1227.

Memon, A., Hope, L., & Bull, R. (2003). Exposure duration: Effects on eyewitness accuracy and confidence. *British Journal of Psychology, 94*, 339–354.

Neil v. Biggers, 409 U.S. 188 (1972).

Nosworthy, G. J., & Lindsay, R. C. L. (1990). Does nominal lineup size matter? *Journal of Applied Psychology, 75*, 358–361.

Olsson, N., Juslin, P., & Winman, A. (1998). Realism of confidence in earwitness versus eyewitness identification. *Journal of Experimental Psychology: Applied, 4*, 101–118.

O'Rourke, T. E., Penrod, S. D., Cutler, B. L., & Stuve, T. E. (1989). The external validity of eyewitness identification research: Generalizing across subject populations. *Law and Human Behavior, 13*, 385–395.

Patterson, K., & Baddeley, A. (1977). When face recognition fails. *Journal of Experimental Psychology: Human Learning and Memory, 3*, 406–417.

Potter, R., & Brewer, N. (1999). Perceptions of witness behaviour–accuracy relationships held by police, lawyers and mock-jurors. *Psychiatry, Psychology, and Law, 6*, 97–103.

Pozzulo, J. D., & Lindsay, R. C. L. (1998). Identification accuracy of children versus adults: A meta-analysis. *Law and Human Behavior, 22*, 549–570.

Pozzulo, J. D., & Lindsay, R. C. L. (1999). Elimination lineups: An improved identification procedure for child eyewitnesses. *Journal of Applied Psychology, 84*, 167–176.

Pryke, S., Lindsay, R. C. L., Dysart, J. E., & Dupuis, P. (2004). Multiple independent identification decisions: A method of calibrating eyewitness identifications. *Journal of Applied Psychology, 89*, 73–84.

R v. Turnbull and others, 3 All ER 549 (1976).

Read, J. D. (1995). The availability heuristic in person identification: The sometimes misleading consequences of enhanced contextual information. *Applied Cognitive Psychology, 9*, 91–121.

Read, J. D., Tollestrup, P., Hammersley, R., H., McFadzen, E., & Christensen, A. (1990). The unconscious transference effect: Are innocent bystanders ever misidentified? *Applied Cognitive Psychology, 4*, 3–31.

Read, J. D., Vokey, J. R., & Hammersley, R. (1990). Changing photos of faces: Effects of exposure duration and photo similarity on recognition and the accuracy–confidence relationship. *Journal of Experimental Psychology: Learning, Memory, and Cognition, 16*, 870–882.

Ross, D. R., Ceci, S. J., Dunning, D., & Toglia, M. P. (1994). Unconscious transference and mistake identity: When a witness misidentifies a familiar with innocent person. *Journal of Applied Psychology, 79*, 918–930.

Sauer, J. D., Brewer, N., & Wells, G. L. (2005). *Diagnosing eyewitness identification accuracy in sequential lineups.* Manuscript in preparation.

Schooler, J. W. (2002). Verbalization produces a transfer inappropriate processing shift. *Applied Cognitive Psychology, 16*, 989–997.

Schooler, J. W., & Engstler-Schooler, T. Y. (1990). Verbal overshadowing of visual memories: Some things are better left unsaid. *Cognitive Psychology, 22*, 36–71.

Searcy, J. H., Bartlett, J. C., & Memon, A. (1999). Age differences in accuracy and choosing in eyewitness identification and face recognition. *Memory and Cognition, 27*, 538–552.

Searcy, J. H., Bartlett, J. C., Memon, A., & Swanson, K. (2001). Aging and lineup performance at long retention intervals: Effects of metamemory and context reinstatement. *Journal of Applied Psychology, 86*, 207–214.

Semmler, C., & Brewer, N. (2004). *Postidentification feedback effects on face recognition confidence: Evidence for metacognitive influences.* Manuscript submitted for publication.

Semmler, C., Brewer, N., & Wells, G. L. (2004). Effects of postidentification feedback on eyewitness identification and nonidentification confidence. *Journal of Applied Psychology, 89*, 334–346.

Shapiro, P. N., & Penrod, S. (1986). Meta-analysis of facial identification studies. *Psychological Bulletin, 100*, 139–156.

Shepherd, J. W. (1983). Identification after long delays. In S. M. A. Lloyd-Bostock & B. R. Clifford (Eds.), *Evaluating witness evidence* (pp. 173–187). Chichester, UK: Wiley.

Shepherd, J. W., Ellis, H. D., & Davies, G. M. (1982). *Identification evidence.* Aberdeen, UK: Aberdeen University Press.

Smith, S. M., Lindsay, R. C. L., & Pryke, S. (2000). Postdictors of eyewitness errors: Can false identifications be diagnosed? *Journal of Applied Psychology, 85*, 542–550.

Smith, S. M., Lindsay, R. C. L., Pryke, S., & Dysart, J. E. (2001). Postdictors of eyewitness errors: Can false identifications be diagnosed in the cross-race situation? *Psychology, Public Policy, and Law, 7,* 153–169.

Smith, S. M., & Vela, E. (1990). Environmental context-dependent eyewitness recognition. *Applied Cognitive Psychology, 6,* 125–139.

Soll, J. B., & Klayman, J. (2004). Overconfidence in interval estimates. *Journal of Experimental Psychology: Learning, Memory, and Cognition, 30,* 299–314.

Sporer, S. L. (1993). Eyewitness identification accuracy, confidence, and decision times in simultaneous and sequential lineups. *Journal of Applied Psychology, 78,* 22–33.

Sporer, S. L. (1994). Decision times and eyewitness identification accuracy in simultaneous and sequential lineups. In D. F. Ross, J. D. Read, & M. P. Toglia (Eds.), *Adult eyewitness testimony: Current trends and developments* (pp. 300–327). New York: Cambridge University Press.

Sporer, S. L., Penrod, S., Read, D., & Cutler, B. (1995). Choosing, confidence, and accuracy: A meta-analysis of the confidence–accuracy relation in eyewitness identification studies. *Psychological Bulletin, 118,* 315–327.

Steblay, N. M. (1992). A meta-analytic review of the weapon focus effect. *Law and Human Behavior, 16,* 413–424.

Steblay, N. M. (1997). Social influence in eyewitness recall: A meta-analytic review of lineup instruction effects. *Law and Human Behavior, 21,* 283–297.

Steblay, N., Dysart, J., Fulero, S., & Lindsay, R. C. L. (2001). Eyewitness accuracy rates in sequential and simultaneous lineup presentations: A meta-analytic comparison. *Law and Human Behavior, 25,* 459–473.

Technical Working Group for Eyewitness Evidence. (1999). *Eyewitness evidence: A guide for law enforcement.* Washington, DC: U.S. Department of Justice, Office of Justice Programs.

Tredoux, C. (2002). A direct measure of facial similarity and its relation to human similarity perceptions. *Journal of Experimental Psychology: Applied, 8,* 180–193.

Tulving, E. (1981). Similarity relations in recognition. *Journal of Verbal Learning and Verbal Behavior, 20,* 479–496.

Tulving, E., & Thomson, D. M. (1973). Encoding specificity and retrieval processes in episodic memory. *Psychological Review, 80,* 358–380.

Valentine, T. (1991). A unified account of the effects of distinctiveness, inversion, and race in face recognition. *Quarterly Journal of Experimental Psychology, 43A,* 161–204.

Valentine, T., & Endo, M. (1992). Towards an exemplar model of face processing: The effects of race and distinctiveness. *Quarterly Journal of Experimental Psychology, 44A,* 671–703.

Valentine, T., & Ferrara, A. (1991). Typicality in categorization, recognition and identification: Evidence from face recognition. *British Journal of Psychology, 82,* 87–102.

Valentine, T., Pickering, A., & Darling, S. (2003). Characteristics of eyewitness identification that predict the outcome of real lineups. *Applied Cognitive Psychology, 17,* 969–993.

Van Zandt, T. (2000). ROC curves and confidence judgments in recognition memory. *Journal of Experimental Psychology: Learning, Memory, and Cognition, 26,* 582–600.

Vickers, D. (1979). *Decision processes in visual perception.* New York: Academic Press.

Vokey, J. R., & Read, J. D. (1992). Familiarity, memorability, and the effect of typicality on the recognition of faces. *Memory and Cognition, 20,* 291–302.

Weber, N., & Brewer, N. (2003). The effect of judgment type and confidence scale on confidence–accuracy calibration in face recognition. *Journal of Applied Psychology*, *88*, 490–499.

Weber, N., & Brewer, N. (2004a). Confidence–accuracy calibration in absolute and relative face recognition judgments. *Journal of Experimental Psychology: Applied*, *10*(3), 156–172.

Weber, N., & Brewer, N. (2004b). *Confidence–accuracy calibration in face recognition*. Unpublished doctoral dissertation, Flinders University, South Australia.

Weber, N., Brewer, N., Wells, G. L., Semmler, C., & Keast, A. (2004). Eyewitness identification accuracy and response latency: The unruly 10–12 second rule. *Journal of Experimental Psychology: Applied*, *10*(3), 139–147.

Wells, G. L. (1984). The psychology of lineup identifications. *Journal of Applied Social Psychology*, *14*, 89–103.

Wells, G. L. (1993). What do we know about eyewitness identification? *American Psychologist*, *48*, 553–571.

Wells, G. L., & Bradfield, A. L. (1998). "Good, you identified the suspect": Feedback to eyewitnesses distorts their reports of the witnessing experience. *Journal of Applied Psychology*, *83*, 360–376.

Wells, G. L., & Bradfield, A. L. (1999). Distortions in eyewitnesses' recollections: Can the postidentification-feedback effect be moderated? *Psychological Science*, *10*, 138–144.

Wells, G. L., Leippe, M. R., & Ostrom, T. M. (1979). Guidelines for empirically assessing the fairness of a lineup. *Law and Human Behavior*, *3*, 285–293.

Wells, G. L., & Murray, D. M. (1984). Eyewitness confidence. In G. L. Wells & E. F. Loftus (Eds.), *Eyewitness testimony: Psychological perspectives* (pp. 155–170). New York: Cambridge University Press.

Wells, G. L., & Olson, E. A. (2002). Eyewitness identification: Information gain from incriminating and exonerating behaviors. *Journal of Experimental Psychology: Applied*, *8*, 155–167.

Wells, G. L., Olson, E. A., & Charman, S. D. (2003). Distorted retrospective eyewitness reports as functions of feedback and delay. *Journal of Experimental Psychology: Applied*, *9*, 42–52.

Wells, G. L., Small, M., Penrod, S., Malpass, R. S., Fulero, S. M., & Brimacombe, C. A. E. (1998). Eyewitness identification procedures: Recommendations for lineups and photospreads. *Law and Human Behavior*, *22*, 603–647.

Windschitl, P. D., & Wells, G. L. (1996). Measuring psychological uncertainty: Verbal versus numeric methods. *Journal of Experimental Psychology: Applied*, *2*, 343–364.

Wright, D. B., & Sladden, B. (2003). An own gender bias and the importance of hair in face recognition. *Acta Psychologica*, *114*, 101–114.

Wright, D. B., & Stroud, J. N. (2002). Age differences in lineup identification accuracy: People are better with their own age. *Law and Human Behavior*, *26*, 641–654.

Yonelinas, A. P. (1994). Receiver-operating characteristics in recognition memory: Evidence for a dual-process model. *Journal of Experimental Psychology: Learning, Memory, and Cognition*, *20*, 1341–1354.

Yonelinas, A. P. (2002). The nature of recollection and familiarity: A review of 30 years of research. *Journal of Memory and Language*, *46*, 441–517.

CHAPTER SEVEN

False Memories

MATTHEW P. GERRIE
MARYANNE GARRY
ELIZABETH F. LOFTUS

In the fall of 1985, a man raped three young teenage girls in three separate incidents, beating them and cursing at them. Two other girls managed to escape before they could be raped. Three days after the last attack, the police visited the home of a young girl, after receiving a complaint that a man was peering into her bedroom window. They searched the nearby area, saw Lonnie Erby, and arrested him for the rape a few days earlier. The next week, all of the girls identified Erby in photographic and live lineups. He was convicted of the three rapes in the era before DNA testing. But when it became available, in 1988, he asked for it. In 1995, the Innocence Project began asking for DNA testing, which the prosecutor opposed as needlessly intrusive and expensive. Eight years later, the judge ordered that DNA testing be carried out, and on August 25, 2003, Lonnie Erby was exonerated—the 136th person the Innocence Project has helped to set free. He lost 17 years of his life in a Missouri prison, a mistake for which the state thus far has offered only an apology (for more information on this case and on the Innocence Project, see *www.innocenceproject.org*).

When the Innocence Project workers took a closer look at their first 70 exonerations, they discovered that in over half of the cases, an eyewitness memory error had led to the wrongful conviction. This finding makes it all the more imperative that we learn what the scientific literature tells us about eyewitness memory. In this chapter, we review the research and show that we can develop false memories for events we see and experiences we have performed, for aspects of events, and even whole events themselves. As we shall see, one theme that encompasses much of this research is that our memories are ever changing.

FALSE MEMORIES OF WHAT WE SEE

Since the 1970s, researchers have typically examined the effect of suggestion on eyewitness memory using a three-stage procedure (Lindsay, 1990; Loftus, 1991; Loftus, Miller & Burns, 1978; McCloskey & Zaragoza, 1985; Tversky & Tuchin, 1989). First, participants watch a simulated crime, a car accident, or some other event that usually requires eyewitness testimony in real life. For example, one study used a simulated robbery (McCloskey & Zaragoza, 1985), and another study used a simulated shoplifting in the campus bookstore (Loftus, 1991). Participants see a man pick up a colored candle, walk past an open elevator, and steal a math book. After a delay designed to allow their memories to fade, participants are exposed to postevent information (PEI) that describes the event. For some participants, the PEI is accurate but generic (the man stole a book), and for others the details are misleading (the man stole a chemistry book). In the final phase, participants answer questions to determine the accuracy of their memory for the event. Compared with control participants, misled participants are more likely to report having seen the suggested details. Since the 1970s, research has reliably demonstrated what has come to be known as the "misinformation effect" (Tousignant, Hall, & Loftus, 1986), which has caused participants to claim they saw buildings in an empty landscape, a thief fiddling with a hammer instead of a screwdriver, or a lost child holding a green instead of a white teddy bear (Belli, 1989; Loftus, 1996; Sutherland & Hayne, 2001; Tverksy & Tuchin, 1989).

Broadly, the misinformation research falls into three categories, each demonstrating a different way to distort eyewitness memory. The first category examines the effects of leading questioning, the second category introduces new details into a scene, and the third transforms details. Below we review each of these memory-altering effects in turn.

LEADING QUESTIONING

The courts have long acknowledged the problem with asking eyewitnesses leading questions and have, in most jurisdictions, strictly limited their use in the courtroom. But the damage done by leading questions may happen long before the eyewitness ever sets foot into a courtroom. Even seemingly innocuous, subtle suggestive questioning can alter people's reports of an event they witnessed just a few minutes earlier.

For example, Loftus and Palmer (1974) showed participants a movie depicting a traffic accident. Later, participants were asked to estimate how fast the cars were traveling at the time of the accident. Some participants were asked "How fast were the cars going when they *smashed into* each other?", whereas others were asked "How fast were the cars going when they *hit* each other?", and still others were asked the same question with the verb *collided*, *bumped*, or *contacted*. The particular verb made a difference in participants' speed estimates. For example, participants estimated that the car traveled faster in response to the word *smashed* than the word *hit*. In a second experiment using a similar method, participants were also asked if they had seen any broken glass at the accident scene. Those participants who had estimated the car's speed after hearing the word *smashed* were more likely to say that they had seen broken glass than those who had heard the word *hit*—yet there was no broken glass in the event. This research shows that leading questions can affect people's reports in the immediate moment and change their memories for event details later. Leading questions can act as PEI, telegraphing new details to participants either directly or indirectly. Later, when participants recall the event, their memories can be distorted by the information embedded in the wording of the questions.

Nonexistent Details

The second category of misinformation research shows that we can implant nonexistent details into people's memories for an event. For example, Loftus and Zanni (1975) provided further evidence that memories can be altered by suggestive questioning. After participants saw a film of a motor accident in which no headlight was broken, they were asked either "Did you see *a* broken headlight?" or "Did you see *the* broken headlight?" By varying the question, Loftus and Zanni found that participants were more likely to answer "yes" when the questioned was posed with the definite article *the* than the indefinite article *a*.

Other research has inserted even larger details into memory. After viewing a videotape of a motor accident, Loftus (1975) asked some of the participants "How fast was the white sports car going while traveling along the country road?", whereas others were asked "How fast was the white sports car going when it passed the barn while traveling along the country road?" In fact, the scene contained no barn; thus, the true purpose of the question was to convey some misleading PEI to one group and not the other. Later, when all participants were asked whether they had seen a barn on the country road, the misled participants were more likely to answer affirmatively than controls.

These studies demonstrate that simply exposing participants to subtle postevent suggestions can lead them to report that they have seen nonexistent details.

Transformed Details

The third category of misinformation research shows that we can transform one kind of detail into another kind. For example, Loftus et al. (1978) showed people a series of slides in which a red car turned a corner and hit a pedestrian on the road. Half the participants saw a stop sign on the corner, whereas the other half saw a yield sign. Participants were then asked if another car had passed the red car while it was at the *stop* sign or the *yield* sign. In the test phase, participants were shown one slide from each version of the event: one with the car at the stop sign, and one with the car at the yield sign. They were asked to choose which slide they had seen. Participants presented with consistent information (e.g., they saw a stop sign and were asked about a stop sign) chose the correct slide much more often than participants presented with inconsistent information (they saw a stop sign and were asked about a yield sign).

Later research examined some of the mechanisms driving the misinformation effect. Although these mechanisms are not the focus of this chapter, it is important to note that the misinformation effect is an umbrella term for the memory-distorting effects of PEI, however those distortions occur. This research produced myriad examples of transformed details in participants' memories. For instance, McCloskey and Zaragoza (1985) showed participants a slide sequence of a robbery in which a repairman steals some items from an office. There were four critical items. For example, at one point, the repairman steals an item and puts it under a hammer in his toolbox. In the PEI phase, participants read a narrative describing the event; the narrative was riddled with misleading information about the critical items (e.g., that the thief had a screwdriver not a hammer). Participants' task was to correctly identify what they had seen in the slide sequence. McCloskey and Zaragoza found that participants were more likely to report inaccurate details when they had read misinformation from the narrative (although later we shall see that these results were not the whole story).

Many researchers used McCloskey and Zaragoza's (1985) robbery event and found similar patterns of results (e.g., see Belli, 1989; Eakin, Schreiber, & Sergent-Marshall, 2003; Lindsay, 1990; Tversky & Tuchin, 1989). Taken together, these studies demonstrate that participants' reports of an event can be altered simply by having them read erroneous information after the fact.

FACTORS THAT INFLUENCE
THE MISINFORMATION EFFECT

Misleading suggestions do not always affect memories the same way. Generally speaking, susceptibility to the misinformation effect is related to the ability to detect discrepancies between event information and PEI. More specifically, as our discrepancy detection increases, the less likely we are to be misled. This finding is called the "principle of discrepancy detection" (Tousignant et al., 1986). Naturally, the question of interest, then, is what kinds of factors enhance (or impair) our ability to detect discrepancies? Some of these factors are discussed elsewhere in this book (e.g., the suggestibility of young children; see Dickinson, Poole, & Laimon, Chapter 5, this volume). In this chapter, we focus on some cognitive and social factors that influence normal adults' ability to detect discrepancies.

Cognitive Factors

Put simply, having a good memory for a particular event and paying attention to later information about that event work to increase the likelihood that we will notice—and ward off—discrepancies between the event and PEI.

Having a Good Memory for the Event

We have known for over 100 years that memories fade, sometimes rapidly, in a function known as the "forgetting curve" (Ebbinghaus, 1885/1913). Thus, as the delay between the witnessed event and PEI increases, memories fade. Loftus et al. (1978) showed that as memories fade, they also become more susceptible to suggestion. In this study, participants witnessed a simulated car accident, then read misleading, consistent, or no postevent information. They took the memory test after a delay of 0 minutes, 20 minutes, 1 day, 2 days, or 1 week, and were fed the PEI either right after the event or just before the test. Loftus et al. reported two important findings. First, as time went by, eyewitness memory diminished, in that control performance decreased. Second, misleading PEI did greater damage with increasing delay.

These findings have serious implications for eyewitness interviewing and testimony. If witnesses do not report their memories as soon as possible, then their ability to detect discrepancies between the event and the PEI decreases. But PEI does not have to involve the deliberate attempt to mislead that it does in psychological research. On the contrary, PEI includes is every instance in which eyewitnesses gain access to, or are exposed to, new information about an event. Discussing the event with other eyewitnesses, talking to a police officer on the scene, making a statement, being interviewed by a detective, seeing newspaper or television accounts, and preparing to testify in court: each of these instances is an opportunity for memory to be corrupted by PEI. Put another way, laboratory studies investigating the misinformation effect are a "best-case scenario." In most studies, participants view the event, receive misinformation, and are tested all within a relatively short time. However, in real life, there are often considerable delays between any one of these three stages, and myriad opportunities to be exposed to PEI.

Other research suggests that having a good memory for the event is not a uniform construct. People often remember some aspects of an event better than others. More specifically, they tend to remember the more central details of an event better than the peripheral details. As a result, the principle of discrepancy detection predicts that PEI should be more likely to affect memory for peripheral details than for central details. That is, in fact, what Wright and Stroud (1998) found. They showed participants a sequence depicting a shoplifting event. The sequence included three types of detail: (1) *central* details (e.g., the pilfered bottle of wine), (2) *peripheral categorical* details (e.g., a coffee maker behind a man in a kitchen), and (3) *peripheral continuous* details (e.g., the color of a bystander's shirt). A short time later, participants read the misleading narrative. Wright and Stroud found a misinformation effect for both kinds of peripheral details but not for central details. They also found that central details were remembered better than peripheral details in controls. In other words, participants were more likely to report misinformation when their memories were weaker—such as for peripheral details—than when their memories were stronger—such as for central details.

The studies show that increased memory strength enhances people's ability to detect discrepancies between the PEI and the original event. However, we cannot consider memory strength by itself; memory strength is directly related to how much attention people pay to an event, and to what they expect to occur during the event.

Paying Attention to the Postevent Information

One way to increase the likelihood that participants detect the discrepancy between the event and the PEI is to increase the attention they pay to the PEI. In other words, when participants scrutinize the PEI more closely, they are more likely to notice the inconsistencies between it and what they saw. Greene, Flynn, and Loftus (1982) found that participants read the postevent narrative more slowly if they were warned just prior that the narrative may be inaccurate, and they were less susceptible to the misinformation effect. Tousignant et al. (1986) showed that this decrease in susceptibility is likely due to increased discrepancy-detection ability. They found that participants who read the narrative more slowly—whether naturally or because they were instructed to do so—were more likely to identify the differences between aspects of the narrative and aspects of the event and therefore less likely to be misled.

More recently, researchers have shown that warnings do not increase participants' ability to detect discrepancies if misleading PEI is highly accessible in memory. Eakin et al. (2003) reasoned that increasing exposure to misinformation should render postevent details more accessible than event details. In such a case, warnings would not help prevent the misinformation effect. To examine their hypothesis, Eakin et al. showed participants McCloskey and Zaragoza's (1985) robbery sequence. Then, *low-accessibility* participants read the PEI once, but *high-accessibility* participants read it twice. Afterward, participants received one of three kinds of warnings: a *general warning* immediately before the test, that they should ignore the erroneous narrative; a *specific warning* immediately following the PEI ("The maintenance man lifted a tool out of his toolbox and placed the calculator beneath it. The tool was not a wrench."), or *no warning*.

Eakin et al. (2003) found two important results. First, warnings just before the test did not help either the low- or high-accessibility participants detect discrepancies: Both groups were equally misled. Second, even specific warnings delivered immediately after the PEI phase did not help the high-accessibility participants detect the discrepancies. They were as misled as participants who were given a general warning just before the test. Even when they were told that *wrench* was the wrong answer, they still went on to say it was the right answer. On the other hand, specific warnings immediately after the PEI did help the low-accessibility participants detect the discrepancies; when they were told that *wrench* was the wrong answer, they used this information to resist misleading suggestions.

On the whole, the research shows us that warnings alone do not account for people's ability to detect discrepancies and resist the misinformation effect. Instead, the effectiveness of warnings is moderated by whether postevent information is more accessible than event information.

Expectations about What Will Happen

Schemas, the organizational cognitive structures that we build from our experiences, help us to organize new information as well. As a result, schemas can promote memory errors by prompting people to fill in missing details with schema-consistent information (e.g., see Alba & Hasher, 1983). To examine how schema relevance affects eyewitness memory for ambiguous details, Tuckey and Brewer (2003) showed participants a video of two people robbing a bank. The video contained a mix of details that were *relevant, irrelevant,* and *inconsistent* with the typical bank robbery schema. In addition, the video contained either *ambiguous* details (a robber holding a bag as if it contained a gun) or *unambiguous* details (a robber holding the bag by his side).

After viewing the robbery, participants were interviewed at intervals from *no delay* to *12 weeks* and given a memory test using free-recall and cued-recall tests. In each interview, Tuckey and Brewer (2003) recorded the number of times each subject reported schema-relevant or -irrelevant details. Results showed that schema-irrelevant details were most likely to be omitted from participants' reports, followed by schema-inconsistent details. Interestingly, however, participants were most likely to report false details that were consistent with the robbery schema for details that were ambiguous in the video. For example, participants were more likely to report seeing a gun when they saw the ambiguous version of the video than the nonambiguous version. Although Tuckey and Brewer did not examine the effect of misleading suggestion, their research shows us that even in the absence of misinformation, eyewitnesses are least likely to remember details that do not fit with their schema for an event, and are more likely to remember ambiguous details that fit with their schema. Put another way, we might be least likely to detect discrepancies that target the atypical aspects of an event.

Social Factors

In addition to cognitive factors that affect susceptibility to the misinformation effect, there are also social factors that tend to operate by influencing cogni-

tive factors, such as the way participants pay attention to the differences between the event and PEI. Below we discuss three such factors: credibility,
power, and social attractiveness.

Credibility

When participants find the source of the PEI less credible, they tend to pay
more attention and are misled less often. Dodd and Bradshaw (1980) showed
participants a slide sequence of two cars involved in an accident and then
asked them to read a summary of the accident. They were told that the summary was prepared by either a neutral witness or the driver that caused the accident. Of course, the narrative was prepared by the experimenter and was
always the same misleading account of the accident. Participants were more
likely to be misled by the neutral account than by the (seemingly biased)
driver's account. These results suggest that when the "misinformation messenger" is a person of questionable reliability, participants show increased discrepancy detection.

Power and Social Attractiveness

In addition to evaluating the credibility of the misinformation messenger by
knowing what role he or she played in an event, participants can also evaluate
the messenger on sociolinguistic factors. Vornik, Sharman, and Garry (2003)
showed that when participants heard the PEI, the extent to which they were
misled was related to two judgments they made about the speaker. The first
judgment was about the speaker's *power*, or the extent to which she was seen
as strong, educated, self-confident, and intelligent. The second judgment was
about the speaker's *social attractiveness*, or the extent to which she was seen
as entertaining, affectionate, good-looking, and likable. Note that the participants never saw the speaker; they made these evaluations based simply on the
sound of her voice. Vornik et al. (2003) found that participants who thought
the speaker was powerful were misled, regardless of whether they also
thought the speaker was socially attractive. But when participants thought the
speaker was not very powerful, social attractiveness mattered: judgments of
high attractiveness caused participants to be more misled. The least misled of
all were those who found the speaker not very powerful and not very socially
attractive. Considered along with Dodd and Bradshaw's (1980) results, these
findings suggest that both the semantic and social content of the PEI can influence people's ability to detect discrepancies between the PEI and the original
event.

Cognitive and Social Factors Considered Together

Assefi and Garry (2003) hypothesized that the misinformation effect has both
a cognitive and a social component. The cognitive component is memory per-

formance in the absence of any misleading PEI. Here, the participants' task was to think back to the original event and report that information on the memory test. By contrast, the social component is memory performance in the face of misleading PEI. For the misinformation effect to occur, participants must capitulate to the misinformation, which is attributed to another person. Assefi and Garry attempted to influence the magnitude of the misinformation effect by drawing on the clinical research showing that when participants drink phony alcoholic drinks, they behave in ways that resemble how they expect alcohol to affect them. Participants became more aggressive, interested in violent and erotic material, and sexually aroused (Cherek, Steinberg, & Manno, 1985; George & Marlatt, 1986; Lang, Searles, Lauerman, & Adesso, 1980; Rohsenow & Marlatt, 1981). In this study, Assefi and Garry gave all their participants plain tonic drinks but told some participants that the drinks were vodka and tonic, and others, that they were plain tonic. After participants consumed their beverages, they took part in a misinformation experiment. Assefi and Garry found that both the "vodka-and-tonic" and "tonic" participants performed equally well on control items, but the vodka-and-tonic participants were more misled than their tonic counterparts. Moreover, although they were more misled, vodka-and-tonic participants were more confident that their wrong answers were right. These results show that we may have more control over our own memory performance than we realize.

SOURCE-MONITORING FRAMEWORK

What happens when participants fail to detect discrepancies? In other words, what mechanism decreases their ability to notice an inconsistency between an event detail and a misleading postevent suggestion? Most forms of discrepancy detection can be accounted for by the source-monitoring framework (Johnson, Hashtroudi, & Lindsay, 1993; Mitchell & Johnson, 2000) that theorizes that we make judgments about memory content and the source of that content. To distinguish between what we did, what we thought, and what we imagined, we monitor the sources when we recall the content. Most of the time, according to Johnson et al., source-monitoring decisions happen effortlessly, without awareness. However, sometimes the decision-making process goes awry: We mistake the source of information, an outcome known as "source confusion." Some source confusions are trivial (e.g., attributing a joke to the wrong person), but some can have significant consequences. For example, Mark may have witnessed a man shoplifting a book, but he may not have noticed what kind of book it was. Later, Mark may have overheard another witness say that it was a chemistry book. When Mark talks to the police, he might say that the thief stole a chemistry book because he has genuinely confused what the other witness said with what he actually saw. Mark's source confusion has resulted in a false memory for what he saw in the bookstore.

Source confusions tend to occur when what we remember fits with our expectations about what our memories should be like. For example, we expect childhood memories to have relatively weak perceptual details (Johnson, Foley, Suengas, & Raye, 1988); we expect memories from yesterday to be vivid and detailed. But, as Mitchell and Johnson (2000) point out, it is not the case that we automatically judge vivid and detailed memories to be real experiences. We also evaluate them on plausibility, emotions, and associated cognitive operations; and we vary our source-monitoring diligence according to our goals, strategies, and biases. Thus, a vivid and detailed memory of an impossible event would probably be judged as a dream, and we would (or should) expend more energy trying to remember the correct citation for a paper than remembering who told us a particular joke (for a more comprehensive review see Mitchell & Johnson).

In a misinformation experiment, source-monitoring ability should be directly related to discrepancy-detection ability. The more participants can distinguish between information that they saw in the event and the PEI they received later, the more they can resist source confusion, and the better they should be at reporting the correct details on the memory test. To examine this hypothesis, Lindsay (1990) varied the discriminability of the phases in an eyewitness experiment. First, he asked all participants to sit in a dark room and watch a slide sequence of a theft while listening to a woman's voice describing the event. Second, the *low-discriminability* group stayed in the dark room and immediately listened to the same woman read the PEI. These participants were also asked to imagine the information in the PEI. By contrast, the *high-discriminability* group met in a brightly lit room on a different day, and—while they were standing—listened to a man read the PEI. Instead of imagining the information in the PEI, this group mentally shadowed what they heard. In the third phase, all participants took the same memory test.

Lindsay (1990) found that low-discriminability participants were more misled than their high-discriminability counterparts. He hypothesized that the high-discriminability participants were better at identifying the sources of suggested versus real details. In other words, participants were better able to distinguish between what they had really seen and what they had been told they had seen. This study shows that eyewitnesses can resist misinformation if their memories of the PEI are distinguishable from memories of the original event.

WHAT HAPPENS TO THE ORIGINAL MEMORY?

Thus far, we have shown that participants can be led to report suggested details about a witnessed event. Early interpretations of the misinformation effect hypothesized that the misleading PEI impaired memory, perhaps "overwriting" it in some way, much like saving a new version of a computer document over an older version (Loftus, 1975). However, McCloskey and Zaragoza (1985) speculated that there are at least two alternative explanations for the misinformation effect. First, they capitulate to the experimenter. Participants who remember, say, that the car was at a stop sign should read that it was a yield sign and be aware of the conflicting information. However, some of them might think, "OK, I thought I saw a stop sign, but you say it was a yield sign, and it's your experiment so you must know what you're talking about. Let's go with yield sign." Second, participants who do not take in certain information about the event, for whatever reasons, may encounter it later at the PEI phase. Thus, participants who do not notice that the car is at a stop sign may later, when reading that it was at a yield sign, adopt that misleading suggestion and report it later on the memory test. Note that both of these scenarios could unfold such that participants choose the misled detail, though they do not necessarily believe what they choose.

To address this issue, McCloskey and Zaragoza (1985) carried out several misinformation studies and used two different kinds of memory tests. Some participants took a *standard* test, in which they chose between the original information (hammer) and the misleading information (screwdriver). The other participants took what McCloskey and Zaragoza referred to as a *modified* test; here, participants chose between the original information (hammer) and completely novel information (wrench). The researchers hypothesized that participants who could remember the original information, but would normally respond with misinformation because of demand, would respond correctly on the modified test. In other words, if the PEI did not impair memory, a modified test would show no evidence of the misinformation effect. Indeed, they found the typical misinformation effect with the standard test, and similar misled and control performances with the modified test. They concluded that misleading PEI did not actually impair eyewitness memory (because there was no memory to impair). Instead, they concluded that participants simply report back the PEI, a process similar to what Belli (1989) would later refer to as "misinformation acceptance."

Of course, as Loftus and Hoffman (1989) pointed out, misinformation acceptance is as interesting and worthy of study as misinformation impairment. Regardless of the route, if the end result of some process is that participants falsely report information about some experience, then it is important to understand that process. In applied settings, the question is not as much about the route as it is about the false report itself. In other words, regardless of impairment, acceptance, or any other route to a false report, if participants truly believe what they say, that is what matters.

DO PARTICIPANTS REALLY BELIEVE
THEIR FALSE REPORTS?

Loftus, Donders, Hoffman, and Schooler (1989) reasoned that measuring participants' reaction times during the test phase as well as their confidence judgments could shed more light on the true belief issue. If participants responded with the suggested details because they were deliberating between the two items they remembered (the first scenario above), we would expect misled participants to be less confident and slower to respond compared with controls. In contrast, Loftus et al. (1989) found that misled participants were not only more confident, they were also faster. In other words, participants who were *wrong* were the fastest and most confident that they were correct. This pattern of results runs contrary to what we would expect to find if participants were deliberating, as McCloskey and Zaragoza (1985) hypothesized. Loftus et al. (1989) also concluded that their results are consistent with McCloskey and Zaragoza's second scenario, in which participants adopted the misleading suggestion, filling in a gap in their memory. However, they noted that the high confidence with which participants held incorrect memories suggests that the mechanism is not as uninteresting as McCloskey and Zaragoza suggested. Instead, the data suggest that these participants believed what they reported.

Once participants adopt the misleading information, do they tend to retain it? That is the question Loftus (1991) asked in one study. Participants watched the McCloskey and Zaragoza (1985) robbery sequence. After they read the PEI, their memory accuracy was measured over two tests. One test was McCloskey and Zaragoza's modified test (which does not allow participants to choose the misled item) and the other was the standard (Loftus et al., 1978) test (which does allow participants to choose the misled item). Participants who took the standard test first and chose the misleading item were more likely to give the wrong answer (choose the novel item) in the modified test that came later. These results suggest that when people are repeatedly asked about an event after being exposed to PEI, their memory performance later is determined by how they performed earlier.

Researchers have used other tools to tap into genuine belief. For example, in an effort to counter the criticism that participants show misinformation effects because they are simply unmotivated to answer correctly, Toland (1990; as cited in Weingardt, Toland, & Loftus, 1994) asked participants to wager that their test responses were correct. Participants were asked to wager up to $10 that each of their memories was correct. If participants bet that they were correct and they were, they would double what they had bet. The person who won the most bets would receive a prize. Toland reasoned that the incentive to be accurate would increase participants' motivation to base their answers only on what they genuinely believed they had seen. However, misled participants were still less accurate than controls, even though their betting patterns did not differ. Thus, even when participants were given an incentive to respond accurately, they were still misled.

Taken together, these studies provide evidence of true belief. That is, they show that the vast majority of participants who have taken part in misinformation studies around the world genuinely do believe that their false memories are true.

THE IMPACT OF STRESS ON MEMORY

In the previous sections we have reviewed several ways in which witnesses' memory can be distorted. However, we have focused on experimental paradigms. Some may criticize the validity of applying experimental research to real-world cases. After all, in these studies, participants watch a simulated crime. They feel no threat to their safety; they can leave whenever they want. Of course, witnesses in real crimes do not enjoy such luxuries. How well, then, does eyewitness memory perform in these stressful, real-life situations? Below we review some of the myriad factors that can contribute to incomplete or inaccurate memories—even in the absence of misleading postevent suggestion.

Many scientists have examined the relationship between stress and eyewitness memory. Both in laboratory and real-world studies, stress has sometimes increased the likelihood of false memories, and other times it has had no effect. As Christianson (1992) observed, the varied findings may be a result of several factors, including inconsistent definitions of what a stressful event really means. Still, in a recent survey, 64% of eyewitness memory experts believed that stress has a negative impact on memory accuracy (Kassin, Tubb, Hosch, & Memon, 2002).

Some of the studies on stress and memory use laboratory methods, whereas others attempt to study real-life witnesses under stress. We review some examples of these two approaches.

Laboratory Studies

Loftus and Burns (1982) showed participants a short movie of a bank robbery that finished either with a robber shooting a boy in the face (the *violent* ending) or a scene from the inside of the bank (the *nonviolent* ending). Later, participants were asked a number of questions about the event, including the number printed on the boy's shirt. Participants who had witnessed the nonviolent version were more likely to recall the number correctly than those who had seen the violent version. On all other questions, participants performed equally well, regardless of whether they had seen the violent or nonviolent version. Loftus and Burns concluded that the shock of the shooting disrupted the memory consolidation process for details seen just before it. This period of retrograde amnesia led to decreased memory performance for participants who had seen the violent version. Put another way, witnessing an emotionally stressful event can impair memory for the stressful event itself.

Stress also seems to affect some details differently from others. For example, Christianson and Loftus (1991) showed participants slides of a woman riding her bicycle. In the nonstressful version of the slides, the woman rides past a car in the background. In the stressful version, the woman is struck off her bicycle when riding near the same car. In five experiments, Christianson and Loftus found that participants who viewed the stressful slides were better at remembering central details (e.g., the woman riding her bicycle) than peripheral details (e.g., the car in the background). On the other hand, participants who had viewed the nonstressful version were better at remembering peripheral details.

A phenomenon related to the finding that stress might *improve* memory for central details goes under the term "weapon focus." This term refers to the attention-capturing effect of being confronted with a weapon: People threatened with a weapon tend to attend to it more than to other aspects of the event. As a result, they do not encode those other details. Loftus, Loftus, and Messo (1987) recorded participants' eye fixations while they watched one of two versions of a slide sequence. One version depicted a man pointing a gun at a cashier in a restaurant; the other showed the man giving a check to the same cashier. Loftus et al. found that the weapon captured participants' attention; they fixated on the gun more than on the check. In a second experiment, participants were given a memory test for the event. "Weapon participants" remembered fewer details than "check participants." These two experiments suggest that the increased attention on the gun affected memory for other details. These results also suggest that what is a central detail at one time (e.g., a gun) may affect memory of details that ultimately become a central issue later. In fact, a meta-analysis of several studies showed a consistent weapon-focus effect that decreased identification accuracy (Steblay, 1992). Thus, eyewitnesses who attend to what might be considered a central event detail (e.g., a gun) may later be less able to remember a different central detail (e.g., the identity of the perpetrator).

A criticism of laboratory research is that it does not reproduce the stress that eyewitnesses experience during real crimes, which can be life-threatening (Christianson, 1992). The "stressful" events, although ethically sound, are not very stressful at all (Wessel & Merckelbach, 1997). This criticism has led some researchers to conduct field studies in which they examine the memories of those who have witnessed real crimes.

Real-World Research

One of the best known examples of eyewitness memory research performed in the field is that of Yuille and Cutshall (1986). They questioned 13 witnesses who had witnessed a fatal shooting, from several different vantage points, during a gun shop robbery. They took the original police interviews and compared them with research interviews carried out 4–5 months later. The research interviews included a misleading question similar to the one used in Loftus and Zanni's (1975) study. The witnesses' reports were compared with police evidence reports and forensic tests to verify their accuracy. Yuille and Cutshall found that witnesses were quite accurate in both the police and research interviews (84% and 81%, respectively) and were rarely misled by PEI. Moreover, witnesses' responses were consistent on the two interviews. Most interesting is that contradictory to laboratory findings, those who reported the highest level of stress during the crime were the most accurate about the information they gave to police. In fact, there was a high correspondence between stress level and accuracy performance.

However, Yuille and Cutshall's (1986) research has not escaped criticism. First, as we noted in an earlier section of this chapter, laboratory research shows that serious memory distortions can occur even in the absence of misinformation; Yuille and Cutshall's witnesses provided real-world evidence in line with these laboratory findings. For instance, three of the 13 witnesses remembered false events. Two of those witnesses were two men who reported a greater role in the robbery than they actually had played. The third witness reported that she had heard another witness say to a man standing next to him, "Did you see me shoot that guy?" in a "menacing" tone (p. 298). Second, Wessel and Merckelbach (1997) rightly pointed out that serious drawbacks prevent us from drawing firm conclusions from the field research genre. For example, the participants who reported the greatest stress in Yuille and Cutshall's study were also closest to the incident. It is not surprising that someone viewing the scene from nearby buildings or passing cars would be less stressed and would not take in as many details compared with someone right on the scene. Put another way, stress and viewing conditions were completely confounded. To account for the uncontrollable factors in field studies, yet still induce genuine stress, Wessel and Merckelbach hit upon an ingenious solution. They exposed people with and without spider phobia to a live spider in a jar. As expected, the people with the spider phobia scored higher on all measures of stress than those with no such phobia. More importantly, in a later memory test, participants were asked about central details (e.g., the spider, the cloth that covered the spider), and peripheral details (e.g., a poster on the wall, a vase of flowers). Both groups of participants performed the same on a memory test of central details, but those with a spider phobia scored significantly lower on a test of peripheral details.

Taken together, both laboratory and real-world research demonstrate that stress can be a threat to memory. In other words, exposing witnesses to stress may further compromise their ability to remember the event accurately. In some cases, furthermore, stress can *increase* memory distortion.

Stress and Expertise

Some researchers believe that certain kinds of people, such as police officers, are better at perceiving and remembering events because of their specialist training (Stanny & Johnson, 2000; Yarmey, 1986). Does this extra training produce better eyewitnesses under stress? To examine this question, Stanny and Johnson (2000) had police officers and civilian controls participate in either an emotionally stressful simulation (a shooting) or a neutral one (no shooting). The simulation was realistic and interactive. The officers carried a laser gun to shoot at perpetrators, if need arose. In addition, a civilian witnessed what happened in both types of simulations. Later, memories of the officers and the civilian controls were tested. Both groups reported less detail in the stressful event than in the neutral event. More to the point, the police officers' memories were no more accurate than the civilians'.

Mechanisms

Researchers have examined the relationship between stress and memory accuracy using two different (yet not mutually exclusive) explanations, the Yerkes–Dodson law and the Easterbrook hypothesis.

Yerkes–Dodson Law

The Yerkes–Dodson law states that as stress increases, so does memory performance—up to a point. Once stress goes past that optimum point, then memory performance declines. In short, a graph of the stress–performance relationship produces an inverted-U pattern, where the tails of the U represent the extreme levels of arousal (high and low) that negatively affect people's memory performance (Deffenbacher, 1983; Loftus, 1996; McNally, 2003; Yerkes & Dodson, 1908). The Yerkes–Dodson law is helpful because it shows how stress can have both good and bad effects; good at moderate levels and bad at the extremes.

Easterbrook Hypothesis

A second way to consider the impact of stress is to investigate its multidimensional nature; stress affects physical, emotional, and cognitive responses (e.g., see Christianson, 1992; McNally, 2003). The Easterbrook hypothesis (Easterbrook, 1959) takes such an approach; it assumes that people can attend to only a limited number of cues at any one time. As stress increases, their attention narrows to the stress-generating features, resulting in the ability to attend to fewer cues. The hypothesis nicely accounts for the research that reports differences in memory performance for central and peripheral details (Christianson, 1992), because it predicts that stress will funnel attention toward central details at the expense of peripheral ones. As a result, memory for central details is better than memory for peripheral details. (For an excellent review of the Yerkes–Dodson law and the Easterbrook hypothesis, see McNally, 2003.)

There are many factors that affect eyewitnesses' memory performance. We have discussed but a small subset of these factors; a more complete examination would fill entire books (Cutler & Penrod, 1995; Memon, Vrij, & Bull, 2003; Wells, 1988). These factors conspire to render memory incomplete or inaccurate, and adding postevent suggestion to the picture only compounds the problem. These inaccurate or false memories can develop for all categories of details: size (e.g., small, large), appearance (e.g., eye color, facial hair), presence or absence of objects, etc. The scientific community has steadily accumulated evidence of these far-ranging memory distortions for over 30 years.

More recently, however, scientists encountered a different kind of memory distortion: one in which the witness was a participant in the events, and one in which the remembered events were horrific, sustained acts of sexual abuse.

FALSE MEMORIES OF WHAT WE DO

In 1988, Ellen Bass and Laura Davis published *The Courage to Heal*, a self-help guide for sexually abused people to help them get past the pain of their sexual abuse. A double-edged sword, this book encouraged reluctant victims of sexual abuse to seek help, but it also encouraged those who simply wondered if they might be victims to believe that they were. The authors were not trained therapists or scientists, yet the book was catapulted into prominence by devoted readers and sympathetic therapists, who coupled a belief in the hidden epidemic of sexual abuse with the Freudian notion that those experiences are often repressed and need to be dug out, so to speak. As McNally (2003) observed, their views reinterpreted the well-known observation that those who have been through trauma do not like to talk about their experiences. "By the end of the decade," he said, "reluctance to disclose became inability to remember" (p. 5). Soon after, we were living in what Carol Tavris (1993) called "the incest survivor machine."

Why dig up long-buried memories? In the neo-Freudian worldview, buried memories exude their toxic content into everyday behavior, contaminating the person's environment and limiting his or her ability to live an emotionally healthy life. Recovering memories, then, is the only way sufferers can begin to heal. Recovered memory techniques became more popular, and stories of repressed sexual abuse experiences found their way into books, television shows, and—most notably—our courtrooms, where millions of dollars were shelled out to those who testified about recently recovered abuse at the hands of parents, grandparents, or neighbors.

Psychological scientists turned their attention to the growing repression phenomenon in the early 1990s. They began with a puzzle that seemed to fly in the face of everything we had learned in 100 years of studying human memory: We remember what is significant better than what is prosaic, and what is repeated better than what is not. The central question, then, was whether there was any scientific support for the validity of a mechanism that, in essence, rounded up a string of horribly abusive experiences and sealed them into some corner of the mind that memory could not reach. Put simply, the answer was (and still is) *no* (for a review, see Holmes, 1995).

The next question was to ask whether people could develop vivid and detailed memories for wholly false events. Loftus and Pickrell (1995; see also Loftus, 1993) described the first attempt to create in people a coherent and detailed memory for something they had never done. The researchers gave participants written descriptions of childhood events: three that were true, obtained from a family member confederate, and one that was false, about getting lost in a shopping mall as a child and eventually being found by an elderly lady who helped the family to reunite. Over two interviews the participants reported what they could remember about each event. About one-quarter of the participants had created a partial or full false memory of being lost in the mall as a child. Even when one subject had been told the real purpose of the study, she found it hard to believe the memory was false and reported, "I totally remember walking around in those dressing rooms and my mom not being in the section she said she'd be in" (p. 723).

In other studies, participants reported traumatic but false experiences such as being attacked by a vicious animal (Porter, Yuille, & Lehman, 1999), causing mayhem at a wedding (Hyman, Husband, & Billings, 1995), and being saved from drowning by a lifeguard (Heaps & Nash, 2001). Still, all of these events can be criticized for being too script-like, too plausible—and thus too easy for people to imagine and confuse with real life. It would be difficult, so this line of criticism goes, to implant a false memory for something implausible. Pezdek, Finger, and Hodge's (1997) results support such a claim. Their unusual event was having a rectal enema as a child; they were unable to plant even a single false memory. Thus, we might be tempted to conclude that an implausible event would be hard to implant.

Yet recent research shows that implausibility is not a fixed quantity, and that people can come to believe that they had implausible experiences. Mazzoni, Loftus, and Kirsch (2001) used an implausible target event—some might say, *impossible*—that as a child, a subject had seen a person being possessed by demons. In four steps, these researchers attempted to increase the plausibility of the demonic scenario. First, participants read a list of various events, including witnessing demonic possession, and rated the plausibility that other people like them had experienced those events. They also rated their confidence that they had experienced the same events in childhood. Some time later, some participants took part in the second phase, in which they read phony articles describing the symptoms of demonic possession. The articles "revealed" that demonic possession is common, as is seeing a possessed person. The third step took place a week later and included only the participants who had taken part in the second step. This time, participants completed a bogus survey about their fears, which were interpreted for them as evidence that they had witnessed a case of demonic possession back in childhood. In the fourth step, all participants completed the same plausibility and confidence measures as in the first step. A key finding was that participants who had been exposed to the phony information about demonic possession thought it was more plausible and more likely that *they* had seen such a phenomenon. However, there was no relationship between plausibility and confidence that the event had happened. Taken together, these findings suggest that events can become more plausible, and even moderate increases in plausibility can morph into increased belief.

On the basis of their results, Mazzoni et al. (2001) proposed a three-stage process by which false memories emerge. In the first stage, people must regard the target event as plausible. In the second stage, they must come to believe they experienced the event. In the third stage, they must reinterpret their narratives and images about the event to produce genuine memories. Put another way, plausibility is not a black-or-white experience, nor is it a fixed quantity. Instead, plausibility can grow into beliefs, and beliefs can grow into false memories.

Let us consider the second step of Mazzoni et al.'s (2001) model: that, over time, people develop a belief that they experienced the false event. The idea that beliefs about our autobiographical experiences can change in response to some manipulation was first examined by Garry, Manning, Loftus, and Sherman (1996). They asked participants how confident they were that a number of childhood events had happened. Later, they asked the participants to imagine some of those events briefly, and then the researchers collected new confidence data. Participants became more confident that they had experienced imagined events than nonimagined events. Garry et al. called the confidence-inflating effect of imagination, "imagination inflation."

Other research reported similar effects (Heaps & Nash, 1999; Paddock et al., 1999). Yet, as Goff and Roediger (1998) pointed out, there was the chance that the imagination component merely helped participants remember events that really had happened. If they were right, then imagination inflation was not very interesting at all. To investigate this issue, Goff and Roediger created a list of simple action statements such as "break the toothpick." In the first phase of their experiment, participants heard some statements from the list. Then they heard and imagined other statements from the list. Next they heard and performed still other actions from the list. In a second session, participants imagined doing some of those actions anywhere from zero to five times. In the final session, participants saw the complete list of action statements and said what actions they had done in the first phase. Goff and Roediger found evidence of imagination inflation: participants were more likely to think they had performed actions when they had only imagined them. Furthermore, the more they had imagined doing those actions, the more imagination inflation they showed.

Thomas and Loftus (2002) adopted Goff and Roediger's method to see if imagination inflation happened for bizarre experiences as well. They asked participants to perform or imagine some ordinary actions (e.g., "flipping a coin") and some bizarre actions (e.g., "sitting on the dice"). Later, participants imagined some of the actions zero to five times. Imagination caused participants to say that they had done actions they had only imagined, even when those actions were bizarre. Repeated imagination produced more inflation than imagining just once. In follow-up work, elaborative imagination in which participants engaged several sensory modalities produced even more inflation (Thomas, Bulevich, & Loftus, 2003). These results demonstrate that repeated imagination can increase false memories, even for actions for which we have no script.

Interestingly, recent research suggests that imagination is not always necessary to produce inflation. Bernstein and colleagues (Bernstein, Godfrey, Davison, & Loftus, 2004; Bernstein, Whittlesea, & Loftus, 2002) have found that surprising fluency—that is, an unexpected wave of understanding—can also increase confidence about life experiences. The researchers used the typical imagination-inflation experiment, but with a few twists. First, they had participants try to solve some anagrams. The anagrams were difficult and should have led participants to expect that they would have a hard time solving other anagrams later in the experiment. Later, when the imagination-inflation part of the experiment began, they asked participants to report their confidence that events on a list of childhood experiences had happened to them. Some of the statements on that list were presented in the correct way ("broke a window playing ball") or with a scrambled (misspelled) word ("broke a nwidwo playing ball"). This time, however, the scrambled words were much easier to solve than the anagrams. The unexpected easiness should have produced a feeling of fluency, and participants should then have attributed that fluency to the familiarity of a real experience (Whittlesea & Williams, 2001). That is what happened: Unscrambling a word increased belief that the event had occurred in the average North American child's life as well as in the participant's own childhood.

Sharman, Garry, and Beuke (2004) demonstrated that other activities can inflate confidence that a hypothetical event actually happened. Their participants took part in a three-stage procedure. First, they rated their confidence that a list of events had happened in their childhood (for example, "When I was young, I gave someone a haircut."). Next, participants imagined or paraphrased those events zero, one, three, or five times. In the third stage, they rated their confidence for the childhood events a second time. Participants became more confident that the fictitious events really did happen in childhood, regardless of whether they were imagined or paraphrased. Unlike Goff and Roediger (1998), there was no repetition effect beyond that of a single exposure. Although the fact that paraphrasing and imagination produced similar effects is not surprising, given Bernstein et al.'s (2002, 2004) results, the lack of a repetition effect is somewhat surprising. Still, Sharman et al.'s study shows that even a single act of paraphrasing a childhood event is enough to inflate confidence that the event was a real experience.

Taken together, these studies show that several factors can increase a person's belief that an unlived childhood event had actually happened. Recall that in Mazzoni et al.'s (2001) three-step model, increased belief can give way to a false memory. Below we discuss three studies illustrating the ways in which belief can morph into memories. These studies are especially important because they also address a criticism of nearly all the false-memory research we have discussed thus far: that the procedures simply help participants to remember an actual experience from their past. By contrast, the next three studies all use impossible target events.

Braun, Ellis, and Loftus (2002) examined the effects of advertising on childhood memory. Their participants were asked to review what they were told was potential advertising copy. Some of the participants saw an advertisement featuring Bugs Bunny at a Disney theme park, whereas others saw an advertisement without cartoon characters. The crucial factor here is that the critical experiences could not have happened; it would have been impossible for participants to have shaken hands with Bugs at a Disney theme park because he is a Warner Brothers' character. There were two important findings from this study. First, participants became more confident that they had shaken hands with Bugs when they had seen the Bugs ad than a control ad. Second, when participants were asked later whether they remembered shaking hands with Bugs, 16% of those who saw the Bugs ad said they had, compared with 7% of participants in the control condition. Braun et al.'s (2002) findings show that exposing people to an impossible event via advertising can create false memories for impossible events.

In a later study (Grinley, 2002), the increased confidence spilled over into memories filled with sensory detail. Participants reported various interactions with Bugs, such has hugging him, shaking his hand, or hearing him utter his tag line, "What's up, Doc?" The problem with these reports? Although Bugs is real and so is Disneyland, he is a Warner Brothers' character and would never "appear" on a Disney property.

Our third example of belief morphing into memory comes from recent work by Mazzoni and Memon (2003). Their research helped to fill a gap in our understanding of the relationship between imagination and memory. As they pointed out, although we knew that imagining an experience could inflate confidence for it, we did not know whether it could also create a false memory. Mazzoni and Memon led their U.K. participants into believing that at age 6, a nurse had taken a skin sample from their little finger to carry out some kind of national health test—but no such test had existed. Imagining the scenario caused participants to become more confident that it had happened to them, and some of them developed false memories. Many of these false memories were filled with sensory detail ("the place smelled horrible," p. 187). These results demonstrate that imagination can cause people to become more confident that a false event happened to them, and some of the individuals will go on to develop rich, detailed narratives about the false event. In other words, they develop what have been called "rich false memories" (Loftus & Bernstein, in press).

We know that simple low-tech means of manipulation, such as imagination, can play havoc with memory. Some research has used more high-tech means to cultivate false memories. What is the effect of seeing a photograph of yourself doing something you thought you had never done? Wade, Garry, Read, and Lindsay (2002) asked exactly this question. They used the Loftus and Pickrell (1995) "lost in the mall" method but replaced the narratives with photographs and changed the content from malls to balloon rides. One of the photos was fake and showed the subject taking a hot-air balloon ride as a child. Family confederates had stated that the balloon ride had never happened. After three interviews in which participants had viewed a fake photo of themselves in a balloon, 50% "remembered" the ride. Often these reports were studded with rich detail:

> I'm certain it occurred when I was [in sixth grade] at um the local school. Um basically for $10 or something you could go up in a hot air balloon and go up about 20 odd meters. . . . it would have been a Saturday and I think we went with, yeah, parents and, no it wasn't, not my grandmother . . . not certain who any of the other people are there. Um, and I'm pretty certain that Mum is down on the ground taking a photo. (Wade et al., 2001).

and

> I'm pretty sure this is um, this happened at home. Like in the weekend there's a kite fair and stuff. Me and [sister] went up when I was pretty young I'd say. I remember the smell and it was really hot . . . the balloon would go up and all the warmth would come down. (Wade et al., 2001)

How do we know that Wade et al.'s (2002) participants believed their hot-air balloon reports? There are several reasons. First, when participants could not remember true events, they said they could not remember them. Why, then, would they go on to make up false stories about the balloon ride? Second, they showed evidence of trying to engage in accurate source monitoring. For example, one subject said, "And I think, no I'm just making it up am I, I was going to say I think it had a beeping. . . . No, I am making that up." Third, when they could not remember the balloon ride, many participants felt bad about causing problems for the experimenter. "I was worried I like stuffed up your study or something like that. I'm sorry about that," one subject said. Finally, participants tended to express what looked like genuine astonishment at debriefing. For instance, one subject exclaimed, "Is that right? Yeah, *truly*? How'd you do *that*?!"

Are photographs more powerful than narratives? Most people think that photographs carry more authority than words alone, and that photographs are better "memory joggers" than stories. That is the proposition Garry and Wade (in press) put to the test in a study examining the effects of false narratives and false photos. Their procedure was almost the same as Wade et al.s (2002), but evidence for the balloon ride was presented either as a photograph or as a narrative, which has been equated with the false balloon photo or a narrative describing the balloon event. Their results were surprising: After three interviews, approximately 80% of narrative participants and half of the photo participants reported something about the balloon event. These narrative-induced reports were just as richly detailed as the photographic ones. For example:

> I think it was at the Wellington School Fair. Um, and I didn't want to go up in a balloon. I vaguely remember being in it and my mum sort of telling me that we weren't actually going to fly away because there were ropes holding it. I didn't believe her, and I was really scared that we were going to fly away and be

stuck up in the air. And my dad was laughing, but I was really mad at him because I just wanted to get out—it was cold and the wind was blowing in my face, and there were quite a few people around. I could see quite a few people. (Garry & Wade, in press)

These findings suggest that photographs may constrain the ability to generate more details about the false event. Another interesting finding was that narrative participants said photographs were better memory joggers, but photo participants said that narratives were better memory joggers. Garry and Wade speculated that this "crossover" pattern reflected the difficulty that participants in each group had recalling the balloon event. Rather than attribute the difficulty to the falseness of the event, they believed that the medium itself was the problem.

Wade and colleagues (Garry & Wade, in press; Wade et al., 2002; Wade & Garry, 2003) have now used variations of this paradigm with close to 150 participants. One particularly striking finding is that participants often try hard to justify why they either initially could not remember the balloon ride, or never came to remember it at all. For example, in the same study cited above (Wade & Garry, 2003), approximately 25% of participants invoked an explanation that sounded very much like a repression mechanism.

Well, I don't remember it happening, unless it was like a repressed fear that I was so scared that I put in the back of my head and thought, "No I don't want to remember it until I go to therapy."

Maybe it was so scary that I just blanked it out! Maybe I didn't like it. If it did happen, I must have blocked it out through trauma.

I sort of have this recollection that I didn't like it. That I basically didn't want to look out of the basket at all. But you know, that could just be something in my mind. You know, I have got a thing about heights now, but I never, it hadn't always been there. But I have this kind of recollection that I didn't actually like it, going up in the balloon, and the height thing just scared me. Being high up. . . . It may just have blocked it out in my own memory, but I don't know.

No. No, I don't remember doing that at all. Probably something bad happened.

These studies provide evidence that doctored photos can cultivate false memories. However, they are subject to the criticism that they lack ecological validity. After all, people do not frequently see photos of themselves doing things they did not do with people they do not know. In response to this criticism, Lindsay, Hagen, Read, Wade, and Garry (2004) used a real photograph to implant a false memory. They obtained descriptions of real childhood experiences from participants' parents. The experiences all took place at school. Then, over two interviews, they asked participants to remember three school experiences that started at age 9 or 10 and went back to age 5 or 6. Two of these experiences were real, and the earliest one was false; the false event described the subject putting Slime (the goopy-green children's toy) into the teacher's desk drawer. All participants were given a narrative describing each event, and half were also given a class photo from the correct year to "help" them remember the event. Slightly fewer than half of the narrative-only participants reported Slime images or images with memories, compared with about three-fourths of the photo participants, who did. These results show that even real photos can lead people to remember unreal events.

IMPLICATIONS

There are both important theoretical and practical issues associated with false memory research. On the theoretical side, psychological science continues to search for mechanisms that cause them. Although we know that false memories can be created with a number of methods, we still do not know what processes underlie their creation. Taken together, however, the research suggests that Mazzoni et al.'s (2001) three-stage model is a recipe for "making" false memories. If we can make something plausible, make people believe that they probably had some experience, and then engage them in imagination or other techniques that add sensory detail, we are well on the way to creating a rich false memory. For example, participants who initially expressed dismay about their childhood hot-air balloon ride tended to believe that it happened because they had "proof" in the form of a photograph or a family member's statement. Those participants might imagine themselves in a hot-air balloon and pack their imagery with sensory detail: feeling the warmth coming down from the gas flame, the sound of the wind whipping through their clothes, and how tiny their parents looked down on the ground. Later, participants might mistakenly attribute the images to a genuine experience, rather than to their imagination, and thereby develop a false memory (see also Mitchell & Johnson, 2000).

The types of false memories discussed here may also be explained by associative network theories of memory (Anderson, 1983; Collins & Loftus, 1975). When a concept is activated, other highly related concepts are also activated, followed by less-related concepts. How might associative network approaches help us make sense of false-memory creation? A man who develops a false memory for riding in a hot-air balloon will report details activated by his thinking about hot-air ballooning and what it entails. Perhaps thinking about the balloon taking off will activiate thoughts about the gas flame and the wicker basket, and the flame will activate thoughts about warmth. Details such as seeing people on the ground, the park where the ride took place, or feeling scared as the balloon rose become activated in a cascade of thoughts associated with a balloon ride. That is not to say, of course, that the associative view is somehow incompatible with a source-monitoring approach to false memories. Indeed, these two viewpoints tend to focus on different levels of resolution, or different steps in the process of false-memory development. For example, the source-monitoring framework helps to guide our thinking about the plausibility of the event and the authoritativeness of the person telling us that an event really happened. It also helps us understand the process by which event details—which may well have been generated by associative processes—are confused with reality. A look at the role of plausibility, in particular, shows us that even modest changes in plausibility can have large consequences for memory.

Research in allied areas continues to support both the long-established and recent psychological research on false memories. For example, a team of neuroscientists explained that their data shows that when we recall an experience, it becomes unstable (Nader, 2003; Nader, Schafe, & le Doux, 2000). In their view, consolidation—which requires protein generation—is not something that happens only during the initial encoding phase; it has to happen *each time* we store the memory. Each reconsolidation sweeps up genuine experience and imagined details into the updated memory and stashes it away via the new proteins. In the cognitive literature, such a process is similar to one proposed by Estes (1997), in his "perturbation" account of memory distortions. It is important to note, however, that Nader and colleagues' reconsolidation interpretation is controversial. For example, Cahill, McGaugh, and Weinberger (2001) note that treatments meant to disrupt "reconsolidation" cause memory deficits only for a short period, after which the memories return—something that does not happen when the same disruptive treatments are given after learning new material.

Another controversial line of research by Anderson and colleagues (Anderson et al., 2004; Anderson & Green, 2001) has shown that being asked to remember a word can improve memory for it, and that sometimes being asked to suppress the word can impair memory for it. They concluded that their results "support a suppression mechanism that pushes unwanted memories out of awareness, as posited by Freud" (Anderson & Green 2001, p. 368). When participants were scanned with fMRI (functional magnetic resonance imaging) to measure brain activity while they tried to either think about or to suppress the target words, they showed a different pattern of brain activity when they were instructed to think about words versus suppress them, and more activity in the frontal cortex when they were successful at the suppression task.

What do these findings tell us about how repression might work? Anderson et al. (2004) claim to have demonstrated a psychological mechanism for "the voluntary form of repression (suppression) proposed by Freud" (p. 232). But other scientists disagree, for several reasons. First, in the Anderson et al. study, when participants tried to suppress a word, their memories were about 10% less accurate than when they did not try to suppress it. Even so, they still remembered about 80% of the target words, compared to about 87% baseline performance (in which they were not asked to think about the word at all). That is a far cry from massive repression. Second, some have questioned whether trying to suppress common words is parallel to suppressing traumatic childhood events (Kihlstrom, 2002; Schacter, 2001): One of the premises of repression is that we banish traumatic experiences from awareness; we do not banish everyday, inconsequential words. Finally, what do the fMRI results tell us? To understand those, let us first try to understand what we might do if we were trying to *not* remember something. We might, as neuropsychologist Larry Squire told the *New York Times*, divert our attention, using up our neural resources to distract ourselves (as cited in O'Connor, 2004). If that is what we do, it is not surprising that asking people to do different things causes activity in different brain regions.

Research from both cognitive neuropsychology and neuroscience investigating the power of imagination is also intriguing. For example, Kosslyn and Thompson (2003) reviewed over 15 years of neuroimaging studies of visual imagery to determine what kinds of imagination tasks cause activation in the early visual cortex (areas 17 and 18). Across these studies, when participants were asked to visualize high-resolution details of objects, they showed activity in areas 17 and 18. More interesting is Kosslyn and Thompson's analysis, which suggests that this activation may not be a by-product of imagery but part of the process of imagery itself. Other recent research suggests that imagining tasks can have real-world effects similar to doing those tasks. In one study, two groups of participants volunteered to wear a cast on their arm for 10 days (Newsom, Knight, & Balnave, 2003). Half the participants did nothing to preserve their hand strength, whereas the other half imagined squeezing a rubber ball three times a day for 5 minutes each. When their casts were removed, the imagined group had kept their strength, but the control group had become significantly weaker. In another study, people were asked to imagine flexing their ankle, do low-intensity strength training, or do nothing (Zijdewind, Toering, Bessem, van der Laan, & Diercks, 2003). After several weeks, the participants who imagined flexing their ankle were stronger than the other two groups. If merely imagining a workout can make you stronger, is it any wonder that imagining a fictitious experience can strengthen a false memory?

On the practical side, new issues give us cause for concern. Those in the area of eyewitness testimony have been heartened by the success of the Innocence Project. However, it looks as though their success is under threat. Recently, prosecutors in the United States have seemingly grown weary of the scores of prisoners freed by the Innocence Project. Florida introduced a 2-year "window" during which prisoners can file petitions asking for DNA analysis. The window ended October 1, 2003, but some prosecutors have said that they will continue to examine petitions. It is not just the state of Florida that seems to have a problem with DNA testing. All across the United States, prosecutors are now starting to oppose DNA testing when a result that does not match the convicted person still does not conclusively prove innocence (Liptak, 2003). In some cases, the opposition has no apparent justification. For example, the prosecutor in Lonnie Erby's case opposed DNA analysis because although there was serological evidence in two of the rapes, there was none in the third. Thus, argued the prosecutor, excluding him as the rapist on two counts would say nothing about the third. Nevermind that the prosecutor had considered the question of guilt by bundling the rapes together—now she wanted to consider the question of innocence by *un*bundling them.

Another area for concern is the current scandal involving sexual abuse by Catholic priests. At the end of the last century, we saw countless casualties in the recovered memory wars. When the battles abated, we asked ourselves, "How did this happen?" and "What can we learn so that it does not happen again?" There are, of course, both differences and similarities. On the one hand, there are clear differences between many of the priest cases and many of the repressed cases. For instance, many Church victims never repressed their abuse, and there is evidence showing that genuine incidents were covered up by Church officials. On the other hand, it is worth bearing in mind that suggested cases of childhood sexual abuse in the 1990s followed on the heels of genuine cases brought to light a few years before; thus, we should not be surprised to see the recent claims of recovered memories for abuse by priests. We should also not be surprised by the pending legislation that gives plaintiffs more time to sue, or by the big-money settlements. If history continues to repeat itself, we will see retractors, lawsuits against those who made false claims, and settlements paid to those who were falsely accused. We will see damage on an enormous scale, and some years from now, we will look back on the "Catholic priest wars" and ask ourselves once more, "How did this happen?" and "What can we learn so that it does not happen again?"

ACKNOWLEDGMENTS

We are grateful to Deryn Strange, Melanie Takarangi, Lauren French, Sophie Parker, Louise Belcher, Kirsty Weir, and Rachel Sutherland for their helpful suggestions and diligent proofreading. Matthew Gerrie was supported by a Victoria University PhD scholarship. Maryanne Garry was supported by a generous Marsden Grant from the Royal Society of New Zealand, Contract No. VUW205.

REFERENCES

Alba, J. W., & Hasher, L. (1983). Is memory schematic? *Psychological Bulletin, 93*, 203–231.

Anderson, J. R. (1983). A spreading activation theory of memory. *Journal of Verbal Learning and Verbal Behavior, 22*, 261–295.

Anderson, M. C., & Green, C. (2001). Suppressing unwanted memories by executive control. *Nature, 410*, 366–369.

Anderson, M. C., Ochsner, K. N., Kuhl, B., Cooper, J., Robertson, S. W., Gabrieli, G. H., et al. (2004). Neural systems underlying the suppression of unwanted memories. *Science, 303*, 232–235.

Assefi, S. L., & Garry, M. (2003). Absolute memory distortions: Alcohol placebos influence the misinformation effect. *Psychological Science, 14*, 77–80.

Bass, E., & Davis, L. (1988). *The courage to heal: A guide for women survivors of child sexual abuse.* New York: Harper & Row.

Belli, R. (1989). Influences of misleading postevent information: Misinformation interference and acceptance. *Journal of Experimental Psychology, 118,* 72–85.

Bernstein, D. M., Godfrey, R. D., Davison, A., & Loftus, E. F. (2004). Conditions affecting the relevation effect for autobiographical memory. *Memory Cognition, 32,* 455–462.

Bernstein, D. M., Whittlesea, B. W. A., & Loftus, E. F. (2002). Increasing confidence in remote autobiographical memory and general knowledge: Extensions of the revelation effect. *Memory and Cognition, 30,* 432–438.

Braun, K. A., Ellis, R., & Loftus, E. F. (2002). Make my memory: How advertising can change our memories of the past. *Psychology and Marketing, 19,* 1–23.

Cahill, L., McGaugh, J. L., & Weinberger, N. M. (2001). The neurobiology of learning and memory: Some reminders to remember. *Trends in Neuroscience, 24,* 578–581.

Cherek, D. R., Steinberg, J. L., & Manno, B. R. (1985). Effects of alcohol on human aggressive behavior. *Journal of Studies on Alcohol, 46,* 321–328.

Christianson, S.-A. (1992). Emotional stress and eyewitness memory: A critical review. *Psychological Bulletin, 112,* 284–309.

Christianson, S.-A., & Loftus, E. F. (1991). Remembering emotional events: The fate of detailed information. *Cognition and Emotion, 5,* 81–108.

Collins A. M., & Loftus E. F. (1975). A spreading-activation theory of semantic processing. *Psychological Review, 82,* 407–428.

Cutler, B. L., & Penrod, S. D. (1995). *Mistaken identification: The eyewitness, psychology, and law.* New York: Cambridge University Press.

Deffenbacher, K. A. (1983). The influence of arousal on reliability of testimony. In. S. M. A. Lloyd-Boystock & B. R. Clifford (Eds.), *Evaluating witness evidence* (pp. 235–251). New York: Wiley.

Dodd, D. H., & Bradshaw, J. M. (1980). Leading questions and memory: Pragmatic constraints. *Journal of Verbal Learning and Verbal Behavior, 19,* 695–704.

Eakin, D. K., Schreiber, T. A., & Sergent-Marshall, S. (2003). Misinformation effects in eyewitness memory: The presence and absence of memory impairment as a function of warning and misinformation accessibility. *Journal of Experimental Psychology: Learning, Memory and Cognition, 29,* 813–825.

Easterbrook, J. A. (1959). The effect of emotion on cue utilization and the organization of behavior. *Psychological Review, 66,* 183–201.

Ebbinghaus, H. (1913). *Memory: A contribution to experimental psychology.* New York: Teachers College, Columbia University. (Original work published 1885)

Estes, W. K. (1997). Processes of memory loss, recovery and distortion. *Psychological Review, 104,* 148–169.

Garry, M., Manning, C. G., Loftus, E. F., & Sherman, S. J. (1996). Imagination inflation: Imagining a childhood event inflates confidence that it occurred. *Psychonomic Bulletin and Review, 3,* 208–214.

Garry, M., & Wade, K. A. (in press). Actually, a picture is worth less than 45 words: Narratives produce more false memories than photographs. *Psychodynamic Bulletin and Review.*

George, W., & Marlatt, G. A. (1986). The effects of alcohol and anger on interest in violence, erotica, and deviance. *Journal of Abnormal Psychology, 95,* 150–158.

Goff, L., & Roediger, H. (1998). Imagination inflation for action events: Repeated imaginings lead to illusory recollections. *Memory and Cognition, 26,* 20–33.

Greene, E., Flynn, M., & Loftus, E. F. (1982). Inducing resistance to misleading information. *Journal of Verbal Learning and Verbal Behavior, 21,* 207–219.

Grinley, M. J. (2002). *Effects of advertising on semantic and episodic memory.* Unpublished master's thesis, University of Washington, Seattle, Washington.

Heaps, C., & Nash, M. (1999). Individual differences in imagination inflation. *Psychonomic Bulletin and Review, 6,* 313–318.

Heaps, C. M., & Nash, M. (2001). Comparing recollective experience in true and false autobiographical memories. *Journal of Experimental Psychology: Learning, Memory, and Cognition, 27,* 920–930.

Holmes, D. S. (1995). The evidence for repression: An examination of sixty years of research. In J. L. Singer (Ed.), *Repression and dissociation: Implications for personality theory, psychopathology, and health. The John D. and Catherine T. MacArthur Foundation series on mental health and development* (pp. 85–102). Chicago: University of Chicago Press.

Hyman, I. E., Husband, T. H., & Billings, F. J. (1995). False memories of childhood experiences. *Applied Cognitive Psychology, 9,* 181–197.

Johnson, M., Foley, M. A., Suengas, A., & Raye, C. (1988). Phenomenal characteristics of memories for perceived and imagined autobiographical events. *Journal of Experimental Psychology: General, 117,* 371–376.

Johnson, M., Hashtroudi, S., & Lindsay, D. S. (1993). Source monitoring. *Psychological Bulletin, 114,* 3–28.

Kassin, S. M., Tubb, V. A., Hosch, H. M., & Memon, A. (2002). On the "general acceptance" of eyewitness testimony research. *American Psychologist, 56,* 405–416.

Kihlstrom, J. F. (2002). No need for repression. *Trends in Cognitive Sciences, 6,* 502.

Kosslyn, S. M., & Thompson, W. L. (2003). When is early visual cortex activated during visual mental imagery? *Psychological Bulletin, 129,* 723–746.

Lang, A. R., Searles, J., Lauerman, R., & Adesso, V. J. (1980). Expectancy, alcohol, and sex guilt as determinants of interest in and reaction to sexual stimuli. *Journal of Abnormal Psychology, 89,* 644–653.

Lindsay, D. S. (1990). Misleading suggestions can impair eyewitnesses' ability to remember event details. *Journal of Experimental Psychology: Learning, Memory, and Cognition, 16,* 1077–1083.

Lindsay, D. S., Hagen, L., Read, J. D., Wade, K. A., & Garry, M. (2004). True photographs and false memories. *Psychological Science, 15,* 149–154.

Liptak, A. (2003, August 29). Prosecutors fight DNA use for exoneration. *New York Times,* p. A1.

Loftus, E. F. (1975). Leading questions and the eyewitness report. *Cognitive Psychology, 7,* 560–572.

Loftus, E. F. (1991). Made in memory: Distortions in recollection after misleading information. *The Psychology of Learning and Motivation, 27,* 187–215.

Loftus, E. F. (1993). The reality of repressed memories. *American Psychologist, 48,* 518–537.

Loftus, E. F. (1996). *Eyewitness testimony* (2nd ed.). Cambridge, MA: Harvard University Press.

Loftus, E. F., & Bernstein, D. M. (in press). Rich false memories: The royal road to success. In A. Healy (Ed.), *Experimental cognitive psychology and its applications: Festschrift in honor of Lyle Bourne, Walter Kintsch, and Thomas Landauer.* Washington, DC: American Psychological Association.

Loftus, E. F., & Burns, T. E. (1982). Mental shock can produce retrograde amnesia. *Memory and Cognition, 10*, 318–232.

Loftus, E. F., Donders, K., Hoffman, H., & Schooler, J. (1989). Creating new memories that are quickly assessed and confidently held. *Memory and Cognition, 17*, 607–616.

Loftus, E. F., & Hoffman, H. G. (1989). Misinformation and memory: The creation of new memories. *Journal of Experimental Psychology: General, 118*, 100–104.

Loftus, E. F., Loftus, G. R., & Messo, J. (1987). Some facts about "weapon focus." *Law and Human Behavior, 11*, 55–62.

Loftus, E. F., Miller, D., & Burns, H. (1978). Semantic integration of verbal information into visual memory. *Journal of Experimental Psychology, 4*, 19–31.

Loftus, E. F., & Palmer, J. (1974). Reconstruction of automobile destruction: An example of the interaction between language and memory. *Journal of Verbal Learning and Verbal Behavior, 13*, 585–589.

Loftus, E. F., & Pickrell, J. (1995). The formation of false memories. *Psychiatric Annals, 25*, 720–725.

Loftus, E. F., & Zanni, G. (1975). Eyewitness testimony: The influence of the wording of a question. *Bulletin of the Psychonomic Society, 5*, 86–88.

Mazzoni, G. A. L., Loftus, E. F., & Kirsch, I. (2001). Changing beliefs about implausible autobiographical events: A little plausibility goes a long way. *Journal of Experimental Psychology: Applied, 7*, 51–59.

Mazzoni, G., & Memon, A. (2003). Imagination can create false autobiographical memories. *Psychological Science, 14*, 186–188.

McCloskey, M., & Zaragoza, M. (1985). Misleading postevent information and memory for events: Arguments and evidence against memory impairment hypothesis. *Journal of Experimental Psychology: General, 114*, 1–16.

McNally, R. J. (2003). *Remembering trauma*. Cambridge, MA: Belknap Press/Harvard University Press.

Memon, M., Vrij, A., & Bull, R. (2003). *Psychology and law: Truthfulness, accuracy and credibility* (2nd ed.). Chichester, UK: Wiley.

Mitchell, K. J., & Johnson, M. K. (2000). Source monitoring: Attributing mental experiences. In E. Tulving & F. I. M. Craik (Eds.), *The Oxford handbook of memory* (pp. 179–195). New York: Oxford University Press.

Nader, K. (2003). Memory traces unbound. *Trends in Neuroscience, 26*, 65–72.

Nader, K., Schafe, G. E., & le Doux, J. E. (2000). Fear memories require protein synthesis in the amygdala for reconsolidation after retrieval. *Nature, 406*, 722–726.

Newsom, J., Knight, P., & Balnave, R. (2003). Use of mental imagery to limit strength loss after immobilization. *Journal of Sport Rehabilitation, 12*, 249–258.

Paddock, J., Noel, M., Terranova, S., Eber, H., Manning, C., & Loftus, E. F. (1999). Imagination inflation and the perils of guided visualization. *Journal of Psychology, 133*, 581–595.

Pezdek, K., Finger, K., & Hodge, D. (1997). Planting false childhood memories: The role of event plausibility. *Psychological Science, 8*, 437–441.

Porter, S., Yuille, J. C., & Lehman, D. R. (1999). The nature of real, implanted, and fabricated memories for emotional childhood events: Implications for the recovered memory debate. *Law and Human Behavior, 23*, 517–537.

Rohsenow, D. J., & Marlatt, G. A. (1981). The balanced placebo design: Methodological considerations. *Addictive Behaviors, 6*, 107–122.

Schacter, D. L. (2001). Suppression of unwanted memories: Repression revisited. *The Lancet, 357,* 1724–1725.

Sharman, S. J., Garry, M., & Beuke, C. J. (2004). Imagination or exposure causes imagination inflation. *American Journal of Psychology, 117,* 157–168.

Stanny, C. J., & Johnson, T. C. (2000). Effects of stress induced by a simulated shooting on recall by police and citizen witnesses. *American Journal of Psychology, 113,* 359–386.

Steblay, N. M. (1992). A meta-analytic review of the weapon focus effect. *Law and Human Behavior, 16,* 413–424.

Sutherland, R., & Hayne, H. (2001). The effect of postevent information on adults' eyewitness reports. *Applied Cognitive Psychology, 15,* 249–263.

Tavris, C. (1993, January 3). Beware the incest survivor machine. *New York Times Book Review,* p. 5.

Thomas, A. K., Bulevich, J. B., & Loftus, E. F. (2003). Exploring the role of repetition and sensory elaboration in the imagination inflation effect. *Memory and Cognition, 31,* 630–640.

Thomas, A. K., & Loftus, E. F. (2002). Creating bizarre false memories through imagination. *Memory and Cognition, 30,* 423–431.

Tousignant, J. P., Hall, D., & Loftus, E. F. (1986). Discrepancy detection and vulnerability to misleading postevent information. *Memory and Cognition, 14,* 329–338.

Tuckey, M. R., & Brewer, N. (2003). The influence of schemas, stimulus ambiguity, and interview schedule on eyewitness memory over time. *Journal of Experimental Psychology: Applied, 9,* 101–118.

Tversky, B., & Tuchin, M. (1989). A reconciliation of the evidence on eyewitness testimony: Comments on McCloskey and Zaragoza. *Journal of Experimental Psychology: General, 118,* 86–91.

Vornik, L. A., Sharman, S. J., & Garry, M. (2003). The power of the spoken word: Sociolinguistic cues influence the misinformation effect. *Memory, 11,* 101–109.

Wade, K. A., & Garry, M. (2003). *Narrative vs. photographs in creating false memories: Effect of order.* Unpublished manuscript.

Wade, K. A., Garry, M., Read, J. D., & Lindsay, D. S. (2001, June). *A picture is worth a thousand lies: Using false photos to create false memories.* Paper presented at the meeting of the Society for Applied Research in Memory and Cognition, Kingston, Ontario, Canada.

Wade, K. A., Garry, M., Read, J. D., & Lindsay, D. S. (2002). A picture is worth a thousand lies: Using false photographs to create false childhood memories. *Psychonomic Bulletin and Review, 9,* 597–603.

Weingardt, K., Toland, H. K., & Loftus, E. F. (1994). Reports of suggested memories: Do people truly believe them? In D. Ross, J. D. Read, & M. P. Toglia (Eds.), *Adult eyewitness testimony: Current trends and developments* (pp. 3–26). New York: Springer-Verlag.

Wells, G. L. (1988). *Eyewitness identification: A system handbook.* Toronto: Carswell Legal Publications.

Wessel, I., & Merckelbach, H. (1997). The impact of anxiety on memory for details in spider phobics. *Applied Cognitive Psychology, 11,* 223–231.

Whittlesea, B. W. A., & Williams, L. M. (2001). The discrepancy-attribution hypothesis: I. Expectation, uncertainty, surprise, and feelings of familiarity. *Journal of Experimental Psychology: Learning, Memory, and Cognition, 27,* 3–13.

Wright, D. B., & Stroud, J. N. (1998). Memory quality and misinformation for peripheral and central objects. *Legal and Criminological Psychology, 3,* 273–286.

Yarmey, A. D. (1986). Perceived expertness and credibility of police officers as eyewitnesses. *Canadian Police College Journal, 10,* 31–51.

Yerkes, R. M., & Dodson, J. D. (1908). The relation of strength of stimulus to rapidity of
habit-formation. *Journal of Comparative Neurology of Psychology, 18,* 459–482.

Yuille, J. C., & Cutshall, J. L. (1986). A case study of eyewitness memory of a crime. *Journal of Applied Psychology, 71,* 291–301.

Zijdewind, I., Toering, S. T., Bessem, B., van der Laan, O., & Diercks, R. L. (2003). Effects of imagery motor training on torque production of ankle plantar flexor muscles. *Muscle and Nerve, 28,* 168–173.

CHAPTER EIGHT

Pretrial Publicity and Its Influence on Juror Decision Making

CHRISTINA A. STUDEBAKER
STEVEN D. PENROD

When a case is being tried, attention is focused on the facts of the case, the nature of the charges, and whether the facts meet the criteria necessary to find the defendant responsible for causing harm or wrongdoing. However, many things happen before the trial that can influence its outcome. These include the selection (or assignment) of attorneys, the selection of jurors, the determination of the trial venue, judicial decisions about what information will be admissible at trial, and the presentation of information about the case (i.e., pretrial publicity) to potential jurors via the local or national media. Although pretrial publicity (PTP) is not available for every case that goes to trial, it can present special challenges when it *is* present because—unlike other pretrial factors—most of what appears in the media is not under the control of the court or the defendant. Even in countries that utilize *sub judice* or statutory law to prevent the dissemination of prejudicial information before trial, PTP is not automatically prevented in every case. Furthermore, once a court has allowed PTP to be presented, it has or may wield little, if any, control over the nature and amount of PTP ultimately presented.

Various aspects of PTP increase its potential to influence juror decision making: (1) the timing of the presentation of PTP compared to the presentation of trial evidence, (2) the amount of PTP that appears, (3) the lack of any procedures to screen for information that would likely be judged inadmissible at trial, and (4) the lack of formal opportunities before trial to rebut information presented via the media (in contrast to cross-examination during trial).

In general, empirical research on PTP effects has shown prejudicial PTP to have broad effects. PTP influences evaluations of the defendant's likability, sympathy for the defendant, perceptions of the defendant as a typical criminal, pretrial judgments of the defendant's guilt, and final verdicts (Bornstein, Whisenhunt, Nemeth, & Dunaway, 2002; Costantini & King, 1980–1981; DeLuca, 1979; Honess, Charman, & Levi, 2003; Hvistendahl, 1979; Kline & Jess, 1966; Kovera, 2002; Moran & Cutler, 1991; Otto, Penrod, & Dexter, 1994; Padawer-Singer & Barton, 1975; Ruva, 2002; Simon & Eimermann, 1971; Sue, Smith, & Gilbert, 1974; Sue, Smith, & Pedroza, 1975; Tans & Chaffee, 1966; Vidmar, 2002). However, it is clear that PTP does not influence evaluations of defendants in all cases in which it is presented. Research has demonstrated the ability of PTP to influence judgments about a case (for a meta-analytic review, see Steblay, Besirevic, Fulero, & Jimenez-Lorente, 1999), but there is no adequate understanding of the factors that moderate these effects, nor of the mechanisms that mediate the effects.

This chapter (1) reviews general legal concerns about PTP effects and the safeguards courts typically apply to guard against them, (2) examines the effects of PTP already demonstrated in research, (3) offers a theoretical framework within which to organize past and current research on PTP effects, (4) uses the framework to identify gaps in our knowledge about PTP effects, and (5) discusses research alternatives to field surveys and experimental laboratory studies (i.e., the dominant forms of existing research) that can help fill the gaps and further our understanding of PTP effects on juror decision making.

LEGAL CONCERNS ABOUT PRETRIAL PUBLICITY

Courts around the world are concerned with ensuring fair trials, but the potential influence of PTP on trials is of greater concern in countries that have an adversarial legal system that allows trials to be decided by juries than in countries that have an inquisitorial legal system. In countries that allow jury trials, the same basic concerns about PTP exist—that is, the potential of PTP (1) to present information to potential jurors that will ultimately be ruled inadmissible or not entered into evidence at trial, and (2) to prevent a fair and impartial trial by biasing potential jurors against a particular party (particularly, the defendant in criminal proceedings) prior to the trial.

Because the vast majority of social science research on PTP effects has been conducted in the United States, that research has examined U.S. law to understand the courts' concerns about PTP and how the courts deal with the potential problems associated with, or caused by, PTP. Consequently, we begin with a discussion of PTP in the context of U.S. law.

PTP concerns the courts because of its potential to create prejudice against defendants in criminal prosecutions. Article III of the U.S. Constitution, the Sixth Amendment, and the Due Process Clause of the Fifth Amendment require fundamental fairness in the prosecution of federal crimes. These rights are the foundation for Federal Rules of Civil Procedure (FRCP) Rule 21(a), which provides for a change of venue to protect from prejudice:

The court upon motion of the defendant shall transfer the proceeding as to that defendant to another district whether or not such district is specified in the defendant's motion if the court is satisfied that there exists in the district where the prosecution is pending so great a prejudice against the defendant that the defendant cannot obtain a fair and impartial trial at any place fixed by law for holding court in that district.

Of course, the Fifth and Sixth Amendments of the U.S. Constitution were devised in an era very different from the present. We need only consider the recent development and convergence of highly mobile broadcasting equipment, widespread access to cable television and satellite broadcasting, 24-hour news networks such as CNN and MSNBC, and specialized cable channels such as Court TV to recognize that the media environment in which people now live is profoundly different from the environment that prevailed 200 years ago. Not only are the media now different, it is clear that at least some trials that took place in the United States in the late 20th century were also profoundly different from those of 200 years ago. The intense public interest and media coverage that accompanied, and are accompanying, cases such as those involving O. J. Simpson, Timothy McVeigh, John Muhammad and Lee Malvo, Michael Jackson, and a host of other cases that garner national attention, raises the question of whether high levels of PTP make it impossible to find any "district" in the United States where a "fair and impartial" jury can be impaneled. Of course, the problem of PTP is not limited to the United States. Vidmar (2002) provides examples of widely publicized cases in Australia, Canada, and New Zealand, and Honess et al. (2003) have conducted research related to a widely publicized case in the United Kingdom.

Although the extensive publicity devoted to high-profile cases makes them instantly recognizable and calls attention to possible media-induced biases, it is important to note that prejudicial information may affect juror decision making in any case that receives substantial PTP, whether that PTP is at the local or national level. As a practical matter, there are a great many more cases that achieve local notoriety than achieve national notoriety. Such cases barely penetrate national consciousness, and yet they are the primary fodder for battles over the effects of PTP, of efforts to change venues, of regionally concentrated public opinion surveys offered in support of those motions, and of the appellate litigation that follows on the heels of such cases.

Appellate case law provides the most important guidelines and legal opinions on the potential threat that PTP poses to fair trial procedures. Several notable U.S. Supreme Court cases touching on PTP—*Irvin v. Dowd* (1961), *Rideau v. Louisiana* (1963), *Sheppard v. Maxwell* (1966), and *Mu'Min v. Virginia* (1991)—have established the framework for judicial evaluations of the prejudicial potential of PTP (due to space constraints we do not review them here, but for a detailed consideration of the case law, see Campbell, 1994, and Studebaker & Penrod, 1997). Hardly a month goes by in which an appellate court does not address PTP issues in a noteworthy case. These cases may involve multiple court hearings and result in changes of venues or changes of venire (i.e., the pool from which potential jurors are selected). The court decisions are often split, with strong dissents raising questions about the impact of PTP on verdicts and sentencing.

The U.S. Supreme Court currently uses a "totality of the circumstances" test to assess claims of prejudicial PTP (*Murphy v. Florida*, 1975). Under this test, the Court examines the atmosphere of the trial and the voir dire transcript as well as other "indicia of impartiality" to determine whether a defendant received a fair trial. Courts also consider jurors' statements about their ability to disregard prejudicial PTP when assessing whether a "substantial likelihood" of prejudice exists. If potentially prejudicial information about a case has appeared in the media, it is not uncommon (although not required) for the judge or attorneys to ask potential jurors during jury selection whether they can disregard the PTP to which they have been exposed and serve as fair and impartial jurors. If prospective jurors report that they are able to do so (as they typically do), their statements are taken as sufficient proof that they can and will do so if selected as jurors.

Potential jurors' knowledge of PTP, in and of itself, is not automatically a problem. In fact, the U.S. Supreme Court stated that "it is not required . . . that the jurors be totally ignorant of the facts and issues involved" in a case (*Irvin v. Dowd*, 1961, p. 722). PTP becomes problematic when it causes potential jurors to be prejudiced against a defendant before trial. Although courts around the world often believe that jurors are able to set aside any preconceived notions about a defendant and base their verdicts solely on the evidence presented at trial, this belief is not supported by the findings from empirical research.

Basic research within social and cognitive psychology underscores the difficulty of setting aside previously acquired information. When making social judgments (such as those involved in deciding whether a defendant is guilty), it is natural for people to process information in an integrative manner. That is to say, people make connections between various pieces of information and base decisions on overall impressions rather than on specific pieces of information (Pennington & Hastie, 1986, 1988; Schul & Burnstein, 1985). Our prejudgments guide our attention, our interpretation of new and old information, and our memories (Bodenhausen, 1988; Hamilton, Sherman, & Ruvolo, 1990). To set aside preconceived notions requires a person to identify previously received information as biasing, to know how that information was eventually processed and stored in memory, and to reverse or control for any biasing effects the information has had. The integrative nature of human information processing makes it very difficult for people to do this successfully.

Within the jury domain, Schum (1993) reported that nearly half of his mock jury participants either ignored testimony that conflicted with prior evidence or reinterpreted it as agreeing with earlier testimony. Schum argued that these results were due to a primacy effect in which early information biases the interpretation given to later information. Pennington and Hastie's (1988,

1993) story model of jury decision making also suggests that early evidence has a greater impact than later evidence. In the story model, jurors start by constructing a story that encompasses information they bring to trial (e.g., PTP) as well as information presented at trial. These stories serve as frameworks within which new trial evidence is interpreted. Thus, by influencing the nature of the initial stories, PTP can influence jurors' later decisions by biasing their interpretation of new evidence.

Clearly, the potential prejudicial influence of PTP on juror decision making causes tension between the First and Sixth Amendments, and some policymaking groups have formulated practice guidelines to address problems posed by prejudicial PTP—see, for example, "Report of the Judicial Conference Committee" (Report, 1968) and the American Bar Association's *Model Rules of Professional Conduct* (2000).

The American Bar Association (2000) identified six specific types of information that lawyers should not disseminate because of their potentially prejudicial impact. These types of information include (1) the prior criminal record of the accused; (2) the character or reputation of the accused; (3) the existence of any confession, admission, or statement given by the accused (or the refusal to make a statement); (4) the performance on any examinations or tests (or the refusal to submit to an examination or test); (5) the possibility of a plea of guilty to the offense charged or to a lesser offense; and (6) any opinion as to the accused's guilt or innocence or as to the merits of the evidence in the case. The American Bar Association's (2000) *Model Rules of Professional Conduct* states that a lawyer should not release potentially prejudicial information if he or she "knows or reasonably should know that it will have a substantial likelihood of materially prejudicing an adjudicative proceeding" (p. 1). The standard of *substantial likelihood* has elicited various interpretations ranging from "reasonably likely to interfere with a fair trial" to "serious and imminent threat to the administration of justice" (Norwood, 1986, p. 175). Even if prejudicial PTP is released, judges may not necessarily see it as producing significant bias against the defendant.

Courts are aware of the potential biasing effects of PTP and have devised safeguards designed to reduce or eliminate those influences. These include continuance, extended voir dire, judicial admonitions, trial evidence, jury deliberation, change of venire, and change of venue. Unfortunately, most safeguards have been shown to be ineffective. The empirical research examining the efficacy of these safeguards is reviewed in more detail later in this chapter.

SOCIAL SCIENCE RESEARCH ON PRETRIAL PUBLICITY AND ITS EFFECTS

Quantities of Pretrial Publicity

Studies examining the nature or content of PTP have typically focused on the prejudicial (i.e., anti-defendant) content, and little information is available concerning the average amount of PTP that appears about particular cases. Imrich, Mullin, and Linz (1995) conducted a content analysis of crime stories in 14 large U.S. newspapers over a period of 8 weeks. Overall, Imrich et al. found that 27% of the suspects in crime stories were described in a prejudicial manner. Negative statements about the suspect's character and opinions of guilt were the most frequent prejudicial statements—followed by prior arrest information, confessions, and prior conviction information. Law enforcement officers and prosecutors were the most common sources of prejudicial information. In short, roughly one-fourth of all suspects in crimes covered by newspaper articles may be subject to prejudicial PTP. Of course, not all cases are covered by the media. Bruschke and Loges (1999) examined reporting from a different perspective: They looked for pretrial newspaper reports focused on 134 first-degree murder cases tried between 1993 and 1995. They found that 46% of the cases received no coverage, 19% were covered in 1–5 articles, 18% were covered in 6–10 articles, and 16% were covered in 11 or more articles. Because their study examined a limited time period and only one type of crime, their data underscore that there is wide variability in the amount of PTP coverage given to individual cases.

Of course, some cases can generate massive amounts of PTP. As we have reported elsewhere (Studebaker & Penrod, 1997; Studebaker, Robbennolt, Pathak-Sharma, & Penrod, 2000), in the 9 months following the bombing of the Murrah Federal Building in Oklahoma City, there were 939 articles published in the *Daily Oklahoman* (i.e., the main newspaper for Oklahoma City)—105 of them on the front page—and these stories were accompanied by 307 pictures. In contrast, the *Denver Post* carried 174 articles—24 on the front page—and just nine pictures. Our content analysis of the *Daily Oklahoman*'s stories also revealed that they carried more statements depicting the emotional impact of the case and reported on subject matter related to the community.

Sometimes cases can be very highly publicized in one location and yet receive virtually no attention in nearby locations. This occurred in relation to an incident in Long Island, New York, in which a minor New York City celebrity, Lizzie Grubman, backed her SUV into a crowd at a nightclub, injuring several bystanders (Penrod, Groscup, & O'Neil, 2002). Coverage of Ms. Grubman in New York City area newspapers was quite intense: Nearly 250 stories appeared in print media in the 3 weeks following the incident. Coverage fell fairly steadily in the following weeks, but at least one story about Ms. Grubman appeared every week for the following 6 months—a total of 505 printed articles (complemented by hundreds of television and radio reports). In contrast, the newspaper in Albany, New York—the state capital located only 150 miles away—generated only nine articles about Ms. Grubman in 6 months. The print coverage took various forms: 111 news stories focused on specific aspects of the incident; 84 stories were longer, in-depth analyses that delved into specific aspects/implications of the incident; another 84 appearances were comprised of columns/articles/letters to the editor, including opinions and assumptions, and 226 columns and editorial comments contained speculation and hearsay about the incident and Ms. Grubman. Coverage of Ms. Grubman continued over the next 10 months as civil and criminal suits proceeded, with another 325 articles appearing in New York newspapers.

Assessing the Impact of Media Coverage

Traditionally, two approaches have been adopted to study the impact of PTP on people's pretrial and trial judgments: field methods and experimental methods (Kerr, 1994; Linz & Penrod, 1992). The field method uses surveys to examine the effects of PTP on pretrial judgments about particular real-life cases. Respondents are typically asked questions about their media exposure, what information they recall or recognize about a case, and their evaluation of the strength of the evidence and the likelihood of the defendant's guilt. Typically, a survey is conducted in the trial venue as well as an alternative venue to which the trial might be moved and where it is believed that PTP exposure and prejudgment will be lower. Comparisons are made between the amounts of exposure and prejudgment in the alternative venues. Analyses are based on correlations between the extent of PTP to which individuals have been exposed and the extent of their prejudgments about the case. Alternatively, laboratory studies using experimental methodology systematically manipulate the amount and nature of PTP presented to individuals. Presentation of PTP is typically followed by simulations of the trial process. Participants are presented evidence about the case and provided with judge's instructions to guide their verdict decision. Analyses focus on the effects of PTP on perceptions of the defendant, evaluation of the evidence, and verdicts.

Survey studies assessing the level of prejudgment among potential jurors in actual cases occur primarily, though not exclusively, in criminal cases. Although such surveys are frequently used to support motions for a change of venue, the results from very few have been published (for one early report, see Vidmar & Judson, 1981, and for a more recent discussion, Vidmar, 2002). Nietzel and Dillehay (1983) reviewed results from their surveys for five murder trials and found that a far greater percentage of respondents in the venue counties had heard or read about the cases than those in other counties. The respondents in venues where cases were scheduled for trial were more likely to know details about the cases, including inadmissible information, and were more likely to believe that defendants were guilty. Similar results were reported by Simon and Eimermann (1971) and by Costantini and King (1980–1981). In related research, Moran and Cutler (1991) surveyed potential jurors in two cases and found that pretrial knowledge was related to prejudgment. Furthermore, regardless of the amount of knowledge, the vast majority of individuals thought they could be fair and impartial.

As an example of the findings that may be produced in a survey, consider the Grubman case noted above. A survey of jury-eligible adults in Suffolk (Long Island), New York (Manhattan), and Albany Counties revealed that over 86% of Suffolk County residents, over 77% of New York County residents, but less than 36% of Albany County residents were familiar with the incident. Residents of Suffolk and New York Counties were significantly more prejudiced against Ms. Grubman than residents of Albany County. Approximately 35%, 34%, and 13% of residents in each county, respectively, reported very or somewhat negative impressions of Ms. Grubman; 32%, 38%, and 13% thought it very or somewhat likely that Ms. Grubman had backed her SUV into a group of people intentionally; 44%, 52%, and 16% thought it somewhat or very likely that Ms. Grubman was intoxicated at the time of the incident; 41%, 43%, and 15% thought her actions were definitely or probably criminal; and 45%, 53%, and 17% believed that plaintiffs should definitely or probably win their lawsuits against Ms. Grubman.

In a change of venue hearing in the case of Timothy McVeigh (*U.S. v. McVeigh*, 1996), results of a public opinion survey were presented to the court, along with results of a content analysis of the pretrial publicity that had appeared in several newspapers (see Studebaker et al., 2000). The public opinion survey was designed to examine the extent of people's knowledge about the case and their attitudes about the case and the parties involved. In general, respondents in cities closer to the bombing site appeared to know more about the bombing, to have been more emotionally affected by the bombing, and to hold more negative opinions about the defendant than respondents in cities farther away. The survey results also indicated a significant amount of prejudgment about the guilt of Timothy McVeigh. Respondents in the Oklahoma venues were more likely to report being absolutely confident of McVeigh's guilt than were respondents in Denver—54% in Lawton (OK) and 47% in Tulsa (OK), as compared to 18% in Denver. As the amount of knowledge about the bombing increased, so did the perceived likelihood of McVeigh's guilt. Similarly, respondents reporting stronger emotional responses to the bombing were more likely to believe that McVeigh was guilty. Thus, the results of this public opinion poll paralleled and complemented the results of the content analysis.

Although survey studies are typically strong in terms of external validity and ecological validity, due to the involvement of real cases, real prospective jurors, and real PTP, it is noteworthy that none have examined (nor does the method really permit examination of) judgments of exposed versus non-exposed individuals in light of trial evidence. That is, these studies do not tell us whether PTP effects persist through the presentation of trial evidence. Experimental studies partially fill that gap—though, typically, at the expense of external and ecological validity.

Experimental Studies

One way to directly test PTP effects is to measure the relationship between the occurrence of PTP and actual jury verdicts. The ideal comparison involves presenting juries with the same trial, unchanged in any way except for the presence and absence of PTP. Of course, that ideal cannot be realized in actual jury trials, but approximations of it can be achieved in experimental studies. In laboratory trial simulations, researchers ensure that the only difference between two sets of jurors or juries is the nature and extent of PTP to which they are exposed. A major advantage of the simulation method is that researchers can vary the PTP presented to participants to determine the effects of different forms of PTP. Of course, the enhanced control comes at the cost of some artificiality, but a number of studies have shown that the artificialities of the typical trial simulation study generally do not bias research results (e.g., Kerr, Nerenz, & Herrick, 1979; Kramer & Kerr, 1989; MacCoun & Kerr, 1988; Miller, 1975; Simon & Mahan, 1971; Stasser, Kerr, & Bray, 1982).

One of the earliest experimental studies of PTP effects in criminal cases was conducted by Tans and Chaffee (1966), who varied the PTP given to participants along a number of dimensions: seriousness of crime, favorable or unfavorable statements by the district attorney, a confession or denial by the suspect, and whether the defendant was released or kept in custody. The suspect in their study was more likely to be judged guilty when all elements of unfavorable information were presented—a finding that suggests a cumulative or "dosage" effect. Subsequent mock-jury experiments by Wilcox and McCombs (1967), Padawer-Singer and Barton (1975), Hvistendahl (1979), and DeLuca (1979) yielded similar results. Some of these early studies used very unrealistic PTP, unrealistic or no case evidence, undergraduate participants, and so on. More recent studies improve on these early ventures in several ways.

Kramer, Kerr, and Carroll (1990) presented participants with either "factual" or "emotional" PTP, then later had participants view a 51-minute reenactment of an actual armed robbery trial. "Emotional" PTP produced a 20% higher conviction rate than "factual" PTP, and the effects were even stronger when hung juries were not considered in the analysis. Analyses of deliberations suggested that PTP increased the persuasiveness of jurors who argued to convict. Judicial instructions were ineffective at reducing the impact of PTP. Penrod and Otto (1992) had student jurors register their verdict preferences both before and after viewing an edited videotape of an actual trial. Jurors' verdicts were significantly affected by the PTP to which they had been exposed, even after they had heard the trial evidence. The strongest effects were demonstrated for the negative PTP about the defendant's character. Otto et al. (1994) employed a case arising from a well-publicized racial incident involving two campus fraternities. They assessed exposure to PTP, and participants then viewed a videotaped trial of the case. There were relationships among measures of PTP recall, bias in recall, pretrial attitudes (e.g., attitudes about fraternities), and ratings of the defendant's culpability.

Overall, these studies reveal that information casting doubt on the character of the defendant is one of the principal vehicles through which PTP exerts its effects. Jurors who have heard about prior bad acts by a party or who have reason to question the character of a party are more likely to convict or find fault with that party.

There are relatively few empirical studies examining the effects of PTP on jurors in civil trials. Kline and Jess (1966) conducted a mock-jury study in which prior record information was embedded in a specially constructed newspaper article. Examination of the statements made during their deliberations indicated that one of four juries referred to the past record, despite the judge's instructions to the contrary. Otto and Penrod (1991) drew upon an edited videotape of an actual 2-day trial of a personal injury case. PTP influenced not only the judgments of negligence but also impressions of the parties, memory, and inferences from the trial. These effects were reflected not only in the participants' verdicts but also in verdict confidence. Furthermore, PTP influenced evaluations of the parties, memory for trial evidence, and inferences from the trial evidence.

In short, field and laboratory studies both reveal an effect of PTP on people's judgments about a publicized case. This result is confirmed by a meta-analysis of PTP effects that examined 23 studies involving a total of 5,755 participants and including reports of 44 effect sizes (Steblay et al., 1999). Overall, the meta-analysis found that research participants exposed to negative PTP were significantly more likely to judge the defendant guilty, compared to participants exposed to less or no negative PTP (average $r = .16$). Other results suggest that experimental studies may, on average, understate the magnitude of PTP effects. Larger effect sizes were produced in studies that used potential jurors (rather than students) as participants, used multiple points of negative PTP, used real PTP, examined crimes involving murder, sexual abuse, or drugs, and had a longer delay between PTP exposure and time of judgment.

Efficacy of Legal Safeguards

It is clear that PTP can and does influence juror judgments about cases. As stated earlier, the courts are aware of this potential influence and rely on a variety of safeguards to avoid, reduce, or eliminate juror bias created by the presentation of PTP. Each safeguard and its effectiveness are reviewed below.

Sub Judice Rule

Several countries, including Canada, the United Kingdom, Australia, and South Africa (but not the United States), use a *sub judice* rule (literally, "under a judge") to prevent or restrict the publication of material that is likely to interfere with the administration of justice by precluding the possibility of a fair trial. The media must exercise care when commenting on matters that are under judicial consideration. Factors that the media should not discuss or with which they should take particular care when discussing are very similar to those included in guidelines provided by the American Bar Association (2003) to aid lawyers in determining what information to share and not share with the media when a case might go to trial. They include whether the accused is

guilty, the accused's prior criminal record, or information illustrative of an accused person's bad character. Although preventing prejudicial PTP from being
distributed is the most reliable way of preventing PTP-induced bias in potential jurors, PTP is not automatically prevented in every case. When prejudicial
PTP has been presented in a community, other safeguards (listed below) are
available. These additional safeguards are utilized by courts in the United
States and other countries.

Continuance

Courts consider the amount of time that has passed between the presentation
of PTP and the start of trial in determining whether the defendant was denied
a fair trial (e.g., *Timmendequas v. New Jersey*, 1999; *United States v. Pfingst*,
1973). Though it is tempting to conclude that the effects of PTP will dissipate
once a case is out of the limelight (assuming it stays out of the limelight), the
Steblay et al. (1999) meta-analysis indicated that longer delays between presentation of PTP and judgments of the defendant's guilt were associated with
larger effect sizes. Specifically, a delay of more than 1 week resulted in a
greater effect size ($r = .36$) than delays of less than a week (no delay, $r = .16$; 1-
day delay, $r = -.11$; 1-week delay, $r = .11$).

Extended Voir Dire

Extended questioning of prospective jurors during jury selection (i.e., voir
dire) and judicial instructions to jurors are commonly used remedies for prejudicial PTP (Weaver, 1983). Use of voir dire reflects a belief that questioning
can effectively identify and eliminate jurors influenced by exposure to PTP. In
a study by Dexter, Cutler, and Moran (1992), mock jurors who either had, or
had not, been exposed to PTP were administered an extensive voir dire (60
minutes) or a minimal voir dire (15 minutes) designed to reduce possible juror
biases. Following voir dire, the participants viewed a 6-hour videotaped trial
and rendered verdicts; the extended voir dire was no more effective at eliminating PTP bias than the minimal voir dire.

Judicial Admonitions

Use of voir dire to identify potential jurors prejudiced by PTP also assumes
that potential jurors who assert during voir dire that they can disregard any
PTP are not only capable of disregarding such information but also will do so
if selected to sit on the jury. Can such assertions of impartiality be trusted? Sue
et al. (1975) asked mock jurors, "Can you, in view of the publicity you have
seen, judge the defendant in a fair and unbiased manner?" (a question that
judges might typically ask potential jurors after instructing them that their
task is to judge the case solely on the information presented at trial and admonishing them against reliance on any information gleaned only from

sources outside the courtroom). Jurors who answered "no" were more likely than jurors who answered "yes" to find the defendant guilty. More interestingly, jurors who answered "yes" were much more likely to convict when they had been exposed to damaging PTP than when they had been exposed to neutral PTP (53% guilty vs. 23% guilty). Kerr, Kramer, Carroll, and Alfini (1991) found that jurors who doubted their ability to decide impartially were just as likely to convict the defendant as jurors with no such doubts.

Presentation of Trial Evidence

The Steblay et al. (1999) meta-analysis revealed an average effect size for field surveys of $r = .39$ versus $r = .13$ for lab experiments. Steblay et al. noted the existence of several significant moderators of this difference (e.g., longer delays between PTP and judgments and use of community members in the survey designs), but they did not directly test presentation of trial evidence as a moderator. Many of the studies that have demonstrated PTP effects have done so using little or no trial evidence (e.g., Sue et al., 1974; Tans & Chaffee, 1966). Those studies that have included a more elaborate trial presentation have sometimes shown mixed results (e.g., Dexter et al., 1992; Kramer et al., 1990), suggesting the possibility that PTP effects may be offset by trial evidence. Studies have not really focused on whether the initial impact of PTP is attenuated by the presentation of trial evidence. Otto et al. (1994) directly examined the impact of trial evidence and found that consideration of trial evidence did not significantly diminish the impact of PTP. Evidence reduced the biasing effect of character PTP somewhat (although not to a statistically significant level), and evidence had no impact on the biasing effects of other forms of PTP.

Jury Deliberation

Jury deliberation as a safeguard is predicated on the assumptions that (1) some jurors will recognize that the discussion or consideration of PTP during deliberation is inappropriate and will reprimand others who begin to discuss it; (2) jurors who are reprimanded will disregard any PTP of which they are aware; and (3) if PTP is not explicitly discussed by the group, it will not affect the jury verdict. Existing research suggests that deliberation may strengthen, not reduce, bias. Otto et al. (1994) found that deliberation did not significantly reduce PTP-induced biases, but Kramer et al. (1990) found that the predeliberation effects of emotionally biased PTP were weaker than the effects after deliberation. The Steblay et al. (1999) meta-analysis also supports the accentuation theory. Participants providing judgments after exposure to trial information *and* after group deliberation were more likely to judge the defendant guilty ($r = .15$) than participants providing judgments posttrial but before group deliberation ($r = .09$).

In sum, it appears that the effects of PTP can find their way into the courtroom, can survive the jury selection process, can survive the presentation of trial evidence, can endure the limiting effects of judicial instructions, and can persevere not only through deliberation, but may also actually intensify.

PRETRIAL PUBLICITY EFFECTS FRAMEWORK: WHO SAYS WHAT, BY WHAT MEANS, TO WHOM

To better understand the complex nature of PTP, the next section examines PTP research findings in more detail by using an analytic framework drawn from persuasion and attitude change research. Research within this framework examines "*who* says *what*, by what *means*, to *whom*." Even though the presentation of PTP may not consist of explicit attempts to persuade the public to think in particular ways about a case or the parties in a case, attitude change is a distinct possibility. To begin with, most people know little, if anything, about a case and therefore have no opinion, or weak opinions, about the case and the parties involved. However, as they learn more, attitude change can occur in the form of attitude formation, strengthening of attitudes, or reversal of attitudes. In this framework, "who" concerns the effect of communicator characteristics (e.g., whether the communicator is an expert) on subsequent changes in a target person's attitude, whereas "what" concerns the effects of the content of the information presented. Characteristics of the target person or persons (i.e., the audience) and whether those characteristics influence the degree and direction of attitude change fall under the "whom" part of the framework, and the "means" concerns the medium by which the information is conveyed (e.g., in print, by radio, by TV, or the Internet). This framework not only conveys the complex nature of PTP, it also can aid our attempts to understand when PTP results in negative bias against a defendant—and when it does not (see Petty & Wegener, 1998).

Who: Effects of Communicator/Source

Communicator characteristics can affect the influence of information presented by that communicator on others' attitudes in several ways. First of all, communicators who are viewed as knowledgeable and having expertise are generally considered more credible than those who are not knowledgeable (Olson & Cal, 1984), and increased credibility can translate into increased persuasiveness. In addition, communicators are more persuasive when they are perceived to be trustworthy (Walster & Festinger, 1962). An interesting way for perceived trustworthiness to be increased is for a communicator to argue or present information against his or her self-interest (Walster & Festinger, 1962). Trustworthiness or credibility of a communicator is likely to be lower when he or she is thought to have a particular opinion or bias and then makes statements or arguments that are consistent with that opinion or bias. Since there are multiple explanations for why the communicator presented the information (i.e., it is true, or it is just what the communicator believes), the persuasiveness of the information may decrease (see Kelley, 1973).

The communicators, or sources, of PTP include the defendant, the victim, other individuals who know the defendant or victim (e.g., friends, family, coworkers, or neighbors), attorneys, law enforcement officials, news reporters, and editors. The credibility and trustworthiness of each of these sources may be perceived differently across individuals in the general population. For example, individuals who have pro-prosecution attitudes may generally view the credibility, expertise, and trustworthiness of the prosecuting attorney as greater than individuals who have pro-defense attitudes. Moreover, most of the sources are likely to be perceived as biased in one way or another (i.e., pro-prosecution, pro-plaintiff, or pro-defense), and much of the information they provide may be discounted accordingly. However, in general, news reporters and editors may be more likely to be perceived as neutral sources of PTP, and consequently they might be the most persuasive sources.

Whether law enforcement officials are perceived as pro-prosecution or neutral could be very important. (It seems very unlikely that they would be perceived as pro-defense.) A content analysis of 14 U.S. newspapers revealed that law enforcement officials such as the police or FBI were the most frequently cited source of PTP statements that were prejudicial against the defendant (Imrich et al., 1995). The influence of these statements on potential jurors may be stronger if the officials are perceived as neutral rather than pro-prosecution. To date, little attention has been given to the role of communicator or source characteristics in PTP effects (but see Imrich et al., 1995, and Studebaker et al., 2000, for some examples).

What: Effects of Message Content

The persuasiveness of a message is affected by several aspects of the message content, including the basic information conveyed, whether the message is based on reason and logic or emotion, whether the message is one-sided or two-sided, and the degree to which the message differs from the target person's existing opinions.

Information Conveyed

The information conveyed in PTP is important because the media are likely to be the public's main source of information about cases going to trial. Relatively few people have access to the parties in a case, their attorneys, or case-relevant documents submitted to the court in order to gather information firsthand about what happened. Therefore, people's pretrial knowledge about a case is likely to largely reflect what has been reported in the media. As Vidmar (2002) has noted, people's pretrial knowledge can also reflect what they have learned via community rumor, gossip, and discussion, but in most instances these "occur in conjunction with media coverage" (p. 86). Consequently, if the fact that a defendant confessed never appears in media reports, that information is unlikely to influence people's opinions about the case.

Much of the PTP research that has been conducted has examined the influence of particular background information about the defendant on people's perceptions of the defendant's blameworthiness. The Steblay et al. (1999) meta-analysis indicates that the presence of potentially biasing content, such as the defendant's prior record, the defendant's confession, and the race of the defendant, has been examined, and very few of these content items have significantly influenced people's opinions about a case. However, when PTP includes multiple content items that are potentially prejudicial to the defendant, the likelihood of a guilty verdict significantly increases compared to a condition in which no PTP has been presented ($r = 0.22$).

Another PTP content item that has been examined is the type of charge being brought against the defendant. The presentation of PTP has been found to significantly increase the likelihood of a guilty verdict when the defendant's alleged crime was drug use, sexual abuse, murder, rape, armed robbery, disorderly conduct, or when the defendant was charged with multiple crimes (Steblay et al., 1999). Of all the crimes that have been examined in empirical research, the only one for which PTP has not been found to significantly influence verdicts is embezzlement. Interestingly, two studies have examined the influence of PTP in civil personal-injury cases, and PTP has significantly decreased the likelihood of a liability verdict in those cases ($r = -0.11$; Steblay et al., 1999).

Consistent with the findings concerning effects of presenting background information about the defendant and information about the nature of the charges against the defendant, PTP is more likely to increase the likelihood of a guilty verdict when it is specific to the defendant ($r = 0.17$) than when it is general in nature, such as publicity about crimes or defendants similar to those involved in a particular case going to trial ($r = 0.09$; Steblay et al., 1999).

Messages Based on Reason versus Emotion

One aspect of message content that can influence the persuasiveness of a message is whether the message is based on logic and reason or emotion. The effect of the nature of the message depends on characteristics of the audience. Individuals who are well educated or analytical are more likely to be persuaded by information and arguments based on reason, whereas less-educated or less analytical individuals are more likely to be persuaded by emotional appeals (Cacioppo, Petty, Feinstein, & Jarvis, 1996; Hovland, Lumsdaine, & Sheffield, 1949). When it comes to knowledge about most legal cases, the general public is likely to be considered uneducated or less educated because relatively little information is reported in the media. This reality suggests that the general public might be more persuaded by emotional PTP than nonemotional

PTP. However, it also suggests that in cases for which large amounts of PTP are disseminated, factual PTP may gain in persuasiveness as the amount of PTP increases over time and the public becomes more educated about a case.

As noted above, Kramer and his colleagues (1990) presented participants with either "factual" PTP, consisting of news reports detailing the defendant's previous convictions for armed robbery and the discovery of incriminating evidence at his girlfriend's apartment, or "emotional" PTP that identified the defendant as a suspect in a hit-and-run killing of a child involving the same motor vehicle used in the robbery. Although both forms of PTP biased mock jurors against the defendant, the "emotional" PTP produced a 20% higher conviction rate. Furthermore, although the biasing effects of the "factual" PTP were removed when there was a continuance between the presentation of the PTP and the presentation of trial evidence, the continuance failed to reduce the biasing effects of "emotional" PTP. In another study of factual and emotional PTP, Wilson and Bornstein (1998) found that both types of PTP biased mock jurors against the defendant, and that there were no significant differences between the two types of PTP.

One-Sided versus Two-Sided Messages

Another aspect of message content that has been found to influence the persuasiveness of the message is whether the message is one-sided or two-sided. As with emotional-versus-rational appeals, the effects depend on characteristics of the audience. Whereas one-sided appeals have been found to be more effective than two-sided appeals with individuals who already agree with a message, two-sided appeals are more effective than one-sided appeals with individuals who initially oppose the message being conveyed (Hovland et al., 1949). This issue is underscored by news reports concerning the case of the pop singer Michael Jackson that is in the news as this chapter is being written (i.e., late 2003)—in contrast to most cases, the allegations of sexual abuse made against Jackson are being met with an active pro-Jackson media campaign involving attorneys and friends of the singer.

There are currently no studies that have compared one-sided and two-sided messages in the context of PTP, but the topic warrants research. It is likely that PTP in many cases is essentially one-sided. Imrich et al. (1995) conducted a content analysis of pretrial crime articles associated with 2,461 suspects and appearing in 14 U.S. newspapers over an 8-week period. Whereas at least one prejudicial statement against the defendant suspect appeared in 27% of the cases reported, statements opining the defendant's innocence appeared in only 5.2% of the cases, and positive statements about the defendant's character appeared in 4.4% of the cases. Given that some people assume (or are at least inclined to think) that a person accused of a crime is guilty of the crime, it may commonly be the case that one-sided, anti-defendant PTP is presented to community members who are already inclined to believe that the defendant is guilty because he or she is charged with a crime. Furthermore, community members' presumptions of the defendant's guilt might be more likely for particularly heinous crimes (e.g., rapes, murders, or acts of terrorism) or those involving victims who provoke much sympathy (e.g., children). The factor of one-sided versus two-sided messages might account for the presence of PTP effects in some cases and the absence of such effects in others.

Amount of Discrepancy between Message and Target Person's Present Attitude

To produce attitude change, the message presented must differ from the attitude of the target person or audience, but the mere presentation of a different attitude does not guarantee that attitude change will occur. When the target's current attitude is very strong or very important to him or her, it is more difficult to change that attitude (Petty & Cacioppo, 1979). Furthermore, the effect of the amount of discrepancy between the message and the target's current attitude on subsequent attitude change is moderated by the credibility of the source. Whereas a message that is slightly different from that of the target results in small attitude change when it is presented by either a highly credible source or a less credible source, a message that is very different from that of the target will result in large attitude change only when it is presented by a highly credible source (Aronson, Turner, & Carlsmith, 1963). Highly discrepant messages presented by a source perceived as having low credibility will result in little or no attitude change.

For most cases the general public will not have prior attitudes about the defendant(s) before PTP is presented. However, in cases that involve a lot of PTP over an extended period of time, initial PTP may be a major source of information with which case-relevant attitudes are formed. The ability or likelihood of later PTP changing those attitudes may depend on the amount of discrepancy between the message/content of the later PTP and individuals' current attitudes. The potential role of message–attitude discrepancy as a mediating factor for PTP effects could be particularly important for defendants. Since initial media reports about criminal cases often come from pro-prosecution sources such as the police or the prosecuting attorney, the likelihood of initial public attitudes leaning in favor of the prosecution may increase. Consequently, the defendant is in the position of trying to change those attitudes. Defendants who attempt to change public attitudes about themselves by initiating pro-defense PTP may be well served by assessing public attitudes beforehand in order to present PTP that is not too discrepant from current attitudes.

In addition, even if the public does not hold prior attitudes about a defendant before PTP is presented, individuals may hold strong prior attitudes about particular sorts of crimes. If individuals tend to view a crime as rather minor, in general (e.g., possession of marijuana) and PTP about a case involving that crime describes the offense as severe, individuals may not believe the PTP. Research on these issues is needed.

Whom: Effects of Audience

It is clear from the discussion above that the effects of numerous factors on attitude change depend on characteristics of the audience. Whether the audience is informed or uninformed about the issues, concerned or unconcerned about the issues, or forewarned or not forewarned about possible opposing arguments have all been found to moderate the influence of factors on attitude change (Aronson et al., 1963; Cacioppo et al., 1996; Hovland et al., 1949). The only aspect of the audience that PTP research has examined is whether the participants in a study are students or community members (Steblay et al., 1999). Examining other audience characteristics may help shed light on the question of why PTP effects occur in some cases and not in others.

Means: Effects of Medium

Persuasion research has examined the effectiveness of information presented in a written format or verbally. Each format has been found to result in attitude change on some occasions but not on others. It appears that rather than the mode of presentation, the key to attitude change is getting the audience or target person to attend to the message. Similar findings have been found in research examining PTP presented by different means. Both print and video presentations of PTP have been found to produce bias against the defendant ($r = .15$ and $r = .16$, respectively), whereas PTP presented by both means (which increases the likelihood of attention being given to at least some part of the message) has an even larger effect ($r = .23$; Steblay et al., 1999).

Although research on PTP effects has examined print and video presentations, there are still many questions concerning the effect of pictures (via print or video presentation) that have not yet been addressed. For instance, does the inclusion of pictures in PTP (e.g., of the defendant or the victim) increase the likelihood that the PTP will be initially attended to or later recalled? Does the way in which the defendant is presented in pictures (e.g., in prison garb vs. street clothes) influence people's presumptions of the defendant's innocence?

How Much: Effects of Amount of Information Presented

A factor that may influence PTP effects but that has not been examined in persuasion and attitude change research is the amount of information presented about a case. It seems reasonable to speculate that the more PTP about a case that appears, the more likely that at least some of the PTP will be attended to and remembered. Even if higher amounts of PTP are associated with more pretrial bias about a case, the relationship may be curvilinear rather than linear. That is, it is possible that, in cases with a lot of PTP presented over an extended period of time, PTP may have diminishing effects over time or may even stop having any effect after a certain point. The difference between 10 stories about a case and 15 stories about a case when it comes to public attitudes may not be the same as the difference between 100 stories about a case and 105 stories. More research is needed for us to better understand the processes by which PTP influences attitudes over time.

FUTURE RESEARCH: METHODOLOGICAL ISSUES

In addition to the review of field surveys and experimental studies that was provided earlier, it can be gleaned from our overall discussion that meta-analysis is a tremendously useful research tool. The Steblay et al. (1999) meta-analysis has begun to piece together the "big picture" of what is known about PTP effects in a way that is more comprehensive and integrated than what can be provided by any individual survey or experiment. However, the picture is by no means complete. As discussed above, there are many factors that have not been examined yet (not even as main effects), and PTP research has just begun to investigate mediating processes and moderating factors that are essential for understanding better why PTP effects occur in some cases and not others.

One of the challenges of understanding real-world PTP effects is that the nature of the PTP can change over time, as can public attitudes about the case and the parties involved. In laboratory studies such changes would be referred to as "extraneous factors" that the experimenters would want to control in order to eliminate their influence. However, PTP research needs to allow changes in PTP to occur in order to understand how PTP operates in the real world. Longitudinal quasi-experiments that take advantage of real-world differences in PTP across various locations and that examine changes in public attitudes over time, as well as changes in the amount and nature of PTP over time, can provide very useful information to researchers and the courts.

REFERENCES

American Bar Association. (2000). *Model rules of professional conduct.* Chicago: Author.

Aronson, E., Turner, J. E., & Carlsmith, J. M. (1963). Communicator credibility and communicator discrepancy as determinants of opinion change. *Journal of Abnormal and Social Psychology, 67,* 31–36.

Bodenhausen, G. V. (1988). Stereotypic biases in social decision making and memory: Testing process models of stereotype use. *Journal of Personality and Social Psychology, 55,* 726–737.

Bornstein, B. H., Whisenhunt, B. L., Nemeth, R. J., & Dunaway, D. L. (2002). Pretrial publicity and civil cases: A two-way street? *Law and Human Behavior, 26,* 3–17.

Bruschke, J., & Loges, W. E. (1999). Relationship between pretrial publicity and trial outcomes. *Journal of Communication, 49,* 104–120.

Cacioppo, J. T., Petty, R. E., Feinstein, J. A., & Jarvis, W. B. G. (1996). Dispositional differences in cognitive motivation: The life and times of individuals varying in the need for cognition. *Psychological Bulletin, 119,* 197–253.

Campbell, D. S. (1994). *Free press v. fair trial: Supreme Court decisions since 1807*. New York: Praeger.

Costantini, E., & King, J. (1980–1981). The partial juror: Correlates and causes of prejudgment. *Law and Society Review, 15*, 9–40.

DeLuca, A. J. (1979). *Tipping the scales of justice: The effects of pretrial publicity*. Unpublished master's thesis, Iowa State University, Ames, Iowa.

Dexter, H. R., Cutler, B. L., & Moran, G. (1992). A test of voir dire as a remedy for the prejudicial effects of pretrial publicity. *Journal of Applied Social Psychology, 22*, 819–832.

Hamilton, D. L., Sherman, S. J., & Ruvolo, C. M. (1990). Stereotype-based expectancies: Effects on information processing and social behavior. *Journal of Social Issues, 46*, 35–60.

Honess, T. M., Charman, E. A., & Levi, M. (2003). Factual and affective/evaluative recall of pretrial publicity: Their relative influence on juror reasoning and verdict in a simulated fraud trial. *Journal of Applied Social Psychology, 33*, 1404–1416.

Hovland, C. I., Lumsdaine, A. A., & Sheffield, F. D. (1949). *Experiments on mass communication: Studies in social psychology in World War II* (Vol. 3). Princeton, NJ: Princeton University Press.

Hvistendahl, J. K. (1979). The effect of placement of biasing information. *Journalism Quarterly, 56*, 863–865.

Imrich, D. J., Mullin, C., & Linz, D. (1995). Measuring the extent of pretrial publicity in major American newspapers: A content analysis. *Journal of Communication, 45*, 94–117.

Irvin v. Dowd, 366 U.S. 717 (1961).

Kelley, H. H. (1973). The process of causal attribution. *American Psychologist, 28*, 107–128.

Kerr, N. L. (1994). The effects of pretrial publicity on jurors. *Judicature, 78*, 120.

Kerr, N. L., Kramer, G., Carroll, J., & Alfini, J. (1991). On the effectiveness of voir dire in criminal cases with prejudicial pretrial publicity: An empirical study. *American University Law Review, 40*, 665–701.

Kerr, N. L., Nerenz, D., & Herrick, D. (1979). Role playing and the study of jury behavior. *Social Methods and Research, 7*, 337–355.

Kline, F. G., & Jess, P. H. (1966). Prejudicial publicity: Its effects on law school mock juries. *Journalism Quarterly, 43*, 113–116.

Kovera, M. B. (2002). The effects of general pretrial publicity on juror decisions: An examination of moderators and mediating mechanisms. *Law and Human Behavior, 26*, 43–72.

Kramer, G. P., & Kerr, N. L. (1989). Laboratory simulation and bias in the study of juror behavior: A methodological note. *Law and Human Behavior, 13*, 89–100.

Kramer, G. P., Kerr, N. L., & Carroll, J. (1990). Pretrial publicity, judicial remedies, and jury bias. *Law and Human Behavior, 14*, 409–438.

Linz, D., & Penrod, S. D. (1992). Exploring the First and Sixth Amendments: Pretrial publicity and jury decisionmaking. In D. K. Kagehiro & W. S. Laufer (Eds.), *Handbook of psychology and law* (pp. 3–20). New York: Springer-Verlag.

MacCoun, R., & Kerr, N. L. (1988). Asymmetric influence in mock jury deliberation: Jurors' bias for leniency. *Journal of Personality and Social Psychology, 54*, 21–33.

Miller, N. (1975). Jurors' responses to videotaped trial materials. *Personality and Social Psychology Bulletin, 1*, 561–569.

Moran, G., & Cutler, B. (1991). The prejudicial impact of pretrial publicity. *Journal of Applied Social Psychology, 21,* 345–352.

Mu'Min v. Virginia, 500 U.S. 415, 111 S.Ct. 1899 (1991).

Murphy v. Florida, 421 U.S. 794, 799–802 (1975).

Nietzel, M., & Dillehay, R. (1983). Psychologists as consultants for changes of venue: The use of public opinion surveys. *Law and Human Behavior, 7,* 309–336.

Norwood, E. A. (1986). The prosecutor and pretrial publicity: The need for a rule. *The Journal of the Legal Profession, 11,* 169–186.

Olson, J. M., & Cal, A. V. (1984). Source credibility, attitudes, and the recall of past behaviours. *European Journal of Social Psychology, 14,* 203–210.

Otto, A. L., & Penrod, S. D. (1991, August). *Assessing mediators of pre-trial publicity effects.* Paper presented at the annual meeting of the American Psychological Association, San Francisco.

Otto, A. L., Penrod, S. D., & Dexter, H. R. (1994). The biasing impact of pretrial publicity on juror judgments. *Law and Human Behavior, 18,* 453–469.

Padawer-Singer, A., & Barton, A. H. (1975). Free press, fair trial. In R. J. Simon (Ed.), *The jury system in America* (pp. 123–139). Beverly Hills, CA: Sage.

Pennington, N., & Hastie, R. (1986). Evidence evaluation in complex decision making. *Journal of Personality and Social Psychology, 51,* 242–258.

Pennington, N., & Hastie, R. (1988). Explanation-based decision making: Effects of memory structure on judgment. *Journal of Experimental Psychology: Learning, Memory, and Cognition, 14,* 521–533.

Pennington, N., & Hastie, R. (1993). The story model for juror decision making. In R. Hastie (Ed.), *Inside the juror: The psychology of juror decision-making* (pp. 192–221). New York: Cambridge University Press.

Penrod, S., Groscup, J. L., & O'Neil, K. (2002). *Report filed on behalf of Elizabeth Grubman, November 6, 2002.*

Penrod, S., & Otto, A. L. (1992, September). *Pretrial publicity and juror decisionmaking: Assessing the magnitude and source of prejudicial effects.* Paper presented at the Third European Conference on Law and Psychology, Oxford, UK.

Petty, R. E., & Cacioppo, J. T. (1979). Effects of forewarning of persuasive intent and involvement on cognitive response and persuasion. *Personality and Social Psychology Bulletin, 5,* 173–176.

Petty, R. E., & Wegener, D. T. (1998). Attitude change: Multiple roles for persuasion variables. In D. Gilbert, S. Fiske, & G. Lindzey (Eds.), *The handbook of social psychology* (4th ed., pp. 323–390). New York: McGraw-Hill.

Report of the Judicial Conference Committee on the Operation of the Jury System on the "Free Press-Fair Trial" Issue, 45 F.R.D. 391, 404–407 (1968).

Rideau v. Louisiana, 373 U.S. 723 (1963).

Ruva, Christine L. (2002). Effects of collaboration and pretrial publicity on juror bias and source monitoring errors. *Dissertation Abstracts International: Section B: The Sciences and Engineering, 63*(2-B), 1062.

Schul, Y., & Burnstein, E. (1985). When discounting fails: Conditions under which individuals use discredited information in making a judgment. *Journal of Personality and Social Psychology, 149,* 894–903.

Schum, D. A. (1993). Argument structuring and evidence evaluation. In R. Hastie (Ed.), *Inside the juror: The psychology of juror decision making* (pp. 175–191). New York: Cambridge University Press.

Sheppard v. Maxwell, 384 U.S. 333, 362 (1966).

Simon, R. J., & Eimermann, T. (1971). The jury finds not guilty: Another look at media influence on the jury. *Journalism Quarterly, 48,* 343–344.

Simon, R. J., & Mahan, L. (1971). Quantifying burdens of proof: A view from the bench, the jury, and the classroom. *Law and Society Review, 5,* 319–330.

Stasser, G., Kerr, N. L., & Bray, R. (1982). The social psychology of jury deliberations: Structure, process, and product. In N. L. Kerr & R. Bray (Eds.), *The psychology of the courtroom* (pp. 221–256). New York: Academic Press.

Steblay, N. M., Besirevic, J., Fulero, S. M., & Jimenez-Lorente, B. (1999). The effects of pretrial publicity on juror verdicts: A meta-analytic review. *Law and Human Behavior, 23,* 219–235.

Studebaker, C. A., & Penrod, S. D. (1997). Pretrial publicity: The media, the law and common sense. *Psychology, Public Policy, and Law, 3,* 428–460.

Studebaker, C. A., Robbennolt, J. K., Pathak-Sharma, M. K., & Penrod, S. D. (2000). Assessing pretrial publicity effects: Integrating content analytic results. *Law and Human Behavior, 24,* 317–336.

Sue, S., Smith, R. E., & Gilbert, R. (1974). Biasing effect of pretrial publicity on judicial decisions. *Journal of Criminal Justice, 2,* 163–171.

Sue, S., Smith, R. E., & Pedroza, G. (1975). Authoritarianism, pretrial publicity, and awareness of bias in simulated jurors. *Psychological Reports, 37,* 1299–1302.

Tans, M., & Chaffee, S. (1966). Pretrial publicity and juror prejudice. *Journalism Quarterly, 43,* 647–654.

Timmendequas v. New Jersey, WL 600519 N.J. (1999).

United States v. McVeigh, pretrial transcript examination of Kent Tedin, 1996 WL 34135 (W.D. Okla. Trans.).

United States v. Pfingst, CA2 N.Y., 477 F.2d 177, cert. den. 412 U.S. 941, 93 S.Ct. 2779 (1973).

Vidmar, N. (2002). Case studies of pre- and midtrial prejudice in criminal and civil litigation. *Law and Human Behavior, 26,* 73–105.

Vidmar, N., & Judson, J. (1981). The use of social sciences in a change of venue application. *Canadian Bar Review, 59,* 76–102.

Walster, E., & Festinger, L. (1962). The effectiveness of "overheard" persuasive communications. *Journal of Abnormal and Social Psychology, 65,* 395–402.

Weaver, F. M. (1983). *Prejudicial publicity: The judge's perspective* (Working Paper). Chicago: American Judicature Society.

Wilcox, W., & McCombs, M. (1967). *Crime story elements and fair trial/free press.* Unpublished paper, University of California.

Wilson, J. R., & Bornstein, B. H. (1998). Methodological considerations in pretrial publicity research: Is the medium the message? *Law and Human Behavior, 22,* 585–597.

CHAPTER NINE

Trial Strategy and Tactics

KIPLING D. WILLIAMS
ANDREW JONES

INTRODUCTION AND ETHICAL CONSIDERATIONS

In this chapter we consider some means by which lawyers might attempt to influence those persons who sit in judgment in a trial. That being the case, it is important that we consider how this knowledge should be used. Being a psychologist brings with it many important responsibilities, and when practicing as a psychologist, ethical issues frequently arise. It is not the intention of this chapter simply to give advice that equips lawyers with a "bag of tricks" with which to manipulate the outcome of trials. Whereas some tactics discussed are legitimate, in that they represent the most effective way to present a case, others, such as unjustifiably impeaching the credibility of an opponent's experts, could be viewed as unethical. It would be wrong, however, not to include discussion of such tactics, because they may be employed by one's opponents and may therefore need to be countered or brought to the attention of the judge or jury. It should also be kept in mind that the first duty of lawyers is to assist the court; if their duty to the court and their duty to their clients come into conflict, the former takes precedence. This hierarchy makes sense: Above all, the community wants the courts to make rulings that are just and fair. So the ethical imperatives of the two professions should be in harmony; both lawyers and psychologists should assist their clients to the best of their abilities (in the case of the psychologist, the lawyer is the client), but both groups should not behave in a way that compromises functions of the court, taints the reputation of their professions, or undermines justice or the interests of the community.

276

THE COURTROOM AS A SOCIAL INFLUENCE ARENA

In many respects the courtroom is a ready-made environment in which to study different forms of social influence. In this setting a social psychologist has the opportunity to observe persuasion: Lawyers try to persuade the triers of fact, whether they be a judge, tribunal, or jury, to agree with their version of events. Attempts at dissuasion also occur; lawyers try to dissuade triers of fact from being persuaded by their opponents' arguments and tactics. Another form of social influence, compliance, might also appear in the courtroom; that is, lawyers may bypass persuasion and directly attempt to make the triers of fact comply with their assumptions and adhere to their wishes. Often social influence, particularly for jurors, is a matter of obedience; a judge is a figure of legitimate authority and may instruct jurors as to what they can and cannot do. In jury trials we may also see conformity; individual jurors may go against their own wishes and opinions in order to conform to those of their fellow jurors.

Social influence operates at many different stages in a trial. From the moment a lawyer appears in the courtroom, the first impressions that he or she conveys are a source of influence. The lawyer may, consciously or otherwise, send nonverbal messages regarding his or her trustworthiness, competence, and confidence in the case. In criminal trials in the United States, jury selection, or voir dire, gives lawyers the opportunity to begin influencing potential jurors before the trial has even commenced. For example, by asking candidate jurors if they "have the strength of character to resist the emotive arguments of the defense," a prosecution team not only begins the process of dissuasion, they also may ask the juror to make a public commitment to the prosecution's line of argument. Once the trial proper has commenced, lawyers will use various forms of social influence on the triers of fact. Influence is exerted during opening statements and closing arguments, in the way the direct examination (in the United Kingdom, Canada, and Australia, this is called "examination in chief") and cross-examination of witnesses are conducted, and how objections are used.

In this chapter we examine some of the tactics that lawyers might adopt in the courtroom in order to influence the decisions of those sitting in judgment. For the sake of simplicity, jurors will be the only triers of fact referred to, although many of the principles and tactics described also may apply to judges, tribunal members, arbitrators, and any other person involved in legal decision making. Three types of social influence form the focus of our discussion: persuasion, compliance, and dissuasion.

PERSUASION

Persuasion is probably the most important means of social influence on display during a trial. First we describe contemporary conceptualizations of persuasion and then examine how persuasion might be employed in court.

Persuasion, Attitudes, and the Tripartite Model

Persuasion can be defined as an attempt to change a person's attitudes. An attitude is a psychological orientation toward a particular stimulus, the attitude-object. An attitude-object might be anything from religion (e.g., "I distrust all organized religions") to corned beef (e.g., "I adore corned beef"). One influential approach to analyzing attitudes is known as the tripartite model. According to this model (Breckler, 1984; Cacioppo, Petty, & Geen, 1989; Rosenberg & Hovland, 1960), attitudes are composed of affective, cognitive, and behavioral components that predispose individuals to feel, think, and act in consistent ways in response to the attitude-object. For example, a person may have an attitude toward street gangs that is characterized by anger (an emotion), a belief that all gang members indulge in criminal activity (a cognition), and a tendency to vote for politicians who endorse tough court action against those charged with gang-related offenses (a behavior). Using a sophisticated statistical method known as covariance structure analysis, Breckler (1984) was able to confirm that emotions, cognitions, and behavioral tendencies are separate components underpinning participants' attitudes, thereby lending empirical support to the tripartite model, by examining the attitudes of research participants toward snakes.

It is important to recognize that within a single attitude, the affective, cognitive, and behavioral components may differ in strength and in the direction of their influence. You may casually believe in the importance of cleaning the bathroom, but hate the behavior involved and therefore rarely do so. Similarly, a juror might find a witness's testimony plausible, but decide to disbelieve and discredit it because he or she dislikes him. Alternatively, jurors may regard a defendant's testimony so unconvincing that despite their sympathy for him or her, they vote to convict. Finally, jurors may have a positive reaction toward a witness and believe what this witness says, yet when it comes to deliberation, this evidence may have little impact on what is said, or on the final verdict. In other words, a persuader must always be mindful of what may be driving a target's attitude. If the evidence of a witness is highly favorable but that witness evokes antipathy in jurors, a lawyer must find a way to make that witness more appealing, lest jurors' attitudes and behavior be driven by emotion rather than reason.

Stable versus Temporary Attitudes in Predicting Behavior

Many attitudes, such as those encapsulating moral values or political ideologies, are long term and relatively unwavering (although less so than personality traits). People typically hold a range of stable, and often strongly felt, attitudes toward aspects of the law and the criminal justice system. For example, research conducted in the United States has shown that Americans are usually either strongly opposed to, or strongly supportive of, the use of the death penalty (Ellsworth & Gross, 1994; Ellsworth & Ross, 1983), disagree on whether crime has social and economic roots, disagree on whether the individual criminal is to blame (Carroll, Perkowitz, Lurigio, & Weaver, 1987), and differ according to whether they have confidence in, or are cynical toward, the legal system generally (Lecci & Myers, 2002).

Other attitudes are temporary and arise in response to a newly encountered object. In the context of the courtroom, for example, jurors will form attitudes toward the main actors involved in the drama and the stories they tell. One obvious attitude is one that is either for or against the defendant. Some jurors might decide they like the defendant, perceive his or her testimony to be believable, and will argue to those ends during the deliberation. What are their attitudes toward the victim? How do they react to the versions of events offered by the defense and prosecution teams? And how do they intend to vote as a consequence of these attitudes? From the perspective of a trial tactician, it is these short-term and context-dependent attitudes that are of most relevance. There are three reasons for this relevance:

1. These attitudes are more specific and therefore more predictive of behavior.
2. They are easier to change than stable, long-term attitudes.
3. Legal restrictions discourage jurors from allowing feelings and beliefs that are not directly related to the case from influencing their decisions.

We explore each of these reasons in more detail.

First, attitudes that are temporary and have arisen in response to aspects of the trial are typically more open to influence than those that jurors bring with them into the courtroom. Because these attitudes are novel, they are less likely to be deeply held than long-term attitudes, and because they are context driven, they are more responsive to new information and new arguments than attitudes that are more general in nature. Stable attitudes, on the other hand, are resistant to change by their very nature.

The second reason for focusing on temporary trial-specific attitudes concerns the relationship between attitudes and behavior. Our earlier description of the tripartite model was a little misleading in one respect. Saying that an attitude includes a behavioral component implies that the holder of a specific attitude will necessarily carry out a specific range of behaviors in response to the attitude-object. But the situation is not so straightforward. It might seem reasonable to expect, say, that a person with an attitude that is strongly anti-immigration would vote for a political party sharing that attitude. But would the same person start an argument about immigration with a total stranger on a bus? Some argue that attitudes are notoriously fickle and unreliable predictors of behaviors. For example, attitude–behavior congruency was first challenged empirically by LaPiere (1934) in a classic study. During a time of notable anti-Chinese sentiment, LaPiere, who was white, toured the United States with a Chinese couple. They stopped at 66 hotels and motor inns and ate in 184 restaurants. Only once were they refused service. Yet in response to surveys later sent by LaPiere to these same enterprises, 92% of the 126 who replied said that they would not serve a Chinese person.

Many have argued that this study demonstrated that behavior was hopelessly inconsistent with attitudes. LaPiere's study was fraught with methodological problems. The couple was not stereotypical Chinese; for one, they were both excellent speakers of English. Thus, LaPiere's observed acquiescence to their presence may not have been representative of behavioral reactions to typical Chinese. Second, the attitudinal measures were taken several months after the behavioral measures were collected. Most importantly, the respondents who were phoned were most likely not the same people who had encountered the couple at the establishments. Despite these problems, subsequent research has supported LaPiere's contention regarding attitude–behavior inconsistency and elaborated the conditions under which it may, or may not, occur (Wicker, 1971).

Because of the often fragile relationship between behavior and the other components of an attitude, many social psychologists choose to define the behavioral aspect of attitudes as a "readiness to act" or a "predisposition to behave." Perhaps a better way of looking at this issue is to recognize that there is a range of behaviors that is consistent with any attitude, and that attitude holders will vary in the degree to which they feel impelled to employ any of these behaviors. For example, a juror who is a dog lover may indeed own a dog (i.e., attitude–behavior consistency) and attend some dog shows (but not others) but may not render a favorable verdict toward a dog-owning man charged with murder (an apparent inconsistency).

So under what circumstances do attitudes best predict actual behavior? This question is critical in the context of the courtroom; a legal team does not wish to concern itself with an attitude that does not have real potential to alter jurors' behavior, whether this alteration is by way of affecting their verdict or by influencing what is said during deliberations. A number of factors, including the conviction with which the attitude is held, affect whether a person behaves in a way that is consistent with his or her attitude. Of particular relevance to us is the notion of attitude specificity (Wicker, 1971). *Specificity* refers to how narrow, exact, or precise an attitude is. For example, "I don't believe in the death penalty for crimes of passion" is far more specific, and probably predictive, than "I don't believe in the death penalty." Typically, attitude–behavior congruence is highest when attitudes are specific rather than broad or general (e.g., see Weigel, Vernon, & Tognacci, 1974; Schuman & Johnson, 1976). Thus, in a courtroom we would expect that specific attitudes toward a particular witness, defendant, or version of events would be more predictive of behavior than a more general orientation for or against criminal defendants.

This factor of predictability is perhaps why research attempts to link stable attitudes with verdicts in response to specific mock trials have typically un-covered only weak, inconsistent, or nonexistent effects (Ellsworth, 1993). But even attitudes that are narrow in scope do not always produce consistent be-havior. A personality variable that can come into play is that of *self-monitoring*, a term that refers to a person's degree of sensitivity to social contexts (Snyder, 1974). A high self-monitor will be more willing than a low self-monitor to ad-just his or her behavior in response to social cues. It has been demonstrated that low-self monitors behave more consistently with their attitudes—or, to put it another way, are "truer" to their beliefs—than high self-monitors, who are more concerned with the impression they make on others (Kraus, 1995). So jurors who have formed attitudes in relation to a case but who are high self-monitors, cannot be relied upon to pursue their position vigorously. If, for example, their views appear discrepant with those of their colleagues, they may choose not to be open in their opinions, or they may even adjust their be-liefs.

The third and final reason for concentrating on short-term attitudes is that the law attempts to ensure that lawyers stick to the facts of the case. Can you imagine a judge sitting idly by while a lawyer delivered a lecture on racial tolerance, the deterioration of family values, or police corruption? So even if such values did influence how jurors reach their verdicts, and even if lawyers could somehow alter such attitudes, they are not given the opportunity to do so.

ELABORATION LIKELIHOOD MODEL

Petty and Cacioppo's (1986a) elaboration likelihood model (ELM) is a use-ful model by which to understand the cognitive processes involved in per-suasion. From a practical standpoint, the ELM provides valuable insights into how best to go about changing the attitudes of others. We therefore ex-plore the basic mechanisms of the model before showing how it can be ap-plied in a legal context. The fundamental assumption of the model is that people can be persuaded by way of one of two routes: the central route, or the peripheral route. (It is possible to consider that both routes can occur independently, but for the sake of explication, we treat them as mutually ex-clusive.) The key difference between the two processes concerns how deeply the target of the persuasive attempt processes the incoming information. Central-route processing entails a high degree of thought and scrutiny, whereas peripheral-route processing is less cognitively effortful. The ELM's creators conceptualize the two routes as poles on a continuum: the elabora-tion continuum. Each point on the continuum represents the extent to which a person is motivated and able to devote cognitive resources to pro-cessing the persuasive message. However, for sake of ease we refer to the two routes as if they were discrete routes. Thus instead of saying, for exam-ple, that "high arousal pushes people toward the central-route end of the elaboration continuum," we would say "high arousal makes people more likely to take the central route."

Central-Route Processing

Attitude change via the central route is a considered and rational process. Persuasion occurs because targets have examined the main arguments presented by the persuader, compared them with their own world knowledge, and found them to be logical and compelling. Moreover, in the process, targets often build on the central arguments, thereby making the final case for attitude change more detailed, more convincing, and of higher quality. For example, targets may supplement the argument "The plaintiff slipped on the supermarket floor because she was preoccupied with planning the luncheon she was due to give later that day" with "Given that she had little remaining time to prepare the luncheon, maybe she slipped because she was anxious and rushing." Petty and Cacioppo (1986a) call this cognitively effortful process of critically examining the arguments and constructing a detailed attitudinal response, *elaboration*. It is expected that individuals converted via the central route—that is, persons who have formed their attitude as a result of elaboration—will truly believe that their new attitude is right.

Peripheral-Route Processing

Unlike their more discerning and contemplative central-route counterparts, individuals who use the peripheral route to evaluate decision-relevant information do not process this information deeply, nor do they reflect upon it to any great degree. They are, as a result, likely to base their decisions on information that is peripheral to the main issues, and to use heuristic ways of thinking. *Heuristics* are mental shortcuts that enable people to interpret situations and make decisions without having to resort to complex analysis and reasoning. For example, if a juror decides that a defendant is culpable because he or she has a "guilty look," then the juror is using heuristic reasoning and has been persuaded via the peripheral route. Rather than critically weighing up the evidence for and against the defendant, the juror has merely based his or her decision on the heuristic "If a person looks guilty, he or she is probably guilty."

Which Route Do Targets Use?

According to Petty and Cacioppo (1986a), two factors determine whether message recipients will go down the central or peripheral paths: ability and motivation. From the target's point of view, central-route processing is, compared to peripheral-route processing, more effortful and cognitively demanding. The target must therefore be able, and motivated, to take this course. Recipients lacking in motivation will travel down the peripheral route by choice, and those lacking ability will travel down it out of necessity.

Motivation

An important factor influencing an individual's motivation to use the central route is the self-relevance of the message. Petty, Cacioppo, and Goldman (1981) demonstrated this effect by asking students to listen to, and evaluate, an argument about introducing comprehensive exams into their curriculum. They varied the degree to which this issue personally impacted upon the students by stating that the university was considering instituting exams either in the short term (the high-relevance condition) or not until later (after the students had graduated; the low-relevance condition). Two other variables were manipulated: the strength of the argument and the putative prestige of the speaker. The authors found that the quality of the speaker's reasoning influenced the evaluations of the high-relevance group more than they did the low-relevance group, an indication that the former group members were examining the arguments more closely and using central-route processing more frequently. Moreover, the low-relevance group was more swayed by a peripheral cue, the prestige of the speaker—a sign of peripheral-route reasoning.

Enthusiasm for taking the central route is also more likely if the recipient is high in a "need for cognition" (NFC), a personality variable that describes the degree to which a person typically feels compelled to understand things; that is, his or her general level of curiosity. We would expect that someone high in NFC would be inherently more motivated to process persuasive messages centrally. To test this hypothesis, Cacioppo, Petty, and Morris (1983) asked students to express their attitude toward either a weak or a strong version of an argument in favor of raising university fees. Participants were also administered the Need for Cognition Scale (Cacioppo & Petty, 1982). Those students rated as high on NFC were persuaded more by the strong argument than those low on NFC, whereas those low on NFC were more persuaded by the weak argument (because they relied on the available peripheral cues associated with persuasiveness). This result offers strong support for the notion that as NFC increases, so does the likelihood of carefully considering arguments via the central route. Unfortunately, it also suggests that in the absence of another strong source of motivation, individuals low on NFC will be unlikely to leave the relatively leisurely peripheral route.

Ability

Even a highly motivated individual, however, will end up taking the peripheral route if he or she is unable to process the information centrally. For example, the target might find the information too difficult to comprehend fully, or even at all. Thus general intelligence, through its impact on a person's ability to understand a message, often influences which form of processing recipients use (Petty & Wegener, 1999). Having working knowledge of the subject area in question is also positively related to the likelihood of elaborate thinking. Those with scant relevant knowledge are likely to revert to heuristic thinking

(Wood, Rhodes, & Biek, 1995). Other factors, such as distractions or competing demands, may also impair the recipient's ability to concentrate on, and embellish, the message, thereby encouraging peripheral processing. In fact, a wide range of variables has been found to affect a target's ability to process information via the central route (for a review, see Petty & Wegener, 1999).

Which Form of Persuasion Most Benefits the Persuader?

Central-route attitude change has several desirable characteristics. By elaborating on the message, the message recipient bolsters his or her attitude, making it more complete and robust and easier to defend. Furthermore, an attitude that has been carefully considered will typically be more memorable and accessible than one that has not been the subject of deep thought (Petty & Cacioppo, 1986b). Effortful consideration should also render more salient those facts and reasons that the attitude holder drew together to support the attitude. This salience should make the facts and reasons more readily available for use, should the attitude come under attack (Petty & Cacioppo, 1986b). Finally, given that the target has put effort and thought into the matter, he or she will probably feel more committed to it than the individual who has given the subject only superficial attention. These ideas point toward the prediction that central-route attitude change will be relatively stable and resilient in the face of attempts at counterpersuasion.

The persistence of central-route attitude change was demonstrated in a study by Petty, Cacioppo, Haugtvedt, and Heesacker (1986; as cited in Petty & Cacioppo, 1986a; see also Haugtvedt & Petty, 1992). The authors used a similar paradigm to that used by Petty, Cacioppo, and Goldman (1981) in the experiment discussed earlier (recall that the attempt at persuasion concerned the implementation of comprehensive exams, and that likelihood of central-route processing was manipulated by making the message more or less self-relevant). Petty, Cacioppo, Haugtvedt, and Heesacker (1986) asked participants to rate their level of agreement with the idea of introducing exams immediately after being exposed to the message. They then assessed participants' attitudes after a delay of 10–14 days. At the first testing, both the low- and high-relevance groups appeared to be favorably persuaded by the message. However, at the second testing only the high-relevance (that is, the central-processing) group stood by their attitude change. Participants in the low-relevance (and, therefore, peripheral-processing) group showed almost no residual effects from the persuasive attempt; their attitude toward exams was no different from a control group who had never received the persuasive attempt. In other words, attitude change in the peripheral processing group simply "wore off."

A study by Haugtvedt and Petty (1992) provides some support for the prediction that, compared to attitude change via the peripheral route, central-route attitude change will also be more resistant to court-persuasive attack. In Study 2 of their research, the authors presented participants with a fictitious article attacking the safety of a specific food additive. They then asked participants to read a second fabricated article refuting the claims of the first. The latter article, however, did not present as strong a case. Haugtvedt and Petty also measured participants' NFC levels. They found that after reading the first article, participants both high and low in NFC formed attitudes that endorsed the criticism of the food additive. However, after reading the second article, individuals low in NFC were prone to changing their attitudes in line with the counterpersuasive arguments. High NFC participants tended to resist the counterattack. As previously discussed, NFC correlates positively with likelihood of central-route processing. The authors therefore proposed that the effect occurred because the high NFC participants used central-route processing when evaluating the first article. In so doing, they would have analyzed the content carefully and elaborated upon it. When exposed to the attempt at counterpersuasion, they would have been able to marshal more counterevidence and counterarguments. To investigate this hypothesis further, the participants were also asked, at the second testing, to recall as much information as they could about the articles, and to write down the reasons for their final attitude. Those high on NFC recalled more facts from the first article and generated more counterarguments when stating their final position. This finding supports a model in which the positive effect of NFC on attitude resistance is mediated by increasing central-route processing.

Finally, there is some evidence that attitude-consistent behavior is more likely when attitude change occurs via the central, rather than peripheral, route. Petty, Cacioppo, and Schumann (1983) found that increasing participants' motivation to process centrally an advertisement for a brand of razor resulted in more participants stating that they intended to switch to that brand of razor.

So, from a persuader's perspective, attitude change via the central route is highly advantageous. Targets thus converted will be more likely to retain, defend, and behave consistently in regard to their new attitude. For those in the business of attitude change, however, encouraging individuals to use the central route is not always realistic or sensible. Firstly, the case for attitude change must be well grounded. If the arguments presented are weak or flawed, the last thing the persuader should want is for the target to scrutinize them too closely. So, as is discussed below, in some circumstances the persuader is better off discouraging central-route processing. Secondly, as we have already seen, if the target audience lacks the motivation or ability to consider the information carefully and to elaborate upon it, peripheral processing is inevitable. The persuader must never put all his or her "eggs" in the central-route "basket," even if the case for attitude change is strong.

Distraction: A Case in Point

To appreciate the usefulness of the ELM, let us consider how two factors might interact to influence the outcome of a persuasive attempt: the strength of the persuasive arguments (i.e., the degree to which they are relevant, logical, and compelling) and the extent to which the message recipients (in this case, the jurors) are distracted from being able to cognitively elaborate upon the message. Common sense might dictate that whenever people are distracted while listening to a persuasive message, the message will fall on deaf ears, rendering it ineffective. However, according to the ELM, distraction reduces persuasion only when the persuasive message could have stood up to close scrutiny: that is, when its arguments are strong. If jurors cannot attend to a well-constructed set of arguments, they will not be able to cognitively elaborate upon the message with favorable, self-generated supportive arguments. Consequently, they will be less persuaded. If jurors have the opportunity to scrutinize the strong messages, they will elaborate upon them and provide additional support, resulting in stronger and more persistent agreement.

The opposite pattern happens if the message is weak. If jurors have the opportunity to scrutinize a weak set of arguments, they will realize that it is a house of cards—the arguments will fall apart with the elaboration of self-generated nonsupportive arguments. If, however, jurors are distracted while trying to process the weak arguments, they will be prevented from realizing the arguments' inherent weaknesses, and will thus be more persuaded by them than if they did have the opportunity to scrutinize them carefully.

Let's take this set of theoretical principles and apply them to a courtroom context. Imagine two courtroom adversaries with a keen understanding of the ELM. The defense attorney has a very weak case, put together with "smoke and mirrors." The prosecuting attorney has a strong case, built on a series of convincing and interlocking pieces of evidence. The prosecutor, a rather ugly-looking gentleman, is able to distract the attention of the jurors by loudly clearing his throat; the defense attorney, on the other hand, is stunningly beautiful, but has a well-controlled and rather exotic wandering eye that onlookers cannot avoid watching when it begins its sojourn through her eye socket. Thus, both attorneys have the ability to distract the jury. Who should employ distraction during their adversary's closing arguments? The prosecutor realizes that the defense attorney's case is weak and hopes the jury will process her closing arguments closely and carefully. If they are distracted, he fears they will rely instead on a rather powerful peripheral cue, her beauty, and ascribe positive attributes to her arguments (taking the easy peripheral route). Hence, the prosecutor refrains from clearing his throat during her closing arguments, allowing the jurors to elaborate (hopefully, by generating a series of counter-arguments) on her message. When the prosecutor gives his closing arguments, the defense attorney, realizing that her opponent's case is strong and that his physical appearance is just short of repulsive, begins to set her eyeball in motion, in a seemingly random orbit. Though the prosecutor is laying out his set of strong arguments in a compelling and logical sequence, its brilliance is lost on the jurors who are transfixed by the defense attorney's wandering eye. To form a quick and easy impression of his arguments, they rely on his ugliness as a cue and devalue what he has said. Thus, both attorneys used their knowledge of the ELM to their advantage. (In case you are wondering, the prosecutor in this case won—good triumphs over evil, and all is well in the world).

The important lesson to draw from this example is that persuaders with strong messages should do their utmost to promote central-route processing, whereas those with flawed or insubstantial material may actually be better off if recipients are diverted down the peripheral route.

PERSUASION IN THE COURTROOM

The above discussion has led us to an important conclusion: How a legal team attempts to persuade a jury should be heavily influenced by the strength of its evidence. If lawyers are presenting strong evidence and potent arguments, they should do their utmost to ensure that the evidence and arguments are processed centrally by jurors. If lawyers are lumbered with weak evidence, they may need to resort to obstructing close analysis by jurors and instead steer them down the peripheral route. To these ends legal teams may wish to employ tactics that either enhance or diminish jurors' motivation and ability to undertake the more effortful and difficult central route. In the next sections we consider some such tactics, but first we must consider several important caveats.

On the whole, the tactics that we discuss are probably of most use when attempting to persuade juries; they are likely to be less successful when the trier of fact is a judge, because the judge's level of expertise and experience would be more likely to immunize him or her to the use of tactics (this is our speculation and not based upon experimental findings). Nor can lawyers be too obvious in their attempts to encourage or prevent elaboration. If they are obvious, they will probably provoke their opponents or the judge to intervene. Furthermore, when message recipients can clearly recognize that they are unable to process the message because of a distraction, they may be inclined to cognitively correct for its influence (Petty & Wegener, 1993). Behavior that is obvious may also result in a loss of credibility for the lawyer, and may cause jurors to turn against him or her. When lowering the likelihood of central-route processing, lawyers must nevertheless give the impression that they are presenting a solid case. Simply to discourage deep thought, without making the most of positive peripheral cues, is unlikely to succeed.

Encouraging or Discouraging Central-Route Processing

At first glance it might seem reasonable to assume that jurors will generally be motivated to take the central route. A trial is, after all, a serious business, the results of which can have very grave consequences for the well-being of real people. However, trials are also often long, demanding, complex, and tedious—so much so that even the most conscientious juror may find his or her motivational resources drained before the trial has reached its conclusion.

There are several ways in which a legal team can, when presenting its evidence, increase jurors' motivation to process centrally. Recall that self-relevance is one of the most effective sources of such motivation. How could lawyers go about making their message more relevant to jurors? Restrictions on how trials are conducted mean that such attempts must be subtle. During direct or cross-examination, the legal team might elicit details that would resonate with jurors. For example, if the witness is a local resident, it could be worth having him or her state that fact for the benefit of the jury. Alternatively, the lawyer could ask the witness how long he or she has lived in the district and where precisely he or she lives. In fact, bringing forth any details that jurors may relate to may serve to heighten motivation. Lawyers should exercise care, however, when their witness is from a starkly different background from the jurors. It would be unwise, for example, to ask a key witness to describe his or her drug-dealing lifestyle; obviously, such a tactic in this instance would not increase relevance for most jurors; instead, it would probably alienate them and create suspicion and hostility. Relevance is probably easiest to create during opening statements and closing arguments. Making these addresses evocative and reflective of jurors' lives will increase their immediacy and render the events described more significant in their eyes. By proceeding in this manner, the hope is that the messages will be more deeply processed and will remain persuasive and memorable.

In a similar vein, a legal team could attempt to provoke central-route processing by presenting their evidence in an engaging style that sparks interest and attention. Even a dutiful juror may "glaze over" during a repetitive and droning cross-examination. Another final option for inciting elaborate thinking is to convey points in the form of questions rather than statements. The effect of rhetorical questions, however, is complex. Petty, Cacioppo, and Heesacker (1981) subjected experimental participants to a persuasive communication concerning proposed changes to their university. The message ended with either a declarative statement or a rhetorical question. The authors also varied the personal relevance of the issue. They reported an interaction in which, in comparison to finishing with a direct statement, the use of a rhetorical question produced more elaborative thinking in participants in the low-relevance condition, but impaired the thinking of individuals for whom the message was highly relevant.

In another study, Burnkrant and Howard (1984) reported similar effects: In a condition of low personal involvement, the use of rhetorical questions led to participants generating more positive thoughts in response to a strong persuasive message and more negative thoughts in response to a weak message. In other words, these individuals carefully considered the quality of the arguments. However, when personal relevance was high, the use of questions only incited negative thoughts, suggesting that such rhetorical devices only served to produce uncertainty. Thus it would appear that when people are already motivated to process a message centrally, asking them to ponder questions only disrupts the natural progress of their thinking. In a trial, then, rhetorical questions might be useful to spark some cognitive life into otherwise inattentive jurors, but if jurors are already concentrating hard, asking them to consider questions may only add to their labors.

In terms of *de*-motivating jurors to use the central route and thereby shepherding them down the peripheral route, many of the factors we have described obviously apply, but in reverse. Lawyers inclined to discourage central-route processing when presenting certain evidence (because they do not want jurors to appreciate its weaknesses) can make this evidence appear remote from the lives of the jurors. For example, the lawyer might ask a witness who is an accountant about minor technical matters. This tactic might also serve to make the evidence less interesting, which will also erode jurors' motivation to reflect deeply upon the information.

A less obvious means of decreasing central-route processing is to make the message source appear as trustworthy as possible. Priester and Petty (1995) found that the lower an individual is in NFC, the more likely he or she is to forgo thoughtful consideration and simply accept the information from a trustworthy and knowledgeable source. In a later study Priester and Petty (2003) repeated this effect: Communications from untrustworthy sources are elaborated on more than those from trustworthy sources.

Enabling or Disabling Central-Route Processing

The presence or absence of distractions, as we have already seen, is an important determinant of whether an audience processes messages in a thorough (i.e., central) manner. Legal teams presenting strong evidence should want jurors to ruminate on it unhindered, and to that end they ought to eliminate as many distractions as possible. Lawyers who wish to avoid close examination of their evidence might consider distracting jurors in some way. They could, for example, wear flashy attire, or squeaky shoes, or perhaps use slightly unusual gestures or interesting turns of phrase. The famous trial lawyer Clarence Darrow has been said to have smoked cigarettes during the trial (long ago, when smoking was not prohibited in government buildings), which was not all that unusual. What was unusual was that the ash on his cigarette would grow ever longer without falling. He accomplished this feat by inserting a wire into his cigarette, to which the ash would longingly cling. During opportune moments in the trial (presumably when his adversaries were trying to make their strongest points), Darrow would display his gravity-defying cigarette to the jury, who would stare, spellbound, at the cigarette and consequently fail to consider Darrow's adversary's compelling arguments. All of these examples are, of course, on the shadier side of ethicality, and it is not our intention to promote such behavior, only to make both sides aware of their effects.

Speed of communication is an important factor in whether targets are able to process the message centrally. Smith and Shaffer (1991) exposed participants to either pro-attitudinal or counterattitudinal persuasive information, but varied the rate at which it was spoken to them. The pro-attitudinal message was less persuasive under the fast condition than under the slow condition, because the speed of transmission hindered elaboration. But the persuasive impact of the counterattitudinal message benefited from increased communication rate, because participants were hampered in their ability to refute the argument. Speed of communication thus appears to hinder central-route processing, presumably because targets do not have the time to process all elements of the message or to reflect sufficiently upon them. However, as Smith and Shaffer's research demonstrates, this effect can be of benefit to the persuader. This was the case in their experiment, because participants would have been motivated to disagree with counterattitudinal messages, but were denied the opportunity to form counterarguments. In a courtroom a legal team could consider delivering messages that are weak in a manner that suggests they are strong, but at a pace that does not facilitate close inspection. Strong messages, however, should be conveyed at a pace that is conducive to proper consideration.

Message complexity has similar effects on ability to process centrally. Hafer, Reynolds, and Obertynski (1996) varied the comprehensibility of language used in a message. Strength of argument was found to have its strongest effect when language was simple, whereas peripheral cues became more important when the language was difficult to understand. Complex messages thus appear to receive more peripheral and less central processing. Again, we could envisage using this effect to advantage: When the arguments are strong, convey them in a simple manner to facilitate central-route processing, and when they are weak, complicate matters and heighten the influence of supporting peripheral cues.

One way of enabling central-route processing is through repetition. Cacioppo and Petty (1980) had participants listen to either a strong or weak persuasive argument, once or multiple times. Compared to individuals who heard the message once, those in the repetition condition were more persuaded by the strong argument and less so by the weak argument. The authors also examined participants' rationales for their attitudes; it appeared that depth of elaboration—that is, the number and sophistication of arguments generated—was responsible for the differences in levels of persuasion (see also Cacioppo & Petty, 1985 and Cacioppo & Petty, 1989). It would appear, then, that repetition helps recipients grasp and elaborate upon messages. But how much repetition should lawyers with strong arguments employ? This depends on how difficult their message is to grasp. If the message is complex, then repetition would probably be welcomed by the jury. As Petty and Cacioppo (1986a) warned, however, excessive reiteration of arguments that jurors already understand might bring about tedium or reactance. *Reactance* occurs when people willfully behave contrary to a manipulative attempt because they feel that their free will is being challenged (Brehm, 1966). If jurors perceive that lawyers are trying to goad them into agreement, this perception may motivate them to reject the persuasive attempt.

Peripheral Cues

Regardless of the strength of their case, lawyers should always maximize peripheral cues that favor them. Even when legal teams are doing their best to encourage central-route processing, trials often include information that is too complex for jurors to comprehend fully. In particular, jurors may be exposed to unfamiliar legal concepts, highly technical expert evidence, and extremely intricate arguments characterized by subtle distinctions. That these jurors enter the trial with little working knowledge—that is, preexisting knowledge that is relevant to the task at hand—makes them more likely to resort to heuristic ways of thinking (Wood et al., 1995). And even if jurors can initially process proceedings via the central route, if the trial continues for too long they may exhaust their cognitive resources and stray onto the peripheral route. So peripheral thinking may, to some degree, be inevitable for a large proportion of even the most motivated jurors. But the jury may also include individuals who are unmotivated to move beyond peripheral processing; for example, those low on NFC and "social loafers" (people who, when in group tasks, allow others to do the work for them; Latané, Williams, & Harkins, 1979). These people also need to be persuaded because they may influence deliberations, and they will vote in the jury room. Finally, according to the ELM, central- and peripheral-route processing is not an either/or matter. Rather, as a person moves toward the central-route end of the likelihood continuum, peripheral cues become less important. But people cannot simply switch off the biases and heuristic ways of thinking associated with peripheral-route processing; although careful consideration of a subject reduces the importance of peripheral cues, their influence never disappears.

However, when the quality of arguments being presented is low, exploitation of peripheral cues becomes indispensable. As we shall see, however, variables that act as peripheral cues can also impact on the target's choice of processing route and lead to unexpected outcomes.

THE SOURCE AND CHARACTERISTICS OF THE PERSUASION ATTEMPT

Source Credibility, Trustworthiness, and Expertise

The attributes of a person conveying persuasive information serve as powerful peripheral cues. In the courtroom, how lawyers and their witnesses appear to the jury can heavily influence their success in swaying jurors' attitudes.

Credibility is a measure of how believable targets find the source. That source credibility is positively related to persuasion was demonstrated by

Hovland and Weiss (1952). They found that participants were, not surprisingly, more likely to be persuaded by medical articles when those articles were said to be from the *New England Journal of Medicine* than from a popular magazine. Hovland, Janis, and Kelley (1953) separated credibility into two independent components, trustworthiness and expertise, both of which have received attention from persuasion researchers.

The positive association between trustworthiness and persuasion was shown by McGinnies and Ward (1980). These researchers found that participants exposed to a persuasive message were more likely to align their attitude with that of the communicator when that communicator was seen to be trustworthy rather than untrustworthy. In fact, they found the effect of trustworthiness to be stronger than that of source expertise, a finding that has also been reported by Lui and Standing (1989). The impact of trustworthiness, however, is complex. As we noted earlier, trustworthiness actually discourages thoughtful elaboration. Perhaps it is such a strong peripheral cue that recipients typically do not feel the need to inspect closely messages from trustworthy sources. This lack of examination could conceivably cause problems for lawyers whose witness's testimony is highly favorable. In such circumstances, central-route processing is desirable, so perhaps it would be advisable for legal teams not to stress trustworthiness to the point that jurors relax their cognitive "muscles."

It is generally well accepted that people are more persuaded by communicators who have relevant expertise than by those who do not (e.g., see Aronson, Turner, & Carlsmith, 1963; Wilson & Sherrell, 1993). Petty, Cacioppi, & Goldman (1981) found a positive relationship between source expertise and persuasion, and perhaps more importantly, found the effect to be at its strongest when the issue in question was of low relevance to participants. This finding implies that decreased likelihood of central processing led to an increased use of the heuristic "He [or she] is an expert, so he [or she] must be right." Similarly, Kiesler and Mathog (1968) showed that when distractions are high, expertise becomes increasingly persuasive. These last two results strongly suggest that expertise is a potent peripheral cue. Matters, however, are not straightforward. In the Petty, Cacioppo, and Goldman (1981) study, the positive effect of expertise on persuasion occurred both when the quality of arguments presented was weak and strong. In another study, by contrast, Heesacker, Petty, and Cacioppo (1983) found that source expertise led to increased persuasiveness only when the message quality was high. When the message quality was low, expertise rendered the communication even less effective. The authors concluded that expert sources provoke elaborate thinking and careful attention in targets. Recent research by Bohner, Ruder, and Erb (2002) also reported that weak arguments attributed to an expert source created more unfavorable attitudes than did the same arguments from a nonexpert source. These researchers, however, did not view the effect as one of elaboration. Rather, they attributed it to a contrast bias: That is, the weak arguments appeared particularly unconvincing when compared to the sorts of arguments one would expect from an expert.

What can we make of these findings in relation to expertise, and how can they be applied in the courtroom? It appears that expertise is a persuasive peripheral cue, so if jurors are unable or unmotivated to take the central route, it could be used effectively. But there is a catch: If we accept the ELM analysis, it would also appear that more expert sources sometimes attract closer scrutiny from their audience. So if a legal team were to attempt to compensate for the weak testimony of a witness by highlighting the witness's expertise, the strategy might backfire: The approach might inadvertently shift jurors into a central-processing mode, thereby enabling them to appreciate the inadequacy of the evidence. (Of course, if jurors are unable to process centrally, perhaps because the evidence is too complex, the team may benefit from expertise as a peripheral cue.) Lawyers with strong cases will win either way. By emphasizing their witness's expertise by, say, asking the witness to trot out his or her achievements for the court, the legal team may encourage jurors to pay close attention to the evidence. And if the lawyers fail in this respect, jurors may nevertheless be seduced by the witness's prestige.

Source Likability

Likability is another source attribute that can serve as a peripheral cue. Wood and Kallgren (1988) had students read a transcript of an interview. The authors varied the likability of the interviewee by having him say complimentary or disparaging remarks about the participants' university. The interviewee then spoke on environmental issues. In terms of their attitudinal response to the environmental message source, likability failed to impact on those participants who performed well on a later recall test (i.e., high elaborators). Low-recall participants (i.e., low elaborators), on the other hand, formed more pro-message attitudes when the source was likable and responded less positively when the source was unlikable. Petty et al. (1983) also found that having popular celebrities endorse a brand of razor blades was effective at eliciting positive attitudes, but only when personal involvement was low. When involvement was high, participants were no more influenced by the famous endorsers than they were by an unknown endorsers. (High involvement was created by telling participants that the brand was about to be tested in a local trial. They were also offered free samples of the razor, or another brand of razor, at the end of the session.)

But, again, the effect is not straightforward, because likability does not appear to act merely as a peripheral cue. As was the case with expertise, it seems that likability may also influence the target's level of processing.

Attractiveness is a cue for likability (Cialdini, 2001; Eagly, Ashmore, Makhijani, & Longo, 1991), and a few studies have examined either physical or social attractiveness within a courtroom setting. Sigall and Ostrove (1975) found that socially attractive "defendants" enjoyed fewer guilty verdicts and lighter sentences than their socially unattractive counterparts, unless the attractiveness was somehow used to commit the crime. If the defendant exploited his or her attractiveness to succeed in the perpetration of the crime, the mock-jurors were more punitive. Kassin (1983) conducted a clever courtroom study examining the cue of social attractiveness—but not that of the defendant or even the witness—investigating responses to a surrogate who simply read the expert's deposition. Sometimes, when expert witnesses cannot appear in court (e.g., because of time conflicts), their depositions are read by a surrogate. Kassin manipulated the variable of surrogate physical attractiveness and found that, despite the fact that the surrogate had nothing to do with the deposition other than to read it, the attractive surrogate was more persuasive.

But, as with most persuasion tactics, the impact of attractiveness is not always so straightforward. Outside the courtroom context, Puckett, Petty, Cacioppo, and Fischer (1983) had participants read essays that were ostensibly by authors of varying degrees of social attractiveness. The researchers found that attractiveness enhanced the persuasiveness of strongly argued essays but diminished the persuasiveness of weakly argued essays. As with the expertise effect, the explanation offered by the ELM is that attractiveness, perhaps through gaining the attention of the audience, may motivate central-route processing. Other accounts are also possible. For example, contrast biases could again be at play: Attractive communicators may make poor arguments look even worse.

So, lawyers who have high-quality messages should attempt to make themselves, their witnesses, and their clients appear as likable and attractive as possible. They are the lucky ones—they do not mind if attractiveness works in their favor via the peripheral route or by increased attention to their arguments. For legal teams with less convincing messages to convey, the situation is more delicate. Excessive attempts at creating a good impression may ultimately work against them by inducing elaborate processing. Nevertheless, it would be unwise for lawyers who have poor cases to make themselves unattractive, by, say, not making eye contact with jurors or bullying witnesses. Nor would they likely benefit by making clients appear unlikable or by putting witnesses who are annoying on the stand.

Confidence

Confidence may serve as a peripheral cue. For example, confidence expressed through nonverbal cues has been found to enhance persuasion (Maslow, Yoselson, & London, 1971). Additional support for this notion can also be extrapolated from the eyewitness research reviewed in Chapter 6. Recall that confident eyewitnesses were found to be more believable than those who appeared uncertain. If confidence renders eyewitnesses more persuasive, perhaps confidence works for other players in court—for example, lawyers and other types of witnesses. However, caution may need to be exercised in order to avoid appearing overconfident. London, McSeveney, and Tropper (1971) found that the relationship between confidence and persuasion is curvilinear: As confidence increases, so does persuasion—initially; but if confidence is too high, targets find the persuader overconfident, and persuasion begins to fall. Perhaps overconfident targets convey smugness or cockiness, and this attitude alienates targets. Another reason to be wary of overconfidence is that it is uncertain whether it will have an effect on the elaboration level of participants. If it were to evoke suspicion, this response might prompt observers to examine the information more closely. In court this approach could lead to adverse consequences for those presenting weak evidence.

Multiple Sources

Using multiple sources to provide support for a persuasive attempt could well be an effective peripheral cue. It might, for example, invite heuristic reasoning along the lines of "Lots of people think that it is the case, so it must be right." Harkins and Petty, in a series of experiments in 1981 and 1987, examined what is known as the "multiple source effect." The researchers found that when the presentation of a collection of strong arguments was divided among different sources, people experienced the arguments as being more persuasive than the same arguments conveyed by a single source. When the arguments were weak, however, the reverse pattern occurred. Harkins and Petty (1987) also subtly varied the degree to which people advocating a similar point of view appeared to be independent from each other, and measured the number of thoughts generated in response to the persuasive attempt. They found that increased independence lead to increased thoughtfulness and persuasion. They were thus able to make a strong case for the multiple source effect: That is, participants perceive that information coming from autonomous sources is more worthy of thoughtful, central-route elaboration than information coming from a single source. The authors argued that targets are impressed by the fact that different people, with differing pools of knowledge and experience, reached similar conclusions, and so are motivated to step up a cognitive gear.

When presenting strong evidence, it would appear, then, that having the information come from more than one source may be a very effective tactic. This does not mean that the evidence must be divided among witnesses—witnesses may, to some degree, repeat the same information (and, as we saw earlier, repetition can also be effective when arguments are convincing). But if the evidence being presented is weak, presenting it via different sources can invite close scrutiny and may therefore be counterproductive. This is not to say that multiple sources are not a positive peripheral cue. If jurors were to remain entrenched in peripheral ways of thinking, exposing them to different people proposing similar ideas would probably be effective. The point is that employing multiple sources may shift people out of the peripheral route and into the central route.

Argument Succinctness

Arguments that are expressed in a concise and "punchy" fashion may be more persuasive than arguments that are more verbose. Wood, Kallgren, and Preisler (1985) found that targets who had little working knowledge on the subject of a persuasive communication were more influenced by the message when it was succinct than when it was wordy. The fact that this same group was not affected greatly by differences in argument strength implies that they used brevity as a peripheral cue. There was no influence among participants with moderate or substantial working knowledge. Lawyers handling complex material should therefore consider using language economically.

Number of Arguments

Petty and Cacioppo (1984) exposed participants to a persuasive message containing arguments that varied in number and strength. They discovered that increasing the number of arguments made the message more persuasive, but only when it was of low personal relevance to the audience. This finding suggests that the quantity of arguments is an effective peripheral cue. When self-relevance was higher (and, presumably, targets were more likely to be carefully attending to the message), the number of arguments only increased the persuasiveness of the message when the quality of the arguments was high. When argument quality was low, increasing the number of arguments only served to dissuade high elaborators.

So when serving up high-quality arguments to attentive jurors, the study's findings suggest that more arguments lead to greater persuasion. The results also imply that for inattentive jurors, number of arguments is a potent peripheral cue. But consistent with the main thrust of the ELM, as the likelihood of jurors' elaboration increases, effectiveness of number of arguments as a peripheral cue diminishes. In fact, if jurors are processing centrally, increasing the number of weak arguments is likely to backfire. Similar lessons may apply to highlighting the number of favorable arguments during a summation. This tactic will be effective if the arguments are strong, regardless of how focused jurors have been. When the arguments are of low quality, it will only work on those who are unable or unmotivated to elaborate on the content of the summation.

The merits of increasing the number of arguments might seem at odds with the previous finding that advocated succinctness. However, it is possible to merely announce the number of arguments without actually listing them, and it is also possible to explicate a long list of arguments more or less succinctly. Thus, both concerns need to be kept in mind when formulating the best way to present arguments.

The Appearance of Winning

One tactic that might prove successful, but which has not yet been tested empirically, is to create the appearance of winning the case. For example, lawyers, by asking witnesses questions to which they know the answers, may convey the impression that they are winning the cross-examination. For example, a lawyer might ask a witness, "Is it true you moved to Black Mountain in 1993?", and "Did you not then establish a pet cemetery known as 'Farewell Fido'"? By eliciting a series of "yes" responses, the lawyer may appear to be successfully on the attack. Similarly, declining to cross-examine an expert witness may be preferable to appearing to lose the cross-examination. It may also create the appearance that the witness's testimony is not worthy of response. This happened to one of us (K.D.W.) in a capital case in Texas when he appeared as an expert on eyewitness testimony. After a rather lengthy direct examination by the defense attorney, the expert prepared himself for the usually grueling experience of cross-examination. Instead, the prosecuting attorney hardly looked up at the witness from his desk, and with a dismissive wave of his hand, said, "I have no questions of this witness." The look on the jurors' faces seemed to indicate that in their perception, the witness was in no way harmful to the prosecutor's case.

Conclusion

Our discussion of peripheral cues has shown that they are not as straightforward as they seem. Many variables not only act as peripheral cues, they are also moderators of information-processing style. Source expertise and source likability, for example, are positive peripheral cues, but their presence also increases the likelihood of elaboration on the part of targets. Trustworthiness, on the other hand, may reduce targets' motivation to scrutinize messages closely. Those advising lawyers on how to present their cases must be aware that what at first glance might seem like a straightforward and effective tactic may have unexpected consequences. Unfortunately, the research literature on these matters is not extensive, so firm conclusions cannot be drawn. Moreover, the findings come from the general field of social psychology. What is lacking is a rigorous examination of how these effects might play out in the courtroom.

THE ELABORATION LIKELIHOOD
MODEL AND JURY DELIBERATIONS

Thus far we have considered how individual jurors form attitudes. Jurors do not, however, operate in isolation; ultimately, they work as a team. An important question is "Does the fact that jurors work as a group in some way predispose them to favor either central- or peripheral-route processing?" One group phenomenon that might erode jurors' motivation to use the central route is social loafing (Karau & Williams, 1993; Latané et al., 1979), which sometimes occurs in conjunction with collective tasks. The term refers to a loss of motivation on the part of the group members to contribute to the team's efforts. A particular type of social loafing, free riding (Kerr & Bruun, 1983), arises when the output of a group consists of the cumulated labors of its constituents, but these constituents are not, or cannot be, held accountable for their contributions. That is, responsibility for the group's performance rests with the group, not the individual. Some team members may therefore loaf because they suppose that their efforts are dispensable, and that their inactivity will be compensated for, and obscured by, the exertions of their colleagues. In a study conducted by Petty, Harkins, and Williams (1980), participants were asked to evaluate the (fictitious) performance of a therapist in a videotaped session. They were led to believe that they were either the sole judge of the performance or that there were 14 other students assessing the therapist. In contrast to participants who thought they were working alone, those who believed they were contributing to a group effort gave less elaborate evaluations and were less sensitive to differences between good and bad therapeutic interviews. This finding strongly suggests that group tasks can induce a form of free riding that reduces thoughtful elaboration.

The jury task seems custom-made to elicit free-riding responses. At the predeliberation stage all jurors share the same task: They are supposed to pay attention to the evidence and commit it to memory. During that time some jurors may assume that a failure to concentrate is of no great consequence, because the efforts others will compensate for their own lapses. There are, after all, usually around 12 people in a jury—plenty to share the load! During deliberations the responsibility for weighing up the evidence and reaching a decision is also shared by the group. Again, there are plenty of team (juror) members to do the hard analysis and to keep the conversation alive. So social loafing and free riding could feasibly affect many jury members, perhaps *all*, to some degree, and this effect is likely to result in less elaborate information processing by jurors.

There is, however, another possibility: The prospect of taking part in deliberations may increase jurors' motivation to attend diligently to proceedings. For example, they may choose to monitor the evidence carefully, so that during deliberations they can gain the approval of their colleagues by appearing conscientious and well informed. Lerner, Goldberg, and Tetlock (1998) asked experimental participants to make judgments about vignettes describing accidents. Prior to undertaking this task, however, some participants were shown a video designed to induce anger. Those individuals who had seen the video attributed greater negligence to parties depicted in the vignettes. On analyzing the reasons individuals gave for their judgments, the authors reported that the anger led participants to generate blame-attributing cognitions and employ more simplistic and heuristic styles of reasoning. But Lerner et al. (1998) also found that, if anger-induced subjects were warned that they would be made to account for their decisions in a later interview with the experimenter, they used higher-quality reasoning. It could be argued that jurors, knowing that they will have to account for their decision during jury deliberations, make similar improvements in their thinking.

So there exist two non-mutually exclusive possibilities: The prospect of deliberations may incite jurors to remain awake and alert, or asleep and inert. Initial evidence for social loafing by jurors who rendered verdicts in a complex trial came from Bourgeois, Horowitz, ForsterLee, and Grahe (1995). They found that, compared to nominal jurors (who did not anticipate group interaction), interactive jurors recalled less evidence (before discussing the evidence).

Henningsen, Cruz, and Miller (2000) took an experimental approach to investigate the effects of anticipated deliberations on jurors' mental exertions. The authors asked participants to adopt the role of mock jurors and told some that they would be required to give their verdicts individually, and others, that they would participate in group deliberations. Participants then read a description of a complex civil litigation. Soon afterward jurors were tested for their recall of witness testimonies. The recall of participants who anticipated rendering an individual verdict was found to be superior to that of jurors expecting to reach a group decision. This finding is consistent with the view that at least some participants in the latter condition engaged in social loafing when processing the evidence, and as a result, did not commit it well to memory. The results of this study suggest that group factors leading to decreased motivation to elaborate may outweigh group factors inciting greater mental effort.

Another important aspect of the jury's task is the deliberation. Does the act of deliberating enhance jurors' level of reasoning? It may be that the deliberation process, in its requirement that different points of view be aired, discussed, and evaluated, is, in itself, a form of central-route processing. Moreover, referring to inadmissible evidence during deliberations may lead to admonishment by juror peers, so deliberations may be effective at reprocessing sloppy peripheral thinking into a more intellectually rigorous output. For example, McCoy, Nunez, and Dammeyer (1999) assessed mock jurors' rationales for reaching their individual verdicts either pre- or postdeliberation. As predicted, the participants from the postdeliberation group gave more complex reasons and cited more supporting evidence. In particular, they showed more awareness of, and willingness to evaluate, opposing points of view.

Furthermore, if juries reason better than individual jurors, one prediction we could make is that juries will be superior at adhering to legal requirements, such as ignoring inadmissible evidence. In this regard, however, the evidence is equivocal. It has been reported that juries are more likely than individual jurors to discount highly volatile evidence that has surfaced in court but then been struck out as inadmissible (Carretta & Moreland, 1983; Kaplan & Miller, 1978; Kerwin & Shaffer, 1994). Kerr, Niedermeier, and Kaplan (1999), however, demonstrate a third possibility: In cases in which the evidence is roughly balanced, discussion may sometimes exacerbate bias. Kerr et al.'s findings reflect those of Myers and Kaplan (1976), who reported that jury deliberations can elicit group polarization. The prejudicing effects of pretrial publicity have also been shown to impact on the decisions of mock juries (Hans & Doob, 1976; Kramer, Kerr, & Carroll, 1990). Thus, the jury is still out regarding the impact of jury deliberations on cognitive processes.

As indicated in Chapter 11, predeliberation juror voting patterns are strong predictors of final outcomes. Say, for example, that at the moment the jury retires to consider its verdict, eight jurors believe that the defendant is guilty and only four consider him or her innocent. If the jury reaches a unanimous verdict, it will almost certainly be one of guilty. This pattern may occur because jurors feel committed to their original positions. In addition, by having already taken a position, they may create biases in how they assess and weigh the arguments of their colleagues. So persuading jurors by the peripheral route may ultimately pay off, if the lawyer can stack the jury in his or her favor.

OTHER PERSUASION TACTICS

Other findings from the fields of social psychology, psychology, and law point toward a range of approaches and tactics that is, or could be, effective in the courtroom. In the following sections we examine some of these.

Presenting a Story

The story model (Pennington & Hastie, 1993; see also Bennett, 1978) proposes that as a trial unfolds, jurors spontaneously construct stories to accommodate the incoming evidence and to fill in any gaps that it might contain. For example, suppose a jury hears evidence that the defendant was seen leaving his girlfriend's house yelling and cursing, and that later he was seen drunk in a bar. Jurors will probably start to form a story in which the accused and his partner quarreled, and as a result, he headed to the bar to drown his sorrows. If story construction is jurors' preferred mode of information processing, it may follow that evidence presented in a manner that facilitates story building will be more persuasive. Indeed, this is what has been found. In an experiment conducted by Pennington and Hastie (1988), mock jurors were presented with trial evidence either in the same chronological order as the events it described or in a completely different order. Jurors found the evidence more compelling and memorable when it was chronologically presented than when it had to be rearranged in order to construct a story. Lawyers should, therefore, always attempt to present their evidence in a way that tells a story. This tactic need not be confined to arranging the order in which they present their evidence. They could, for example, elicit details from witnesses that may not have any evidentiary value but may help in terms of setting a scene, adding action to the story, or rounding out the characters.

Primacy Effects, Opening Address, and Promising More Than the Evidence Can Show

The primacy and recency effects describe the fact that information that appears first or last, respectively, within a presentation is, in comparison to information appearing in the middle, better remembered by recipients and experienced as more persuasive. These types of biases are known as order effects. Information presented first is the most effective overall, whereas information presented last is only more effective if the recipient needs to make his or her decision soon afterward.

To investigate whether primacy and recency effects occur in trials, Pennington (1982) conducted a study involving a simulated rape trial. The author rated each witness's testimony according to how beneficial or damaging it was to the defendant. He also classified every statement made in each witness's testimony along similar lines. Pennington then manipulated the sequence in which both the prosecution and defense witnesses were called; the order went from the most beneficial witnesses first to the most damaging last (the primacy-effect order), or from most the damaging first to the most beneficial last (the recency-effect order). The sequence of evidence given by each witness was similarly arranged. The author found that when it came to the most serious charge laid against the defendant, that of rape, ordering witnesses and testimony along primacy effect lines (that is, from good to bad) led to the least number of guilty verdicts. The results suggest that, at least when it comes to the order in which evidence is presented, primacy effects reign supreme.

It must be kept in mind that simply discussing order of presentation of arguments does not include a consideration of the strength of the arguments. Research has shown that, generally speaking, it is best to use as many strong arguments as possible, but not to mix weak with strong arguments because doing so lowers the overall persuasiveness of the message (e.g., see Anderson, 1968).

Primacy effects have also been reported in research investigating the influence of opening addresses on verdicts. In a mock-trial study, Pyszczynski and Wrightsman (1981) varied the extensiveness of both the prosecution's and the defense's opening statements: A lawyer either simply introduced him- or herself and promised that he or she would present a convincing case, or the lawyer provided a comprehensive outline of the evidence he or she would present. The results reported by the authors provide compelling evidence of primacy effects. They found that strength of the defense's opening statement only influenced verdicts when the prosecution's opening statement was brief: When the prosecution waived its right to preview its case, long opening addresses by the defense were associated with low rates of conviction. But when the prosecution began with an extensive introduction, the scope of the defense's opening address no longer influenced verdicts!

Bear in mind that the prosecution opens first. Given this fact, one explanation of these findings is that jurors were prejudiced by the first strong statement they heard, and that this prejudice biased them from then on. That is to say, when the prosecution started with a strong opening statement, jurors aligned themselves with this statement. However, when the prosecution's introduction was weak, and the subsequent defense introduction was strong, jurors seized upon the defense's opening address, and this influence endured. And what happens when both statements are weak? Pyszczynski and Wrightsman observed that under those circumstances, jurors voted *guilty* as often as when the prosecution's introduction was strong. Why? The authors argued that because the prosecution presents its evidence first, the initial strong message that jurors receive after the introductions are over comes from the prosecution. Overall the authors found that strong messages, initially encountered, have a lasting persuasive influence. This impact is the very essence of the primacy effect.

Pyszczynski and Wrightsman (1981) argued that, in the case of opening statements, it may be that if jurors are provided with a broad overview of a party's case, they will sometimes adopt this framework as a schema. (*Schemas* are cognitive structures that describe how beliefs, memories, and behaviors are organized in relation to specific subjects.) Incoming subject-relevant information is then interpreted according to, and incorporated into, the schema. If jurors accept a legal team's preview of the case as a schema, they may modify or assimilate newly arriving evidence to fit in with this initial account. They may also bump up or discount the evidence's importance, depending on how compatible it is with the schema. For example, by accepting the prosecution's description of how the accused planned to kill his victim, a juror might decide, upon hearing that the victim was stabbed with a knife in his kitchen, that it is most likely that the accused brought the knife with him, rather than grabbing it from a drawer. If opening statements do act as schemas, it is easy to see how they could lead to biased information processing and judgment making by jurors.

Promising more than can be shown is perhaps the best example of exploiting an opening address. In his or her opening statements, the lawyer claims that as the trial unfolds, he or she will show X, Y, and Z, but ultimately only X and Y are demonstrated. Pyszczynski, Greenberg, Mack, and Wrightsman (1981) revealed that making such unmet claims can actually influence final verdicts. In a mock criminal trial, mock jurors exposed to false promises were more likely to vote in line with those promises. Moreover, by asking participants to rate guilt at different points in the trial, the authors were also able to ascertain that the biasing impact of the unmet claims grew in influence as the trial progressed; that is, the judgments of those who did and did not hear the promises grew further apart. Again, the best account for this effect centers on the schemas used by jurors. By including unfulfillable claims, the lawyer provided jurors with schema and expectations about his or her case that were more substantial and more positive. Subsequent evaluations of each side's evidence may thus have been biased in favor of the side that "dressed up" the opening statement with bogus claims. However, the tactic can be countered, and as a result, it may boomerang. Pyszczynski et al. (1981) found that if lawyers alerted the jury that their opponents had made false claims, the effect was reversed: Jurors became less sympathetic to the case of those who promised more than they could deliver.

From the preceding discussion we can draw some tentative conclusions. Primacy effects appear to emerge in trials. (Unfortunately, those acting for the defendant may therefore be at a disadvantage, because they are always second to make their opening address, present their witnesses, and close their case.) It is therefore imperative that legal teams open their case as strongly as possible. In terms of presenting evidence, lawyers should also put their best foot forward first. For example, during direct examination, or in giving closing arguments, it is probably beneficial for legal teams to open with their winning arguments and evidence, while pushing weaker and less convincing material further back. There remains doubt, however, about whether recency effects occur. It is therefore difficult to say whether information heard last by jurors is granted extra weight. Perhaps the fact that jurors do not make their final judgment until well after most evidence is heard would wipe out any recency effects.

Emotional versus Rational Persuasion

A lesson learned from memory research is that compared to emotionally bland information, emotive material is processed more deeply and integrated within wider cognitive (and probably neural) networks. It is, therefore, more easily primed and remembered, or more accessible. Does this fact mean that emotional information has a persuasive edge? Within psychology and law fields there is a large body of work suggesting that highly emotive stimuli that is damaging to defendants—such as affectively charged pretrial publicity (Kramer et al., 1990; Ogloff & Vidmar, 1994; Wilson & Bornstein, 1998), powerfully emotive language (Edwards & Bryan, 1997) or graphic video or photographic images (Douglas, Lyon, & Ogloff, 1997; Kassin & Garfield, 1991)—can bias jurors toward conviction, even when that information has no evidentiary value.

There is also research suggesting that jurors find it particularly difficult to suppress the impact of such material in order to reach an objective verdict. For example, Edwards and Bryan (1997) found that attempts to stifle negative affect aroused by emotive language resulted in mock jurors being even more biased by the information. Kramer et al. (1990) demonstrated that mock jurors have less success at countering the effects of pretrial publicity that is unfavorable to a defendant when the content of the publicity is emotive rather than merely factual. The authors also found that the impact of affect-laden stimulus material persisted for far longer than did that of the factual stimulus. It would appear that, at least for prosecutors in criminal cases, affect can be a powerful weapon. However, emotion must be used with subtlety and caution; overt emotional pleas or sensationalist tactics are unlikely to be tolerated by judges.

Crime Heinousness

Some crimes are more than merely emotional; they are horrific, involving torture and an apparent inhumanness that evokes a sense of disgust and moral outrage. The heinousness of a crime is, and ought to be, a factor in determining the sentence. For instance, in the United States, heinousness is an aggravating factor that legally facilitates penalty of death. However, heinousness should not affect verdicts. Verdicts should be based on judgments of whether or not the prosecution has proved the defendant's guilt beyond a reasonable doubt, and this determination ought to be the result of the convincedness of the evidence. Nevertheless, our recent exploratory research (Jones & Williams, 2004; see also Bright & Williams, 2001; Chew & Williams, 2000; Koletti & Williams, 2001) has demonstrated that even if the evidence is held constant, crimes that are more heinous result in higher percentages of guilty verdicts. Interestingly, measures of the probability of guilt do not differ, just the verdicts. Our internal analyses suggest that the threshold for "beyond a reasonable doubt" slips downward when the crime is more heinous. That is, mock jurors require less evidence when they feel a sense of disgust and moral outrage at the crime itself. How this effect may be relevant to trial tactics is still speculative, but we believe that different reasons for conviction (McFatter, 1982) might play a role. If people are so disgusted and enraged by a crime, the most salient reason for conviction might change from clear and convincing evidence of guilt to one of restoring a sense of calm and order to the community, or of sending a message to anyone else who might consider carrying out such a crime. For these latter two motives, getting the right person might be secondary to getting someone, anyone. Thus, tactics aimed at either heightening the apparent heinousness of the crime or of shifting the motives for conviction might ultimately affect verdicts.

Vivid Testimony

Information can be described as vivid when it stimulates the imagination in a lifelike, interesting, and immediate manner. Presenting evidence in a way that enhances its vividness may make the information more engaging and relevant, and the audience may devote more cognitive resources to attending to it, thereby processing the message more thoroughly. Many (but certainly not all) studies investigating the impact of message vividness have found vivid messages to be more persuasive and memorable than their pallid equivalents, a phenomenon known as the vividness effect (Smith & Shaffer, 2000). In a study on how the vividness of evidence affects its persuasiveness, Bell and Loftus (1985) presented mock jurors with eyewitness testimony that either contained substantial evocative but irrelevant detail, or testimony that, although it included the same critical evidence, was less colorful. The vivid testimony was found to be more persuasive than its pallid equivalent, an effect that went on to impact the verdicts and the level of "damages" awarded. The authors argued that the effect on verdicts occurred because the vividness added to the credibility of the testimony. The finding in relation to damages was perhaps even more interesting, because it cannot be attributed to mediation via witness credibility; instead it suggests that vividness, in itself, can add to the persuasive power of a message. In two other psychology and law studies, vividness was also found to increase later recall of testimony (Bell, 1983, as cited in Bell & Loftus 1985; Reyes, Thompson, & Bower, 1980). That is, vividness may make information more memorable.

The vividness effect, however, is far from predictable. In fact, some researchers have found that vividness can actually make messages less persuasive (Collins, Taylor, Wood, & Thompson, 1988; Frey & Eagly, 1993; Kisielius & Sternthal, 1984). The keys to predicting if a vividness effect will arise may be whether there is vividness congruency (that is, the vivid elements of the message are congruent with the message's main themes [Smith & Shaffer, 2000]), and whether recipients are motivated to process the message. Smith & Shaffer (2000, Experiment 2) examined the difference between the persuasiveness of vivid and pallid messages concerning the benefits of a healthy lifestyle. They observed that when messages containing strong arguments were accompanied by relevant images, these communications were, in comparison to their unembellished equivalents, found to be more persuasive, but only by participants low on NFC. However, when images were disharmonious with the main thrust of the message, this effect disappeared.

Frey and Eagly (1993) manipulated both the colorfulness of language used in two messages and the extent to which participants would be motivated to attend carefully to these messages. They found that when motivated to be more diligent, participants were not affected by the luridness of the communications. However, recipients unmoved to pay close attention were less persuaded by the vivid messages. On examining the experimental materials used, it would appear that the vivid elements of the messages may have been incongruent with the message's themes. In one instance, one message was an argument in favor of not warning passengers of terrorist threats. In its vivid version it was punctuated with fear-arousing images that could serve to heighten anxiety at the prospect of terrorist attacks. The other communication concerned falling education standards and the need for the privatization of schools. Vividness was increased by adding colloquial and sensationalist elements—language that could undermine the credibility of an argument about education. Emphatic, but incongruent components of a message may hinder its effectiveness, perhaps because such features seize cognitive resources that should be devoted to processing the main themes of the message. Or it could be that they give the message the appearance of being inconsistent and of low quality.

Bringing the discussion back to the law, it may be that enhancing the vividness of evidence is sometimes effective at making it more persuasive and memorable. Lawyers might consider increasing vividness by using more expressive language, by including information that enriches the testimony, or by employing visual representations. Such tactics are most likely to influence jurors who are low on NFC, or who are otherwise unmotivated to elaborate carefully on the evidence. However, lawyers should avoid enhancing vividness in ways that appear distracting and irrelevant to the case. For example, lawyers should feel free to ask a witness what he or she was doing on the day he or she saw the crime, or to ask him or her what the defendant was wearing, because this level of information will only help increase the realism of the events described and may aid in story construction. However, they should avoid discussing the merits of nonstick cookware and other irrelevant matters (even if the judge were to allow it), in the hopes of vivifying the story, because then they would be straying just a little too far from the main themes of the evidence! Similarly, emphatic and colorful language may be called for when presenting evidence that is vital, but the same language might backfire if used to introduce evidence that is necessary, but less dramatic.

Use of Visual Aids

Do visual aids such as photos, PowerPoint presentations, and videotapes add to the persuasiveness and memorability of evidence? Intuitively this proposition seems likely, and research from disciplines outside of psychology and law has demonstrated that when people are shown information in addition to simply listening to it, they are better able to retrieve the information at another time (Weiss & McGrath, 1963). Surprisingly little empirical attention has been paid to the topic by researchers in psychology and law (Feigenson & Dunn, 2003). Here we review studies that do cast some light on the subject.

Whalen and Blanchard (1982) issued experimental participants transcripts of a personal injury case. Some individuals were also given either color or black-and-white photographs of the injuries sustained. When the injuries were severe and the defendant clearly at fault, jurors in the color photograph condition awarded considerably higher damages. Other research has demonstrated that gruesome photographic images have the power to alter mock verdicts in criminal matters (Douglas et al., 1997). In both these studies, however, the emotionally arousing nature of the materials may have mediated the effect. Whether photographs increase the persuasiveness of evidence that is blander remains to be tested.

Some researchers have examined the persuasiveness of computer-generated simulations. Over two experiments Kassin and Dunn (1997) exposed mock jurors to a trial concerning an insurance claim. The case hinged on how a man had fallen to his death from a building: A finding that the fall was the result of an accident would result in a decision for the plaintiff; a finding that it was suicide would lead to verdict for the defendant. The authors manipulated the distance from the base of the building that the body was found. In the pro-plaintiff condition, the body was between 5 to10 feet from the building, a gap that was compatible with the victim having accidentally slipped and fallen, more or less, straight down. In the pro-defendant condition the body landed 20–25 feet from the building, a distance consistent with the man having run and jumped outward from the structure. In both conditions expert evidence was introduced concerning the positioning of the body. In Experiment 1 half of the participants were also shown an animated portrayal of the fall. Kassin and Dunn found that the presence of the simulation led to more findings for the plaintiff in the pro-plaintiff condition, and more findings for the defendant in the pro-defendant condition. In other words, the visual aid helped jurors to interpret correctly which party the point-of-impact evidence favored, and rendered this evidence more persuasive.

Can such simulations also persuade jurors to interpret evidence inaccurately? That is, can simulations be used to mislead and prejudice jurors? In Experiment 2 (Kassin & Dunn, 1997) jurors were shown a computer animation that also included the moments before the fall. In one version the victim was depicted as having slipped accidentally, whereas in the other version the person was shown running and jumping. Participants viewing the "jumping" video still interpreted the distance evidence accurately: The closer the body had landed to the building, the more likely they were to find for the plaintiff. For jurors viewing the "slipping" depiction, however, the video simulation distorted judgments. Specifically, jurors who saw the victim depicted as slipping and accidentally falling showed elevated rates of finding for the plaintiff, even when the body was found 20–25 feet from the building. In fact, these jurors did not distinguish between the two distance-of-impact conditions at all. Between them, the two experiments imply that not only can visual representations help lawyers when the evidence in question is supportive; sometimes it can be used to make unfavorable evidence appear favorable.

Binder and Bourgeois (2004) conducted a study wherein they had an eyewitness expert testify with no visual aids, a flip pad, or PowerPoint. They found that overall, jurors recalled more of the testimony with either visual aid. Additionally, they found a NFC × mode interaction on credibility: Low-NFC jurors rated the expert more credible when he used visual aids.

Other research casts doubt on how much extra weight jurors apportion computer-simulation evidence. Bennett, Leibman, and Fetter (1999) also employed computer-generated recreations to augment expert testimony in a mock civil trial. Across a range of measures, the authors could not detect any indication that the judgments of jurors shown the electronic representations differed from the judgments of those who were exposed only to oral testimony accompanied by more traditional pictorial aids. Interestingly, participants rated the computer simulation as a high-quality piece of evidence, even though it failed to affect their decisions. One possibility not explored by the authors is that exposing jurors to any form of well-chosen visual representation, including the charts and photographs used in the control condition, may be sufficient to make the testimony more persuasive. That is to say, one form of visual medium may not be any more effective than another.

The influence on video evidence has also been the subject of empirical investigation. But, as with computer simulations, the evidence is mixed. Fishfader, Howells, Katz, and Teresi (1996) compared the effect of video recreations on mock jurors' decisions in a civil matter concerning wrongful death. Compared to controls, participants exposed to the video evidence assigned more liability to the defendant. This effect was mediated by changes in jurors' moods: Those exposed to the video experienced more mood change, and the size of this change was positively related to the liability estimates. Surprisingly, however, the average damages awarded did *not* vary between the two groups. In a mock murder trial, Douglas et al. (1997) showed that shocking video evidence can bias jurors against the accused. But, again, the effect was mediated by the negative emotion it provoked in participants.

What can we conclude about the use of visual stimuli in the courtroom? Not much, unfortunately. We cannot be sure how and when illustrating evidence visually may make it more persuasive and memorable. Nor do we know whether there are factors that moderate the effect. For example, do factors such as size, realism, and color alter a display's impact? How important are movement and sound? Other issues that need to be resolved concern how the perspective from which a display is shown might affect jurors' thinking. For example, in relation to videotaped confessions, it has been demonstrated that the presence or absence from view of the questioning detective and the angle from which the video was shot can influence observers' perceptions of whether the confession was voluntarily given or the result of coercion (Lassiter et al., 2002). How might differences in the way scenes are depicted affect, say, the attributions of observers? For example, would showing a car accident from different angles make people shift blame between the actors involved, or between the actors and external factors such as the curvature of the road? Would shooting a scene from the point of view of a particular party create, as we might expect, empathy for that party? (Feigenson & Dunn, 2003). Many such questions remain unanswered but should be contemplated when choosing ways of displaying evidence.

Metaphors

Metaphors are particularly powerful linguistic devices; they are evocative words that can turn a complex proposition into a concept that is more concrete, comprehensible, and recognizable. When used to reinforce an argument, they can be very persuasive (for a review of the literature on the persuasiveness of metaphors, see Sopory & Dillard, 2002). Metaphors might therefore be useful in court, both because they can elucidate complex evidence and arguments, and because they are, in themselves, persuasive. Metaphors are particularly influential when introduced early in a communication (Sopory & Dillard, 2002). Early in their case lawyers might therefore consider introducing an overarching metaphor that jurors could use as a framework or schema around which to build the story of the case. However, caution should be exercised when employing metaphors. If the metaphor is too far-fetched, it might be the subject of an objection. The effectiveness of metaphors also diminishes as they become increasingly complex, and if they are overextended (Sopory & Dillard, 2002); a metaphor should not be stretched too far in an effort to encompass too much of the evidence.

Sometimes metaphors are so powerful that they may require a response from the opposing attorneys. One of us (K.D.W.) once visited a trial in which, during closing arguments, the defense attorney asked the jury to imagine that she was holding a bunch of helium-filled balloons. She pinched her fingers together and looked up at her imaginary balloons, as did the jury. For each piece of prosecution evidence that she countered, she took one of the imaginary strings with her other hand, and let the balloon go. She (and the jury) watched the balloon rise in the air. At the end of her closing argument, she held no more balloons, and the jury was watching the ceiling. When the prosecutor attempted to deliver his closing argument, the jurors persisted in watching the ceiling. Although the attorney would not like to feel bound to continue the use of his adversary's metaphors, he might have been well advised to have dealt with the metaphor rather than ignoring it (maybe by saying, "I'll agree with the defense council that her explanations, like the balloons, are filled with hot air").

Counterfactual Reasoning

Counterfactual reasoning occurs when a person imagines how an outcome would have been different, had some factor or behavior been changed. People usually generate counterfactuals in response to bad events: "If only I hadn't stopped off at the shop . . . " or "If only she hadn't decided to take a shortcut through the park. . . ." Branscombe, Owen, Garstka, and Coleman (1996) asked participants to imagine how hypothetical scenarios of rape and a motor vehicle accident would have turned out if the behavior of specific actors had been different in the moments leading up to the events. Surprisingly, such reasoning altered how participants later attributed blame to the different parties. When participants had imagined how changing the actions by a particular person would have led to a better outcome, that person was found to be more at fault. Thus, when cross-examining a witness, a shrewd lawyer might ask a seemingly innocuous question such as, "So if you had not rung your sister that morning, you would never have left the house"—and thereby initiate in jurors a process of counterfactual reasoning that would ultimately lead to the witness being judged more harshly.

Naked Statistics

An interesting phenomenon emerging from persuasion research is that two pieces of statistical evidence that are equally strong in terms of establishing the occurrence of an event, or the truth of a fact, may not be equally persuasive. In a hypothetical civil case involving a bus hitting a dog, Wells (1992) asked jurors to give verdicts based on one of several alternative pieces of evidence. All items of evidence suggested that it was 80% likely that the defendant was liable. Rates of finding for the plaintiff, however, varied widely. Wells found that jurors shied away from condemning the defendant based purely on naked statistics, which is probabilistic evidence that is true irrespective of the crime. For example, few jurors found for the plaintiff based on the fact that 80% of the buses in the area were owned by the defendant's company. Jurors, however, were far more readily persuaded by probabilistic evidence concerning the reliability of information. For example, the results of forensic tests on tire tracks at the accident scene that favored the plaintiff led to high rates of finding against the defendant, even though jurors were told that these tests were only 80% reliable. These findings, labeled the "Wells effect," have been replicated (Niedermeier, Kerr, & Messé, 1999). The mechanics of the effect remain unclear, but legal teams should be wary of relying on naked statistics—no matter how convincing they believe them to be.

COMPLIANCE

Compliance differs from persuasion in that compliance involves behaviors rather than attitudes. A person seeking compliance wants to make his or her target perform a certain act or actions, such as buying a car or taking out the garbage. In the words of Robert Cialdini (1994) "the process of generating compliance . . . refers to the process of getting others to say yes to a request" (p. 196). For some seekers of compliance, having the target perform the desired act may be the extent of their ambitions. Others trying to generate compliance may, however, be driven by an ulterior motive: to change their target's attitudes. That people often change their attitudes to make them consistent with their behavior has been revealed by research on the phenomena known as cognitive dissonance (Festinger, 1957) and self-perception (Bem, 1967). To give an example of behavior-consistent attitudinal change, consider Jane, a person who strongly opposes tax evasion. Jane is talked into taking advantage of a loophole in tax law and, as a consequence, changes her attitude toward tax evasion to one of "you should get away with whatever you can." From the perspective of cognitive dissonance theory, Jane changed her attitude in order to resolve the incompatibility of her behavior and her initial attitude. A self-perception theorist would interpret the situation differently; Jane inferred her new attitude from observing her behavior. In other words, "I avoided tax, so I must be a person who thinks that that is OK." Either way, compliance is a very powerful form of manipulation; it can change both behavior and, consequently, the attitude underpinning it (which, in turn, will influence future behavior).

There are many different compliance techniques (e.g., see Cialdini, 2001). Few, however, are applicable, ethical, or permissible in a courtroom setting. One tactic that could be used, while maintaining a clear conscience, involves the idea of commitment and consistency. Imagine, for example, that during the voir dire leading up to a criminal trial, a lawyer asks each potential juror, "If the prosecution fails to prove its case beyond a reasonable doubt, will you find the accused not guilty, even if deep down you believe that he [or she] is guilty?" Obtaining a public commitment in the affirmative will make it very difficult for people to behave subsequently in a manner that is inconsistent with this commitment. It may also cause jurors to form the attitude that the behavior advocated by the lawyer is correct and admirable. In a trial attended by K.D.W., the defense attorney asked the group of potential jurors during voir dire, "Even if you feel the defendant is guilty, if there is not sufficient proof against my client, what will your verdict be?" He waited patiently as the jurors murmured, "Not guilty." He said, "What? I can't hear you." They said, "Not guilty." He said, "Excuse me?" and they answered, almost shouting, "NOT GUILTY!" Talk about public commitment; what better way to begin a trial than having the jury chant "NOT GUILTY, NOT GUILTY, NOT GUILTY!" Similarly, a legal team might ask jurors to commit to setting aside their revulsion at a crime, and to make their decision in an objective manner. Even if jurors are only asked to make the commitment silently to themselves, doing so may be a sufficient behavioral incentive to cause attitudinal change.

DISSUASION

Dissuasion is a form of social influence whereby the influencer attempts to prevent the target from being persuaded by other potential influencers. In a courtroom a lawyer might use dissuasion tactics to increase the jury's resistance to persuasion from his or her opponents. In the following section we consider a number of such tactics that could be used in a trial.

Forewarning

The gist of the forewarning tactic is that "forewarned is forearmed." The tactic involves alerting targets to the fact that someone intends to persuade them. People do not like the idea that they are malleable, that they can be pushed around. If individuals are, through forewarning, made aware that someone plans to manipulate them, it is likely that they will prepare to resist this attack. By using forewarning, a lawyer may thereby encourage jurors to mount their own resistance to the persuasive efforts of the opposition. A lawyer might tip off jurors by saying something like "My learned friend will try to persuade you that. . . ." Such a statement might prompt jurors to defy this message when it eventually arrives. We are unaware of any research demonstrating the effectiveness of forewarning in the courtroom, although it has been shown to increase resistance to attitude change in other social contexts (e.g., see Chen, Reardon, Rea, & Moore, 1992; Jacks & Cameron, 2003; Jacks & Devine, 2000; Petty & Cacioppo, 1977).

Inoculation

Inoculation involves giving targets a weak version of the opponent's arguments, so that they will be easily able to construct counterarguments. The hope is that the targets will build up a bank of such ripostes, so that by the time that the opposition introduces his or her arguments, targets will be prepared to counter them. (Thus the analogy with medical inoculation: In medicine, inoculation involves giving patients a weak version of a disease, so that they can develop antibodies for it; then, if they are exposed to the full-blown disease later, they will be prepared to resist it.) For instance, imagine a case of fraud involving many complicated transactions. To begin the process of inoculation, the prosecution might open with "The defense will try to convince you that somehow an accountant with 20 years of experience simply forgot that balance sheets must balance," thereby reducing a complex tangle of evidence into a simple and easily countered proposition. Again, published research on the usefulness of the inoculation as a trial tactic appears to be nonexistent, although its effectiveness has been demonstrated in other settings (e.g., see the classic work of McGuire, 1964).

Stealing Thunder

Stealing thunder describes a tactic whereby a lawyer explicitly and preemptively reveals some attribute of his or her client, or some aspect of the case, that should be greatly disadvantageous. This, of course, would be an exception to the general rule of primacy, discussed earlier. For example, the defense begins its opening address with "My client is a prostitute and a welfare cheat." Stealing thunder appears to have the effect of stripping the volatile information of its negative impact and removing its influence on jury verdicts (Williams, Bourgeois, & Croyle, 1993; Williams & Dolnik, 2001). In order for the tactic to work, the damaging material must be revealed before the opposition has had a chance to introduce it. The tactic does not, however, require that the stealers of thunder put a positive spin on the material. Rather, stealing thunder works for at least two reasons. First, it acts as a peripheral cue for credibility; the thunder stealer is perceived to be forthright and honest, hence, more believable in general. Second, it seems that jurors find it so perplexing that a lawyer would act in such an apparently self-destructive way that they resolve this conundrum by devaluing the information's importance (Dolnik, Case, & Williams, 2003). In other words, they decide, either consciously or otherwise, that the facts revealed must not be so bad after all, or else the side that revealed them would not have revealed them. However, Dolnik et al. found that if the prosecution informs the jury during closing arguments that the defense manipulated them with the stealing thunder tactic, then their verdicts were no longer affected by the stealing thunder factor.

Impeaching the Credibility of the Other Side's Witnesses

Attacking the standing of an opponent's expert witnesses is particularly damaging to jurors' perceptions of those witnesses' credibility. In a mock-jury study by Kassin, Williams, and Saunders (1990), an expert under cross-examination was asked "Isn't it true that your work is poorly regarded by your colleagues?" and "Hasn't your work been sharply criticized in the past?" Despite the accusations being unfounded and uncorroborated, jurors ratings' of the witness's credibility were significantly lowered. This effect occurred even when the questions were met with a denial or a sustained objection.

Reactance

One tactic that seems appealing at first glance but is likely to backfire is that of making demands of the jury. We often hear in court, especially during closing arguments, phrases such as "It is your duty to find the defendant guilty . . . " and "You have no choice but to acquit the accused. . . ." Unfortunately, such appeals are likely to evoke reactance. *Reactance* (Brehm, 1966) is a phenomenon wherein individuals interpret demands made, or restrictions placed, upon them by others as an impingement on their freedom. In order to reassert their independence, they do the converse of what was demanded of them. This effect has been demonstrated experimentally and is considered robust (Brehm & Brehm, 1981).

Reactance might be particularly prominent within juries, given that jurors are always told by judges that they are the sole triers of fact and that theirs is a particularly weighty role. Any attempt at appropriating these powers may be interpreted by jurors as a form of effrontery and a sign of disrespect. For example, if a lawyer tells jurors how they should vote, this injunction may motivate them to vote in the opposite direction. An instance of courtroom reactance was observed by Wolf and Montgomery (1977) in an experimental setting. In that study, mock jurors were exposed to key testimony that was then ruled either inadmissible or admissible by the judge. To make matters more interesting, for some of the jurors in the inadmissible condition the ruling was also accompanied by an admonishment by the judge to disregard the evidence. Wolf and Montgomery (1977) found that jurors only discounted the inadmissible testimony when they were *not* admonished to do so. The authors concluded that otherwise conscientious jurors were provoked into reactance by the perceived authoritarian behavior of the judge.

CONCLUSION

Most jury decisions are based on the evidence and the way it is presented. Trial tactics are therefore of utmost importance. In this chapter we discussed how, from an elaboration likelihood model perspective, persuasion can occur via two different routes: one that requires careful attention and cognitive elaboration on the part of the jurors, and the other that takes advantage of jurors' cognitive shortcuts. We examined how this model of persuasion might influence the approach that lawyers take in court. Compliance tactics were also discussed, specifically, how lawyers might ask jurors to make a commitment and behave in a manner consistent with that commitment. Finally, we considered how dissuasion tactics can be used to undermine the other side's persuasiveness.

Having explored some of the ways in which social influence may be exerted on decision makers, it is worth restating the importance of using this knowledge ethically. It is not the intention of the authors simply to provide instructions on how to manipulate jurors. Unfortunately, there is a fine line between presenting a case as effectively as possible and deliberately impeding jurors from considering the evidence in an unbiased matter. Practices such as distracting jurors or sullying the reputations of an opponent's experts are clearly not ethical. Perhaps the best guide as to whether you think a tactic is ethical would be to ask yourself the question, "How would I feel if I were a party in a case and my opponents used such a tactic? Would I be outraged, or would I feel that the strategy was justified?"

ACKNOWLEDGMENTS

Portions of this chapter were facilitated by Australian Research Council Discovery Grant No. DP0343548 to N. Brewer, K. Williams, and L. ForsterLee. We thank Marty Bourgeois for his comments on a previous draft of the chapter.

REFERENCES

Anderson, N. H. (1968). A simple model of information integration. In R. B. Abelson, E. Aronson, W. J. McGuire, T. M. Newcomb, M. J. Rosenberg, & P. H. Tannenbaum (Eds.), *Theories of cognitive consistency: A sourcebook*. Chicago: Rand McNally.

Aronson, E., Turner, J. A., & Carlsmith, J. M. (1963). Communicator credibility and communication discrepancy as determinants of opinion change. *Journal of Abnormal and Social Psychology, 67*, 31–36.

Bell, B. E., & Loftus, E. F. (1985). Vivid persuasion in the courtroom. *Journal of Personality Assessment, 49*, 659–664.

Bem, D. J. (1967). Self-perception: An alternative interpretation of cognitive dissonance phenomena. *Psychological Review, 74*, 183–200.

Bennett, L. (1978). Storytelling in criminal trials: A model of social judgment. *The Quarterly Journal of Speech, 64,* 1–22.

Bennett, R. B., Leibman, J. H., & Fetter, R. E. (1999). Seeing is believing; or is it? An empirical study of computer simulations as evidence. *Wake Forest Law Review, 34,* 257–294.

Binder, D. M., & Bourgeois, M. J. (2004). *Effects of the use of PowerPoint by expert witnesses.* Unpublished manuscript, University of Wyoming.

Bohner, G., Ruder, M., & Erb, H. (2002). When expertise backfires: Contrast and assimilation effects in persuasion. *British Journal of Social Psychology, 41,* 495–519.

Bourgeois, M. J., Horowitz, I. A., ForsterLee, L., & Grahe, J. 1995). Nominal and interactive juries: Effects of preinstruction and discussion on decisions and evidence recall in a complex trial. *Journal of Applied Psychology, 80,* 87–96.

Branscombe, N. R., Owen, S., Garstka, T. A., & Coleman, J. (1996). Rape and accident counterfactuals: Who might have done otherwise and would it have changed the outcome? *Journal of Applied Social Psychology, 26,* 1042–1067.

Breckler, S. J. (1984). Empirical validation of affect, behavior, and cognition as distinct components of attitude. *Journal of Personality and Social Psychology, 47,* 1191–1205.

Brehm, J. W. (1966). *A theory of psychological reactance.* New York: Academic Press.

Brehm, J. W., & Brehm, S. S. (1981). *Psychological reactance.* New York: Wiley.

Bright, D. A., & Williams, K. D. (2001). When emotion takes control of jury verdicts. *Clio's Psyche: Special Issue on Crime, Punishment, and Incarceration, 8*(2), 68–70.

Burnkrant, R., & Howard, D. J. (1984). Effects of the use of introductory rhetorical questions versus statements on information processing. *Journal of Personality and Social Psychology, 47,* 1218–1230.

Cacioppo, J. T., & Petty, R. E. (1980). Persuasiveness of communications is affected by exposure frequency and message quality: A theoretical and empirical analysis of persisting attitude change. In J. H. Leigh & C. R. Martin (Eds.), *Current issues and research in advertising* (pp. 97–122). Ann Arbor, MI: University of Michigan Graduate School of Business Administration.

Cacioppo, J. T., & Petty, R. E. (1982). The need for cognition. *Journal of Personality and Social Psychology, 42,* 116–131.

Cacioppo, J. T., & Petty, R. E. (1985). Central and peripheral routes to persuasion: The role of message repetition. In A. Mitchell & L. Alwitt (Eds.), *Psychological processes and advertising effects* (pp. 91–112). Hillsdale, NJ: Erlbaum.

Cacioppo, J. T., & Petty, R. E. (1989). Effects of message repetition on argument processing, recall, and persuasion. *Basic and Applied Social Psychology, 10,* 3–12.

Cacioppo, J. T., Petty, R. E., & Geen, T. R. (1989). Attitude structure and function: From the tripartite to the homeostasis model of attitudes. In A. R. Pratkanis, S. J. Breckler, & A. G. Greenwald (Eds.), *Attitude structure and function.* Hillsdale, NJ: Erlbaum.

Cacioppo, J. T., Petty, R. E., & Morris, K. J. (1983). Effects of need for cognition on message evaluation, recall, and persuasion. *Journal of Personality and Social Psychology, 45,* 805–818.

Carretta, T. R., & Moreland, R. L. (1983). The direct and indirect effects of inadmissible evidence. *Journal of Applied Social Psychology, 13,* 291–309.

Carroll, J. S., Perkowitz, W. T., Lurigio, A. J., & Weaver, F. M. (1987). Sentencing goals, causal attributions, ideology, and personality. *Journal of Personality and Social Psychology, 52,* 107–118.

Chen, H. C., Reardon, R., Rea, C., & Moore, D. (1992). Forewarning of content and involvement: Consequences for persuasion and resistance to persuasion. *Journal of Experimental Social Psychology, 28,* 523–541.

Chew, J., & Williams, K. D. (2000, April). *The effectiveness of crime heinousness on juror decision-making: A case of jury vilification.* Paper presented at the Society for Australasian Social Psychology, Fremantle, Western Australia.

Cialdini, R. B. (1994). Interpersonal influence. In S. Shavitt & T. C. Brock (Eds.), *Persuasion: Psychological insights and perspectives* (pp. 195–217). Boston: Allyn & Bacon.

Cialdini, R. B. (2001). *Influence: Science and practice* (4th ed.). Boston: Allyn & Bacon.

Collins, R. L., Taylor, S. E., Wood, J. V., & Thompson, S. C. (1988). The vividness effect: Elusive or illusory? *Journal of Experimental Social Psychology, 24,* 1–18.

Dolnik, L., Case, T. I., & Williams, K. D. (2003). Stealing thunder as a courtroom tactic revisited: Processes and boundaries. *Law and Human Behavior, 27,* 265–285.

Douglas, K. S., Lyon, D. R., & Ogloff, J. R. P. (1997). The impact of graphic photographic evidence on mock jurors' decisions in a murder trial: Probative or prejudicial? *Law and Human Behavior, 21,* 485–501.

Eagly, A. H., Ashmore, R. D., Makhijani, M. G., & Longo, L. C. (1991). What is beautiful is good, but . . . : A meta-analytic review of research on the physical attractiveness stereotype. *Psychological Bulletin, 110,* 109–128.

Edwards, K., & Bryan, T. S. (1997). Judgmental biases produced by instructions to disregard: The (paradoxical) case of emotional information. *Personality and Social Psychology Bulletin, 23,* 849–864.

Ellsworth, P. C. (1993). Some steps between attitudes and verdicts. In R. Hastie (Ed.), *Inside the juror: The psychology of juror decision making* (pp. 42–64). Cambridge, UK: Cambridge University Press.

Ellsworth, P. C., & Gross, S. R. (1994). Hardening of the attitudes: Americans' views on the death penalty. *Journal of Social Issues, 50,* 19–52.

Ellsworth, P. C., & Ross, L. (1983). Public opinion and capital punishment: A close examination of the views of abolitionists and retentionists. *Crime and Delinquency, 29,* 116–169.

Feigenson, N., & Dunn, M. A. (2003). New visual technologies in court: Directions for research. *Law and Human Behavior, 27,* 109–126.

Festinger, L. (1957). *A theory of cognitive dissonance.* Evanston, IL: Row, Peterson.

Fishfader, V. L., Howells, G. N., Katz, R. C., & Teresi, P. S. (1996). Evidential and extralegal factors in juror decisions: Presentation mode, retention, and level of emotionality. *Law and Human Behavior, 20,* 565–572.

Frey, K. P., & Eagly, A. H. (1993). Vividness can undermine the persuasiveness of messages. *Journal of Personality and Social Psychology, 65,* 32–44.

Hafer, C. L., Reynolds, K. L., & Obertynski, M. A. (1996). Message comprehensibility and persuasion: Effects of complex language in counterattitudinal appeals to laypeople. *Social Cognition, 14,* 317–337.

Hans, V. P., & Doob, A. N. (1976). Section 12 of the Canada evidence act and the deliberations of simulated jurors. *Criminal Law Quarterly, 18,* 235–253.

Harkins, S. G., & Petty, R. E. (1981). Effects of source magnification of cognitive effort on attitudes: An information-processing view. *Journal of Personality and Social Psychology, 40,* 401–413.

Harkins, S. G., & Petty, R. E. (1987). Information utility and the multiple source effect. *Journal of Personality and Social Psychology, 52,* 260–268.

Haugtvedt, C. P., & Petty, R. E. (1992). Personality and persuasion: Need for cognition moderates the persistence and resistance of attitude changes. *Journal of Personality and Social Psychology, 63,* 308–319.

Heesacker, M., Petty, R. E., & Cacioppo, J. T. (1983). Field dependence and attitude change: Source credibility can alter persuasion by affecting message-relevant thinking. *Journal of Personality, 51,* 653–666.

Henningsen, D. D., Cruz, M. G., & Miller, M. L. (2000). Role of social loafing in predeliberation decision making. *Group Dynamics: Theory, Research, and Practice, 4,* 168–175.

Hovland, C. I., Janis, I. L., & Kelley, H. H. (1953). *Communication and persuasion.* New Haven, CT: Yale University Press.

Hovland, C. I., & Weiss, W. (1952). The influence of source credibility on communication effectiveness. *Public Opinion Quarterly, 15,* 635–650.

Jacks, J. Z., & Cameron, K. A. (2003). Strategies for resisting persuasion. *Basic and Applied Social Psychology, 25,* 145–161.

Jacks, J. Z., & Devine, P. G. (2000). Attitude importance, forewarning of message content, and resistance to persuasion. *Basic and Applied Social Psychology, 22,* 19–30.

Jones, A., & Williams, K. D. (2004). *Let the verdict fit the crime: The biasing effects of crime heinousness on juror verdicts.* Unpublished manuscript, Macquarie University, Sydney, Australia.

Kaplan, M. F., & Miller, L. E. (1978). Reducing the effects of juror bias. *Journal of Personality and Social Psychology, 36,* 1443–1455.

Karau, S. J., & Williams, K. D. (1993). Social loafing: A meta-analytic review and theoretical integration. *Journal of Personality and Social Psychology, 65,* 681–706.

Kassin, S. M. (1983). Deposition testimony and the surrogate witness: Evidence for a "messenger effect" in persuasion. *Personality and Social Psychology Bulletin, 9,* 281–288.

Kassin, S. M., & Dunn, M. A. (1997). Computer-animated displays and the jury: Facilitative and prejudicial effects. *Law and Human Behavior, 21,* 269–281.

Kassin, S. M., & Garfield, D. A. (1991). Blood and guts: General and trial-specific effects of videotaped crime scenes on mock jurors. *Journal of Applied Social Psychology, 21,* 1459–1472.

Kassin, S. M., Williams, L. N., & Saunders, C. L. (1990). Dirty tricks of cross-examination: The influence of conjectural evidence on the jury. *Law and Human Behavior, 14,* 373–384.

Kerr, N. L., & Bruun, S. E. (1983). Dispensability of member effort and group motivation losses: Free-rider effects. *Journal of Personality and Social Psychology, 44,* 78–94.

Kerr, N. L., Niedermeier, K. E., & Kaplan, M. F. (1999). Bias in jurors vs. bias in juries: New evidence from the SDS perspective. *Organizational Behavior and Human Decision Processes, 80,* 70–86.

Kerwin, J., & Shaffer, D. R. (1994). Mock jurors versus mock juries: The role of deliberations in reactions to inadmissible testimony. *Personality and Social Psychology Bulletin, 20,* 153–162.

Kiesler, S. B., & Mathog, R. B. (1968). Distraction hypothesis in attitude change: Effects of effectiveness. *Psychological Reports, 23,* 1123–1133.

Kisielius, J., & Sternthal, B. (1984). Detecting and explaining vividness effects in attitudinal judgments. *Journal of Marketing Research, 21,* 54–64.

Koletti, C., & Williams, K. D. (2001, February). *The effects of trial heinousness and victim's reputation on mock juror verdicts.* Presented at the First International Conference on Forensic Psychology, Sydney, Australia.

Kramer, G. P., Kerr, N. L., & Carroll, J. S. (1990). Pretrial publicity, judicial remedies, and jury bias. *Law and Human Behavior, 14,* 409–438.

Kraus, S. J. (1995). Attitudes and the prediction of behavior: A meta-analysis of the empirical literature. *Personality and Social Psychology Bulletin, 21,* 58–75.

LaPiere, R. T. (1934). Attitudes vs. actions. *Social Forces, 13,* 230–237.

Lassiter, G. D., Beers, M. J., Geers, A. L., Handley, I. M., Munhall, P. J., & Weiland, P. E. (2002). Further evidence of a robust point-of-view bias in videotaped confessions. *Current Psychology: Developmental, Learning, Personality, and Social, 21,* 265–288.

Latané, B., Williams, K., & Harkins, S. G. (1979). Many hands make light work: The cases and consequences of social loafing. *Journal of Personality and Social Psychology, 37,* 322–332.

Lecci, L., & Myers, B. (2002). Examining the construct validity of the original and revised JBS: A cross-validation of sample and method. *Law and Human Behavior, 26,* 455–463.

Lerner, J. S., Goldberg, J. H., & Tetlock, P. E. (1998). Sober second thought: The effects of accountability, anger, and authoritarianism on attributions of responsibility. *Personality and Social Psychology Bulletin, 24,* 563–574.

London, H., McSeveney, D., & Tropper, R. (1971). Confidence, overconfidence and persuasion. *Human Relations, 24,* 359–369.

Lui, L., & Standing, L. G. (1989). Communicator credibility: Trustworthiness defeats expertness. *Social Behavior and Personality, 17,* 219–221.

Maslow, C., Yoselson, K., & London, H. (1971). Persuasiveness of confidence expressed via language and body language. *British Journal of Social and Clinical Psychology, 10,* 234–240.

McCoy, M. L., Nunez, N., & Dammeyer, M. M. (1999). The effect of jury deliberations on jurors' reasoning skills. *Law and Human Behavior, 23,* 557–575.

McFatter, R. M. (1982). Purposes of punishment: Effects of utilities of criminal sanctions on perceived appropriateness. *Journal of Applied Psychology, 67,* 255–267.

McGinnies, E., & Ward, C. D. (1980). Better liked than right: Trustworthiness and expertise as factors in credibility. *Personality and Social Psychology Bulletin, 6,* 467–472.

McGuire, W. J. (1964). Inducing resistance to persuasion: Some contemporary approaches. In L. Berkowitz (Ed.), *Advances in experimental psychology* (Vol. 1, pp. 191–229). New York: Academic Press.

Myers, D. G., & Kaplan, M. F. (1976). Group-induced polarization in simulated juries. *Personality and Social Psychology Bulletin, 2,* 63–66.

Niedermeier, K. E., Kerr, N. L., & Messé, L. A. (1999). Jurors' use of naked statistical evidence: Exploring bases and implications of Wells effect. *Journal of Personality and Social Psychology, 76,* 533–542.

Ogloff, J. R. P., & Vidmar, N. (1994). The impact of pretrial publicity on jurors: A study to compare the relative effects of television and print media in a child sex abuse case. *Law and Human Behavior, 18,* 507–525.

Pennington, D. C. (1982). Witnesses and their testimony: Effects of ordering on juror verdicts. *Journal of Applied Social Psychology, 12,* 318–333.

Pennington, N., & Hastie, R. (1988). Explanation-based decision making: Effects of memory structure on judgment. *Journal of Experimental Psychology: Learning, Memory, and Cognition, 14,* 521–533.

Pennington, N., & Hastie, R. (1993). The story model for juror decision making. In R.

Hastie (Ed.), *Inside the juror: The psychology of juror decision making* (pp. 192–221). Cambridge, UK: Cambridge University Press.

Petty, R. E., & Cacioppo, J. T. (1977). Forewarning, cognitive responding, and resistance to persuasion. *Journal of Personality and Social Psychology, 35,* 645–655.

Petty, R. E., & Cacioppo, J. T. (1984). The effects of involvement on responses to argument quantity and quality: Central and peripheral routes to persuasion. *Journal of Personality and Social Psychology, 46,* 69–81.

Petty, R. E., & Cacioppo, J. T. (1986a). *Communication and persuasion: Central and peripheral routes to attitude change.* New York: Springer-Verlag.

Petty, R. E., & Cacioppo, J. T. (1986b). The elaboration likelihood model of persuasion. In L. Berkowitz (Ed.), *Advances in experimental social psychology* (Vol. 19, pp. 123–205). New York: Academic Press.

Petty, R. E., Cacioppo, J. T., & Goldman, R. (1981). Personal involvement as a determinant of argument-based persuasion. *Journal of Personality and Social Psychology, 41,* 847–855.

Petty, R. E., Cacioppo, J. T., Haugtvedt, C., & Heesacker, M. (1986). *Consequences of the route to persuasion: Persistence and resistance of attitude changes.* Unpublished manuscript, University of Missouri, Columbia, MO.

Petty, R. E., Cacioppo, J. T., & Heesacker, M. (1981). Effects of rhetorical questions on persuasion: A cognitive response analysis. *Journal of Personality and Social Psychology, 40,* 432–440.

Petty, R. E., Cacioppo, J. T., & Schumann, D. (1983). Central and peripheral routes to advertising effectiveness: The moderating role of involvement. *Journal of Consumer Research, 10,* 135–146.

Petty, R. E., Harkins, S. G., & Williams, K. D. (1980). The effects of group diffusion of cognitive effort on attitudes: An information-processing view. *Journal of Personality and Social Psychology, 38,* 81–92.

Petty, R. E., & Wegener, D. T. (1993). Flexible correction processes in social judgment: Correcting for context induced contrast. *Journal of Experimental Social Psychology, 29,* 137–165.

Petty, R. E., & Wegener, D. T. (1999). The elaboration likelihood model: Current status and controversies. In S. Chaiken & Y. Trope (Eds.), *Dual-process theories in social psychology* (pp. 37–72). New York: Guilford Press.

Priester, J. R., & Petty, R. E. (1995). Source attributions and persuasion: Perceived honesty as a determinant of message scrutiny. *Personality and Social Psychology Bulletin, 21,* 637–654.

Priester, J. R., & Petty, R. E. (2003). The influence of spokesperson trustworthiness on message elaboration, attitude strength, and advertising effectiveness. *Journal of Consumer Psychology, 13,* 408–421.

Puckett, J. M., Petty, R. E., Cacioppo, J. T., & Fischer, D. L. (1983). The relative impact of age and attractiveness stereotypes on persuasion. *Journal of Gerontology, 38,* 340–343.

Pyszczynski, T. A., Greenberg, J., Mack, D., & Wrightsman, L. S. (1981). Opening statements in a jury trial: The effect of promising more than the evidence can show. *Journal of Applied Social Psychology, 11,* 434–444.

Pyszczynski, T. A., & Wrightsman, L. S. (1981). The effects of opening statements on mock jurors' verdicts in a simulated criminal trial. *Journal of Applied Social Psychology, 11,* 301–313.

Reyes, R. M., Thompson, W. C., & Bower, G. H. (1980). Judgmental biases resulting from differing availabilities of arguments. *Journal of Personality and Social Psychology, 39,* 2–12.

Rosenberg, M. J., & Hovland, C. I. (1960). Cognitive, affective, and behavioral components of attitude. In M. H. Rosenberg, C. I. Hovland, W. J. McGuire, R. P. Abelson, & J. W. Brehm (Eds.), *Attitude organization and change: An analysis of consistency among attitude components* (pp. 1–14). New Haven, CT: Yale University Press.

Schuman, H., & Johnson, M. P. (1976). Attitudes and behavior. *Annual Review of Sociology, 2,* 161–207.

Sigall, H., & Ostrove, N. (1975). Beautiful but dangerous: Effects of offender attractiveness and nature of the crime on juridic judgment. *Journal of Personality and Social Psychology, 31,* 410–414.

Smith, S. M., & Shaffer, D. R. (1991). Celerity and cajolery: Rapid speech may promote or inhibit persuasion through its impact on message elaboration. *Personality and Social Psychology Bulletin, 17,* 663–669.

Smith, S. M., & Shaffer, D. R. (2000). Vividness can undermine or enhance message processing: The moderating role of vividness congruency. *Personality and Social Psychology Bulletin, 26,* 769–779.

Snyder, M. (1974). The self-monitoring of expressive behavior. *Journal of Personality and Social Psychology, 30,* 526–537.

Sopory, P., & Dillard, J. P. (2002). The persuasive effects of metaphor: A meta-analysis. *Human Communication Research, 28,* 382–419.

Weigel, R. H., Vernon, D. T., & Tognacci, L. N. (1974). Specificity of the attitude as a determinant of attitude–behavior congruence. *Journal of Personality and Social Psychology, 30,* 724–728.

Weiss, H., & McGrath, J. B. (1963). *Technically speaking: Oral communication for engineers, scientists, and technical personnel.* New York: McGraw-Hill.

Wells, G. L. (1992). Naked statistical evidence of liability: Is subjective probability enough? *Journal of Personality and Social Psychology, 65,* 739–752.

Whalen, D. H., & Blanchard, F. A. (1982). Effects of photographic evidence on mock juror judgment. *Journal of Applied Social Psychology, 12,* 30–41.

Wicker, A. W. (1971). An examination of the "other variables" explanation of attitude–behavior inconsistency. *Journal of Personality and Social Psychology, 19,* 18–30.

Williams, K. D., Bourgeois, M. J., & Croyle, R. T. (1993). The effects of stealing thunder in criminal and civil trials. *Law and Human Behavior, 17,* 597–609.

Williams, K. D., & Dolnik, L. (2001). Revealing the worst first: Stealing thunder as a social influence strategy. In J. P. Forgas & K. D. Williams (Eds.), *Social influence: Direct and indirect processes* (pp. 213–231). Philadelphia: Psychology Press.

Wilson, E. J., & Sherrell, D. L. (1993). Source effects in communication and persuasion research: A meta-analysis of effect size. *Journal of the Academy of Marketing Science, 2,* 101–112.

Wilson, J. R., & Bornstein, B. H. (1998). Methodological considerations in pretrial publicity research: Is the medium the message? *Law and Human Behavior, 22,* 585–597.

Wolf, S., & Montgomery, D. A. (1977). Effects of inadmissible evidence and level of judicial admonishment to disregard on the judgments of mock jurors. *Journal of Applied Social Psychology, 7,* 205–219.

Wood, W., & Kallgren, C. A. (1988). Communicator attributes and persuasion: Recipients' access to attitude-relevant information in memory. *Personality and Social Psychology Bulletin, 14,* 172–182.

Wood, W., Kallgren, C. A., & Preisler, R. M. (1985). Access to attitude-relevant information in memory as a determinant of persuasion: The role of message attributes. *Journal of Experimental Social Psychology, 21*, 73–85.

Wood, W., Rhodes, N., & Biek, M. (1995). Working knowledge and attitude strength: An information-processing analysis. In R. E. Petty & J. A. Krosnick, (Eds.), *Attitude strength: Antecedents and consequences. Ohio State University series on attitudes and persuasion* (Vol. 4, pp. 283–313). Mahwah, NJ: Erlbaum.

CHAPTER TEN

Simulation, Realism, and the Study of the Jury

NORBERT L. KERR
ROBERT M. BRAY

Over 20 years ago, rather early in the modern era of psycholegal scholarship (Ogloff, 2000), we published two articles (Bray & Kerr, 1979, 1982) that considered the utility of experimental simulations for the study of jury behavior. These articles represented our response to a growing drumbeat of criticism of such jury simulation research. The major themes of this criticism were (1) that typical jury simulations were highly artificial, (2) that the nature of these artificialities called into serious question the ecological validity of such studies, (3) that field research on juries was likely to be much more informative and ecologically valid than simulation research, and (4) that if experimental jury simulations were to be employed at all, they must achieve a much higher level of verisimilitude. (Similar criticisms can be, and were, raised in other areas of psycholegal research, such as eyewitness performance and child testimony.) Our view then was that although this criticism raised some valid concerns, those concerns were far too sweeping, had little theoretical or empirical foundation, failed to reflect a proper appreciation for the trade-offs inherent in any choice of method, and could, if widely influential, deprive the nascent field of psycholegal studies of one of its most powerful methodological tools.

Now, over two decades later, these same methodological issues are still being discussed and debated (e.g., Bornstein, 1999; Diamond, 1997)—which is, no doubt, why the editors of this volume invited us to prepare the present chapter that attempts both to reiterate many of our original arguments[1] for a new generation of scholars and, when appropriate, to update them by incorporating relevant research and commentary from the past two decades. Our hope now, as it was back then, is that our arguments may contribute to a fuller discussion and appreciation of the advantages and disadvantages of all available methods for the study of human behavior in legal settings.

METHODOLOGY, VALIDITY, AND UTILITY

Behavioral research has been drawn on increasingly by the judiciary, courts, and law enforcement (e.g., Monahan, Walker, Kelly, & Monohan, 2001; Wells et al., 1998; Wrightsman, Greene, Nietzel, & Fortune, 2002). A recent four-volume work by Faigman, Kaye, Saks, and Sanders (2002), a comprehensive attempt to assemble current empirical evidence from scientific studies to assist the judiciary in making legal decisions, illustrates this trend. Clearly, the utility of such research depends, in good measure, upon the methods it uses. Hence, it is vital in interpreting the validity and utility of such research to understand the strengths and limitations of alternative research methodologies. In most of the extant research, particularly that on juror and jury behavior, experimental simulations have emerged as a common research method. Despite their popularity, such simulations have been the target of considerable criticism (Bermant, McGuire, McKinley, & Salo, 1974; Colasanto & Sanders, 1976; Diamond, 1997; Dillehay & Nietzel, 1980, 1981; Foss, 1975; Konečni & Ebbesen, 1979, 1991, 1992; Konečni, Mulcahy, & Ebbesen, 1980; Miller, Fontes, Boster, & Sunnafrank, 1983; Ogloff, 2000; Weiten & Diamond, 1979). Although such criticisms have raised important issues that deserve thoughtful consideration, we see a need for an analysis that identifies and balances the many strengths of the simulation methodology against its weaknesses. In this chapter, we discuss alternative methodologies for studying behavior in legal contexts, giving special attention to the use of laboratory experiments and simulations.

We begin by examining the range of procedures actually in use for juror/jury research, followed by a general consideration of laboratory, simulation, and field methodologies, coupled with an examination of their strengths and limitations. Special emphasis is given to the problem of establishing generality. In the next two sections of the chapter, we examine basic themes inherent in methodological criticisms of simulation studies and offer responses to those criticisms. Finally, we draw several conclusions and present some recommendations regarding the scientific study of behavior in legal contexts.

THE MOCK TRIAL: STATE OF THE ART

Because the simulated or mock trial is one of the most widely used research strategies in psycholegal research, and because it has, in particular, drawn considerable criticism, it is of some preliminary interest to describe the range of procedures employed within this method. In one set of analyses (Bray & Kerr,

1979, 1982), we considered published investigations of juror/jury behavior, the most active area of research in the psychology of the courtroom (cf. Ogloff, 1999, Table 4). We examined over 70 studies published during the preceding two decades. Although that overview was not exhaustive, it was substantial enough to be representative of the techniques used, both then and today (Bornstein, 1999).

Bray and Kerr (1979, 1982) classified the studies with respect to subject population (students, jurors from actual jury pools, others), research setting (classroom, laboratory, courtroom), mode of trial stimulus presentation (written fact summary, audiotaped reenactment, videotaped reenactment, live presentation), trial elements that were included (voir dire, opening statements, witness testimony, closing arguments, judge's instructions, and jury deliberation), dependent variables examined (dichotomous verdict, continuous guilt rating, sentence recommendation, damage award), and primary unit of analysis (individual juror vs. jury). The modal strategy (37.5%) in these studies was that of students responding to a written summary of the facts in an experimental laboratory. Courtrooms were the setting for fewer than 20% of the studies. The written (54%) and audiotaped (29%) modes of presentation were the most popular, by far. Furthermore, jury deliberations were routinely omitted (in 48% of the studies), but even when deliberation was included, researchers frequently did not use group data in their analyses. The jury appeared as the unit of analysis (always along with individual jurors) only 28.8% of the time. Examination of the dependent variables showed (1) that dichotomous guilt scales and continuous guilt scales were each used in about half of all studies, (2) that sentence recommendations were collected somewhat less often (43% of all studies), and (3) that analysis of interaction among jurors was fairly rare (less than 10% of studies).

More recently, Bornstein (1999) has performed a similar analysis focusing on the 113 simulation studies published during the first 20 years of *Law and Human Behavior* (L&HB; 1977–1996), which covers most of the period since the Bray and Kerr (1979) piece. In this sample of studies, nearly two-thirds (i.e., 65%) used students as mock jurors and over half (i.e., 55%) used written trials. Bornstein also examined temporal trends over this period. Simulation studies represented an increasing share of L&HB's output during this period (rising, roughly, from about 10% at the journal's inception to about 20% two decades later). Likewise, examination of simulation studies showed that the percentage using relatively artificial subject populations (e.g., students) and stimulus materials (e.g., written summaries or transcripts) has also tended to increase over the past two decades.

Thus, although a few jury experiments have been quite "realistic" (e.g., live presentation in a courtroom with jury-pool jurors; e.g., Borgida, DeBono, & Buckman, 1990; Miller et al., 1975), most of the studies examined by Bray and Kerr and by Bornstein appear to be quite "unrealistic" (e.g., students responding to a written summary in the classroom or laboratory), and the clear trend has been for fewer rather than more realistic simulations. When consid-

ering other topics in psycholegal research, this same range of procedures—
from the highly artificial (i.e., laboratory) to the highly realistic (i.e., field)—is
also evident. Some topics place even greater reliance on artificial methods
(e.g., eyewitness testimony, witness credibility) than observed in the jury literature, whereas other topics place greater emphasis on the field methods (e.g.,
judges' and attorneys' behavior, courtroom innovation).

In general, it seems that when behavior is largely governed by formal legal rules, procedures, or strong social norms, or enacted by actors with extensive legal experience, then research tends to rely less on artificial laboratory or
simulation methods and more on field methods. For example, judges' behavior may more often be studied in the field, because in laboratory or simulated
conditions judges may be inclined to give responses in line with legal and social norms about how they are supposed to make judgments. In contrast,
when there are few formal rules that specify behavioral expectations, when
the actors within the legal system are laypersons without extensive legal
knowledge or experience (e.g., witnesses, eyewitnesses, jurors), and when
there are few theoretical reasons to doubt the external validity of experimental
findings (e.g., there is little reason to suspect that drastically different processes will operate in a study of eyewitness reliability posed as a memory task
in the laboratory or classroom vs. as an eyewitness task at an actual crime),
then more highly controlled and hence artificial methods are more often employed.

LABORATORY EXPERIMENTS VERSUS
SIMULATIONS VERSUS FIELD STUDIES

As we have discussed, simulation and laboratory experiments are widely used
research strategies in the study of jury behavior as well as in the study of the
behavior of other courtroom participants. Although not nearly as prevalent,
many field studies and experiments have also been conducted. In fact, field research is generally the corrective preferred by critics of simulation and laboratory research. In this section, we contrast the simulation strategy with its most
commonly proposed alternative, the field study. Then we consider the advantages of laboratory research and "unrealistic" simulations to understand
better why they have been so widely used. We conclude by addressing the major limitation of nonfield research: the problem of establishing generality.

First, however, it is useful to draw some broad distinctions among the
simulation, laboratory, and field methods of research. In an experimental simulation, according to Runkel and McGrath (1972), the researcher seeks to
construct a behavior setting that mirrors, in certain respects, some naturally
occurring behavior system (e.g., the jury system). Thus, a simulation attempts
to capture the essential features of a specific, existing behavioral system. This
methodology contrasts with the laboratory experiment, which is concerned
with a generic or abstract class of systems that are deliberately isolated from

any particular behavioral system. For example, a jury simulation might study the influence of defendant attractiveness on judgments of guilt or innocence. A laboratory experiment, in contrast, would be more concerned with the general processes of making judgments (perhaps on a variety of dimensions) about others as a function of their attractiveness (regardless of the particular setting).

The most popular alternative research strategy to simulations and experiments is the field study, in which the systematic observation of behavior takes place in a naturally occurring behavior system (as opposed to the artificial ones created for the experiment or simulation). In the present discussion, by *field studies* we mean any form of systematic observation of the behavior of actual participants in a legal context (e.g., actual jurors in a courtroom). Thus, we include direct in-court observations, postdeliberation interviews with jurors, analyses of court records or archives, and so on. By realistic experimental simulations, we mean those that closely reconstruct the actual behavior setting. For example, a model realistic simulation of the jury task would draw its participants from actual jury rolls and would present an entire actual case using live actors (or actual judges, lawyers, etc.) in a courtroom setting. Furthermore, it would collect group verdicts after a deliberation period largely unconstrained by time limitations, from a jury that believed its verdict would have real consequences for the defendant. (The studies by Brekke, Enko, Clavet, & Sellau, 1991; Diamond, Casper, Heiert, & Marshall, 1996; and Miller et al., 1975, include many aspects of such a realistic simulation.)

Each of these research strategies has particular strengths and limitations (for detailed discussions, see Runkel & McGrath, 1972, Chapter 4; McGrath, 1982). Unfortunately, a strength of one strategy is often a limitation of another. Regardless of which method is used, researchers always face dilemmas in that they cannot (in a given study) simultaneously maximize (1) realism (i.e., the concreteness of the behavioral system), (2) precision of control and measurement, and (3) generality over actors, behaviors, and situations. A decision to strengthen one feature (e.g., precision of control or measurement) by the adoption of a particular strategy (e.g., using a laboratory experiment) invariably weakens one or both of the other features.

Advantages of Experiments and Simulations

Advantages of Experimental Simulations over Field Studies

The advantages of experimental simulations over field studies are both methodological and practical. Methodological advantages are the familiar ones implied by the term *experimental control*. Foremost among these is the ability to obtain unconfounded replications (cf. Strodtbeck, 1962). Since no two actual trials are exactly alike, each courtroom behavior is a response to a unique and highly complex stimulus. A comparison of the outcomes of pairs (or sets) of trials that are demonstrably different on some variable of interest is constantly plagued by the strong likelihood that they also differ on some other variables as well. For example, one study that compared the sentences received by black and white defendants (Bullock, 1961) seemed to show that blacks received longer sentences than whites for interracial crimes. Another study (Green, 1964), however, suggested that these effects may have been attributable to differences in the prior criminal history of the defendants and the seriousness and repetitiveness of their criminal act, and not to the defendant's race, per se. Usually it is possible to guess at the existence of some such confounding variables, but we can rarely anticipate, control, and/or measure all of them. Thus, establishing empirical relationships with a high degree of confidence is much more challenging in field studies. In the experimental simulation, however, researchers can exercise more control and construct trial elements so that they differ only on the variable(s) of interest.

A related methodological advantage of simulations is the ability to perform multiple replications using the same trial stimulus materials. The same simulated case can be shown to many jurors or juries, whereas it is possible to observe the response of only one single jury to any unique actual trial. By performing multiple replications, the effects of extraneous subject characteristic variables (e.g., juror personality variables) can be removed through random assignment and, at the same time, the reliability of observed differences can be statistically assessed.

Another familiar advantage of the experimental method is the ability to establish causal relationships. By comparing experimental conditions whose only differences are created by the experimenter prior to the performance of the behavior of interest, we can conclude with some confidence that these created differences caused any obtained behavioral differences. In theory, of course, it is possible to manipulate factors of interest within the courtroom setting (i.e., to do field experiments on courtroom behavior or bring the laboratory into the courtroom). In practice, however, there may be many serious legal, ethical, and practical barriers. For example, the constitutional requirement of equal protection under the law may require an equal treatment of defendants that would prohibit experimentation on many procedural questions. Furthermore, the courts have their own traditional methods of analysis and evaluation, which are not, by and large, experimental in nature. Thus, policymakers whose cooperation would be essential for field experimentation in the courts (e.g., judges, legislators, lawyers) are often neither familiar with, nor reliant upon, the experimental method of analysis.

Even when it is possible to win the active cooperation of the court and avoid serious ethical difficulties, a variety of thorny problems still exists. For example, adequate experimental control may be compromised in unpredictable and uncontrollable ways; organizational procedures may come into conflict with experimental requirements; decision makers may exercise discretionary powers in selective or arbitrary ways; or court leadership or cooperativeness may change in the middle of the experiment. (For a description of an attempted field experiment on sentencing, which provides an excellent illustration of the difficulty of field experimentation, even under ideal conditions, see Ross & Blumenthal, 1975.) Although such problems are daunting, they are not, in principle, insurmountable (see Heuer & Penrod, 1988, 1994a, 1994b, or Hannaford, Hans, & Munsterman, 2000, for ambitious attempts to overcome such obstacles). The problem of multiple confounds in field research can often be dealt with, in part, through sophisticated methods of analysis (e.g., multiple partial correlations). Only rarely and indirectly (e.g., by the use of cross-lag panel correlation techniques, structural equation models, and longitudinal designs) can field data be analyzed to establish causal relationships, and even then, such inferences are usually inconclusive.

A final important aspect of the utility of experimental control is the investigator's greater ability to observe in the context of experimental simulation. Many interesting aspects of actual jurors' behavior are inaccessible to observation. Jurors may not discuss their opinions of the case during a trial, and jury deliberations are—both by tradition and by law—also secret. Attempts to question jurors directly during a trial or to secretly observe their deliberations would be both illegal and unethical. One notorious attempt to tape-record jury deliberations clandestinely (Strodtbeck, 1962) precipitated a storm of protest and a federal law barring such observation. Other topics for which simulations afford greater ability to observe than does the actual setting include plea bargaining (e.g., to examine the impact of alternate strategies), fairness of lineups (e.g., to see what variables are related to selection bias), and eyewitness behavior (e.g., to determine the factors that limit accuracy).

Several less direct methods of assessment have been applied with some degree of success. These include conducting posttrial interviews with trial participants (e.g., Broeder, 1959), asking some knowledgeable participants what they think influenced the behavior of other participants (e.g., Heuer & Penrod, 1994a, and Kalven & Zeisel, 1966, both of whom surveyed judges' inferences about jury behavior), correlating observations of in-court behavior (e.g., Kerr, 1981, who examined relationships between attorney and judge in-court behaviors and jury verdicts), and archival analyses (e.g., Dillehay & Nietzel, 1981; Kerr, Harmon, & Graves, 1982; Konečni & Ebbesen, 1979). However, each of these methods is typically subject to serious difficulties of measurement reliability and validity. For example, posttrial interviews with jurors run several risks: (1) Jurors may forget or distort their recollection of their predeliberation opinions and jury deliberations; (2) jurors' conclusions about other jurors' motives are usually subjective inferences based on fragmentary information; and (3) judges' inferences of the basis for a jury's verdict (e.g., Kalven & Zeisel, 1966) are probably based on even less information.

In contrast to these drawbacks, the experimental simulation permits systematic examination of any private or public behavior of interest. One may not only observe the product of individual and group judgment but also examine the processes of individual and group decision making that lead to those judgments. These factors are particularly crucial when attempting to competitively test theories of individual or group decision making.

In addition to the methodological problems we have been considering, there are also practical drawbacks to field studies. All of the field study methods mentioned above tend to be fairly costly. Archives are often inaccessible and are rarely organized in ways that yield the desired data without laborious and expensive distillation; comprehensive in-court observation is difficult and time consuming; courtroom participants may be hard to contact, set meetings with, and interview; and working with expert observers (e.g., judges or lawyers) can also be expensive (e.g., in terms of the time to cultivate contacts). Because the complexity of real trials produces so much "noise," field studies may require many more observations than experimental simulations to detect a "signal" (i.e., a relationship of interest). After initial laboratory setup costs, the experimental simulation tends to have a far lower cost per replication.

Advantages of "Unrealistic" Simulations/Laboratory Studies over More "Realistic" Simulations

The foregoing discussion focused on the advantages of an experimental over a field methodology. However, even if we are convinced of the merits of an experimental approach, we may still question why an experimental simulation should, or should not, be "realistic." Whereas the most compelling reasons for choosing an experimental over a field strategy are methodological ones, the popularity of "unrealistic" simulations and laboratory experiments derives more from practical considerations.

The key practical considerations are research costs and ethics. For example, the ready accessibility of a student population to academicians often governs the choice of participants. The expense of using samples more representative of actual jurors may be prohibitive for many investigators. Likewise, the widespread use of classrooms or laboratory rooms instead of actual or simulated courtrooms is attributable to their greater accessibility and lower cost. Highly artificial stimuli (e.g., written case summaries, staged crimes for eyewitnesses) are chosen for similar reasons. The equipment, production, and personnel costs of stimulus preparation and presentation usually increase rapidly as we move from more to less artificial modes of stimulus presentation (e.g., written to audiotaped to videotaped to live trial enactments). The brevity of most simulated case materials may be traced to the costs of producing lengthy trials and of having participants sit through them. If groups (e.g., judicial panels, juries rather than individual jurors) are used as experimental replicates, the cost per replicate increases by a factor of n (i.e., group size) at the minimum; these costs are further inflated by the additional expenses of scheduling groups and by participant no-shows (when fewer than n subjects appear at an experimental session). Finally, we can lead participants to believe that their decisions will have real consequences, but the deception required must be thorough and elaborate, especially for student participants familiar with experimental deception (cf. Kerr, Nerenz, & Herrick, 1979; Miller et al., 1983). In addition to the material costs of such a deception, many significant ethical questions may be raised by the use of what is likely to be an elaborate deception about a personally significant behavior for the participant (e.g., see Elwork & Sales, 1980; Kelman, 1967).

In addition to these practical and ethical considerations, there are also several good methodological reasons to prefer relatively unrealistic simulations. Consider, for example, stimulus mode. The most realistic mode of stimulus presentation, a live trial, can never be replicated exactly. Like a stage play, a live trial simulation can vary from performance to performance, conceivably in ways that may alter the behavior under study. We could have all participants attend a single live presentation, but this approach still has problems that the use of recorded trials can avoid. For example, even with this procedure, the live trial can never be reproduced by the same or different experimenters hoping to replicate or extend the original findings. Furthermore, the presence at a trial of large numbers of jurors or juries can create another kind of artificiality with potentially important effects (Kerr et al., 1979).

Another reason to use abbreviated transcripts or case summaries is to increase the prominence and, hence, the impact of an experimental treatment. The less complex and lengthy the case materials are, the more sharply the independent variables will typically stand out (Baumeister & Darley, 1982; Linz & Penrod, 1982). This consequence is particularly desirable when the primary research objectives are to demonstrate whether some variable *can* have an effect or to test a hypothesis of a psychological theory or model. Whereas we suggest that this can be an asset, others count it as a liability. We return to this issue when we discuss reactions to simulation research.

Judgments other than, or in addition to, those normally made in a real trial (e.g., sentencing recommendations or probability of guilt judgments from mock jurors) are commonly collected for several methodological reasons:

1. The statistical analysis of dichotomous dependent variables can present difficulties (although log-linear models have made this less problematic).
2. Multivalued or continuous response scales should, in general, be more sensitive than simple dichotomous ones (cf. Diamond, 1997).
3. Some theory-guided research has sought to test hypotheses framed in terms of conceptual variables (e.g., punitiveness), for which several operationalizations are reasonable.

Of course, the unit of analysis should be dictated by the purpose of the research. Naturally, individual mock jurors rather than juries have been studied where theories of individual juror decision making are being tested (e.g., Hastie, 1993; Thomas & Hogue, 1976). Finally, for some situations the use of an unrepresentative population for respondents may be preferred over the use of a more representative population (e.g., college students rather than actual jury panel members). This preference may be the case, for example, when one participant population has greater familiarity or facility with experimental stimuli or response instruments. Students, for example, may show greater comprehension and reading speed than a more representative participant sample.

Summary

In summary, there are a number of practical and methodological reasons for the use of simulations instead of field studies and for the greater popularity of laboratory experiments and/or unrealistic simulations over more realistic simulations. The practical advantages are primarily associated with available resources and research costs in securing participants, stimulus materials, facilities, and the like. Methodological advantages include the ability to obtain unconfounded and multiple replications, to effect precision and control in establishing causal relationships, to more thoroughly observe all individual and group behaviors of interest, to increase the impact of explanatory variables, and to use measures maximally sensitive to statistical methods.

Disadvantages of Experiments and Simulations: Establishing Generality

The main limitation of experiments and simulations is the extent to which results obtained using these methods are generalizable to the behaviors of interest in actual legal contexts. If generalizability is sufficiently poor, the control and affordability of these methods could be purchased at too high a price (at least, for some purposes). This issue leads us to consider just how we can establish the generality of any research finding.

A familiar distinction, proposed by Campbell (1957), is a useful one for the present discussion. He suggested that there are two fundamental problems with drawing inferences from experimental studies. The first problem is establishing that the effects observed in the experiment can be attributed, with confidence, to the experimental treatment. The more firmly this link is established, the greater the *internal validity* of the study. We can specify many threats to internal validity, such as variables confounded with the experimental treatment (Campbell & Stanley, 1966), procedural or instructional artifacts, experimental demand characteristics (Orne, 1962), experimenter effects (Rosenthal, 1964), and so on. A quite separate problem is establishing that the effects observed in an experiment are generalizable beyond the particular conditions of that experiment. The more broadly the results generalize, the greater the *external validity* of the study. Although these two kinds of validity are conceptually distinct, they are not wholly independent of one another. An experiment must have high internal validity to have high external validity. As Carlsmith, Ellsworth, and Aronson (1976) state, "If random or systematic error makes it impossible for the experimenter to draw any conclusions from the experiment, the question of the *generality* of these conclusions never arises" (p. 85, emphasis in original). On the other hand, high internal validity is never sufficient to establish high external validity; there may be a genuine effect that occurs only under the particular conditions of the experiment (see Cook & Campbell, 1979, for an expanded discussion of these distinctions). The issue presently at hand is how to establish the external validity of psycholegal research that uses experimental and simulation methods. Our discussion draws extensively from Runkel and McGrath (1972).

Runkel and McGrath conceptualized the science of behavior as dealing with *actors* who engage in *behavior toward an object* in a *context*. This view suggests that researchers must be concerned with generality in (at least) three forms. The first is the concern with generality over actors, that is, with the range of people over whom results will recur. For example, we need to be concerned that the results found with college student mock jurors will also occur in the general population of actual jurors and juries. The second is the concern with the generality over variations in the particulars of experimental treatment and measurement. For example, will the physical attractiveness of a defendant in a live trial have a similar effect to that of a photographed defendant in a written trial summary? In this category we might also include questions concerning variation over the type of response (e.g., dichotomous verdicts vs. continuous ratings of guilt vs. sentences) and the consequentiality of the response to the participant. Finally, researchers need to be concerned with the extent of generality across contexts or settings. For example, will a phenomenon that is observed in a university classroom also occur in a criminal courtroom?

Before specifying ways to establish generality across actors, behaviors, and contexts, two fundamental points should be made. They are obvious, perhaps, but frequently seem to be overlooked in evaluations of experimental and simulation research. The first point is that we can firmly establish that a result will, or will not, generalize from one investigated set of conditions (e.g., an experimental jury simulation) to another, new set of conditions (e.g., an actual trial situation) only by investigating the phenomenon in question under the new conditions. In other words, external validity ultimately must be established empirically. The second point is that high external validity cannot be established within the confines of a single study. Since any study is necessarily carried out under particular conditions (i.e., actors, contexts, and behaviors toward objects), we can assume with confidence that its results hold only under those particular conditions. Runkel and McGrath (1972) made these points in the following way:

> Any single study, even the most grandly planned, can yield only a very limited degree of external validity. If, in an initial study, we obtain a substantial and interesting finding within an internally valid experiment, we can be proud of having composed a hypothesis that predicted the fall of the data. However, our finding cannot have any practical influence on the wider world until this first study is followed by other studies that explore the range of treatments, . . . measurements, . . . and actors over which the obtained results will hold.

. . . Only after we have demonstrated that the effect holds over a range of variations in treatments, observations, and actors can we begin to have confidence that it will hold in other cases under conditions not yet tested. And even then, we cannot know with certainty that it will hold under any given set of not-yet-tested conditions. (pp. 46–47)

This second point warrants some discussion. It is (contrary to some suggestions; cf. Konečni & Ebbesen, 1992) wholly impractical to empirically test the generality of an effect over all conceivable conditions of interest. Strictly speaking, since no two observations are exactly alike, it is impossible to test, in principle. Such certainty is precluded by the inductive nature of scientific reasoning. We can never be absolutely certain that a result will generalize to new conditions (or even, for that matter, recur under conditions as unchanging as we can make them), although we can take steps to increase our confidence that it will.

There are at least two ways to increase our confidence in a result's external validity within the confines of a single study. The first approach is to increase the diversity of the populations of actors, contexts, and behaviors toward objects from which an investigator randomly samples. For example, instead of using a single criminal case, as is the norm in experimental jury simulations, a random sample of such cases could be used. Obtaining comparable results across cases would increase our confidence that the results were not case specific. We are not justified in assuming that the observed effects will be identical or even similar for all of the cases in the sample or population. By random sampling of cases (or subjects, treatments, etc.), we estimate only the "average" response for the entire population of cases. The second approach is to vary the actor, context, or behavior toward objects systematically within the study, rather than permitting them to vary unsystematically. For example, we might include a case factor with several levels (e.g., rape, murder, robbery, and burglary) as a variable in the experimental design. If the same effect occurred with each type of case, the external validity of the result would be increased; if not, then something about the limits of generalization might be learned.

Despite the utility of these methods for increasing a study's external validity, both require more resources. Increasing the diversity of actors, contexts, or behaviors toward objects in a study also increases the error variation and hence reduces the power of the study's tests. The power can be restored, but only by increasing the number of observations and, hence, the cost. Likewise, for any particular total sample size, the more design factors included, the lower the number of observations per experimental treatment, and the lower the power of the experiment to detect effects. Thus, increases in external validity of a study may be purchased at the cost of the study's power to detect any effects at all. We are not suggesting that studies with more costly designs should be avoided (e.g., simulations, field experiments, naturalistic field studies, probability-based population surveys); indeed, they should not be avoided and may be critical for establishing some aspects of external validity. We are simply pointing out that these approaches to increasing external validity can be very costly.

Of course, researchers need not, or rarely do, attempt to establish a result's external validity within the confines of a single study. Rather, normally a systematically planned series of studies would be carried out. Consider an example of the relationship between a criminal defendant's physical attractiveness and the punitiveness of jurors established in an experiment or unrealistic simulation (e.g., Efran, 1974; Lieberman, 2002; Sigall & Ostrove, 1975). A first step in external validation might be an attempt to replicate the findings using a longer videotaped trial, mock juries instead of mock jurors, and participants solicited from current jury rolls. This step might be followed (or preceded) by a field study to test for an association between actual defendants' attractiveness and jury verdicts. The results of such a series of investigations would provide the data needed to assess the limits of external validity. Unfortunately, the cost considerations that militate against "grandly planned" single studies have also discouraged this kind of systematic work among those interested in jury behavior. Other important factors are many investigators' theoretical (rather than applied) interests and a widespread and unfortunate attitude that because such external validation research lacks originality, it also lacks value (Neuliep & Crandall, 1990, 1993). Consequently, few investigators have made attempts at external validation (for exceptions to this rule, see Ebbesen & Konečni, 1975; Hans & Lofquist, 1992).

Given that research in this area can be very costly (particularly field studies or highly realistic simulation research), it seems evident that only the most important simulation research findings could be externally validated in anywhere near a thorough fashion. What, then, besides our intuition is to guide us in judging how complete or accurate an understanding of actual courtroom behavior is provided by the experimental and simulation literature? One general principle is that the more similar two situations (i.e., actors behaving toward objects in a context) are, the more likely it is that results obtained in one will also be obtained in the other. This principle lies at the heart of the frequently heard exhortations that more realistic simulations be used in jury research. (As noted more fully below, we should keep in mind that apparent similarity is neither a sufficient nor a necessary condition for the generality of a result.)

Another springboard for the inferential leap from examined to unexamined conditions is psychological theory (see Davis, 1980). It is often possible to extend a well-validated theory or model to as yet unstudied or practically unexaminable conditions. Psychological or other theory can also suggest limitations on the external validity of a result. One concrete illustration is the research on jury size using J. H. Davis's (1973) social decision scheme model. Application of this model involves specifying a combinatorial function or *social decision scheme* that summarizes a group's (e.g., a jury's) movement from disagreement to consensus. A number of studies have suggested that some kind of high-order majority decision scheme can fairly well account for the distribution of student mock juries' verdicts (Stasser, Kerr, & Davis, 1989). This type of decision scheme has direct implications for the effect on verdicts of changing jury size. For example, it has been shown (Davis, Kerr, Atkin, Holt, & Meek, 1975) that if juries operate under such decision schemes, permissible variation in jury size between 6 and 12 members (*Ballew v. Georgia*, 1978; *Johnson v. Louisiana*, 1972) should have only very small effects on jury verdicts. Furthermore, the model predicts that the effect of jury size should depend on such factors as the strength of the prosecution and defense cases. Of course, theoretical predictions of this sort must make several assumptions, the most central of which is the validity and generality of the theory itself. Before we can confidently pursue the predictions of the theory, its predictive power must be demonstrated. In the case of the social decision scheme model, we are encouraged by the number and consistency of its findings, corroborative results from jury field research (Kalven & Zeisel, 1966, Chapter 38), and the confirmation of some of its predictions in experimental studies (e.g., Kerr & MacCoun, 1985; Kerr, Niedermeier, & Kaplan, 1999; Myers & Kaplan, 1976).

Summary

Attempts to establish generality or external validity presume that the research of interest is internally sound or valid (i.e., results are attributable to experimental treatments rather than to uncontrolled or confounding factors). External validity must be demonstrated empirically, in the final analysis, through a series of carefully conducted studies that demonstrate generality across actors, contexts, and behaviors; it cannot be established by any single study's use of particular actors, contexts, and behaviors. Nonetheless, we can increase our confidence in the generality of any single study's findings by (1) sampling a diverse set of actors, contexts, and behaviors toward objects, and/or (2) systematically incorporating the variation of actors, contexts, and behaviors into the experimental design rather than letting them vary randomly. Such elaborations of a study, however, are often constrained by cost considerations. An alternate and more favored approach to establishing generality is to conduct a series of carefully planned studies that collectively provide data that determine the limits of generalizability. Regrettably, the high costs of such a research program often limit the number of issues that will be thoroughly assessed. When systematic data are unavailable, a well-validated theory may provide useful information about the likelihood and limits of the external validity of research findings.

BASIC THEMES IN CRITICISMS OF SIMULATION RESEARCH

With few exceptions (e.g., Kaplan, 1977; Kerr, 1994; Sigall & Ostrove, 1975; Studebaker et al., 2002), most of those who have evaluated the experimental simulation methodology for the study of the psychology of the courtroom have been highly critical of it. In this section we outline the most common themes running through this criticism; in the next section we discuss some of the key assumptions and implications of these themes. We focus on methodological criticisms and omit discussion of another common criticism (e.g., Konečni & Ebbesen, 1992; Ogloff, 1999): that psycholegal research has been excessively preoccupied with certain topics (i.e., juror/jury behavior and eyewitness behavior).

Experiments and Simulations Tell Us Little about Actual Courtroom Behavior

The artificiality of most laboratory experiments and experimental simulations has led many observers to argue that the findings of this literature are of limited or no value in describing or understanding actual behavior in the courtroom. For example, Miller et al. (1983), in discussing the common use of student mock jurors, state that "researchers should stop deluding themselves with the wishful thought that the exclusive reliance on the species, *akademia moros*, will yield empirical generalizations which will meet the predictive tests of the [judicial] marketplace" (p. 38). Likewise, in their discussion on the common use of brief, nondetailed case materials, Miller et al. (1983) conclude that "it may well be an act of scientific and social folly to read much practical import into the findings of such truncated simplified studies" (p. 42). Some writers question the utility of simulation research because subjects are often asked to play the role of trial participants. Dillehay and Nietzel (1980), for example, note that

> in the experimental research on jurors/juries, subjects are sometimes asked to behave "as if" they were real jurors. This is role playing research. As a method it has generated a share of debate . . . and generally appears to be inadequate to the task of understanding real juries. (p. 250)

Similarly, Weiten and Diamond (1979), in critiquing the jury simulation paradigm, note:

> In jury simulations, subjects are asked to speculate about how they would behave *if they were real jurors*. Thus role-playing represents the very essence of the jury simulation paradigm. Yet, role-playing has been the target of much criticism, . . . which has questioned the premise that subjects can predict with substantial accuracy how they would behave in various situations. (p. 81, emphasis in original)

Such reservations about typical simulation research are fairly representative of social scientists who have criticized this methodology. The skepticism that characterizes these critics, who are well versed in research methodology, often becomes outright dismissal among those less grounded in the social sciences. For example, Justice Powell of the Supreme Court asserted in *Ballew v. Georgia* (1978) that the many studies of jury size (for a review, see Lempert, 1975) "merely represent the unexamined findings of persons interested in the jury system" (p. 246). (For similar reactions by judges in other court cases, see Ellsworth, 1988; Thompson, 1989.)

Typical Simulation Treatments Are Worthless or Misleading

Several observers (e.g., Colasanto & Sanders, 1976; Dillehay & Nietzel, 1981; Elwork & Sales, 1980) have pointed out that experimental treatments sometimes fail to recognize legal realities. For example, some researchers have examined the effects of types of evidence that are excluded from actual trials by the rules of evidence (e.g., see critiques of the Landy & Aronson, 1969, study by Colasanto & Sanders, 1976, and Dillehay & Nietzel, 1981), and many researchers have collected sentences from mock jurors—a judgment that few actual noncapital juries make.

A second complaint is that the experiment's independent variable is often more prominent in the simulation than in actual trials, either because the accompanying trial materials are very abbreviated or because the independent variable is accentuated in an unrepresentative fashion. This situation causes concern for several reasons. It has been asserted that studies with unduly prominent treatments may well arouse strong demand characteristics (i.e., provide clues that allow participants to infer the hypothesis or purpose of the study), especially if their participants are experimentally sophisticated (Miller et al., 1983). Jurors' evaluation of the independent variable might also be altered, qualitatively or quantitatively, by the complexity and content of the context within which it is presented (Miller et al., 1983). Therefore, an effect obtained within one bare-bones context might not obtain or might be altered in a more complicated context.

Finally, when the experimental treatment is highly prominent, the effect it produces on behavior may be much stronger than the effect it would have in actual trials, either because the variable does not show as much variation in actual trials or because the manipulation constitutes a disproportionate share of the total stimulus in the simulation (see Colasanto & Sanders, 1976; Konečni et al., 1980; Miller et al., 1983). The basic thrust of this argument is that the proportion of behavioral variance accounted for by the experimental treatment may not accurately estimate the proportion of variance this variable accounts for in actual courtroom behavior.

"Unrealistic" Simulations or Laboratory Experiments Are Inappropriate to Study Applied Questions

Several observers have suggested that because psycholegal research has an obvious potential for application, simulations or experiments that contain artificial elements are not appropriate research methods. At the heart of this argument is the premise that applied issues require different ways of choosing a problem and conducting research than are appropriate for basic research. For example, Miller et al. (1983) argue that "in an applied area such as juror behavior, research should aim for results which shed light on the consequences of various policy alternatives" (p. 2). Or, as an anonymous reviewer of one of our own jury simulation studies opined:

> [My] objection is the implicit assumption that one can understand complex, real-life events by doing laboratory research using "rigorous experimental control" and then "adding up" the results. This assumption is widely made among experimental social psychologists, and it may be appropriate for study of certain psychological "processes." But the raison d'etre of research on jury decision making is to understand better the behavior of actual jurors making decisions which will affect participants in court cases.

Interestingly, critics of the typical simulation differ on the "correct" method for doing "applied," "real-life" research. Some seem to favor field studies. As Konečni and Ebbesen (1992) express it, "In psycho-legal research, the first step should *always* be that the existence of a relationship . . . be established on real-world data by means of archival or observational research methods" (p. 420, emphasis added); they suggest that simulations can be useful subsequently, but only if they are "finely honed (in terms of the type of subjects, instructions given to them, method of presentation of stimuli, supposed consequences of the subject's decisions, and so on)" (p. 421) and all variables examined exhibit the same range of values observed originally in the field data.

Others, like Colasanto and Sanders (1976), seem to favor realistic simulations: "We hope to show that typical simulation methods do indeed greatly distort the laboratory findings, and that a clearer conception of how real juries decide may *only* be obtained through more realistic simulation and refined conceptualization" (p. 2, emphasis added). But all would probably agree with an anonymous reviewer who stated (in a review of one of our papers), "I think that the *minimum* starting point for research intended to be directly generalized to the real world is an experiment modeled after the 'actual' conditions" (emphasis added).

Some critics suggest that the method and type of research being conducted require certain matches. Dillehay and Nietzel (1981), for example, argue that experiments and simulations might be acceptable methods for research aimed at testing basic psychological theory (in which all reference to legal terms should be avoided) or for theory specific to the psychological and social processes of the courtroom (the bases of which are best derived from astute observation in actual courtrooms), but see little value in most mock trial research because it may not accomplish either of these. Furthermore, they suggest that experiments and simulations are unacceptable for applied research with policy implications. Similarly, Lind and Walker (1979) say that if a (presumably) general theory guides the research, then the closely controlled laboratory method is an acceptable and even necessary research strategy. Without such theory, they argue, realism is needed.

"Unrealistic" Simulations or Laboratory Experiments Should Not Be Conducted

A number of critics have prescribed the specific conditions under which experiments or simulation methods can provide useful information. For example, Miller et al. (1983) advance the following methodological caveat: "If trial simulations are to provide much practical guidance concerning juror behavior, they should use persons whose demographic characteristics and perceptual and attitudinal sets approximate those of actual venirepersons" (p. 38). Miller et al. also advise that simulations should be "conducted under informational and presentational conditions closely approximating the actual courtroom trial" (p. 42).

Different critics identify different features as essential to a sufficiently realistic simulation. For example, Colasanto and Sanders (1976) emphasize the importance of deliberations in studying juries: "Our feeling is that having a deliberation is by far the most crucial consideration in the design of a jury simulation (beyond the obvious necessity of a proper simulation)" (p. 31). Weiten and Diamond (1979) indicate that "insofar as future researchers are interested in the generalizability of their findings, they should procure more representative samples, employ more realistic trial simulations such as lengthy and complex audio and videotaped trials, and focus more on collective verdicts arrived at by deliberating juries" (p. 83). Most critics would probably agree with Colasanto and Sanders (1976) that unrealistic simulations are proscribed:

> If researchers are going to try to exert influence in areas outside of social psychological theory, they must begin to conduct their research more responsibly and be aware of the requirements of external validity before making broad generalizations from their results. If this research is to be done, it must be done *correctly*. (p. 32, emphasis added)

Unrealistic Research Is Unpersuasive to the Target Consumers for Psycholegal Research

Although some psycholegal research is purely basic research, much of it is undertaken to inform and influence real legal institutions and actors. Another recent theme in the criticism of simulation research is that—regardless of its internal validity, regardless of what theory and data currently might suggest about ecological validity—legal policymakers (e.g., appellate judges, legislators, court administrators) will require very high verisimilitude in such research before they will accept and apply any of its findings. Diamond (1997) notes that

> even if researchers are prepared to believe that simulation findings provide valuable insights about jury behavior, courts need not agree with that evaluation. . . . Are courts skeptical about the weight they should give simulation research? Absolutely. (pp. 566, 568)

Similarly, Studebaker et al. (2002) note that

> unfortunately, . . . the verisimilitude of research conditions is often used as a proxy for external validity by both researchers and other decision makers. . . . Although research low in verisimilitude may be high in external validity, when social science research is proffered in court, low verisimilitude can provide the court with a ready justification for dismissing the research, especially when there is little data concerning external validity. . . . The courts tend (rightly or wrongly) to discount research that does not approximate real-world conditions. (pp. 21, 23)

The moral of this story, for many, is that high verisimilitude may be a necessary (although not a sufficient) condition for psycholegal work to have real impact in the courts.

ASSUMPTIONS AND IMPLICATIONS OF CRITICISMS

The themes we have outlined above run through much of the critical discussions of simulation methods. They all share a single implication that discourages the use of laboratory research or nonrealistic simulations, at least as they are typically conducted. From personal experience, we also know that these themes are often overriding concerns of journal editors, journal reviewers, and the members of advisory panels to funding agencies. Thus, they represent more than considerations in individual investigators' choice of research method; they may fundamentally affect the funding and dissemination of research in this area. Hence, these themes deserve careful scrutiny and evaluation. We now examine what we perceive to be the key questions arising from these themes.

Does Low Realism Necessarily Equate with Low External or Ecological Validity?

As our overview of the existing literature has documented, the usual jury simulation study is different from an actual courtroom trial in many ways. Many critics of the simulation method conclude that these differences make generalization impossible. Some critics are bothered by the large number of differences, whereas others argue that any differences make generalization impermissible. In one sense they are correct, since, as noted previously, a study's results are always conditional on the particular choice of actors, contexts, and behaviors toward objects. But some of the critics go one step further. They imply that the very existence of such differences makes it implausible or impossible that results will generalize. They fail to recognize that identifying such differences only *raises* the question of generalizability; it does not *settle* the question.

There are, we think, two extreme positions that are often taken when it comes to making judgments about external validity. One position holds that results observed under one set of conditions *will* generalize to any other set of conditions unless there are clear empirical or theoretical reasons to the contrary. (It is this too sanguine viewpoint, we suspect, that many critics of simulation work see as rampant among those who conduct psycholegal experimental simulations; the critics think that such investigators too often make strong and unqualified recommendations for changes in legal policy based on little more than the results of those simulations.) Like most extreme positions, this one is hard to defend. Simple observation as well as the history of science give ample proof that there are nearly always boundary conditions on phenomena and that overhasty or overbroad generalization is perilous. This position is also subject to the "appeal to ignorance" logical fallacy (e.g., Gray, 1991): That is, it can make the *absence* of contradictory evidence (i.e., our ignorance of possible boundary conditions) affirmative evidence for generalization.

The other position holds that results obtained under one set of conditions can never be generalized to any other set of conditions until they have been well replicated under these new conditions. On its surface, this position looks more tenable, because for any important external validity question (e.g., will an anti-cancer drug that works on lab animals also work on humans?), a direct, empirical external validation will be attempted. But as a working set of assumptions, this view is no more defensible than the other extreme. Because no two sets of conditions (actors, contexts, behaviors) are strictly identical, researchers can never confidently generalize when taking this position. Scientific progress and useful application will require (cautious) inferential leaps from extant data to other conditions of interest. Requiring exhaustive replication under all possible conditions of interest is a prescription for paralysis. Moreover, this position is equally vulnerable to the appeal to ignorance fallacy. Here, our failure to directly examine generalization under some conditions is advanced as affirmative evidence for a result's lack of generality (for illustrations, see Konečni & Ebbesen, 1992).

As in many situations, the most viable position is likely to fall somewhere between these extremes. We must be very cautious about assuming external validity, particularly when much is at stake and direct, empirical validation is possible. On the other hand, such caution should not preclude tentative exploration of the broader implications of research results to conditions other than those under which they were first obtained. Nor should it preclude the use of any particular research method.

Is There Overreaction to an Apparent Lack of Realism?: The Case of "Role Playing"

In some instances the arguments raised against use of the unrealistic simulation turn out, on closer inspection, to be less serious than portrayed. A case in point is the criticism that jury simulations are not useful because subjects are merely role playing or anticipating how they might behave as jurors in a real trial (e.g., Dillehay & Nietzel, 1980; Weiten & Diamond, 1979). Since such expectations often turn out to be considerably different from actual behavior, the role-playing results are deemed questionable. (For example, in his classic studies on obedience, Milgram, 1965, found large discrepancies between subjects' estimates of how many individuals would administer the maximum level of shock to a learner and the number who did.)

One should, however, keep in mind the important distinction between active role playing and passive role playing (Mixon, 1977). In active role playing, the participants do more than passively speculate about how they might behave—they actively engage in the behavioral situation. As Krupat (1977) has noted:

> By having subjects actively participate in a situation, active role playing envelopes [sic] them in a set of circumstances which elicits the high degree of realism and spontaneity which critics have found missing in other role playing models. In active role playing subjects do not sit passively and predict what they might do in a situation that is selectively summarized and interpreted for them as in what Mixon calls role taking or non-active role playing. Rather, they actively participate, they "go to the moon." (p. 501)

Our own experience with mock jury research suggests that simulated jurors typically engage in active, rather than passive, role playing; they become highly involved and take their role as jurors very seriously. Simon (1967) has offered a similar observation: "The mock jurors became so involved in defending their own interpretation of the case and in convincing others of the correctness of their views that they forgot that their verdicts would have no practical significance" (p. 38). Of course, even though our experience with role-playing jurors has led us to feel more optimism than do many critics, this external validity question cannot and should not be settled by intuition; it must be demonstrated empirically (more on this below).

When Is Lack of Realism Important?: Conceptual Analysis

The question of external validity is not dissimilar to the problem of ruling out alternative explanations for an experimental result. We can, with a little thought, come up with alternatives to almost any explanation for a result (Kerr, 1998). But advocates of one explanation will not usually be equally concerned with every such alternative; rather, they will attempt to collect the data needed to rule out the most plausible alternatives to the proposed explanation. The point is that our confidence in the validity of alternative explanations rests on their *plausibility* and not their mere existence. In the same way, we can always identify differences (if only temporal) between any study and the settings to which we would hope to generalize its results. Without direct empirical evidence, our confidence in a result's external validity largely depends on whether it is plausible that such differences limit its generality, in the light of what else we know. When there are many differences, our confidence is lowered, just as our confidence in an explanation is lowered when there are many, instead of a few, alternative explanations. But even when there are many differences, we can still have some confidence that the result may generalize if existing theory and data erect few plausible obstructions.

Do existing theory and research plausibly suggest that any or all of the artificialities of the standard courtroom simulation limit its value for describing actual courtroom behavior? There is little doubt that college students often behave differently from the general adult population, that individual behavior often differs from group behavior, and so on. The null hypothesis is rarely, if ever, valid. But which of these differences represent plausible reasons to question the informativeness of the simulation's results? Or, as the title of this section asks, when is lack of realism important?

Some differences are much more important than others, in our judgment. To illustrate, let us imagine a simulation study that examines the effect of the defendant's physical attractiveness on mock jurors' verdicts. Furthermore, let us suppose we have here our generic "unrealistic" simulation: college students, reading brief, written trial summaries that include photos of the defendant, making individual judgments afterwards. Finally, let us assume, for the sake of argument, that there are no internal validity problems with the study. Suppose we find that the mock jurors are more likely to convict the unattractive than the attractive defendant. Now, the question is, what kind of difference between our unrealistic jurors' behavior and realistic mock or actual jurors' behavior would be important? That is, if we consider two factors—an independent variable (defendant attractiveness, in our example) and a "realism" factor (e.g., student vs. nonstudent subject population)—what effects of the latter factor limit our ability to generalize the effect of the independent variable observed under the "low-realism" conditions?

The first and least important difference would be if the "high-realism" participants were more (or less) likely to convict; that is, there could be a main effect on the "realness" factor. This effect would be least important because it would suggest that the jurors in both settings are reacting to attractiveness similarly, both qualitatively and quantitatively, although they do differ in their general evaluation of the case or perhaps in their criteria for reasonable doubt (Simon & Mahan, 1971).

The second and next most important difference might be a "realism ×amp; attractiveness" interaction, indicating that *attractiveness* and *acquittals* were positively related in both settings but that the relationship was stronger in one of the two settings. Here the relationship differs in degree but not in kind. The difference may suggest that attractiveness was manipulated more powerfully, that it was noticed more, or that there were other, more powerful factors operating in one of the settings. But the *way* the attractiveness information is used is apparently the same. Much of the research on the differences between individual and group decisions seems to follow this pattern (e.g., Kerr, MacCoun, & Kramer, 1996; more on this topic below).

A third kind of difference could be an interaction that shows an attractiveness effect for the unrealistic conditions but no effect for the more realistic ones (or vice versa). This difference might indicate that the attractiveness factor is salient in the one condition but not in the other. This type of outcome might be illustrated by Kerr's (1978) finding that the severity of the prescribed penalty affected verdicts but not judgments of the probability of guilt.

The fourth and most serious difference we might find is an interaction indicating that the jurors in the two settings differing in realism both react to attractiveness but in opposite ways. This difference is the most serious because it suggests that the attractiveness information may be evaluated and/or processed very differently in the two settings. For example, Konečni and Ebbesen (1979) observed a number of such crossover effects in their study of judges' sentencing decisions, which compared several different research methods. Results based on interviews, questionnaires, experimental simulations, and archival records suggested that a different overall pattern of factors influenced judges' sentencing decisions (although some of the same factors emerged from several methods).

We suspect that such "realism × independent variable" crossover interactions may sometimes reflect reactive measurement effects (Webb, Campbell, Schwartz, & Sechrest, 1966). In reactive situations, participants' awareness of, or sensitivity to, their participation in a research project often systematically influences or affects their responses. In legal contexts, such reactive situations appear most problematic for such behaviors as those of judges or lawyers that are governed by rules or norms and for which there are a clear set of socially desirable (or "politically correct") responses. For example, Konečni and Ebbesen's (1979) questionnaire and interview methods, which asked judges to identify the factors that influenced their sentencing decisions, may have elicited responses about the factors judges thought they were *expected* to employ (e.g., severity of the crime, prior record, family background, etc.). In contrast, Konečni and Ebbesen's finding from the archival analysis—that judges relied primarily on the recommendation of the probation officer (who relied on the factors of prior record, severity of the crime, and status)—may reflect a heuristic strategy judges use to deal with the pressures of heavy caseloads in the courtroom. The research methods compared by Konečni and Ebbesen (1979) basically distinguish self-report (e.g., interview, questionnaire, simulation) and behavioral measures (or some trace evident in archival records). These researchers favor the latter measures as valid but decry the former as misleading. We agree that when strong norms exist that are likely to result in reactive situations (e.g., in the study of judges' decisions), then behavioral or unobtrusive measurement, such as archival analyses, are generally to be favored over self-report or laboratory methods (see Webb et al., 1966). But we disagree with the implication that, because different methods produced different results in the study of one behavior (e.g., judges' sentencing decisions), different methods will necessarily or routinely produce different results for all behaviors in the courtroom. In particular, the behaviors of jurors, juries, and eyewitnesses do not seem to engage the strong social desirability norms apparent for judges' behavior. There are few rules, for example, that dictate how jurors should behave. Prior to deliberations jurors are prohibited from discussing the case; during deliberations they are sheltered from external intrusions; after deliberations they are protected from any sanctions relative to their verdicts. Thus, a wider range of methods—including laboratory and simulation methods—is likely to produce comparable results for the study of such behaviors.

When Is Lack of Realism Important?: Empirical Analyses

Although the relevant literature is not extensive, a reasonable number of studies have compared relatively less realistic with relatively more realistic conditions, often while examining respondents' sensitivity to independent variables of interest. We turn now to an examination of this literature.

More versus Less Realistic Subject Populations

Bornstein (1999) identified 26 separate studies that compared the responses of student-versus-nonstudent mock jurors. These studies examined a wide variety of experimental treatments (e.g., variations in expert testimony, pretrial publicity, defendant status, hypnotically refreshed memories) for a wide variety of trials (e.g., murder, robbery, assault, civil cases). What we have characterized as the relatively unimportant "realism" main effect—i.e., the comparison of students versus nonstudents—was significant for only 5 of the 26 studies. Among these, the modal effect (for 3 studies) was for students to be more lenient than nonstudents; the other two effects could not be described simply in these terms (i.e., one study [Finkel, Meister, & Lightfoot, 1991] found that students were less receptive to a claim of self-defense, but only for one of three cases they examined; another study [Casper, Benedict, & Perry, 1989] found that students awarded larger compensatory damages in a civil case but showed no effect on punitive damages). What we have characterized as the more important "realism × treatment" interaction effects emerged in only 1 of the 26 studies. Specifically, Cutler, Penrod, and Dexter (1990) found that experienced jurors were relatively more sensitive to two aspects of an eyewitness's testimony (i.e., whether a weapon was present and whether the witness had looked through a mugshot book) than student mock jurors. However, such interactions were observed for none of eight other treatment variables examined in this study (e.g., perpetrator disguise, confidence of the eyewitness). Bornstein and Rajki (1994) found that two variables likely to be associated with student/nonstudent status (i.e., race and education level) did moderate reactions to plaintiff injury; however, the student/nonstudent variable did not.

Bornstein (1999) also reviewed a set of papers that made between-experiment comparisons of student and nonstudent samples. In five of the six papers cited, the results obtained with student samples were replicated with nonstudent samples. The single exception (Halverson, Hallahan, Hart, & Rosenthal, 1997) found a complex (Treatment 1 × Treatment 2) interaction effect in a study with nonstudents that was not found for the student sample; the individual treatments examined showed no overall main effects for either sample.

Thus, it appears to be the rare exception rather than the rule that student mock jurors react differently to trial information than do samples of mock jurors more representative of actual jurors. We agree with Bornstein's (1999) conclusion that the overall pattern of these studies provides "strong evidence that factors at trial affect students and nonstudents in the same way" (p. 135).

More versus Less Realistic Modes of Stimulus Presentation

Bornstein (1999) conducted a similar analysis of the effects of trial presentation medium. He identified 11 studies that systematically varied the mode of stimulus presentation from relatively more to less realistic (i.e., contrasted two or more of the modes: live, video, audio, transcript, and written summary). Five of these studies also manipulated some treatment variables (e.g., number of eyewitnesses, expert testimony). The general pattern was similar to that reported for the subject population. "Mode" main effects occurred in only 3 of the 11 studies. Moreover, in those 3 studies, there was no consistent pattern (e.g., more convictions with a more realistic mode of presentation). Of the 5 studies that included treatments, only 1 (Borgida, 1979) found a significant mode × treatment interaction (i.e., the number of character witnesses affected verdicts for a videotaped version of a trial but not when the transcript was read aloud).

A complication in such comparisons is that it can be difficult to manipulate the mode of presentation without confounding the actual trial content. For example, in a transcript version of a trial, all nonverbal behavior, paralinguistic behavior, verbal emphases, and witness appearance/expression information are lost. Thus, it can be difficult to determine whether an apparent mode × treatment interaction is really attributable to different treatments in the modes being compared *per se*.

A related issue of stimulus trial presentation is the length or level of detail presented. Kramer and Kerr (1989) contrasted a longer (100 minute) videotaped version of a trial with a condensed (10 minute) version. Much of the testimony in the longer version was summarized in the shorter version, but care was taken to ensure that all evidence and the images of all trial participants were included in both versions. Experimental treatments were two types of prejudicial pretrial publicity. Although both types of publicity affected juror judgment, neither effect was moderated by the length of the trial.

An increasingly popular mode of stimulus presentation and response collection is the Internet. As a medium for research, the Internet offers a number of distinctive advantages over alternatives (e.g., laboratory settings), including access to a larger, more diverse subject population, convenient access for participants, relatively low cost, and excellent control of stimulus presentation and data collection (O'Neil & Penrod, 2002; Studebaker et al., 2002). With more sophisticated programming and media options becoming available, investigators can randomly assign participants to conditions, functionally interact with respondents (e.g., using responses on one item to decide what other questions will be posed), use multimedia for stimulus trials (including video and audio), and even permit jury deliberation (conveniently via "chat room" formats today; via Internet conferencing in the not-too-distant future). These many advantages, and encouraging trends in nonlegal research domains (cf. Krantz & Dalal, 2000), have led to several systematic contrasts of Internet versus non-Internet versions of trial simulations. For example, O'Neil and Penrod (2002) reported the results of four studies that were both run under typical laboratory conditions (with responses collected via paper-and-pencil self-reports) and on the Internet. Each study included manipulations of variables of substantive interest (e.g., status of a corporate representative-witness, aggravating and mitigating factors, defendant testimony, method of recovery of witness memory). Across these four studies, tests on nine different dependent variables showed only one main effect (fewer negligence verdicts on the Internet for one study) and one interaction effect (accepting personal responsibility for faulty design affected responsibility ratings only on the Internet in that same study) involving the Internet/non-Internet variable. O'Neil and Penrod note that, given the large number of statistical tests being conducted, at least this many effects would be expected by chance alone. Elsewhere, O'Neil (2002) has reported a pair of studies that functionally attempted to replicate paper-and-pencil simulation studies with several independent variables on the Internet. These comparisons were somewhat difficult, since such factors as length of trial and subject population (student vs. nonstudent) were confounded with the contrast of Internet versus non-Internet versions. Nevertheless, O'Neil reported that "the substantive results between the two versions were compared and no main effects on verdicts or interactions with other variables were found" (p. 126).

There are, to be sure, a number of potential disadvantages of using the Internet to mount simulation studies, including lack of respondent representativeness, repeat participation, obtaining consent, and guaranteeing anonymity. However, solutions for many of these problems are being developed and tested (see Birnbaum, 2000). In addition, there are many possible methodological variations of Internet-based simulations (e.g., the use of unpaid vs. paid volunteer participants; elaborate vs. simple consent procedures; seeking vs. not seeking personal information from participants), which can affect response rate, dropout rate, and sample representativeness. Research has begun to explore whether, when, and to what degree such methodological variations might affect the substantive findings of Internet-based research (O'Neil, 2002; O'Neil, Penrod, & Bornstein, 2002; O'Neil & Penrod, 2001). Given its potential for research rigor, efficiency, and verisimilitude, the prospects for the Internet as a tool for psycholegal research look bright.

More versus Less Realistic Dependent Variables

Vidmar (1979), among others, has noted that the dependent variables collected in simulation studies often bear little resemblance to the judgments made by the legal actors to whom the simulations' results would be generalized. Sometimes this lack of resemblance reflects a justified desire to improve the sensitivity of a measure (e.g., when a rating of guilt rather than a dichotomous verdict is obtained), sometimes it reflects an investigator's interest in a general evaluative response (e.g., using evaluations of a defendant rather than verdicts), but sometimes it reflects legal naivete and/or carelessness (e.g., when juror sentencing recommendations are equated with juror verdicts; cf. Kerr, 1978). Although Diamond (1997) suggests that the latter departures from realism have become less frequent, there have been (to our knowledge) no empirical confirmations of this decline, nor systematic attempts to identify just when such artificialities in simulation studies might lead to misleading, ecologically invalid conclusions. On the other hand, there have been interesting demonstrations that unrealistic dependent variables can shed interesting light on more realistic behaviors. For example, although actual jurors are never asked to disclose their level of confidence in their verdicts, such data (1) can be used to compute a more sensitive verdict + confidence index (Diamond, 1997), (2) identify jurors who are more likely to change verdict preference during deliberation (Diamond et al., 1996; Stasser & Davis, 1981), or (3) can be used to estimate jurors' standard of proof (Kerr, 1993).

Consequential versus Inconsequential Decisions

Two studies have compared mock jurors who know that their decisions are inconsequential with those who are led to believe that their verdicts will have real consequences for a defendant. In a student discipline case, Kerr et al. (1979) found no detectable differences between these two conditions on juror verdicts, jury verdicts, deliberation time, or group decision-making process. In contrast, Kaplan and Krupa's (1986) real jurors were more likely to convict and more certain of their verdicts, but the real/hypothetical factor did not interact with the two other substantive variables manipulated in their study (i.e., source of punishment decision and strength of evidence). The latter null effect is particularly interesting; if making a consequential decision made jurors attend more carefully to the trial evidence, dual-process models of attitude change (e.g., the elaboration likelihood model) would clearly predict an interaction with strength of evidence.

Juror versus Jury Verdicts

There has been no comprehensive empirical review comparing juror with jury judgments. Based on certain results, some have suggested that juries are generally less susceptible to extralegal biases than are individual jurors (Kaplan & Miller, 1978; Kerwin & Shaffer, 1994). Kerr et al. (1996) reviewed the extant literature and found 13 potentially relevant studies examining both jurors' and juries' reactions to a variety of biasing factors (e.g., exposure to pretrial publicity, defendant physical attractiveness, joinder of charges, spurious attorney arguments). For four of these studies, various methodological problems precluded a meaningful juror/jury comparison. For example, Kerwin and Shaffer's (1994) study, which has been touted as showing that juries are less likely than jurors to use inadmissible testimony, failed to include a no-inadmissible-testimony control condition. Of the remaining nine studies, five found larger bias effects among juries than among jurors, three found comparable biases, and only one (Kaplan & Miller, 1978) found a smaller bias among juries. The modal pattern, consistent with group polarization research, is that the effects observed at the individual level tend to be larger at the group level.

Kerr et al. (1996) also presented a theoretical analysis, based on J. H. Davis's (1973) social decision scheme model, which suggests that there can be no general answer to this question: Depending on a number of factors (including group size, the nature and magnitude of the bias, and, most important, the group decision-making process), groups will sometimes be more and sometimes less biased than individuals. However, if a serviceable summary of the way group members combine individual preferences into a group decision (i.e., a social decision scheme) is available, it is then possible to specify when groups will be more or less biased than individuals. We have such a summary for criminal juries—predeliberation majorities usually prevail in deliberations (e.g., Kalven & Zeisel, 1966; Stasser et al., 1989), and when criminal juries are evenly divided initially, pro-acquittal factions are more likely to prevail, due to certain advantages they have under the reasonable doubt standard (e.g., defendants must be given the benefit of any doubts; MacCoun & Kerr, 1988). Such a social decision scheme not only provides accurate predictions of jury verdicts (see Stasser et al., 1989), it also makes a number of other verified predictions (e.g., that juries generally are more lenient than individual judges, Kalven & Zeisel, 1966; that juries tend to polarize individual juror sentiment, Myers & Kaplan, 1976). The model also can explain apparent anomalies in the literature. For example, consider the only study in the literature that found a weaker bias among juries than among jurors: Kaplan and Miller (1978, Experiment 3). This study included a manipulation of strength of evidence: The stimulus trial had either very strong or very weak evidence against the defendant. Kerr et al.'s (1996) theoretical analysis showed (1) that it is precisely for such "extreme" cases that jury deliberation should attenuate juror bias (through the combination of polarization and a kind of floor/ceiling effect), and (2) that exactly the reverse should occur for less extreme cases. To test this prediction, Kerr et al. (1999) compared jurors' and juries' reactions to biasing information (i.e., prejudicial pretrial publicity [PTP]) for two versions of the same case: one with an extremely low rate of conviction and another with a moderate rate of conviction. As the social decision scheme analysis predicted, juries were less biased (than jurors) by PTP for the extreme case and were more biased by PTP for the moderate case. In summary, although jury and juror judgments routinely differ, those differences are orderly and predictable.

Summary of Empirical Contrasts

Empirical work evaluating the external validity of the mock-jury literature has identified very few factors that consistently produce either the less serious (e.g., "realism" main effect) or the more serious (e.g., crossover realism × treatment interaction effect) kinds of realism effects. Nor, in our judgment, have there been any compelling theoretical arguments advanced that make such effects likely. It is also important to remember that it is no more reasonable to conclude that simulation studies of legal systems are often misleading, based on isolated studies that do find a "serious" difference (cf. Colasanto & Sanders, 1976, p. 14; Konečni et al., 1980, p. 89), than it would be to conclude that simulation studies are not misleading, based on a single (or even many) studies that fail to find a serious difference. Given the current state of theory and research, it clearly seems unjustified to dismiss the utility of standard simulations (i.e., to presume that serious differences are, in fact, the rule).

Is There a Right Way and a Wrong Way to Study Juries?

Runkel and McGrath (1972) have suggested that

> the choice among the [research] strategies should be made with an eye to their respective advantages and weaknesses and on the basis of (1) the nature of the problem the investigator wants to study, (2) the state of prior knowledge about this problem, and (3) the amount and kind of resources available to the investigator. (p. 89)

Much of the criticism of the standard jury simulation is implicitly founded on the assumption that all those who use it are, or should be, concerned with the same problem, that is, how juries behave in situ. If this issue is indeed the researcher's sole or overriding objective, then the importance placed on simulation realism is better founded. However, there are many other legitimate objectives being pursued in such research. Some investigators are testing a psychological theory or model for which juries are but one interest-ing application. Others hope to test the validity of some of the psychological assumptions of the law or court procedure and may or may not have wanted also to determine the probable extent or impact of the violation of that as-sumption on the operation of the real system. Still others have been doing ba-sic research on more general psychological processes that are also manifest in juries. Many, including us, have pursued both theoretical and applied interests and have tried to wound (if not able to kill) two birds with one stone. We dis-agree with those who feel that experimenters must always choose either one objective or another in their research (e.g., Dillehay & Nietzel, 1980); useful knowledge about courtroom behavior as well as general psychological knowl-edge can often be gained while pursuing several objectives simultaneously.

But even if the researcher's objectives are purely applied, we disagree with the notion that an optimal research method exists for him or her to employ. To borrow a metaphor from Runkel and McGrath (1972), researchers are continually faced with a multihorned dilemma. In choosing to avoid one horn, they invariably are gored by another. The investigator who chooses the field setting to maximize realism must sacrifice experimental control and opportu-nity for observation. The investigator who chooses the standard simulation buys control, opportunity to observe, and affordability, but at a cost of real-ism. No choice of method is free from such compromises, including the realis-tic simulation. Making a jury simulation more realistic by removing such artificialities as predeliberation polling of jurors, experimenter observation of deliberation, rehearsed testimony, and knowledge that verdicts have no real consequences requires sacrifices of control, opportunities to observe, or ethi-cal principles. Runkel and McGrath (1972) make our key point well: "The trick is not to search for the 'right' strategy but to pick the strategy that is best *for your purposes and circumstances* and then use all the strengths of that strategy and do whatever can be done to limit or offset its inherent weak-nesses" (p. 117, emphasis in original). Given the range of objectives and re-sources of those interested in the study of psychology and the law, many strat-egies, including the standard simulation, can be "optimal."

Triandis (1978) suggests a similar view in arguing the need for basic re-search when studying applied problems: "As soon as you break a practical problem into its more basic elements you are faced with numerous fundamen-tal questions, requiring basic research. You cannot make progress in the situa-tion of the practical problem unless you solve the basic problems" (p. 385). In proposing a general paradigm for conducting research in applied areas, Triandis advocates both basic laboratory research, which is usually empha-sized more during the study of the initial phases of a problem, and field re-search, which is usually more prevalent later in the study of the problem.

Finally, there is the implicit (sometimes explicit, e.g., Konečni et al., 1980) assumption that the relevance of basic laboratory research for relatively concrete and well-defined "real-world" systems (such as the jury) is not as great as it is for more general and diffuse topics (e.g., aggression). There are differences between the two, to be sure. One difference is that the jury is certainly a much more specific, delimited system. Another difference may be a greater temptation to apply laboratory results prematurely because the potential for application is so tangibly manifest. Clearly, there is a need for caution in discussing findings for an area such as jury research. Such caution, of course, is manifested differently depending on the audience. Research published in scientific journals for an audience trained in research methodology should not require constant reminders of the limits of generalization. Research described in law journals or the popular press should probably draw conclusions much more carefully. Caution in describing findings, however, should not preclude discussion of potential implications for actual jury behavior suggested by those findings. Some (e.g., Ellsworth & Ross, 1976) have counseled social scientists to preempt misinterpretation and misapplication of their findings by actively disseminating their research findings among the appropriate policymakers. This suggestion has much to recommend it when the strength of the data justifies such an advocacy role. However, we are not persuaded that there are basic differences in the suitability or utility of the various research methodologies for delimited, applied topics and for more abstract topics. The relative concreteness of courtroom behavior only makes ecological validation of laboratory research more tractable. Rather than presenting an impediment to laboratory research, this concreteness presents, in our opinion, an opportunity for checking the generality of such research to the real-world settings of interest.

Is Half a Loaf Better Than None?

Several critics have argued that if psycholegal research cannot be done "correctly" (i.e., with highly realistic simulations or in the field), it should not be done at all. This is a policy of "no loaf is better than half a loaf." But, as we have noted previously, different researchers may (straining our metaphor) have very different tastes or nutritional needs, and in any case, researchers can never buy the whole loaf in a single purchase. Some (e.g., Konečni et al., 1980) argue that the power of the simulation as a method with which to test and develop psychological theory is of little use in describing legal decision makers' behavior. In effect, they argue that this part of the loaf has no nutritional value: "We do not question the *possibility* of generating 'mediational' explanations for the decisions under study but merely doubt that they *add* anything to the ability to predict and understand the future behavior of the participants in the real legal system" (p. 90, emphasis in original). In an even stronger statement, Konečni and Ebbesen (1979) seem to reject all but field research as acceptable:

> It is impossible for researchers to be present during jury deliberations and it is extremely difficult to obtain access to files containing information that leads to certain decisions (e.g., prosecutor's files). Many would probably think that

simulation research in these cases is fully justified even if all of our criticisms are correct. A more cautious point of view, and one that we favor, is that erroneous information obtained by scientific methods (and therefore having an aura of truth) *is more harmful than no information at all* . . . especially when issues as sensitive as legal ones are being dealt with, and people's futures are quite literally at stake. (p. 68, emphasis added)

Others argue that increased quality of the "loaf" justifies a drop in quantity. For example, Miller et al. (1983) noted that the production of more realistic simulations

is sure to increase the economic and energy costs of conducting research; the sheer volume of research conducted is likely to shrink dramatically. This reduction in quantitative output can be justified by the added potential for ecological validity. Although researchers may not know as much, they should be able to place more confidence in the social applicability of what they do know. In an applied area such as juror behavior, we view this change in priorities as a step in the right direction. (p. 17)

These viewpoints suggest that the body of knowledge regarding courtroom behavior can best grow on a steady diet of realistic research. We feel, on the other hand, that theory development is essential if we are to move beyond description to an explanation of behavior, and that abandonment of the controlled research methods upon which such theory development relies is no wiser a course than complete reliance on highly controlled, and thus unrealistic, methods.

As Runkel and McGrath (1972) noted, choice of research strategy must inevitably take into account "the amount and kind of resources available to the investigator" (p. 89). We do not stand to gain much knowledge by prohibiting all research except that which is prohibitively expensive for most investigators. We concur with Kalven and Zeisel's (1966) view that "in new efforts it must be better to learn something, however imperfectly, than to withdraw from inquiry altogether when preferred methods are as a practical matter not available" (p. 39). In other words, a good half loaf is better than no loaf. We are not applying the drunkard's logic of looking for his key under a distant streetlamp because the light is better there, when he knows he lost it by his darkened doorway. That is, we are not advocating employing a method with little value just because it is all we can afford. Rather, we are suggesting that beginning our inquiry where the light is good (i.e., where research is practical and powerful) is a reasonable strategy when it can provide useful clues to the key's location.

Can "Unrealistic" Simulations Be Informative?

Naturally, this issue will be fully resolved only through a great deal more research, but we think that experimental simulations can make several valuable contributions to our understanding of psychology and law. As we have noted previously, much of this research has added to our general body of knowledge and to theory development on the processes of interpersonal perception, attribution, group decision processes, and so on, which are part and parcel of jurors', judges', witnesses', and lawyers' tasks. Small-scale and quickly conducted simulation studies can also be an efficient way of developing and checking tentative, working hypotheses about actual behavior; in essence, they can serve as pilot studies for more ambitious simulations or field studies. Davis, Bray, and Holt (1977) have also suggested that such studies can be viewed "as 'demonstrations' that may reveal that assumptions inherent in the law do not always hold or that the legal system works in a way other than that officially prescribed" (p. 327). Finally, we are not persuaded that simulation studies must accurately estimate the strength of an effect or that the effect must account for large amounts of variability in the behavior of actual legal actors in order to be interesting or useful. If our interest is exclusively predictive, weak effects may not be terribly useful. But if our interest extends to the ability of courtroom participants to carry out their responsibilities, even small or infrequently applied biases may be important, particularly when they are based on extralegal factors or might be remedied through minor procedural safeguards. Nor is it essential that an experimental treatment in a simulation study accurately mirror the range in variation or prominence of that same variable in "typical" trials. In this regard, we might draw an analogy between the use of strong manipulations in simulations and feeding massive doses of a substance to laboratory rats to determine possible carcinogenic effects of that substance. Even if saccharine is not a major cause of human bladder cancer, demonstrating that massive saccharine doses reliably lead to bladder cancers in rats can alert us to possible risks and can guide future research. Demonstrations that artificially powerful treatments reliably affect simulated courtroom behavior can serve similarly valuable functions.

Dillehay and Nietzel (1980) have objected to our use of this analogy as applied to mock-jury research (e.g., see Bray & Kerr, 1979):

> A close examination of this analogue reveals significant differences from the experimental juror/jury research. A main difference concerns the inducing agent or treatment variable. In drug research using animal models the drug of interest, not a substitute or facsimile, is used as the inducing agent. In experimental juror/jury research typically there is low fidelity to the events of the trial that are targeted for research. (p. 252)

Their criticism seems based on their failure to distinguish between passive and active role playing (discussed earlier). In jury simulations, we maintain that the stimuli that subjects are exposed to are, in fact, real and not a substitute or facsimile. For example, if defendant attractiveness is manipulated, it is accomplished by actually exposing subjects to defendants of varying attractiveness, not by asking them to imagine a defendant who is attractive or unattractive, as would be the case in passive role playing. It is true that the laboratory presentation does not always mirror what occurs in the courtroom (e.g., pictures of defendants may be used instead of live defendants), but the extent to which that difference is a serious problem is the issue of external validity. In defense of our analogy, we would also point out that there are a number of differences between the way a drug is administered in research settings and how it is handled in real settings (e.g., the size and frequency of dosage, the method of ingestion). Despite these differences, which primarily exploit the advantages of control offered by the laboratory, such drug research is still considered very useful.

Must We Strive for Realism to Meet Policymakers' Ideal of Relevant Research?

The uses (and misuses) of scientific evidence by legal practitioners and policymakers is a fascinating and complex topic. It is well beyond our goals (and powers) to analyze it in any thorough way here (for more extensive treatments, see Erickson & Simon, 1998; Kerr, 1986; Monahan et al., 2001; Rosen, 1972). However, we briefly consider the argument that high verisimilitude in psycholegal research is essential for such work to have influence on policy and practice by focusing, in particular, on realism in simulation studies (e.g., of the jury) and influence on appellate court rulings (e.g., the U.S. Supreme Court).

It is quite true that we can find instances in which judges dismiss studies explicitly because of low realism (e.g., *Ballew v. Georgia*, 1978; *Lockhart v. McCree*, 1986). Judges are not immune to the common error of using *verisimilitude* as a direct proxy for *ecological validity* (Studebaker et al., 2002). Thus, lack of realism would indeed appear to be a barrier to the use of scientific research by the courts. The question is, just how serious a barrier is it? If we examine the history of the court's reactions to science—not just to laboratory simulations of juror behavior but to scientific empirical research more generally—our assessment is (1) that lack of verisimilitude is not a major barrier, (2) that overemphasis on avoiding it carries very high costs, and (3) that there are other (and better) ways to overcome it than by imposing broad prohibitions on "unrealistic" research. Let's briefly consider each of these points.

We can find exceptions to any generalization we could make about the courts' use of scientific evidence. Nevertheless, certain patterns have emerged. The courts do not tend to evaluate such evidence as scientists do, even when that evidence is accompanied by authoritative scientific opinion (cf. *Barefoot v. Estelle*, 1983; *Lockhart v. McCree*, 1986). This reality is perhaps not surprising; judges are not trained as scientists, nor do they typically pursue the same goals (e.g., in addition to the scientist's preoccupation with establishing what is true, judges must also consider other matters such as precedent, the wording of constitutions or legislation, the net impact of their decisions). So, if it is not the scientific rigor of a piece of research that weighs most heavily with judges, what is it that they value especially?

A few scholars (e.g., Haney, 1979; Monahan, 1983; Rosen, 1972) have suggested that judges only rely strongly on scientific evidence when other, more traditional grounds are unavailable. And many scholars (e.g., A. L. Davis, 1973; Ellsworth, 1988; Grofman & Scarrow, 1980; Haney, 1979; Lochner, 1973; Mason, 1931; Rosen, 1972; Rosenblum, 1975; Studebaker et al., 2002; Wasby, 1980) have suggested that judges tend to accept scientific evidence if, and only if, it bolsters the decision that they already favor on other grounds. The same justices who in one case blithely accept empirical claims that are based on flimsy and demonstrably incorrect "evidence" but that happen to bolster their own positions (e.g., that the death penalty is an effective deterrent in *Gregg v. Georgia*, 1976; that clinicians can provide useful information to jurors about a convicted defendant's future dangerousness in *Barefoot v. Estelle*, 1983) will reject much stronger scientific evidence in another case when the evidence happens to contradict their positions (e.g., that reducing jury size has predictable effects on jury verdicts and deliberation in *Ballew v. Georgia*, 1978; that excluding jurors who oppose the death penalty results in more pro-conviction juries in *Lockhart v. McCree*, 1986). These patterns of use suggest that questions about the quality of research (including its realism) are likely to arise in very few cases—those for which (1) judges are otherwise uncommitted or indifferent, and (2) there are no more traditional bases for decision available.

It could be argued that, regardless of the number of such cases, high realism could still contribute to the persuasiveness of research in the courts. But at what cost? As we have noted, achieving high degrees of realism is costly in many ways—for example, in experimental control, in opportunities for observation, as well as in terms of money, time, and effort. Mounting a few highly realistic simulations could easily consume as many resources as a much larger number of less realistic studies. It is unclear to us that the several advantages of doing many more studies (e.g., for obtaining converging evidence, for developing methods and procedures, for establishing stability and boundary conditions of phenomena, etc.) should routinely be sacrificed in the (usually vain) hope that the few realistic studies might be more readily accepted by nonscientists. In sum, the costs for satisfying the courts' preference for highly realistic research may be too high in many instances.

Of course, we want to maximize the impact of our research. Our judgment is that this impact is usually best achieved by conducting the very best science possible with the limited resources available—*best* by the standards of science. This is not to say that we should always be indifferent to how realistic our studies are; there will be times when realism will be a priority. For example, when the quality of a body of research justifies strong confidence in its conclusions, and its relevance for some legal question is high, establishing the research's ecological validity might well be the most sensible next step. And, when possible, we in the scientific community should continue to explain the bases of our confidence to the courts by every means possible—as expert witnesses, as authors of *amicus curiae* briefs, as consultants, as educators. The relationship between science and the courts is an evolving one, and there is much we can do to reduce misunderstanding and misuse of science by the courts (as well as our own misunderstanding of legal realities and constraints).

In the past decade there has been notable movement toward greater use of empirical evidence in judicial decisions, a movement that we expect will continue and grow. Much of this movement stems from the U.S. Supreme Court ruling in the case of *Daubert v. Merrell Dow Pharmaceuticals, Inc.* (1993). The court considered the standard for evaluating admissibility of scientific expert testimony and ruled that trial court judges must evaluate the merits of scientific research supporting an expert's opinion before permitting experts to testify. Clearly, for this ruling to be followed, both judges and lawyers must have at least a basic understanding of the logic and methods of scientific research. Although the ruling does not expect members of the legal profession to become scientists, it does expect them to be familiar with scientific methods and key evidence from scientific studies bearing on a range of legal issues. Indeed, the *Daubert* ruling has heralded the law's accession to the world of science. One outgrowth of this ruling is a four-volume work compiled by Faigman et al. (2002) that is designed to acquaint judges and lawyers with scientific fields that are crucial to their practices or to particular cases. It attempts to bring together an understanding of the law into which the methodological principles and reasoning that underlie various types of scientific evidence must be integrated. In addition, Faigman et al. provide a summary of key scientific findings surrounding a series of topics. It is of particular interest to note that Volume 1 of this series is devoted to a discussion of scientific methods.

CONCLUSIONS AND RECOMMENDATIONS

The fundamental conclusion of the present chapter is that the standard mock-trial simulation is one of several viable methods for the study of behavior in legal contexts. Although it clearly would not be the preferred method in every situation, we maintain that social scientists should not, in their zeal for realism, dismiss the utility of closely controlled experimental simulations, nor be unmindful of the practical and methodological drawbacks of more realistic methods. Realizing that our research methods are imperfect tools for answering empirical questions, we recommend methodological diversity in the study of the psychology of the courtroom. This point of view also leads us to urge rejection of the counsel to limit the range of "acceptable" methods. Unless the need for such closure can be established empirically, we urge mutual tolerance of differences in research methodologies when these reflect honest differences in research objectives, resources, and style.

A second conclusion, related to the first, is that the study of the psychology of the courtroom is not qualitatively different from the study of other social phenomena, although the potential for application of the findings may be considerably greater. To prevent misapplication or misinterpretation of findings, we recommend that investigators be as explicit as possible about the objectives of their research and use great care in noting the limits on generalization of their results. Findings derived from unrealistic simulations should be appropriately qualified (depending on the audience and outlet for the material) and should not be forwarded as the primary basis for policy changes. This does not mean, however, as some have suggested (e.g., Dillehay & Nietzel, 1980), that investigators must be so cautious that they fail to explore *potential* implications of their data.

The need for explicitness of purpose and qualification of findings seems particularly important, given that the potential consumers of such research crosscut the disciplines of social science and law. Members of both disciplines share a joint interest in how legal institutions and the people within them operate. There is, though, a need for greater education of, and cooperation between, participants in both camps. Social scientists with clear applied interests need training in the law and legal realities, and legal professionals need to acquire greater sophistication in the methods and theories of scientists. It is our hope that such training may help us view, in proper perspective, the value of data obtained through all methods.

ACKNOWLEDGMENT

This material is based upon work supported by the National Science Foundation under Grant No. 0214428.

NOTE

1. Portions of R. M. Bray and N. L. Kerr (1982), "Methodological Issues in the Study of the Psychology of the Courtroom." In N. L. Kerr and R. M. Bray (Eds.), *The Psychology of the Courtroom* (pp. 287–323). New York: Academic Press. Reprinted with permission from Elsevier.

REFERENCES

Ballew v. Georgia (1978). *U.S. Supreme Court Reports, 435*, 223.
Barefoot v. Estelle (1983). *U.S. Supreme Court Reports, 463*, 880.
Baumeister, R. F., & Darley, J. M. (1982). Reducing the biasing effect of perpetrator attractiveness in jury simulation. *Personality and Social Psychology Bulletin, 8*, 286–292.
Bermant, G., McGuire, M., McKinley, W., & Salo, C. (1974). The logic of simulation in jury research. *Criminal Justice and Behavior, 1*, 224–233.

Birnbaum, M. (2000). *Psychological experiments on the Internet*. San Diego, CA: Academic Press.

Borgida, E. (1979). Character proof and the fireside induction. *Law and Human Behavior, 3,* 189–202.

Borgida, E., DeBono, K. G., & Buckman, L. A. (1990). Cameras in the courtroom: The effects of media coverage on witness testimony and juror perceptions. *Law and Human Behavior, 14,* 489–509.

Bornstein, B. H. (1999). The ecological validity of jury simulations: Is the jury still out? *Law and Human Behavior, 23,* 75–91.

Bornstein, B. H., & Rajki, M. (1994). Extra-legal factors and product liability: The influence of mock jurors' demographic characteristics and intuitions about the cause of an injury. *Behavioral Sciences and the Law, 12,* 127–147.

Bray, R. M., & Kerr, N. L. (1979). Use of the simulation method in the study of jury behavior. *Law and Human Behavior, 3,* 107–119.

Bray, R. M., & Kerr, N. L. (1982). Methodological issues in the study of the psychology of the courtroom. In N. L. Kerr & R. M. Bray (Eds.), *The psychology of the courtroom* (pp. 287–323). New York: Academic Press.

Brekke, N. J., Enko, P. J., Clavet, G., & Sellau, E. (1991). Of juries and court-appointed experts: The impact of nonadversarial versus adversarial expert testimony. *Law and Human Behavior, 15,* 451–475.

Broeder, D. W. (1959). The University of Chicago jury project. *Nebraska Law Review, 38,* 744–761.

Bullock, H. A. (1961). Significance of the racial factor in the length of prison sentences. *Journal of Criminal Law, Criminology, and Police Science, 52,* 411–417.

Campbell, D. T. (1957). Factors relevant to the validity of experiments in social settings. *Psychological Bulletin, 54,* 297–312.

Campbell, D. T., & Stanley, J. C. (1966). *Experimental and quasi-experimental designs for research*. New York: Houghton Mifflin.

Carlsmith, J. M., Ellsworth, P. C., & Aronson, E. (1976). *Methods of research in social psychology*. Reading, MA: Addison-Wesley.

Casper, J. D., Benedict, K., & Perry, J. L. (1989). Juror decision making, attitudes, and the hindsight bias. *Law and Human Behavior, 13,* 291–310.

Colasanto, D., & Sanders, J. (1976). *From laboratory to jury room: A review of experiments on jury decision making*. Unpublished manuscript, University of Michigan, Ann Arbor, MI.

Cook, T. D., & Campbell, D. T. (1979). *Quasi-experimentation: Design and analysis issues for field settings*. Chicago, IL: Rand McNally.

Cutler, B. L., Penrod, S. D., & Dexter, H. R. (1990). Juror sensitivity to eyewitness identification evidence. *Law and Human Behavior, 14,* 185–191.

Daubert v. Merrell Dow Pharmaceuticals, Inc. (1993). 509 U.S. 579, 113 S.Ct. 2786, 125 L.Ed.2d 469.

Davis, A. L. (1973). *The United States Supreme Court and the uses of social science data*. New York: MSS Information Corp.

Davis, J. H. (1973). Group decision and social interaction: A theory of social decision schemes. *Psychological Review, 80,* 97–125.

Davis, J. H. (1980). Group decision and procedural justice. In M. Fishbein (Ed.), *Progress in social psychology* (pp. 157–229). Hillsdale, NJ: Erlbaum.

Davis, J. H., Bray, R. M., & Holt, R. W. (1977). The empirical study of decision processes in juries: A critical review. In J. L. Tapp & F. J. Levine (Eds.), *Law, justice, and the individual in society: Psychological and legal issues* (pp. 326–361). New York: Holt.

Davis, J. H., Kerr, N. L., Atkin, R. S., Holt, R., & Meek, D. (1975). The decision processes of 6- and 12-person mock juries assigned unanimous and 2/3 majority rules. *Journal of Personality and Social Psychology, 32*, 1–14.

Diamond, S. S. (1997). Illuminations and shadows from jury simulations. *Law and Human Behavior, 21*, 561–571.

Diamond, S. S., Casper, J. D., Heiert, C., & Marshall, A. M. (1996). Juror reactions to attorneys at trial. *Journal of Criminal Law and Criminology, 87*, 17–47.

Dillehay, R. D., & Nietzel, M. T. (1980). Constructing a science of jury behavior. In L. Wheeler (Ed.), *Review of personality and social psychology* (pp. 246–264). Beverly Hills: Sage.

Dillehay, R. D., & Nietzel, M. T. (1981). Conceptualizing mock jury-juror research: Critique and illustrations. In K. S. Larsen (Ed.), *Psychology and ideology*. Monmouth, OR: Institute for Theoretical History.

Ebbesen, E. B., & Konečni, V. J. (1975). Decision making and information integration in the courts: The setting of bail. *Journal of Personality and Social Psychology, 32*, 805–821.

Efran, M. G. (1974). The effect of physical appearance on the judgment of guilt, interpersonal attraction, and severity of recommended punishment in a simulated jury task. *Journal of Research in Personality, 8*, 45–54.

Ellsworth, P. C. (1988). Unpleasant facts: The Supreme Court's response to empirical research on capital punishment. In K. C. Haas & J. A. Inciardi (Eds.), *Challenging capital punishment: Legal and social science approaches* (pp. 177–211). Newbury Park, CA: Sage.

Ellsworth, P., & Ross, L. (1976). Public opinion and judicial decision making: An example from research on capital punishment. In H. A. Bedau & C. M. Pierce (Eds.), *Capital punishment in the United States*. New York: AMS Press.

Elwork, A., & Sales, B. D. (1980). Psychological research on the jury and trial processes. In C. Petty, W. Curran, & L. McGarry (Eds.), *Modern legal, medicine, and forensic science* (pp. 927–962). Philadelphia: Davis.

Erickson, R. J., & Simon, R. J. (1998). *The use of social science data in Supreme Court decisions*. Champaign, IL: University of Illinois Press.

Faigman, D. L., Kaye, D. H., Saks, M. J., & Sanders, J. (Eds.). (2002). *Modern scientific evidence: The law and science of expert testimony* (Vols. 1–4). St. Paul, MN: West.

Finkel, N. J., Meister, K. H., & Lightfoot, D. M. (1991). The self-defense defense and community sentiment. *Law and Human Behavior, 15*, 585–602.

Foss, R. D. (1975, August). *A critique of jury simulation research*. Paper presented at the annual meeting of the American Psychological Association, Chicago.

Gray, W. D. (1991). *Thinking critically about New Age ideas*. Belmont, CA: Brooks/Cole.

Green, E. (1964). Inter- and intra-racial crime relative to sentencing. *Journal of Criminal Law, Criminology, and Political Science, 55*, 348–358.

Gregg v. Georgia (1976). *U.S. Supreme Court Reports, 428*, 153.

Grofman, B., & Scarrow, H. (1980). Mathematics, social science, and the law. In M. Saks & C. Baron (Eds.), *The use/nonuse/misuse of applied social research in the courts* (pp. 117–127). Cambridge, MA: Abt.

Halverson, A. M., Hallahan, M., Hart, A. J., & Rosenthal, R. (1997). Reducing the biasing effects of judges' nonverbal behavior with simplified jury instruction. *Journal of Applied Psychology, 82*, 590–598.

Haney, C. (1979). Psychology and legal change: On the limits of a factual jurisprudence. *Law and Human Behavior, 4,* 147–200.

Hannaford, P. L., Hans, V. P., & Munsterman, G. T. (2000). Permitting jury discussions during trial: Impact of the Arizona Reform. *Law and Human Behavior, 24,* 359–382.

Hans, V. P., & Lofquist, W. S. (1992). Jurors' judgments of business liability in tort cases: Implications for the litigation explosion debate. *Law and Society Review, 26,* 101–115.

Hastie, R. (1993). *Inside the juror: The psychology of juror decision making.* New York: Cambridge University Press.

Heuer, L., & Penrod, S. (1988). Increasing jurors' participation in trials: A field experiment with jury notetaking and question asking. *Law and Human Behavior, 12,* 231–261.

Heuer, L., & Penrod, S. (1994a). Juror notetaking and question asking during trials: A national field experiment. *Law and Human Behavior, 18,* 121–150.

Heuer, L., & Penrod, S. D. (1994b). Instructing jurors: A field experiment with written and preliminary instructions. *Law and Human Behavior, 13,* 409–430.

Johnson v. Louisiana (1972). *United States Reports, 406,* 356–403.

Kalven, H., Jr., & Zeisel, H. (1966). *The American jury.* Boston: Little, Brown.

Kaplan, M. F. (1977). Judgments by juries. In M. Kaplan & S. Schwartz (Eds.), *Human judgment and decision processes in applied settings* (pp. 31–55). New York: Academic Press.

Kaplan, M. F., & Krupa, S. (1986). Severe penalties under the control of others can reduce guilt verdicts. *Law and Psychology Review, 10,* 1–18.

Kaplan, M. F., & Miller, L. E. (1978). Reducing the effects of juror bias. *Journal of Personality and Social Psychology, 36,* 1443–1455.

Kelman, H. C. (1967). Human use of human subjects: The problem of deception in social psychological experiments. *Psychological Bulletin, 67,* 1–11.

Kerr, N. L. (1978). Severity of prescribed penalty and mock jurors' verdicts. *Journal of Personality and Social Psychology, 36,* 1422–1431.

Kerr, N. L. (1981). Trial participants' characteristics/behaviors and juries' verdicts: An exploratory field study. In V. Konečni & E. Ebbesen (Eds.), *Social psychological analyses of legal processes* (pp. 261–290). San Francisco: Freeman.

Kerr, N. L. (1986). Social science and the Supreme Court. In M. F. Kaplan (Ed.), *The impact of social psychology on procedural justice* (pp. 56–79). Springfield, IL: Thomas.

Kerr, N. L. (1993). Stochastic models of juror decision making. In R. Hastie (Ed.), *Inside the juror: The psychology of juror decision making* (pp. 116–135). New York: Cambridge University Press.

Kerr, N. L. (1994). The effects of pretrial publicity on jurors. *Judicature, 78,* 120–127.

Kerr, N. L. (1998). HARKing (Hypothesizing After the Results are Known). *Personality and Social Psychology Review, 2,* 196–217.

Kerr, N. L., Harmon, D., & Graves, J. (1982). Independence of verdicts by jurors and juries. *Journal of Applied Social Psychology, 12,* 12–29.

Kerr, N. L., & MacCoun, R. (1985). The effects of jury size and polling method on the process and product of jury deliberation. *Journal of Personality and Social Psychology, 48,* 349–363.

Kerr, N. L., MacCoun, R., & Kramer, G. P. (1996). Bias in judgment: Comparing individuals and groups. *Psychological Review, 103,* 687–719.

Kerr, N. L., Nerenz, D., & Herrick, D. (1979). Role playing and the study of jury behavior. *Sociological Methods and Research, 7,* 337–355.

Kerr, N. L., Niedermeier, K., & Kaplan, M. (1999). Bias in jurors vs. juries: New evidence from the SDS perspective. *Organizational Behavior and Human Decision Processes, 80,* 70–86.

Kerwin, J., & Shaffer, D. R. (1994). Mock jurors versus juries: The role of deliberations in reactions to inadmissible testimony. *Personality and Social Psychology Bulletin, 20,* 153–162.

Konečni, V. J., & Ebbesen, E. B. (1979). External validity of research in legal psychology. *Law and Human Behavior, 3,* 39–70.

Konečni, V. J., & Ebbesen, E. B. (1991). *Methodische Probleme in der Forschung ueber juristische Entscheidungsprozesse—unter besonderer Beruecksichtigung experimenteller Simulationen* [Methodological problems in research on legal decision-making processes: Special consideration of experimental simulations]. *Gruppendynamik, 22,* 175–188.

Konečni, V. J., & Ebbesen, E. B. (1992). Methodological issues in research on legal decision-making, with special reference to experimental simulations. In F. Loesel, D. Bender, & T. Bliesener (Eds.), *Psychology and law: International perspectives* (pp. 413–423). Oxford, UK: de Gruyter.

Konečni, V. J., Mulcahy, E. M., & Ebbesen, E. B. (1980). Prison or mental hospital: Factors affecting the processing of persons suspected of being "mentally disordered sex offenders." In P. D. Lipsitt & B. D. Sales (Eds.), *New directions in psycholegal research* (pp. 87–124). New York: van Nostrand-Reinhold.

Kramer, G. P., & Kerr, N. L. (1989). Laboratory simulation and bias in the study of juror behavior: A methodological note. *Law and Human Behavior, 13,* 89–100.

Krantz, J. H., & Dalal, R. (2000). Validity of Web-based psychological research. In M. H. Birnbaum (Ed.), *Psychological experiments on the Internet* (pp. 35–60). San Diego, CA: Academic Press.

Krupat, E. (1977). A re-assessment of role playing as a technique in social psychology. *Personality and Social Psychology Bulletin, 3,* 498–504.

Landy, D., & Aronson, E. (1969). The influence of the character of the criminal and his victim on the decisions of simulated jurors. *Journal of Experimental Social Psychology, 5,* 141–152.

Lempert, R. O. (1975). Uncovering "nondiscernible" differences: Empirical research and the jury-size cases. *Michigan Law Review, 73,* 643–708.

Lieberman, J. D. (2002). Head over the heart or heart over the head? Cognitive experiential self-theory and extralegal heuristics in juror decision making. *Journal of Applied Social Psychology, 32,* 2526–2553.

Lind, E. A., & Walker, L. (1979). Theory testing, theory development, and laboratory research on legal issues. *Law and Human Behavior, 3,* 5–19.

Linz, D., & Penrod, S. (1982). *A meta-analysis of the influence of research methodology on the outcomes of jury simulation studies.* Paper presented at the Academy of Criminal Justice Sciences, Louisville, KY.

Lochner, P. (1973). Some limits on the application of social science research in the legal process. *Law and the Social Order, 5,* 815–848.

Lockhart v. McCree (1986). *U.S. Supreme Court Reports, 476,* 162.

MacCoun, R. J., & Kerr, N. L. (1988). Asymmetric influence in mock jury deliberation: Jurors' bias for leniency. *Journal of Personality and Social Psychology, 54,* 21–33.

Mason, A. (1931). *Brandeis: Lawyer and judge in the modern state.* Princeton, NJ: Princeton University Press.

McGrath, J. E. (1982). Dilemmatics: The study of research choices and dilemmas. In J. E.

McGrath, J. Martin, & R. A. Kulka (Eds.), *Judgment calls in research* (pp. 69–102). Beverly Hills: Sage.

Milgram, S. (1965). Liberating effects of group pressure. *Journal of Personality and Social Psychology, 1,* 127–134.

Miller, G. R., Bender, D. C., Boster, F., Florence, B. T., Fontes, N., Hocking, J., & Nicholson, H. (1975). The effects of videotape testimony in jury trials. *Brigham Young University Law Review, 1975,* 331–373.

Miller, G. R., Fontes, N. E., Boster, F. J., & Sunnafrank, M. J. (1983). Methodological issues in legal communication research: What can trial simulations tell us? *Communication Monographs, 50,* 33–46.

Mixon, D. (1977). Temporary false belief. *Personality and Social Psychology Bulletin, 3,* 479–488.

Monahan, J. (1983, October). *The identification of future, present, and past criminal offenders.* Paper presented at the biennial meeting of the American Psychology–Law Society, Chicago.

Monahan, J., Walker, L., Kelly, L. G., & Monohan, J. (2001). *Monahan and Walker social science in law (University Casebook;* 5th ed.). Westbury, NY: Foundation Press.

Myers, D. G., & Kaplan, M. F. (1976). Group-induced polarization in simulated juries. *Personality and Social Psychology Bulletin, 2,* 63–66.

Neuliep, J. W., & Crandall, R. (1990). Editorial bias against replication research. *Journal of Social Behavior and Personality, 5,* 85–90.

Neuliep, J. W., & Crandall, R. (1993). Reviewer bias against replication research. *Journal of Social Behavior and Personality, 8,* 21–29.

Ogloff, J. R. P. (1999). *Law and Human Behavior*: Reflecting back and looking forward. *Law and Human Behavior, 23,* 1–8.

Ogloff, J. R. P. (2000). Two steps forward and one step backward: The law and psychology movement(s) in the 20th century. *Law and Human Behavior, 24,* 457–483.

O'Neil, K. M. (2002). *Web-based experimental research in psychology and law: Methodological variables that may affect dropout rates, sample characteristics, and verdicts.* Unpublished doctoral dissertation, University of Nebraska, Lincoln, NE.

O'Neil, K. M., & Penrod, S. D. (2001). Methodological variables in Web-based research that may affect results: Sample type, monetary incentives, and personal information. *Behavior Research Methods, Instruments, and Computers, 33,* 226–233.

O'Neil, K. M., & Penrod, S. D. (2002, October). *Jury research meets the World-Wide Web: Assessing the impact of research methods on substantive findings.* Paper presented at the annual convention of the Society of Experimental Social Psychology, Columbus, OH.

O'Neil, K. M., Penrod, S. D., & Bornstein, B. H. (2002). Web-based research: Methodological variables' effects on dropout and sample characteristics. *Behavior Research Methods, Instruments, and Computers, 35,* 217–226.

Orne, M. T. (1962). On the social psychology of the psychological experiment: With particular reference to demand characteristics and their implications. *American Psychologist, 17,* 776–783.

Rosen, P. (1972). *The Supreme Court and social science.* Urbana, IL: University of Illinois Press.

Rosenblum, V. G. (1975). *Report on the uses of social science in judicial decision making.* Final report on NSF Grant No. 74-17572 to the Panel on Law and Social Sciences, National Science Foundation, Evanston, IL.

Rosenthal, R. (1964). Experimental outcome-orientation and the results of the psychological experiment. *Psychological Bulletin, 61,* 405–412.

Ross, H. L., & Blumenthal, M. (1975). Some problems in experimentation in a legal setting. *American Sociologist, 10,* 150–155.

Runkel, P. J., & McGrath, J. E. (1972). *Research on human behavior: A systematic guide to method.* New York: Holt.

Sigall, H., & Ostrove, N. (1975). Beautiful but dangerous: Effects of offender attractiveness and nature of the crime on juridic judgment. *Journal of Personality and Social Psychology, 31,* 410–414.

Simon, R. J. (1967). *The jury and the defense of insanity.* Boston: Little, Brown.

Simon, R. J., & Mahan, L. (1971). Quantifying burdens of proof: A view from the bench, the jury and the classroom. *Law and Society Review, 5,* 319–330.

Stasser, G., & Davis, J. H. (1981). Group decision making and social influence: A social interaction sequence model. *Psychological Review, 88,* 523–551.

Stasser, G., Kerr, N. L., & Davis, J. H. (1989). Influence processes and consensus models in decision-making groups. In P. Paulus (Ed.), *Psychology of group influence* (2nd ed., pp. 279–326). Hillsdale, NJ: Erlbaum.

Strodtbeck, F. (1962). Social processes, the law, and jury functioning. In W. M. Evan (Ed.), *Law and sociology: Exploratory essays* (pp. 144–164). New York: Free Press.

Studebaker, C. A., Robbennolt, J. K., Penrod, S. D., Pathak-Sharma, M. K., Groscup, J. L., & Devenport, J. L. (2002). Studying pretrial publicity effects: New methods for improving ecological validity and testing external validity. *Law and Human Behavior, 26,* 19–41.

Thomas, E. A. C., & Hogue, A. (1976). Apparent weight of evidence, decision criteria, and confidence ratings in juror decision making. *Psychological Review, 83,* 442–465.

Thompson, W. C. (1989). Death qualification after *Wainwright v. Witt* and *Lockhart v. McCree. Law and Human Behavior, 13,* 185–215.

Triandis, H. C. (1978). Basic research in the context of applied research in personality and social psychology. *Personality and Social Psychology Bulletin, 4,* 383–387.

Vidmar, N. (1979). The other issues in jury simulation research: A commentary with particular reference to defendant character studies. *Law and Human Behavior, 3,* 95–106.

Wasby, S. L. (1980). History and state of the art of applied social research in the courts. In M. Saks & C. Baron (Eds.), *The use/nonuse/misuse of applied social research in the courts* (pp. 15–16). Cambridge, MA: Abt.

Webb, E. J., Campbell, D. T., Schwartz, R. D., & Sechrest, L. (1966). *Unobtrusive measures: Nonreactive research in the social sciences.* Chicago, IL: Rand McNally.

Weiten, W., & Diamond, S. S. (1979). A critical review of the jury simulation paradigm: The case of defendant characteristics. *Law and Human Behavior, 3,* 71–93.

Wells, G. L., Small, M., Penrod, S., Malpass, R. S., Fulero, S. M., & Brimacombe, C. A. E. (1998). Eyewitness identification procedures: Recommendations for lineups and photospreads. *Law and Human Behavior, 22,* 603–647.

Wrightsman, L. S., Greene, E., Nietzel, M. T., & Fortune, W. H. (2002). *Psychology and the legal system* (5th ed.). Belmont, CA: Wadsworth.

CHAPTER ELEVEN

The Psychology of Jury
and Juror Decision Making

LORA M. LEVETT
ERIN M. DANIELSEN
MARGARET BULL KOVERA
BRIAN L. CUTLER

In 1988, the Carmichael family was involved in a car accident that killed one family member and injured seven others. The family sued the tire manufacturer, and the result was the landmark case *Kumho Tire v. Carmichael* (1999). In *Kuhmo*, a tire failure expert was called to testify on behalf of the plaintiff. The defense argued that the testimony was inadmissible under current standards for admitting expert testimony, and the plaintiff argued that those standards did not apply. The U.S. Supreme Court heard the case, and the competence of jurors to evaluate expert testimony was called in to question. How do jurors evaluate experts? Are they able to understand technical testimony? Or do they defer to the expert, deciding in favor of whichever side the expert represents? Psychologists weighed in on both sides of the debate, filing amicus curiae briefs about the competence of juries as decision makers (see Vidmar et al., 2000). Two arguments emerged. One side viewed jurors as competent decision makers, and the other viewed jurors as biased against wealthy defendants and corporations in civil cases and asserted that jurors have a natural tendency to defer to experts (Vidmar et al., 2000). Who is correct? Are jurors competent decision makers?

There is no question that juries have made decisions that others may find controversial or outrageous. For example, in one well-known lawsuit, *Liebeck v. McDonald's* (1992), a jury awarded $2.9 million to a woman who was burned when she spilled coffee from a McDonald's restaurant in her lap. In another lawsuit, a jury awarded plaintiffs suing BMW $4 million seemingly for a bad paint job (*BMW of North America, Inc. v. Gore*, 1996). Many were also shocked when the jury returned a not guilty verdict, despite substantial physical evidence, in the high-profile O.J. Simpson criminal case, in which the former football star was charged with murdering his ex-wife and a male acquaintance (*People v. Orenthal James Simpson*, 1995). Each of these decisions was scrutinized by the public and led the public to question the competency of the jury system. These three cases are obviously not entirely representative of all cases decided by juries, but they lead to questions concerning jury competence. As illustrated by the *Kuhmo* debate, even experts disagree on the competence of the jury. In this chapter, we explore the empirical psychology of jury decision making to address the issues necessary to answer the question: Are juries competent decision makers?

To best answer our question, we first explore *how* juries and jurors make decisions. We explore several different models of jury and juror decision making, discussing each of the models' strengths and weaknesses. Second, we examine how jurors use different types of evidence, such as eyewitness evidence, statistical evidence, and confession evidence in their decision-making process. We explore whether jurors use the evidence presented to them in trial correctly. Third, we learn how jurors make decisions in civil cases, and whether jurors follow the law when determining liability and awarding damages. Fourth, we explore extraevidentiary information jurors may use in their decision making. Do characteristics of the defendant affect jurors' decisions? Finally, we discuss procedural reforms and other methods of improving the quality of jury decisions.

MODELS OF JURY AND JUROR DECISION MAKING

Researchers have traditionally studied jury decision making within two contexts: the group decision and the individual juror decision. First, we examine jury decision making at the group level. We describe the typical decision-making process observed in many juries, discuss the effects of majority and minority influences, and answer questions raised by Supreme Court cases, such as: Do juries make better decisions unanimously or non-unanimously? How many people need to serve on a jury to produce the best decision? Second, we examine juror decision making at the individual level by considering different models of juror decision making and exploring the strengths and weaknesses of each.

Jury Decision Making

Deliberation generally consists of a discussion of the evidence presented at trial and the judge's instructions about the law. Generally, jurors spend about 70–75% of deliberation time discussing the evidence and 20% discussing the law (Ellsworth, 1989). A typical jury moves through three stages during deliberation (Costanzo, 2003; Stasser, 1992): orientation, open conflict, and reconciliation. In the orientation stage, the jurors elect their foreperson, discuss procedures, and raise general trial issues. Juries generally use one of two deliberation styles: verdict driven or evidence driven (Hastie, Penrod, & Pennington, 1983). Verdict driven juries comprise about 30% of juries. These juries begin deliberation by taking an initial public poll, also known as a straw poll. The jurors then orient their deliberation around that poll, sorting evidence into categories in support of their respective positions. In verdict driven juries, jurors generally advocate one particular verdict at a time and take frequent straw polls to monitor other jurors' opinions. Conversely, evidence driven juries begin discussions by focusing on the evidence presented at trial. The jurors discuss different verdict categories until they have thoroughly reviewed the evidence, and individual jurors may relate testimony or evidence to several verdicts at one time. After jurors have agreed upon the best story accounting for all of the evidence, they often take a straw poll, but only late in the deliberation.

Do these differences in orientation result in differences in jury decision making? Generally, the evidence driven jury is more vigorous in its examination of the evidence than the verdict driven jury, which may not discuss all the evidence completely (Hastie et al., 1983). Verdict driven juries reach decisions faster and rate their task as less serious than evidence driven juries, and jurors report feeling less satisfied with their contribution to the decision-making task.

The second stage in jury deliberation is open conflict, in which jurors attempt to persuade their fellow jurors to reach a verdict (Costanzo, 2003; Stasser, 1992). Small groups such as juries are swayed by means of two processes: normative and informational influence (Kaplan & Miller, 1987). Jurors swayed by informational influence privately accept the change, converting their personal views because of a compelling argument or set of facts presented by another juror. Conversely, jurors swayed by normative influence publicly conform to the other jurors but still maintain their private beliefs. In a mock civil trial, Hans (1992) found that jurors were more likely to rely on informational influence when making fact-based decisions, such as determining liability. When making a more subjective decision, such as damage-award decisions, jurors were more likely to rely on normative influences. Furthermore, juries compelled to reach unanimity through a dynamite charge were more likely to be swayed by normative influence than informational influence (Smith & Kassin, 1993). After the jury reaches a verdict, jurors enter the final stage of decision making: reconciliation. During reconciliation, juries attempt to ensure that every jury member is satisfied with the verdict (Costanzo, 2003; Stasser, 1992).

Who has the most influence during deliberation? Are juries more likely to be swayed by the minority, after listening to different opinions? Or are juries more likely to decide with the majority, convincing those in the minority of the popular opinion? Given that the best predictor of verdict is the initial individual verdicts of the jurors (Kalven & Zeisel, 1966), it follows that the majority generally prevails. In one study, of the 215 juries that showed a clear majority, 209 of those juries eventually produced a verdict congruent with that of the majority (Kalven & Zeisel, 1966). Thus, when groups begin discussion with a clear preference, discussion tends to strengthen those opinions—a phenomenon called "group polarization" (Burnstein, 1983; Lamm & Myers, 1978).

Jury research has demonstrated that a slight modification to the general rule of group decision making is needed in criminal trials. A review of 45 years of jury decision making research suggests that for juries of 12 persons, when 7 or fewer jurors initially favor conviction, the jury is likely to acquit (Devine, Clayton, Dunford, Seying, & Pryce, 2001). If 10 or more jurors initially favor conviction, the jury is likely to convict. If 8 or 9 jurors initially favor conviction, it is difficult to predict whether the jury will acquit or convict. The tendency of criminal juries to favor the accused is known as the "leniency bias" (Kerr, MacCoun, & Kramer, 1996; MacCoun & Kerr, 1988). Generally, the majority does prevail; however, the standard of guilt beyond a reasonable doubt and the deliberation process tend to produce the leniency bias. Those jurors in favor of acquittal only need to produce a reasonable doubt in their fellow jurors; those in favor of conviction need to produce a plausible reason for conviction that eliminates reasonable doubt. When there is no clear majority, the jury is more likely to acquit.

Jury Size

How many jurors are required for good decision making? In *Williams v. Florida* (1970), the U.S. Supreme Court held that a 6-person jury was acceptable in noncapital cases. They later clarified their decision in *Ballew v. Georgia* (1978), ruling that a 5-person jury was too small, and that a 6-person jury is the constitutional minimum. These decisions spurred research seeking to answer the question: Do 6-person juries make the same decisions as 12-person juries?

A meta-analysis of this body of research on jury size reviewed 17 studies that tested whether 6-person juries make decisions that differ from the decisions of 12-person juries (Saks & Marti, 1997). Juries of 12 people deliberated longer, recalled more evidence accurately, generated more arguments, and were more demographically representative of the community than 6-person juries. Although juries of 12 deliberate longer than juries of 6, this difference in deliberation length may be a function of the 12-member juries containing more people. One study found that the average juror contribution to the deliberation was the same for 6-member and 12-member juries (Hastie et al., 1983). The other differences between 6-member and 12-member juries cannot be explained so easily. Minority views are more likely to be represented, and those holding minority views are more likely to have an ally in a 12-member jury. Because the group holding the minority position is fewer in number in a

6-person jury, the minority may feel greater pressure to conform compared to a 12-person jury. Furthermore, because a 12-person jury is more representative of the larger community than a 6-person jury, it is more likely to contain a range of juror opinions and expertise. Based on these findings, it appears that the deliberation process is affected by jury size; however, verdicts of 6-and 12-person juries do not differ significantly (Saks & Marti, 1997).

Decision Rule

At the same time the U.S. Supreme Court was making decisions regarding jury size, it was also making decisions about the decision rules that juries should use; the court ruled that non-unanimous decisions made by juries were constitutional (*Apodaca, Cooper, & Madden v. Oregon*, 1972; *Johnson v. Louisiana*, 1972). Presently, 27 U.S. states still require unanimity in all types of trials, 44 states require unanimity in criminal felony trials, and all states require unanimity in capital murder trials. Furthermore, if the state is using a 6-person jury, the court ruled that the decision must be unanimous (*Burch v. Louisiana*, 1979). Why did the court abandon the age-old requirement for unanimity? A jury deliberating with a unanimous decision rule "hangs" twice as often as a jury deliberating with a majority decision rule (Kalven & Zeisel, 1966; Padawer-Singer, Singer, & Singer, 1977), and the court made the landmark decisions to reduce the number of hung juries. However, it is important to consider whether the costs of a non-unanimous decision rule are worth the benefit of reducing the number of hung juries.

Minority group members may not be heard as often or as thoroughly when the jury is under a majority decision rule. In one study, 6-member mock juries deliberated to either a unanimous verdict or to majority of 5 out of 6 (Hans, 1978). Those with minority opinions played a larger role in the deliberations of juries using a unanimous decision role than they did in juries deliberating under a majority rule. In another study, 12-member mock juries watched a murder trial and then deliberated to either a unanimous verdict, a 10-to-2 verdict, or an 8-to-4 verdict (Hastie et al., 1983). The decision-making processes used by unanimous juries differed from the processes used by majority rule juries. Specifically, majority rule juries took votes earlier, spent more time voting (and therefore less time discussing the evidence), were more likely to use normative influence to sway fellow jurors, and were more verdict driven than unanimous rule juries. In majority rule juries, once the correct number of votes was reached, deliberation ceased, regardless of whether the majority had swayed the views of the minority.

Hastie et al. (1983) recognized four major themes in decision rule research. First, unanimous juries are more likely to hang compared to non-unanimous juries. Second, the unanimous jury tends to take more time examining the evidence, whereas the non-unanimous jury focuses more on polling and normative influence. Third, overall juror satisfaction is higher in unanimous juries compared to non-unanimous juries. Last, jurors with minority viewpoints are more likely to be heard and perceived as more influential in a unanimous jury compared to a non-unanimous jury. Thus, the cost of having a non-unanimous jury (i.e., less thorough examination of the evidence, disregard of minority viewpoints) may not outweigh the benefit that non-unanimous juries are less likely to hang.

We have examined how the deliberation process affects jury decision making and considered the pressures of conformity, the different types of juries, and how different Supreme Court rulings have affected jury decision making. However, we have not yet asked, What determines how a single juror interprets the evidence? Recall that the single best predictor of postdeliberation *jury* verdict is predeliberation *individual juror* verdict. How do individual jurors arrive at conclusions? Do jurors make decisions about verdict before the trial is over, or do they wait until they hear all the evidence? In the next section, we examine these questions as we consider different models of juror decision making.

Models of Juror Decision Making

Although juries make decisions as groups, much of the literature on jury decision making has examined the decision-making processes of individual jurors. There are several reasons for this emphasis on individual decision making. The cognitive revolution within psychology has produced an interest in the mental processes underlying decision making, which is best studied at the individual level. Moreover, studying groups (i.e., juries) presents logistical and methodological difficulties (e.g., extra time for deliberations, more participants required to maintain statistical power) that are not present for the study of individual decision making. Finally, many studies have demonstrated that the best predictor of postdeliberation verdicts is individual jurors' predeliberation verdicts (Davis, 1980; Kalven & Zeisel, 1966; Sandys & Dillehay, 1995; Stasser, Kerr, & Bray, 1982), which has led some to question the necessity of conducting costlier studies that include deliberating juries.

The prevailing models of juror decision making generally fall into one of two categories: the mathematical approach and the explanation-based or cognitive approach (Greene et al., 2002). There are generally three types of mathematical models: probability theory models (e.g., Moore & Gump, 1995), algebraic models (e.g., Slovic & Lichtenstein, 1971), and stochastic process models (e.g., Kerr, 1993). The most popular model for explanation-based juror decision making is the story model (Pennington & Hastie, 1986). First, we discuss the various mathematical approaches for studying juror decision making and then discuss the story model and the research supporting it.

Probabilistic Approach

The most dominant probabilistic model of juror decision making is Bayesian probability theory. Bayesian theory rests on the assumption that jurors make decisions using a single "mental meter" that measures their belief in the defendant's guilt or innocence. This meter adjusts as the juror hears and evaluates trial evidence and other relevant information. The primary assumption of Bayesian theory is that the mental meter represents the juror's belief in the probability that an event occurred or is true (Hastie, 1993). At the beginning of a trial, jurors are thought to have an initial opinion about the likelihood that the defendant is guilty or innocent. During the course of the trial, jurors interpret each piece of evidence as a unit of information. Jurors interpret each unit of information by assigning it a probability and then combining that probability with their prior belief—a process described by Bayes theorem, which uses an equation derived from the axioms of probability theory (Hastie, 1993). This combinatorial process may move the mental meter, producing a new belief in the probability that the defendant committed the crime. If the mental meter reaches a probability of 0 or 1, it will stop moving. At the end of the deliberations, jurors compare their final belief with their threshold for conviction. If their beliefs about the likelihood of guilt exceed their thresholds for conviction, they will vote to convict the defendant. Otherwise, they will vote to acquit. The use of Bayes theorem as a model of juror decision-making processes has not garnered much empirical support. Indeed, several studies have found that jurors do not make trial judgments according to Bayes theorem (e.g., Schklar & Diamond, 1999; Smith, Penrod, Otto, & Park, 1996). These studies have found that compared to Bayesian norms, jurors generally underuse probabilistic evidence.

Algebraic Approach

Similar to the Bayesian approach, the algebraic model of juror decision making also rests on the assumption that there is a single mental meter representing the juror's belief in the defendant's guilt or innocence; however, the algebraic approach differs from the Bayesian approach in two ways. First, because the mental meter reading does not freeze at extreme probabilities, as it does in Bayes theorem, extreme judgments (in Bayes theorem, judgments of 0 or 1) can be adjusted when new evidence is introduced. Second, jurors update their mental meter by *adding* the value of each piece of evidence to their overall belief, whereas Bayesian theory uses *multiplication* (Hastie, 1993).

Jurors begin the trial with an initial opinion, or anchor. When new pieces of evidence are identified, jurors derive an implication of guilt (i.e., whether the evidence indicates the defendant was the perpetrator) from each piece of evidence. That implication is multiplied by the weight that the juror assigns to the evidence. For example, when an eyewitness positively identifies the defendant, the implication is that the defendant is the perpetrator. The weight the juror assigns to that implication will ultimately determine the impact of the implication on the juror's overall belief in the defendant's guilt. For example, if the eyewitness saw the perpetrator under poor viewing conditions, the juror may assign less weight to the implication than if the eyewitness saw the perpetrator under good viewing conditions. After jurors weight an implication, they adjust their belief in the defendant's guilt or innocence by adding it to, or averaging it with, their prior belief in the defendant's guilt. The mental meter may or may not move, based on the addition of each new piece of evidence. At the end of the trial, jurors create their conviction criterion using the judge's instructions on the standard of proof, the severity of the crime, and their general attitudes toward the criminal justice system. They then compare their belief in the defendant's guilt or innocence with their conviction criterion. Ultimately, if a juror's final mental meter rating exceeds his or her conviction criterion, he or she will vote to convict the defendant. The algebraic model of juror decision making has some empirical support (e.g., Moore & Gump, 1995). An interesting implication of this model for jury decision making is that it may be advantageous for attorneys to only present their strongest evidence.

Stochastic Process Model

The stochastic process model differs from the algebraic and probability approaches in that it accounts for error variance in the juror decision-making process. Furthermore, the decisions that jurors make about evidence occur in real time; that is, jurors interpret and weigh each piece of evidence as they receive it and then adjust their mental meters before considering the next piece of evidence (Hastie, 1993). The weight given to each piece of evidence varies by individual, accounting for the randomness of individual jurors seated on a particular jury. As in the other mathematical models, the stochastic process begins with jurors' initial opinions about the guilt or innocence of the defendant. Then jurors undertake an evidence evaluation process, in which they extract implications from each piece of evidence, weigh them, and apply the evidence to their mental meter in real time. Another unique feature of the stochastic process model is that it employs a "critical event" feature: At some point in the trial, a critical event occurs for each juror, whether it is an eyewitness, a particular person's testimony, or another piece of evidence. This event freezes the mental meter into a permanent position, and it cannot be changed. For example, if jurors listen to several eyewitnesses each identify the perpetrator in a convenience store robbery, their mental meters may freeze, and any other evidence that follows this identification would not affect their beliefs about the defendant's guilt.

After the critical event, jurors then compare their final opinion of the defendant's guilt with their decision criterion for guilt. If the jurors' ratings of the defendant's guilt fall within their decision criterion to convict, they will convict. The last unique feature of the stochastic process model approach is that, in addition to verdict, the output includes a confidence level based on the distance between the threshold for conviction and the jurors' final belief in the defendant's guilt. As the distance between the jurors' conviction threshold and their final belief in the defendant's guilt decreases, so too will jurors' confidence in their verdict decrease. The stochastic model of juror decision making has garnered some empirical support. In one study, the model successfully predicted changes in jurors' ratings of probability of guilt at several different points in the trial (Crott & Werner, 1994).

Several critiques of the mathematical models of jury decision making have been offered (e.g., Ellsworth & Mauro, 1998; Pennington & Hastie, 1981). The most serious criticism stems from the use of the single-meter postulate in the mathematical models. Specifically, the law assumes that the jurors' task is multidimensional, in that jurors are asked to determine whether the defendant committed each element of a crime beyond a reasonable doubt. However, the single-meter postulate of the mathematical approaches only account for a single decision (Hastie, 1993). Therefore, the mathematical approaches do not fully address the complicated process of juror decision making.

Explanation-Based Approaches: The Story Model

Explanation- or cognitive-based approaches for studying juror decision making account for the jurors' active role in the decision-making process (Greene et al., 2002). Instead of viewing the juror as a passive listener, recording and weighing evidence, explanation-based approaches view the juror as an active participant, struggling to make sense of the trial evidence. These models incorporate jurors' unique experiences, knowledge, beliefs, and attitudes that may affect how they interpret the evidence and ultimately decide whether the defendant is guilty; the models also account for jurors' cognitive organization, or mental representation, of the information they heard during the trial (Bennett & Feldman, 1981; Hastie, 1993; Pennington & Hastie, 1986).

The story model is the most sophisticated of the explanation-based models (Pennington & Hastie, 1986) and posits three separate processes in juror decision making. First, the juror integrates the evidence into a story or a causal chain of events (Pennington & Hastie, 1986). In constructing a story, the juror uses three types of knowledge: (1) evidence learned through the trial, (2) personal knowledge about events similar to the event in question, and (3) expectations or knowledge about what constitutes a complete story. During the trial, evidence is generally presented in a disconnected format; that is, different witnesses offer different elements of the story, and these elements are unlikely to be presented in chronological order. Furthermore, witnesses are often prohibited from elaborating on why particular events happened. For these reasons, jurors must play an active role in story construction in that they organize the evidence into stories, infer motivation or goals of the event's participants, infer causal relations between the pieces of evidence in the story, and may fill in missing information based on their knowledge of similar events.

One of the assets of the story model is that it incorporates the unique experiences of the juror into a model of the juror decision-making process. These unique experiences may influence how the jurors interpret the evidence. Thus, one juror may create a different story from a fellow juror, based solely on his or her unique experiences. If a juror creates a different story, he or she may arrive at a different verdict. The jurors then bring their unique stories to the deliberation process, where they come to a shared understanding of the evidence.

Jurors may construct more than one story while they evaluate the evidence during the course of the trial; however, one story usually emerges as the best story (Pennington & Hastie, 1986). Three "certainty principles" contribute to the acceptability of a story and a juror's subsequent confidence in that story: coverage, coherence, and uniqueness. A story's *coverage* refers to "the extent to which the story accounts for all the evidence presented at trial" (Pennington & Hastie, 1993, p. 198). If a story explains most or all of the evidence, a juror is more likely to be confident in the story. Conversely, if a story does not explain most, if not all, of the evidence, it is less likely to be chosen as the acceptable story, and confidence in the story will decrease.

A story's *coherence* has three separate components: consistency, plausibility, and completeness. If a story does not contradict itself or other pieces of evidence that the juror deems true, then it is consistent. A story is plausible if it is similar to the juror's knowledge of what generally happens in similar situations. A story is complete when it has all the parts that jurors expect a story to have (i.e., it fills jurors' expectations of what constitutes a complete story). If a story is missing key parts, jurors' confidence in the story will decrease, and they will be less likely to accept the story. These three components combine to form the story's coherence.

Last, if more than one story covers the trial evidence and jurors judge both stories to be coherent, then the stories lack *uniqueness* and the jurors' confidence in either of the stories is likely to be low. However, if only one story emerges as the most coherent and high in coverage, the confidence in that story is likely to be higher because it is unique.

After jurors create stories through listening to evidence and constructing an explanation based on their world experiences and knowledge about what makes a complete story, they learn the different verdict definitions and decision alternatives available to them. Judges typically provide this information to jurors at the end of the trial, and mastering this information is generally a difficult, one-trial learning task (Pennington & Hastie, 1993). The story model posits that jurors represent the possible verdict definitions as categories with lists of the various features of that category. Jurors' prior knowledge (correct or incorrect) of the law may interfere with their ability to comprehend the different verdict definitions. One study showed that jurors held incorrect representations of verdict definitions, and did not discard those verdict definitions when a judge instructed them about the proper verdict definitions (Smith, 1991). Thus, jurors may not use the law correctly because of their prior knowledge of verdict definitions. In the last stage of the story model, the jury reaches a verdict decision. To make a decision, jurors match the accepted story with the various verdict definitions. Jurors will choose the verdict that best matches the story they constructed while interpreting the evidence.

The story model has been successfully used to explain juror decision making in several different studies. Pennington and Hastie (1992) tested the story model in three different experiments. In the first experiment, participants read two cases. The cases were either organized by story (i.e., each witness told a complete story) or by issue (e.g., testimony addressing motive was presented together, testimony addressing character was presented together). In addition, the researchers also varied the credibility of one of the witnesses (i.e., high, low, or no information). The evidence was designed to favor innocence in the first case and guilt in the second case. They found that participants' memory for evidence was the same in all cases. However, verdict decisions were stronger in the conditions in which jurors read the evidence in story form; that is, jurors were more likely to find the defendant guilty in those cases in which the evidence favored guilt when they read the evidence in story form. Therefore, when it was easier for the jurors to create a story, they were more likely to decide in accordance with the preponderance of evidence.

In the second and third experiments, jurors rendered a global guilt judgment at the end of a case, assessed each piece of evidence as it was presented, or read a block of evidence and provided a guilt likelihood ratio for each block. In those conditions in which jurors rendered a global judgment, the story model described their decision-making processes better than did linear and Bayesian models. When jurors made item-by-item assessments, linear models best described the decision-making process, but story completeness did not have as great an effect on decisions. Thus, in those conditions most similar to a real juror's task (i.e., global judgments), the story model best described the process of juror decision making. The story model has also been used to describe juror decision making in rape cases (Olsen-Fulero & Fulero, 1997) and sexual harassment cases (Huntley & Costanzo, 2003).

The stories that jurors construct also influence the verdicts that they choose. For example, Pennington and Hastie (1981) had jurors render verdicts in a murder case. They then interviewed the jurors, assessing how they arrived at their verdicts. They found a central story for each verdict group. That is, those jurors who reached a verdict of guilty of first-degree murder shared several common themes in their stories. Those jurors who reached a verdict of not guilty also shared several common themes. Thus, the decisions jurors reached varied with the story they constructed.

ARE JURORS COMPETENT DECISION MAKERS?

Thus far we have explored how juries and jurors arrive at decisions. However, we have not addressed the ability of jurors to make correct decisions. How accurate are jurors in their decision making? Do they understand statistical evidence such as DNA or fingerprint evidence? Are they able to detect when an expert's testimony is flawed? What happens when judges instruct jurors to disregard evidence? Do they use that evidence in their decision making? Do juries award outrageous damages in civil cases? Is a defendant more likely to be found guilty if he or she is from a particular background? In the next section, we explore whether jurors competently evaluate the evidence and follow the law as they are instructed.

Jurors' Evaluations of Evidence

Eyewitness Evidence

Jurors are more likely to convict a defendant of a crime if an eyewitness positively identifies him or her than if only circumstantial evidence points to the defendant (Loftus, 1980). However, research has demonstrated that several factors influence the accuracy of eyewitness identifications (e.g., viewing conditions, weapon focus, lineup instructions). Do jurors take these factors into account when making decisions about eyewitness evidence presented to them at trial? Research has demonstrated that the answer may be no, at least not without additional guidance.

In one trial simulation, mock jurors heard eyewitness testimony that varied several factors that influenced the reliability of eyewitness identification (e.g., weapon focus, viewing conditions, lineup instructions, retention interval, stressfulness; Cutler, Penrod, & Stuve, 1988). They also varied the confidence of the eyewitness. The only factor to influence juror judgments was eyewitness confidence. Similar results were found in another study examining the effects of different factors influencing eyewitness identification and juror decision making, in that, again, only eyewitness confidence affected juror judgments (Cutler, Penrod, & Dexter, 1990). Thus, it appears that jurors are not particularly adept at evaluating eyewitness evidence.

Hearsay Evidence

Hearsay evidence is testimony from a witness about a fact or statement relayed to the witness by another person, known as the declarant (*Federal Rules of Evidence*, 1984). With the exception of special circumstances (e.g., deathbed statements, spontaneous utterances), hearsay evidence is generally excluded from trial (Park, 1987). In most cases, this evidence is excluded because the declarant is not available for cross-examination. Courts are concerned that hearsay information is unreliable, and jurors' decisions may be influenced by the unreliable information. Are these concerns valid? How much weight do jurors assign hearsay evidence? Are jurors able to evaluate hearsay evidence correctly? Some legal scholars have argued that jurors should be allowed to evaluate hearsay evidence, arguing that jurors regularly evaluate secondhand information in their lives and therefore should be allowed to evaluate such information at trial (Park, 1987).

Several studies have examined the effects of hearsay evidence on juror judgments. Generally, these studies have found that juror judgments are not influenced by hearsay evidence (Landsman & Rakos, 1991; Miene, Park, & Borgida, 1992; Pagilia & Schuller, 1998; Rakos & Landsman, 1992). One study found that hearsay evidence influenced juror decisions (Schuller, 1995); however, in this study, an expert, rather than a layperson, presented the hearsay evidence, and this difference in source may account for the difference in findings (Greene et al., 2002).

Despite the seeming absence of influence of hearsay evidence on juror decisions, the courts' concern that jurors may be influenced by inaccurate information has still not been addressed. In one study, mock jurors evaluated hearsay witnesses who had been interviewed either 1 day or 1 week after watching an eyewitness interview (Kovera, Park, & Penrod, 1992). Those hearsay witnesses who were interviewed 1 day after watching the eyewitness interview were more accurate than those who were interviewed a week later. Jurors reported that the testimony of the good hearsay witness was more accurate and useful than the testimony of the poor hearsay witness. Although this research suggests that jurors may be more sensitive to variations in the reliability of hearsay evidence than in the reliability of eyewitness evidence, future research is needed to examine whether jurors' evaluations of hearsay witnesses influence the decisions they make in trial.

Confession Evidence

How much weight do jurors assign to confession evidence? According to the U.S. Supreme Court, confession evidence should be treated similarly to other types of evidence (*Arizona v. Fulminante*, 1991). Do jurors treat it as such? In an investigation of the impact of confession evidence, eyewitness evidence, and character testimony on juror judgments, mock jurors read one of four different types of trials: murder, assault, rape, and theft (Kassin & Neumann, 1997). Cases that contained a confession had the highest conviction rates, indicating that jurors assign more weight to confession evidence than to the other types of evidence. In a second experiment, all three types of evidence were presented at different points in the trial, and jurors rendered a mid-trial judgment. Again, the researchers found that confession evidence was the most incriminating of all the types of evidence (Kassin & Neumann, 1997). Confession evidence is compelling evidence. However, what happens when that confession was coerced? Are jurors sensitive to the possibility that a coerced confession may be a false confession?

False confessions are a recognized problem in the criminal justice system (Gudjonsson, 2003). The techniques employed by police officers (e.g., the Reid technique) may increase the likelihood of a false confession, and some confessions have been ruled inadmissible because of the techniques used to obtain them (Gudjonsson, 2003). Are jurors able to disregard an inadmissible confession? If they know the confession was coerced, do jurors assign it less weight? Although jurors perceive high-pressure confessions as less voluntary and less influential than low-pressure confessions, the presence of a high-pressure confession still increases conviction rates (Kassin & Sukel, 1997). This effect obtained even when the confession was ruled inadmissible and jurors reported that it had no influence on their decision. Thus, jurors seem to have difficulty discounting confession evidence that is likely to be unreliable.

Statistical Evidence

Research in social psychology suggests that laypeople may not be successful in detecting errors in scientific research (Nisbett, 1993). People do not recognize that the results obtained from smaller samples are less reliable than those obtained by using larger samples (Tversky & Kahneman, 1974). Individuals ignore sample-size information when making probability judgments; they tend to see small and large samples as equally representative of the larger population (Kahneman & Tversky, 1972; Tversky & Kahneman, 1971). Other studies have demonstrated that individuals often have a flawed perception of chance; that is, they may not understand probabilistic information (e.g., Gilovich, Vallone, & Tversky, 1985; Tversky & Kahneman, 1971). These experiments demonstrate that individuals often are unable to evaluate statistics properly. In recent years, the use of probabilistic scientific evidence in trial has increased (Smith et al., 1996). Therefore, it is important to examine how jurors perceive such evidence. Given what we know about laypersons' perceptions of statistical information, it is reasonable to assume that individuals (e.g., jurors) may not use statistical information correctly in court. How do jurors react when presented with complicated statistics associated with certain types of tests (e.g., fingerprints, DNA testing)? Do they use the information properly to make a fair decision?

Courts have expressed concerns that jurors may give too much weight to the scientific testimony about a DNA report (e.g., Commonwealth v. Curnin, 1991). The primary concern is that jurors may perceive such evidence as infallible and therefore disregard information provided by other conflicting evidence. Compared to predictions made from normative Bayesian models, jurors generally underweight probabilistic information about blood and enzyme types (Smith et al., 1996); this finding is consistent with those of other studies examining jurors' use of probabilistic information (Faigman & Baglioni, 1988; Goodman, 1992; Schklar & Diamond, 1999; Thompson & Schumman, 1987).

Jurors are sensitive to variations in the weight of the statistical evidence. That is, in those cases in which the probability that the match was shared in the population was high, jurors' guilt judgments were lower than in those cases in which the match was shared with a lower portion of the population. Evidence that was not probabilistic in nature (e.g., eyewitness confidence) affected juror verdict (i.e., higher eyewitness confidence resulted in more convictions than lower eyewitness confidence). Thus, the use of probabilistic information did not overwhelm other evidence presented (Smith et al., 1996).

Overall, this research presents a promising picture of jurors' abilities to evaluate probabilistic evidence. However, further research is needed to examine the variation in the use of probabilistic evidence.

Complex Evidence

We have addressed how jurors use statistical evidence; however, we have not yet addressed how jurors evaluate other complex evidence. How do jurors evaluate evidence in cases with multiple defendants or plaintiffs? Does complex language inhibit the ability of jurors to evaluate the evidence presented? First, it is important to define *trial complexity*, which generally has been studied in the civil law realm. The term has been operationalized as the presence of multiple or overlapping legal issues in one trial, technical evidence, or merely as having a large amount of information for jurors to process (Horowitz, ForsterLee, & Brolly, 1996). Trial complexity can be viewed as consisting of two components: decision complexity and evidence complexity (Helgeson & Ursic, 1993; Horowitz et al., 1996). *Decision complexity* refers to the complexity of the legal principles in question at the trial (Horowitz et al., 1996). *Evidence complexity* refers to the amount of information, or "information load," present in the trial; it includes the number of witnesses, the number of plaintiffs, the number of injuries, and the sum of those injuries (Helgeson & Ursic, 1993). It also includes the clarity of the evidence and the general complexity (i.e., technicality, difficulty) of the evidence.

In one field study, as the amount of trial information increased, jurors reported that their ability to understand the issues in the trial and confidence in their verdict decreased (Heuer & Penrod, 1994). Experimental research also supports the hypothesis that as information load increases, juror comprehension decreases (Horowitz et al., 1996). In the context of a mock civil case with multiple defendants, researchers varied the complexity of the evidence and information load. Even though the evidence favored the plaintiffs, jurors in the high-information-load condition were more likely to blame the plaintiffs for their situation and were less able to distinguish among plaintiffs than were those in the low-information-load condition. Although language complexity did not directly affect jurors' decisions about liability, it affected jurors' abilities to distinguish among the plaintiffs (Horowitz et al., 1996).

How might we help jurors better comprehend difficult information? Preinstructed jurors appear to make better decisions about complex evidence than jurors who were only instructed after the evidence was presented (ForsterLee, Horowitz, & Bourgeois, 1993). It is also possible that providing jurors with a trial transcript will increase their ability to focus on the relevant evidence in a complex trial (Bourgeois, Horowitz, & ForsterLee, 1993). Thus, although jurors may struggle with complex evidence, there are procedures that can be used to increase their ability to interpret such evidence.

Expert Evidence

Several studies have examined the effect of expert testimony on juror verdict (e.g., Brekke & Borgida, 1988; Cutler & Penrod, 1995; Kovera, Gresham, Borgida, Gray, & Regan, 1997; Kovera, Levy, Borgida, & Penrod, 1994; Schuller, 1992; Schuller & Cripps, 1998). Collectively, these studies demonstrated that expert evidence influences juror decisions across a variety of case types, including child sexual abuse, rape, eyewitness identification, and battered women who kill their partners. Expert testimony has a greater effect on juror judgments when it is presented early in the trial (Brekke & Borgida, 1988; Schuller & Cripps, 1998) and when the expert testimony is clearly related to the case facts (Brekke & Borgida, 1988; Fox & Walters, 1986; Kovera et al., 1997; Schuller, 1992). Expert testimony can also serve as an educational tool that helps the jurors evaluate the reliability of other evidence (e.g., Cutler, Dexter, & Penrod., 1989; Cutler, Penrod, & Dexter, 1989; Kovera et al., 1997).

The above studies presented jurors with valid scientific evidence. *Daubert v. Merrell Dow Pharmaceuticals* (1993) established judges as the gatekeepers of scientific evidence, but judges may admit flawed scientific evidence to trial (Kovera & McAuliff, 2000b). What happens when jurors are presented with invalid evidence? Are they able to evaluate it as such and weigh it appropriately (Kovera, Russano, & McAuliff, 2002)? Several studies have examined the ability of eligible jurors to evaluate scientific evidence presented by an expert. In the first of these studies, researchers manipulated the construct validity, general acceptance, and the ecological validity of the research presented by the plaintiff's expert in a sexual harassment case (Kovera, McAuliff, & Hebert, 1999). Although jurors noticed information provided about construct validity in the expert evidence, they did not use this information in their legal decision making. However, if the evidence was generally accepted in its respected field and the methods that produced the evidence were ecologically valid, participants judged that the expert testimony was valid.

In additional studies, jurors evaluated expert testimony proffered by the plaintiff in a hostile work environment case (McAuliff & Kovera, 2003). In the first part of this investigation, researchers manipulated the internal validity of the evidence (i.e., the research presented by the expert was valid, contained a confound, or had a confederate who was not blind to condition). The validity of the expert evidence did not significantly influence juror decisions about liability or the reliability of the expert evidence. In a second experiment, researchers again manipulated the internal validity of the research presented by the expert, describing the research as valid or as missing a control group. Jurors did not detect threats to the validity of an expert's research unless they scored high, as opposed to low, in need for cognition (i.e., how much people enjoy engaging in effortful cognitive activities; Cacioppo & Petty, 1982). It is unclear whether increased motivation to engage in cognitive processes leads to more scientifically sound decisions or whether high need for cognition people, because they tend to be heavier consumers of news and other information than low need for cognition people, are more likely to possess the knowledge that would enable them to make sound decisions about scientific validity.

Given that some jurors are not able to evaluate scientific evidence, it is important to examine whether the legal safeguards established in *Daubert* will prevent flawed expert testimony from influencing jurors' decisions. The *Daubert* ruling noted that trials may contain at least three safeguards that would prevent jurors from basing their decisions on unreliable evidence: cross-examination, the presentation of contrary evidence (e.g., opposing experts), and judicial instruction on the burden of proof. Are these safeguards an effective way of educating jurors about the factors that they should consider when judging the reliability of scientific evidence?

Thus far, results are not promising. For the opposing expert and cross-examination safeguards to be effective, the opposing attorney must first recognize that the expert testimony is flawed. One study found that they might not be successful in doing so (Kovera & McAuliff, 2000a). Furthermore, in those studies that tested the safeguards, opposing experts and cross-examination were unsuccessful in alerting jurors to "junk science" (Kovera et al., 1999; Levett & Kovera, 2003). Judicial instruction on the burden of proof may prove to be more promising. One study found that revised judicial instructions helped jurors detect scientific flaws in expert testimony (Groscup & Penrod, 2002). So although jurors may have difficulty dealing with evaluating the reliability of evidence presented to them, researchers are finding that some safeguards are effective in assisting jurors to make better decisions about the evidence they hear in court.

Juror Decision Making in Civil Cases

Until recently, researchers investigating juror decision-making processes focused their attention on issues relevant to decision making in criminal trials, relatively neglecting the different issues that arise when jurors decide civil cases (Greene, 2003; Greene & Bornstein, 2003; Nietzel, McCarthy, & Kern, 1999). In the past decade, however, psychologists have investigated how jurors decide issues of liability and damage awards in civil litigation (Wilbanks, Dunn, & Penrod, 2002). Criticisms about the competence of the civil jury include concerns that these juries (1) rely on sympathy rather than legally relevant factors when deciding liability, (2) are biased against wealthy defendants, and (3) are more likely to make outrageous damage awards than are legal professionals (Hastie, Schkade, & Payne, 1999; Vidmar, 1995). Using a variety of methodologies, researchers have investigated empirically whether jurors are capable of considering only legally relevant factors when deciding liability and awarding damages.

Liability Judgments

When deciding liability, jurors should attend to issues such as (1) whether the defendant has a duty to the plaintiff, (2) whether the defendant breached that duty, and (3) whether the defendant's conduct caused the plaintiff's injuries (Keeton, Dobbs, Keeton, & Owen, 1984). A number of extralegal factors may influence jurors' determinations of liability—but should not do so according to the law. These factors include the reprehensibility of the defendant's conduct, defendant wealth (the "deep pockets" hypothesis), defendant status as a corporation or an individual, and the severity of the plaintiff's injury. If jurors render decisions based on sympathy for the plaintiff, as some critics claim they do, then we might expect injury severity to inappropriately influence liability decisions. Similarly, jurors may be more willing to find a defendant liable if that defendant has the wealth to pay a damage award or would not be personally responsible for paying the award. The question is whether these concerns are well founded.

Several studies have demonstrated that the reprehensibility of the defendant's conduct inappropriately influences mock jurors' judgments of defendant liability (Greene, Johns, & Bowman, 1999; Greene, Johns, & Smith, 2001). Although jurors should be determining *whether* the defendant is at fault, they inappropriately factor in *the degree* to which the defendant is at fault (MacCoun, 1996). In contrast, wealthy defendants are no more likely to be found liable than are less wealthy defendants (MacCoun, 1996); however, corporate defendants are more likely to be found liable than are individual business owners (Bornstein, 1994; Hans & Ermann, 1989; MacCoun, 1996). The findings regarding the influence of injury severity judgments on jurors' liability judgments are more mixed, with some studies reporting that defendants were more likely to be found liable for severe injuries than for less severe injuries (Bornstein, 1998; Greene, Johns, et al., 2001; Horowitz et al., 1996) and others finding no relationship between injury severity and liability judgments (Greene et al., 1999). A meta-analysis examining the relationship between outcome severity and responsibility attributions in both archival and experimental research found that the relationship between injury severity and liability judgments appears to be stronger in experimental research than in field studies (Robbennolt, 2000). A different meta-analysis that was limited to studies in which actual liability judgments were rendered also found no relationship between injury severity and liability judgments; however, defendant reprehensibility, defendant fault, and corporate status all inappropriately influenced liability judgments (Wilbanks et al., 2002).

Damage Awards

Once a jury finds a defendant liable, jurors must determine whether the plaintiff should be awarded damages. Two types of damages may be awarded. The purpose of compensatory damages is to return plaintiffs to the state that they experienced prior to the wrongful actions of the defendant. These damages are intended to compensate a plaintiff for economic damages that they incurred because of the defendant's actions, including medical expenses and lost wages. Compensatory damages may also compensate a plaintiff for noneconomic losses, such as pain and suffering. Punitive damages, which are less frequently awarded, are intended to punish the defendant for reprehensible behavior and to deter the defendant, and others, from engaging in similar actions in the future. Researchers have explored whether jurors attend to legally relevant variables when assessing both types of damages.

Compensatory Damages. Injury severity is the only factor that should influence the size of compensatory damage awards. Because the severely injured are likely to have more medical expenses and to suffer more than those who are less severely injured, they deserve to receive greater compensation for their injuries. With rare exception (Bornstein, 1998), the results of trial simulation studies reveal that jurors award higher compensatory damages to severely injured plaintiffs than to those less severely injured (Feigenson, Park, & Salovey, 1997; ForsterLee, Horowitz, Athaide-Victor, & Brown, 2000; Greene, Johns, et al., 2001; Horowitz et al., 1996; Robbennolt & Studebaker, Study 2, 1999; Wissler, Evans, Hart, Morry, & Saks, 1997).

To examine whether jurors make legally appropriate decisions about compensatory damages, researchers have also examined whether other inappropriate factors (e.g., defendant reprehensibility, defendant fault, corporate status) influence jurors' compensatory damage awards. Defendant wealth seems unrelated to compensatory damages (Greene, Woody, & Winter, 2000; MacCoun, 1996). Studies exploring the alternative hypothesis that compensatory damage awards are driven not by defendant wealth but rather by the corporate status of the defendant have produced mixed results, with some studies finding no relationship between corporate status and award amount (Bornstein, 1994; Carpenter, 2000), and others finding that corporations were assessed larger awards than were individuals (Hans & Ermann, 1989; MacCoun, 1996). The findings regarding the influence of defendant reprehensibility on compensatory awards are similarly mixed. Some studies find no relationship between defendant reprehensibility and the size of compensatory awards (Anderson & MacCoun, Study 2, 1999; Cather, Greene, & Durham, 1996), whereas others find that jurors make larger awards when the defendant is reprehensible, at least under some circumstances (Greene et al., 2000).

Empirical evidence supports the notion that juries will make larger compensatory damage awards when the defendant is clearly at fault than when defendant fault is ambiguous (ForsterLee & Horowitz, 1997; MacCoun, 1996). This influence of defendant fault is inappropriate, unless the case is being tried under comparative negligence laws and the plaintiff bears some responsibility for his or her own injury. Even in these circumstances, jurors should not decrease the plaintiff's award to account for the plaintiff's role in the injury, because the judge will adjust the award to reflect the plaintiff's contribution to the harm. However, research suggests that jurors do decrease their awards under these circumstances, a phenomenon known as "double discounting" (Wissler, Kuehn, & Saks, 2000; Zickafoose & Bornstein, 1999).

Punitive Damages. Given that the purpose of punitive damages is to punish the defendant and to deter others from engaging in similar wrongful actions, the reprehensibility of the defendant's conduct should influence the size of a punitive damage award. That is, if a defendant's behavior is particularly bad, it is appropriate for a jury to assess a greater punitive award so that the award is likely to have a greater deterrent effect. In one study, defendant reprehensibility influenced jurors' decisions to award punitive damages but did not influence the size of the award (Anderson & MacCoun, Study 2, 1999). In another study, defendant reprehensibility influenced total damages awards (i.e., an aggregate of compensatory and punitive damage awards) but not compensatory damages when analyzed individually (Cather et al., 1996). A third study found the predicted relationship between defendant conduct and punitive damage awards, but only for a product liability case and not for other types of cases (Greene et al., 2000). A recent meta-analysis suggests that defendant reprehensibility does influence punitive damage awards, although this effect is moderated by participant type, such that the effect only holds for college-student participants (Wilbanks et al., 2002).

In contrast, injury severity should not influence jurors' punitive damage awards because the purpose of these awards is not to compensate the plaintiff for his or her loss but to penalize the defendant for misbehavior, irrespective of the severity of the plaintiff's outcome. Although some studies have found that jurors award higher punitive damages to more severely injured plaintiffs than to those with milder injuries (Kahneman, Schkade, & Sunstein, 1998; Robbennolt & Studebaker, Study 2, 1999), at least one other study found no effect of injury severity on punitive damages (Cather et al., 1996). This finding (i.e., no relationship between injury severity and punitive damage awards) is supported by recent meta-analytic findings (Wilbanks et al., 2002).

Procedural Reforms

Because of concerns surrounding the competency of the civil jury, a variety of reforms has been suggested to improve decision making regarding damage awards (Greene et al., 2002). These reforms include statutory caps on the size of both noneconomic (e.g., pain and suffering) and punitive damage awards, changing the burden of proof for deciding the issue of damages, and bifurcating the trial to separate liability, compensatory damages, and punitive damages phases. Empirical evaluation of these proposed and/or enacted reforms has begun.

In response to perceptions that awards for pain and suffering and punitive damage awards are outrageously high, legislators have proposed monetary caps, either recommending a total dollar award that cannot be exceeded, or, in the case of punitive awards, mandating that punitive awards may not exceed a specific ratio of the compensatory award (Robbennolt & Studebaker, 1999). One study (Saks, Hollinger, Wissler, Evans, & Hart, 1997) found that rather than decreasing variability in damage awards, caps may increase both the variability and the size of noneconomic damage awards for mildly and moderately injured plaintiffs. In another study, higher caps increased the variability and size of punitive damage awards in comparison to awards made by jurors in a no-cap condition (Robbennolt & Studebaker, 1999). Finally, limitations of punitive awards may have the unintended effect of increasing compensatory damage awards. When jurors had no option to award punitive damages, they inflated their compensatory awards (Anderson & MacCoun, 1999; Greene, Coon, & Bornstein, 2001).

Bifurcation can be used to prevent jurors from using information that is relevant for one phase of a civil trial from influencing another phase for which the information is legally irrelevant and potentially prejudicial. For example, bifurcating the liability and compensatory damages phases from the punitive damages phase would allow jurors to consider issues of liability and compensation before hearing evidence about defendant reprehensibility or defendant wealth, eliminating the potential for this evidence to inappropriately influence those decisions (Ghiardi & Kircher, 1995; Landsman, Diamond, Dimitropoulos, & Saks, 1998). Does bifurcation affect liability decisions? It does appear that defendants are more likely to be found liable in a unitary trial than in a bifurcated trial (Horowitz & Bordens, 1990; Landsman et al., 1998). The findings for compensatory damage awards are less clear, with some studies finding no differences between unitary and bifurcated trials (Greene et al., 2000; Landsman et al., 1998), one study finding decreased awards for plaintiffs in unitary trials (Horowitz & Bordens, 1990), and a fourth study reporting an increase in awards in unitary trials (Robbennolt & Studebaker, 1999).

Mixed findings also characterize the research on the effects of bifurcation on punitive damage awards, with some studies showing no effect (Horowitz & Bordens, 1990; Robbennolt & Studebaker, 1999), and others finding that bifurcation increases punitive damage awards (Greene et al., 2000; Landsman et al., 1998). A meta-analysis of this literature indicates that bifurcation does not influence any of these judgments (Wilbanks et al., 2002), suggesting that this trial procedure does not assist jurors in making better or worse decisions. Thus, neither bifurcation nor award caps appear to produce the effects desired by proponents of civil jury reform.

Extraevidentiary Influences

Thus far, we have examined how jurors use different types of evidence to make decisions. Several different types of evidence influence juror decision making, and under many circumstances, jurors appropriately use evidence when rendering a verdict. We also learned that there are types of evidence that jurors generally do not evaluate and weigh appropriately. Are there other factors that could influence jury decision making? Elsewhere we learn that pretrial publicity affects jurors' decisions (see Studebaker & Penrod, Chapter 8, this volume). Are there other extraevidentiary factors that can influence jurors? For example, does the race or socioeconomic status of the defendant influence whether the jury finds him or her guilty? If evidence is ruled inadmissible, do jurors appropriately disregard it? In the next sections, we examine these questions and explore the effects of extraevidentiary information on jurors' decisions.

Defendant Characteristics

At times, jurors may use information irrelevant to the trial to make trial judgments. Personal attributes, such as physical attractiveness, race, and socioeconomic status, of a defendant can influence a juror's decision-making process and affect the verdict. Many empirical studies have now explored whether these extraevidentiary factors bias jurors' decisions (e.g., Kalven & Zeisel, 1966; MacCoun, 1990).

Defendant Attractiveness. According to the results of a meta-analysis exploring the influence of defendant characteristics on jurors' judgments, one of the greatest advantages a defendant can have is simply being physically attractive (Mazzella & Feingold, 1994). The researchers examined 25 studies that assessed the effects of physical attractiveness on jurors' judgments. Mock jurors were less likely to find physically attractive defendants guilty than those who were physically unattractive (Mazzella & Feingold, 1994). There is some evidence that unattractiveness is related to criminality (Bull & Rumsey, 1988), which may explain why attractiveness is advantageous (i.e., jurors may relate unattractiveness to criminality and, therefore, to guilt). If attractive defendants do get convicted, they may receive more lenient punishments than unattractive defendants (Mazzella & Feingold, 1994). However, the punishment jurors assigned to the defendant differed significantly depending on the type of crime. Overall, the attractiveness bias extends to punishments for crimes such as robbery, rape, and cheating; however, attractive defendants received harsher punishments than did unattractive defendants in cases of negligent homicide and swindling (Bray, 1982; Efran, 1974; Jacobson, 1981; Jacobson & Popovich, 1983; MacCoun, 1990; Mazzella & Feingold, 1994; Skinner, 1978).

Defendant Race. Several studies have examined the effects of defendant race on the jury decision process. Scholars and scientists have claimed that white jurors often exhibit a bias against black defendants (Fairchild & Cowan, 1997; Parloff, 1997). In addition, concern has also been voiced about black jurors treating black defendants more leniently than would white jurors. Are jurors' decisions influenced by the race of the defendant? A meta-analysis of 37 studies exploring this question revealed that defendant race did not significantly influence verdict; however, once convicted, blacks and whites received different punishment, depending on the type of crime they had committed (Mazzella & Feingold, 1994). Specifically, blacks received harsher punishments for negligent homicide, whereas whites were given harsher punishments for fraud and embezzlement. It is possible that when defendants commit crimes that are stereotypically associated with their race, jurors view them in a more negative light, consequently punishing those defendants more severely (Gordon, Bindrim, McNicholas, & Walden, 1988).

Defendant Socioeconomic Status. How does the socioeconomic status (SES) of a defendant influence juror decisions? Are defendants who jurors perceive to be wealthy or who hold a white-collar job judged differently from those who are poor or hold blue-collar jobs? A meta-analysis revealed that jurors rendered more guilty verdicts and gave harsher punishments when the defendant had low SES than when the defendant was a member of a higher social class (Mazzella & Feingold, 1994). However, the effect sizes were small because of the conflicting results of some studies. For example, one study found that low-SES defendants were assigned significantly longer sentences than high-SES defendants (Osborne & Rappoport, 1985), one study found no effect for defendant SES on punishment (Gleason & Harris, 1976), and two studies found that high-SES defendants were given harsher sentences (Bray, Struckman-Johnson, Osborne, MacFarlane, & Scott, 1978; Gray & Ashmore, 1976).

Why are there so many conflicting results in studies that investigate the effects of SES on jurors' judgments? Conflicting results have also been found when examining other defendant characteristics, including education, gender, and income. Disparities in verdict and sentencing may be based on the relationship between the characteristics of the juror and the defendant (Daudistel, Hosch, Golmes, & Graves, 1999; McGowen & King, 1982; Nagel & Weitzman, 1972; Perez, Hosch, Ponder, & Trejo 1993). Therefore, it is difficult to identify any clear-cut rules governing which of the defendant's characteristics jurors will view negatively; the characteristics of a defendant can only be considered an advantage or disadvantage when the attributes of individual jurors are known.

Interactions of Defendant Characteristics with Other Variables. How might jurors' characteristics moderate the influence of defendant characteristics on juror judgments? The most straightforward and widely accepted idea explaining the way in which jurors view the defendant is called the "similarity principle" (Brehm, Kassin, & Fein, 1999). Simply put, people prefer others who are similar to them. This principle governs how we choose our friends and partners in everyday life, and it also appears to explain a juror's preference to render an innocent or guilty verdict. Many empirical studies have found that mock jurors render fewer guilty verdicts in cases in which the defendant resembles their background, ethnicity, and beliefs (Amato, 1979;

Griffitt & Jackson, 1973; Kerr, Hymes, Anderson, & Weathers, 1995; Stephan & Stephan, 1986). However, there is evidence that jurors can react negatively to a defendant who is similar to them but has committed a crime or acted in a shameful manner, therefore leading jurors to judge the defendant more harshly (Kerr et al., 1995).

In addition to a juror's similarities to the defendant, certain aspects of the crime can also determine whether a juror will be biased against a defendant of a particular race. For example, one study examined the effects of defendant race on judgments of white and black mock jurors (Sommers & Ellsworth, 2000). The researchers manipulated whether racial issues were salient. They found that when racial issues were salient, the defendant's race did not influence white participants' decisions about the defendant. However, when racial issues were not salient, white participants rated the black defendant to be more guilty, violent, and aggressive than the white defendant. Black participants were more likely to be more lenient toward the black defendant than the white defendant. The researchers concluded that whites were more motivated to appear nonprejudiced when racial issues were emphasized than when they were not emphasized. Thus, extralegal factors affect juror decisions, and the presentation of the case facts may also interact with the extralegal factors to produce bias (Sommers & Ellsworth, 2000).

Jury Nullification

Although judges inform jurors that they must apply the law and make a decision on the basis of the evidence provided, jurors are also responsible for taking on a second, historical role of representing the "conscience of the community." This role allows the jury to acquit defendants who are legally guilty but morally correct in their actions (Becker, 1980). Although the majority of states do not inform juries of this power, all juries possess the right to nullify, or disregard, the law, to uphold the values of the community (DiPerna, 1984). Jurors have nullified several times in U.S. courts, typically in cases in which there was strong and unmistakable evidence of the defendant's guilt, according to the law, but where widespread public resistance to the defendant's conviction led to an acquittal (e.g., Rembar, 1980). Furthermore, because the verdict does not require a rational explanation, various extralegal factors can contribute to jury nullification. Research suggests that jurors' attitudes, sentiments, and interpretations of the defendant's motives influence the decision to nullify (Horowitz, 1985, 1988; Pfeiffer & Ogloff, 1991; Wiener, Habert, Shkodriani, & Staebler, 1991).

Jurors may choose to nullify because their conscience does not allow them to convict the defendant for the crime with which he or she has been charged. They may apply the "reasonable person" standard, reasoning that the defendant's behavior was technically illegal but that any reasonable person would have behaved similarly (Finkel, 1995). Jurors may also believe a defendant's actions were admirable in intent (Finkel, 1995). Euthanasia is a prime example of a well-publicized crime in which jurors may acquit because they feel that the intentions of the defendant were honorable (Kalven & Zeisel, 1966; Meissner, Brigham, & Pfeifer, 2003; Scheflin & Van Dyke, 1980). For example, a well-known example of jury nullification in a case involving euthanasia is the trial of Jack Kevorkian, or "Dr. Death." Kevorkian was tried and acquitted on charges of assisted suicide, although the evidence was substantial enough to convict him of the crime (Battin, Rhodes, & Silvers, 1998).

Juries may also exercise their right to nullify if they believe that the punishment is too harsh or disproportionate to the offense (Horowitz & Willging, 1991). For example, in one study mock jurors were presented with a case in which a physician was accused of knowingly transfusing a patient with blood that was unscreened for the HIV virus. Although the charges and evidence were held constant, they found that the mock jurors were less likely to find the physician guilty when the penalty prescribed by the law was severe than when it was mild (Niedermeier, Horowitz, & Kerr, 1999). Thus, as the severity of the penalty increases, the probability of criminal conviction declines and jurors apply a higher standard of proof (Kerr, 1978).

Although classic cases, juror interviews, and experimental research demonstrate that juries may use their power to nullify, there is minimal evidence to indicate that they are aware that they wield this power. One survey of jury-eligible adults found that only 5% of those asked were aware of their nullification powers (Brody & Rivera, 1997). Many argue that this small percentage may be due to the fact that in only three states (Georgia, Indiana, and Maryland) are juries directly informed that they have the right to nullify (DiPerna, 1984). Opponents of nullification posit that instructing the jury that it has the power to disregard the law would invite anarchy (Simson, 1976), whereas proponents argue that there is no evidence of anarchy in the three states in which jurors are currently instructed on their nullification rights (Becker, 1980).

Research suggests that nullification instructions may alter both jury functioning and verdicts (Horowitz, 1985, 1986, 1988). For example, in one study, mock juries were provided with three levels of judicial instructions: standard pattern instructions that make no reference to nullification, nullification instructions used in the state of Maryland, and radical nullification instructions that explicitly inform the jury of their nullification rights (Horowitz, 1985). Only those juries receiving the radical instructions differed significantly from baseline outcomes and functioning, rendering fewer guilty verdicts in cases in which technically guilty defendants could be viewed as meriting leniency, and rendering more guilty verdicts in a drunk-driving case when the defendant was unsympathetic (Horowitz, 1985). The overall effect, however, appears to depend on a multitude of factors, including sympathy for the defendant, case content (Horowitz, 1985), and who provides the nullification reminder (Horowitz, 1988). Furthermore, nullification instructions increase acquittals in trial simulations when strict application of the law would violate some mock jurors' senses of justice (Horowitz, 1985; Wiener et al.,

1991). In summary, these findings indicate that mock jurors' verdicts appear to reflect community sentiment. That is, mock jurors were willing to be merciful to morally upright defendants with whom they could sympathize, but were more severe when dealing with less worthy, dangerous defendants. This pattern of findings suggests that informing jurors of their right to nullify does not induce a general inclination to acquit, but rather influences the jury's interpretation of the defendant's behavior within the context of the community's values.

In the past several sections, we learned that jurors' decisions may be unduly influenced by extralegal factors. We also learned that the influence of these characteristics might vary based on the individual characteristics of the juror. Thus, jurors may use information they are not supposed to use when making a decision. What other information do jurors use when making decisions? If jurors learn about the crime before the trial (i.e., through newspapers or television), does this knowledge affect their decision making? If a police officer illegally obtains evidence in a case and the jury is instructed to disregard the evidence, does it do so? In the next section, we examine the effects of inadmissible evidence on jury decision making.

Inadmissible Evidence

One of a juror's tasks during trial is to integrate evidence that is presented to the jury and form an opinion about the guilt or innocence of the defendant based on the law that is given by the judge. For information to be admitted into evidence, at least in the United States, it must be relevant to the case at hand, reliable, and its probative value must outweigh its potential for prejudice (*Federal Rules of Evidence* 401, 402, and 403; 1984). Thus, although a piece of evidence may be probative, judges may rule it inadmissible if they feel that the jury may not evaluate it appropriately or may be confused by it. It is possible that a jury may hear testimony during the course of the trial that is subsequently ruled inadmissible by the presiding judge. For example, a witness may make a statement in his or her testimony that is considered inadmissible hearsay. The opposing lawyer will object, and the judge will rule that the jury is to disregard the witness's statement. Information can be deemed inadmissible for a variety of reasons: It has been illegally obtained, is redundant, could be misleading or confusing to the jury, or could interfere with a defendant's right to due process.

The Effects of Inadmissible Evidence on Juror Judgments. Jurors may learn about inadmissible evidence from a variety of sources. For example, before a trial begins, jurors may be exposed to publicity regarding the case or the defendant that may bias or prejudice their decisions (Kramer, Kerr, & Carroll, 1990; Moran & Cutler, 1991; Otto, Penrod, & Dexter, 1994). During trial, a witness may inadvertently reveal a defendant's prior conviction during a statement (Doob & Kirshenbaum, 1973; Greene & Dodge, 1995; Hans & Doob,

1976; Wissler & Saks, 1985), or a witness may provide some inadmissible hearsay evidence in his or her testimony (Kovera et al., 1992; Miene et al., 1992; Schuller, 1995). Finally, illegally obtained evidence may influence jurors' decisions (Kassin & Sommers, 1997). Knowing that inadmissible evidence has ample opportunities to be presented at trial and that thousands of jury trials take place each year, it is necessary to consider the effects that this information can exert on the jury decision-making process.

Pretrial publicity may be one of the most common vehicles through which jurors are exposed to inadmissible evidence. Through television, newspapers, and the Internet, potential jurors have numerous opportunities to obtain information about the crime in question. A meta-analytic review examining 44 pretrial publicity studies found that mock jurors exposed to pretrial publicity were significantly more likely to find a defendant guilty compared to those participants who were exposed to less or no negative pretrial publicity (Steblay, Besirevie, Fulero, & Jimenez-Lorente, 1999; for a detailed summary of the effects of pretrial publicity, see Studebaker & Penrod, Chapter 8, this volume).

To the extent that extraevidentiary factors can change a juror's perception of the defendant's culpability, they may have a biasing effect on the decision-making process (Green & Dodge, 1995; Kassin, Williams, & Saunders, 1990; Schuller, 1995; Wissler & Saks, 1985). How do the courts propose to remedy this problem? Judges have a variety of methods at their disposal with which to reduce the potential impact that inadmissible evidence can have on jurors' decisions. First, a judge can declare a mistrial. This procedure is typically avoided, however, because it is both costly and time consuming. The second, and most common, remedy is for the judge to instruct the jurors to ignore or limit their use of the evidence. The assumption is that admonishing the jurors will reduce or eliminate the biasing effects of the inadmissible information. A limiting instruction may be used in a trial when a defendant's prior record has been exposed (i.e., the jury can use the defendant's prior record to determine intent, motive, or identity, but cannot use the defendant's prior record to make inferences about the defendant's character; *Federal Rule of Evidence* 404, 1984). Similarly, an expert psychologist testifying about a defendant's mental state may discuss the defendant's reports of being beaten by her partner, for example, if the expert used this information in forming his or her opinion, although this information would ordinarily be treated as inadmissible hearsay (*Federal Rule of Evidence* 703, 1984). In this situation, the judge would instruct jurors to use the hearsay evidence in their judgments about how much weight to give to the expert's testimony, but not to use it to judge the guilt of the defendant (Schuller, 1995).

The Effectiveness of Instructions to Disregard. Are admonishments to disregard information successful at eliminating the influence of inadmissible evidence on jurors' decisions? The courts cannot agree on this issue; some describe admonishment as a "powerful tool" (*Carter v. Kentucky*, 1981, p. 303), whereas others express very little faith in its effectiveness (*Krulewitch v. United States*, 1949; *United States v. Grunewald*, 1956). Empirical research has examined the effects of both admonishing and limiting instructions, yielding mixed results.

There is substantial research demonstrating that judges' admonitions are not successful at preventing jurors from using the inadmissible evidence when deciding the verdict (Doob & Kirshenbaum, 1973; Hans & Doob, 1976; Saks & Wissler, 1984). In one study, mock jurors read trial summaries that contained a false confession. Although the judge instructed jurors to ignore the evidence because the confession was coerced and therefore inadmissible, jurors used the confession information when rendering a verdict (Kassin & Sukel, 1997). Furthermore, admonitions may not only be ineffective, but may also result in jurors giving greater emphasis to the inadmissible evidence. In an early study, mock jurors read about a defendant charged with robbery and murder (Sue, Smith, & Caldwell, 1973), then listened to a taped phone conversation in which the defendant admitted committing the crime. This evidence was obtained using an illegal wiretap, and the defense objected to it. The evidence was either deemed admissible or inadmissible; in the inadmissible condition, the judge instructed the jury to disregard the evidence. Those participants who were given instructions to ignore the wiretap evidence rendered more guilty verdicts than did those who were told that they were allowed to use the information (Sue et al., 1973). Thus, the judge's admonition increased jurors' use of the inadmissible evidence. Several studies investigating the effectiveness of admonitions on jurors' abilities to ignore the information have demonstrated this backfire effect (Broeder, 1959; Cox & Tanford, 1989; Pickel, 1995). The findings of other studies suggest that jurors may be able to discount inadmissible evidence and overcome biases when given proper instructions (e.g., Elliot, Farrington, & Manheimer, 1988; Hatvany & Strack, 1980; Kerwin & Shaffer, 1994; Landsman & Rakos, 1994; Weinberg & Baron, 1982).

In addition, limiting instructions may not provide jurors with effective guidance on how to use certain pieces of evidence correctly (e.g., Wissler & Saks, 1985). Although studies have shown that mock jurors who were aware of the defendant's past criminal record were more likely to find the defendant guilty than were those who were not aware of the defendant's record (Doob & Kirshenbaum, 1973), a follow-up study showed that deliberation does not help limit jurors' inappropriate use of a defendant's prior criminal record (Hans & Doob, 1976). Jurors commonly misuse the defendant's prior criminal record when deciding verdict, consequently increasing the likelihood that they will find the defendant guilty (Baldus, Pulaski, & Woodworth, 1983; Barnett & Field, 1978; Blanck, 1985; Greene & Dodge, 1995; Myers, 1979; Sealy & Cornish, 1973; Wissler & Saks, 1985).

Whether jurors use a defendant's prior record in rendering a verdict may depend on the similarity of the past crime to the crime in question. In one study, participants in one condition were informed of the defendant's previous conviction of a separate yet similar crime and were instructed to ignore that information. A control group, which received no information about the defendant's past criminal activity, rendered lower conviction rates then those who were told details of the defendant's past criminal activity (Wissler & Saks, 1985). Mock jurors were able to follow the judge's admonition to ignore inadmissible prior conviction records when the prior convictions were for dissimilar offenses (Sealy & Cornish, 1973), suggesting that the nature of the previous crime influences whether jurors can ignore information about a defendant's prior record, even with judicial admonishment.

Other factors may contribute to a juror's inability to ignore inadmissible evidence. For example, the extent to which inadmissible evidence affects juror decision making may depend on how the evidence was obtained, the overall strength of the evidence, the seriousness of the crime, and the direction of the evidence (e.g., Kassin & Sommers, 1997; Rind, Jaeger & Strohmetz, 1995; Sealy & Cornish, 1973; Sue et al., 1973; Thompson, Fong, & Rosenthal, 1981). In a trial simulation in which jurors heard an audiotaped telephone conversation of the defendant confessing to the crime, the defense attorney objected to the admission of the tape (Kassin & Sommers, 1997). The judge ruled in one of three ways: the evidence was (1) admissible, (2) inadmissible because the tape was barely audible (i.e., the tape was unreliable), or (3) inadmissible because it was obtained in an investigation unrelated to the crime in question (i.e., a legal reason). Participants rendered more guilty verdicts in the admissible evidence condition compared to the inadmissible evidence conditions. However, when the tape was inadmissible because it was unreliable, participants rendered more not-guilty verdicts than when the tape was inadmissible because of a legal reason (Kassin & Sommers, 1997). Thus, an admonition instruction may function as expected in cases of unreliability but not in cases of illegally obtained evidence. Another study found that the strength of the evidence in the case influenced mock jurors' abilities to disregard additional inadmissible evidence (Sue et al., 1973). Specifically, when the case evidence was weak, jurors were more likely to use the inadmissible evidence when rendering a verdict, compared to when the case evidence was strong. Inadmissible evidence also has a greater effect on mock jurors' decisions in simulated trials for less serious crimes (i.e., vandalism) as opposed to more serious crimes (i.e., rape, murder; Rind et al., 1995; Sealy & Cornish, 1973).

Overall, the research in this area has yielded mixed results; however, there is strong evidence that in at least some situations, jurors may find it difficult to ignore information once they have been exposed to it. Unless jurors strictly adhere to the instructions to disregard inadmissible evidence, the defendant's Sixth Amendment right to a fair trial in the United States may be endangered. Thus far, researchers have focused their efforts on the outcomes and consequences of exposing mock jurors to inadmissible evidence. More research is needed that investigates the process by which inadmissible evidence influences the jurors' decision-making processes, so that we can develop remedies to successfully counter these prejudicial biases. For example, perhaps a defendant's prior record or an illegally taped confession influences jurors' decisions because this information remains accessible when they are deliberating. Admonishment to disregard may only serve to increase the accessibility of the inadmissible evidence, resulting in the ineffectiveness of the judicial instruction to disregard as a remedy. This hypothesis has not been directly tested, but if tested, it could provide us with valuable information in developing a countermeasure to decrease the effects of inadmissible evidence on juror verdicts.

Judges versus Juries

Since the introduction of juries, there has been a relentless controversy over who is the better decision maker: the judge or the jury? Use of a jury has many advantages as a decision-making system. First, some scholars argue that the group deliberation process, by exposing jurors to different views on the trial evidence, provides some protection against inaccurate recollections of evidence (Ellsworth, 1989). Group deliberations may foster jurors' recall of trial facts. Although individual jurors' memories for trial facts and legal instructions were not particularly strong in one study, the collective pooled memories of the jurors produced a 90% accuracy rate for recall of trial facts, and an 80% accuracy rate for recall of instructions (Hastie et al., 1983). The jury also brings community standards and morals to bear on trial decisions, which can produce a just result even when strict adherence to the law would not (e.g., Horowitz, 1985, 1988; Pfeiffer & Ogloff, 1991; Wiener et al., 1991). Others have defended the jury's role in the legal system by positing that not all judges are diligent and capable of rendering more rational decisions than juries (Lempert, 1999). In addition to not having the advantage of collective recall, judges are more likely to be influenced by the political implications of their decisions (Lempert, 1999). And although some jurors may be overwhelmed by complex cases, judges are likely to have similar problems (Sperlich, 1980, 1982).

There are also many advantages to a judge as the sole decision maker. The judge can often see the long-range implications of the judgment in a case (Lilly, 2001). Furthermore, it may be easier for attorneys to confuse or distract a jury than it would be to divert a judge's attention from the primary issues in a trial (Lilly, 2001). Judges also have a major advantage over juries in that they cost much less. Jury selection can be time consuming and costly. Once the jurors are selected, they must be protected from extralegal information that could potentially bias their decisions. Providing this protection can prove difficult, and in some cases, impossible. In addition, research has shown that juries often misunderstand the legal terminology of judicial instructions (e.g., Charrow & Charrow, 1979; Goodman & Greene, 1989; Reifman, Gusick, & Ellsworth, 1992; see also Ogloff & Rose, Chapter 12, this volume). Such misunderstanding can result in a misuse of the law.

Given the advantages and disadvantages of both judges and juries, do verdicts rendered by juries differ from verdicts rendered by judges? In a classic comparison of judges and juries, researchers mailed questionnaires to trial judges and asked them to report the jury's verdict in the case and the decision that the judge would have made had the trial been a bench trial (Kalven & Zeisel, 1966). After examining 4,000 civil jury trials and 3,576 criminal jury trials, they found that for 78% of the trials, the jury and the judge agreed on the verdict. Although this groundbreaking project suffered from some obvious methodological flaws (e.g., the heavy reliance on self-report and recollections from judges, a possible hindsight bias in the judges' verdicts), this study provided one of the first significant empirical insights into the jury system, and it helped to establish an optimistic view of juries' decision-making capabilities. A few additional studies have examined the judge–jury agreement issue; the results of these studies have not provided empirical foundation for the conclusion that judges are better legal decision makers than juries (Robbennolt, 2002; Wissler, Hart, & Saks, 1999).

Although the consensus among most social scientists, judicial professionals, and legal experts is that the collective fact-finding jury system is superior to bench trials, most also agree that our current system has ample room for renovation and improvement (Heuer & Penrod, 1989; Lempert, 1981). Several mechanisms have been proposed to improve the overall performance of juries. These measures include, but are not limited to (1) rewording judicial instructions, (2) instructing jurors before and after the presentation of evidence, (3) allowing jurors to take notes during trial, (4) giving jurors the opportunity to ask questions of witnesses, (5) allowing jurors to discuss the case throughout the course of the trial, and (6) increasing the diversity of jury pools (Abramson, 1994; Adler, 1994; Dann, 1993; Ellsworth, 1999). Some social scientists have posited that these reforms could facilitate rational decisions and increase juror participation and satisfaction, which may improve the overall quality of the jury decision-making process (Heuer & Penrod, 1994).

CONCLUSION

We began this chapter by asking the question, Are juries competent decision makers? To answer this question, we reviewed the empirical literature on jury decision making, including research on the process by which juries arrive at their verdicts, jurors' abilities to evaluate the reliability of a variety of evidence types, extraevidentiary influences on juror decisions, and the effectiveness of the procedural safeguards in place to help jurors make better decisions. Before discussing the conclusions that can be drawn from these reviews, it is important to note the limitations of the studies on which these conclusions rest.

With rare exception (e.g., Hans, 2000; Vidmar, 1995), researchers use trial simulation methodologies to investigate jury and juror decision making (Bornstein, 1999). Some have raised concerns about the ecological and external validity of trial simulation research, questioning whether college-student participants make the same decisions as real jurors, whether minimal written fact patterns convey the same complexity as the evidence presented in an actual trial, and whether the lack of real consequences of the simulated juries' decisions cause mock jurors to make different decisions than real-world jurors (see Kerr and Bray, Chapter 10, this volume, for a more detailed discussion of the criticisms of trial simulation research). Certainly, triangulating on an empirical question using multiple methods of data collection (e.g., archival data, juror interviews, experimental studies of real juries, and trial simulation) is a desirable goal. Even so, the latest investigations of the generalizability of trial simulation findings reveal that increasing realism of methods does not influence the results obtained (Bornstein, 1999), and importantly, methodological features of jury research rarely interact with the independent variables under investigation to influence juror decisions (Dunn, Wilbanks, & Penrod, 2002).

Methodological issues aside, what have we learned about the jurors' decision-making abilities? Jurors do seem to have some problems evaluating the reliability of some types of evidence (e.g., eyewitness evidence, confession evidence, expert evidence), and the procedural safeguards intended to assist their discernment of reliability appear to be relatively ineffective. Jurors are also influenced by extraevidentiary factors, for example, considering inadmissible evidence even after judicial admonishments to disregard it. Nevertheless, juror decision making in civil cases appears to be relatively competent, with jurors generally attending to legally relevant factors when deciding liability, compensatory damages, and punitive damages.

Some procedural variables do appear to increase the decision-making capabilities of juries. Twelve-person juries and those deliberating under a unanimous decision rule appear to be more affected by informational influence than normative influence. The opposite is true for smaller juries and those deliberating under a majority decision rule.

Perhaps the ultimate question is whether juries perform their decision-making tasks any differently from their most likely alternative: judges. The limited evidence addressing this question suggests that they do not. However, more research is needed to elucidate the differences between judge and jury decisions, to identify the weaknesses in jurors' decision-making abilities, and to evaluate procedural reforms that might assist jurors perform their important task of rendering fair decisions in our justice system.

REFERENCES

Abramson, J. (1994). We, the jury: The jury system and the ideal of democracy. New York: Basic Books.

Adler, S. J. (1994). The jury: Trial and error in the American courtroom. New York: Times Books.

Amato, P. R. (1979). Juror-defendant similarity and the assessment of guilt in politically motivated crimes. Australian Journal of Psychology, 31, 79–88.

Anderson, M. C., & MacCoun, R. J. (1999). Goal conflict in juror assessments of compensatory and punitive damages. Law and Human Behavior, 23, 313–330.

Apodaca, Cooper, & Madden v. Oregon, 406 U.S. 404 (1972).

Arizona v. Fulminante, 500 U.S. 938 (1991).

Baldus, D. C., Pulaski, C., & Woodworth, G. (1983). Comparative review of death sentences: An empirical study of the Georgia experience. *Journal of Criminal Law and Criminology, 74,* 661–753.

Ballew v. Georgia, 435 U.S. 223 (1978).

Barnett, N. J., & Field, H. S. (1978). Character of the defendant and length of sentence in rape and burglary crimes. *Journal of Social Psychology, 104,* 271–277.

Battin, M. P., Rhodes, R., & Silvers, A. (Eds.). (1998). *Physician-assisted suicide: Expanding the debate.* New York: Routledge.

Becker, B. C. (1980). Jury nullification: Can a jury be trusted? *Trial, 16,* 18–23.

Bennett, W. L., & Feldman, M. S. (1981). *Reconstructing reality in the courtroom: Justice and judgment in American culture.* New Brunswick, NJ: Rutgers University Press.

Blanck, P. D. (1985). The appearance of justice: Judges' verbal and nonverbal behavior in criminal jury trials. *Stanford Law Review, 38,* 89–164.

BMW of North America, Inc. v. Gore, 116 S.Ct. 1589 (1996).

Bornstein, B. H. (1994). David, Goliath, and Reverend Bayes: Prior beliefs about defendants' status in personal injury cases. *Applied Cognitive Psychology, 8,* 233–258.

Bornstein, B. H. (1998). From compassion to compensation: The effect of injury severity on mock jurors' liability judgments. *Journal of Applied Social Psychology, 28,* 1477–1502.

Bornstein, B. H. (1999). The ecological validity of jury simulations: Is the jury still out? *Law and Human Behavior, 23,* 75–91.

Bourgeois, M. J., Horowitz, I. A., & ForsterLee, L. (1993). Effects of technicality and access to trial transcripts on verdicts and information processing in a civil trial. *Personality and Social Psychology Bulletin, 19,* 220–227.

Bray, R. M. (1982). Defendant attractiveness and mock juror judgments. *Replications in Social Psychology, 2,* 25–28.

Bray, R. M., Struckman-Johnson, C., Osborne, M. D., MacFarlane, J. B., & Scott, J. (1978). The effects of defendant status on the decisions of student and community juries. *Social Psychology, 41,* 256–260.

Brehm, S. S., Kassin, S. M., Fein, S. (1999). *Social psychology* (4th ed.). Boston: Houghton-Mifflin.

Brekke, N., & Borgida, E. (1988). Expert psychological testimony in rape trials: A social cognitive analysis. *Journal of Personality and Social Psychology, 55,* 372–386.

Brody, D. C., & Rivera, C. (1997). Examining the Dougherty "all knowing assumption": Do jurors know about their nullification power? *Criminal Law Bulletin, 151,* 161–165.

Broeder, D. (1959). The University of Chicago jury project. *Nebraska Law Review, 38,* 744–760.

Bull, R., & Rumsey, N. (1988). *The social psychology of facial appearance.* New York: Springer-Verlag.

Burch v. Lousiana, 99 S.Ct. 1623 (1979).

Burnstein, E. (1983). Persuasion as argument processing. In M. Brandstatter, J. H. Davis, & G. Stocker-Kriechgauer (Eds.), *Group decision processes.* London: Academic Press.

Cacioppo, J. T., & Petty, R. E. (1982). The need for cognition. *Journal of Personality and Social Psychology, 42,* 116–131.

Carpenter, T. (2000, March). *Countering the consideration of extra-legal factors in dam-*

age award decisions. Poster session presented at the biennial meeting of the American Psychology-Law Society, New Orleans, LA.

Carter v. Kentucky, 110 S.Ct. 3282 (1981).

Cather, C., Greene, E., & Durham, R. (1996). Plaintiff injury and defendant reprehensibility: Implications for compensatory and punitive damage awards. *Law and Human Behavior, 20,* 189–205.

Charrow, R. P., & Charrow, V. R. (1979). Making legal language understandable: A psycholinguistic study of jury instructions. *Columbia Law Review, 79,* 1306–1374.

Commonwealth v. Curnin, 565 N.E. 2d 440, 441 (Mass. 1991).

Costanzo, M. (2003). *Psychology applied to law.* Belmont, CA: Wadsworth.

Cox, M., & Tanford, S. (1989). Effects of evidence and instructions in civil trials: An experimental investigation of rules of admissibility. *Social Behaviour, 4,* 31–55.

Crott, H. W., & Werner, J. (1994). The norm–information–distance model: A stochastic approach to preference change in group interaction. *Journal of Experimental Social Psychology, 30,* 68–95.

Cutler, B. L., Dexter, H. R., & Penrod, S. D. (1989). Expert testimony and jury decision making: An empirical analysis. *Behavioral Sciences and the Law, 7,* 215–225.

Cutler, B. L., & Penrod, S. D. (1995). *Mistaken identification: The eyewitness, psychology, and the law.* Cambridge, UK: Cambridge University Press.

Cutler, B. L., Penrod, S. D., & Dexter, H. R. (1989). The eyewitness, the expert psychologist, and the jury. *Law and Human Behavior, 13,* 311–322.

Cutler, B. L., Penrod, S. D., & Dexter, H. R. (1990). Juror sensitivity to eyewitness identification evidence. *Law and Human Behavior, 14,* 185–191.

Cutler, B. L., Penrod, S. D., & Stuve, T. E. (1988). Juror decision making in eyewitness identification cases. *Law and Human Behavior, 12,* 41–55.

Dann, B. M. (1993). "Learning lessons" and "speaking rights": Creating educated and democratic juries. *Indiana Law Journal, 68,* 1229–1279.

Daudistel, H. C., Hosch, H. M., Golmes, M. D., & Graves, J. B. (1999). Effects of defendant ethnicity on juries' dispositions of felony cases. *Journal of Applied Social Psychology, 29,* 317–336.

Daubert v. Merrell Dow Pharmaceuticals, Inc. 113 S.Ct. 2786 (1993).

Davis, J. H. (1980). Group decision and procedural justice. In M. L. Fishbein (Ed.), *Progress in social psychology* (Vol. 1, pp. 157–229). Hillsdale, NJ: Erlbaum.

Devine, D. J., Clayton, L. D., Dunford, B. B., Seying, R., & Pryce, J. (2001). Jury decision making: 45 years of empirical research on deliberating groups. *Psychology, Public Policy, and Law, 7,* 622–727.

DiPerna, P. (1984). *Juries on trial: Faces of American justice.* New York: Dembner Books.

Doob, A. N., & Kirshenbaum, H. M. (1973). Some empirical evidence on the effect of S. 12 of the Canada evidence act upon an accused. *The Criminal Law Quarterly, 15,* 88–96.

Dunn, K. F., Wilbanks J. C., & Penrod S. D. (2002, September). *Assessing the external validity of jury decision making research methodologies: A meta-analysis.* Paper presented at the annual meeting of the European Association of Psychology and Law, Leuven, Belgium.

Efran, M. G. (1974). The effect of physical appearance on the judgment of guilt, interpersonal attraction, and severity of recommended punishment in a simulated jury task. *Journal of Research in Personality, 8,* 45–54.

Elliott, R., Farrington, B., & Manheimer, H. (1988). Eyewitness credible and discredible. *Journal of Applied Social Psychology, 44,* 20–33.

Ellsworth, P. C. (1989). Are twelve heads better then one? *Law and Contemporary Problems, 52,* 205–224.

Ellsworth, P. C. (1999). Jury reform at the end of the century: Real agreement, real changes. *University of Michigan Journal of Law Reform, 32,* 213–225.

Ellsworth, P. E., & Mauro, R. (1998). Psychology and law. In D. T. Gilbert., & S. T. Fiske (Eds.), *The handbook of social psychology* (4th ed., Vol. 2, pp. 684–732). New York: McGraw-Hill.

Faigman, D. L., & Baglioni, A. J. (1988). Bayes' theorem in the trial process: Instructing jurors on the value of statistical evidence. *Law and Human Behavior, 12,* 1–17.

Fairchild, H. H., & Cowan, G. (1997). The O. J. Simpson trial: Challenges to science and society. *Journal of Social Issues, 53,* 583–591.

Federal rules of evidence, (1984). St. Paul, MN: West.

Feigenson, N., Park, J., & Salovey, P. (1997). Effect of blameworthiness and outcome severity on attributions of responsibility and damage awards in comparative negligence cases. *Law and Human Behavior, 21,* 597–617.

Finkel, N. J. (1995). *Commonsense justice: Jurors' notions of the law.* Cambridge, MA: Harvard University Press.

ForsterLee, L., & Horowitz, I. A. (1997). Enhancing juror competence in a complex trial. *Applied Cognitive Psychology, 11,* 305–319.

ForsterLee, L., Horowitz, I., Athaide-Victor, E., & Brown, N. (2000). The bottom line: The effects of written expert witness statements on juror verdicts and information processing. *Law and Human Behavior, 24,* 259–270.

ForsterLee, L., Horowitz, I. A., & Bourgeois, M. J. (1993). Juror competence in civil trials: Effects of preinstruction and evidence technicality. *Journal of Applied Psychology, 78,* 14–21.

Fox, S. G., & Walters, H. A. (1986). The impact of general versus specific expert testimony and eyewitness confidence upon mock juror judgment. *Law and Human Behavior, 10,* 215–228.

Ghiardi, J., & Kircher, J. (1995). *Punitive damages law and practice.* Deerfield, IL: Clark, Boardman, & Callaghan.

Gilovich, T., Vallone, R., & Tversky, A. (1985). The hot hand in basketball: On the misperception of random sequences. *Cognitive Psychology, 17,* 295–314.

Gleason, J. M., & Harris, V. A. (1976). Group discussion and defendant's socio-economic status as determinants of judgments by simulated jurors. *Journal of Applied Social Psychology, 6,* 186–191.

Goodman, J. (1992). Jurors' comprehension and assessment of probabilistic evidence. *American Journal of Trial Advocacy, 16,* 361–389.

Goodman, J., & Greene, E. (1989). The use of paraphrase analysis in the simplification of jury instructions. *Journal of Social Behavior and Personality, 4,* 237–251.

Gordon, R. A., Bindrim, T. A., McNicholas, M. L., & Walden, T. L. (1988). Perceptions of blue-collar and white-collar crime: The effect of defendant race on simulated juror decisions. *Journal of Social Psychology, 128,* 191–197.

Gray, D. B., & Ashmore, R. D. (1976). Biasing influence of defendants' characteristics on simulated sentencing. *Psychological Reports, 38,* 727–738.

Greene, E. (2003). Psychology in civil litigation: An overview and introduction to the special issue. *Law and Human Behavior, 27,* 1–4.

Greene, E., & Bornstein, B. H. (2003). *Determining damages: The psychology of jury awards.* Washington, DC: American Psychological Association.

Greene, E., Chopra, S. R., Kovera, M. B., Penrod, S. D., Rose, V. G., Schuller, R., et al.

(2002). Jurors and juries: A review of the field. In J. R. P. Ogloff (Ed.), *Taking psychology and law into the twenty-first century* (pp. 225–284). New York: Kluwer/Plenum.

Greene, E., Coon, D., & Bornstein, B. (2001). The effects of limiting punitive damage awards. *Law and Human Behavior, 19,* 67–78.

Greene, E., & Dodge, M. (1995). The influence of prior record evidence on juror decision making. *Law and Human Behavior, 19,* 67–78.

Greene, E., Johns, M., & Bowman, J. (1999). The effects of injury severity on jury negligence decisions. *Law and Human Behavior, 23,* 675–693.

Greene, E., Johns, M., & Smith, A. (2001). The effects of defendant conduct on jury damage awards. *Journal of Applied Psychology, 86,* 228–237.

Greene, E., Woody, W. D., & Winter, R. (2000). Compensating plaintiffs and punishing defendants: Is bifurcation necessary? *Law and Human Behavior, 24,* 187–205.

Griffitt, W., & Jackson, T. (1973). Simulated jury decisions: The influence of jury–defendant attitude similarity–dissimilarity. *Social Behavior and Personality, 1,* 1–7.

Groscup, J., & Penrod, S. D. (2002, March). *Limiting instructions' effects on juror assessments of scientific validity and reliability.* Paper session presented at the biennial meeting of the American Psychology–Law Society, Austin, TX.

Gudjonsson, G. H. (2003). *The psychology of interrogations and confessions: A handbook.* Chichester, UK: Wiley.

Hans, V. P. (1978). *The effects of the unanimity requirement on group decision processes in simulated juries.* Unpublished doctoral dissertation, University of Toronto, Toronto, Canada.

Hans, V. P. (1992). Jury decision making. In D. K. Kagehiro & W. S. Laufer (Eds.), *Handbook of psychology and law* (pp. 56–76). New York: Springer-Verlag.

Hans, V. P. (2000). *Business on trial: The civil jury and corporate responsibility.* New Haven, CT: Yale University Press.

Hans, V. P., & Doob, A. N. (1976). Section 12 of the Canada Evidence Act and the deliberation of simulated juries. *Criminal Law Quarterly, 18,* 235–253.

Hans, V. P., & Ermann, M. D. (1989). Responses to corporate versus individual wrongdoing. *Law and Human Behavior, 13,* 151–166.

Hastie, R. (1993). Algebraic models of juror decision processes. In R. Hastie (Ed.), *Inside the juror: The psychology of juror decision making* (pp. 84–115) New York: Cambridge University Press.

Hastie, R., Penrod, S. D., & Pennington, N. (1983). *Inside the jury.* Cambridge, MA: Harvard University Press.

Hastie, R., Schkade, D. A., & Payne, J. W. (1999). Juror judgments in civil cases: Effects of plaintiff's requests and plaintiff's identity on punitive damage awards. *Law and Human Behavior, 23,* 445–470.

Hatvany, N., & Strack, F. (1980). The impact of a discredited key witness. *Journal of Applied Social Psychology, 10,* 490–509.

Helgeson, J. G., & Ursic, M. L. (1993). Information load, cost/benefit assessment and decision strategy variability. *Journal of the Academy of Marketing Science, 21,* 13–20.

Heuer, L., & Penrod, S. D. (1989). Instructing jurors: A field experiment with written and preliminary instructions. *Law and Human Behavior, 13,* 409–421.

Heuer, L., & Penrod, S. D. (1994). Trial complexity: A field investigation of its meaning and its effect. *Law and Human Behavior, 18,* 29–52.

Horowitz, I. A. (1985). The effect of jury nullification instructions on verdicts and jury functioning in criminal trials. *Law and Human Behavior, 9,* 25–36.

Horowitz, I. A. (1986). *Effects of lawyers' arguments on juries' nullification tendencies.* Unpublished manuscript.

Horowitz, I. A. (1988). Jury nullification: The impact of judicial instructions, arguments, and challenges on jury decision making. *Law and Human Behavior, 12,* 439–453.

Horowitz, I. A., & Bordens, K. S. (1990). An experimental investigation of procedural issues in complex tort trials. *Law and Human Behavior, 14,* 269–285.

Horowitz, I. A., ForsterLee, L., & Brolly, I. (1996). Effects of trial complexity on decision making. *Journal of Applied Psychology, 81,* 757–768.

Horowitz, I. A., & Willging, T. E. (1991). Changing views of jury power, *Law and Human Behavior, 15,* 165–182.

Huntley, J. E., & Costanzo, M. (2003). Sexual harassment stories: Testing a story-mediated model of juror decision-making in civil litigation. *Law and Human Behavior, 27,* 29–51.

Jacobson, M. B. (1981). Effects of victim's and defendant's physical attractiveness on subjects' judgments in a rape case. *Sex Roles, 7,* 247–255.

Jacobson, M. B., & Popovich, P. M. (1983). Victim attractiveness and perceptions of responsibility in an ambiguous rape case. *Psychology of Women Quarterly, 8,* 100–104.

Johnson v. Louisiana, 406 U.S. 356 (1972).

Kahneman, D., Schkade, D., & Sunstein, C. R. (1998). Shared outrage and erratic awards: The psychology of punitive damages. *Journal of Risk and Uncertainty, 16,* 49–86.

Kahneman, D., & Tversky, A. (1972). Subjective probability: A judgment of representativeness. *Cognitive Psychology, 3,* 430–454.

Kalven, H. Jr., & Zeisel, H. (1966). *The American jury.* Boston: Little, Brown.

Kaplan, M. F., & Miller, C. E. (1987). Group decision making and normative versus informational influence: Effects of type of issue and assigned decision rule. *Journal of Personality and Social Psychology, 53,* 306–313.

Kassin, S. M., & Neumann, K. (1997). On the power of confession evidence: An experimental test of the fundamental difference hypothesis. *Law and Human Behavior, 21,* 469–484.

Kassin, S. M., & Sommers, S. R. (1997). Inadmissible testimony, instructions to disregard, and the jury: Substantive versus procedural considerations. *Personality and Social Psychology Bulletin, 23,* 1046–1054.

Kassin, S. M., & Sukel, H. (1997). Coerced confessions and the jury: An experimental test of the "harmless error" rule. *Law and Human Behavior, 21,* 27–46.

Kassin, S. M., Williams, L. N., & Saunders, C. L. (1990). Dirty tricks of cross-examination: The influence of conjectural evidence on the jury. *Law and Human Behavior, 14,* 373–384.

Keeton, W. P., Dobbs, D. B., Keeton, R. E., & Owen, D. G. (1984). *Prosser and Keeton on the law of torts* (5th ed.). St. Paul, MN: West.

Kerr, N. L. (1978). Severity of prescribed penalty and mock jurors' verdicts. *Journal of Personality and Social Psychology, 36,* 1431–1442.

Kerr, N. L. (1993). Stochastic models of juror decision making. In R. Hastie (Ed.), *Inside the juror: The psychology of juror decision making* (pp. 116–135). New York: Cambridge University Press.

Kerr, N. L., Hymes, R. W., Anderson, A. B., & Weathers, J. E. (1995). Defendant–juror similarity and mock juror judgments. *Law and Human Behavior, 19,* 545–567.

Kerr, N. L., MacCoun, R. J., & Kramer, G. O. (1996). Bias in judgment: Comparing individuals and groups. *Psychological Review, 103*, 687–719.

Kerwin, J., & Shaffer, D. R. (1994). Mock jurors versus juries: The role of deliberations in reactions to inadmissible testimony. *Personality and Social Psychology Bulletin, 20*, 153–162.

Kovera, M. B., Gresham, A. W., Borgida, E., Gray, E., & Regan, P. C. (1997). Does expert psychological testimony inform or influence juror decision making? A social cognitive analysis. *Journal of Applied Psychology, 82*, 178–191.

Kovera, M. B., Levy, R. J., Borgida, E., & Penrod, S. D. (1994). Expert testimony in child sexual abuse cases: Effects of expert evidence type and cross-examination. *Law and Human Behavior, 18*, 653–674.

Kovera, M. B., & McAuliff, B. D. (2000a). Attorney evaluations of psychological science: Does evidence quality matter? In M. B. Kovera & B. D. McAuliff (Chairs), *Judge, attorney, and juror decisions about scientific and statistical evidence*. Symposium conducted at the biennial meeting of the American Psychology–Law Society, New Orleans, LA.

Kovera, M. B., & McAuliff, B. D. (2000b). The effects of peer review and evidence quality on judge evaluations of psychological science: Are judges effective gatekeepers? *Journal of Applied Psychology, 85*, 574–586.

Kovera, M. B., McAulliff, B. D., & Hebert, K. S. (1999). Reasoning about scientific evidence: Effects of juror gender and evidence quality on juror decisions in a hostile work environment case. *Journal of Applied Psychology, 84*, 362–375.

Kovera, M. B., Park, R. C., & Penrod, S. D. (1992). Jurors' perceptions of eyewitness and hearsay evidence. *Minnesota Law Review, 76*, 703–722.

Kovera, M. B., Russano, M. B., & McAuliff, B. D. (2002). Assessment of the commonsense psychology underlying *Daubert*: Legal decision makers' abilities to evaluate expert evidence in hostile work environment cases. *Psychology, Public Policy, and Law, 8*, 180–200.

Kramer, G. P., Kerr, N. L., & Carroll, J. S. (1990). Pretrial publicity, judicial remedies, and jury bias. *Law and Human Behavior, 14*, 409–438.

Krulewitch v. United States, 336 U.S. 440 (1949).

Kumho Tire Co. v. Carmichael, 526 U.S. 137 (1999).

Lamm, H., & Myers, D. G. (1978). Group-induced polarization of attitudes and behavior. In L. Berkowitz (Ed.), *Advances in experimental social psychology* (pp. 145–195). New York: Academic Press.

Landsman, S., Diamond, S., Dimitropoulos, L., & Saks, M. J. (1998). Be careful what you wish for: The paradoxical effects of bifurcating claims for punitive damages. *Wisconsin Law Review*, 297–342.

Landsman, S., & Rakos, R. F. (1991). A research essay: A preliminary empirical enquiry concerning the prohibition of hearsay evidence in American courts. *Law and Psychology Review, 15*, 65–85.

Landsman, S., & Rakos, R. F. (1994). A preliminary inquiry into the effect of potentially biasing information on judges and jurors in civil litigation. *Behavioral Sciences and the Law, 12*, 113–126.

Lempert, R. O. (1981). Civil juries and complex cases: Let's not rush to judgment. *Michigan Law Review, 68*, 117–121.

Lempert, R. O. (1999). Juries, hindsight, and punitive damage awards: Failures of a social science case for change. *DePaul Law Review, 38*, 867–894.

Levett, L., & Kovera, M. B. (2003). Can opposing experts educate jurors about unreliable expert evidence on child eyewitness memory? In B. Cutler & L. VanWallandael (Chairs), *Expert psychological testimony on eyewitness memory.* Symposium conducted at the meeting of the International Interdisciplinary Conference on Psychology and the Law, Edinburgh, Scotland.

Liebeck v. McDonald's Restaurants, Inc. (1992), No. CV-93-02419.

Lilly, G. C. (2001). The decline of the American jury. *University of Colorado Law Review, 72,* 53–91.

Loftus, E. F. (1980). Impact of expert psychological testimony on the unreliability of eyewitness identification. *Journal of Applied Psychology, 65,* 9–15.

MacCoun, R. J. (1990). The emergence of extralegal bias during jury deliberation. *Criminal Justice and Behavior, 17,* 303–314.

MacCoun, R. J. (1996). Differential treatment of corporate defendants by juries: An examination of the "deep-pockets" hypotheses. *Law and Society Review, 30,* 121–161.

MacCoun, R. J., & Kerr, N. L. (1988). Asymmetric influence in mock jury deliberation: Jurors' bias for leniency. *Journal of Personality and Social Psychology, 54,* 21–33.

Mazzella, R., & Feingold, A. (1994). The effects of physical attractiveness, race, socioeconomic status, and gender of defendants and victims on judgments of mock jurors: A meta-analysis. *Journal of Applied Social Psychology, 24,* 1315–1344.

McAuliff, B. D., & Kovera, M. B. (2003). *Need for cognition and juror sensitivity to methodological flaws in psychological science.* Unpublished manuscript, Florida International University, Miami, FL.

McGowen, R., & King, G. D. (1982). Effects of authoritarian, anti-authoritarian, and egalitarian legal attitudes on mock juror and jury decisions. *Psychological Reports, 51,* 1067–1074.

Meissner, C. A., Brigham, J. C., & Pfeifer, J. E. (2003). Jury nullification: The influence of judicial instruction on the relationship between attitudes and juridic decision making. *Basic and Applied Social Psychology, 25,* 243–254.

Miene, P., Park, R., & Borgida, E. (1992). Juror decision making and the evaluation of hearsay evidence. *Minnesota Law Review, 76,* 51–94.

Moore, P. J., & Gump, B. B. (1995). Information integration in juror decision making. *Journal of Applied Social Psychology, 25,* 2158–2179.

Moran, G., & Cutler, B. L. (1991). The prejudicial impact of pretrial publicity. *Journal of Applied Social Psychology, 21,* 345–367.

Myers, M. A. (1979). Rule departures and making law: Juries and their verdicts. *Law and Society Review, 13,* 781–797.

Nagel, S., & Weitzman, L. (1972). Sex and the unbiased jury. *Judicature, 56,* 108–111.

Niedermeier, K. E., Horowitz, I. A., & Kerr, N. L. (1999). Informing jurors of their nullification powers: A route to a just verdict or judicial chaos. *Law and Human Behavior, 23,* 331–351.

Nietzel, M. T., McCarthy, D. M., & Kern, M. J. (1999). Juries: The current state of the empirical literature. In R. Roesch, S. D. Hart, & J. R. Ogloff (Eds.), *Psychology and law: The state of the discipline* (pp. 23–52). New York, NY: Kluwer/Plenum.

Nisbett, R. E. (1993). *Rules for reasoning.* Hillsdale, NJ: Erlbaum.

Olsen-Fulero, L., & Fulero, S. M. (1997). Commonsense rape judgments: An empathy–complexity theory of rape juror story making. *Psychology, Public Policy, and Law, 3,* 402–427.

Osborne, Y. H., & Rappaport, N. B. (1985). Sentencing severity with mock jurors: Predictive validity of three variable categories. *Behavioral Sciences and the Law, 3,* 467–473.

Otto, A. L., Penrod, S., & Dexter, H. (1994). The biasing impact of pretrial publicity on juror judgments. *Law and Human Behavior, 18,* 453–470.

Padawer-Singer, A. M., Singer, A. N., & Singer, R. L. (1977). Legal and social–psychological research in the effects of pre-trial publicity on juries, numerical makeup of juries, and non-unanimous verdict requirements. *Law and Psychology Review, 3,* 71–79.

Pagilia, A., & Schuller, R. A. (1998). Jurors' use of hearsay evidence: The effects of type and timing of instructions. *Law and Human Behavior, 22,* 501–518.

Park, R. (1987). A subject approach to hearsay reform. *Michigan Law Review, 86,* 51–94.

Parloff, R. (1997). Speaking of junk science . . . *American Lawyer, 19,* 5–8.

Pennington, N., & Hastie, R. (1981). Juror decision-making models: The generalization gap. *Psychological Bulletin, 89,* 246–287.

Pennington, N., & Hastie, R. (1986). Evidence evaluation in complex decision making. *Journal of Personality and Social Psychology, 51,* 242–258.

Pennington, N., & Hastie, R. (1992). Explaining the evidence: Tests of the story model for juror decision making. *Journal of Personality and Social Psychology, 62,* 189–206.

Pennington, N., & Hastie, R. (1993). The story model for juror decision making. In R. Hastie (Ed.), *Inside the juror: The psychology of juror decision making* (pp. 192–221) New York: Cambridge University Press.

People v. Orenthal James Simpson, No. BA097211, 1995 WL 672664, at *11 (Cal. Super. Trans. Sept. 21, 1995).

Perez, D. A, Hosch, H. M., Ponder, B., & Trejo, G. C. (1993). Ethnicity of defendants and jurors as influences on jury decisions. *Journal of Applied Social Psychology, 23,* 1249–1262.

Pfeiffer, J. E., & Ogloff, J. R. P. (1991). Ambiguity and guilt determinations: A modern racism perspective. *Journal of Applied Social Psychology, 21,* 1713–1725.

Pickel, K. L. (1995). Inducing jurors to disregard inadmissible evidence: A legal explanation does not help. *Law and Human Behavior, 19,* 407–424.

Rakos, R. F., & Landsman, S. (1992). Researching the hearsay rule: Emerging findings, general issues, and future directions. *Minnesota Law Review, 76,* 655–681.

Reifman, A., Gusick, S. M., & Ellsworth, P. C. (1992). Real jurors' understanding of the law in real cases. *Law and Human Behavior, 16,* 539–554.

Rembar, C. (1980). *The law of the land.* New York: Simon & Schuster.

Rind, B., Jaeger, M., & Strohmetz, D. B. (1995). Effect of crime seriousness on simulated jurors' use of inadmissible evidence. *Journal of Social Psychology, 135,* 417–424.

Robbennolt, J. K. (2000). Outcome severity and judgments of "responsibility": A meta-analytic review. *Journal of Applied Social Psychology, 30,* 2–39.

Robbennolt, J. K. (2002). Punitive damage decision making: The decisions of citizens and trial court judges. *Law and Human Behavior, 26,* 315–314.

Robbennolt, J. K., & Studebaker, C. A. (1999). Anchoring in the courtroom: The effects of caps on punitive damages. *Law and Human Behavior, 23,* 353–373.

Saks, M. J., Hollinger, L. A., Wissler, R. L., Evans, D. L., & Hart, A. J. (1998). Reducing variability in civil jury awards. *Law and Human Behavior, 21,* 243–256.

Saks, M. J., & Marti, M. W. (1997). A meta-analysis of the effects of jury size. *Law and Human Behavior, 21,* 451–467.

Saks, M. J., & Wissler, R. L. (1984). Legal and psychological bases of expert testimony: Surveys of the law and of jurors. *Behavioral Sciences and the Law, 2,* 435–449.

Sandys, M., & Dillehay, R. C. (1995). First-ballot votes, predeliberation dispositions, and final verdicts in jury trials. *Law and Human Behavior, 19,* 175–195.

Scheflin, A., & Van Dyke, J. (1980). Jury nullification: The contours of a controversy. *Law and Contemporary Problems, 43,* 52–115.

Schklar, J., & Diamond, S. S. (1999). Juror reactions to DNA evidence: Errors and expectancies. *Law and Human Behavior, 23,* 159–184.

Schuller, R. A. (1992). The impact of battered woman syndrome evidence on jury decision-processes. *Law and Human Behavior, 16,* 597–620.

Schuller, R. A. (1995). Expert evidence and hearsay: The influence of "secondhand" information on jurors' decisions. *Law and Human Behavior, 19,* 345–362.

Schuller, R. A., & Cripps, J. (1998). Expert evidence pertaining to battered women: The impact of gender of expert and timing of testimony. *Law and Human Behavior, 22,* 17–31.

Sealy, A. P., & Cornish, W. R. (1973). Juries and the rules of evidence. *Criminal Law Review,* 208–223.

Simson, G. (1976). Jury nullification in the American system: A skeptical view. *Texas Law Review, 54,* 488–526.

Skinner, L. J. (1978). Physical attractiveness of the defendant and the defense attorney in jury simulations with high and low structural verisimilitude. *Dissertation Abstracts International, 39,* 2019B. (UMI No. 7819220)

Slovic, P., & Lichtenstein, S. (1971). Comparison of Bayesian and regression approaches to the study of information processing in judgment. *Organizational Behavior and Human Decision Processes, 6,* 649–744.

Smith, B. C., Penrod, S. D., Otto, A. L., & Park, R. C. (1996). Jurors' use of probabilistic evidence. *Law and Human Behavior, 20,* 49–82.

Smith, V. L. (1991). Prototypes in the courtroom: Lay representations of legal concepts. *Journal of Personality and Social Psychology, 61,* 857–872.

Smith, V. L., & Kassin, S. M. (1993). Effects of the dynamite charge on the deliberations of deadlocked mock juries. *Law and Human Behavior, 17,* 625–643.

Sommers, S. R., & Ellsworth, P. C. (2000). Race in the courtroom: Perceptions of guilt and dispositional attributions. *Personality and Social Psychology Bulletin, 26,* 1367–1379.

Sperlich, P. W. (1980). . . . And then there were six: The decline of the American jury. *Judicature, 63,* 262, 275–277.

Sperlich, P. W. (1982). The case for preserving trial by jury in complex civil litigation. *Judicature, 65,* 395–419.

Stasser, G. (1992). Information salience and the discovery of hidden profiles by decision-making groups: A "thought experiment." *Organizational Behavior and Human Decision Processes, 52,* 156–181.

Stasser, G., Kerr, N. L., & Bray, R. M. (1982). The social psychology of jury deliberations: Structure, process, and product. In N. L. Kerr & R. Bray (Eds.), *The psychology of the courtroom* (pp. 221–256). New York: Academic Press.

Steblay, N. M., Besirevie, J., Fulero, S. M., & Jimenenz-Lorente, B. (1999). The effects of pretrial publicity on juror verdicts: A meta-analytic review. *Law and Human Behavior, 23,* 219–235.

Stephan, C. W., & Stephan W. G. (1986). *Habla Ingles?* The effects of language translation on simulated juror decisions. *Journal of Applied Social Psychology*, *16*, 577–589.

Sue, S., Smith, R. E., & Caldwell, C. (1973). Effects of inadmissible evidence on the decisions of simulated jurors: A moral dilemma. *Journal of Applied Social Psychology*, *3*, 345–353.

Thompson, W. C., Fong, G. T., & Rosenthal, D. L. (1981). Inadmissible evidence and juror verdicts. *Journal of Personality and Social Psychology*, *40*, 453–463.

Thompson, W. C., & Schumman, E. (1987). Interpretation of statistical evidence in criminal trials. *Law and Human Behavior*, *11*, 167–187.

Tversky, A., & Kahneman, D. (1971). Belief in the law of small numbers. *Psychological Bulletin*, *76*, 105–110.

Tversky, A., & Kahneman, D. (1974). Judgment under uncertainty: Heuristics and biases. *Science*, *185*, 1124–1131.

United States v. Grunewald, 77 S.Ct. 963 (1956).

Vidmar, N. (1995). *Medical malpractice and the American jury*. Ann Arbor, MI: University of Michigan.

Vidmar, N., Lempert, R. O., Diamond, S. S., Hans, V. P., Landsman, S., MacCoun, R., et al. (2000). Amicus brief: Kumho Tire v. Carmichael. *Law and Human Behavior*, *24*, 387–400.

Weinberg, H. I., & Baron, R. S. (1982). The discredible eyewitness. *Personality and Social Psychology Bulletin*, *8*, 60–67.

Wiener, R. L., Habert, K., Shkodriani, G., & Staebler, C. (1991). The social psychology of jury nullification: Predicting when jurors disobey the law. *Journal of Applied Social Psychology*, *21*, 1379–1401.

Wilbanks, J., Dunn, K., & Penrod, S. (2002, March). *A meta-analysis of civil juror decisions*. Paper presented at the biennial meeting of the American Psychology–Law Society, Austin, TX.

Williams v. Florida, 399 U.S. 78 (1970).

Wissler, R. L., Evans, D. L., Hart, A. J., Morry, M. M., & Saks, M. J. (1997). Explaining "pain and suffering" awards: The role of injury characteristics and fault attributions. *Law and Human Behavior*, *21*, 181–207.

Wissler, R. L., Hart, A. J., & Saks, M. J. (1999). Decision-making about general damages: A comparison of jurors, judges, and lawyers. *Michigan Law Review*, *98*, 751–826.

Wissler, R. L., Kuehn, P., & Saks, M. J. (2000). Instructing jurors on general damages in personal injury cases: Problems and possibilities. *Psychology, Public Policy, and Law*, *6*, 712–742.

Wissler, R. L., & Saks, M. J. (1985). On the inefficacy of limiting instructions: When jurors use prior conviction evidence to decide on guilt. *Law and Human Behavior*, *9*, 37–48.

Zickafoose, D. J., & Bornstein, B. H. (1999). Double discounting: The effects of comparative negligence on mock juror decision making. *Law and Human Behavior*, *23*, 577–596.

CHAPTER TWELVE

The Comprehension
of Judicial Instructions

JAMES R. P. OGLOFF
V. GORDON ROSE

> The purpose of the jury is to guard against the exercise of arbi-
> trary power—to make available the commonsense judgment of
> the community as a hedge against the overzealous or mistaken
> prosecutor and in preference to the professional or perhaps
> over-conditioned or biased response of a judge.
> —*Taylor v. Louisiana* (1975, p. 530)

As the previous chapters on the jury process make clear, the jury—although commonly referred to as the hallmark of the legal system—plays a narrowly defined role in the legal system. Specifically, it is the role of the jury to serve as the finder of fact in the case. This task requires jurors to listen to the evidence admitted into evidence, to learn the relevant procedural and substantive law to be considered, and to arrive at a verdict. Although seemingly straightforward, this task, in practice, requires at least three unique functions of the jury. First, jurors must be able to evaluate, fairly and impartially, the evidence presented; to this end, their decisions must not be influenced, to any inappropriate extent, by "extralegal" factors such as pretrial publicity, discrimination, etc. Second, jurors must be able to comprehend the law as instructed by the judge and counsel at trial. Third, jurors must be able to systematically consider the evidence in light of the law in order to come to a verdict. The first function was evaluated in earlier chapters. Here we limit our discussion to the latter two functions: jurors' comprehension of the law (i.e., judicial instructions) and their ability to employ the law in a systematic way when deliberating to reach a verdict.

The value of the jury is seen to be among the strengths of the commonlaw legal system. King John's signing of the *Magna Carta* on June 15, 1215 guaranteed, among other things, the right to a free and fair trial and set in motion the development of the jury system that has evolved to be a hallmark of our legal system. As Blackstone commented, "trial by jury ever has been, and I trust ever will be, looked upon as the glory of English law" (Blackstone, 1765, Vol. 1, p. 379). Despite such affirmations and various constitutional and common-law guarantees, legal commentators, social scientists, and the public have subjected the jury system to critical scrutiny. Moreover, it has been noted that the increased complexities of evidentiary matters as well as the law only serve to make the jury's task all the more difficult (Adler, 1994; Bouck, 1993).

Given the complexity of the law, concern has been expressed that jurors are unable to comprehend adequately the judge's instructions. Indeed, if jurors do not understand the judge's instructions, "there can be no assurance that the verdict represents a finding by the jury under the law and upon the evidence presented" (*Warren v. Parks*, 1976, p. 687). Steele and Thornburg (1988–1989) document several cases in which courts have affirmed erroneous verdicts despite the fact that the jurors misunderstood the judge's instructions. Because jury deliberations take place in secrecy, and, in most countries, not including the United States, jurors are not permitted to discuss their deliberations after the trial, it is impossible to know in how many cases jurors have made errors based on their misunderstanding or lack of knowledge concerning the jury instructions they received.

Aside from historical and philosophical justifications, do jury instructions matter? Certainly, there is much experimental evidence that jury instructions are *capable* of influencing jury behavior. The presence or absence of instructions can affect conviction rates by mock juries (e.g., Reed, 1980). Nullification instructions[1] have been shown to affect mock jury decisions (Horowitz, 1985, 1988; Wiener, Halbert, Shkodriani, & Staebler, 1991), as have reasonable doubt instructions (Koch & Devine, 1999) and joinder instructions (Tanford, Penrod, & Collins, 1985). Shaw and Skolnick (1995) demonstrated that the manner of instruction (prohibitive vs. informational) can impact verdicts. Furthermore, when asked, real-world jurors are apt to report that the judicial instructions on the law were the most important factor in their decisions (e.g., Flango, 1980; Jackson, 1992). Accordingly, there is reason to believe that instructions can and do influence jury behavior, and as a result, it becomes important to know whether those instructions are capable of being— or are actually—understood and applied by jurors.

Popular and anecdotal evidence suggests that there are problems with the jury format. For example, Burnett (2001), a historian at Princeton University, wrote about his experiences as the jury foreman in a murder trial. He described the experience as "the most intense sixty-six hours of my life" (p. 12). He wrote that "the jury room is a most remarkable—and largely inaccessible—space in our society, a space where ideas, memories, virtues, and prejudices clash with the messy stuff of the big, bad world. We expect much of this room, and we think about it less often than we probably should" (p. 13). In another matter, Berger (1997), a Michigan psychiatrist reflecting on the trial of a malpractice suit against him, including the results of posttrial juror interviews, concluded that juries do not necessarily understand or follow the jury instructions, and may decide cases on issues that are different from those they are instructed to consider. In a more scholarly appraisal, Adler (1994) interviewed jurors in several high-profile cases and attempted to reconstruct the jury deliberations. The picture that resulted is one of jurors who are typically genuinely motivated to do a good job, but who feel abandoned by the system in terms of how to go about doing so; jurors cannot understand the legal issues upon which they are supposed to decide cases, and they are therefore left to their own devices.

Ferguson and Bouck (1987) pointed out that, of the 98 cases that were appealed in Ontario, Canada, between 1981 and 1989, based on the inadequacies of the jury charges given, the court found the instructions unsatisfactory and ordered a new trial in 50% of the cases. Between 1974 and 1984, 53 cases were appealed to the Supreme Court of Canada for review of jury charges. The reversal rate requiring a new trial was 34%. Bouck (1993) later reported a reversal rate among appellate courts as high as 70%. Aside from the deficiency of the current process for charging juries, these reversal rates are particularly problematic because of the added pressure they place on the legal system and the uncertainty defendants face regarding their fate. The high standard and precision of instructions that must be presented to juries also create a particular difficulty for judges (Bouck, 1993; Eames, 2003; Young, 2003).

In this chapter, we review the research on the comprehension of judicial instructions, or the jury charge, as it is also known. We begin with a series of points that are important to consider when evaluating the research findings. Because research on judicial instructions has utilized a variety of methodologies and approaches, we review research based on several sources: (1) data from actual jurors (i.e., data obtained by questioning jurors and reviewing questions jurors have asked judges), (2) data from judges, (3) data from comprehension studies considering judicial instructions out of context, and (4) the results of comprehension studies within the context of simulated trials. We then consider the methods of assessing jurors' comprehension of judicial instructions. In addition to the research assessing jurors' comprehension of instructions, we also provide an overview of the research that has been conducted on strategies and approaches that have been considered to enhance jurors' comprehension of instructions. Such approaches have included attempts to simplify instructions by using "plain language," allowing jurors to take notes, providing jurors with instructions prior to the evidence portion of the trial, and providing juries with a copy of the jury charge. In addition to these strategies, there has been a movement in the United States for each state to adopt "pattern" (or standardized) jury instructions. Also, some attention has been paid by both scholars and judges to the possible benefits of providing jurors with decision trees or flow charts to improve comprehension instructions.

RESEARCH ON THE COMPREHENSION
OF JUDICIAL INSTRUCTIONS

In this section, we consider data from various sources, including actual jurors and judges, and from the laboratory. As we do so, it is worth bearing in mind several points:

1. What is comprehension? Is memory for instructions a suitable measure of comprehension? It is certainly possible for a juror to correctly remember an instruction, yet to be completely mistaken about its meaning. Is willingness to apply the instruction a valid measure of comprehension? Or should we distinguish those jurors who understand an instruction but choose not to apply it?

2. As a closely related issue, how should we measure comprehension? The ability to paraphrase or recall instructions assumes a basic understanding. Recognition (true/false) tests examine memory for instructions, presumably on the basis that if a person understands an instruction, then he or she is more likely to store and retrieve information about it accurately. Tests of the ability to apply instructions to a novel hypothetical fact situation more closely resemble the task real juries undertake. Some might argue that in practical terms, differences in understanding instructions are unimportant unless they have an effect on verdict.

3. What level of comprehension is good enough? The research has predominantly focused on determining how *poor* comprehension of instructions is among jurors. As research findings (hopefully) facilitate improvement in the comprehensibility of instructions, the legal and political policy question arises of what standard of comprehension should be expected of jurors. Should we expect all jurors to meet the implicit legal assumption of perfect comprehension, recall, and application? Is it sufficient if some specified majority of jurors can reach some reasonable but imperfect standard of comprehension on some kind of laboratory test (Elwork, Alfini, & Sales, 1987; Elwork & Sales, 1985)? As Koenig, Kerr, and Van Hoek (1987) correctly point out, at the very least, an instruction should not make things worse!

4. As a related issue, is there some (essentially) maximum level of juror comprehension? In other words, is there a ceiling on juror comprehension? Some researchers have implied that there may be (Diamond, 1993; Smith, 1991, 1993; Wiener, Pritchard, & Weston, 1995), although others maintain that there is as yet insufficient evidence to draw that conclusion (English & Sales, 1997).

5. Do we need to distinguish between findings that pertain to criminal juries and those that pertain to civil juries? Are there fundamental differences in

the ways that the two types of juries are instructed? Are there differences in the tasks they must carry out in applying their instructions? Greene and Bornstein (2000) argue that it is harder to understand civil instructions, and it is consequently harder to improve them, because the legal standards involved are not as clear. Can the findings from research in one context be applied to the other?

Although a discussion of all of these matters is beyond the scope of the present chapter, it is essential to keep these practical issues in mind when assessing the importance and the implications of the research data.

Findings from Research with Actual Jurors

Data on jury instructions from real jurors have been gathered in three main ways: through surveys or interviews, by an examination of jury questions, and in the course of field studies. Researchers have considered jurors' subjective assessments of their understanding, their verdicts and behavior in real trials, and the questions on the law that they submit to the trial courts in seeking clarification of the instructions.

Questioning Jurors

A number of studies have been conducted in which jurors who have served on a trial are questioned about a number of matters, including the extent to which they feel that the judge's instructions were helpful to them in their task. Following an extensive study of 48 jury trials in New Zealand, 85% of the 312 jurors interviewed indicated that they found the jury charge "clear," and more than 80% answered that the judge's instructions were "helpful" to them in their task (Young, Cameron, & Tinsley, 2001). Despite the fact that such a high percentage of jurors reported finding the jury charge clear and helpful, the researchers found that at least some of the jurors in 72% (35/48) of the cases demonstrated a misunderstanding of the law. Most often, this misunderstanding concerned the elements of the offense (i.e., the particular legal requirements needed to be proven beyond a reasonable doubt in order to find the accused guilty). The researchers concluded that the misunderstanding of the law led to questionable verdicts or hung juries in only four cases—two of which resulted in the whole or partial acquittal of the accused. As a result of the report, New Zealand has been implementing a number of sweeping changes to their jury system (see Eames, 2003).

Reifman, Gusick, and Ellsworth (1992) mailed out questionnaires to jurors in Michigan shortly after the completion of their jury service. They received responses from 40% of the people they solicited, resulting in a sample of 224 people who had been called for jury service, including 140 who had actually served on a jury. Respondents were asked to complete a series of true/false questions relating to procedural duties and to the substantive law for various crimes. On the procedural questions, respondents performed better if they had been instructed than if they had not, and better if they had served on a criminal jury than a civil jury, but at best, the mean performance was below chance ($M = 47.8\%$). Regarding substantive legal issues, jurors' responses were considered in light of the specific type of crime they had judged. Reifman et al. found that jurors of criminal cases were correct on only 41% of issues related to their case—not significantly different from their performance on issues that were not related to their case, and not significantly better than those who had never received legal instructions. Two of the jurors who responded were lawyers, and even they did no better than 70% correct. Jurors who reported having been on juries that had asked for help from the judge on points of law did better than those who had not, and this effect was even more pronounced if the assistance provided went beyond simply rereading or replaying the instructions. This finding suggests that jurors should be instructed on their right to ask questions. On the other hand, addresses by counsel did not enhance juror performance.

Steele and Thornburg (1988–1989) found that people who had previously served on juries almost always indicated that they discussed the judge's instructions, and frequently reread the entire set of instructions aloud. Thus, jurors genuinely try to use the instructions as they are intended to be used. On this issue, Jackson (1992) described a survey conducted of all jurors in England and Wales over a 2-week period in February 1992. Jurors reported a high level of comprehension of the communications of various parties in the trial; for example, 65% said they understood "all" of what was said by the judge, and 25% understood "most," with only 10% reporting that they understood only "some" or "none." In the same vein, 97% said they understood the summing up, and 93% claimed it was useful. Unfortunately, this seemingly bright picture held by jurors of their understanding of judicial instructions is tarnished by the observation that of the 32% of jurors who reported that they had been told to disregard evidence, despite the fact 84% said they understood why, only 68% claimed they had been successful in disregarding the evidence. Furthermore, several respondents criticized other jurors as incompetent, prejudiced, and so on.

Cutler and Hughes (2001) surveyed jurors and venire persons in North Carolina (4,654 venire persons, including 1,478 jurors from both criminal and civil cases). Again, 96.6% of jurors indicated that they thought their judges' instructions were "clear and understandable." Respondents claimed to have had a generally positive reaction to their experiences as venire persons or jurors.

Rose, Chopra, and Ogloff (2001) conducted semistructured interviews of persons who had served as criminal jurors in the previous 2 years in the lower mainland of British Columbia, and concluded that levels of juror comprehension of judicial instructions were very low and very consistent with laboratory results. Also, as discussed below, Saxton (1998) warned that despite jurors' confidence in having understood the judge's instructions, their confidence is not a good measure of actual understanding, which was found to be significantly lower than the participants had believed.

Field Studies

Several field studies have been conducted under the auspices of the courts. Saxton (1998) presented the results of a field experiment conducted in the courts in Wyoming, using real criminal and civil jurors from real trials. Before being discharged, jurors completed questionnaires, along with the judges and counsel. Saxton concluded that jurors spent considerable time and effort in considering and trying to apply their instructions—they did not merely disregard them, as is sometimes suggested. In all, 94% of jurors reported that the instructions were generally helpful, and 97% felt that they had understood their instructions. However, in response to case-relevant comprehension questions, criminal jurors scored 74% correct, and civil jurors only 58%. Furthermore, juror confidence was not an indicator of accuracy. As compared to a control group of jury-eligible participants who did not actually serve on a jury, instructed jurors did better on their performance test (70 vs. 53%), implying that instructions do help but fail to instill adequate levels of comprehension. Specific problems involved instructions on circumstantial evidence, burden and standard of proof, and the use of expert evidence.

Heuer and Penrod (1988, 1989, 1994; also Penrod & Heuer, 1997) have been involved in a long-running series of field studies in Wisconsin and throughout the United States. These studies concentrated on the effects of various proposed solutions for increasing juror comprehension, and are discussed later, in that context.

The general picture that emerges from real jurors is that they genuinely seem to believe they understand and follow judicial instructions, but also, that it is unlikely that they really do so.

Juries' Questions

Severance and Loftus (1982, 1984) studied the questions submitted by actual juries in trials in King County, Washington, over the period of a year. They concluded that it was clear that juries were not being provided with sufficient guidance to properly carry out their duties. Juries seem to have particular problems with the notions of "intent" and "reasonable doubt," suggesting that even the general, introductory jury instructions are not well understood. Severance and Loftus also noted that trial judges typically responded to jury questions by simply referring the jury back to the original instructions, without additional comment.

Research Data Obtained from Judges

In their classic work on the Chicago jury project, Kalven and Zeisel (1966) asked trial judges to reflect on their most recent jury trials and indicate whether they agreed with their juries' verdicts. The results indicated that judges agreed with their juries' decisions 75.4% of the time, and that most disagreements (16.9%) occurred when the judge would have convicted but the jury acquitted. Furthermore, if a jury hung, it was more likely to be the case that the judge would have convicted than acquitted. Whether or not the jurors understood their instructions, then, they most often come to the "correct" conclusion, in that their decisions are likely to be consistent with the trial judge's view of the case.

Reflecting on the above study, it is important to note that, given the limited number of decision options available to judges and jurors (e.g., guilty or not guilty, or some limited variation thereof), chance agreement is high. Therefore, a more salient finding perhaps is that that of the 1,083 cases on which the juries acquitted, judges would have convicted on 604 or 57% of these cases (even though this would be only 16.9% of all cases).

In Saxton's (1998) field experiment in Wyoming, criminal judges agreed with their juries' decisions 76% of the time, and reported believing that their juries had understood the key facts (97%) and law (100%). In civil trials, judges agreed with their juries' verdicts 50% of the time, although 100% of civil trial judges claimed to believe that their juries had correctly understood the key facts and law.

Interestingly, the methodology employed in the above studies has typically involved asking judges to recall, retrospectively, the past several jury trials over which they have presided and to indicate whether they agreed with the verdicts reached by the juries. Of course, such a methodology can easily be criticized because a judge's recollection of "correct" past trial verdicts can be affected by the jury's verdict. Using a more valid methodology in the New Zealand study mentioned above, Young and colleagues (2001) met with the trial judges at the close of the trial but before the deliberations were returned. At that time they asked, among other things, what the judge's verdict would be. The results showed that judges agreed with the jury verdicts in 24 out of 48 jury trials (50%—no better than chance). Of course, it is impossible to determine which verdicts were "correct." Nonetheless, the degree of agreement, or disagreement, between judges and juries provides some information about the relative convergence of trial outcome, at least in criminal cases.

Sand and Reiss (1985) reported on a court-sponsored field experiment in the United States Second Circuit. Judges responded to questions concerning various proposed remedies for problems with jury comprehension. Unfortunately, the study was essentially qualitative, and it is difficult to discuss the "bottom line" in the absence of statistics; individual findings are discussed later in this chapter. Similarly, a discussion of judges' views on note taking, written instructions, and other suggested remedies, as discussed in the Heuer and Penrod (1988, 1989, 1994) field experiments, are treated later under the appropriate headings.

In an experiment on jury instructions regarding eyewitnesses, Greene (1988) prepared revised instructions and circulated both the original pattern instructions and revised instructions to several judges. Of the 37 who responded, most thought that both sets of instructions were biased in favor of the defendant, and most (78% pattern, 53% revised) thought that neither set was proper to leave with a jury.

Koenig et al. (1987) surveyed trial judges in Michigan regarding the standard criminal jury instructions used in that jurisdiction, and specifically about particular instructions they were concerned jurors did not understand adequately. They found that 44% of responding judges were concerned about the instructions regarding intent in specific intent offenses, although 87% "usually" or "always" used it, and 82% used it verbatim. Additionally, 29% were concerned about the instruction regarding general intent, 45% about lesser included offenses, 29% about limiting instructions (one judge reportedly responded, "Useful to sophists only," p. 354), 27% about criminal sexual conduct, 26% about assault, 31% about reasonable doubt, and 25% of responding judges were concerned that various other instructions were not comprehensible to jurors. Despite that substantial level of concern, however, the instructions continue to be used, because they could be expected to survive appellate review. (For an additional discussion of so-called limiting instructions, see Lieberman and Arndt [2000].)

Although judges may believe, in general, that judicial instructions are understood, they are more skeptical when they consider particular instructions. Despite that skepticism, however, they continue to use instructions that they doubt effectively communicate the law to the jury.

Comprehension Studies of Instructions Alone

Several studies have examined the ability of people to understand jury instructions, divorced from the context of an actual trial. In fact, a trial context may not be necessary for testing the comprehensibility of instructions (Elwork, Sales, & Alfini, 1977). For instance, in a more general situation, Mason and Waldron (1994) found that people generally had difficulty understanding various legal documents, even when archaic terms were removed, and that comprehension continued to be low even when the documents were redrafted in "plain language" and legal terms were defined.

Strawn and Buchanan (1976) played a 25-minute videotape of Florida's standard jury instructions on burglary for participants, who then completed a 40-item true/false comprehension test. Following the instructions, only 57% of participants understood that circumstantial evidence was admissible and capable of constituting proof of a crime, and 23% thought that in a circumstantial case in which the circumstances permit two equally reasonable interpretations, one pointing to guilt and one to innocence, the defendant must be convicted. Only half the participants understood that the defendant need not present any evidence to prove innocence, and 10% did not understand the meaning of the presumption of innocence. Over a quarter of respondents incorrectly thought that out-of-court statements by the defendant must be ignored. Furthermore, the instructions did virtually nothing to increase comprehension of the legal jargon used in them, suggesting that instructions do not adequately define the terms involved. In fact, in some instances, comprehension was actually worse after instruction.

Buchanan, Pryor, Taylor, and Strawn (1978) presented the same 25-minute videotape of jury instructions on "breaking and entering with intent" to real jury panel members. Performance was assessed on a 40-item comprehension questionnaire. Subjects who received the instructions outperformed noninstructed participants on the comprehension test but still achieved scores of only 72% correct. The concepts of "information," "reasonable doubt," "material allegation," and the application of reasonable doubt and witness credibility were the biggest problem areas.

Charrow and Charrow (1979), using an oral paraphrase test to assess comprehension of various target instructions from the California pattern jury instructions, found very low levels of performance and concluded that standard jury instructions are not well understood. Steele and Thornburg (1988–1989) used the same methodology, reporting that over a set of five instructions, correct paraphrases for pattern instructions amounted to only 12.85% of all paraphrases, and redrafting the instructions increased the proportion of correct paraphrases to an average of only 24.59%. Similarly, but less dramatically, Elwork, Sales, and Alfini (1977) found that rewriting Michigan pattern instructions on negligence raised performance on a comprehension test from 60 to 80.8%. The apparently higher comprehension scores here, as compared to those in the Steele and Thornburg study, are likely a function of the manner in which comprehension was measured (recognition vs. paraphrase/recall).

In relation to death-penalty instructions in U.S. jurisdictions, Haney and Lynch (1997) found that participants receiving the standard California penalty instructions could not provide accurate definitions of "aggravating," "mitigating," and "extenuating"; in fact, only 18% of participants could provide even a partially correct definition for "extenuating." Even using revised pattern instructions from North Carolina, only 53% of participants answered all eight questions correctly (Luginbuhl, 1992).

In sum, the results of studies that are not set within the context of a trial generally suggest low levels of juror comprehension of judicial instructions. Such studies have been criticized as unrealistic, since in an actual trial, the jurors are provided with a rich evidentiary context for the judicial instructions they will receive. Moreover, in the course of their arguments, lawyers may also educate the jury about the law—though this practice varies across jurisdictions.

Comprehension Studies within the Context of a Simulated Trial

The most common way of studying juror and jury comprehension of judicial instructions is through some sort of experimental simulation. Methodologies in these studies have ranged from providing participants with a very brief written trial synopsis (as little as a paragraph) to thorough presentations of videotaped trial reenactments of 2 or 3 hours in length, containing all the major elements of a real trial, including opening and closing statements by counsel, preliminary and final instructions by the judge, and direct and cross-examination of witnesses for both sides. Generally, despite the exact nature of the stimulus materials, experimental findings have consistently shown low levels of juror and jury comprehension of judicial instructions.

Severance and Loftus (1982; see also Severance, Greene, & Loftus, 1984; Severance & Loftus, 1984) showed participants a 1-hour videotaped trial reenactment, along with either no instructions, general instructions only, or general instructions plus additional specific instructions. They measured verdict, responses to a multiple-choice questionnaire, and responses to application questions requiring participants to apply the law to new fact patterns. Overall, the error rates were very similar among conditions: 35.6% errors for the no-instruction condition, 34.7% errors for the condition of general instructions only, and 29.6% errors for the condition of general plus specific instructions; results did not differ significantly among the groups. In the case of only one question on the application test (concerning "reasonable doubt"), the specific instructions helped participants, whereas in one other case, the specific instructions actually lowered performance. Deliberation did not generally affect individual jurors' comprehension, aside from reducing errors on "intent" from 40 to 34.1%. Thus, the authors concluded, jurors have considerable difficulty understanding and applying legal instructions.

In Canada, using a murder/manslaughter with provocation case, Jones and Myers (1979) found 61.8% comprehension on 11 questions concerning the instructions used in the actual case upon which the stimulus materials were based, and 71.6% comprehension after redrafting the instructions according to psycholinguistic principles (discussed below). In regard to the Canadian instructions on conspiracy and the co-conspirator exception to the hearsay rule, Rose and Ogloff (2001) found that comprehension levels in samples from various populations were in the 60–70% range (although first-year law students did slightly better). Furthermore, they found that participants were equally confident in their correct and incorrect answers, suggesting that the option of asking the judge questions is likely an unreliable remedy for lack of juror understanding, because jurors are just as likely to be incorrect when they believe they understand the instruction when, in fact, they do not. In the context of death-penalty instructions, Diamond (1993) reported that on a series of application questions, between 40 and 68% of participants answered each question correctly.

Simulation studies have shown poor comprehension of instructions relating to eyewitnesses. For example, Greene (1988) found only 59.8% accuracy on eight comprehension questions using the standard "Telfare" instruction (i.e., an instruction judges are permitted to give concerning eyewitness reliability), not significantly different from giving no instruction at all. Participants, however, rated those instructions as an average of 3.51 on a 5-point scale for their effectiveness in helping them to understand the law. As noted previously, it is not uncommon for jurors to perceive that the judicial instructions were very useful in helping them to understand the law, yet when measured objectively, their level of understanding was limited. Indeed, Cutler, Penrod, and Dexter (1990) found the same Telfare instructions to be ineffective at sensitizing jurors to frailties in eyewitness evidence, and at producing skepticism of eyewitness identifications (see also Greene, 1987).

Using externally valid procedures (e.g., lengthy trial videotapes, comprehensive jury instructions, complete verdict choice, insanity disposition information), Ogloff (1991) employed two studies to investigate the effect of various insanity defense standards on mock jurors. In particular, randomly assigned mock jurors were presented with identical videotaped trials in which only the insanity defense standard was varied (i.e., the M'Naghten standard, the American Law Institute standard, or the Guilty But Mentally Ill standard). This study also included conditions that measured the effect that burden and standard of proof had on juror decision making about insanity. The results suggested that neither the insanity defense standard nor the assignment of burden or standard of proof differentially affected the insanity acquittal rate. Given that different insanity standards and standards of proof did not affect decisions, Ogloff also investigated mock jurors' comprehension of the insanity defense standards and the standard of proof (e.g., beyond a reasonable doubt, preponderance of the evidence). He found that the participants had difficulty correctly recalling or identifying the insanity defense standards (30% accuracy rate) and standard of proof instructions (64% accuracy rate). The mean accuracy rate for burden of proof was also low (69%).

In a more recent study, Ogloff (1998) engaged more than 500 jury-eligible people from the community in a day-long experimental procedure in which they viewed a 2½-hour videotaped trial based on an actual case. The videotape included extensive jury instructions, and mock jurors deliberated together in juries to arrive at a verdict. The results show that jurors have a very low level of comprehension of judicial instructions, as measured by recall and recognition tasks. For example, when asked to specify an exact estimate of how sure one must be of the accused's guilt to be satisfied "beyond a reasonable doubt," the mean estimate provided by participants was quite reasonable 94.97% (SD = 43.83). The mean or average level of accuracy may be misleading, however, because the majority of people believe that, to be found guilty beyond a reasonable doubt, jurors must be 100% certain of a defendant's guilt. This is an unrealistically high standard; it means that there is *no doubt whatsoever* that the accused is not guilty. At the other end of the extreme, almost one out of every six participants (15% of the sample) believed that they need only be 80% certain or less to find an accused guilty beyond a reasonable doubt. This is arguably too low a standard, because it suggests that there is *at least* 20% doubt that the accused is guilty—is such a level of doubt "reasonable"? Anecdotally, when addressing a group of judges on the subject, one of us (J.R.P.O.) surveyed judges about what they thought the percent of certainty ought to be in order to find an accused guilty beyond a reasonable doubt. Although a small majority of judges complained that answering this question was an impossible task, the judges that did participate believed that jurors ought to be approximately 95–99% certain in order to find a defendant guilty beyond a reasonable doubt.

Finally, the videotaped deliberations obtained from this study were reviewed to assess the frequency, duration, and degree of accuracy with which mock jurors referred to judicial instructions during deliberation. The juries, on average, spent only 8% of the deliberation time discussing the judicial instructions. Out of a maximum 2-hour deliberation period, mock juries spent only 73.09 seconds, on average, discussing the judicial instructions they were given. On average, the instructions were mentioned or discussed only 3.17 times during the deliberation period. Finally, on those rare occasions when jurors actually attempted to define the judicial instructions ($M = 1.78$ times per deliberation), they did so correctly 61% of the time.

In addition to assessing overall comprehension of instructions, Ogloff (1998) also investigated the extent to which mock jurors comprehend judicial instructions and whether strategies to increase comprehension are effective. Five separate experiments were conducted to determine whether the following strategies increased jurors' comprehension of judge's instructions: (1) "plain language" instructions, (2) juror note taking, (3) instructing jurors both prior to, and following, the trial, (4) providing jurors with a copy of the judge's instructions for their consideration during deliberation, and (5) a decision-tree jury deliberation model. Although none of the alternative strategies was particularly effective at increasing jurors' comprehension of the instructions, providing instructions to jurors prior to, and following, the trial and the decision-tree jury deliberation model did produce a slight increase in comprehension. Such strategies are discussed later in this chapter.

As discussed previously, in some studies providing instructions has reduced the conviction rate or increased the chances of simulated jurors being unable to reach a verdict (Reed, 1980). Nullification instructions also affected jury deliberations and verdicts, specifically increasing acquittals (Horowitz, 1985, 1988; see Devine, Clayton, Dunford, Rasmy, & Price, 2001). Similarly, judicial instructions on joined trials reduced conviction rates in at least one laboratory study (Tanford et al., 1985).

In a study by Kerr et al. (1976) that used a 50-minute videotaped trial simulation, small differences in the wording of the legal definition of reasonable doubt ("any doubt," "substantial doubt," and undefined) were found to have considerable effect on individual verdicts (43%, 60.5%, and 42.1% convictions, respectively), although the different definitions had no effect on judgments of factual guilt. Furthermore, ignoring hung juries, the definitions of reasonable doubt also affected group verdicts (any doubt, 10.5% convictions; substantial doubt, 42.1% convictions). A related study by Horowitz and Kirkpatrick (1996) also found that variations in reasonable doubt instructions affected both verdicts and quantified subjective standards of reasonable doubt; in some conditions, participants reported needing, on average, less than 50% confidence in guilt in order to find guilt "beyond a reasonable doubt."

In some judicial instructions, the judge notifies the jurors to either ignore information they have heard or to limit the use of the information to a particular purpose. Such instructions are sometimes called "limiting instructions." Results from laboratories investigating limiting instructions have been mixed. For example, instructions have been found insufficient to prevent pretrial publicity effects (Kramer, Kerr, & Carroll, 1990) or to affect verdicts in light of a coerced confession (Kassin & Wrightsman, 1981). Paglia and Schuller (1998) reported that the nature and timing of limiting instructions or prohibitions on the use of hearsay evidence had no effect on verdicts. In terms of trial testimony containing both direct and implied assertions, instructions warning of the dangers of treating implied information as if it were fact were ineffective in changing juror behavior (Harris, 1978).

In a simulated murder trial in which inadmissible evidence was presented, the judge's instructions to ignore the evidence did not vary in their effect whether the judge emphasized due process or accuracy (Thompson, Fong, & Rosenhan, 1981). Generally, participants were more likely to follow the instructions when informed that not to do so would reduce the accuracy of their decisions than when they were told that due process required it. Contrary results were obtained by Kassin and Sommers (1997), who found that jurors were swayed not by the ruling, but by the reason for that ruling, such that they were more likely to ignore evidence ruled inadmissible because it was unreliable than because it was illegally obtained (due process).

Generally, the law allows any witness, including an accused who testifies in his or her own defense, to be cross-examined about his or her criminal record. This evidence, however, may only be used for the purpose of assessing the credibility of the witness and not for the purpose of determining character (i.e., whether the accused is the type of person who would likely have committed the offense charged). Several studies have found that limiting instructions on the use of criminal record evidence are ineffective in preventing jurors from using that evidence in evaluating the defendant's guilt (e.g., Sealy & Cornish, 1973; Wissler, Kuehn, & Saks, 2000), and that in fact, such instructions may produce a "backfire" effect, actually increasing the influence of the impugned evidence (Tanford & Cox, 1987).

In a recent study, Rose (2003) presented almost 150 participants with a videotaped reenactment of an actual trial. He randomly assigned participants to one of four conditions, varying only in terms of the evidence presented regarding the accused's criminal record (character related, credibility related, neutral, or no record). In contrast to other studies, the nature of the criminal record evidence that was presented to participants had no effect on participants' individual verdicts, nor on their confidence in the verdict and their belief in the factual (as opposed to legal) guilt of the accused. Those participants who convicted expressed different views on various aspects of the evidence, the accused, and on the impact of criminal record evidence than did those who acquitted, and these differences were independent of criminal record condition. Clearly, additional research is required to study further whether jurors are necessarily affected by the accused's criminal record.

Although we have focused thus far on studies involving criminal law, a number of studies have examined juror comprehension in civil cases. Not surprisingly, the results also show that people have a great deal of difficulty comprehending the jury charge in civil cases. In fact, extant research suggests that people may have a greater level of difficulty understanding civil instructions, perhaps due to the fact that they are more likely to be exposed to concepts from criminal law than civil law in the media, on television, or in film. It is important to note, however, that Smith (1991) found that although jurors have some preexisting knowledge of the law, their knowledge is often incorrect. As such, she noted that "the objective of jury instruction, then, must be concept revision, not merely concept formation" (Smith, 1991, p. 869). Greene and Johns (2001) asked participants to read a 10-page transcript of a civil negligence trial and then answer 10 multiple-choice questions about the definition of negligence. The overall comprehension rate was 63.7%, and performance on individual questions ranged from 31 to 84%.

Hastie, Schkade, and Payne (1998) presented videotapes of civil trials (11–15 minutes in length), along with realistic 500-word jury instructions to participants. In these trials courts of appeal had ruled that consideration of punitive damages was unwarranted—so, in a sense, an objective standard existed for assessing juror responses. Participants were divided into 120 six-person juries, which were assessed on their responses to questions about five relevant legal issues. Results showed that comprehension of the judicial instructions on liability was extremely low ($M = 9\%$). Despite the fact that there were almost no blank responses, 30% of participants scored zero on the comprehension test, and the highest score obtained was 67%. During deliberations, many juries did not consider any of the five relevant legal issues. More importantly, the greater the number of the five legal issues discussed during deliberations, the more likely the jury would (correctly) not assess punitive damages. Thus, 100% of the juries that discussed none of the legal elements awarded punitive damages, but only 45% of those that considered all five elements did so (although, of course, they were still incorrect). When asked to justify their decisions, fully 49% of jurors made no reference to the judge's instructions.

Finally, Shaffer and Kerwin (1992) present evidence that juries composed of "dogmatic" jurors are more likely to be influenced by instructions than juries of "nondogmatic" jurors, although the authors point out that this finding does not necessarily mean that nondogmatic juries ignore judicial instructions. There is also some tentative evidence that judges' outcome expectations may affect verdicts; in a study by Halverson, Hallahan, Hart, and Rosenthal (1997), judicial expectations directly affected verdicts when standard instructions were given, although the influence was weaker and inverted when simplified instructions were used. This finding was interpreted as indicating that the simplified instructions increased juror comprehension and thereby reduced juror reliance on the judge's nonverbal behavior.

Before leaving this section, it is worth considering one of the usual legal responses to trial simulation studies. Inasmuch as the majority of simulation studies are actually studies of *juror* behavior, and not *jury* behavior, their results are often dismissed by the courts as lacking ecological validity. Indeed, courts typically believe that a virtue of having several jurors (depending on the jurisdiction) is that at least one juror will understand the law and help explain it to other jurors. Certainly, there seem to be consistent differences in simulation studies in the rates at which jurors and juries convict (e.g., Shaw & Skolnick, 1995). There are also a few instances in which deliberation has been found to improve comprehension. Kerwin and Shaffer (1994) reported that juries (but not jurors) followed instructions to ignore inadmissible evidence. Severance and Loftus (1984) found that deliberation decreased errors on one question but not on any others. The overwhelming weight of the experimental evidence, however, is that deliberation is not sufficient to overcome the incomprehensibility of judicial instructions (Elwork & Sales, 1985; Harris, 1978; Hastie et al., 1998; Rose & Ogloff, 2001). Recall, for example, that Ogloff (1998) found that jurors rarely mentioned the judicial instructions, spent very little time discussing them, and were correct in less than two out of three times when they did.

Ellsworth (1989) had participants view a 2½-hour videotaped homicide trial, including 30 minutes of instructions, and then deliberate as 12-person juries. She found that juries spent an average of 21% of their time discussing the judge's instructions. However, postdeliberation juror performance on 18 comprehension questions was only 65%, and there were no differences between deliberating and nondeliberating participants regarding their understanding of judicial instructions. These results suggest that although deliberations may serve to correct errors of fact, they do not succeed in correcting errors of law. Analyzing the contents of the deliberations, Ellsworth found that even with a lenient marking scheme, references to the law in deliberations were only clearly correct 51% of the time, and were clearly incorrect 21% of the time. When juries changed position during deliberations on a legal issue, 52% of the time they changed from an incorrect to a correct position, and 48% of the time they moved from a correct position to an incorrect one. During deliberations, although jurors typically defended their correct views of the facts, they did not defend their correct views of the law. Rather, in regard to the law, the most forcefully stated position usually prevailed. Thus, confident jurors were most likely to be followed on questions of law, irrespective of the accuracy of their comprehension. Of the unclear or incorrect statements of law expressed during deliberations, only 12% were corrected. Although 7% of jury discussions of the law involved the issue of reasonable doubt and 10% considered the procedural instructions, no juror actually raised the issue of the *definition* of reasonable doubt. Both reasonable doubt and the procedural instructions were primarily used as "arguing tactics" and were at least as likely as not to be used incorrectly. In fact, as Ellsworth opined, "jurors may also use the judge's cautionary instructions to stifle discussion of unpalatable, but clearly relevant, evidence" (p. 223).

Thus, based on the experimental evidence from jury simulations, it is clear that juror comprehension of legal instructions is generally poor. Furthermore, based on those studies that have directly examined the issue, *jury* comprehension of the law is unlikely to be much better than that of individual *jurors*. Inadequate comprehension is a general finding across various types of instructions on substantive law, both criminal and civil, and in regard to essential general issues such as reasonable doubt, the use of evidence, the presumption of innocence, and so on.

Methods of Assessing Comprehension

Based on the evidence discussed above, it seems clear that jury instructions are not well understood. A legal acceptance of this result must necessarily lead to efforts to improve the comprehension of instructions, as is discussed in the next major section of this chapter. In doing so, of course, it is essential that some satisfactory methodology be used to systematically examine and evaluate whether revised instructions or procedural changes actually serve to increase comprehension of the law. As Wissler et al. (2000) suggest, "before courts or legislatures replace current instructions with alternative instructions or procedures, jurors' understanding, interpretation and use of both the current instructions and the 'improvements' should be carefully tested. Some treatments can be more harmful than the neglect they were designed to replace" (p. 737; see also Diamond, 1993). Fixing instructions must be an interdisciplinary and collaborative effort, and instructions must be tested and retested as they are revised, until jury performance is satisfactory (Koenig et al., 1987).

Charrow and Charrow (1979) suggested the use of a paraphrase test in studying juror comprehension of legal instructions, on the premise that a person cannot paraphrase an instruction that he or she does not understand. In a criminal trial simulation Goodman and Greene (1989) used a paraphrase test for elements of guilt beyond a reasonable doubt, intent, burglary, and the use of prior conviction evidence. They found that fewer than half of the paraphrases were correct and often failed to include fundamental aspects of the concepts being paraphrased. For instance, fewer than 40% of jurors correctly defined "burglary"—a concept with a commonly used legal definition not exclusive to the legal context. This lack of accurate comprehension, in turn, causes problems with other instructions that presume an understanding of the elements of the offense, such as reasonable doubt. Goodman and Greene point out that paraphrase analysis can be used to suggest ways of revising instructions to increase comprehensibility. For example, many key terms from judicial instructions ("element," "plea") are never used in juror paraphrases and are good candidates for replacement in revised instructions.

Steele and Thornburg (1988–1989) also used a paraphrase test but noted that the most frequent response on that test was no response—participants were unable to paraphrase the instructions because, the authors contended, they could not understand them. This, of course assumes that the failure to paraphrase an instruction means a failure to understand it. However, failure to paraphrase an instruction may just be a recall failure—if something in the test had made the element salient, it is possible that the memory of the instruction relevant to that element would have been retrieved.

Another type of comprehension test, which avoids this memory problem, is the application test. Such tests have considerable merit because assessing the extent to which participants can apply the law correctly to a fact pattern provides a more accurate evaluation of their comprehension than tests that require jurors to recall or paraphrase the law. Severance and Loftus (1982) correctly pointed out that the real task of jurors is to apply the law, as instructed by the judge, to the facts of the case. Rose and Ogloff (2001) provided an illustration of how an application test (involving a relatively fast and inexpensive method) can be used to determine those areas of a set of instructions that are generally understood and those that are not. In doing so, they demonstrated that several traditional methodological concerns (lack of deliberation, the use of students as participants, etc.) may not be a problem, at least when demonstrating that instructions are not well understood.

It should be noted that Severance and Loftus (1982) developed their application test after studying actual questions submitted by juries in Washington State to their trial judges. The study of jury questions might seem, on its face, a fruitful way of assessing the comprehensibility of instructions. However, those authors correctly pointed out that this technique is likely to produce a conservative view of the jury comprehension problem, because jurors will only ask questions when they know they are unclear on the law, and they may often think they are clear on the law when, in fact, they are mistaken. Indeed, the picture is likely to be very conservative, because it only examines the questions jurors realize they have, only the questions jurors think matter to their final decision, and only those questions they are prepared to ask formally. Considering that in the Severance and Loftus study, of 405 jury trials studied, only 99 juries submitted written questions to the judge (apparently, usually one question each), and comparing those figures to the experimental and other evidence showing overall jury comprehension to be very low, this technique is not useful for assessing jury comprehension for specific instructions, although it may be very useful for identifying instructions in need of improvement.

It is also possible to use field studies as a systematic method for assessing instructions. Although such studies are less useful than laboratory studies in testing individual instructions, due to the variability in real trials and the lack of random assignment and experimental control, they are capable of providing convergent validity for laboratory results. Furthermore, such studies, necessarily involving the courts' approval and involvement, will serve to increase the judicial acceptance of research results on the issue of jury instructions (see Penrod & Heuer, 1997).

Although each of the techniques discussed has particular advantages and weaknesses, and on balance, some may be preferable to others for particular purposes, it is likely that a combination of techniques is the most useful for providing convincing evidence of juries' abilities to understand particular instructions.

Summary

Evidence gathered from real jurors and judges and from the laboratory has produced convergent results demonstrating that no matter how it is measured, jurors appear largely incapable of understanding judicial instructions as they are traditionally delivered by the judge. Judges and jurors both seem to believe that jurors generally understand legal instructions, and that those instructions are helpful. However, despite those beliefs, the overwhelming weight of the evidence is that the instructions are not understood and therefore cannot be helpful.

Does it matter whether juries correctly understand and apply the law? Does it matter if they come to the "right" verdict for the "wrong" reasons? According to Elwork and Sales (1985), "the law is clear on this issue. A jury cannot be said to have reached a correct verdict unless it understands the relevant law" (p. 281). Similarly, in Canada, the inability of juries to understand their legal instructions brings two constitutional rights—the right to a trial by jury and the right to be presumed innocent until proven guilty according to law—into conflict (Rose & Ogloff, 2001). Steele and Thornburg (1988–1989) suggest that "the use of incomprehensible instructions sends a message to jurors that the law is an undecipherable mystery and that juror understanding of the law is not important" (p. 94). They maintain that juries' genuine efforts to properly use judicial instructions "are seriously undermined because of the badly organized, jargon-filled, convoluted prose used by lawyers and judges who write jury instructions" (p. 98). According to Elwork and Sales (1985), failure to understand instructions can affect deliberations in several ways: by making it more likely that one or two strong jurors dominate the deliberations, by increasing the likelihood that deliberations will discuss legally inappropriate topics, and by making it more likely that the jury will fail to discuss important points of law.

In the past, much criticism has been leveled at the methodology used in the various avenues of research. Laboratory studies are artificial and often use unrealistically simple stimulus materials, but such research typically does not merit the criticisms made by the courts—criticisms that frequently reflect a lack of understanding of the scientific method. Certainly, the laboratory studies are necessary for their benefits of control and causal inference. The courts tend not to appreciate the importance of those benefits and simply dismiss the results of such studies as ungeneralizable. In fact, due to its reliance on precedents, the law is more likely to be convinced by a single compelling anecdote than any amount of experimental data. Having said that, however, the results using various methodologies and in a variety of contexts have been remarkably consistent in showing that most jury instructions cannot be well understood. Accordingly, it may be time that the burden of establishing that instructions *are* understood should shift to those who wish to maintain the status quo.

It is possible to consider whether the data suggest *why* jury instructions seem to be poorly understood. One explanation that shows great promise is the concept of "common sense justice" (CSJ; Finkel, 1995). A full consideration of this issue is beyond the scope of this chapter, but recent work by Finkel and others has made it clear that people have naive prototypes for various legal concepts, based on the media and popular culture, etc., which tend to emphasize the extreme and bizarre cases, thereby leading to extreme prototypes (Finkel, 2000). The law and CSJ may analyze the same cases quite differently. If legal instructions contradict jurors' "prior knowledge" about the law, jurors are likely to continue to rely upon their prototypes and to ignore the judge's instructions (Smith, 1991; see also Devine et al., 2001; Hastie et al., 1998). Ogloff's (1991) work investigating mock jurors' understanding of insanity defense instructions led to similar conclusions. He found that whereas legal instructions concerning the insanity defense did not affect jurors' decisions, and jurors demonstrated poor levels of understanding of the legal instructions, jurors nonetheless had relied upon their own common-sense understanding of legal insanity and concocted their own standards—again, based on their common-sense understanding of legal insanity—to arrive at a decision.

According to the above research on what has come to be known as "common-sense justice," judicial instructions must go beyond merely providing the correct legal concepts; instead, the instructions must inform jurors that their natural decision strategy is inappropriate, advise them of the appropriate strategy, and clearly present the necessary and sufficient condition for conviction (Smith, 1991). A failure to take jurors' notions of CSJ into account may mean that other efforts to improve the comprehensibility of instructions are bound to fail (Diamond, 1993; Mason & Waldron, 1994).

With an understanding of the importance of the objective evaluation of efforts to measure and improve the comprehension of instructions, we now turn our attention to suggestions for improving juror and jury understanding.

RESEARCH ON STRATEGIES/MECHANISMS TO INCREASE COMPREHENSION OF JUDICIAL INSTRUCTIONS

Having established that jurors and juries apparently have a great deal of difficulty understanding judicial instructions, the question becomes whether anything can be done to improve the situation. Answers to this question may depend on whether the problem is characterized as a deficiency in jurors or a deficiency in instructions. In light of the results discussed above, consistent across research methods and legal contexts, it seems likely that the fault is not that of jurors; rather, it may be that we are asking jurors to perform a task structured in such a way as to make it virtually impossible for them to carry out in a legally appropriate manner. Ellsworth (1989) listed the factors impeding juror comprehension as including technical legal language and uninspired presentation of the law, a failure to instruct jurors until after they have heard all the evidence, a refusal to provide juries with copies of the instructions, the lack of juror training, the failure to help (or to adequately help) juries with questions, and "the general failure to discover and correct jurors' preconceptions about the law" (p. 224).

Many solutions have been proposed, including massive revision of jury instructions and various procedural changes, including the allowance of juror note taking, providing preinstruction, and providing juries with a copy of the charge. At the outset, it is worth noting that Ogloff (1998) found that none of these strategies significantly enhanced mock jurors' comprehension of the instructions.

"Plain Language" or Redrafted Instructions

One of the easiest targets for critics of the current manner of instructing juries is the use of technical, complex legal language. Several authors have presented psycholinguistic principles upon which they advocate the redrafting of jury instructions (Charrow & Charrow, 1979; Goodman & Greene, 1989; Imwinkelried & Schwed, 1987; Jones & Myers, 1979; Myers & Jones, 1979; Sales et al., 1977). As Charrow and Charrow argue, standard jury instructions are not well understood, various linguistic factors are responsible for that deficit in understanding, and fixing those factors will improve comprehension. Such a redrafting of instructions would include revision of syntax, grammar, vocabulary and register, increased redundancy, and the elimination of known impediments to comprehension (Goodman & Greene, 1989).

A great number of studies have examined the effect of redrafting instructions in the manner suggested by these authors, and generally reported improved comprehensibility but still relatively low levels of understanding. For example, Mason and Waldron (1994) examined lay comprehension of legal documents and concluded that removing archaic legal terms or defining legal terms had little effect on comprehension. Plain-language drafting helped, but performance remained fairly poor.

Some other efforts have had a somewhat greater degree of success. For example, in the context of instructions on eyewitness evidence, Ramirez, Zemba, and Geiselman (1996) found that revision of the standard "Telfaire" instructions enhanced memory for the factors to be considered, but even so, produced only 29% recollection of the 13 factors. Greene (1987, 1988) found that revising the Telfaire instructions reduced conviction rates as compared to the original version, but a majority of the judges she consulted felt that neither version of the instructions was proper to leave to the jury. Frank and Applegate (1998) also reported that linguistically revised penalty-phase capital-case instructions were better understood than the prerevision instructions (68.4 vs. 49.7% performance). Rewritten Michigan negligence instructions raised juror comprehension from 60 to 80.1%, and in the context of a videotaped trial simulation, juror comprehension rose from 62.5 to 70.1% (Elwork et al., 1977). In a Canadian study involving a murder/manslaughter case with provocation, Jones and Myers (1979) found that linguistically revised instructions raised comprehension levels from 61.8 to 71.6%.

Severance and Loftus (1984; also 1982; Severance et al., 1984) found that revised instructions improved juror comprehension but still produced many errors in understanding. Wiener et al. (1995) reported that revisions of pattern instructions from Missouri produced only modest improvements in poor levels of comprehension. Halverson et al. (1997) studied the influence of trial judge's expectations on jury verdicts, and found that the effect was reduced when juries received simplified instructions, apparently because increased juror comprehension resulted in reduced reliance on the judge's nonverbal behavior.

Thus, it seems that there are gains in juror comprehension to be achieved from rewriting jury instructions according to psycholinguistic principles, but those gains seem to be limited. Two general reasons have been advanced to explain the limits on the success of plain-language instructions. The first explanation relies on the notion, introduced above, that jurors have their own common-sense notions of the law. If the legal instructions are consistent with jurors' intuitive ideas, comprehension will be higher (Morier, Borgida, & Park, 1996). If, on the other hand, the legal instructions conflict with jurors' prior knowledge, they are likely to ignore the instructions; as a result, plain-language instructions, by themselves, will not necessarily solve the problem of poor juror comprehension (Smith, 1991; see also, Mason & Waldron, 1994; Smith, 1993).

A second explanation involves the complexity of legal concepts. Even when such concepts are expressed in plain language, they may remain complex and difficult to understand (Mason & Waldron, 1994). As well, this complexity results in a conflict of interest for trial judges, who are not only concerned with the ability of their juries to understand their charge but also (and perhaps more so) with the ability of their charge to withstand appellate review (Perlman, 1986). It may also be that the law is not so much complex as it is unclear, and that any attempt to deviate from approved methods of explaining it will highlight differences in interpretation and lead to problems (Elwork & Sales, 1985).

Not all problems in comprehension of instructions stem from the complexity of the language. Hamilton, Hunter, and Stuart-Smith (1992) found that the use of the "masculine generic" pronoun, as opposed to some gender-neutral approach, had adverse effects for female defendants in a case involving self-defense. Accordingly, the use of male-biased language may itself suffice to impede understanding and affect jury verdicts.

In sum, it appears that plain-language instructions may be a promising technique for increasing juror comprehension of instructions, but they are unlikely to be a panacea. Although the use of plain language techniques may serve to help increase the comprehension of judicial instructions, existing research shows that the increase is a limited one and that additional factors should be taken into account.

Before proceeding to the next section, we feel compelled to comment briefly on so-called pattern jury instructions. Beginning in the 1930s in California, states began adopting "pattern" jury instructions, which are now available in most states (see Bouck, 1993; Perlman, 1986). The instructions enable judges to rely on standardized instructions when preparing jury charges. The adoption of pattern instructions has resulted in reduced reversal rates for cases in which the jury instructions have been challenged (Bouck, 1993). Although the reduced reversal rates indicate that the appellate courts find the instructions that were provided to the jury to be legally correct, appellate court satisfaction does not ensure that jurors will comprehend the instructions (Charrow & Charrow, 1979; Elwork et al., 1977; Severance et al., 1984). Indeed, many of the studies described in this chapter have employed pattern instructions as the instructions that were tested. Therefore, although the use of pattern jury instructions certainly has advantages for judges—given that the instructions of judges who rely strictly on the patterned versions are, in essence, "appeal proof"—advantages to jurors seem limited, in that their use provides no assurance of juror comprehension to any satisfactory extent. Indeed, we would submit that if pattern instructions are to be developed for use in jurisdictions, they must be carefully tested for comprehension by jurors (see Rose & Ogloff, 2001).

Juror Note Taking

Many U.S. jurisdictions prohibit jurors from taking notes during both the evidence and the instruction portions of jury trials. In other countries, such as Australia and Canada, judges have considerable discretion in permitting jurors to take notes. Although practices vary, there is ongoing disagreement about the possible advantages and disadvantages of allowing jurors to take notes. In support of such a prohibition, it is argued that note taking is an acquired skill, so that note takers will appear more knowledgeable and have more influence in deliberations; notes may be inaccurate, focusing deliberations on unimportant evidence; note taking may be distracting to the note taker and others; notes may be incomplete, due to the pace of the trial; jurors are likely to make notes at the beginning, and then reduce or stop the note taking altogether, giving undue emphasis to the evidence of the side that goes first (Flango, 1980). In questioning real jurors following civil and criminal trials, in the course of a field experiment, Flango discovered that everyone who was allowed to take notes did so; furthermore, note takers claimed that their cases were easier to understand, involved higher-quality deliberations, and that they relied less on other jurors. They also reported that their notes served as memory enhancers and helped convince other jurors regarding factual issues. In another field experiment on note taking, U.S. Second Circuit judges generally had a positive reaction to juror note taking, and most negative responses merely involved doubts about its effectiveness (Sand & Reiss, 1985).

It would appear that jurors clearly *want* to take notes. In a survey of jurors in North Carolina, Cutler and Hughes (2001) found that 39.1% of jurors reported being allowed to take notes, and of the remainder, 38.9% thought that taking notes would have helped their decisions. In an experimental study, Rosenhan, Eisner, and Robinson (1994) observed that note takers reported they were more involved in the proceedings (that is, more attentive).

Heuer and Penrod (1988, 1994) have reported on a series of field experiments in Wisconsin and across the United States. They found no support for any of the supposed drawbacks to juror note taking, but also no clear support for most of the anticipated benefits: memory aid, increased juror involvement and satisfaction, and juror confidence in recall of instructions and in verdict (Heuer & Penrod, 1988). Similar results were obtained by Heuer and Penrod (1994), in a repetition of the 1988 study with greatly increased statistical power. Jurors were found to have taken an average of 0.6 pages of notes per hour, both in civil and criminal trials, and for both the plaintiff/prosecution and the defense cases. Furthermore, the notes, when examined, proved to be accurate, and to not favor either side.

Based on these results, Penrod and Heuer (1997) argued that, in the absence of support for either the suggested advantages or disadvantages of juror note taking, trial judges should permit it, because jurors are favorably disposed to it, judges and counsel are more favorably disposed toward it as they are exposed to it, and there seems to be little risk in allowing it (see also, Devine et al., 2001; Sales et al., 1977). Flango (1980) also concluded that jurors should be permitted (but not required) to take notes and suggested that jurors (1) should be given assurances of the confidentiality of their notes, (2) should be told to destroy them at the end of the trial, and (3) should be instructed to be as tolerant of each other's notes as of each other's recollections.

A final point to bear in mind is that the benefits of note taking may interact with other variables, such that the benefits may not be obvious in single-factor studies. For example, ForsterLee and Horowitz (1997) discovered that note taking enhanced the beneficial effect of preinstruction (discussed below). Thus, when jurors were provided with an initial cognitive framework, note taking improved their performance. Although performance was measured here primarily by recall of evidence, it is suggestive to note that preinstructed jurors took more notes about the jury instructions than postinstructed-only jurors.

It seems that (1) permitting jurors to take notes may assist them in understanding their instructions, (2) doing so will not otherwise impede the proper progress of the trial, and (3) jurors want to be able to take notes and will generally choose to take notes, if permitted to do so.

Preinstruction of Juries

Jurors are typically not instructed on the relevant law to any significant extent until the end of the evidence portion of the trial. Although many courts deliver preliminary instructions about the role of the jury, and so on, substantive and evidentiary law specifically related to the case at bar is withheld until the end of the trial. This practice is presumably in place because of the belief that the relevant legal issues will not be definitively known to counsel and the court until after all the evidence has been presented. Indeed, in criminal cases, the defenses that will be invoked most often cannot be known by any other parties until after the defense has presented its case. Although such an approach is likely to maximize recall for the instructions, it limits jurors' abilities to assess the evidence in light of the law they are supposed to use to interpret the evidence; it relies on the implicit legal assumption that jurors store but do not evaluate the evidence until the end of the trial, and it ignores the probability that jurors are actively evaluating the evidence as they hear it—despite the lack of a legal framework to use in doing so (Elwork & Sales, 1985). The argument for providing jurors with instructions on the law prior to the trial is based on the belief that allowing jurors to become aware of the law prior to hearing the evidence will provide them with some framework—or schema—with which they can consider and process the evidence, as it is presented during the course of the trial.

In a simulated grand larceny trial, Cruse and Browne (1987) discovered that the timing of the legal instructions had no effect on verdicts, but the frequency of those instructions did. Apparently, as might be expected, multiple exposures to the law helped ensure that all jurors had a grasp of the rules and therefore needed to rely less, or not at all, on their implicit legal concepts.

In a survey of jurors in North Carolina (Cutler & Hughes, 2001), 49.8% of those responding reported that it would have been helpful if the judge had provided instructions on the law before the trial began. In another field study, a majority of judges and counsel favored preinstructing juries on the law, more so in criminal than civil cases (Sand & Reiss, 1985). In presenting their field study, Heuer and Penrod (1989) reported that jurors expected preinstructions to be helpful, then found them to be even more helpful than expected, although there was no clear evidence that the procedure helped them recall the judge's instructions or clarified their confusion about trial procedure. Preinstructions did increase juror satisfaction and appeared to assist the jury in evaluating the evidence according to the correct legal principles. Interestingly, judges did not feel that preinstruction was impractical because of not knowing what law would be relevant until after the evidence was presented, and they did not find it disruptive to the trial process.

In tests of preinstructions, Elwork et al. (1977) failed to find an effect for timing of instructions (preevidence, postevidence, or both) on comprehension, although it did affect jurors' beliefs on two of three factual issues. On the other hand, Kassin and Wrightsman (1979) showed that preinstruction on the requirements of proof, presumption of innocence, and reasonable doubt reduced conviction rates and ratings of probability of factual guilt, and did so immediately. It appears that the preinstructions caused jurors to adopt, in fact, a presumption of innocence, as compared to the other groups, which presumed guilt.

Preinstruction may be even more important in civil trials, because jurors are less familiar with, or knowledgeable about, the relevant areas of law than in criminal cases (ForsterLee, Horowitz, & Bourgeois, 1993). Indeed, through media and television, jurors may gain some understanding of concepts in criminal law; however, they would have far less exposure to concepts of civil law. ForsterLee and colleagues found that preinstruction in a simulated tort trial provided jurors with a legally relevant schema into which to fit the evidence, and as a result, jurors were better able to correctly distinguish between plaintiffs when assessing damages. Preinstructed jurors were also better able to reject "lures" (i.e., to avoid false positive errors) on recognition items.

Preinstruction seems to interact with other variables. ForsterLee and Horowitz (1997) found that preinstructed juries performed better in a simulated civil "toxic tort" case, and that this effect was enhanced by permitting juror note taking. Bourgeois, Horowitz, ForsterLee, and Grahe (1995) reported that in a complex civil negligence trial simulation, preinstruction helped produce proper verdicts in cases where the evidence was of moderate complexity, and therefore comprehensible, although in cases where the evidence was highly complex, preinstruction resulted in a pro-plaintiff bias, probably due to a confirmatory bias.

The concept of CSJ may have a useful relevance to preinstruction. Smith (1991) argues that, as with plain-language instructions, preinstruction is not, by itself, likely to cause jurors to abandon or revise their preexisting "knowledge" about trial-relevant law. She suggests, however, that preinstruction *combined with* plain-language instructions may lead to substantial improvement in juror comprehension (Smith, 1993). As with plain-language instruction, preinstruction seems to offer some measure of promise in improving juror comprehension, but, by itself, will not completely address the issue.

Providing Juries with Copies of the Jury Charge

A survey of judges in Michigan revealed that only 7% of respondents always provided a written copy of their instructions to jurors, while 61% of respondents never did so; those who did felt it aided jury deliberation, and those who did not were concerned that it would represent an added burden for the jurors (Koenig et al., 1987). Another survey of judges in the U.S. Second Circuit produced mixed reactions on this issue (Sand & Reiss, 1985). On the other hand, a survey of 1,478 jurors in North Carolina found that whereas only 18.2% reported receiving a written copy of the judge's charge, 52.2% of the remaining jurors thought that it would have been helpful (Cutler & Hughes, 2001).

The results of a field experiment in Wisconsin (Heuer & Penrod, 1989) showed that jurors in real trials expected written instructions to be helpful, and those who received them reported that they were even more helpful than expected—although there is no evidence that they really were helpful. There was no clear effect of written instructions on juror satisfaction or on the length of deliberations. The written version did assist in reducing and resolving disputes about the instructions. As well, there was no evidence that jurors spent too much time studying them, or less time studying the evidence, and no evidence that the trial process was disrupted as a result of the provision of written instructions.

In a survey of 140 jurors responding shortly after their service, Reifman et al. (1992) found that those who had received written copies of instructions were no better at answering case-relevant substantive questions than those who had not been given copies of the instructions. In a jury simulation experiment using a civil negligence context, Greene and Johns (2001) found that providing written instructions did not affect either predeliberation or post-deliberation juror verdicts.

Jurors seem to want copies of the jury instructions to which they can refer, and there seems to be no good reason not to provide them (Diamond, 1993). However, there also seems to be no clear evidence that doing so will affect juror comprehension of those instructions. As Greene and Johns (2001) caution, "Even when jurors are looking directly at the instructions, they sometimes lack understanding. Providing jurors with a copy of abstract and convoluted instructions will grant them neither clarity nor wisdom" (p. 853).

Summary

Several measures have been suggested to attempt to address the problem of juries' apparent inability to understand legal instructions. Some procedural remedies, such as providing a copy of the judge's charge and perhaps permitting juror note taking, have relatively little evidence supporting their effectiveness, but also run little risk of harm and can be implemented with very little trouble. Even if they do not appreciably improve juror performance, these steps should improve juror satisfaction with the trial process. Other measures show more promise, such as drafting or revising jury instructions according to psycholinguistic principles in order to increase comprehensibility, and preinstructing juries before evidence is presented.

Unfortunately, the evidence is persuasive that any remedies which do not take into account jurors' naive concepts of the law—their so-called common-sense justice—will be limited in their ability to improve juror comprehension to acceptable levels. Just as a combination of methods is necessary to make a compelling case to the legal system that juries do not understand their instructions, it is likely to take a combination of remedies to maximize their comprehension. In the next section of this chapter, we turn to a discussion of novel or more comprehensive approaches to charging the jury that may be more effective than the attempts that have been made thus far.

WHERE DO WE GO FROM HERE?: COMPREHENSIVE APPROACHES TO INSTRUCTING THE JURY

Most of the research discussed thus far has either sought to measure jurors' (or mock jurors') understanding of judicial instructions or assessed relatively benign approaches to changing the jury charge so as to increase jurors' understanding of the judge's instructions. After many years of studying the matter, though, we have come to believe that rather than merely tinkering with minor changes to the status quo, a more comprehensive approach is required to ensure that jurors are able to use the law as their guidepost for coming to a decision within the parameters of that law. Fortunately, this view is shared by some on the bench and, as indicated, some jurisdictions, such as New Zealand, are making widespread changes that may result in true progress in the challenge of ensuring an effective jury system. In a comprehensive article, Ellsworth and Reifman (2000) provide an overview of a number of the reforms that have been recommended and, in some cases, implemented and/or tested.

To determine how to improve the jury charge, we must consider the problems with the current methods by which jurors are instructed. The research reviewed in this chapter suggests that there are two major difficulties with jury instructions. First, the law is novel, and any given trial may last for a few days or a few weeks or even months, during which time a range of difficult issues may arise, which must be considered and decided by the jury. Second, many legal concepts are somewhat amorphous and difficult to understand, even for law students and lawyers. To date, most attempts to increase jurors' comprehension of judicial instructions have been directed toward the second difficulty and have helped make it easier for jurors to understand the legal concepts.

Compounding the difficulties referred to above is the fact that the cognitive task required of jurors is complex. They enter a novel situation, filled with some degree of anxiety (Chopra & Ogloff, 2000). Typically, jurors are given relatively little direction by judges about the process of being a juror, let alone any systematic preliminary legal instructions. They then are presented with evidence and arguments in the manner of the adversarial system, wherein competing arguments and perspectives on the facts are presented. As noted, a jury trial may last for weeks or months, and jurors are often exposed to a considerable amount of technical information, followed by hours of jury instructions that embody the complex nature of the law. After listening to all of the evidence and instructions, jurors usually are asked to provide the court with the answer to a simple question: Is the accused guilty or not guilty? From a psychological perspective, Semmler and Brewer (2002) point out that barriers to increased comprehension of judicial instructions may be caused by limitations to working memory as a result of the nature of the task required of jurors. Indeed, as indicated above, the cognitive tasks required of jurors are quite broad and demanding. As such, it is not simply a difficulty with understanding the law that makes the comprehension of judicial instructions such a difficult task.

Beyond the obvious problem of needing to help jurors understand complex legal principles, jurors require some overall direction and assistance in learning to organize the material with which they are presented in a manner that will enable them to apply the law to come to a verdict. Such a comprehensive revision to the way in which jurors are charged has been suggested before, at least as early as 1980 (Law Reform Commission of Canada, 1980); however, as Eames (2003) notes, "it has not been generally or consistently applied" (p. 49). More recently, Eames (2003) described a process, introduced by Justice Bernard Teague of the Supreme Court of Australia, designed to assist jurors in their decision-making tasks.[2] In short, Justice Teague provides jurors with a printed overview that contains "a summary of the charge or charges, and a list of proposed witnesses, . . . headings as to foreperson selection . . . [and] a list of headings to which he refers only after the jury is empanelled" (p. 50). Once the jury is impaneled, the judge provides the jurors with instructions on a range of useful background information. He allows them to take notes and to ask questions (in an appropriate manner).

Prior to deliberating and charging the jury, Justice Teague also provides jurors with an outline of the charge, which has been agreed to by counsel. The outline "contains a list of headings for the participants within the charge, a short statement of elements of a charge or like matters, and a list of witnesses called" (p. 50). After delivering the charge, but prior to deliberation, jurors are provided with a final document that "addresses the methodology which they might employ in conducting their deliberations and in determining the verdicts on each charge" (p. 50).

Beyond the need to provide the sort of guidance that Justice Teague provides to juries, there is some support for the use of flow charts or decision trees to assist jurors in understanding the law during the deliberation (see Dattu, 1998; Heuer & Penrod, 1994; Ogloff, 1998; Wiggins & Breckler, 1990). The use of flow charts and decision models has been recommended in a report prepared by Young and colleagues (2001) for the New Zealand Law Reform Commission. Despite the permissibility of using such aids in a number of jurisdictions, it is still apparently rare for judges to do so (Eames, 2003).

While considerable faith has been placed in the potential power of the flow chart or decision-tree models, there have been few empirical investigations of the utility of such an approach. In the United States, jurors in civil proceedings can be asked to provide a special verdict or a general verdict with interrogatories. A special verdict requires the jury to provide a written finding on each issue of fact presented to it by the judge. A general verdict with inter-rogatories requires the jury to answer specific questions in writing, in addition to providing an overall verdict. It is believed that such verdict options "may help juries adhere to the law when strong emotional factors might otherwise interfere with their ability to objectively decide cases" (Wiggins & Breckler, 1990, p. 36).

In an evaluation of special verdict options, Wiggins and Breckler (1990) used a mock juror paradigm to compare special-verdict versus general-verdict options. They found that mock jurors who were presented with special-verdict options were able to provide more correct answers on questions pertaining to burden of proof than those participants who were presented with the general-verdict option. However, the differences did not extend to verdict determina-tions. The authors concluded that this finding suggested that the jurors had relied upon general impressions of the evidence rather than any specific con-sideration of relevant issues.

As part of a larger study exploring the extent to which trial complexity affected the ability of the jury to properly do its job, Heuer and Penrod (1994) obtained information from 160 actual jury cases in the United States. Al-though not experimentally manipulated, they did find that

> the use of special verdict forms was most consistently beneficial. In trials where special verdict forms were used, the jurors reported feeling better in-formed, more satisfied, more confident that their verdict was correct, more confident that their verdict reflected a proper understanding of the judge's in-structions. . . . Furthermore, . . . jurors found the use of special verdict forms to be the most helpful for dealing with large quantities of information. (p. 50)

In the study by Ogloff (1998), one group of jurors/juries was presented with a flow chart (decision tree) that showed the legal questions that needed to be addressed and the order in which they could reasonably be dealt with, in order to arrive at a verdict in a criminal case. Unfortunately, Ogloff (1998) found, at least in the context of the day-long mock-juror paradigm employed, that the group that received the flow chart did not demonstrate significantly greater comprehension of the judicial instructions. However, it appeared that jurors did not routinely refer to, or use, the decision tree during their delibera-tions. This lack of use highlights the need to clearly instruct—and perhaps to direct—the jury in the use of decision-making aids such as decision trees.

Finally, in a recent study, Semmler and Brewer (2002) used a mock-juror paradigm to experimentally investigate whether the use of a flow chart de-signed to aid the jurors in understanding the legal questions to be answered in the deliberation would enhance their comprehension of jury instructions. Par-ticipants included 234 adults from the general community who were ran-domly assigned to the experimental groups. Participants listened to a short summary of a case in which the accused was charged with murder but raised the affirmative defense of self-defense. Participants were then presented with a summary of judicial instructions delivered by an actual justice of the Supreme Court of South Australia. Participants were not permitted to take notes. Jury comprehension was measured by having participants summarize the instructions they were given as well as having them complete an application measure designed to assess their ability to identify a fact pattern that satisfied the legal elements from those that did not.

Results showed that allowing participants to refer to a flow chart while deciding on the case helped increase both their comprehension and application scores. With regard to the comprehension scores, allowing participants to read the judge's instructions also served to enhance comprehension. While acknowledging the limitations of using a mock-juror paradigm on their findings, the authors concluded that

> it seems worthwhile to explore more closely alternative interventions that involve a more structured presentation of the key information elements. . . . It is possible that a useful approach might involve supplementing the verbal presentation of instructions with a visual representation of key concepts, an approach that has been shown to be particularly useful for reducing the load on working memory when there are complex interactions between the different elements of the instructional material. (p. 267)

The final suggestion appears to be consistent with the practice of Justice Teague, outlined above.

In a perhaps even more innovative approach, Brewer and his colleagues (Brewer, Harvey & Semmler, 2004) have developed computer-animated conceptualizations of legal constructs to increase jurors' understanding of the concepts. Using this technology, Brewer et al. conducted a study that employed an audio–visual presentation of the legal concepts pertaining to self-defense. In the study, they used a mock-jury paradigm to compare the use of traditional instructions (audio), enhanced instructions (audio-elaborated with a verbal flow chart to describe the self-defense elements) that made use of additional examples, and instructions that used computer animations (audio–visual) to help explain legal concepts. In the audio–visual condition, participants were presented with the same information as the audio-elaborated condition, except that the examples used to illustrate the self-defense elements and flow chart were shown using a computer animation. For example, to depict the legal concept of "reasonable possibility" that the accused acted in self-defense, the animation employed the example of the likelihood that various types of balls would shatter a pane of glass: tennis ball ("a chance"), steel ball ("almost certain"), and baseball ("reasonable possibility").

The findings showed that the novel approach of using audio–visual animations significantly improved jurors' comprehension of the judicial instructions. In addition, subjects that were instructed with the novel audio–visual

approach were better able to generalize the knowledge obtained to other conditions. Although promising, the results indicate, unfortunately, that the level
of comprehension obtained using the audio–visual approach was still limited.
For example, participants, on average, obtained a correct recognition score of
5.15 out of a possible 8 points (64.4%) on a recognition task, 3.75 out of 7
(53.6%) on a recall measure, and 8.58 out of 21 (40.9%) on an application/
transfer measure.

Only with ongoing research and cooperation by judges, counsel, and legislatures can we continue to learn the extent to which jurors understand judicial instructions and, more importantly, devise strategies for assisting them in
becoming better able to apply the law to the facts presented at trial to come to
a verdict that is just and right.

SUMMARY AND CONCLUSIONS

In this chapter, we have attempted to provide an overview of the current empirical understanding of jurors' comprehension of judicial instructions. As
pointed out, it is critical that jurors demonstrate some basic understanding
and appreciation of the legal principles and elements with which the judge
provides them in order to determine whether the evidence presented in the
trial meets the legal requirements for a verdict. A number of approaches have
been taken to learning whether jurors do, in fact, understand the judge's
charge.

Generally, surveys of jurors show that jurors who have served on a trial
believe that the judge's instructions were helpful. Moreover, those studies that
have asked the question suggest that jurors believe, and have some confidence
in, the "fact" that they understand the judge's instructions. By contrast, virtually all of the existing empirical research, primarily employing a mock-juror
paradigm, shows that, at best, jurors or participants have a very limited understanding of the law. Field studies of actual jurors suggest that although instructions do help jurors, at least to some extent, jurors still demonstrate considerable difficulty understanding the jury charge.

Given the concern that has existed among researchers and those in the legal profession regarding jurors' comprehension of judicial instructions, a
number of solutions have been proposed to help enhance the level of comprehension. Most of the solutions have been relatively benign attempts to tinker
with the language of the instructions or the way in which they are delivered.
Among such alternative approaches, some strategies have been more successful than others—although none is a panacea individually or even when used in
combination. Certainly, drafting judicial instructions using a plain-language
approach and clear grammar help to increase jurors' comprehension of the instructions, to some extent. Unfortunately, although the United States has
adopted standardized or "pattern" jury instructions that are mandated for use

by all judges, there is very little empirical support that such instructions, although generally "appeal proof," are significantly better understood by jurors than the instructions they were designed to replace.

Although jurors appear to want to take notes, there is surprisingly little support that allowing them to do so helps to significantly increase their comprehension of the instructions. However, it must be emphasized that there is no evidence that allowing note taking is detrimental. Similarly, providing jurors with copies of the charge to refer to during deliberation does not seem to hinder—or to help, particularly—their understanding of the instructions.

Perhaps more useful is providing the jury with instructions about the law prior to hearing the evidence, rather than only at the close of the case. This finding is not surprising, because the instructions provide a legal framework with which jurors may be able to get some idea of the questions they should consider before they evaluate the evidence presented at trial.

In addition to merely reviewing the literature, we show that various matters, such as how comprehension is construed or measured, serve to affect the outcome of the research. Indeed, whereas most researchers have measured comprehension by having jurors or participants summarize the legal instructions they were given, research—and common sense—suggests that measures that assess the extent to which jurors can apply the instructions correctly to a fact pattern are perhaps more valid measures of comprehension, because they more closely approximate the juror's task.

Of greatest significance, however, are the efforts that have been made more recently to rethink the way in which juries are instructed from the beginning to the end of the trial. In addition, systematic approaches to assisting jurors to better understand the nature of their task, as well as providing them with strategies for approaching their task, make a great deal of sense and are beginning to be used in some jurisdictions. Some support has been found for using flow charts, decision trees, special verdicts, and other strategies that break down the complexity of the cognitive tasks required of the juror into meaningful bits. Only with ongoing research and cooperation from judges, counsel, and legislatures can we continue to identify the extent to which jurors understand judicial instructions and, more importantly, devise strategies for assisting them in becoming better able to apply the law to the facts presented at trial to come to a verdict that is just and right.

NOTES

1. Nullification instructions are those that inform the jurors that they have the power to ignore the law, should they believe that the law is incorrect or invalid. Typically, though, judges are prohibited from informing the jury about this power.
2. In his article, Eames (2003) provides an example of the information that Justice Teague provides to jurors. Readers are referred to the appendices of the article for detailed information about the information provided.

REFERENCES

Adler, S. J. (1994). *The jury: Disorder in the courts.* New York: Doubleday.

Berger, S. H. (1997). Do juries listen to jury instructions? *Journal of the American Academy of Psychiatry and the Law, 25,* 565–570.

Blackstone, W. (1765). *Commentaries on the laws of England,* Vol. 1–4. London: Strathan, Cadell, & Prince.

Bouck, J. C. (1993). Criminal jury trials: Pattern instructions and rules of procedure. *Canadian Bar Review, 72,* 129–161.

Bourgeois, M. J., Horowitz, I. A., ForsterLee, L., & Grahe, J. (1995). Nominal and interactive groups: Effects of preinstruction and deliberations on decisions and evidence recall in complex trials. *Journal of Applied Psychology, 80,* 58–67.

Brewer, N., Harvey, S., & Semmler, C. (2004). Improving comprehension of jury instructions with audio-visual presentation. *Applied Cognitive Psychology, 18,* 765–776.

Buchanan, R. W., Pryor, B., Taylor, K. P., & Strawn, D. V. (1978). Legal communication: An investigation of juror comprehension of pattern jury instructions. *Communications Quarterly, 26,* 31–35.

Burnett, D. G. (2001). *A trial by jury.* New York: Knopf.

Charrow, R. P., & Charrow, V. R. (1979). Making legal language understandable: A psycholinguistic study of jury instructions. *Columbia Law Review, 79,* 1306–1374.

Chopra, S. R., & Ogloff, J. R. P. (2000). Evaluating jury secrecy: Implications for academic research and juror stress. *Criminal Law Quarterly, 44,* 190–222.

Cruse, D., & Browne, B. A. (1987). Reasoning in a jury trial: The influence of instructions. *Journal of General Psychology, 114,* 129–133.

Cutler, B. L., & Hughes, D. M. (2001). Judging jury service: Results of the North Carolina administrative office of the courts juror survey. *Behavioral Sciences and the Law, 19,* 305–320.

Cutler, B. L., Penrod, S. D., & Dexter, H. R. (1990). Nonadversarial methods for sensitizing jurors to eyewitness evidence. *Journal of Applied Social Psychology, 20,* 1197–1207.

Dattu, F. (1998). Illustrated jury instructions: A proposal. *Psychology and Law Review, 22,* 67–102.

Devine, D. J., Clayton, L. D., Dunford, B. B., Rasmy, S., & Price, J. (2001). Jury decision making: 45 years of empirical research on deliberating groups. *Psychology, Public Policy, and Law, 7,* 622–727.

Diamond, S. S. (1993). Instructing on death: Psychologists, juries, and judges. *American Psychologist, 48,* 423–434.

Eames, J. (2003). Towards a better direction: Better communication with jurors. *Australian Bar Review, 24,* 35–78.

Ellsworth, P. C. (1989). Are twelve heads better than one? *Law and Contemporary Problems, 52,* 205–224.

Ellsworth, P. C., & Reifman, A. (2000). Juror comprehension and public policy: Perceived problems and proposed solutions. *Psychology, Public Policy, and Law, 6,* 788–821.

Elwork, A., Alfini, J. J., & Sales, B. D. (1987). Toward understandable jury instructions. In L. S. Wrightsman & S. M. Kassin (Eds.), *In the jury box: Controversies in the courtroom* (pp. 161–179). Thousand Oaks, CA: Sage.

Elwork, A., & Sales, B. D. (1985). Jury instructions. In S. Kassin & L. Wrightsman (Eds.), *The psychology of evidence and trial procedure* (pp. 280–297). Beverly Hills: Sage.

Elwork, A., Sales, B. D., & Alfini, J. J. (1977). Juridic decisions: In ignorance of the law or in light of it? *Law and Human Behavior, 1,* 163–189.

English, P. W., & Sales, B. D. (1997). A ceiling or consistency effect for the comprehension of jury instructions. *Psychology, Public Policy, and Law, 3,* 381–401.

Ferguson, G. A., & Bouck, J. C. (1987). *Canadian criminal jury instructions.* Vancouver, BC: Law Society of British Columbia.

Finkel, N. J. (1995). *Commonsense justice: Jurors' notions of the law.* Cambridge, MA: Harvard University Press.

Finkel, N. J. (2000). Commonsense justice and jury instructions: Instructive and reciprocating connections. *Psychology, Public Policy, and Law, 6,* 591–628.

Flango, V. E. (1980). Would jurors do a better job if they could take notes? *Judicature, 63,* 436–443.

ForsterLee, L., & Horowitz, I. A. (1997). Enhancing juror competence in a complex trial. *Applied Cognitive Psychology, 11,* 305–319.

ForsterLee, L., Horowitz, I. A., & Bourgeois, M. J. (1993). Juror competence in civil trials: Effects of preinstruction and evidence technicality. *Journal of Applied Psychology, 78,* 14–21.

Frank, J., & Applegate, B. K. (1998). Assessing juror understanding of capital-sentencing instructions. *Crime and Delinquency, 44,* 412–433.

Goodman, J., & Greene, E. (1989). The use of paraphrase analysis in the simplification of jury instructions. *Journal of Social Behavior and Personality, 4,* 237–251.

Greene, E. (1987). Eyewitness testimony and the use of cautionary instructions. *University of Bridgeport Law Review, 8,* 15–20.

Greene, E. (1988). Judge's instructions on eyewitness testimony: Evaluation and revision. *Journal of Applied Social Psychology, 18,* 252–276.

Greene, E., & Bornstein, B. (2000). Precious little guidance: Jury instructions on damage awards. *Psychology, Public Policy, and Law, 6,* 743–768.

Greene, E., & Johns, M. (2001). Jurors' use of instructions on negligence. *Journal of Applied Social Psychology, 31,* 840–859.

Halverson, A. M., Hallahan, M., Hart, A. J., & Rosenthal, R. (1997). Reducing the biasing effects of judges' nonverbal behavior with simplified jury instructions. *Journal of Applied Psychology, 82,* 590–598.

Hamilton, M. C., Hunter, B., & Stuart-Smith, S. (1992). Jury instructions worded in the masculine generic: Can a woman claim self-defense when "he" is threatened? In J. C. Crisler & D. Howard (Eds.), *New directions in feminist psychology: Practice, theory, and research* (pp. 169–178). New York: Springer-Verlag.

Haney, C., & Lynch, M. (1997). Clarifying life and death matters: An analysis of instructional comprehension and penalty phase closing arguments. *Law and Human Behavior, 21,* 575–595.

Harris, R. J. (1978). The effect of jury size and judge's instructions on memory for pragmatic implications from courtroom testimony. *Bulletin of the Psychonomic Society, 11,* 129–132.

Hastie, R., Schkade, D. A., & Payne J. W. (1998). A study of juror and jury judgments in civil cases: Deciding liability for punitive damages. *Law and Human Behavior, 22,* 287–314.

Heuer, L., & Penrod, S. D. (1988). Increasing jurors' participation in trials: A field experiment with jury notetaking and question asking. *Law and Human Behavior, 12,* 231–261.

Heuer, L., & Penrod, S. D. (1989). Instructing jurors: A field experiment with written and preliminary instructions. *Law and Human Behavior, 13,* 409–430.

Heuer, L., & Penrod, S. D. (1994). Trial complexity: A field investigation of its meaning and its effects. *Law and Human Behavior, 18*, 29–51.

Horowitz, I. A. (1985). The effect of jury nullification instructions on verdicts and jury functioning in criminal trials. *Law and Human Behavior, 9*, 25–36.

Horowitz, I. A. (1988). Jury nullification: The impact of judicial instructions, arguments, and challenges on jury decision making. *Law and Human Behavior, 12*, 439–453.

Horowitz, I. A., & Kirkpatrick, L. C. (1996). A concept in search of a definition: The effects of reasonable doubt instructions on certainty of guilt standards and jury verdicts. *Law and Human Behavior, 20*, 655–670.

Imwinkelried, E. J., & Schwed, L. R. (1987). Guidelines for drafting understandable jury instructions: An introduction to the use of psycholinguistics. *Criminal Law Bulletin, 23*, 135–150.

Jackson, J. (1992). Juror decision-making and the trial process. In G. Davis & S. Lloyd-Bostock (Eds.), *Psychology, law, and criminal justice: International developments in research and practice* (pp. 327–336). Oxford, UK: de Guyter.

Jones, C. S., & Myers, E. (1979). Comprehension of jury instructions in a simulated Canadian court. In Law Reform Commission of Canada (Eds.), *Studies on the jury* (pp. 301–392). Ottawa: Law Reform Commission of Canada.

Kalven, H., & Zeisel, H. (1966). *The American jury.* Boston: Little, Brown.

Kassin, S. M., & Sommers, S. R. (1997). Inadmissible testimony, instructions to disregard, and the jury: Substantive versus procedural considerations. *Personality and Social Psychology Bulletin, 23*, 1046–1054.

Kassin, S. M., & Wrightsman, L. S. (1979). On the requirements of proof: The timing of judicial instruction and mock juror verdicts. *Journal of Personality and Social Psychology, 37*, 1877–1887.

Kassin, S, M., & Wrightsman, L. S. (1981). Coerced confessions, judicial instruction, and mock juror verdicts. *Journal of Applied Social Psychology, 11*, 489–506.

Kerr, N., Atkin, R., Stasser, G., Meek, D., Holt, R., & Davis, J. G. (1976). Beyond a reasonable doubt: Effects of concept definition and assigned role on the judgments of mock jurors. *Journal of Personality and Social Psychology, 34*, 282–294.

Kerwin, J., & Shaffer, D. R. (1994). Mock jurors versus mock juries: The role of deliberations in reactions to inadmissible testimony. *Personality and Social Psychology Bulletin, 20*, 153–162.

Koch, C. M., & Devine, D. J. (1999). Effects of reasonable doubt definition and inclusion of a lesser charge on jury verdicts. *Law and Human Behavior, 23*, 653–674.

Koenig, D. M., Kerr, N. L., & Van Hoek, D. (1987). Michigan standard criminal jury instructions: Judges' perspectives after ten years' use. *Cooly Law Review, 4*, 347–373.

Kramer, G. P., Kerr, N. L., & Carroll, J. S. (1990). Pretrial publicity, judicial remedies, and jury bias. *Law and Human Behavior, 14*, 409–438.

Law Reform Commission of Canada. (1980). *The jury in criminal trials* (Working Paper No. 27). Ottawa, Ontario: Author.

Lieberman, J. D., & Arndt, J. (2000). Understanding the limits of limiting instructions: Social psychological explanations for the failures of instructions to disregard pretrial publicity and other inadmissible evidence. *Psychology, Public Policy, and Law, 6*, 677–711.

Luginbuhl, J. (1992). Comprehension of judges' instructions in the penalty phase of a capital trial: Focus on mitigating circumstances. *Law and Human Behavior, 16*, 203–218.

Mason, M. E. J., & Waldron, M. A. (1994). Comprehension of legal contracts by non-experts: Effectiveness of plain language redrafting. *Applied Cognitive Psychology, 8,* 67–85.

Morier, D., Borgida, E., & Park, R. C. (1996). Improving juror comprehension of judicial instructions on the entrapment defense. *Journal of Applied Social Psychology, 26,* 1838–1866.

Myers, E. R., & Jones, C. S. (1979). Language and jury instructions. In Law Reform Commission of Canada (Eds.), *Studies on the jury* (pp. 301–392). Ottawa: Law Reform Commission of Canada.

Ogloff, J. R. P. (1991). A comparison of insanity defense standards on juror decision-making. *Law and Human Behavior, 15,* 509–531.

Ogloff, J. R. P. (1998). *Judicial instructions and the jury: A comparison of alternative strategies. Final Report.* Vancouver, British Columbia: British Columbia Law Foundation.

Paglia, A., & Schuller, R. A. (1998). Jurors' use of hearsay evidence: The effects of type and timing of instructions. *Law and Human Behavior, 22,* 501–518.

Penrod, S. D., & Heuer, L. (1997). Tweaking commonsense: Assessing aids to jury decision making. *Psychology, Public Policy, and Law, 3,* 259–284.

Perlman, H. S. (1986). Pattern jury instructions: The application of social science research. *Nebraska Law Review, 65,* 520–557.

Ramirez, G., Zemba, D., & Geiselman, R. E. (1996). Judges' cautionary instructions on eyewitness testimony. *American Journal of Forensic Psychology, 14,* 31–66.

Reed, R. (1980). Jury simulation: The impact of judges' instructions and attorney tactics on decision-making. *Journal of Criminal Law and Criminology, 71,* 68–72.

Reifman, A., Gusick, S. M., & Ellsworth, P. C. (1992). Real jurors' understanding of the law in real cases. *Law and Human Behavior, 16,* 539–554.

Rose, V. G. (2003). *Social cognition and section 12 of the Canada Evidence Act: Can jurors "properly" use criminal record evidence?* Unpublished doctoral dissertation, Simon Fraser University, Burnaby, British Columbia.

Rose, V. G., Chopra, S. R., & Ogloff, J. R. P. (2001, June). *The perceptions and reactions of real Canadian criminal jurors.* Paper presented at the annual convention of the Canadian Psychological Association, Ste.-Foy, Quebec.

Rose, V. G., & Ogloff, J. R. P. (2001). Evaluating the comprehensibility of jury instructions: A method and an example. *Law and Human Behavior, 25,* 409–431.

Rosenhan, D. L., Eisner, S. L., & Robinson, R. L. (1994). Notetaking can aid juror recall. *Law and Human Behavior, 18,* 53–61.

Sales, B. D., Elwork, A., & Alfini, J. J. (1977). Improving comprehension for jury instructions. In B. D. Sales (Ed.), *Perspectives in law and psychology: The criminal justice system* (Vol. 1, pp. 23–90). New York: Plenum Press.

Sand, L. B., & Reiss, S. A. (1985). A report on seven experiments conducted by district court judges in the second circuit. *New York University Law Review, 60,* 423–497.

Saxton, B. (1998). How well do jurors understand jury instructions? A field test using real juries and real trials in Wyoming. *Land and Water Law Review, 33,* 59–189.

Sealy, A. P., & Cornish, W. R. (1973). Juries and the rules of evidence. *Criminal Law Review,* 208–223.

Semmler, C., & Brewer, N. (2002). Using a flow-chart to improve comprehension of jury instructions. *Psychiatry, Psychology, and Law, 9,* 262–270.

Severance, L. J., Greene, E., & Loftus, E. F. (1984). Toward criminal jury instructions that jurors can understand. *Journal of Criminal Law and Criminology, 75,* 198–223.

Severance, L. J., & Loftus, E. F. (1982). Improving the ability of jurors to comprehend and apply criminal jury instructions. *Law and Society Review, 17,* 153–197.

Severance, L. J., & Loftus, E. F. (1984). Improving criminal justice: Making jury instructions understandable for American jurors. *International Review of Applied Psychology, 33,* 97–119.

Shaffer, D. R., & Kerwin, J. (1992). On adhering to judicial instructions: Reactions of dogmatic and nondogmatic juries to the judge's charge in an entrapment case. *Journal of Applied Social Psychology, 22,* 1133–1147.

Shaw, J. L., & Skolnick, P. (1995). Effects of prohibitive and informative judicial instructions on jury decisionmaking. *Social Behavior and Personality, 23,* 319–325.

Smith, V. L. (1991). Prototypes in the courtroom: Lay representations of legal concepts. *Journal of Personality and Social Psychology, 61,* 857–872.

Smith, V. L. (1993). When prior knowledge and law collide: Helping jurors use the law. *Law and Human Behavior, 17,* 507–536.

Steele, W. W., & Thornburg, E. G. (1988–1989). Jury instructions: A persistent failure to communicate. *North Carolina Law Review, 67,* 77–119.

Strawn, D. J., & Buchanan, R. W. (1976). Jury confusion: A threat to justice. *Judicature, 59,* 478–483.

Tanford, J. A., & Cox, M. (1987). Decision processes in civil cases: The impact of impeachment evidence on liability and credibility judgments. *Social Behavior, 2,* 165–182.

Tanford, S., Penrod, S., & Collins, R. (1985). Decision making in joined criminal trials: The influence of charge similarity, evidence similarity, and limiting instructions. *Law and Human Behavior, 9,* 319–337.

Taylor v. Louisiana, 419 U.S. 522 (1975).

Thompson, W. C., Fong, G. T., & Rosenhan, D. L. (1981). Inadmissible evidence and juror verdicts. *Journal of Personality and Social Psychology, 40,* 453–463.

Warren v. Parks, 230 S.E.2d 684 (1976).

Wiener, R. L., Halbert, K., Shkodriani, G., & Staebler, C. (1991). The social psychology of jury nullification: Predicting when jurors disobey the law. *Journal of Applied Social Psychology, 21,* 1379–1402.

Wiener, R. L., Pritchard, C. C., & Weston, M. (1995). Comprehensibility of approved jury instructions in capital murder cases. *Journal of Applied Psychology, 80,* 455–467.

Wiggins, E. C., & Breckler, S. J. (1990). Special verdicts as guides to jury decision making. *Law and Psychology Review, 14,* 1–41.

Wissler, R. L., Kuehn, P., & Saks, M. J. (2000). Instructing jurors on general damages in personal injury cases: Problems and possibilities. *Psychology, Public Policy, and Law, 6,* 712–742.

Young, W. (2003). Summing-up to juries in criminal cases: What jury research says about current rules and practice. *Criminal Law Review,* 665–689.

Young, W., Cameron, N., & Tinsley, Y. (2001). *Juries in criminal trials* (Report 69). Wellington, New Zealand: New Zealand Law Commission.

CHAPTER THIRTEEN

Dealing with the Guilty Offender

JANE GOODMAN-DELAHUNTY
LYNNE FORSTERLEE
ROBERT FORSTERLEE

Sentencing is the imposition of a legal sanction on a person convicted of a criminal offense. The typical participants in sentencing decisions are the sentencer (judge or magistrate), counsel for the prosecution, the offender, and his or her legal representative(s). In some instances, community and family members may participate, including the crime victim or his or her representatives. By and large, judges and magistrates impose most criminal sentences in the context of a sentencing hearing, but in some circumstances laypersons render the sentence. For example, in Canada and Australia, indigenous community members and the crime victim, as well as representatives of the defendant, contribute to "circle sentencing decisions" (e.g., when the court incorporates aspects of traditional tribal justice into its proceedings). In addition, within the United States, several states allow juries to issue noncapital sentences, although in some of these states the jury's power is limited (Nadler & Rose, 2003), and in 38 states jurors serve on capital cases to determine whether a death penalty will be imposed.

Compared with the amount of psycholegal research that has investigated pretrial issues and litigation over guilt determinations in criminal cases, there is relatively little empirical research on sentencing. A small proportion of cases goes to trial in comparison with the number that are settled or disposed of out of court; thus investigations confined to studies of the trial process ignore the majority of cases and more normative dispositional processes. Relatively few cases in which criminal culpability is determined proceed to a sentencing hearing. In the United States, as many as 90% of all criminal cases are determined by means of a plea bargain between the offender and the state (Haney, 2002).

The percentage of cases resolved by plea bargains is lower in other countries (e.g., in New South Wales, Australia, 32% of cases are resolved by pleas; Samuels, 2002). The salient point is that research focused only on a contested, adversarial hearing neglects a process by means of which a substantial number of criminal sentences is determined.

Plea bargaining remains controversial, but its abolition is unlikely (Mirsky & Kahn, 1997). Plea-bargaining negotiations are often conducted in private, confidential meetings between the parties—which hinders research access. Thus, little is known about types of offenders who may benefit from entering a guilty plea, and the advantages and disadvantages of alternate pleas, where allowed, such as nolo contendere or Alford pleas (Alschuler, 2003). By entering a plea of nolo contendere, the accused does not accept or deny responsibility for the charges but agrees to accept punishment. Unlike a plea of "not guilty," the plea of nolo contendere cannot be used against the defendant in any future cause of action. By entering an Alford plea, the accused pleads guilty but asserts factual innocence (*North Carolina v. Alford*, 1970). Observers have noted that (1) defendants receive confusing, mixed messages about the merits of pleading guilty, on the one hand, and refusing to admit guilt or to discuss the offense, on the other; and (2) the far-reaching consequences of entering a guilty plea are poorly appreciated by most defendants at the time of negotiation. Concerns have been expressed that the system of plea bargaining can be coercive, encouraging guilty defendants to feign remorse and persuading a number of innocent defendants to plead guilty because of overestimating their chance of conviction at trial (Bibas, 2003). Plea bargaining within the Australian legal system typically results in reductions of 25–35% of the sentence (Law Reform Commission of Western Australia, 1999).

In the past decade, dissatisfaction with judicial sentences (e.g., Canadian government officials reported that the public perceptions, attitudes, and understanding of the legal system were at a nadir; Alberta Summit on Justice, 1999) has led most legal communities to engage in some type of sentencing reform, particularly reforms that supplement or limit the discretion of judges and magistrates (Smith & Pollack, 1999). Implicated in many reforms and innovations are psychological theories about punishment. Sentencing reforms have heightened scrutiny and evaluation of sentencing theories and systems, and also serve to underscore the need for empirical research that examines the relationship between theory, practice, and policy formulation and application

THEORIES OF PUNISHMENT

Most sentences imposed are intended to inhibit criminal behavior or to reform the individual defendant in light of a particular philosophy or goal of punishment and sentencing. Five major goals of punishment have been distinguished, each of which is linked to assumptions about the causes of criminal conduct: incapacitation, retribution, deterrence, rehabilitation, and restoration (Carroll,

Perkowitz, Lurigio, & Weaver, 1987). Sentences imposed to prevent the commission of future offenses depend, in part, on beliefs about the causes of crime and how blame is allocated for criminal conduct. To the extent that free will, individual choice, or internal, dispositional factors are regarded as the essential causal factors, the motive for retribution in sentencing increases (Carroll et al., 1987). When external factors are seen to shape criminal conduct, mitigation is extended to offenders, and a wider causal context is examined to deter future criminal conduct (Clark, 2003). The major objectives of sentencing, and research findings and trends on the psychological underpinnings in support thereof, are outlined next.

Incapacitation

As a goal or theory of punishment, incapacitation is closely associated with the notion of criminal propensity, or the likelihood that an offender will reoffend. Incarceration specifically deters criminal conduct by means of imprisonment or by isolating offenders from the rest of society so that they are unable to commit offenses during their confinement. There are two types of incapacitation: selective and collective. Selective incapacitation is the prevention of crime through the physical restraint of persons selected for confinement on the basis of a prediction that they, and not others, will engage in forbidden behavior unless physically prevented from doing so. That is, sentencing practices emphasizing selective incapacitation promote longer sentences for high-rate offenders, based on predictions of the likelihood of reoffending (Chan, 1995).

Those emphasizing collective incapacitation promote longer sentences for all offenders regardless of their criminal history. Collective incapacitation, although appealing to communities wanting to "get tough" on crime, involves costs that outweigh its benefits. For example, to achieve a 10% reduction in crime through incarceration, a doubling of the prison population is necessary (Chan, 1995). At best, selective incapacitation offers modest crime-reduction benefits (Chan, 1995).

Theories of incapacitation rely extensively on techniques to predict reoffending (Chan, 1995) and do not always entail custodial detention. Although their predictive accuracy is debated, the two major approaches used to estimate the effect of incapacitation are actuarial risk assessments and structured clinical judgments (Sjostedt & Grann, 2002). Actuarial approaches are more technically sophisticated; they are based on mathematical models that use various individual and social characteristics, along with behaviors, to predict recidivism in offenders. The notion of a criminal career is postulated by models developed by Shinnar and Shinnar (1975) and the closely associated Poisson model (Maltz, 1996). Among the various static or unchanging predictors of recidivism such as offender gender, criminal history, and early family factors (Gendreau, Goggin, & Little, n.d.), the models incorporate age to predict future offenses. For example, 65–70% of violent crimes are committed by males under age 30 (Greenwood et al., 1994). The second approach by which to assess the effect of incapacitation, structured clinical judgment, is based on the dynamic or present circumstances and behaviors of the offender (Gendreau et al., n.d.), which may be affected through treatment. The accuracy of either of these predictive measures has been the subject of ongoing debate (Sjostedt & Grann, 2002).

Selective incapacitation is most effective for high recidivists such as sex offenders and violent offenders (Chan, 1995). Psychologists are often consulted to assess whether a sex offender or a violent offender is likely to reoffend in order to assist a court in determining whether to impose an incapacitating sentence. In some jurisdictions, preventive sentencing options may be applied to sex and violent offenders. For example, in New Zealand preventive detention—for all practical purposes, a life sentence—has been adapted to encompass a broad scope of sexual and violent offenses, such as conspiracy to murder, aggravated robbery, and kidnapping (Ministry of Justice, 2002). An alternative means of selective incarceration was implemented because offenders were routinely released, for good behavior or due to prison overcrowding, prior to completing the imposed period of detention. That is, truth in sentencing laws was aimed primarily at violent offenders, both to eliminate uncertainty concerning the length of their sentences and to ensure that dangerous offenders serve a larger portion (at least 85%) of their sentence (Sabol, Rosich, Kane, Kirk, & Dubin, 2002).

In some communities, including 27 states in the United States (Costanzo, 2004) and Western Australia, laws mandating lengthy prison sentences for offenders convicted three times have proliferated. Since California initiated the first "Three Strikes and You're Out" legislation in 1994 to incapacitate recidivists, in excess of 7,300 offenders—presently 4.7% of the prison population—have been incarcerated under that law (California Department of Corrections, 2004; King & Mauer, 2001, p. 3). Many "three strikes" prisoners are serving sentences of 25 years to life for potentially minor offenses such as shoplifting or drug possession (Hoppin, 2003). In a case in which the offender had a drug habit, no record of violence, and minor past shoplifting offenses, the U.S. Supreme Court upheld the view that a 50-year sentence for shoplifting was not cruel or unusual (*Lockyer v. Andrade*, 2003). Each petty-theft conviction triggered a separate application of the three strikes law, culminating in two consecutive terms of 25 years to life in prison for the offender. Thus, a law enacted to "isolate and punish the most serious, habitual offenders" (King & Mauer, 2001, p. 3) is applied equally to those committing relatively petty crimes with little likelihood of continued criminal activities.

Three strikes laws ignore the fact that criminal career trajectories are not monotonic. A criminal convicted of a first offense at age 15 and a second and third offense 10 years apart is likely to have reached the end of his or her criminal activities. The longer the third sentence, the greater the proportion of incarcerated individuals who would have retired from crime before the sentence expires. If so, increased incarceration is an inefficient means to achieve incapacitation (Caulkins, 2001). Commentators have noted that mandatory sentencing laws that limit judicial discretion have resulted in prisons filled with young, nonviolent, low-level drug offenders serving long sentences at enormous cost to taxpayers (Greenwood et al., 1994). Critics of incapacitation argue that offenders are not punished based on the seriousness of their past conduct but on imperfect predictions about their future conduct (Bartol & Bartol, 2004; von Hirsch, 1985). Decisions about who is to be imprisoned need not entail predictions as to future conduct (Chan, 1995) but may consider factors such as "just deserts" and proportionality of the offenses, concepts fundamental to retributive goals of sentencing.

Retributive Justice

Retributive justice is motivated by the theory of just deserts and dictated by moral outrage. It is the underlying foundation of a number of Western criminal legal systems, including those in Australia, Canada, and the United States (Jeffery, 1990; Price, 1997; Sallman & Willis, 1984). It is often a default sentencing strategy employed in the absence of other guidelines (McFatter, 1978). When asked to rank the philosophies they believe should guide sentencing, many people select retribution as the most important principle (Graham, Weiner, & Zucker, 1997; Hamilton & Sanders, 1988). The punishments proposed are seen as vital to satisfy the people's desire for justice and fairness (Feather, 1996).

Different perspectives on the goals of justice in sentencing lead to different sentencing procedures and outcomes. To some, justice is served by equality in sentencing based on the crime committed; that is, the severity of the punishment appears consistent with the severity of the crime (Hamilton & Rotkin, 1979). To others, justice is served when a sentence is individually tailored to the offender, based on the unique aspects of the offender's background and the effect of punishment on the offender and his or her family (Tonry, 1996). Both types of retributive sentences are not concerned with future outcomes, only that the severity of the punishment is proportionate to the crime committed (Carlsmith, Darley, & Robinson, 2002).

The basic premise of justice motivated by vengeance is that the penalty must be equivalent to the vileness of the crime, and that the community demands redress in the form of harsh punishment (Ho, ForsterLee, ForsterLee, & Crofts, 2002). Retribution is "concerned with the moral nature of the offense," (Vidmar, 2001, p. 35), driven by perceived harm to society, in general, and to the victim, in particular. Studies have shown that judges and laypeople would accord less severe punishment to a person who steals $5 from a church poor box than to someone who embezzles $50,000 from the same church (Wheeler, Mann, & Sarat, 1988). The fact that judges pay particular attention to harm in determining punishment judgments is evidenced in their own descriptions of their sentencing practices for white-collar crimes (Wheeler et al., 1988). The emphasis on retributive justice has given rise to victim participation in the criminal justice system (Hills & Thomson, 1999). Some commentators have argued that this kind of participation promotes vengeance (Joh, 2000) by encouraging sentencers to respond to the victim's pain rather than the relevant points of law.

Critics of retributive justice note that attempts to control an offender's behavior via punishment "leave it up to him to discover how to behave well" (Skinner, 1971, p. 66), as well as leaving unanswered the question, "will he, if punished, behave in a different way when similar circumstances again arise?" (p. 72). The result of punishment is not necessarily a reduction in the maladaptive behavior but, rather, that the offender "learns how to avoid punishment" (p. 81). Sentences awarded on this basis do not offer viable long-term solutions to reduce criminal behavior.

Retributive sentencing leads to overcrowded prisons, a factor underlying the early releases that, in turn, produce sentencing disparities. This cycle of threatened lengthy incarceration followed by early release may act as reinforcement for the offenders to maintain criminal behaviors, because the punishment is not fully meted out. Concern over apparent or superficial disparities between sentences for the same crime are voiced primarily by persons who oppose individually tailored sentences. Nonetheless, in the United States and Australia, trial judges are allowed considerable latitude in sentencing, within the constraints of legislatively imposed guidelines. For instance, the Sentencing Act of 1991 in Victoria, Section 6(D), allows sentencers to give more weight to the protection of the community, thereby negating the principle of proportionality by making it possible to impose sentences disproportionate with the offense (Brown & Pratt, 2000).

Disparities in judicial sentencing decisions have long been observed by means of experimental methods involving sentence simulations (Doob & Beaulieu, 1992), and by the compilation of archival data from court records (Hogarth, 1971; Roberts, 1999). In one study, a number of case descriptions were provided to over 200 provincial court judges, who were asked to state what sentence they would impose. Results showed a high degree of variation in the judges' decisions (Palys & Divorski, 1986). For example, in response to a case of armed robbery, sentences varied from a suspended sentence to 13 years in prison. In a second case involving theft, the sentence varied from a fine to 3 years in prison. Similar sentencing variability emerged in a study of district court judges who responded to hypothetical cases by recommending verdicts and sentences (Austin & Utne, 1977).

Perceived or documented disparities in sentencing have led many Western legal systems to propose uniformity of sentences based on the facts of the case (e.g., the heinousness of the crime, whether violence and/or cruelty was present in the commission of the crime), and to reduce the scope of judicial discretion to tailor sentences to offenders (Smith & Pollack, 1999). For instance, federal sentencing guidelines issued in the United States (Ruback & Wroblewski, 2001; Smith & Pollack, 1999) mandate specific sentences based on features of the crime. Laws imposing mandatory sentences, determinate sentences, and maximum sentences reflect a theory of retributive justice in which just deserts are determined by the number of past convictions rather than the nature of the offenses. Mandatory sentences, determinate sentences, and maximum sentences also reflect a deterrent objective in sentencing. When the offender's punishment is seen to be deserved by the community, it may also accomplish a secondary purpose of deterring possible future criminal actions by that offender or by others.

Deterrent Sentencing

This theory is based on the notion that the punishment of the offender should be sufficient to prevent future instances of the offense (Carlsmith et al., 2002). Two types of deterrence are distinguished: (1) specific deterrence, which aims to dissuade or prevent a particular offender from committing crimes; and (2) general deterrence, which aims to discourage other potential offenders from engaging in similar unlawful conduct.

The most common deterrents in Western criminal justice systems are incarceration, probation supervision, electronic monitoring, boot camps (shock incarceration), and short periods of incarceration followed by intense surveillance. Recently, the number of criminals incarcerated and the length of prison terms have increased despite empirical studies repeatedly demonstrating that incarceration is ineffective in deterring offenders from reoffending (Bartol & Bartol, 2004; Bohm, 1999). An additional trend in the United States is application of the death penalty.

Use of the Death Penalty

Despite conflicting evidence as to whether the death penalty deters individuals from committing homicide, capital punishment applies in cases of aggravated murder in 38 states in the United States (Costanzo, 1997). Some statistical models indicate that each execution saves between 5 and 18 lives (Dezhbakhsh, Rubin, & Shepherd, 2002; Mocan & Gittings, 2003) attributed to the deterrent effect on the offender and those who might engage in violent behavior. Conversely, various scholars have noted that the use of a death penalty supports the premise that killing is an acceptable response to provocation and, as a legitimized action, increases its occurrence within society (Bandura, 1986; Bowers & Pierce, 1980; Huesmann, Moise-Titus, Podolski, & Eron, 2003). That is, authorized executions, rather than increasing deterrence, may foster homicidal behavior through the legitimization of lethal vengeance, referred to as the "brutalization effect" (Cochran, Chamlin, & Seth, 1994).

Shortcomings of Deterrence

Several shortcomings of deterrent theories of sentencing are acknowledged. First, there is often a gap between the theory and the implementation of specific deterrent goals. A series of studies by Carlsmith et al. (2002) demonstrated that although participants (in this case, university students) agreed with the theory of specific deterrence, in practice they imposed punishments in conformity with notions of just deserts. Participants expressed support for deterrence but failed to assign punishment consistent with a deterrent objective.

Second, empirical uncertainty exists as to the extent to which punishment prevents future offending. A meta-analytic review of 117 studies, dating from the 1950s to the present, on the effects of criminal sanctions on 442,471 offenders' recidivism demonstrated a lack of support for criminal justice policies based on the belief that "getting tough" serves as a specific deterrent (Smith, Goggin, & Gendreau, 2002). The analysis included different types of offenders (e.g., juveniles, men, and women) and varying sanctions (e.g., imprisonment; intermediate, such as electronic surveillance) and sentence lengths (e.g., more than 2 years vs. 6 months). Overall, harsher sanctions had no deterrent effect on recidivism, and more severe sanctions actually produced a slight increase in recidivism (Smith et al., 2002). Compared with community sanctions, lengthier sentences increased recidivism more so than shorter sentences. Finally, intermediate sanctions demonstrated no relationship with reoffending. These findings were consistent across all ages, genders, and races (Smith et al., 2002).

Third, ongoing emphasis on high-visibility enforcement is needed to counteract psychological uncertainty of apprehension (Homel, 1988). Offenders generally underestimate the risks of being caught. Personal experience in breaking rules (i.e., the experiential effect) tends to lower their perception that offending behavior is risky (Indermaur, 1996). One example of highly visible law enforcement is the use of random breath testing to deter drunk-driving offenses. Many Western societies, including Australia, introduced roadside random breath testing of drivers in the early 1980s. In New South Wales, Australia, this program commenced in 1980. A comprehensive time-series analysis of daily accident data over a 10-year period, from 1982–1992, showed that a 24% decrease in single-vehicle accidents was maintained for approximately 5 years; there were 12% fewer such accidents for every 1,000 drivers tested. These findings support the view that offenders must perceive the likelihood of apprehension as high in order for deterrence to work (Homel, McKay, & Henstridge, 1995). Put simply, it is not the sentence, per se, that is effective in deterring criminal conduct but the likelihood of apprehension *plus* imposition of the sentence. However, social psychological research has shown that people reject the notion that punishment should vary with the probability of crime commission detection (Sunstein, Schkade, & Kahneman, 2000).

Finally, the failure of general deterrent measures has also been observed as it applies to corporate offenders. Fines are the most common sentencing penalty for corporate offenders, but these penalties are often inadequate. For example, a fine of £3,000 for violating regulations requiring packaging recycling was imposed on a large importer of bananas to the United Kingdom;

however, the company saved £50,000 by ignoring the regulations (Brown, 2003). Large corporations often treat fines as mere business losses that can be passed on to shareholders, employees, or consumers of products. Fines tend to trivialize corporate crime, transmitting a message to the community that corporate crime is not serious. Because corporate offenders are organizations, not individuals, no direct action may be taken against the corporation, and there is no rehabilitative aspect to the sentence. Thus, the deterrent effect of a prison sentence is difficult to achieve when monetary punishments are the only deterrents.

Alternate sentencing options for corporate crime, such as equity fines, publicity orders, corporate probation, community service, and disqualification and dissolution are rarely imposed (Fisse, 1990). However, the collapse of large corporations in the United States, for example, has led to recent federal legislation that dramatically increased the financial penalties and potential for criminal prosecution of executives guilty of financial crimes (O'Donnell & Willing, 2003). The existing empirical support for the deterrent effect of the threat of sanctions on corporate crime has been limited and conditional. For example, in a cross-sectional study of 410 managers of nursing homes in Australia, only the probability of state detention had the expected deterrent effect on compliance with nursing home regulations. This finding was not uniform; a deterrent effect was observed only among nursing home managers who tested low on emotionality (Makkai & Braithwaite, 1994). The researchers noted that deterrence failed to explain compliance with regulatory law.

At best, general deterrence works for some offenders and some crimes. Many citizens are ignorant about the penalties attached to various crimes (Haney, 2002). Unless offenders fully appreciate the possible sanctions for criminal behaviors, the philosophy of deterrence is likely to be only weakly supported.

Rehabilitation

Rehabilitative approaches to punishment emphasize changes that can and should be brought about in the criminal's behavior in the interests of both the community and the criminal. Rehabilitative theories are based on the assumption that social, psychological, psychiatric, or other factors outside a person's direct control, which have wholly or partly determined or influenced an offender's actions (e.g., to commit a crime), can be accurately identified. Once these factors are known, treatment or assistance can be prescribed that provides the individual with alternatives to the undesirable behavior. Juvenile courts have typically espoused noncustodial rehabilitative sentencing goals for young offenders. For example, the resolution of criminal issues might involve the imposition of the least restrictive environmental option, avoidance of criminal proceedings if viable alternatives exist, and the involvement of members within the juvenile's community (i.e., parents, community groups) and possibly the crime victims.

Rehabilitative sentencing goals for adult offenders were largely abandoned in the 1970s, following publication of an extensive review of 234 studies on psychological and nonpsychological interventions, which concluded that few programs decreased the rate of recidivism. The catch phrase "nothing works" (Martinson, 1974, p. 25) resulted. Although the author stated that many programs showed successful rehabilitative results (Martinson, 1979), the emphasis on recidivism reduction—perhaps too stringent a criterion for success—led policymakers and researchers to concur with the infamous pronouncement.

More recent reviews, however, contain more encouraging conclusions about rehabilitation programs for offenders (Lipton, Pearson, Cleland, & Yee, 2002; MacKenzie, 2000). Cognitive-behavioral interventions that incorporate features such as problem-solving skills, interpersonal skills, social learning, and communication skills have had the greatest success in reducing criminal propensities (Lipton et al., 2002). Effective juvenile court-ordered rehabilitation programs contain elements that (1) focus on altering behavior and developing prosocial skills, (2) integrate the juveniles' families into problem-solving efforts, (3) maintain a flexibility to engage a variety of intervention approaches, and (4) are well structured and intensive in their application (Kurlychek, Torbet, & Bozynski, 1999).

The distinction between rehabilitation and treatment often blurs. Some rehabilitative programs seek "to reduce criminal propensities by changing the attitudes, cognitive patterns, social relationships, and/or resources of offenders" (Cullen & Applegate, 1998, p. xiv). Other programs aim to treat offenders by addressing their underlying cognitive deficiencies and adjustment problems. For example, some psychologists regard sex offenders as persons with deviant conceptions, which can be treated (Ward, 2002). Model forensic treatment approaches used in the United States and The Netherlands were reviewed by Heilbrun and Griffin (1999). Incarceration-based treatment programs for sex offenders, violent offenders, and domestic abusers address offenders individually, in groups, or combinations of individual and group settings. Evaluations indicate that cognitive-behavioral programs have been effective in treating both sexual (Laws, 1996) and violent offenders (Arias, Dankwort, Douglas, Dutton, & Stein, 2002; Kemshall, 2002).

Applications of Therapeutic Jurisprudence

The concept of therapeutic jurisprudence emerged in the United States in the late 1980s, seeking to make the law a therapeutic agent (Wexler & Winick, 1996). Among the contentions of therapeutic jurisprudence is the notion that the legal system, at all stages of contact, should encourage prosocial lifestyles by incorporating social science knowledge to determine methods that would promote the offender's psychological well-being (Birgden & Ward, 2003). Put another way, therapeutic jurisprudence contends that the legal system is better served if certain offenders (e.g., recidivist drunk drivers, drug addicts, and kleptomaniacs) are encouraged to plead guilty and accept treatment, where such options are available, rather than seeking acquittal (Bibas, 2003). In such cases the emphasis is on rehabilitation outside of jails and prisons and involves noncustodial sentences (Wexler, 2002). To assist judges in considering alternatives to prison or parole for nonviolent offenders, programs in the United States such as The Sentencing Project (2003) offer expert advice to courts from lawyers and social workers on rehabilitative sentencing packages tailored to the criminal and the crime.

Principles of therapeutic jurisprudence have been applied in drug courts established in the United States and Australia. In these courts, the drug offender's addiction is considered a central element of the criminal act, and the sentences aim not to punish but to treat (Senjo & Leip, 2001). Since the first drug court was established in Miami, Florida, in 1989 (Eleventh Judicial Circuit of Florida, n.d.), more than 65,000 individuals in the United States have received treatment (Drug Strategies, 1998). Studies confirm a reduction in drug use by offenders whose cases are processed in drug courts versus traditional courts (Senjo & Leip, 2001). For example, an evaluation of the drug court in Kalamazoo, Michigan, indicated that the specialized programs for female offenders were graduating more than half of those participating, and the recidivism rate among those who had graduated was only 10% (Drug Strategies, 1998). A study of the Orange County, Florida, drug court revealed that as few as 10% of participants were rearrested during participation in the program (Applegate, Reuter, McCarthy, & Santana, 1999).

Eligibility criteria for drug-court participation vary from one jurisdiction to another. For instance, in the New South Wales Drug Court in Australia, established in 1998, drug dealers, violent offenders, and sex offenders are excluded from participating (*Regina v. Buttigieg*, 2002). Immediate entry into a drug-treatment program subsequent to an arrest increases the chances of program success (Long, 1996), as does the length of time spent under drug-court supervision. A key feature in the success of many programs is the ongoing involvement of the same judge in monitoring the progress of offenders (Freeman, 2003). In one study, more than half of the 157 drug-court participants felt that the opportunity to discuss their progress and problems with the judge was important, and 65% attributed their completion of the program to frequent appearances before the same judge (Cooper & Bartlett, 1996). Separate drug courts for juveniles have been established along similar lines to those dealing with adults (Belenko & Dembo, 2003).

Other noncustodial rehabilitation schemes include the Court Referral Evaluation for Drug Intervention and Treatment (CREDIT) and Magistrates Early Referral into Treatment (MERIT), bail schemes started in Australia in 1998, under which arrestees charged with drug-related, nonviolent but indictable offenses are brought before a magistrate and assessed for suitability for treatment (Freiberg, 2003). If suitable, they are released on bail for periods of up to 4 months or more. Eligible offenders must have a drug problem and must not be subject to a community-based disposition. This bail scheme deals with first-time offenders as well as those with criminal histories (Freiberg, 2003). The pre-plea opportunity for offenders to access treatment without first admitting guilt was significant: MERIT participants were more responsive to treatment and more willing to address lifestyle issues known to promote drug-abuse recovery (Scantleton, Boulton, & Didcott, 2002). A recent evaluation showed that offenders, 90% of whom had previous criminal convictions, who successfully completed the MERIT program were more likely to receive good behavior bonds and suspended sentences. In addition, they were less likely to be fined or be sent back to prison, compared to offenders who did not complete the treatment program. Recidivism reduction was positive over the first 20 months. The majority who completed the program (62%) were not charged with further offenses. Most reoffenses that did occur were minor *cannabis* charges. Offenders who entered the methadone program or residential treatment tended to continue their treatment after finishing MERIT (Flaherty & Jousif, 2002).

Psychological research suggests that the expression of remorse may inhibit future criminal conduct (Hayes & Daly, 2003). One problem with many rehabilitative, noncustodial sentencing options, and with some custodial sentences, is the insistence that the offender enter a guilty plea as a condition of eligibility. This requirement clouds the assessment of the genuineness of any remorse expressed. Numerous studies indicate that when remorse is lacking, recidivism is higher (Indermaur, 1996). Some investigations of therapeutic jurisprudence have examined the importance of psychological factors such as trust, procedural fairness, emotional intelligence, and relational interactions. These factors are also prominent in restorative justice programs.

Restorative Justice

Restorative justice aims to reestablish victims, offenders, and communities following an offense. Among the major forms of restorative justice are circle sentencing, reintegrative shaming, and victim–offender mediation. The South African Truth and Reconciliation Commission pioneered the use of restorative justice methods with numerous positive outcomes (Allan & Allan, 2000).

Sentencing Circles

Among the best-known examples of restorative justice programs is circle sentencing, originated by the First Nations in Canada, in which tribal dispute resolution practices are incorporated into sentencing practices. Community members actively assist justice authorities by participating in discussions about available sentencing options and plans to reintegrate the offender into the community (Melton, 1995). An evaluation of 30 circles undertaken in Southern Ontario demonstrated positive results. Measures of sexual and violent recidivism (Structured Anchored Clinical Judgment; Rapid Risk Assessment for Sex Offence Recidivism Average) and the STATIC-99 confirmed the high-risk status of offenders entering the program (Hanson & Thornton, 2000). The mean length of time spent in the program was 36 months, ranging from 9 months to 7 years. Comparisons of the expected and the observed recidivism rate, using STATIC-99 survival data, showed that recidivism was reduced by more than 50% (Wilson, Huculak, & McWhinnie, 2002). From a harm-reduction perspective (Laws, 1996; Marlatt, 1998), each act of sexual recidivism was categorically less invasive and less severe than the offense for which the offender had been most recently apprehended (Wilson et al., 2002). A separate evaluation of the Circles of Support and Accountability (COSA) pilot project in Canada showed that offenders receiving assistance via a circle reoffended at a lower rate incrementally, in comparison with a matched control sample (Wilson, Picheca, & Serin, 2001).

Indigenous Courts

Several alternative forms of justice are presently being considered for sentencing Aboriginal offenders in Australia and Maori offenders in New Zealand (Cunneen, 2001). Circle sentencing has been proposed for certain offenses in courts reserved specifically for Aborigines in New South Wales, Australia (New South Wales Law Reform Commission, 2000). An initiative for a Koori Court in Victoria, Australia, is being developed by the Department of Justice jointly with the Aboriginal Justice Forum. It is anticipated that a tribal elder will sit on the bench with a magistrate and offer advice about the offender, but not play a direct role in the sentence. Eligible offenses (e.g., property crimes) can receive customary punishments or community service orders as an alternative to incarceration (Cunneen, 2001).

The Nunga Court in Murray Bridge, Port Adelaide, and Port Augusta (all in the state of South Australia) has been in effect since 1999. In this alternative setting, the magistrate, along with an indigenous justice officer who provides advice about cultural and community issues, sit at eye-level with the offender, not on the bench. To assist with the sentencing options the offender may have a family member present at the bar table while the magistrate asks questions of the offender, possibly the victim, and any other community or family member (Cunneen, 2001). The Nunga Court increased the rate of attendance by Aboriginal people (80%) compared to attendance in other courts (less than 50%).

Although research has demonstrated that circle sentencing and the integration of traditional tribal processes can be effective in reducing crime, their use has been criticized as a form of reverse racism: Certain groups within the community are treated differently based on their ethnic background. Additional criticisms are that costs of circle sentencing and integrating indigenous elements into the courts exceed those of standard court sentencing (News in Review, 2001), and that some communities may have unstructured discretion in dealing with offenders, leading to inconsistent outcomes (Roberts & Laprairie, 1997).

Reintegrative Shaming

In Western judicial systems the offender may be denigrated, shamed, and re-garded as inherently bad by peers, resulting in a stigmatic shaming. This type of stigmatization threatens individual identity and weakens individuals' moral bonds with society, leading to an amplification of deviance apparent in the of-fenders' rejection of those who shame them (e.g., judges or police officers). By comparison, restorative justice promotes reintegrative shaming, in which the offender is seen as a good person who engaged in bad conduct (Braithwaite, 2000). The social well-being of those affected by the crime and the general goal of healing take priority over punishment (Presser & van Voorhis, 2002). This emphasis is present throughout the process as well as the outcome. The theory of reintegrative shaming predicts that restorative justice processes are more effective than criminal trials in reducing crime, because the emphasis on the problem rather than the person avoids direct denunciation of the offender. The underlying assumption of reintegrative shaming is the avoidance of stig-matization that hinders reintegration of the offender into the community (Braithwaite, 2000). Offenders, victims, and representatives of the community are given an opportunity to participate in the sentencing process, express their viewpoints, and hear from others involved in the crime.

An additional core feature of reintegrative shaming is providing an op-portunity for the offender to apologize. Experimental studies of the effects of apology and expressions of remorse by offenders demonstrated that they dif-fused punitive attitudes. In one study, participants read either about a lock-smith who considered stealing or about a locksmith who actually completed a theft. The locksmith was remorseful in some conditions and attempted to re-turn the coins, whereas in others he was not (Robinson & Darley, 1995). The remorseful locksmith was less likely to be considered guilty, even if he com-mitted theft, compared with the locksmith who lacked remorse (Vidmar, 2001). In one review of youth justice conferences, reduced recidivism was as-sociated with expressed remorse on the part of the offender and participation in consensual decision making (Hayes & Daly, 2003).

The value of an apology to victims and offenders was examined in an evaluation of family-group conferencing for young offenders charged with property (60% shoplifting) and assault crimes. Admission of guilt was a con-dition of eligibility for the diversionary program. Thirty percent of offenders stated that offering the victim an apology was the reason they chose to partici-pate in the conference; 26% cited that they wanted "to make things right" by taking responsibility for their conduct (Fercello & Umbreit, 1998, p. 7). More than 90% of the victims reported that it was important to receive an apology (92% received apologies), and an equal number felt that family-group conferencing was effective in holding the offenders accountable (Fercello & Umbreit, 1998). Victim–offender mediation programs in which the offender and victim are brought face to face in the presence of a trained facilitator have also given priority to apologies. An analysis of victim–offender mediation programs in three states in the United States disclosed that 9 out of 10 offenders listed apologizing to the victim, negotiating restitution, paying restitution, and telling the victim what happened as the most important issues in the process (Umbreit & Coates, 1992).

Numerous juvenile justice systems have implemented alternatives to traditional criminal proceedings such as restorative justice. Most evaluations of youth justice conferences reveal more positive outcomes than juvenile courts, but some mixed results have also been reported. The length of the follow-up period and small sample sizes may not allow for subtle differences in reoffending levels to emerge (Luke & Lind, 2002). Additionally, most evaluations employ nonexperimental survey designs that assess factors such as (1) conference participants' satisfaction with the process, (2) their satisfaction with the outcomes of the proceedings, and (3) the acceptance of responsibility by the offender. An example can be seen in the assessment of 391 conferences convened by the New South Wales Youth Justice Conferencing scheme in Australia in 1999. Overall, the study reported that 79% of participants who went through the conferencing process were satisfied with the way their case was handled by the justice system, and 89% were satisfied with the outcomes (Trimboli, 2000). In addition, 94.2% of offenders reported that "after the conference, they had a proper understanding of the harm caused to the victim" and 77.7% of victims reported believing that "after the conference, the offender had a proper understanding of the harm caused to the victim" (Trimboli, 2000, p. 54). These types of results are promising, but it must also be noted that all offenders who attended the conferences were assigned by the courts, possibly biasing the sample. Levels of satisfaction with the process may decrease when a more representative group of offenders participates in the process.

Evaluations of conferencing schemes often demonstrate reductions in recidivism and increases in participant satisfaction. For instance, an evaluation of the New Zealand Family Group Conferencing (FGC) scheme by Maxwell and Morris (2001) reported that when offenders showed remorse and agreed with the outcomes, recidivism was lower. A 6-year follow-up of 108 participants revealed that 29% had no further convictions, and a further 14% had one reconviction. Multivariate analyses distinguishing between predictors of reconviction and pathways to reoffending confirmed that family group conferencing can decrease recidivism, even when factors such as adverse early experiences and subsequent life events are present. Similarly, victim–offender mediation has been shown to reduce the victim's fears, to hold the offender accountable, to increase client satisfaction and restitution, and to decrease recidivism and crimes of violence (Umbreit, Coates, & Vos, 2001). Restitution is an element included in most victim–offender agreements, and more than 8 out of 10 agreements are completed. Currently, there is interest in developing victim–offender programs to address very violent crimes (Umbreit et al., 2001).

A recent review of restorative justice programs by Poulson (2003) spanned four continents and examined outcomes in five countries (Israel, Australia, Canada, the United Kingdom, and the United States). On measures such as perceived fairness, accountability, increased respect, and reduction of fear, victims and offenders rated the restorative justice programs as superior to traditionally adjudicated sentences. Recidivism rates among 619 participants in restorative justice programs were lower than those receiving traditional sentences (19% vs. 28%), and the types of offenses were less severe than those of offenders who did not experience restorative justice. An additional meta-analytical review of 8 conferencing and 27 victim–offender mediation programs showed that conferences yielded higher levels of participant satisfaction and lower levels of recidivism than nonrestorative approaches to criminal behavior (Latimer, Dowden, & Muise, 2001). These findings have been presented to the United Nations Working Party on Restorative Justice, with the goal of extrapolating restorative justice principles across cultures. Notably, considerable variability exists in conferencing from one context or another; thus caution must be exercised in using these results to establish conferencing procedures across situations and across cultures in which group values may differ (Tyler, Degoey, & Smith, 1996).

Questions have been raised as to the criteria and attributes of an effective or successful conference (Daly, 2003). For instance, offenders who perceive legal procedures as fair may increase their compliance with the law and their cooperation with legal authorities. However, cross-cultural differences exist in preferences for procedural fairness and justice. Restorative justice programs such as police- and civilian-convened conferences are popular alternatives in sentencing juveniles (Sivasubramaniam & Goodman-Delahunty, 2003). One concern is that police conveners versus civilian conveners may be perceived differently by ethnic minorities because of differences in their trustworthiness, which in turn influences the perceived fairness of the conference. Two psychologically relevant variables to consider when making decisions about appropriate conferencing models to be implemented in multicultural societies are power-distance and perceptions of police trustworthiness (Tyler, Lind, & Huo, 2000). "Power-distance refers to the distance people believe is appropriate between authorities and subordinates. People high on power-distance tend to favor a large distance between authorities and their subordinates and believe that societies and organizations function better when there is a more hierarchical structure of power. In contrast, people low on power-distance favor small distance between authorities and their subordinates and believe that people who hold positions of power should display a more consultative relationship with people who do not hold power" (Sivasubramaniam & Goodman-Delahunty, 2003, p. 2).

In sum, a contemporary contextual model of human behavior requires crime control policies such as sentences that are less dependent on prisons as a solution to the offender's behavior (Haney, 1997, 2002). Many rehabilitation and restorative justice programs show promise in reducing recidivism and are less costly in the long term than incarceration. The relative novelty and structure of these programs have not allowed the psychological aspects underlying their success to be fully evaluated and understood. The implications for legal systems across numerous countries warrant the further study of the underlying principles and applications of these alternative models, along with the dynamics of those (both victims and offenders) who may benefit from the use of such processes. Realistically, no known psychological interventions have been found that universally reduce criminality (McGuire, 2003). However, research on therapeutic jurisprudence and restorative justice demonstrates that interactions between lawyers, judges, and defendants during the sentencing phase are linked to more positive outcomes (Petrucci, 2002; Winick, 2000).

LEGAL DECISION MAKING IN DEALING WITH OFFENDERS

Many facts deemed inadmissible in determining whether the defendant is culpable of the crime charged may be admitted into evidence and given consideration during the penalty phase of the trial when a judge determines the appropriate sentence. For example, the judge may consider whether the offender is a first-time or frequent offender, the nature and scope of prior convictions, and historical and family background facts such as character references and psychological evaluations of the offender (Sallman & Willis, 1984). Fairness and impartiality dictate that judges weigh factors that lessen or increase the responsibility of the guilty party (Hebenton & Pease, 1995). That is, judges must consider mitigating circumstances that lessen the responsibility of the offender and potentially reduce the sentence, as well as aggravating factors that heighten the serious nature of the crime and increase the severity of the sentencing consideration (Hebenton & Pease, 1995; Ho et al., 2002). A guilty plea by an offender may reduce a sentence (Albonetti, 1998); similarly, a defendant who displays remorse and confesses may receive a reduced sentence (*Regina v. Pensini*, 2003).

In reaching a decision about an appropriate sentence, trial judges depend on precedents, case law, and formal sentencing guideline principles (Ainsworth, 2000). The possession and expression of differing perspectives on points of law are fundamental elements of the justice system. This encouragement of autonomy within the court is a major contributor to the variance in the application of the law (Feldman, 1993). Some researchers posit that judges may arrive at their sentencing determinations "by adding or subtracting the effects of aggravating or mitigating case factors" (Hebenton & Pease, 1995, p. 381). Formalization of such a method would reflect a "numerical guideline" (Warner, 2002, p. 13), a system that has not been adopted in Australia. A form of numerical sentencing guidelines that applies in the instance of rape was established in England (*Regina v. Billam*, 1986). These judgment guidelines include mitigating and aggravating case factors, along with a basic beginning sentence for a sexual assault committed by an adult. The federal sentencing guidelines within the United States are similar in concept but complex to use, requiring consideration of 43 factors and allocating points for aggravating and mitigating factors (Ruback & Wroblewski, 2001). An aggravating factor considered to aid in the balancing of sentencing decisions is a victim-impact statement (*Payne v. Tennessee*, 1991).

The Influence of Victim-Impact Statements

A recent innovation during the sentencing determination is the admission of victim-impact statements, which are presented to the court, orally or in writing, during the sentencing phase of trials in Australia and the United States (Erez & Rogers, 1999; Myers & Greene, 2004). For example, the Criminal Offence Victims Act (1995) in Queensland, Australia, primarily compels counsel for the prosecution to notify the judge of the impact of the convicted offender's actions on the victims or their survivors (Robertson & Mackenzie, 1998). Victim-impact testimony, typically expressed in written form, followed by oral statements in court, provide the trial judge or capital jury with an account of the emotional trauma, psychological, physical, and/or financial harm suffered by the victims or their immediate families (Jerin & Moriarty, 1998; Nadler & Rose, 2003). Victim-impact testimony permits victims to articulate their feelings about the crime and potentially influences the punishment meted to the convicted offender (Erez, 1991). Victim involvement in the criminal trial process increases victim satisfaction with the legal system, because the full impact of the crime becomes known to the sentencing judge through these statements (Henley, Davis, & Smith, 1994). However, the goal of the judicial system is the dispensation of justice, not satisfaction of the victim; therefore, victim input remains contentious (Blumenthal, 2001). Proponents such as U.S. Supreme Court Chief Justice Rehnquist emphasize the importance for the court to understand the full effects of the criminal's actions upon the victims or their families to render an appropriate sentence (Nadler & Rose, 2003). Opponents suggest that sentencers should remain dispassionate and impartial, and should not impose differential penalties for the same offense based on victim input (Erez, 1991) or the perceived relative worth of the victim (Nadler & Rose, 2003). The problematic issue for the prosecution is "not to be seen as promoting the interests of the victim at the expense of the interest of justice . . . vengeance is not equated with justice" (Robertson & Mackenzie, 1998, p. 19,054).

Paramount is the consideration of whether the emotional content of victim-impact evidence is relevant in determining a sentence. The U.S. Supreme Court deemed victim-impact testimony relevant in capital cases (*Payne v. Tennessee*, 1991); however, the relevance or weight of such a statement is difficult to determine (Robertson & Mackenzie, 1998). For instance, testimony by a victim often fails to adequately convey the brutality of an offense, nor can it reflect upon the status of the convicted offender's future dangerousness (Sullivan, 1998). Indeed, the potentially biasing effects of victim input due to the emotive content inherent in victim-impact evidence has led a number of critics to express cautionary warnings about the use of potentially prejudicial and inflammatory factors (Bandes, 1996), particularly when presented to juries in capital cases. Most of the states (32 of the 38) in the United States that allow for capital punishment permit the admission of victim-impact statements in the penalty phase of the trials (Logan, 1999; Nadler & Rose, 2003).

Emotionally Arousing Evidence

Victim-impact statements are not the only potential sources of emotional arousal within the trial process. Evidence or testimony presented throughout the process may provoke emotional arousal, which, in turn, produces augmented estimates of the probability of the guilt of the defendant. The potentially prejudicial impact of visual evidence was demonstrated in a study that found that gruesome photographic evidence influenced mock-juror emotional states and mock-juror decision making regarding culpability (Douglas, Lyon, & Ogloff, 1997). Heightened emotional arousal in response to gruesome evidence has been shown to evoke more conviction-prone decision-making in mock jurors (Kassin & Garfield, 1991). When evidence arouses jurors to experience strong negative affective states, such as anger, their perceptions of the strength of particular items of evidence may be enhanced (Bright & Goodman-Delahunty, 2004). The research concerned with the impact of emotionally arousing testimony and/or evidence that impedes rational juror decision making and leads to excessively severe sentencing judgments (Myers & Greene, 2004) appears to support the dissenting opinion of U.S. Supreme Court Justice Stevens, who commented that victim-impact testimony evidence serves no function other than encouraging jurors to determine in favor of a death penalty by substituting their emotions for their ability to reason (*Payne v. Tennessee*, 1991).

Judgments about sentences may be influenced by sentimental reactions to the personal characteristics of the victims and their families embedded in victim-impact evidence (Greene, 1999). For instance, mock jurors believed that the immediate family of the victim suffered more when the victim's personal character was described in more respectable ways (a loyal husband vs. a loner). Similarly, mock jurors punished a defendant more severely when the victim was characterized as innocent versus a dangerous criminal, even though the defendant had no information about the victim when the crime was committed (Alicke & Davis, 1989). Anger over the deaths of police officers in the line of duty reflects the impact that victim identity can exert on sentence severity.

A powerful influence on the extent of sentences imposed appears to derive from the severity of harm inflicted on the victim. In one Western Australian study, 250 participants read case files about a robbery or a rape, which varied in their description of how well the victim coped subsequent to the crime (Hills & Thomson, 1999). Victim coping styles are not foreseeable and may not be relevant to sentencing determinations. However, in response to information provided by the prosecution that victims were coping poorly, sentences were more punitive than in response to information provided by the defense that victims were coping well. Although in this study, the information source (prosecution or defense) was confounded with coping responses, the data showed that the sentencing decision may be influenced by perceived harm to the victim.

A recent study in the United States examined the influence of harm severity on sentencing to test the theory that the outcome of a criminal act serves as a heuristic for the perpetrator's culpability and other factors that are difficult for the fact finder to ascertain (Nadler & Rose, 2003). Participants indicated what prison sentence, if any, the defendant should receive, ranging from probation to 18 years or more in prison, for either a burglary or robbery, and answered questions about the perceived seriousness of the crime and the extent of injury to the victim. Participants imposed a higher prison term, on average, when the victim-impact evidence described severe emotional injury (4.4 years) than when it described mild emotional injury (2.7 years). A similar pattern emerged for robbery: Participants assigned more severe sentences, on average, when the victim-impact testimony expressed severe emotional injury (4.8 years) than when the victim-impact statement expressed mild emotional injury (3.1 years). Participants rated their own feelings of sympathy higher when the victim-impact evidence described severe versus mild emotional injury.

Mortality Salience and Terror Management Theory

Whereas the impact of emotional information may certainly influence sentencing and penalty decisions, Rosenblatt, Greenberg, Solomon, Pyszczynski, and Lyon (1989) wondered about the impact of exposing judges to thoughts about their own death. Twenty-two municipal court judges were asked to set bail for a prostitute. They were given the usual information pertaining to her arrest and past behavior, and were asked to set a dollar amount for bail. Prior to assessing the prostitute's case, half the judges were asked to think about their own death. Specifically, they were asked to imagine what would happen to them as they physically died and how they would feel. The judges in the control condition were not asked to consider their own death. The differences in bail between these groups was large: Judges who had thought about their own death set bail averaged at $450; judges who had not thought about their own death set bail averaged at $50.

This difference was predicted by terror management theory (Rosenblatt et al., 1989), which states that humans are unique in knowing that they will die and that this knowledge is terrifying. People do several things to buffer the terror; the one most pertinent here is that they are more likely to hold firmly to their cultural worldview. In other words, they defend against the terror of death by thinking that their perspective is right and that others who are different are wrong. Hence, when forced to consider their own deaths, judges held more firmly to their worldview that people who violate the law—a prostitute, in this instance—should be punished.

Mortality salience encourages people to invest in and defend their cultural world view and stimulates in-group identification. Individuals who are perceived as out-group members, such as offenders who are not law-abiding and whose conduct may threaten the identity of the in-group, are treated more punitively as a consequence. This phenomenon has been replicated in more than a hundred studies in several different countries. Mortality salience has been shown to increase punitive judgments across many types of crimes and is moderated by individual differences and contextual features (Florian, Mikulincer, & Hirschberger, 2002). Individuals who have high self-esteem, which serves a buffering mechanism against the anxiety provoked by mortality salience, are less prone to the effects of mortality salience than are individuals with moderate or low self-esteem (Harmon-Jones et al., 1997). Interestingly, when the victim is seen as a member of the out-group and the offender is a member of the in-group, the sentence imposed on the offender is more lenient in response to mortality salience. In those instances, presumably, the act of the offender in attacking the transgressor is seen to support the world view of the judge or jury, so the offense is viewed as less serious and less deserving of punishment (Greenberg, Schimel, Martens, Solomon, & Pyszczynski, 2001; Lieberman, Arndt, Personius, & Cook, 2001).

In summary, research supports the contention that the presence of emotionally evocative information may lead to the imposition of harsher sentences by mock jurors (ForsterLee, Fox, ForsterLee, & Ho, 2004; Hills & Thomson, 1999; Myers & Arbuthnot, 1999) and judges (Rosenblatt et al., 1989). This effect may result from the influence of victim-impact and mortality-salient evidence in sentencing decisions. Additional factors that have been found to coincide with the decisions rendered in the courtroom concern characteristics of the offender relative to the judge. Specifically, a review of sentences rendered in 160,000 cases revealed that the severity of the offense along with the defendant's race, ethnicity, gender, and age were significant factors used by judges to decide whether or not to incarcerate the offender, and the length of the sentence to impose (Ulmer, 1997). Thus, the research and court decision analyses converge to support the "severity effect," which may underlie the influence of victim-impact evidence in sentencing decisions.

THE INFLUENCE OF JUDICIAL CHARACTERISTICS ON SENTENCING OFFENDERS

One constraint on judicial decision making that is underresearched is the influence of potential reversals of judges' decisions by courts of appeal. Trial judges carefully consider their sentencing comments, including discussion of mitigating and aggravating case factors, to avoid challenge on appeal (Wrightsman, Greene, Nietzel, & Fortune, 2002). Indeed, any comments that indicate the possibility of bias against the defendant are grounds for disqualification of the judge (*Rucks v. Florida*, 1997). When judges impose a sentence that they believe may attract public criticism, they usually take pains to explain why the particular penalty was imposed. However, a content analysis of newspaper reports of sentences imposed revealed the omission of the reasons underlying the punishment by three-quarters of the papers (Roberts, 1995).

Race, Gender, and Age Influences

Some researchers have examined the tendency for judges to exhibit biases based on factors such as race and gender (Coontz, 2000; Feldman, 1993; Kapardis, 2003; Mulhausen, 2004). The biasing effect of gender has been observed in regard to the gender of the judge as well as that of the offender. Male and black offenders are 50% more likely to receive longer prison sentences than those awarded to similarly situated women and white offenders (Ulmer, 1997). The impact of gender is not unexpected; one survey of 10,500 felony cases in California revealed that male judges sentenced female offenders less harshly than similarly situated male offenders (Associated Press, 1984). However, Mulhausen's (2004) analyses of the interactions between the characteristics of judges and offenders displayed more distinctive findings. That is, although female defendants received more lenient sentences than males, the most lenient sentences were given to females by female judges. Concerning racial aspects, it was demonstrated that "black offenders could expect to receive longer sentences when black judges presided over their cases" (Mulhausen, 2004, p. 21). It must be noted that the African American judges presided in counties where the crime rates were twice those of counties overseen by white judges. It was speculated that the higher victimization rates may have led to a greater concern "for the plight of minority victims than for the rights of minority criminals" (Mulhausen, 2004, p. 21).

Although the scales of justice are supposed to be blind, studies indicate that sentencers cannot set aside their own experiences, values, and attitudes in applying legal principles (Costanzo, 2004). Judicial characteristics such as the judge's age, years of experience on the bench, previous employment as a prosecutor, and political viewpoint and philosophy about punishment may account for some of the observed disparities in sentences (Wrightsman et al., 2002). Early experimental findings based on an in-depth analysis of a number of sentencing decisions, measuring variables associated with the case, characteristics of the offender, and characteristics of the judge confirmed that less than 10% of the proportion of the variation in sentencing could be explained by objectively defined facts of the case, whereas over half of the variance was attributable to certain features of the presiding judge (Hogarth, 1971). Finally, a study of gender bias sampled 378 Illinois judges and found that the male judges were more likely than their female counterparts to believe gender bias was a tactic used in the courtroom, rather than a discriminatory phenomenon. Additionally, age was associated with the belief that gender bias did not occur in the courtroom. That is, older officers of the court tended to believe that problems with gender bias did not arise during proceedings (Riger, Foster-Fishman, Nelson-Kuna, & Curran, 1995).

Individual Decision Styles

Personal factors of officers of the court (judges) rather than factors relating to the case have been demonstrated to impact sentencing decisions. An analysis of the cognitive processes involved in sentencing revealed that a magistrate's decision style involves individualized strategies for selecting and interpreting case information (Lawrence, 1988). These cognitive processes that mediate judges' sentencing decisions often occur without their awareness. Indeed, an early study of judicial sentencing decisions showed that although judges claimed to take into account a series of items in evidence, in 84% of the cases they used a conservative heuristic and simply accepted the parole officer's recommendation (Ebbesen & Konečni, 1981).

Judgmental Biases and Heuristics

A *heuristic* is a rule that describes the process, not simply the result, of problem solving (Gigerenzer, 2004). As such, it utilizes developed and learned behavioral and cognitive capacities along with the organization of environments, making its engagement effortless and intelligent (i.e., speedy problem solving). A recent groundbreaking examination of judicial decisions highlighting the impact of heuristics, undertaken in the United Kingdom, demonstrated a reliance by magistrates on fast and frugal heuristics in reaching bail or confinement determinations (Dhami & Ayton, 2001). Magistrates' decision strategies were modeled best by the matching heuristic. That is, each magistrate tended to utilize only a single criterion in reaching decisions, and different magistrates used different criteria. For example, one might rely on the prosecutor's recommendation, whereas another considered the age of the defendant, leading to an inconsistency across the magistrates' decisions.

Another judgmental bias that has been shown to influence fact finders is that of illusory causation, which occurs when individuals attribute baseless causality to a stimulus because of its salience over other stimuli. A series of recent studies examined whether the perspective of the camera angle used to videotape confessions and courtroom testimony could produce illusory causation (Lassiter, 2002). The results consistently demonstrated that the point of view (camera angles) from which participants observed interactions (i.e., interrogations or testimony) influenced their perceptual organization of information from the interaction, which in turn directly influenced their causal attributions and related judgments. For example, when the camera was focused solely on the accused, participants rated the confession as more voluntary, perceived the offender to be more culpable, and issued more severe sentencing recommendations than in experimental conditions where the camera focused equally on the interrogator and suspect. This robust effect was present for videotaped conversations lasting 5 minutes, 30-minute interrogations, and extensive trial simulations lasting 3–5 hours. The importance of overreliance on heuristic processing is further highlighted in models that focus on the sentencer's attitudes.

The possible influence of heuristic processing was suggested as a source of bias in a study of mock-jury responses to expert testimony on the risk of future dangerousness of an offender in a simulated capital sentencing hearing (Krauss & Sales, 2001). Mock jurors viewed videotaped examinations of the experts, simulated by actual lawyers and clinical psychologists. The expert testimony on the future dangerousness of the offender was presented in one of two ways, using either clinical or actuarial methods of risk assessment. Mock jurors' ratings of dangerousness were measured after reading the trial facts, after the testimony of the expert witness, and after the cross-examination or testimony by an opposing expert. Irrespective of the presence of cross-examination or competing expert testimony, the clinical testimony was more persuasive and influential. Nonetheless, actuarial methods using statistical techniques produced increased ratings of dangerousness. One explanation for this finding was that jurors may have perceived the actuarial expert's testimony as more involved and technical, leading them to process the information more peripherally compared to the testimony of the clinical expert (Krauss & Sales, 2001). Additional sources of bias may have involved preexisting beliefs about the validity of the actuarial instruments and the accuracy of clinical judgments, with a preference for clinical over statistical information.

Since the 1970s, psychologists have focused an ever-increasing amount of attention on conducting research related to jury functioning (Devine, Clayton, Dunford, Seying, & Pryce, 2001; Guthrie, Rachlinski, & Wistrich, 2001), with considerably fewer studies of judges, magistrates, parole officers, and others involved in different phases and aspects of the sentencing process (Guthrie et al., 2001; Hebenton & Pease, 1995). When researchers have included judges as participants, their findings have generally confirmed that most judges are susceptible to the same judgmental errors and biases as jurors. For example, a study of 167 federal magistrates and judges confirmed their susceptibility to five common cognitive illusions: anchoring, framing, the hindsight bias, the representativeness heuristic, and egocentric biases (Guthrie et al., 2001). Additionally, the evidence gathered demonstrated that judges rely on the same decision-making processes as laypersons—a reliance that makes them vulnerable to systematic mental shortcuts (Guthrie et al., 2001). Furthermore, the few available empirical comparisons of judges and juries do not confirm the superiority of judges in resisting bias, and the verbal or nonverbal communication of bias by judges affects jury decision making (Costanzo, 2004). The importance of overreliance on heuristic processing is further highlighted in models that focus on the sentencer's attitudes.

MODELS OF JUDICIAL DECISION MAKING

The various psychological theories and approaches to punishment and alternative sentencing options reviewed do not account for the processes used in reaching sentencing decisions. As the previous sections demonstrated, the characteristics and biases of the participants within the court setting impact judicial decisions. The systematic study of these variables is accounted for within models of judicial sentencing.

A desirable goal in judicial decision making is impartiality, detachment from emotion and bias, and a logical analysis of the case facts (Costanzo, 2004). However, the legal system does not expect judges to function in a mechanistic, inhuman fashion in dispensing justice, as would a robot or a computer. Judges and magistrates are expected to take into account the appropriate legal sentencing criteria, the specifics of a particular case, and to draw on their experience and wisdom in rendering an appropriate decision. Currently, there is no widely accepted model of judicial information processing and decision making. Several models by which to elucidate judicial decision making have been proposed, drawing from research on decision-making processes in other domains of cognitive and social psychology. These include decision style, attitudinal, and various heuristic models (i.e., fast and frugal, emotion as information, and harm-severity-blame justification).

The attitudinal model posits that judges interpret trial facts in reference to their own ideological viewpoints and value systems. In addition, they rely on personal intuition and then "work backward" to check that the decision is not logically flawed (Wrightsman, 1999, p. 48). This model emphatically rejects the assumption that judges are emotionally detached and consider only the application of the law to the case at hand. Instead, it proposes that each judge's ideological attitudes and personal intuition most likely contain bias and prejudice, which will influence the decision. Along similar lines, the social–cognitive process model takes into account individual differences in personality variables, especially "right-wing" authoritarianism and value priorities of the decision maker. This model has been applied to examine whether sentences are based on retributive justice motives by examining four elements: perceived responsibility, perceived seriousness or negative valence, deservingness, and affective and cognitive reactions (Feather, 1996). Researchers presented participants with hypothetical scenarios involving offenses such as domestic violence, plagiarism, shoplifting, and resisting police. Results indicated that perceived responsibility for an offense influenced its perceived seriousness (or negative valence) and together, responsibility and seriousness influenced the degree to which the offender was seen to deserve the penalty imposed (Feather, 1996).

Another promising model of judicial reasoning draws from attribution theory on the grounds that judicial analysis of the offender's behavior and the appropriate punishment, guided by sentencing guidelines (Ainsworth, 2000), is ultimately based upon each judge's unique attributions. Attribution theory accounts for ways in which individuals appraise the causes of behavior (Weiner, 1980). In their decisions judges attempt to determine the distinction between internal causes (i.e., character, motives) and external causes (i.e., situational and/or social pressures) of behavior (Kelly, 1967). They further assess the level of controllability (e.g., whether the crime was under the offender's control or not) and stability (e.g., whether the crime was accidental or intentional), which are the essential components of this decision-making model (Costanzo, 2004; Kapardis, 2003). The basic premise is that attributions are made about the accused, and the combination of his or her traits and motives, as well as legal considerations, are factored into the sentencing decision (Costanzo, 2004).

When the criminal act is attributed to internal, controllable, stable causes, the accused is viewed as more responsible and is treated in a less neutral fashion. For example, a judge may be strict with evidentiary submissions and award a harsher punishment. Conversely, the theory posits that criminal acts attributed to external, less controllable, and unstable causes should evoke more empathy and consequently result in more leeway in allowing mitigating testimony, a wider scope within cross-examination, and possibly in acquittal or a lighter sentence (Costanzo, 2004; Kapardis, 2003; Weiner, Graham, & Reyna, 1997).

A more recent model of judicial decision making that extends attribution theory and encompasses identity assessment, behavior, attributions, and emotions draws on affect-control theory (Heise, 1987; Tsoudis & Smith-Lovin, 1998). This model suggests that legal decision making is influenced not only by an attributional analysis of the causes of the criminal act, but by the sentencer's affective reaction to the appraisal of the identity assessment (e.g., remorsefulness of the accused; Tsoudis, 2000). Following this logic, if a convicted criminal displays appropriate emotional (i.e., contriteness) behavior, judicial negative affect should be lessened. An appropriate emotional response coupled with the knowledge, for example, that it is a first-time offense for the accused should, in turn, disconfirm the criminal's negative identity and increase positive affect, leading to an increase in judicial sympathy (Heise, 1987; Vidmar, 2001). This model suggests emotion as a core component in decisions, and has been applied to examine the social–psychological dynamics of retribution. If an offense is seen as blameworthy and the violation threatens or actually harms values related to the judge's personal self, status, or internalized group, anger is aroused and the judge's cognitions and emotions foster reactions against the violator. This reaction can be viewed as similar to the terror management response. During or following punishment, the anger dissipates, and rule or norm violation is perceived to be vindicated.

The effects of altering evidentiary standards, shaping perceptions, or guiding jurors "to search selectively for information that supports a desired blame attribution" are considered to reflect blame-validation processing (Alicke, 2000, p. 568). In the model of this processing style, particularly severe emotional harm suffered by the victim or the murder victim's family members is seen as promoting an exaggerated view of the offender's culpability, because decision makers use the cue of severe harm to systematically increase the relevance of mundane aspects of the crime (Nadler & Rose, 2003). Thus, the emotional arousal induced by the level of harm to the victim may lead to a number of systematic biases toward the offender, in which "human agency attributions are favored over explanations involving mitigating circumstances" (Alicke, 2000, p. 568). Additionally, it seems likely that considerations of aggravating circumstances would be enhanced even when the relevant causal factors were accidental.

Nonetheless, a closer inspection of the role of emotion in decision making reveals conflicting findings applicable to sentencing. Inducing a negative mood state, for instance, can increase prejudice, because an angry mood can activate the use of stereotypes in judgment tasks (Forgas & Fiedler, 1996). By comparison, negative emotions, such as sadness, are less likely to invoke stereotypes (Bodenhausen, Gabriel, & Lineberger, 2000) and may induce more systematic information processing (Clore, Schwartz, & Conway, 1993).

CONCLUSIONS

Despite the significant reliance on plea bargaining, there has been a paucity of research on participants in plea-bargaining and post-sentencing decisions (e.g., conditionally released offenders, day parole, full parole, and statutory releases). Identifying strategies to manage the successful reintegration of offenders into society should be a research priority. Rather than concentrating on the causes and consequences of the maladaptive behavior of criminals, researchers should focus attention on adaptive prosocial behaviors by examining issues such as sentencing options that permit offenders to continue their employment, education, and home life. Additional research is needed on the value of various nontraditional sentencing methods to the offender, the victim, and the community.

Empirical studies have established that punishments based on traditional conceptualizations of retribution, deterrence, and incapacitation have not effectively decreased recidivism or enhanced the public's satisfaction with the legal system. In spite of the apparent rise in the popularity of these traditional forms of punishment (i.e., longer periods of incarceration), contemporary theories focusing on situational or contextually determined factors contributing to crime, rather than merely on individual dispositions, have been implemented with apparent success. Given the lower recidivism rates and increased victim satisfaction with the outcome of the legal process in response to some rehabilitation and restorative justice programs, further research and evaluation of these programs are warranted. Future studies can take advantage of improved research designs (i.e., longer postprogram periods, randomized samples) and more stringent measures (i.e., normative rather than qualitative and idiographic).

In many respects, the opportunities for psychologists to have an impact on sentencing recommendations and policy formulation in the determination of the future of sentencing have never been stronger. For instance, a study of juvenile court dispositions demonstrated that judges were likely to incorporate recommendations derived from extensive psychological evaluations (Hecker & Steinberg, 2002). Specifically, recommendations drawn from reports containing the juvenile's history of drug and alcohol usage and the results of the interview with the juvenile were likely to influence dispositions. Future research should evaluate how juvenile and other court judges use information derived from psychological evaluations.

Additionally, contributions can be made both in terms of assessing and fine-tuning existing systems. Analyses of sentencing guidelines designed to simplify the sentencing process in Pennsylvania revealed how "judges, prosecutors, and defense attorneys use the formal decision-making criteria set by the guidelines in an interpretative, situationally contingent manner to aid them in coping with uncertainty in case processing and sentencing, and furthering their own and their sponsoring agencies' organizational and political interests" (Ulmer & Kramer, 1998, p. 263).

This study also demonstrated that the guidelines afforded a systematic method through which pleas of guilty were rewarded, whereas offenders who went to trial and lost were punished. In addition to revealing flaws in the systems and methods currently being utilized, psychological research may support the proposition and evaluation of innovative sentencing systems, such as rehabilitation, restorative justice programs, and decision aids. For instance, as shown by the drug-court studies, sentences aimed at reducing recidivism would benefit from efforts that directly address situational causes of crime, rather than modifying the terms of punishment.

Although we have reviewed some of the contributions from psychology to the law, we must also be cognizant of the nature of this relationship. As we uncover the underlying psychological and social mechanisms that may influence the decision-making processes of those involved in legal procedures, we must keep in mind the relevance and applicability of the findings. That is, it is not enough for research to demonstrate that judges, correctional staff, and jury-eligible individuals are not immune to unreliability, the use of heuristics, and biases while making decisions on legal matters. There remains the need to examine and assess potential remedies to such factors to substantiate the merit of adopting psychological methods and procedures in the legal system.

ACKNOWLEDGMENTS

We gratefully acknowledge the invaluable contribution of Misia R. Temler, a student in the University of New South Wales M. Psychol. (Forensic) program, for the many dedicated hours she spent researching source materials for this chapter, drafting sections on the theories of punishment, and checking references. Preparation of parts of this chapter was facilitated by Grant No. A00104516 from the Australian Research Council to Neil Brewer, Kipling D. Williams, and Lynne ForsterLee.

REFERENCES

Ainsworth, P. B. (2000). *Psychology and crime: Myths and reality.* Harlow: Longman.

Alberta Summit on Justice. (1999). Submission to the Law Society of Alberta to the Alberta Summit on Justice: Legal Community. Retrieved May 21, 2004, from *http:// www.justice.gov.ab.ca/publications/justicesummit/consult/crep5.htm.*

Albonetti, C. A. (1998). Direct and indirect effects of case complexity, guilty pleas and offender characteristics on sentencing for offenders convicted of a white-collar offense prior to sentencing guidelines. *Journal of Quantitative Criminology, 14,* 353–377.

Alicke, M. D. (2000). Culpable control and the psychology of blame. *Psychological Bulletin, 126,* 556–574.

Alicke, M. D., & Davis, T. L. (1989). The role of *a posteriori* victim information in judgments of blame and sanction. *Journal of Experimental Social Psychology, 25,* 362–377.

Allan, A., & Allan, M. M. (2000). The South African Truth and Reconciliation Commission as a therapeutic tool. *Behavioral Sciences and the Law, 18,* 459–477.

Alschuler, A. W. (2003). Straining at gnats and swallowing camels: The selective morality of Professor Bibas. *Cornell Law Review, 88,* 1412–1424.

Applegate, B., Reuter, D., McCarthy, B., & Santana, S. (1999). *Evaluation of the Orange County juvenile substance abuse treatment court program.* Paper presented at the University of Central Florida, Orlando, FL.

Arias, I., Dankwort, J., Douglas, U., Dutton, M., & Stein, K. (2002). Violence against women: The state of batterer prevention programs. *Journal of Law, Medicine, and Ethics, 30,* 157–169.

Associated Press. (1984, November 23). Judicial leniency toward women found. *Kansas City Times,* p. A15.

Austin, W., & Utne, M. K. (1977). Sentencing discretion and justice in judicial decision-making. In B. D. Sales (Ed.), *Psychology in the legal process* (pp. 163–196). New York: Spectrum.

Bandes, S. (1996). Empathy, narrative, and victim impact statements. *University of Chicago Law Review, 63,* 361.

Bandura, A. (1986). *Social foundations of thought and action: A social cognitive theory.* Englewood Cliffs, NJ: Prentice-Hall.

Bartol, C. R., & Bartol, A. M. (2004). *Psychology and law: Theory, research and application.* Belmont, CA: Wadsworth/Thomson Learning.

Belenko, S., & Dembo, R. (2003). Treating adolescent substance abuse problems in juvenile drug court. *International Journal of Law and Psychiatry, 26,* 87–110.

Bibas, S. (2003). Bringing moral values into a flawed plea-bargaining system. *Cornell Law Review, 88,* 1425–1432.

Birgden, A., & Ward, T. (2003). Pragmatic psychology through a therapeutic jurisprudence lens: Psycholegal soft spots in the criminal justice system. *Psychology, Public Policy, and Law, 9,* 334–360.

Blumenthal, J. A. (2001). The admissibility of victim impact statements at capital sentencing: Traditional and non-traditional perspectives. *Drake Law Review, 50,* 67–92.

Bodenhausen, G. V., Gabriel, S., & Lineberger, M. (2000). Sadness and susceptibility to judgmental bias: The case of anchoring. *Psychological Science, 11,* 320–323.

Bohm, R. M. (1999). *Deathquest: An introduction to the theory and practice of capital punishment in the United States.* Cincinnati, OH: Anderson.

Bowers, W. J., & Pierce, G. (1980). Deterrence or brutalization: What is the effect of executions? *Crime and Delinquency, 26,* 453–484.

Braithwaite, J. (2000). Shame and criminal justice. *Canadian Journal of Criminology, 42,* 281–299.

Bright, D. A., & Goodman-Delahunty, J. (2004). Heinous evidence and mock jury decisions. *Psychiatry, Psychology, and Law, 11,* 159–166.

Brown, M., & Pratt, J. (2000). *Dangerous offenders: Punishment and social order.* New York: Routledge.

Brown, P. (2003). *Pollution still pays as firms shrug off fines.* Retrieved October 23, 2003, from *http://www.guardian.co.uk/waste/story/ 0,12188,1009470,00.html.*

California Department of Corrections. (2004). *Offender information reports.* Retrieved May 21, 2004, from *http://www.cdc.state.ca.us/OffenderInfoServices/Reports/ OffenderInformation.asp.*

Carlsmith, K. M., Darley, J. M., & Robinson, P. H. (2002). Why do we punish? Deterrence and just deserts as motives for punishment. *Journal of Personality and Social Psychology, 83,* 284–299.

Carroll, J. S., Perkowitz, W. T., Lurigio, A. J., & Weaver, F. M. (1987). Sentencing goals, causal attributions, ideology, and personality. *Journal of Personality and Social Psychology, 52,* 107–118.

Caulkins, J. P. (2001). How large should the strike zone be in "three strikes and you're out" sentencing laws? *Journal of Quantitative Criminology, 17,* 227–246.

Chan, J. (1995). *The limits of incapacitation as crime control strategy.* Retrieved September 6, 2003, from *http://www.lawlink.nsw.gov.au/bocsar1. nsf/pages/cjb25text.*

Clark, T. W. (2003). Against retribution. *Human Nature Review, 3,* 466–479.

Clore, G. L., Schwartz, N., & Conway, M. (1993). Affective causes and consequences of social information processing. In R. S. Wyer & T. K. Srull (Eds.), *Handbook of social cognition,* (2nd ed., pp. 323–417). Hillsdale, NJ: Erlbaum.

Cochran, J. K., Chamlin, M. B., & Seth, M. (1994). Deterrence or brutalization? An impact assessment of Oklahoma's return to capital punishment. *Criminology, 32,* 107–133.

Coontz, P. (2000). Gender and judicial decisions: Do female judges decide cases differently than male judges? *Gender Issues, 18,* 59–73.

Cooper, C. S., & Bartlett, S. R. (1996, March). *Drug courts: Participant perspectives.* SJI National Symposium on the Implementation and Operation of Drug Courts, Portland, OR.

Costanzo, M. (1997). *Just revenge: Costs and consequences of the death penalty.* New York: St. Martin's.

Costanzo, M. (2004). *Psychology applied to law.* Belmont, CA: Wadsworth.

Cullen, F. T., & Applegate, B. (1998). *Offender rehabilitation: Effective correctional intervention.* Darmouth, UK: Ashgate.

Cunneen, C. (2001). *The impact of crime prevention on aboriginal communities.* Retrieved October 13, 2003, from *http://www.lawlink.nsw.gov.au/ajac.nsf/pages/reports.*

Daly, K. (2003). Mind the gap: Restorative justice in theory and practice. In A. V. Hirsch, J. Roberts, A. E. Bottoms, K. Roach, & M. Schiff (Eds.), *Restorative justice and criminal justice: Competing or reconcilable paradigms?* (pp. 219–236). Oxford, UK: Hart Publishing.

Devine, D. J., Clayton, L. D., Dunford, B. B., Seying, R., & Pryce, J. (2001). Jury decision-making: 45 years of empirical research on deliberating groups. *Psychology, Public Policy, and Law, 7*, 622–727.

Dezhbakhsh, H., Rubin, P. H., & Shepherd, J. M. (2002). Does capital punishment have a deterrent effect? New evidence from post-moratorium panel data (Emory University Economics Working Paper No. 01-01). Retrieved March 23, 2004, from *http:// ssrn.com/abstract=259538.*

Dhami, M. K., & Ayton, P. (2001). Bailing and jailing the fast and frugal way. *Journal of Behavioral Decision Making, 14*, 141–168.

Doob, A. N., & Beaulieu, L. A. (1992). Variation in the exercise of judicial discretion with young offenders. *Canadian Journal of Criminology, 34*, 35–50.

Douglas, K. S., Lyon, D. R., & Ogloff, J. R. P. (1997). The impact of graphic photographic evidence on mock juror decisions in a murder trial: Probative or prejudicial. *Law and Human Behavior, 21*, 485–501.

Drug Strategies. (1998). *Keeping score: Women and drugs: Looking at the federal drug control budget.* Retrieved May 6, 2004, from *http://www.drugstrategies.org/.*

Ebbesen, E. B., & Konečni, V. J. (1981). The process of sentencing adult felons: A causal analysis of judicial decision. In B. D. Sales (Ed.), *The trial process* (pp. 413–458). New York: Plenum Press.

Eleventh Judicial Circuit of Florida. (n.d.). *Miami–Dade County drug court.* Retrieved March 29, 2004, from *http://www.jud11.flcourts.org/programs_and_services/ drug_court.htm.*

Erez, E. (1991). Victim impact statements. *Trends and Issues in Crime and Criminal Justice, 33*, 1–4.

Erez, E., & Rogers, L. (1999). Victim impact sentencing outcomes and processes: The perspectives of legal professionals. *The British Journal of Criminology, 39*, 216–239.

Feather, N. T. (1996). Reactions to penalties for an offense in relation to authoritarianism, values, perceived responsibility, perceived seriousness, and deservingness. *Journal of Personality and Social Psychology, 71*, 571–587.

Feldman, P. (1993). *The psychology of crime.* New York: Cambridge University Press.

Fercello, C., & Umbreit, M. S. (1998). *Client evaluation of family group conferencing in 12 sites in 1st Judicial District of Minnesota.* St Paul, MN: University of Minnesota, Center for Restorative Justice and Mediation.

Fisse, B. (1990). Sentencing options against corporations. *Criminal Law Forum, 1*, 211–258.

Flaherty, B., & Jousif, J. (2002, September). *MERIT-conference paper: Magistrate's early referral into treatment.* Paper presented at the Australian Institute of Criminology National Crime Prevention Conference, Sydney, New South Wales, Australia.

Florian, V., Mikulincer, M., & Hirschberger, G. (2001). An existentialist view on mortality salience effects: Personal hardiness, death-thought accessibility, and cultural worldview defenses. *British Journal of Social Psychology, 40*, 437–453.

Forgas, J. P., & Fiedler, K. (1996). Us and them: Mood effects on intergroup discrimination. *Journal of Personality and Social Psychology, 70*, 28–40.

ForsterLee, L., Fox, G. B., ForsterLee, R., & Ho, R. (2004). The effects of a victim impact statement and gender on juror information processing in a criminal trial: Does the punishment fit the crime? *Australian Psychologist, 39,* 57–67.

Freeman, K. (2003, March). *Evaluating Australia's first drug court: Research and challenges.* Paper presented at the conference on Evaluation in Crime and Justice: Trends and Methods, Canberra, Australia.

Freiberg, A. (2003). *Therapeutic jurisprudence in Australia: Paradigm shift or pragmatic incrementalism?* Paper presented at the 28th International Congress on Law and Mental Health Congress, Sydney, New South Wales, Australia.

Gendreau, P., Goggin, C., & Little, T. (n.d.). *Predicting adult offender recidivism: What works! 1996-07.* Retrieved May 21, 2004, from *http://www.psepc-sppcc.gc.ca/publications/corrections/pdf/199607_e.pdf.*

Gigerenzer, G. (2004). Fast and frugal heuristics: The tools of bounded rationality. In D. Koehler & N. Harvey (Eds.), *Blackwell handbook of judgment and decision making.* Oxford, UK: Blackwell.

Graham, S., Weiner, B., & Zucker, G. S. (1997). An attributional analysis of punishment goals and public reaction to O. J. Simpson. *Personality and Social Psychological Bulletin, 23,* 331–346.

Greenberg, J., Schimel, J., Martens, A., Solomon, S., & Pyszczynski, T. (2001). Sympathy for the devil: Evidence that reminding whites of their mortality promotes more favorable reactions to white racists. *Motivation and Emotion, 25,* 113–133.

Greene, E. (1999). The many guises of victim impact evidence and effects on juror's judgments. *Psychology, Crime, and Law, 5,* 331–348.

Greenwood, P. W., Rydell, C. P., Abrahamse, A. F., Caulkins, J. P., Chiesa, J., & Model, K. E. (1994). *Three strikes and you're out: Estimated benefits and costs of California's new mandatory sentencing law.* Santa Monica, CA: Rand.

Guthrie, C., Rachlinski, J. J., & Wistrich, A. J. (2001). Inside the judicial mind. *Cornell Law Review, 86,* 777–830.

Hamilton, V. L., & Rotkin, L. (1979). The capital punishment debate: Public perception of crime and punishment. *Journal of Applied Psychology, 9,* 350–376.

Hamilton, V. L., & Sanders, J. (1988). Punishment and the individual in the United States and Japan. *Law and Society Review, 28,* 301–328.

Haney, C. (1997). Coming crisis in the Eighth Amendment law. *Psychology, Public Policy, and Law, 3,* 499–588.

Haney, C. (2002). Making law modern: Toward a contextual model of justice. *Psychology, Public Policy, and Law, 8,* 3–63.

Hanson, K., R., & Thornton, D. (2000). Improving risk assessments for sex offenders: A comparison of three actuarial scales. *Law and Human Behavior, 24,* 119–136.

Harmon-Jones, E., Simon, L., Greenberg, J., Pyszczynski, T., Solomon, S., & McGregor, H. (1997). Terror management theory and self-esteem: Evidence that increased self-esteem reduced mortality salience effects. *Journal of Personality and Social Psychology, 72,* 24–36.

Hayes, H., & Daly, K. (2003). Youth justice conferencing and reoffending. *Justice Quarterly, 20,* 725–764.

Hebenton, B., & Pease, K. (1995). Weighing the pound of flesh: The psychology of punishment. In R. Bull & D. Carson (Eds.), *Handbook of psychology in legal contexts* (pp. 375–391). New York: Wiley.

Hecker, T., & Steinberg, L. (2002). Psychological evaluation at juvenile court disposition. *Professional Psychology: Research and Practice, 33,* 300–306.

Heilbrun, K., & Griffin, P. (1999). Forensic treatment: A review of programs and research. In R. Roesch, S. D. Hart, & J. R. P. Ogloff (Eds.), *Psychology and law: The state of the discipline* (pp. 242–278). New York: Kluwer/Plenum.

Heise, D. R. (1987). Affect control theory: Concepts and model. *Journal of Mathematical Sociology, 13*, 1–33.

Henley, M., Davis, R., & Smith, B. (1994). The reactions of prosecutors and judges to victim impact statements. *International Review of Victimology, 3*, 83–93.

Hills, A., & Thomson, D. (1999). Should victim impact influence sentences? Understanding the community's justice reasoning. *Behavioral Sciences and the Law, 17*, 661–671.

Ho, R., ForsterLee, L., ForsterLee, R., & Crofts, N. (2002). Justice versus vengeance: Motives underlying punitive judgments. *Personality and Individual Differences, 33*, 365–377.

Hogarth, J. (1971). *Sentencing as a human process.* Toronto: Toronto University Press.

Homel, R. (1988). *Policing and punishing the drinking driver: A study of general and specific deterrence.* New York: Springer-Verlag.

Homel, R., McKay, P., & Henstridge, J. (1995). The impact on accidents of random breath testing in New South Wales: 1982–1992. In C. Kloeden & A. McLean (Eds.) *Alcohol, drugs, and traffic safety* (Vol. 2, pp. 849–855). Adelaide, Australia: NHMRC Road Accident Research Unit.

Hoppin, J. (2003, May 28). Judge bucks third-strike rules. *The Recorder: Cal Law California's Legal News Source.* Retrieved March 24, 2003, from *http://www.law.com/ jsp/pubarticleCA.jsp?id=1052440794273.*

Huesmann, L. R., Moise-Titus, J., Podolski, C. L., & Eron, L. D. (2003). Longitudinal relations between children's exposure to TV violence and their aggressive and violent behavior in young adulthood: 1977–1992. *Developmental Psychology, 39*, 201–221.

Indermaur, D. (1996). Offender psychology and sentencing. *Australian Psychologist, 31*, 15–19.

Jeffery, C. R. (1990). *Criminology: An interdisciplinary approach.* Englewood Cliffs, NJ: Prentice Hall.

Jerin, R. A., & Moriarty, L. J. (1998). *Victims of crime.* Chicago: Nelson Hall.

Joh, E. E. (2000). Narrating pain: The problem with victim impact statements. *Southern California Interdisciplinary Law Journal, 10*, 17–37.

Kapardis, A. (2003). *Psychology and law: A critical introduction* (2nd ed.). New York: Cambridge University Press.

Kassin, S., & Garfield, D. (1991). Blood and guts: General and trial specific effects of videotaped crime scenes on mock jurors. *Journal of Applied Social Psychology, 21*, 1459–1472.

Kelly, H. H. (1967). Attribution theory in social psychology. In D. Levine (Ed.), *Nebraska symposium on motivation* (Vol 15., pp. 192–238). Lincoln, NE: University of Nebraska Press.

Kemshall, H. (2002). *Risk assessment and management of serious violent and sexual offenders: A review of current issues.* Edinburgh: Scottish Executive.

King, R. S., & Mauer, M. (2001). Aging behind bars: "Three Strikes" seven years later. *The Sentencing Project.* Retrieved March 31, 2004, from *http://www.sentencingproject. org/pubs_06.cfm.*

Krauss, D. A., & Sales, B. D. (2001). The effects of clinical and scientific expert testimony on juror decision making in capital sentencing. *Psychology, Public Policy, and Law, 7*, 267–310.

Kurlychek, M., Torbet, P., & Bozynski, M. (1999). Focus on accountability: Best practices for juvenile court and probation. In S. Bilchik (Ed.), *Juvenile accountability incentive block grants program bulletin* (MCJ 177611, pp. 1–11). Washington, DC: U.S. Department of Justice.

Lassiter, G. D. (2002). Illusory causation in the courtroom. *Current Directions in Psychological Research, 11*, 204–208.

Latimer, J., Dowden, C., & Muise, D. (2001). *The effectiveness of restorative practices: A meta-analysis.* Canada: Research and Statistics Division Methodological Series, Department of Justice, Canada.

Law Reform Commission of Western Australia. (1999). Review of the criminal and justice system: Final report. Retrieved March 23, 2004, from *http://www.lrc.justice.wa.gov.au/RevCCJS-p92/finalreport/freportindex.htm*.

Lawrence, J. A. (1988). Expertise in judicial decision making. In M. T. H. Chi, R. Glaser, & M. Farr (Eds.), *Informal reasoning and education* (pp. 59–82). Hillsdale, NJ: Erlbaum.

Laws, D. R. (1996). Relapse prevention or harm reduction. *Sexual Abuse, 8*, 243–247.

Lieberman, J. D., Arndt, J., Personius, J., & Cook, A. (2001). Vicarious annihilation: The effect of mortality salience on perceptions of hate crimes. *Law and Human Behavior, 25*, 547–566.

Lipton, D. S., Pearson, F., Cleland, C., & Yee, D. (2002). The effects of cognitive-behavioural methods on recidivism: CDATE analyses. In J. McGuire (Ed.), *Offender rehabilitation and treatment: Effective programmes and policies to reduce re-offending* (pp. 79–112). Chichester, UK: Wiley.

Lockyer v. Andrade, 538 U.S. (2003).

Logan, W. (1999). Through the past darkly: A survey of the uses and abuses of victim impact evidence in capital trials. *Arizona Law Review, 41*, 143–192.

Long, G. F. (1996). Denver drug court: New approaches to old problems. *Colorado Lawyer, 25*, 29.

Luke, G., & Lind, B. (2002). Reducing juvenile crime: Conferencing versus court. *Crime and Justice Bulletin: Contemporary Issues in Crime and Justice, 69*. New South Wales: Bureau of Crime Statistics and Research. Retrieved September 15, 2003, from *http://www.lawlink.nsw.gov.au/bocsar1.nsf/pages/cjb69text*.

MacKenzie, D. L. (2000). Evidence-based corrections: Identifying what works. *Crime and Delinquency, 46*, 457–471.

Makkai, T., & Braithwaite, J. (1994). The dialectics of corporate deterrence. *Journal of Research in Crime and Delinquency, 31*, 347–373.

Maltz, M. D. (1996). From Poisson to the present: Applying operations research to problems of crime and justice. *Journal of Quantitative Criminology, 12*, 3–61.

Marlatt, G. A. (1998). *Harm reduction: Pragmatic strategies for managing high-risk behaviors.* New York: Guilford Press.

Martinson, R. (1974). What works? Questions and answers about prison reform. *The Public Interest, 35*, 22–54.

Martinson, R. (1979). New findings, new views: A note of caution regarding sentencing reform. *Hofstra Law Review, 7*, 243–258.

Maxwell, G., & Morris, A. (2001). Restorative justice and reoffending. In H. Strang & J. Braithwaite (Eds.), *Restorative justice: Philosophy and practice* (pp. 93–103). Burlington, VT: Ashgate.

McFatter, R. M. (1978). Sentencing strategies and justice: Effects of punishment philosophy on sentencing decisions. *Journal of Personality and Social Psychology, 36,* 1490–1500.

McGuire, J. (2003). Maintaining change: Converging legal and psychological initiatives in a therapeutic jurisprudence framework. *Western Criminology Review, 4,* 108–123.

Melton, A. P. (1995). Indigenous justice systems and tribal society. *Judicature, 79,* 126–133.

Ministry of Justice. (2002). *Reforming the criminal justice system: Sentencing Act 2002 Parole Act 2002.* Retrieved May 21, 2004, from *www.justice.govt.nz/pubs/other/ pamphlets/ 2002/sentence-parole-2002/qa.html.*

Mirsky, C. L., & Kahn, G. (1997). No bargain. *The American Prospect, 32,* 56–45.

Mocan, H. N., & Gittings, R. K. (2003). Getting off death row: Commuted sentences and the deterrent effect of capital punishment. *Journal of Law and Economics, 46,* 453–478.

Mulhausen, D. B. (2004). *The determination of sentencing in Pennsylvania: Do the characteristics of judges matter?* Washington, DC: The Heritage Foundation.

Myers, B., & Greene, E. (2004). The prejudicial nature of victim impact statements: Implications for capital sentencing policy. *Psychology, Public Policy, and Law, 10,* 492–515.

Myers, R., & Arbuthnot, J. (1999). The effects of victim impact evidence on verdicts and sentencing judgments of mock jurors. *Journal of Offender Rehabilitation, 29,* 95–112.

Nadler, J., & Rose, M. R. (2003). Victim impact testimony and the psychology of punishment. *Cornell Law Review, 88,* 419–438.

New South Wales Law Reform Commission. (2000). *Report 96 (2000) sentencing: Aboriginal offenders.* Retrieved March 23, 2003, from *http://www.cjc.nsw.gov.au/ lrc.nsf/pages/R96CHP4.*

News in Review. (2001). *The Aboriginal dilemma: Conditional sentencing: Effective or not?* Retrieved February 18, 2004, *from http://www.cbc.ca/newsinreview/may2000/ sentence/aborig.html.*

North Carolina v. Alford, 400 U.S. 25 (1970).

O'Donnell, J., & Willing, R. (March 12, 2003). *Prison time gets harder for white-collar crooks.* Retrieved March 23, 2003, from *http://www.cjcj.org/press/white_collar. html.*

Palys, T., & Divorski, S. (1986). Explaining sentence disparity. *Canadian Journal of Criminology, 28,* 347–362.

Payne v. Tennessee, 501 U.S. 808 (1991).

Petrucci, C. J. (2002). Respect as a component in the judge–defendant interaction in a specialized domestic violence court that utilizes therapeutic jurisprudence. *Criminal Law Bulletin, 38,* 263–295.

Poulson, B. (2003). A third voice: A review of empirical research on psychological outcomes of restorative justice. *Utah Law Review, 1,* 167–203.

Presser, L., & van Voorhis, P. (2002). Values and evaluation: Assessing processes and outcomes of restorative justice programs. *Crime and Delinquency, 48,* 162–188.

Price, M. (1997). Can mediation produce justice? A restorative justice discussion for mediators. *Signal, 1,* 1–6.

Regina v. Billam, 1WLR 349 (1986).

Regina v. Buttigieg, Drug Court of New South Wales (2002).

Regina v. Penisini, NSWSC 892 (2003).

Riger, S., Foster-Fishman, P., Nelson-Kuna, J., & Curran, B. (1995). Gender bias in court-room dynamics. *Law and Human Behavior, 19,* 465–480.

Roberts, J. V. (1995). New data on sentencing trends in provincial courts. *Criminal Reports, 34,* 181–196.

Roberts, J. V. (1999). Sentencing trends and sentencing disparity. In J. V. Roberts & D. Cole (Eds.), *Making sense of sentencing* (pp. 139–159). Toronto: University of Toronto Press.

Roberts, J. V., & Laprairie, C. (1997). Sentencing circles: Some unanswered questions. *Criminal Law Quarterly, 39,* 69.

Robertson, J., & Mackenzie, G. (1998). *Queensland sentencing manual.* Sydney, Australia: Law Book Company.

Robinson, P. H., & Darley, J. M. (1995). *Justice, liability, and blame: Community views of the criminal law.* Boulder, CO: Westview Press.

Rosenblatt, A., Greenberg, J., Solomon, S., Pyzczynski, T., & Lyon, D. (1989). Evidence for terror management theory, I: The effects of mortality salience on reactions to those who violate or uphold cultural values. *Journal of Personality and Social Psychology, 57,* 681–690.

Ruback, B., & Wroblewski, J. (2001). The federal sentencing guidelines: Psychological and policy reasons for simplification. *Psychology, Public Policy, and Law, 7,* 739–775.

Rucks v. Florida, 692 So.2d 976 (1997).

Sabol, W. J., Rosich, K., Kane, K. M., Kirk, D. P., & Dubin, G. (2002, April). *The influences of truth-in-sentencing reforms on changes in states' sentencing practices and prison populations.* Retrieved March 29, 2004, from the Urban Institute website: *http://www.urban.org/urlprint.cfm?ID=7810.*

Sallman, P., & Willis, J. (1984). *Criminal justice in Australia.* Melbourne, Australia: Oxford University Press.

Samuels, G. (2002). *Review of the New South Wales Director of Public Prosecutions' policy and guidelines for charge bargaining and tendering of agreed facts.* Retrieved August 7, 2004, from *www.lawlink.nsw.gov.au/report/lpd_reports.nsf/files/Report%201.PDF/$FILE/Report%201.PDF.*

Scantleton, J. J. L., Boulton, B., & Didcott, P. (2002, May). *MERIT: A cooperative approach addressing drug addiction and recidivism.* Paper presented at the 2nd Australasian Conference on Drugs Strategy, Perth, Western Australia.

Senjo, S., & Leip, L. A. (2001). Testing therapeutic jurisprudence theory: An empirical assessment of drug court process. *Western Criminology Review, 3*(1). Retrieved October 3, 2003, from *http://wcr.sonoma.edu/v3n1/senjo.html.*

Sentencing Project, The. (2003). *U.S. prison populations: Trends and implications.* Retrieved March 31, 2004, from *http://www.sentencingproject.org/pubs_06.cfm.*

Shinnar, R., & Shinnar, S. (1975). The effect of the criminal justice system on the control of crime: A quantitative approach. *Law and Society Review, 9,* 581–612.

Sivasubramaniam, D., & Goodman-Delahunty, J. (2003, December). *Perceptions of justice among minority cultures: Implications for youth justice conferencing.* Paper presented at Conference of the Australian Institute of Criminology and the Department of Juvenile Justice, New South Wales, "Juvenile Justice: From the Lessons of the Past to a Road Map for the Future," Sydney, Australia: Retrieved August 28, 2004, from *http://www.aic.gov.au/conferences/2003-juvenile/sivasubramaniam.html.*

Sjostedt, G., & Grann, M. (2002). Risk assessment: What is being predicted by actuarial prediction instruments? *International Journal of Forensic Mental Health*, *1*, 179–183.

Skinner, B. F. (1971). *Beyond freedom and dignity*. New York: Vintage Press.

Smith, A. B., & Pollack, H. (1999). Curtailing the sentencing power of trial judges: The unintended consequences. *Court Review: The Journal of the American Judges Association*, *6*, 4–7. Retrieved May 21, 2004, from *http://aja.ncsc.dni.us/courtrv/cr36-2/CR36-2SmithPol.pdf*.

Smith, P., Goggin, C., & Gendreau, P. (2002). *The effects of prison sentences and intermediate sanctions on recidivism: General effects and individual differences* (User Report 2002-01). Ottawa, Ontario: Solicitor General of Canada.

Sullivan, B. E. (1998). Harnessing Payne: Controlling the admission of victim impact statements to safeguard capital sentencing hearings from passion and prejudice. *Fordham Urban Law Journal*, *25*, 601–638.

Sunstein, C. R., Schkade, D. A., & Kahneman, D. (2000). Do people want optimal deterrence? *Journal of Legal Studies*, *29*, 237–253.

Tonry, M. (1996). *Sentencing matters*. Oxford, UK: Oxford University Press.

Trimboli, L. (2000). *An evaluation of the NSW Youth Justice Conferencing scheme*. Sydney, Australia: New South Wales Bureau of Crime Statistics and Research, Attorney General's Department.

Tsoudis, O. (2000). Relation of affect control theory to the sentencing of criminals. *Journal of Social Psychology*, *140*, 473–486.

Tsoudis, O., & Smith-Lovin, L. (1998). How bad was it? The effects of victim and perpetrator emotions on responses to criminal court vignettes. *Social Forces*, *77*, 695–722.

Tyler, T. R., Degoey, P., & Smith, H. J. (1996). Understanding why the justice of group procedures matters: A test of the psychological dynamics of the group-value model. *Journal of Personality and Social Psychology*, *70*, 913–920.

Tyler, T. R., Lind, E. A., & Huo, Y. J. (2000). Cultural values and authority relations: The psychology of conflict resolution across cultures. *Psychology, Public Policy, and Law*, *6*, 1138–1163.

Ulmer, J. T. (1997). *Social worlds of sentencing: Court communities under sentencing guidelines*. Albany, NY: State University of New York Press.

Ulmer, J. T., & Kramer, J. H. (1998). The use and transformation of formal decision-making criteria: Sentencing guidelines, organizational contexts, and case processing strategies. *Social Problems*, *45*, 248–267.

Umbreit, M. S., & Coates, B. V. (1992). The impact of mediating victim offender conflict: An analysis of programs in three states. *Juvenile and Family Court Journal*, *43*, 21–28.

Umbreit, M., Coates, R., & Vos, B. (2001). The impact of victim–offender mediation: Two decades of research. *Federal Probation*, *65*(3), 29–35.

Vidmar, N. (2001). Retribution and revenge. In J. Sanders & V. L. Hamilton (Eds.), *Handbook of justice research in law* (pp. 31–63). New York: Kluwer/Plenum.

von Hirsch, A. (1985). *Past of future crimes: Deservedness and dangerousness in the sentencing of criminals*. New Brunswick, NJ: Rutgers University Press.

Ward, T. (2002). Good lives and rehabilitation of offenders: Promises and problems. *Aggression and Violent Behavior*, *7*, 513–528.

Warner, K. (2002, October). *Sentencing guidelines for rape*. Paper presented at the Eighth

International Criminal Law Congress of the Criminal Lawyers Association of Australia and New Zealand, Melbourne, Australia.

Weiner, B. (1980). *Human motivation.* New York: Holt, Rinehart, & Winston.

Weiner, B., Graham, S., & Reyna, C. (1997). An attributional examination of retributive versus utilitarian philosophies of punishment. *Social Justice Research, 10,* 431–452.

Wexler, D. B. (2002). Some reflections on therapeutic jurisprudence and the practice of criminal law. *Criminal Law Bulletin, 38,* 205–243.

Wexler, D. B., & Winick, B. (1996). *The law in a therapeutic key: Developments in therapeutic jurisprudence.* Durham, NC: Carolina University Press.

Wheeler, S., Mann, K., & Sarat, A. (1988). *Sitting in judgment: The sentencing of white-collar criminals.* New Haven, CT: Yale University Press.

Wilson, R. J., Huculak, B., & McWhinnie, A. (2002). Restorative justice innovations in Canada. *Behavioral Sciences and the Law, 20,* 363–380.

Wilson, R. J., Picheca, J. E., & Serin, R. C. (2001, November). *Circles of support and accountability: Evaluating the efficacy of professionally supported volunteerism in the long-term reintegration of high-risk sexual offenders.* Paper presented at the 20th Annual Conference of the Association for the Treatment of Sexual Abusers, San Antonio, TX.

Winick, B. (2000). Redefining the role of the criminal defense lawyer at plea bargaining and sentencing: A therapeutic jurisprudence/preventive law model. In D. P. Stolle, D. B. Wexler, & B. J. Winick (Eds.), *Practicing therapeutic jurisprudence: Law as a helping profession* (pp. 245–305). Durham, NC: Carolina Academic Press.

Wrightsman, L. S. (1999). *Judicial decision making: Is psychology relevant?* New York: Kluwer/Plenum.

Wrightsman, L. S., Greene, E., Nietzel, M., & Fortune, W. (2002). *Psychology and the legal system* (5th ed.). Belmont, CA: Wadsworth.

CHAPTER FOURTEEN

Helping Experimental
Psychology Affect Legal Policy

GARY L. WELLS

Any scientific psychologist who has interacted extensively with police, law-yers, or trial judges has learned that scientific psychology and the legal system are very different beasts. The differences run much deeper than mere language and instead represent different types of thinking—a clash of cultures. This clash is particularly apparent when psychologists attempt to use research find-ings to affect legal policies and practices. In order for scientific psychologists to work effectively in applying psychological science to the legal system, they will need to develop a better understanding of the concept of policy and the contingencies that exist for policymakers.

Much of what I have to say in this chapter might seem obvious. For ex-ample, I describe how, in order to affect legal policies, you have to know who the policymakers are, you have to know something about how they think, and you have to overcome their preconceptions of social scientists and social sci-ence. As obvious as these points might seem, however, I have been surprised at how little thought and appreciation some scientific psychologists seem to have given to these matters. The training and reward contingencies within scientific psychology are poor preparation for the challenges of applying psychological science to the reform of legal practices and policies.

The examples that I use in this chapter are derived from my experience in trying to reform eyewitness lineup policies and procedures in the United States. The problem of trying to reform lineup policies in this country is an enormous one. Eyewitness identification procedures in the United States are not controlled by any central authority; instead, they are under local control, usually at the level of the individual law enforcement agency. There are over 19,000 independent law enforcement agencies in the United States and almost any conceivable set of lineup procedures can be found somewhere in the country. Furthermore, these procedures are commonly in considerable opposition to the procedures that are recommended on the basis of research findings. Not only is there wide variation in procedures and practices across local jurisdictions, but there is also wide variation in who controls those procedures, and there is wide variation in the attitudes of policymakers who could reform the procedures. At the time of this writing, only a small minority of U.S. jurisdictions has made policy changes based on eyewitness identification research conducted by psychologists, and almost all of this change has occurred within the last 2 years. I have been directly involved in almost all of these changes and each is unique in certain ways. Because some attempts to implement lineup reform have been successful and others have not, I have been able to extract some ideas about what works and what does not work.

There are two important caveats that readers should keep in mind regarding this material. First, the general ideas here are based on my experience with lineup reform, which is but one of many areas in which psychological science can be applied to legal policies. Although similar issues are likely to be encountered in attempting to apply psychological science to other legal reforms, there are likely to be some important differences as well. For example, attempts to reform how juries are selected would have little or no involvement of police. Second, the experiences noted here are based on attempts to reform policies in the United States, and it is likely that some of this information will not generalize to other countries. The United States is quite different from countries where there is more central control of eyewitness identification procedures, such as occurs in England and Wales. In fact, in England and Wales the issue of lineup ("identity parades") procedure has been addressed repeatedly and at regular intervals by legislators and police. The result of this attention is that the procedures are not only more uniform in England and Wales than in the United States, but also more sophisticated. Of course, historical revisions of lineup procedure in England and Wales generally have not been guided by experimental research on eyewitness identification because most of these reforms preceded any such research. Some of the written procedures in England, for example, date back to the 1800s (Police Orders, 1860), and the Home Office Circulars in eyewitness identification procedures date back to the early 1900s (Home Office, 1905).

There is nothing like this historical basis in the U.S. experience with eyewitness identification procedures. In fact, other than some very narrow and questionable rulings by the U.S. Supreme Court in the 1970s (e.g., *Neil v. Biggers*, 1972), procedural and policy issues concerning eyewitness identification have not been seriously addressed by legislators, police, or courts in this country. There simply is no counterpart in the United States to the Home Office approach in England and Wales. It is interesting to speculate that this difference might account for why DNA evidence has uncovered large numbers of innocent people who were convicted based on mistaken eyewitness identification in the United States (see Scheck, Neufeld, & Dwyer, 2000), whereas comparable numbers have not emerged in England or Wales. In any case, readers should keep in mind that some of the matters discussed in the current chapter might be unique to the U.S. experience or might be unique to the issue of eyewitness identification reform. Most matters, however, are likely to be broadly true for any research psychologist who is involved in trying to apply research findings to legal policy reform.

This chapter is not about expert testimony. It is true that legal policies regarding the admissibility of expert testimony by psychological scientists have evolved considerably over the last two decades. The general direction of this change in the United States has been toward increased acceptance of expert testimony on eyewitness issues. However, when I refer to the idea of using psychological science to affect legal policies and practices, I do not mean legal policies and practices regarding the admissibility of psychological scientists as experts in trials. Instead, I mean the use of psychological science to address such matters as policies and practices on how to best collect eyewitness evidence, how to interrogate suspects in ways that minimize the chances of false confessions, how to make judicial instructions more comprehensible for jurors, or how to select juries that will have fewer or less extreme biases. Although expert testimony by psychological scientists can be a mechanism or a tool for promoting such reforms, increases in the admissibility of expert testimony by psychological scientists, per se, is not what I mean by *legal policy reform*.

Readers will notice that in this chapter I offer no advice to policymakers, such as police, prosecutors, judges, or legislators, regarding their need to be receptive to findings in scientific psychology. That would be a different chapter. My purpose in writing this chapter is to increase the effectiveness of research psychologists who might attempt to apply scientific psychology to legal policy reform. Generally, I contend that research psychologists are somewhat naive about how to affect legal policies and practices. I base this contention on my own history of wrongheaded thinking and my gradual discovery of more productive ways of thinking about legal policy.

The term *legal policy* is used loosely here to refer to any formalized practice within the legal system. Sometimes these practices are grounded in a written document that was broadly scrutinized and officially sanctioned by a government body. The current guidelines for conducting lineups in the state of New Jersey, for example, are clearly written, broadly available over the Internet, and were officially sanctioned by the Department of Criminal Justice of the State of New Jersey under the authority of the Attorney General of New Jersey. In other cases, however, these practices might be no more than informal understandings about acceptable procedures that are not even written down. The Louisville, Kentucky Police Department, for example, frequently permits detectives to conduct show-ups (rather than lineups; defined below) for identification purposes long after the commission of a crime. The permissibility of show-ups in Louisville is not a written procedure and, in fact, there is almost nothing at all written down in the Louisville Police Department procedures manual regarding eyewitness identification procedures. In such cases, we generally infer policy from practices.

There are, of course, many levels at which to ponder the issue of using psychological science to affect legal policies and practices. For example, there is the question of whether the research findings are reliable and then the question of whether the findings can be generalized outside of the research setting. Those are important questions, but that is not what this chapter is about. Instead, this chapter presumes that there are reliable and generalizable findings in scientific psychology that are relevant to legal policy and the question is how to use those findings to promote meaningful policy reform in the legal system. This task requires a different set of skills and a different type of thinking than the type usually engaged in by scientific psychologists. Indeed, the first problem I describe here, which I call the "single-effects" problem, is perhaps the biggest difference between psychological scientists' usual ways of thinking and the kind of thinking that necessarily characterizes policymakers.

THE SINGLE-EFFECTS PROBLEM

Experimental psychologists are generally quite good at identifying individual effects from the manipulation of variables. The problem is that policymakers must consider a much broader range of possible effects, many of which are totally outside the domain of measurement and often are fully outside the thoughtful consideration of psychological researchers. These other possible effects include financial costs, public safety concerns, and various unintended consequences of specific policies and procedures. The tendency of experimental psychologists to focus intently on a specific dependent variable is important in conducting psychological science, but a restricted focus on a single variable can lead to a myopic view of policy.

In eyewitness identification research, the primary focus tends to be on the dependent variable of eyewitness accuracy. Eyewitness researchers are concerned about procedures that seem to produce less accurate results, especially procedures that increase the rate of mistaken identifications. Consider, for example, the effect of using a lineup versus a show-up procedure for obtaining eyewitness identifications. A lineup is a procedure in which the suspect, who might or might not be the culprit, is embedded among known-innocent fillers. A show-up is a procedure in which the suspect is presented alone to the eyewitness. Research has shown that a lineup tends to be a more effective procedure for protecting an innocent suspect from being mistakenly identified than does a show-up, especially if the innocent suspect happens to resemble the culprit (see meta-analysis by Steblay, Dysart, Fulero, & Lindsay, 2003). Nevertheless, U.S. policies and practices routinely permit the use of show-ups when a suspect who fits the description is detained shortly after crime in a geographic area that would have made it possible for the person to be the perpetrator in question. So, there appears to be a discrepancy between the type of procedure that experimental psychologists have shown to be best and the type of procedure that law enforcement often uses.

The great temptation for psychologists, given this state of affairs, is to call for the abolition of show-ups. But such a conclusion assumes that a policy on show-ups versus lineups is purely a matter of which one produces the fewest mistaken identifications. It would be a mistake, however, to use current data on show-ups versus lineups to argue for the abolition of show-ups. Even if we assume that the research is totally compelling and that it is definitively the case that a show-up procedure is more dangerous to an innocent suspect than is a lineup, the fact remains that policymakers must ponder a much broader set of effects that might result. Two considerations are particularly important: public safety, and the rights of individuals to be quickly freed from suspicion. In the United States, an individual cannot be arrested without probable cause, but an individual can be detained for a relatively short period of time for questioning—a period of time sufficient for conducting a show-up procedure. Consider now a policy that does not permit show-ups. Suppose a person has been detained who fits the description of the perpetrator and is in the proximity of the crime. From a practical perspective, there is no time to do a lineup unless the individual is arrested. Furthermore, merely fitting the description and being in the general area of the crime is not sufficient grounds for arrest. If show-ups are not permitted, then a potentially dangerous person must be released, perhaps endangering the public. A policy that would routinely permit perpetrators to escape this situation would appear to be bad policy in relation to issues in public safety. Alternatively, consider a situation in which the detained individual is, in fact, innocent of the crime. Both the detained individual and the police have an interest in quickly removing innocent persons from suspicion. Field data from actual show-ups and data from controlled experiments indicate that the dominant response to a show-up is a rejection response (Steblay et al., 2003). Hence, show-ups are relatively effective in freeing individuals from suspicion, and they do so in a quick and efficient manner without the need to arrest a detained individual.

The fact that there are policy reasons to permit show-ups does not mean that show-ups are acceptable under all circumstances. Consider the situation in Louisville, Kentucky, where police often use show-ups days or even weeks after the commission of a crime. In these cases, the policy reasons that are used to justify show-ups (public safety and the need to quickly free a detained person from suspicion) are no longer applicable. Under these circumstances, the research indicating that show-ups are less accurate and therefore more dangerous than lineups, especially after a delay interval (see Yarmey, Yarmey, & Yarmey, 1996), should hold considerably more weight in guiding legal policy.

The general point here has nothing to do with lineups versus show-ups, per se. Instead, the general point is that policymakers often have very good reasons for not being highly influenced by research data, because the research usually measures only one effect rather than the broad effects that might result from a change in policy. The propensity of experimental psychologists to focus narrowly on a specific effect contrasts sharply with the policymaker's need to analyze all possible effects. As a result, what sometimes appears to be recalcitrance or neglect by policymakers to consider the findings of scientific psychology is not recalcitrance or neglect at all, but rather a consideration of other factors that manage to outweigh the single effect observed by psychological researchers. These other factors are diverse and vary from one policy or practice to another policy or practice. They can include such factors as financial cost, public safety, victims' rights, and the need to balance the risks of falsely convicting the innocent against the risk of falsely freeing the guilty. By understanding these policy concerns, research psychologists can better understand why the research findings can sometimes be trumped by other considerations in the setting of legal policy.

One of the obvious implications of this real-world situation is that psychological scientists need to ask policymakers a lot of questions to identify the foundations for their policies. Conducting experiments and measuring a narrow set of variables could very well miss the mark regarding the critical foundations underlying the policy or practice. This is not to say that the existing policies and practices in the legal system are always well grounded. It is to say, however, that psychologists must first learn about the broad foundations for a particular policy before arguing that an experimental result ought to result in adjustments to it.

WHO ARE THE POLICYMAKERS?

In order to affect legal policy, we have to know who the real policymakers are. That would seem to be a straightforward problem that is easily answered, but this is not always the case. For example, who are the policymakers in the area of lineup reform? For many years, the general presumption of most eyewitness researchers, including myself, was that policies and procedures regarding lineups were under the control of the courts. Accordingly, expert testimony geared at criticizing how lineups were conducted in individual cases was presumed to be the best mechanism to effect changes in those procedures. In fact, however, despite a considerable amount of such expert testimony spanning over 25 years, no genuine success has been achieved in getting U.S. courts to issue guidelines for reforming lineup procedures. The reason for this appears to be that judges in the United States do not think it is their role to tell police how to collect evidence. Instead, U.S. judges consider their role to be interpreters of the law. To the extent that the manner in which evidence is collected violates the U.S. constitution, such as searching a home without a legal search permit, then judges are willing to concern themselves with the procedure that was used to collect the evidence. But the use of a poor lineup procedure, or the failure to use the best lineup procedures, is not a constitutional right. As a result, judges have played no significant role at all in promoting lineup reform in the United States.

Intuitively, it makes sense to assume that police are the policymakers when it comes to lineup procedure issues in the United States. However, it is not strictly true that police control policies on lineup procedures. Although police conduct most of the lineup procedures, it has become increasingly clear that it is prosecutors who carry the greatest weight in determining policies and procedures on lineups. The extent to which this is true varies somewhat across jurisdictions, but no lineup reforms in the United States have yet been implemented without the blessings or encouragement of the chief prosecutors in their jurisdictions. This makes sense when we consider the fact that police turn their evidence over to prosecutors. It is the prosecutors who then decide whether to proceed with charges, and it is the prosecutors who then have to use this evidence in court in any attempt to convict the identified person.

Working with police and with prosecutors on reforming lineup procedures in the United States has revealed some interesting differences between police and prosecutors. Because police and prosecutors have different roles and responsibilities, they tend to have different experiences that shape their views. For instance, while working on the U.S. Department of Justice eyewitness guidelines project, it was our experience that police were more likely to perceive a problem with eyewitness evidence than were prosecutors (Wells et al., 2000). Furthermore, police were more receptive to recommendations for improving lineup procedures than were prosecutors. I was surprised by this difference, as were the other psychologists in the working group. We had anticipated the reverse: that police would be the ones most resistant to change. After all, it is the police, not the prosecutors, who would have to change their policies and practices. As it turns out, however, police are in a much better position than prosecutors to observe frequent instances of eyewitness misidentification and other eyewitness errors. A major source of this difference in experience occurs at the level of the photographic lineup. Lineups, when properly constructed, have one suspect (who might or might not be the culprit) and the remaining lineup members are known-innocent persons (fillers). Police with broad experience in administering photo lineups have learned that witnesses frequently pick known-innocent lineup fillers and often do this with high confidence. Field research shows that eyewitnesses pick fillers 20–25% of the time in actual cases (Behrman & Davey, 2001; Wright & McDaid, 1996).

Prosecutors, on the other hand, are not the ones administering these lineups to eyewitnesses. What prosecutors see are the "successful" cases in which the eyewitness picked the suspect, rather than a filler, from the lineup. Compounding this problem is a tendency for lineup administrators to simply note that the eyewitness "could not make a positive identification of the suspect," rather than clearly noting the instances in which the eyewitness picked a filler from a lineup. When this kind of record is passed along to a prosecutor, the impression is that the witness did not even attempt an identification, rather than that the witness picked a filler. In hindsight, it now makes good sense to me that police would have a better appreciation of the frequency of eyewitness error than would prosecutors.

In addition, it has been my experience that police have been more receptive to the idea of detailed procedural policies for lineups than have prosecutors. In part, this view reflects differences in perceptions of the reliability of eyewitnesses, but it also reflects other differences. Having a well-defined procedural policy protects the police investigators from criticism as long as they simply follow the procedural policy that has been adopted. For prosecutors, on the other hand, having a well-defined procedural policy for police represents one more area in which to grapple with troublesome discrepancies between what the police did and what the procedural policy says they should have done. Any difference between the procedural policy and the practice followed by police is potentially a huge problem for the prosecution. Accordingly, it has been my experience that many prosecutors prefer to have unclear, informal procedural policies for lineups so that, no matter how the lineup was conducted, it could never have violated the procedural policy. Of course, this view would be most likely to be held by prosecutors who have low opinions of the ability of police to follow procedural policies—and, therefore, rarely will a prosecutor explicitly articulate this reason for resisting the development of clearer lineup procedural policies. But the more general lesson here is that different actors in the legal system have different roles, different backgrounds, and different experiences. Do not expect that groups that work together (such as police and prosecutors) will always think alike.

Legal policymakers in the United States also include those who hold the title of attorney general. Each state has an attorney general, usually an elected office. Unfortunately, in only one state does the attorney general have significant authority over prosecutors and police within that state. It is not coincidental that this one state, New Jersey, also happens to be the first state to adopt research-based recommendations for how police should conduct lineups. In fact, New Jersey is still the only state to have adopted these reforms statewide. In other states, there is no single authority that can set policy for individual police departments within that state on matters such as lineup procedure. Accordingly, there are no good wide-scale mechanisms for reforming lineup policy in the United States, even at the level of the individual states, and local control (at the level of counties, cities, and towns) remains the rule on such matters.

One mechanism that is theoretically available to change legal policies on a large scale is at the level of state legislatures. With regard to reforming lineup procedures, for example, state legislatures could legally impose such reforms on police within their respective states. Unsuccessful attempts to impose lineup reform have been made in the states of Iowa, Missouri, and Illinois, among others. To be successful, this type of approach requires a sophisticated understanding of the political process that includes the basic reality that the recommended reforms have to fit the complex political agenda of the legislature. The kinds of legal reform that scientific psychologists tend to press generally do not fit into the legislative political arena in the United States.

In domains where there are thousands of individual policymakers operating largely independently of each other, it is important to not overlook key individuals who, although not in direct control of policy, have a "bully pulpit" by virtue of their position. The Attorney General of the United States, for instance, cannot dictate policies and procedures to individual states or local jurisdictions but does have the ear of law enforcement and prosecutors. In the area of lineup reform, former U.S. Attorney General Janet Reno was concerned about eyewitness identification problems based on the fact that the DNA exoneration cases were showing that mistaken identification was the cause of most of these convictions of innocent persons. This finding gave scientific psychology a chance to be heard, and the result was the development of the first set of national guidelines for the collection and preservation of eyewitness evidence (Technical Working Group for Eyewitness Evidence, 1999). Five psychological scientists were included in this effort, and the guide tended to follow, rather closely, the recommendations based on eyewitness identification research (see Wells et al., 2000). It is important to note that the guide has no legal force on how states and local jurisdictions collect eyewitness evidence. Nevertheless, this was clearly the most significant role that psychological science has played in trying to shape legal policies in the United States, and the fact that it was initiated and endorsed by the U.S. Attorney General has given it some force in encouraging states and local jurisdictions to reform their policies and procedures on eyewitness evidence.

THE PERCEPTION OF A SOCIAL AGENDA

Research psychologists in academia sometimes have to persuade others that their research is valuable, but that usually means persuading other psychologists or students. Selling psychology to other psychologists and students, however, is rather easy compared to selling psychology to people in the legal system. Brewer, Wilson, and Braithwaite (1995) have provided a useful description of steps to be taken in selling research in police organizations for purposes of collecting data in such settings. But what about selling research findings to actors in the legal system? Very few actors in the legal system have a conception of psychology as a science. Generally, their contact with psychologists is restricted to clinical forensic expert testimony. Indeed, to some in the legal system, the term *scientific psychology* is an oxymoron. To the extent that no conception of psychology as a science exists within the legal system, there is a great deal of room for those in the legal system to believe that psychological conclusions and ideas are heavily biased toward a social agenda.

In the United States there is a relatively wide perception that academics, especially those in the social sciences and humanities, are politically and socially motivated by a liberal agenda. Among other things, this means that academics are perceived to be opposed to the death penalty, opposed to strong penalties for drug use, and generally more concerned with the rights of the accused than they are with law and order. Along with this cluster of social and political attitudes is the perception that academics would prefer a much higher ratio of the number of guilty going free to the number of innocent being convicted than would most people. I know of no data that speak directly to this perception, but there is almost certainly some validity to it, especially if the attitudes of academics were contrasted with those of prosecutors or people in law enforcement. Clearly, this is an overgeneralization of academics, just as it is an overgeneralization of police and prosecutors to presume that they are more concerned about making sure they convict the guilty than they are about making sure that they do not convict the innocent. Nevertheless, this perception harms the credibility of experimental psychologists in the minds of some policymakers.

Experimental psychologists are no different from other people in the sense that their values creep into their language and the nature of the questions that they ask. For instance, eyewitness identification researchers are much more likely to frame their work in terms of a concern with lowering false identification rates rather than a concern with lowering the rate of misses (i.e., failures to identify the perpetrator). Indeed, none of the four major recommendations of the American Psychology–Law Society "White Paper" on lineups (Wells et al., 1998) was described as a mechanism to reduce miss rates or enhance hit rates. I, of course, recognize the apparent irony of that criticism, given that I was an author of the recommendations. It turns out that we could make the argument that implementing the recommendations would have positive effects on reducing misses and enhancing hit rates, but we simply did not make that case as effectively as we could have in the article. The case is easily made by pointing out how the identification of an innocent suspect leads to the cessation of a search for the actual perpetrator. Anything that stops the search for the actual perpetrator must, by definition, increase the rate of misses (i.e., reduce hit rates). Had the "White Paper" focused on the ways that poor lineup procedures help a guilty person go undetected (because the witness mistakenly identified someone else) as much as it focused on preventing mistaken identifications, it might have had a more productive impact on U.S. police and prosecutors. I would write the recommendations article differently today—but such is the nature of hindsight.

Success in obtaining policy change requires that experimental psychologists somehow manage to show policymakers that the effect of the changes is to reduce the chances of the innocent being convicted, without harming the chances that the guilty will be convicted—or, better yet, to reduce the chances that the innocent will be convicted and also increase the chances that the guilty will be convicted. Unfortunately, many experimental psychologists have not managed to show this kind of balance. For instance, many experimental psychologists are eager to provide expert testimony on eyewitness identification issues at trial, and this testimony is almost invariably testimony for the defense. Granted, the reason that such testimony is for the defense resides primarily in the fact that it is almost always defense attorneys, not prosecuting attorneys, who have sought the assistance of eyewitness experts. Regardless of the reason, however, consistent alignment with the defense serves to brand the experimental psychologist as having a defense bias—a bias that is consistent with an already-existing stereotype of academics. If policies and practices are controlled by prosecutors or police—which they are, in the case of lineup procedures—those who testify consistently for the defense have little chance of working effectively with these policymakers. This is, of course, a page right out of social psychology. Recipients of persuasion attempts are quite sensitive to the question of whether the persuader understands the problems, needs, and interests of the recipient. Whether correct or not, police and prosecutors are going to assume that someone who works closely and consistently with the defense does not understand the problems, needs, and interests of prosecutors and police.

Because of my role in dealing with prosecutors, police, and judges on issues regarding lineup policy, several years ago I declared a moratorium on giving expert testimony for the defense in eyewitness cases. That is a rather extreme measure, and it is not one I am advocating for others. Nevertheless, I believe that it has helped immensely in my ability to work effectively with policymakers to effect lineup reforms in Massachusetts, New Jersey, Wisconsin, Minnesota, and North Carolina, among other states. Today, I get asked to talk to police, prosecutors, and judges across the United States on a regular basis regarding eyewitness identification issues and these venues permit me to educate them about the research and to appeal to them to make lineup reforms. I do not believe that this level of effectiveness regarding lineup policy change could have been achieved if I were routinely giving expert testimony for the defense.

Legal systems such as the U.S. legal system are, by design, adversarial systems: It is the prosecution team versus the defense team. Those who enter this system as outsiders, as experimental psychologists clearly are, tend to get cast on one side or the other; few can straddle both sides. Because academics are generally thought to have a socially liberal agenda, psychological scientists have to work particularly hard to overcome this preconception. There is probably more to this social agenda labeling than mere stereotyping of academics. Having a social agenda is perhaps the reason why many psychologists became involved in trying to change policy in the first place. There is nothing inherently wrong with being motivated by a social agenda. Many prosecutors probably became prosecutors because of their social agenda. Nevertheless, if psychological scientists want to be effective in changing policy, then pushing a social agenda is going to interfere with that effectiveness.

In addition to the concern that social scientists have a biased social agenda, the very fact that social science is outside of the legal system permits those in the legal system to dismiss social scientists as people who are out of touch with the "real world" of crime. This dismissal appears truer of police perceptions of social scientists than it is of lawyers' perceptions—and in either case, it should not be taken personally. Police tend to see lawyers as out of touch with the real world of crime as well. The social scientist who rides around in a squad car for a week or month can overcome this perception a bit, but it is foolish for the social scientist to pretend to know what it is like to actually be a crime investigator. Social scientists who refuse to concede this point will be shut out of the interaction process. The best approach is to concede this point up front and use it constructively. You have research information to share with them, and they have real-world experiences to share with you; it is a two-way street and there is something to be learned by listening to their experiences and ideas.

DATA DRIVE SCIENCE BUT INDIVIDUAL CASES DRIVE POLICYMAKERS

An important event that occurred in the 1990s in the United States in the eyewitness identification area is instructive about one of the fundamental differences in thinking between the legal system and science. Before the 1990s, eyewitness identification research was almost completely ignored by legal policymakers except as it related to expert testimony and the issue of the admissibility of such testimony. In spite of numerous calls by psychologists for reform of eyewitness identification procedures, no serious efforts were undertaken by legal policymakers to reform eyewitness identification procedures. By the mid 1990s, however, the legal system was beginning to take notice of eyewitness identification research with an eye toward reform. The big event that caused this nascent attention to eyewitness identification research was the use of postconviction forensic DNA testing to uncover convictions of innocent persons. An analysis of the first 28 cases revealed that mistaken eyewitness identification was the primary evidence driving most of these wrongful convictions (Connors, Lundregan, Miller, & McEwan, 1996). Analyses of later DNA exoneration cases have continued to show that mistaken eyewitness identification is responsible for more of these convictions of innocent people than all other causes combined (Scheck et al., 2000; Wells et al., 1998).

From a scientific perspective, the DNA exoneration cases told us almost nothing. Although the DNA exoneration cases told eyewitness scientists that mistaken identifications do happen, eyewitness scientists already felt that this was a well-established reality, based on their extensive experiments. Importantly, the DNA cases tell us nothing about how often mistaken identifications occur, what variables are causing mistaken identifications, what psychological processes are involved, or how to prevent mistaken identifications. To eyewitness identification scientists, the DNA exoneration cases were simply case studies, not hard data, due to their uncontrolled nature. Hence, from a scientific point of view, the DNA exoneration cases were not of great significance.

To the legal system, on the other hand, these cases were powerful because they represented individual, real-world cases of miscarriages of justice. Whereas the psychological scientists were writing about numbers from their experiments and reporting pallid statistical analyses regarding research participants, the DNA exoneration cases began to put real faces on the victims of misidentification. Newspapers and television news programs began to report vivid stories of individuals who had served many years in prison, some of whom had been on death row awaiting execution, and the common theme was that mistaken identification had been responsible for the miscarriage of justice. It has been these individual cases and the publicity surrounding them, not the research experiments themselves, that have led the justice system in the United States to become interested in eyewitness identification research experiments and their findings.

There is a general lesson in this for psychological scientists who are interested in using their research findings to affect the legal system. Whereas scientists are impressed by hard data and controlled experiments, actors in the legal system are impressed by vivid individual cases in which the outcome went awry (e.g., conviction of an innocent person). Of course, psychologists should not be surprised by this fact because long ago social psychologists demonstrated that people are more likely to be persuaded by a single, vividly recounted story of an individual than they are by statistical data (e.g., Nisbett, Borgida, Crandall, & Reed, 1976). Nevertheless, it is easy for psychological scientists to underestimate the extent to which actors in the legal system seemingly require concrete, individual, real-world case examples in order to take seriously the science that is directed at the problem. The real-world individual case is important for policymakers not simply because it is more vivid than the experimental data; the real-world case demonstrates that the event in question can, in fact, happen in the real world and that it is not restricted to the laboratory or to the college sophomore.

There is another lesson in this as well. It appears as though the legal system entertains the idea of change or reform only in response to significant negative events that become a focus of attention. For example, the not-guilty verdict in the O. J. Simpson case was a major impetus for the development of standard protocols for the collection and preservation of DNA evidence, even though experts had long warned that such protocols were needed. Similarly, it was the bungling of the crime scene in the Jon Bonnet murder case in Boulder, Colorado, that facilitated the development of guidelines for U.S. police in the investigation of murder scenes. Sometimes an event has to be catastrophic to trigger reform. Consider the longstanding warnings from experts about the lack of security on airlines, and yet almost nothing was done to address airline security until the World Trade Center attacks of September 11, 2001. In each of these examples, experts had to wait until something negative happened before the system became receptive to their reform recommendations. It is possible that this reactive pattern for reform is characteristically American and that legal reforms in other countries are more proactive rather than reactive. But I suspect that there is something more universal about this pattern because it seems so characteristically human.

One of the implications of the catastrophe–reform link is the existence of certain windows of opportunity for attempting to apply psychological science to legal reform. Outside of this window, the psychological science is often ignored, no matter how strong or sophisticated the efforts. No matter how solid and extensive the research was in 1985, for example, the time was not right for implementing reform in how lineups are conducted in the United States. As it turns out, the time for such reform was dependent on the development and acceptance of forensic DNA testing, which then uncovered dramatic instances of serious miscarriages of justice. Notice, however, that it is difficult, if not impossible, to predict when these critical negative events will occur and, hence, when the window of opportunity will present itself. The idea is for psychological science to be ready when windows of opportunity arise, which they inevitably do, albeit it can be years or decades down the road.

Even when there are windows of opportunity, lack of progress often reflects a shortage of time, energy, and other resources that academics have available to devote to policy endeavors. Other demands on time, such as teaching, conducting research, and publishing are themselves full-time endeavors, and policy change activities tend to be something that is done "on the side." Furthermore, academic psychology departments generally do not recognize applications of science to policy as something that their faculty ought to be doing.

MAKING THE RESEARCH POLICY RELEVANT

No matter how effective an individual might be as someone who can work with legal policymakers, attempts to apply psychological science to legal policy are fruitless if the research is not policy relevant. Generally, policy relevance is not an either/or matter but, rather, a matter of degree or type. This difference in degree or type of policy relevance was recognized early in eyewitness identification research via the distinction between estimator variables and system variables (Wells, 1978). *Estimator variables* are those that affect the accuracy of eyewitness identification, over which the legal system has no control. These would include variables such as lighting conditions during witnessing, the weapon-focus effect, whether the witness and culprit were of the same race, and so on. *System variables*, in contrast, are those that affect the accuracy of eyewitness identification over which the legal system does (or could) have control. These would include variables such as the instructions given to witnesses prior to their viewing a lineup, methods for choosing the fillers who will appear in the lineup, whether the lineup members are presented simultaneously or sequentially, and so on. Although both estimator and system variables could be policy relevant under some circumstances, it is system variables that have the strongest and most direct implications for policy. Recognition of the "extra value" of system variables for purposes of making eyewitness identification research relevant to legal policy probably accounts for the relatively greater emphasis on system variables than on estimator variables over the last 20–25 years in eyewitness identification research.

The system-variable versus estimator-variable distinction is primarily a distinction between whether the information can be used by the legal system to improve outcomes, or whether the information is only useful to the legal system as a post-hoc estimator of a problem. We need not restrict the distinction to eyewitness identification research. For instance, we could conduct research showing that jurors are not capable of disregarding testimony that they have been instructed to disregard—and leave it at that. But such research would not have much "policy punch" because it fails to tell the legal system what alternative might work better. For example, the idea that all testimony could be videotaped and played to a jury, so that any inadmissible portions could be edited out before the jury hears it, is perhaps a radical idea and it might or might not be practical or desirable on other accounts. But research directed at this kind of potential solution to the ineffective "disregard" instructions from a judge is much more policy relevant than research that merely identifies the problem. In general, policymakers are not going to find useful a body of research that undermines their current policies and practices, unless there are clear demonstrations of better policies and practices to take their place. Policy-relevant research is research that examines one set of policies or practices versus another, not research that merely shows weaknesses of current policies and practices.

When there exists a body of research in scientific psychology that has clear legal policy implications, it can be useful to take the White Paper approach. This was the approach taken under the auspices of the American Psychology–Law Society by eyewitness identification researchers. The American Psychology–Law Society has a scientific review paper committee that is capable of appointing a subcommittee to review all that is known about some topic and reach conclusions that appear to have good scientific consensus. An open process is created that permits psychology and law researchers to provide input based on drafts of a manuscript. The resulting manuscript is peer reviewed and widely publicized, and any dissenting views can be printed alongside the resulting White Paper when it is published in the journal *Law and Human Behavior*. The so-called White Paper on lineups was published in 1998 (Wells et al., 1998), and it has had a remarkable effect in the United States. Among other things, drafts of this paper were read by U.S. Attorney General Janet Reno and by the entire working group that was charged with developing the U.S. Justice Department's Guide for Law Enforcement on eyewitness evidence. Furthermore, this article has become widely distributed among practicing lawyers, police, and judges through workshops and continuing education seminars across the United States. It could be argued that any article, regardless of whether it was endorsed as a White Paper by the American Psychology–Law Society, could have had this kind of impact. But I strongly suspect that the scientific consensus process and the endorsement by a scholarly body gave this article a special boost. A similar process might be done in other areas of scientific psychology and the law for which there is good consensus among scientists, such as some aspects of jury selection, jury instructions, or the detection of deception.

The White Paper approach can be an effective way of bridging scientific psychology findings and legal policy. Some "rules of thumb" about how such papers need to be written are useful. First, as noted earlier, there needs to be a consensus among the scientists that the findings are reliable and relevant to legal policy recommendations. This is not a format in which to present recommendations that are not fully endorsed among the scientists. Second, the recommendations need to have been scrutinized at the policy level to ensure that such matters as costs, benefits, and unintended consequences have been thoroughly examined and included. This domain is where the authors of the White Paper have to be able to think on levels that may be unfamiliar to psychological scientists. Third, the number of recommendations should generally be small, perhaps three to five recommendations, rather than expansive. This focus on a limited number of recommendations helps guarantee that the policy implications can be thoroughly examined for each, that recommendations with lower levels of consensus among scientists will not creep onto the list, and that each recommendation can be sufficiently explained and properly documented. There will inevitably be some psychological scientists who want to add recommendations, but it is better to have a limited set that are compelling than to risk counterargumentation on a subset of the recommendations. Later, additional recommendations can be made either in a follow-up White Paper or through other means. For instance, the White Paper on lineups had only four recommendations, each of which is compelling. However, this paper has opened the door to dispersing other recommendations for lineups via workshops, seminars, and consultations. A fourth rule of thumb is that the White Paper needs to be written in a manner that is easily read by nonpsychologists. Although it should include an extensive bibliography that permits readers to access original sources, psychological jargon and most inferential statistics must be jettisoned from the article. This does not mean that the article should be purged of science, but rather that the scientific foundations (methods) must be written for comprehension by the public.

SUMMARY

Although the long-term prospects for psychological science to have a lasting impact on legal policy are very promising, the effectiveness of psychological science at this point has tended to be rather limited. Most of this limited impact is probably due to the relative newness of the interface between psychological science and legal policy. As more research that is relevant to legal policies and practices emerges, the impact of psychological science on legal policies and practices undoubtedly will increase. Meaningful impact on the legal system, however, does not depend solely on the quality and relevance of the research. The impact of psychological science on the legal system also depends on the ability of psychological scientists to communicate clearly with legal policymakers and with an understanding that legal policymakers must consider a broad range of factors, not just the research. Furthermore, in order to be highly effective with policymakers, psychological scientists will have to overcome the perception that they have a socially liberal agenda or an agenda that strongly favors one or the other side of the adversarial legal system. When a scientific consensus develops regarding a legal policy matter, a White Paper approach can be an effective way to proceed. Finally, psychological scientists need to be patient about reform, because legal reform is a slow process and usually requires negative events or catastrophes of one sort or another to catalyze it.

ACKNOWLEDGMENT

Preparation of portions of this chapter was facilitated by Australian Research Council Grant No. A00104516 to Neil Brewer and Gary L. Wells.

REFERENCES

Behrman, B. W., & Davey, S. L. (2001). Eyewitness identification in actual criminal cases: An archival analysis. *Law and Human Behavior, 25,* 475–491.

Brewer, N., Wilson, C., & Braithwaite, H. (1995). Psychological research and policing. In N. Brewer & C. Wilson (Eds.), *Psychology and policing* (pp. 395–412). Hillsdale, NJ: Erlbaum.

Connors, E., Lundregan, T., Miller, N., & McEwan, T. (1996). *Convicted by juries, exonerated by science: Case studies in the use of DNA evidence to establish innocence after trial.* Alexandria, VA: National Institute of Justice.

Home Office. (1905). *Identification of criminals—metropolitan police regulations.* Home Office Circular to the Police, His Majesty's Stationary Office, London.

Neil v. Biggers, 409 U.S. 188 (1972).

Nisbett, R. E., Borgida, E., Crandall, R., & Reed, H. (1976). Popular induction: Information is not necessarily informative. In J. S. Carroll & J. W. Payne (Eds.), *Cognition and social behavior* (Vol. 2, pp. 227–236). Hillsdale, NJ: Erlbaum.

Police Orders. (1860). *Identification of persons charged with offences.* Metropolitan Police Office.

Scheck, B., Neufeld, P., & Dwyer, J. (2000). *Actual innocence.* New York: Random House.

Steblay, N. M., Dysart, J., Fulero, S., & Lindsay, R. C. L. (2003). Eyewitness accuracy rates in police showup and lineup presentations: A meta-analytic comparison. *Law and Human Behavior, 27,* 523–540.

Technical Working Group for Eyewitness Evidence. (1999). *Eyewitness evidence: A guide for law enforcement.* Washington, DC: United States Department of Justice, Office of Justice Programs.

Wells, G. L. (1978). Applied eyewitness testimony research: System variables and estimator variables. *Journal of Personality and Social Psychology, 36,* 1546–1557.

Wells, G. L., Malpass, R. S., Lindsay, R. C. L., Fisher, R. P., Turtle, J. W., & Fulero, S. (2000). From the lab to the police station: A successful application of eyewitness research. *American Psychologist, 55,* 581–598.

Wells, G. L., Small, M., Penrod, S., Malpass, R. S., Fulero, S. M., & Brimacombe, C. A. E. (1998). Eyewitness identification procedures: Recommendations for lineups and photospreads. *Law and Human Behavior, 22,* 603–647.

Wright, D. B., & McDaid, A. T. (1996). Comparing system and estimator variables using data from real lineups. *Applied Cognitive Psychology, 10,* 75–84.

Yarmey, A. D., Yarmey, M. J., & Yarmey, A. L. (1996). Accuracy of eyewitness identifications in showups and lineups. *Law and Human Behavior, 20,* 459–477.

Index